Elizabeth A. Kennedy

MW01698464

# ALBERT BIERSTADT

## Art & Enterprise

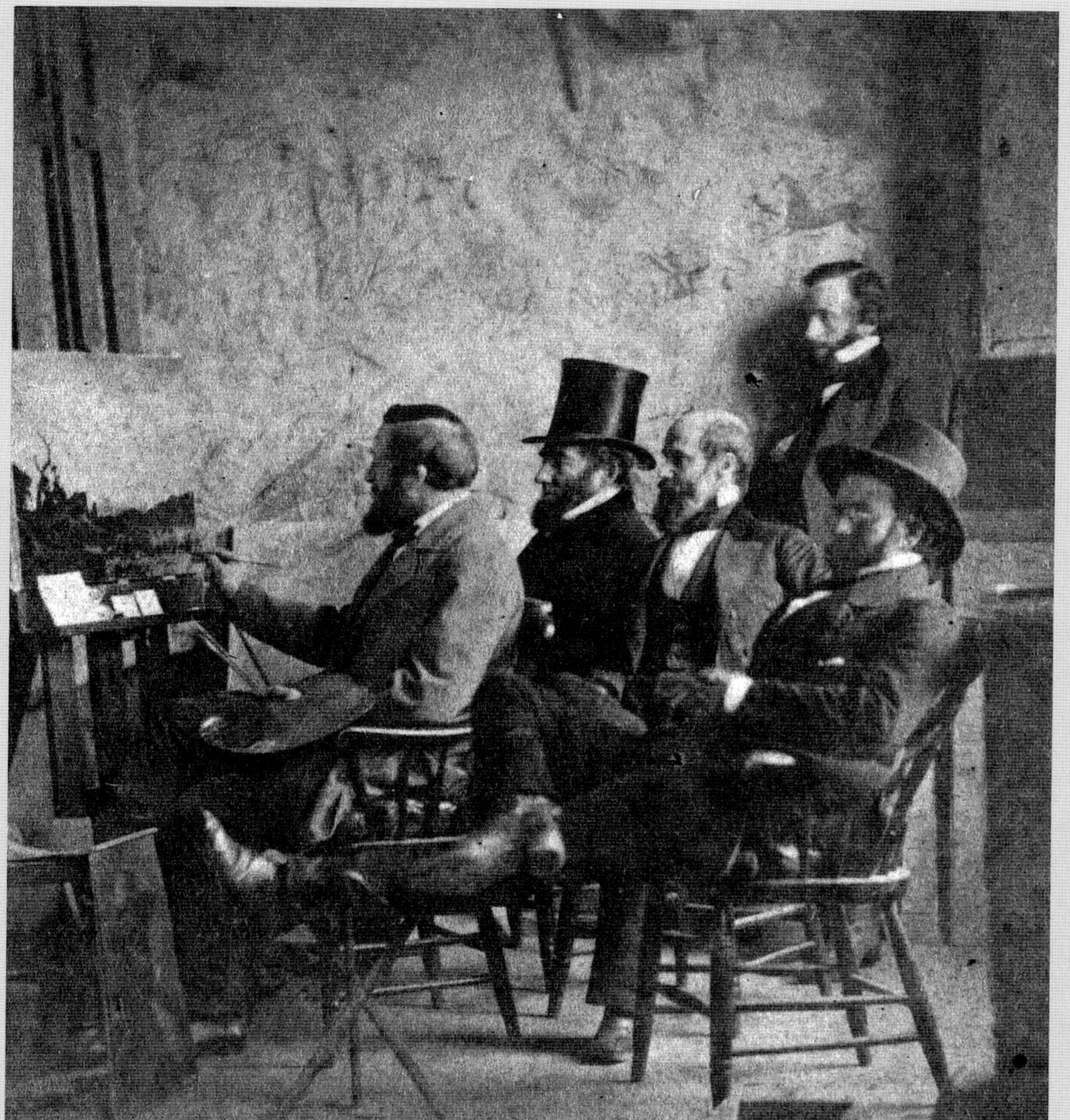

# ALBERT BIERSTADT
## Art & Enterprise

NANCY K. ANDERSON

LINDA S. FERBER

with a contribution by Helena E. Wright

THE BROOKLYN MUSEUM
IN ASSOCIATION WITH HUDSON HILLS PRESS, NEW YORK

Published on the occasion of the exhibition *Albert Bierstadt: Art & Enterprise*, organized by The Brooklyn Museum in association with the National Gallery of Art, Washington, D.C.

**Exhibition Itinerary:**

The Brooklyn Museum: February 8–May 6, 1991
The Fine Arts Museums of San Francisco: June 8–September 1, 1991
National Gallery of Art, Washington, D.C.: November 3, 1991–February 17, 1992

The exhibition is made possible by Philip Morris Companies Inc.

Critical support was also provided by The Henry Luce Foundation, Inc. Additional funds were provided by the National Endowment for the Humanities and the National Endowment for the Arts, Federal agencies, by the New York State Council on the Arts, and by Mr. and Mrs. Wilbur L. Ross, Jr.

First Edition

© 1990 by The Brooklyn Museum

All rights reserved under International and Pan-American Copyright Conventions.

Assistant Director for Publications: Elaine Koss

Editor: Joanna Ekman

Published in the United States by Hudson Hills Press, Inc., Suite 1308, 230 Fifth Avenue, New York, NY 10001-7704.

Editor and Publisher: Paul Anbinder

Designer: Binns & Lubin/Martin Lubin

Composition: Trufont Typographers

Manufactured in Japan by Toppan Printing Company

Distributed in the United States, its territories and possessions, Canada, Mexico, and Central and South America by Rizzoli International Publications, Inc.

Distributed in the United Kingdom and Eire by Thomas Heneage & Co. Ltd.

Distributed in Japan by Yohan (Western Publications Distribution Agency).

**Library of Congress Cataloguing-in-Publication Data**

Anderson, Nancy K.
Albert Bierstadt : art & enterprise / Nancy K. Anderson and Linda S. Ferber.
p. cm.
Includes bibliographical references.
1. Bierstadt, Albert, 1830–1902—Exhibitions. 2. West (U.S.) in art—Exhibitions. I. Ferber, Linda S.
II. Brooklyn Museum.
III. Title.
ND237.B585A4 1991 90-39692
759.13—dc20 CIP
ISBN: 0-87273-125-1 (alk. paper)
Cover illustration: *The Last of the Buffalo*, 1888 (detail)

Frontispiece: Bierstadt Brothers, New Bedford, Massachusetts. *Albert Bierstadt Painting "Thunderstorm in the Rocky Mountains" in His New Bedford Studio*, 1859. Stereograph. Collection of William L. Schaeffer. Inscription identifies figures as, left to right, Bierstadt, Edward Merrill, John Hopkins, C. B. H. Fessenden, and Elisha C. Leonard

# CONTENTS


List of Colorplates 7

Preface 11

Directors' Foreword 13
ROBERT T. BUCK, HARRY S. PARKER III, AND J. CARTER BROWN

Lenders to the Exhibition 14

Acknowledgments 15

List of Abbreviations 18

ALBERT BIERSTADT: ART & ENTERPRISE

Albert Bierstadt: The History of a Reputation 21
LINDA S. FERBER

"Wondrously Full of Invention": The Western Landscapes of Albert Bierstadt 69
NANCY K. ANDERSON

Chronology and Colorplates
NANCY K. ANDERSON

*1830–1858: New Bedford Youth, European Apprenticeship* 111
*1859–1862: Rocky Mountain Reconnaissance* 139
*1863–1870: Overland to California, Return to Europe* 171
*1871–1879: New Subjects, New Patrons* 219
*1880–1902: Late Years* 245

Bierstadt and the Business of Printmaking 267
HELENA E. WRIGHT

*Checklist of Nineteenth-Century Prints After Paintings by Albert Bierstadt* 271
*Colorplates* 289

Selected Bibliography 295

Appendix A: Catalogue of the New Bedford Art Exhibition 304

Appendix B: Reminiscences of an Overlander 306
FITZ HUGH LUDLOW

Index 322

Photograph Credits 327

# COLORPLATES


| | | |
|---|---|---|
| Fig. 8 | *Mount Washington*, 1862, oil on canvas | 31 |
| Fig. 16 | *View of the Hudson Looking Across the Tappan Zee Towards Hook Mountain*, 1866, oil on canvas | 37 |
| Fig. 33 | *The Emerald Pool*, 1870, oil on canvas | 59 |
| Fig. 55 | *Mount Hood, Oregon*, 1865, oil on canvas | 86 |
| Fig. 58 | *The Domes of the Yosemite*, 1867, oil on canvas | 90 |
| Fig. 61 | *Donner Lake from the Summit*, 1873, oil on canvas | 95 |
| No. 1 | *A Rustic Mill*, 1855, oil on canvas | 125 |
| No. 2 | *Sunlight and Shadow: Study*, 1855, oil on paper mounted on canvas | 126 |
| No. 3 | *Pioneers of the Woods*, oil on paper mounted on canvas | 127 |
| No. 4 | *The Old Mill*, 1855, oil on canvas | 128 |
| No. 5 | *The Wetterhorn*, 1857, oil on canvas | 129 |
| No. 6 | *Lake Lucerne (Switzerland)*, 1858, oil on canvas | 131 |
| No. 7 | *Fishing Boats at Capri*, 1857, oil on paper mounted on canvas | 132 |
| No. 8 | *Capri*, c. 1857, oil on paper mounted on masonite | 133 |
| No. 9 | *Italian Costume Studies*, oil on paper mounted on board | 134 |
| No. 10 | *Costume Study of Seated Woman*, oil on paper mounted on board | 134 |
| No. 11 | *The Arch of Octavius (The Roman Fish Market)*, 1858, oil on canvas | 135 |
| No. 12 | *Wharf Scene with Ship at Dock*, oil on paper mounted on board | 136 |
| No. 13 | *Gosnold at Cuttyhunk, 1602*, 1858, oil on canvas | 137 |
| No. 14 | *The Marina Piccola, Capri*, 1859, oil on canvas | 151 |
| No. 15 | *Thunderstorm in the Rocky Mountains*, 1859, oil on canvas | 152 |
| No. 16 | *The Wolf River, Kansas*, c. 1859, oil on canvas | 153 |
| No. 17 | *Sweetwater River, Wind River Mountains, Wyoming Territory*, 1859, oil on board | 154 |
| No. 18 | *Nebraska [Territory]: Wasatch Mountains*, 1859, oil on paper mounted on board | 155 |
| No. 19 | *Wind River Country*, 1859, oil on paper mounted on board | 156 |
| No. 20 | *Surveyor's Wagon in the Rockies*, c. 1859, oil on paper mounted on masonite | 157 |
| No. 21 | *Mounted Trapper*, oil on paper | 158 |
| No. 22 | *Grizzly Bears*, c. 1859, oil on paper mounted on canvas | 159 |
| No. 23 | *Ox*, oil on cardboard | 160 |
| No. 24 | *Five Indians*, c. 1859, oil on paper | 161 |
| No. 25 | *Four Indians*, c. 1859, oil on paper | 162 |
| No. 26 | *Indians Traveling near Fort Laramie*, 1861, oil on canvas | 163 |
| No. 27 | *The Trappers' Camp*, 1861, oil on millboard | 164 |
| No. 28 | *Wind River Mountains, Nebraska Territory*, 1862, oil on composition board | 165 |
| No. 29 | *Sunlight and Shadow*, 1862, oil on canvas | 166 |
| No. 30 | *Guerrilla Warfare (Picket Duty in Virginia)*, 1862, oil on panel | 167 |
| No. 31 | *Fir Trees and Storm Clouds*, oil on paper mounted on canvas | 168 |
| No. 32 | *White Mountains, New Hampshire*, oil on paper | 169 |
| No. 33 | *Moat Mountain, Intervale, New Hampshire*, c. 1862, oil on canvas | 170 |
| No. 34 | *Haying, Conway Meadows*, 1864, oil on canvas | 191 |
| No. 35 | *White Mountains, New Hampshire*, 1863, oil on board | 192 |
| No. 36 | *The Mountain Brook*, 1863, oil on canvas | 193 |

| | | |
|---|---|---|
| No. 37 | *The Rocky Mountains, Lander's Peak*, 1863, oil on canvas | 195 |
| No. 38 | *On the Plains*, 1863, oil on paper mounted on board | 196 |
| No. 39 | *North Fork of the Platte, Nebraska*, 1863, oil on canvas | 197 |
| No. 40 | *Cho-looke, The Yosemite Fall*, 1864, oil on canvas | 198 |
| No. 41 | *Valley of the Yosemite*, 1864, oil on board | 199 |
| No. 42 | *Looking Down Yosemite Valley, California*, 1865, oil on canvas | 201 |
| No. 43 | *The Sierras near Lake Tahoe, California*, 1865, oil on panel | 202 |
| No. 44 | *Yosemite Valley*, 1866, oil on canvas | 203 |
| No. 45 | *Storm in the Rocky Mountains, Mt. Rosalie*, 1866, oil on canvas | 205 |
| No. 46 | *Yosemite Valley*, 1868, oil on canvas | 206 |
| No. 47 | *Sunset in the Yosemite Valley*, 1868, oil on canvas | 207 |
| No. 48 | *Among the Sierra Nevada Mountains, California*, 1868, oil on canvas | 209 |
| No. 49 | *Buffalo Trail: The Impending Storm*, 1869, oil on canvas | 210 |
| No. 50 | *The Oregon Trail*, 1869, oil on canvas | 211 |
| No. 51 | *Niagara*, c. 1869, oil on paper mounted on canvas | 212 |
| No. 52 | *Passing Storm over the Sierra Nevada*, 1870, oil on canvas | 213 |
| No. 53 | *Puget Sound, on the Pacific Coast*, 1870, oil on canvas | 214 |
| No. 54 | *Canoes*, oil on paper | 215 |
| No. 55 | *Stormy Lake Scene (Pacific Northwest)*, oil on paper mounted on board | 216 |
| No. 56 | *Snowcapped Mountains (Pacific Northwest)*, oil on paper mounted on board | 217 |
| No. 57 | *Snowcapped Mountains (Pacific Northwest)*, oil on paper mounted on board | 217 |
| No. 58 | *View of Donner Lake, California*, 1871–72, oil on paper | 233 |
| No. 59 | *Mountain Scene*, oil on cardboard | 234 |
| No. 60 | *Sunrise in the Sierras*, oil on paper mounted on board | 235 |
| No. 61 | *Cathedral Rocks, Yosemite Valley, California*, 1872, oil on paper | 236 |
| No. 62 | *Bridal Veil Falls, Yosemite*, c. 1871–73, oil on canvas | 237 |
| No. 63 | *Seal Rock, California*, c. 1872, oil on paper mounted on canvas | 238 |
| No. 64 | *Seal Rock*, c. 1872, oil on canvas | 239 |
| No. 65 | *The Great Trees, Mariposa Grove, California*, 1876, oil on canvas | 241 |
| No. 66 | *The Shore of the Turquoise Sea*, 1878, oil on canvas | 243 |
| No. 67 | *Nassau Harbor*, after 1877, oil on paper mounted on board | 244 |
| No. 68 | *The Last of the Buffalo*, 1888, oil on canvas | 259 |
| No. 69 | *Studies of Bison*, oil on paper | 260 |
| No. 70 | *Buffalo Head*, oil on paper mounted on board | 261 |
| No. 71 | *Canadian Rockies*, c. 1889, oil on canvas | 262 |
| No. 72 | *Wreck of the "Ancon" in Loring Bay, Alaska*, 1889, oil on paper mounted on panel | 263 |
| No. 73 | *Moose*, oil on cardboard | 264 |
| No. 74 | *Butterfly*, 1900, oil on paper with graphite pencil | 265 |
| No. 75 | *Butterfly*, 1900, oil on paper with graphite pencil | 265 |
| No. 76 | *Sunlight and Shadow*, published 1864, chromolithograph | 289 |
| No. 77 | *The Rocky Mountains, Lander's Peak*, published 1866, steel engraving | 290 |
| No. 78 | *The Rocky Mountains, Lander's Peak*, published 1869, chromolithograph | 291 |
| No. 79 | *Storm in the Rocky Mountains, Mt. Rosalie*, published 1869, chromolithograph | 292 |
| No. 80 | *The Domes of the Yosemite*, published 1870, chromolithograph | 293 |
| No. 81 | *The Last of the Buffalo*, copyrighted 1891, photogravure, hand-colored | 294 |

During the 1860s, Albert Bierstadt painted a series of heroic landscapes of the American West that today, a century and a half later, still command attention, captivate audiences, and demonstrate the hold of this mythic region on our collective imagination.

Bierstadt's visionary images of the Rocky Mountains, Sierra Nevada, and Yosemite Valley—conceived during a period of astonishing technological and social change—have continued to shape American consciousness and the perspectives from which we still understand many of the natural wonders of our country.

Thanks to The Brooklyn Museum's initiative in assembling this exhibition, the spectacular landscapes that gained Bierstadt his lasting fame, as well as lesser-known and newly discovered paintings of great beauty and importance, are brought together for the first time. This exhibition presents a unique opportunity to explore and to enjoy a body of extraordinary work that offers valuable insight toward an understanding of American civilization and of an exciting period in our nation's history.

Philip Morris is pleased to help present this tribute to the enduring vision of an artist whose sense of adventure and enterprise, wed to talent and the extraordinary capacity to reach an audience, are qualities that we think are as important to business as they are to the arts.

HAMISH MAXWELL
*Chairman and Chief Executive Officer*
*Philip Morris Companies Inc.*

The Henry Luce Foundation is pleased to support The Brooklyn Museum's project *Albert Bierstadt: Art & Enterprise*. This important exhibition and its publication bring together for the first time Bierstadt's most important works, focusing on the richest period of his career from the mid-1850s to the mid-1870s. The paintings included demonstrate a variety of subjects that may surprise those familiar only with Bierstadt's western landscapes.

The catalogue examines Bierstadt's works in the context of his reputation as a painter who not only produced some of the most important landscapes in the history of nineteenth-century American art, but also promoted himself and his works with remarkable skill. Both aspects of Bierstadt's career—his art and his enterprise—reflect the cultural and social values of the second half of the nineteenth century.

This project has been a felicitous partnership between Dr. Linda S. Ferber, Chief Curator and Curator of American Painting and Sculpture at The Brooklyn Museum, and Dr. Nancy K. Anderson, Assistant Curator of American Art at the National Gallery of Art in Washington, D.C. Their research will make a lasting contribution to the field.

I am delighted to greet this latest accomplishment of the program that the Luce Foundation began in 1982. Since that year, the foundation has made more than one hundred grants for scholarship in American art to some fifty museums for a total commitment of more than twenty million dollars. We are also pleased that this is the fourth project at The Brooklyn Museum in which we have participated.

HENRY LUCE III
*President*
*The Henry Luce Foundation, Inc.*

# PREFACE

By the time of his death in February 1902, Albert Bierstadt had become so completely identified with an older and, by implication, outmoded generation of artists that a contemporary painter remarked, "I did not know he was alive until I saw he had died." The large panoramic landscapes that had brought Bierstadt such success during the 1860s and 1870s had, in fact, passed from fashion long before the turn of the century.

Despite the steady decline in his reputation during the 1880s and 1890s, Bierstadt was not entirely ignored by those writing the early histories of American art. He was remembered, often begrudgingly, for the monumental western landscapes that had captured the nation's attention during the decade of the Civil War. Ironically, however, the paintings that actually sparked the twentieth-century revival of interest in Bierstadt were not the grand nationalistic landscapes of the American West, but rather the small plein air oil sketches that the artist had produced primarily as preparatory works.

As early as 1949, John I. H. Baur suggested that Bierstadt's oil sketches should be reevaluated, but it was not until 1963, when the Florence Lewison Gallery in New York mounted the first of three exhibitions devoted to the plein air sketches, that such a reappraisal began. In that same year, Richard Shafer Trump completed his pioneering dissertation on the artist. The first to attempt a comprehensive view of Bierstadt's entire career, Trump faced the difficult task of gathering the facts and sorting through the paintings for the first time.

In 1964 the Santa Barbara Museum of Art mounted the first major exhibition of Bierstadt's work and Gordon Hendricks published the first of several articles on the artist. Following up on Trump's groundbreaking work, Hendricks spent a decade gathering information and locating paintings. In the early 1970s, his efforts culminated in a traveling exhibition (1972) organized by the Amon Carter Museum and in *Albert Bierstadt: Painter of the American West* (1974), the second study to consider the artist's career in its entirety. Hendricks's biography of the artist included the most comprehensive collection of illustrations of Bierstadt's work to date and a valuable listing of paintings by the artist in American public collections.

As interest in nineteenth-century American landscape painting grew during the 1970s, valuable contributions to Bierstadt studies were made by Elizabeth Lindquist-Cock ("Stereoscopic Photography and the Western Paintings of Albert Bierstadt," 1970), Barbara Novak ("Grand Opera and the Still Small Voice," 1971), Rena Coen ("The Last of the Buffalo," 1973), and Donald Strong ("Albert Bierstadt, Painter of the American West," 1975).

In 1981 Catherine Campbell published a valuable study of Bierstadt's White Mountain paintings and Matthew Baigell included a thoughtful essay on the development of the artist's style in his book *Albert Bierstadt*. Two years later, Alexander Gallery in New York mounted an exhibition of forty works by Bierstadt and published a catalogue with an introductory essay by Gerald Carr. In 1983 Patricia Trenton and Peter Hassrick included a chapter on Bierstadt in their publication *The Rocky Mountains: A Vision for Artists in the Nineteenth Century*. Nancy Anderson completed her dissertation on the artist in 1985 and discussed Bierstadt's Yosemite paintings in an exhibition catalogue published the following year by the Timken Art Gallery in San Diego. Donald Keyes took a similarly focused look at Bierstadt's paintings of Yellowstone in an article published in 1986. Bierstadt's international activities were also discussed in articles by Allan Pringle ("Albert Bierstadt in Canada," 1985) and Gerald Carr ("Albert Bierstadt, Big Trees, and the British: A Log of Many Anglo-American Ties," 1986).

Renewed interest in Frederic Edwin Church, the master of the panoramic landscape and Bierstadt's contemporary, has also served Bierstadt scholarship. David Huntington's insightful study and recent publications by Franklin Kelly, Gerald Carr, Katherine Manthorne, and others have done much to enrich our understanding of the cultural milieu in which both Church and Bierstadt worked. Important thematic exhibitions, including *American Paradise: The World of the Hudson River School* (Metropolitan Museum of Art, 1987), have also placed Bierstadt's work in historical and cultural contexts that confirm the richness of his imagery.

Almost two decades have passed, however, since the last museum exhibition devoted solely to the work of this artist. During these years, interest in Bierstadt's art and career has grown steadily. The varied researches noted above, the appearance of new documents, and, especially, the rediscovery of important works underscore the timeliness of the present exhibition. *Albert Bierstadt: Art & Enterprise* gathers together a full range of the artist's work, including a number of paintings that have not been seen publicly in this century, so that the measure of Bierstadt's achievement may be newly assessed and appreciated. The title of the exhibition reflects our interest not only in Bierstadt's paintings, but also in the inventive strategies that the artist developed to promote those paintings during a long and active career. Both are central to a full understanding of Bierstadt's place in the history of American art.

The core of the publication accompanying this exhibition is an extensive illustrated and documented chronology of Bierstadt's life and career drawn from primary sources including letters, diaries, government publications, and official records, as well as newspaper and journal articles. It is hoped that this data not only will provide a full profile of an active life and career, but also will correct a number of often repeated errors of fact and date. The chronology is divided into five sections corresponding to the main periods in Bierstadt's career. Each of the sections is introduced by a short essay highlighting the most important events and key works of that period. Colorplates illustrating those works in the exhibition that fall within each chronological division conclude each section. The plates are accompanied by brief quotations from contemporary critics and observers; some of the excerpts testify to the widespread popular appeal of the paintings, while others demonstrate the sharp divisions of critical opinion inspired by some of Bierstadt's most famous works. This central section of the book is preceded by two interpretive essays, dealing with the dynamics of the rise and fall of Bierstadt's reputation and with the genesis and significance of the major western landscapes. An essay on Bierstadt's involvement with printmaking, including an illustrated and annotated checklist of all known engravings, chromolithographs, woodcuts, and illustrations after works by the artist produced during his lifetime, follows the chronology. Through these works, Bierstadt reached his widest audience. Two appendices are also included: the first reproduces the catalogue Bierstadt published when he mounted New Bedford's first art exhibition in 1858; the second reprints in their entirety six letters (originally published in the *Golden Era*) by Fitz Hugh Ludlow describing his overland journey with Bierstadt in 1863. Both the catalogue and the letters have been relatively inaccessible to scholars until now.

Although Bierstadt has attracted increased scholarly attention during the last decade, much work remains to be done. The authors hope that this volume will provide a sound base upon which future Bierstadt scholarship may be built.

# DIRECTORS' FOREWORD

The participating museums are proud to offer this landmark exhibition to a wide audience on both coasts. Organized by The Brooklyn Museum, in association with the National Gallery of Art, the exhibition was initially inspired by the acquisition by Brooklyn of a great painting, *Storm in the Rocky Mountains, Mt. Rosalie. Albert Bierstadt: Art & Enterprise* appraises the career of one of the most important landscape painters of the nineteenth century. The exhibition offers an opportunity to study familiar works by the artist in a new context and to discover brilliant paintings never before exhibited in this century.

The Brooklyn Museum has a long tradition of organizing important exhibitions on the history of nineteenth-century American painting. The Museum presented the first modern reappraisals of artists Eastman Johnson (1940), William Sidney Mount (1942), John Quidor (1942), Theodore Robinson (1946), John F. Peto (1950), James Hamilton (1966), and William T. Richards (1973). Major movements in painting have also been investigated in pioneering exhibitions including *Leaders of American Impressionism: Mary Cassatt, Childe Hassam, John H. Twachtman, J. Alden Weir* (1937), *The Eight* (1944), and *The New Path: Ruskin and the American Pre-Raphaelites* (1985). For many years, the National Gallery's exhibition program was devoted almost exclusively to monographic shows on American artists; and especially since the coming of the Rockefeller Collection, San Francisco has played an important role in the appreciation of American painting on the West Coast. All have inspired further research, contributing to the growing body of scholarship dealing with the rich and complex history of American art.

Linda S. Ferber, Chief Curator and Curator of American Painting and Sculpture at The Brooklyn Museum, and Nancy K. Anderson, Assistant Curator of American Art at the National Gallery of Art, have traveled the country over the past four years to assess Bierstadt's work. The results surely represent the most comprehensive and exhaustive attempt to date to evaluate the artist in terms of his goals and achievements as well as his place in American art. The National Gallery's extraordinary conservation and research facilities have also played a key role in this effort. We extend to Dr. Ferber and Dr. Anderson admiring gratitude and appreciation for this important exhibition and its equally major publication.

The magnificent generosity of the Philip Morris Companies Inc. will ensure that the exhibition and its programs are made available to a wide national audience. The farsighted support of the Luce Foundation for Scholarship in American Art was fundamental for exhibition research and travel and for the realization of this important publication; the support of the National Endowment for the Arts and the National Endowment for the Humanities was also essential to the Museum's undertaking the project. We are also grateful for the support of the New York State Council on the Arts and Mr. and Mrs. Wilbur L. Ross, Jr.

ROBERT T. BUCK
*Director*
*The Brooklyn Museum*

HARRY S. PARKER III
*Director*
*The Fine Arts Museums of San Francisco*

J. CARTER BROWN
*Director*
*National Gallery of Art*

# LENDERS TO THE EXHIBITION

Albright-Knox Art Gallery, Buffalo, New York
Amon Carter Museum, Fort Worth, Texas
Berry-Hill Galleries, Inc., New York
Birmingham Museum of Art, Birmingham, Alabama
The Brooklyn Museum, Brooklyn, New York
Buffalo Bill Historical Center, Cody, Wyoming
The Butler Institute of American Art, Youngstown, Ohio
The Century Association, New York
The Cleveland Museum of Art, Cleveland, Ohio
Ryan M. Cooper
The Corcoran Gallery of Art, Washington, D.C.
The Currier Gallery of Art, Manchester, New Hampshire
The Detroit Institute of Arts, Detroit, Michigan
Dr. Howard P. Diamond
Duke University Museum of Art, Durham, North Carolina
Elliott Galleries, New York
The Fine Arts Museums of San Francisco, San Francisco, California
Jo Ann and Julian Ganz, Jr.
Garzoli Gallery, San Rafael, California
The Thomas Gilcrease Institute of American History and Art, Tulsa, Oklahoma
The Haggin Museum, Stockton, California
High Museum of Art, Atlanta, Georgia
Manoogian Collection, Grosse Pointe, Michigan
The Metropolitan Museum of Art, New York
Gil Michaels
Mr. and Mrs. Leonard L. Milberg
Milwaukee Art Museum, Milwaukee, Wisconsin
Museum of Fine Arts, Boston, Massachusetts
National Gallery of Art, Washington, D.C.
National Museum of American Art, Smithsonian Institution, Washington, D.C.
National Museum of American History, Smithsonian Institution, Washington, D.C.
New Britain Museum of American Art, New Britain, Connecticut
The New-York Historical Society, New York
The New York Public Library, New York
The Newark Museum, Newark, New Jersey
North Carolina Museum of Art, Raleigh, North Carolina
The Oakland Museum, Oakland, California
The Phelan Collection
Private collections
The San Antonio Museum Association, San Antonio, Texas
The Saint Louis Art Museum, Saint Louis, Missouri
Timken Art Gallery, San Diego, California
The Warner Collection of Gulf States Paper Corporation, Tuscaloosa, Alabama
The Whaling Museum, New Bedford, Massachusetts
Edward T. Wilson
Nicholas Wyeth
Yale University Art Gallery, New Haven, Connecticut

# ACKNOWLEDGMENTS

From the outset, *Albert Bierstadt: Art & Enterprise* has been a collaborative effort. As co-curators of the exhibition, we welcome the opportunity to acknowledge the generous assistance of the many curators, collectors, dealers, and scholars who opened their files, galleries, and homes to us as we searched for paintings and information. Our initial thanks go to the three institutions whose support and encouragement allowed the project to go forward: The Brooklyn Museum, The Fine Arts Museums of San Francisco, and the National Gallery of Art. For enlightened and generous financial support, we are equally grateful to Philip Morris Companies Inc.; The Henry Luce Foundation, Inc.; the National Endowment for the Humanities; the National Endowment for the Arts; the New York State Council on the Arts; and Mr. and Mrs. Wilbur L. Ross, Jr. Finally, our special gratitude is extended to the fifty-three lenders, whose generosity in sharing their treasures with the public has made the exhibition and catalogue possible.

At The Brooklyn Museum, we are grateful to Robert T. Buck, Director; Roy R. Eddey, Deputy Director; and Serena Rattazzi, Associate Director, for their encouragement and unfailing administrative support. Larry K. Clark, Curatorial Administrator, has been an invaluable ally, both in the planning of the exhibition and in the preparation of the catalogue. The editorial expertise of Joanna Ekman and Elaine Koss as well as the advice of Rena Zurofsky have been critical to the successful publication of this volume. Paul Anbinder of Hudson Hills Press has been unstinting in his support of the book, which has been beautifully designed by Martin Lubin and Mariana Francis. We must also thank members of the Department of American Paintings and Sculpture—Barbara Dayer Gallati, Teresa Carbone, Barbara H. Millstein, and Elizabeth Murphy—as well as Principal Librarian Deirdre Lawrence and her able staff for assistance with endless research and reference questions. Kenneth Moser, Chief Conservator, has provided advice and information—not only about the physical condition of many works examined, but also about Bierstadt's working methods—that have greatly enriched our study of the artist. In the Development Office, Vice Director Karen Putnam and Managers Robin Rosenbluth and Eileen Lanihan have worked closely with the curators and the venues in securing the funding necessary to mount a project of this scale. Sally Williams, Assistant Director for Public Information, has coordinated efforts to promote the exhibition and its programs with expertise and diplomacy. Chief Exhibition Designer Jeffrey Strean has most ably planned the installation, while Collections Manager Cathryn Anders and the art handlers and technicians have mounted the exhibition with their usual skill and efficiency. Chief Photographer Patricia Laymon Bazelon and her staff have been unfailing in meeting myriad needs. Deborah Schwartz, Missy Sullivan, Diana Linden, and Sonnet Takahisa are to be thanked for their excellent work on public and school programs associated with the exhibition. Registrars Elizabeth Reynolds, Tamra Yost, and the late Barbara LaSalle planned the tour of the exhibition with great care.

At The Fine Arts Museums of San Francisco, we gratefully acknowledge the support of Harry S. Parker III, Director, and Steven A. Nash, Associate Director and Chief Curator. In the

Department of American Art, we extend our special thanks to Marc Simpson and Sally Mills, who brought paintings to our attention and shared with us their research on the many works by Bierstadt in the permanent collection. We are grateful as well for the assistance of Paula March, Manager of Corporate Relations, and Jim Wright, Chief Conservator of Paintings. For their assistance with the installation of the exhibition, we thank Debra Pughe, Connie King, William White, Virginia Kelly, and the technical crew.

At the National Gallery of Art, we extend our thanks to J. Carter Brown, Director, and Roger Mandle, Deputy Director, for their early and continued support. Nicolai Cikovsky, Jr., Franklin Kelly, Deborah Chotner, and Charles Brock of the American Art Department have assisted us in countless ways during the five years the exhibition and catalogue have been in preparation. Elizabeth Weil, Corporate Relations Officer, provided enthusiastic support and expert assistance from the beginning. D. Dodge Thompson and Trish Waters of the Exhibition Department have been unfailingly thorough in seeing to the myriad details associated with planning for the exhibition. For their care and expertise in installing the exhibition, we are indebted to Gaillard Ravenel, Mark A. Leithauser, Gordon Anson, John Olson, Linda Heinrich, Barbara Keyes, and Kathleen Buckalew. For their help in locating even the most obscure references, we extend our thanks to the entire library staff and especially to Thomas McGill, Jr., Ted T. Dalziel, Jr., Frances P. Lederer, and Lamia Doumato. In the Photographic Services Department, our special thanks go to Richard Amt, Bill Wilson, Philip Charles, Richard Carafelli, James Locke, Jose A. Naranjo, and Desiree Miller. In the Slide Library, we thank Bill Taylor and Mary S. Wassermann for anticipating our needs before we did. Susan Arensberg and Kathleen Walsh-Piper of the Education Department have assisted with teacher and public programs. Michelle Fondas, Assistant Registrar, John Poliszuk, Andrew Krieger, and their expert crew of art handlers have transported, received, and hung the paintings with exemplary care. Katie Ziglar, of the Information Office, has answered numerous public inquiries on our behalf. Ross Merrill, Head of Conservation, has offered invaluable assistance throughout the project, sharing with us the results of his ongoing study of Bierstadt's painting technique.

We are deeply indebted to our professional colleagues who directed our attention to important paintings, photographs, and documents. In particular we wish to thank: Jeremy Adamson, Michael R. Aldrich, Nancy E. Allyn, Gail Anderson, M.D., Marjorie Arkelian, Joanne Avant, Kevin Avery, Lynne Baer, Matthew Baigell, Joseph Armstrong Baird, Jr., Deborah Balken, Lydia Barker, Joan Barnes, Susan Barnes, Madeline Fidell Beaufort, Kathie Bennewitz, Barbara Beroza, Bruce Bieneman, Jennifer A. Bienstock, Annette Blaugrund, Doreen Bolger, Lynn Bonfield, Anne Françoise Bonnardel, Morton C. Bradley, Jr., Arthur J. Breton, Elizabeth Broun, Cheryl A. Brutvan, Catherine H. Campbell, Gerald L. Carr, Joanne D. Chaison, Cecilia Chin, Helen Cooper, James P. Crain, Barbara Smillie Curtis, Paul Cyr, Daphne Deeds, Carole Drachler, Janice Driesbach, Stephen R. Edidin, Lisa B. Eckerman, Bill Eloe, Elizabeth Evans, Betsy Fahlman, Susan Farr, Lois Fink, David M. Forgang, Abigail Booth Gerdts, William H. Gerdts, Barbara K. Gibbs, Linda Jones Gibbs, Susan W. Glenn, William H. Goetzmann, Alden R. Gordon, Barbara Groseclose, Anne Halpern, John Hand, Jonathan P. Harding, Alfred C. Harrison, Jr., Dare Myers Hartwell, Peter H. Hassrick, Cheryl Hauser, Louis C. Hawes, Barry Heisler, Christine Hennessey, Erica E. Hirschler, Martha Hoppin, Holly Hotchner, Perry Houston, John K. Howat, Mary Itsell, Anthony F. Janson, Harvey Jones, Nan and Roy Farrington Jones, Alexander Katlan, Donald Keyes, Joni Kinsey, Anthony Kirk, Allan Kollar, Elizabeth and Stephen Kornhauser, Diane Wetmore Kotowski, Richard C. Kugler, Gary Kurutz, Judy Larson, Laura C. Luckey, Patricia M. Lynagh, Ann Madonia, Mary E. Manion, Katherine E. Manthorne, Garnett M. McCoy, Howard

Merritt, Michael P. Mezzatesta, Betty Monkman, Anne Morand, Caroline Mortimer, Ed Muno, Amy R. W. Myers, Milo Naeve, Kate Nearpass, Edward J. Nygren, Carol M. Osborne, Lloyd Ostendorf, Wendy Owens, Peter E. Palmquist, Helen Mar Parkin, Sara Parrott, Vernon Pascal, Sandra Phillips, Ruth N. Post, Allan Pringle, Jan Seidler Ramirez, Jane Reed, the late Gary A. Reynolds, Bruce Robertson, Betsy Rosasco, Talbot B. Ruhstaller, Rachel Sadinsky, Patricia Sanders, William L. Schaeffer, Ruta Schuller, Ellen Schwartz, Nancy Rivard Shaw, Ellen Simak, Louis H. Smaus, Tom Smith, Theodore E. Stebbins, Jr., Katharine F. Stewart, Susan E. Strickler, Donald S. Strong, Bonita N. Sweet, Joyce M. Szabo, William S. Talbot, Ellen Tenentes, Nicki Thiras, Judith E. Throm, Ellen Todd, Arthur C. Townsend, Patricia Trenton, Carol Troyen, William H. Truettner, Evan and Brenda Turner, Peter Vogel, Leonard A. Walle, Wendy Watson, H. Barbara Weinberg, Ila Weiss, Thurman Wilkins, Cumbee Wilson, Barbara Wolanin, James L. Yarnall, Alice Yelen, and Judith K. Zilczer.

Many private collectors, museum colleagues, galleries, and auction houses have assisted us in our search for paintings and documents. We are especially grateful to: Alexander Acevedo, Warren Adelson, Mr. and Mrs. Randolph J. Agley, C. Douglass Alves, William N. Banks, Fred Bernaski, James Berry-Hill, Michael Botwinick, Mr. and Mrs. John C. Bullard, Russell Burke, Jay Cantor, Phil Carll, Guido Castelli, Bruce N. Chambers, the late Robert Coggins, M.D., Ted Cooper, James L. Coran, Barbara Curtis, Carl David, Peter H. Davidson, Mark Davis, Roy and Cecily Davis, John Driscoll, Beverly G. Dunne, Michael Dwyer, Peter Fairbanks, Stuart P. Feld, Sandra Feldman, Lawrence A. Fleischman, Debra Force, Jeffrey Fraenkel, Roger Friedman, Michael Frost, John H. Garzoli, Sanford Gifford, M.D., Florence Glickman, Ed Goldfield, Ralph Gosse, Eldon Grupp, David Henry, Judith Hernstadt, Frederick D. Hill, Ay Whang Hsia, Mary N. Hunter, Vance Jordan, Paul Kossey, Nancy Little, Donald Loker, Mary Lublin, Mr. and Mrs. Thomas Mann, James Maroney, Robert Mayo, Lee R. Minton, M.D., M. P. Naud, Jon Nelson, Walter Nelson-Rees, Bettina A. Norton, Bernard Osher, Peter Rathbone, Christina Ryan, Robert D. Schonfeld, M. R. Schweitzer, Edward Shein, Ira Spanierman, Dr. and Mrs. Jacob Y. Terner, Mr. and Mrs. John Turner, Paul H. Viets, Abbott W. Vose, Robert C. Vose, Jr., Robert C. Vose III, Edward Weekes, Edward Weekes, Jr., Joe Weider, Eric Widing, Mrs. Donald Winbigler, the late Catharine Morris Wright, and Richard York. Joyce Randall Edwards and Evan Hopkins Turner deserve special thanks for allowing us to study the Bierstadt family documents, photographs, and memorabilia in their keeping, as does Alfred Hummerich for making the Bierstadt album in his collection accessible to us.

At crucial stages during the course of the project, we enjoyed the able assistance of several museum interns, research assistants, and volunteers. For their energetic efforts on our behalf, we wish to thank Joan Blume, Elizabeth Chew, Diane Dillon, Mary Ellen Connor Fraser, Michael Godfrey, Megan Granda, Nanni Kaps, Lisa Mariam, and Andrew Walker. Our special thanks to Merl M. Moore, Jr., who cheerfully tracked down numerous obscure references, searched for photographs, and shared with us his comprehensive files on Bierstadt's contemporaries.

# LIST OF ABBREVIATIONS

AAA
Archives of American Art, Smithsonian Institution, Washington, D.C.

*Alta*, San Francisco
Title varies: *Alta California*, *Daily Alta California*

*Boston Transcript*
Title varies: *Boston Daily Evening Transcript*, *Boston Evening Transcript*, *Boston Transcript*, *Daily Evening Transcript*

*Bulletin*, San Francisco
*Daily Evening Bulletin*

Corcoran Archives
Corcoran Gallery of Art Archives, Washington, D.C.

CPR Archives
Canadian Pacific Railway Corporate Archives, Montreal

Downs Collection
Joseph Downs Manuscript and Microfilm Collection, Henry Francis du Pont Winterthur Museum, Winterthur, Del.

Edwards Collection
Joyce Randall Edwards Collection, Dobbs Ferry, N.Y.

FVH Papers
Ferdinard V. Hayden Papers, National Archives, Washington, D.C.

GH Papers
Gordon Hendricks Papers, Archives of American Art, Smithsonian Institution, Washington, D.C.

Hannover Album
Bierstadt Album, private collection, Hannover, Germany

Hayden Survey Records
Records of the Geological Survey; Records of the Hayden Survey. Letters Received 1871–79, National Archives, Washington, D.C.

Hayes Presidential Center
Rutherford B. Hayes Presidential Center, Fremont, Ohio

HL Papers
Henry Lewis Papers, William L. Clements Library, University of Michigan, Ann Arbor

*Mercury*, New Bedford
*Daily Mercury*

NAD
National Academy of Design, New York

National Archives
National Archives, Washington, D.C.

*New Bedford Standard*
*New Bedford Evening Standard*

*NY Herald*
*New York Herald*

*NY Leader*
*New York Leader*

*NY Times*
*New York Times*

*NY Tribune*
*New York Tribune*

*Post*, New York
*Evening Post*

ROM/MFA Corresp.
Correspondence of Rosalie Osborne Mayer and Mrs. Ross Taggart, Museum of Fine Arts, Boston

SRG Letters
Sanford Robinson Gifford Letters, Archives of American Art, Smithsonian Institution, Washington, D.C.

Turner Collection
Evan Hopkins Turner Collection, Cleveland, Ohio

# ALBERT BIERSTADT

## Art & Enterprise

# *Albert Bierstadt*

## THE HISTORY OF A REPUTATION

LINDA S. FERBER

FEW NINETEENTH-CENTURY American artists enjoyed as meteoric a rise to fame as Albert Bierstadt did during his short heyday in the 1860s. Then, as now, Bierstadt's dramatic panoramas of the American West captured the public imagination and commanded record prices. After these initial boom years, however, his reputation suffered an equally rapid and public decline. By the time of his death in 1902, Bierstadt's work had nearly been forgotten. His passing prompted art historian and critic William Howe Downes to take a thoughtful look back at the art world in which Bierstadt had conducted a long and eventful career. Downes described the rapidly changing styles of landscape painting that had, each in its turn, successively dominated American taste during the turbulent decades of Bierstadt's activity. "It is a far cry from Dusseldorf to Barbizon," he wrote, "and a still farther cry from Dusseldorf to Giverny: art history is made so rapidly in these swift times."[1] The times were "swift," indeed, and during Bierstadt's most productive years, from the sixties until the end of the eighties, the artist developed inventive strategies to promote his work and his reputation in the face of rising competition from newer styles and European masters. Bierstadt's career, conducted on a grand scale, especially dramatizes some of the issues and problems that confronted an entire generation of American artists as they grappled with an international market and with patrons of increasingly cosmopolitan taste.

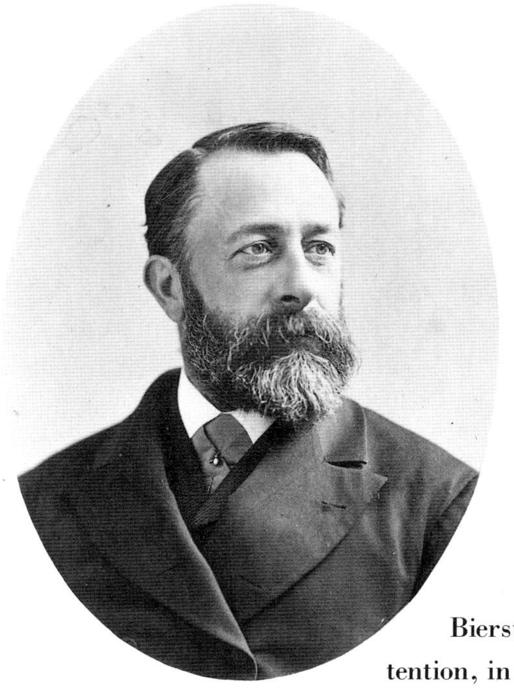

Figure 1

Watkins Yosemite Art Gallery, San Francisco. *Albert Bierstadt*, c. 1873. Cabinet card. Rutherford B. Hayes Presidential Center, Fremont, Ohio.

Bierstadt's successes and disappointments attracted wide attention, in no small part because of the artist's own strong instinct for self-promotion. Indeed, Bierstadt's career is instructive not only as a chapter in art history, but also as an example of the American success story, chronicling the rise of an ambitious and indefatigable self-made man. At the height of his fame, Bierstadt's rags-to-riches saga was almost as captivating to his audience as his paintings.[2] While his model and early rival, the American-born Frederic Church (1826–1900), scion of a prominent Hartford family and also a brilliant self-promoter, was perceived as "fortune's favorite from the beginning," Bierstadt's personal triumph over early adversity was always deemed central to his character and achievement.[3] In fact, he was an energetic businessman, whose candor in seeking not only professional recognition, but also the material rewards of success, challenged many contemporary conventional pieties about the artist's life as remote from the world of commerce. Bierstadt's interests were not confined to his career as a landscape painter. Over the years, his business ventures ranged from participation in his brothers' photographic endeavors; land and mining speculation; investment in the development of an "acetylene invention"; and his own invention, the Expansion Railway Car (p. 257). At Bierstadt's death, the National Academy of Design in New York paid tribute to him as a man of large ideas, "ambition," and "boldness."[4] Decades before, the critic James Jackson Jarves had recognized that Bierstadt's (and Church's) special genius for landscape was fueled not only by talent and artistic ambition, but also by "speculating blood" and the "zest of gain."[5] Indeed, this high-profile entrepreneurial persona has figured as prominently in the history of Bierstadt's reputation as the larger forces of change affecting both styles of painting and American responses to the national landscape in the second half of the nineteenth century.

## A Self-Made Man

Albert Bierstadt's humble origins were widely noted in his time. His father, a German cooper, emigrated with his family to New Bedford, Massachusetts, from Prussia in 1832, when Albert was just two years old. As a youth, Bierstadt was permitted to pursue artistic interests, although he gave no hint of any remarkable talent in that direction; on the contrary, we are told, he displayed a businesslike "probity, application, and mastery of practical affairs" that gave his family ample reason to believe that he would succeed in more "remunerative" occupations.[6] In fact, through application of these natural talents to the "precarious" livelihood of an artist, Bierstadt would succeed financially, professionally, and socially far beyond the fondest dreams of his immigrant parents.

Though we know little of his earliest years, from first record Bierstadt seems to have manifested an unusual degree of industry. By 1851, having himself mastered only the most basic rudiments of image making, he was already offering lessons in monochromatic painting at "$3 for 24 hours."[7] The following year, Bierstadt contracted with artist George Harvey (1801–1878) to tour the latter's "Dissolving Views" of American scenery "illustrating the progress of our country." Harvey's landscape images, painted on glass, were projected at a grand scale (fifteen by seventeen feet) in a theater setting by means of a device called a Drummond Light. Admission was twenty-five cents (children half-price), and the New Bedford hall where the Views were shown was "nightly thronged with admiring spectators." Pamphlets describing the pictures were sold for twelve and a half cents. Advertised by Bierstadt as "the greatest exhibition of the kind ever offered to the American public," the Dissolving Views enterprise taught valuable lessons of showmanship the artist would apply with success a decade later in his "Great Picture" exhibitions.[8]

In 1853, with the modest proceeds of these endeavors, Bierstadt went to Düsseldorf for three years of highly productive study. The academy in this German city on the Rhine was then the nucleus of a famous international artists' colony. The manner of painting taught there was especially admired by Americans for its technical strengths: "good composition, accurate drawing, and faithful and elaborate finish."[9] Although Bierstadt was not enrolled as a formal student at the academy, he learned a great deal from fellow artists in Düsseldorf. Eastman Johnson (1824–1906), Emanuel Leutze (1816–1868), and Worthington Whittredge (1820–1910) were among the many Americans who preceded Bierstadt there; the last two were still in residence when he arrived. Bierstadt's remarkable industry and ambition were noted by Whittredge (with whom he shared a studio) and by fellow student Henry Lewis (1819–1904), who thought him "a noble fellow, and one who deserves to succeed, for no one ever worked harder, or against more adverse circumstances than he did." "You have a striking example in him, of what travel can do for a man," he continued, writing in 1858 after Bierstadt's return to New Bedford. "When he first came here some 4 years ago he was the most timid, awkward, unpolished specimen of a Yankee you can well imagine. Now I expect he has the manners and bearing of a well bred gentleman. He will make his mark in the world of Art, and for this reason that he has no other aim, pursuit, pleasure but *to paint*."[10] The vivid plein air studies and paintings based upon Bierstadt's European experience are striking evidence of that pleasure and of his rapid and complete mastery of his craft.

Soon after his return from Düsseldorf, Bierstadt and a local New Bedford businessman and patron, John Hopkins, organized an ambitious exhibition of some one hundred fifty paintings by American and European artists (see Appendix A). The project was both a gesture of support for the arts and a financial speculation, with an admission charge of twenty-five cents. Hopkins and Bierstadt served as sales agents, and Bierstadt himself was the largest exhibitor, with fourteen paintings of German, Swiss, and Italian subjects.

While the exhibition proved a commercial failure, the venture brought Bierstadt and his work to the attention of artists, collectors, and dealers in Boston, New York, and Philadelphia.[11] New Bedford was becoming too limited a stage for Bierstadt, and like many ambitious young Americans, he headed west—in search of not material wealth, but visual riches. In the spring of 1859, he departed on an adventurous trip, the first of many, to the Rocky Mountains. This pivotal journey provided the critical visual and emotional experiences that launched his career as Bierstadt enthusiastically embraced the role of the artist-explorer.

Soon after his return east in September 1859, Bierstadt moved to what was then the acknowledged center of the American art world, New York City, and to the hub of that community, the new Tenth Street Studio Building (Fig. 2). There he furnished a studio with his remarkable plein air oil sketches (Nos. 18–25) and "a great number of Indian trophies" and began to lay claim to the subject matter that would make him famous.[12] As he rapidly produced an impressive series of large and small paintings based upon his recent western experience, Bierstadt also manifested a well-developed talent for capturing and holding the public's attention. He was adept, as well, at the assiduous cultivation of patronage, realizing early on that big pictures often attracted big patrons.[13]

## The "Great Picture"

Bierstadt's fame and fortune would be based upon a series of panoramas of the American West shown widely through the 1860s, beginning with the now-unlocated *Base of the Rocky Mountains, Laramie Peak*, 1860 (see Fig. 3), followed by *The Rocky Mountains, Lander's Peak*, 1863 (No. 37), and including *Mount Hood, Oregon*, 1865 (Fig. 55), *Looking Down Yosemite Valley, California*, 1865 (No. 42), *Storm in the Rocky Mountains, Mt. Rosalie*, 1866 (No. 45), *The Domes of the Yosemite*, 1867 (Fig. 58), and *Among the Sierra Nevada Mountains, California*, 1868 (No. 48). These large landscape paintings, like those of Frederic Church, represented a brilliant orchestration of the landscape vocabulary of the Romantic sublime and capitalized upon public curiosity about the geography of the New World.

The convention of the "Great Picture"—a very large painting exhibited publicly and conceived in subject to appeal to a wide spectrum of popular taste—was well established in America by midcentury. In the conception, presentation, and promotion of their "Great Pictures,"

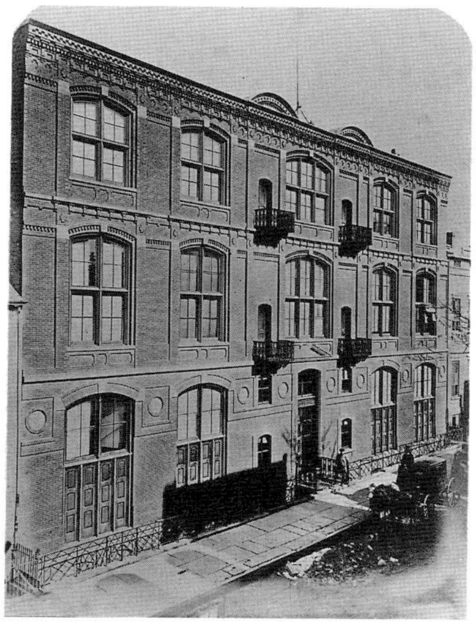

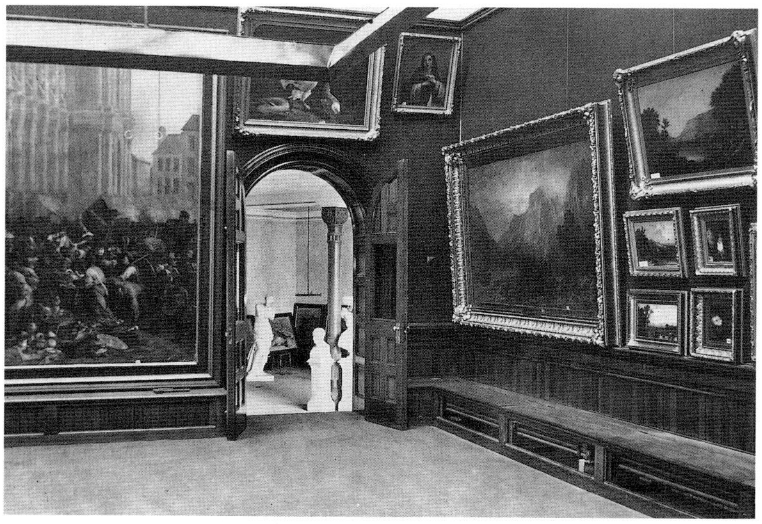

Figure 2 *(left)*

*Studio Building, 15 West 10th Street, New York City* (demolished), 1857. Photograph. Octagon Museum, Prints and Drawings Collection, The American Architectural Foundation, Washington, D.C.

Figure 3 *(right)*

*Fine Arts Academy. Southwest Corner Galleries*, c. 1887. Photograph published in *The Buffalo Library and Its Building* (Buffalo, N.Y.: 1887). Bierstadt's painting *Base of the Rocky Mountains, Laramie Peak* (unlocated) is visible near the door on the right.

Bierstadt and Church, like other artists, employed many of the devices and strategies associated with the diorama and the moving panorama, highly popular forms of public entertainment. These presentations combined large-scale scenery with dramatic effects of light in a kind of precinematic theater experience. In some instances, Bierstadt and Church exhibited their "Great Pictures" independently of the National Academy of Design and the regular studio receptions as profit-making ventures, depending upon paid advertising, press coverage, and other forms of promotion to attract an audience. That audience paid admission to see enormous and highly detailed oil paintings, sometimes exhibited in darkened rooms under controlled lighting conditions that enhanced the optical impact. The public was also invited to purchase and read pamphlets offering explanatory and interpretive texts to complement the imagery and, frequently, to purchase reproductions after the paintings by subscription. These exhibitions—like the moving panoramas—frequently traveled to other cities after opening in New York, establishing national (and international) reputations for the artists and providing financial returns as well.[14]

*The Rocky Mountains, Lander's Peak* (No. 37) was the first of Bierstadt's "Great Pictures" to be promoted with all the trappings—single-picture exhibition, pamphlet, engraving, and tour—used so successfully by Church. The huge popular success of this painting instantly placed Bierstadt in a league with his illustrious rival. A student of Thomas Cole (1801–1848), Church had established a reputation as a brilliant painter of North American landscapes by the late 1840s and had gone on to claim South America with *Heart of the Andes*, 1859 (Fig. 40), and the Far North with *Icebergs*, 1861 (Dallas Museum of Fine Arts). His celebrity status, record sale prices, and financial return from "Great Picture" exhibitions offered a powerful model of professional and material success.[15] While Church's "Great Pictures" of the 1850s and 1860s represented the crowning achievement of a long and successful career, however, Bierstadt's monumental 1863 painting of an entirely different kind of subject was a bold and aggressive bid for public attention by a relative newcomer.

First with *Base of the Rocky Mountains, Laramie Peak*, and then with *The Rocky Mountains, Lander's Peak*, Bierstadt effectively appropriated the American West, tapping public curiosity and excitement about these remote national territories. This interest was fueled, even during the apprehensive years of the Civil War, by the powerful idea of Manifest Destiny. The prevalent belief that Americans were divinely ordained masters of the continent lent special significance to Bierstadt's choice of subjects. The direct correlation between the imagery of his "Great Pictures" and the promise of Manifest Destiny was amply demonstrated by the rhetoric these paintings stimulated. Bierstadt's own pamphlet for *The Rocky Mountains, Lander's Peak* concluded with the hope that, upon the painting's foreground plain, "a city, populated by our descendants, may rise, and in its art-galleries this picture may eventually find a resting-place." The *Leader* expressed the opinion that "He who lays his ear to the wild grass may perhaps hear the distant tramp, not of the buffaloes, but of civilization, coming like an army with banners." The power and appeal of Bierstadt's "Great Pictures" of the 1860s were perhaps best summarized in this simple newspaper endorsement of *The Domes of the Yosemite* in 1867: "We recommend our readers to go at once and see the work. They will feel that the world is progressing and the Americans are a great people." Popular praise had so escalated with each large western painting that, with the debut of *The Domes of the Yosemite* just four years after that of *The Rocky Mountains, Lander's Peak*, the same enthusiast could claim: "This picture will advance Mr. Bierstadt's reputation still more. He is ascending the throne, and [with] a few more strides, he will seat himself as the monarch of landscape painters."[16]

## The Boom Years

The 1860s, when Bierstadt produced his series of much-lauded "Great Pictures," were the years of his greatest professional and financial success. By the summer of 1863, Leutze informed friends in Düsseldorf that the Civil War had stimulated the demand for pictures and noted that Bierstadt "is now a comparatively *rich man*."[17]

When Leutze passed on this happy news, Bierstadt himself was far from the war. The artist was in California, on his second trip west, with writer Fitz Hugh Ludlow, whose vivid and exciting accounts of their journey were being published regularly in the New York *Evening Post* as "Letters from Sundown." Ludlow's narratives of the trip were widely circulated, and these highly descriptive texts proved to be among the most effective vehicles in firmly establishing Bierstadt as the preeminent artist-interpreter of the western landscape in the 1860s. His domination of the subject matter was such that a reviewer of the 1868 Annual Exhibition at the National Academy of Design, appreciating the alternative vision of a Rocky Mountain scene by Whittredge, could lament in jest that Bierstadt had already "copyrighted nearly all of the principal mountains."[18]

Surveying the artist's career in 1878, the writer George W. Sheldon recognized that Bierstadt had indeed been the right man in the right place at the right time. "The impulse which the late war gave to American picture-making reached Mr. Bierstadt at the most favorable moment," wrote Sheldon. "He had more studies of fine and novel scenery than any other artist in this country, and he knew how to use them in the most effective style. It soon became fashionable for gentlemen of means, who were founding or enlarging their private galleries, to give Mr. Bierstadt an order for a Rocky Mountain landscape, and during at least ten years the artist's income from that source was princely."[19] The most spectacular series of commissions at prices buoyed by the war boom came in 1865. It began early in the year with the reported sale of *The Rocky Mountains, Lander's Peak* to a buyer from England, later identified as railroad entrepreneur James McHenry, for the staggering sum of $25,000.[20] Only seven years before, in 1858, Alvin Adams, founder of the Adams Express Company and among Bierstadt's first patrons of great wealth, had purchased the young artist's then-largest painting, *Lake Lucerne (Switzerland)*, 1858 (No. 6), for the very respectable price of $925 (Frederic Church had, the year before, received a total of only $5,500 for his internationally acclaimed *Niagara*, 1857 [Corcoran Gallery of Art, Washington, D.C.]).[21] Bierstadt had reportedly refused an earlier offer of $10,000 for *The Rocky Mountains, Lander's Peak*—a record sum for an American painting in 1859, when Church had received that amount from William T. Blodgett for *Heart of the Andes*.[22] Church had matched (or exceeded) his own record in 1864 with the sale of *Icebergs* to another railroad entrepreneur from England, Edward William Watkin, for between $10,000 and $15,000.[23]

Bierstadt's sales in the banner year of 1865 broke Church's records several times over. That fall, a Bierstadt buying frenzy erupted among visiting "English capitalists" to the delight of the press, which reported that the artist had received from them "two commissions at the same price" ($25,000) that McHenry had paid.[24] While one such commission may not have materialized, the other transaction was completed, apparently for *Storm in the Rocky Mountains, Mt. Rosalie* (No. 45), based upon studies made on the 1863 journey. Bierstadt evidently accepted $20,000 (rather than the reported $25,000) for the painting from McHenry's business associate, Thomas William Kennard, despite a rumored counteroffer of $30,000 "by a New York merchant," possibly the department-store magnate A. T. Stewart.[25] Between 1864 and 1869, Stewart, who was described as a man who "thinks money; makes money; lives money," built the first of the new millionaires' mansions on Fifth Avenue.[26] This marble palace included a lavish picture gallery that eventually housed at least three of Bierstadt's works (Fig. 4).[27] The artist figured in the gallery's

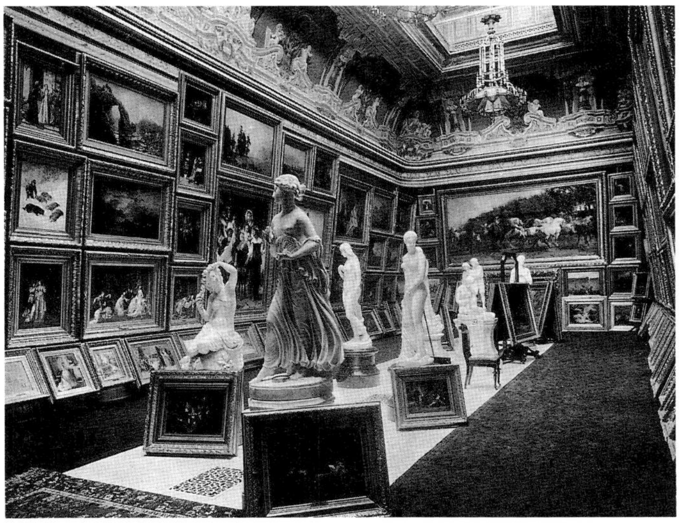

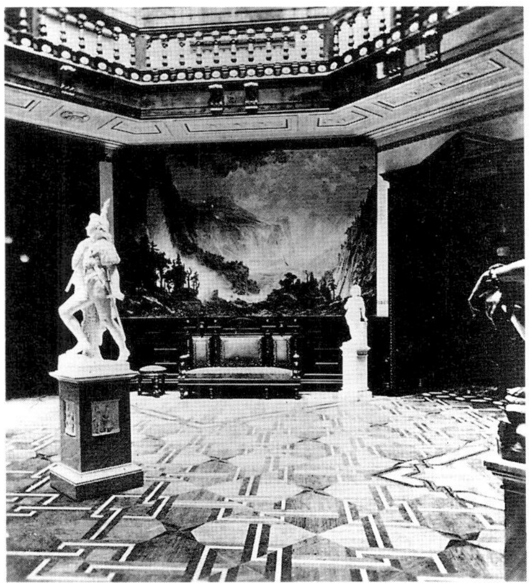

Figure 4 *(left)*

*The Picture-Gallery of the A. T. Stewart House, Fifth Avenue at Thirty-fourth Street* (demolished), c. 1883. Photograph published in *Artistic Houses: Being a Series of Interior Views of a Number of the Most Beautiful and Celebrated Names in the United States with a Description of the Art Treasures Contained Therein* (New York: 1883). The Brooklyn Museum Library Collection, Gift of Paul F. Walter. A version of Bierstadt's *Seal Rock* (private collection) is at the top left.

Figure 5 *(right)*

*"The Domes of the Yosemite" in the rotunda of the Lockwood Mansion*, c. 1869. Photograph. The Lockwood-Mathews Mansion Museum, Norwalk, Connecticut.

program of ceiling decoration as one of a company of "portrait-heads" that also included Church and other American and European artists who were the stars of Stewart's large collection.[28] In about 1865, New York financier Le Grand Lockwood commissioned for $25,000 what would be Bierstadt's largest painting, *The Domes of the Yosemite*, for Elm Park, his mansion then being built in Norwalk, Connecticut (Fig. 5).[29] All these fabulous prices quickly became legend, to be repeated over and over in the press and by the artist.

## Mounting Critical Censure

Even as Bierstadt's triumphs accumulated, however, strong negative reaction to his works developed. While his paintings enjoyed great success, the critical climate grew increasingly chilly, signaling certain changes under way in American taste and attitudes toward landscape painting. Two of the major critical voices of the decade were James Jackson Jarves and Clarence Cook (Figs. 6, 7). Jarves authored two important volumes on art history and criticism (published in 1864 and 1869), while Cook assumed the powerful role of art critic for the *New York Tribune* in 1864.[30] Their criticism of Bierstadt during the 1860s—from their initial responses to *The Rocky Mountains, Lander's Peak* to the end of the decade—yields insights into the dynamics of taste that made the artist's reputation rise and fall.

Like the English critic John Ruskin, whose eloquent works were a model for their prose styles, both Jarves and Cook were not only critics, but reformers, concerned about the future development of American art and taste. They differed in the stylistic models they favored—Jarves was an early admirer of the Barbizon-inspired landscapes of George Inness (1825–1894), while Cook, at the time, was a fanatical champion of the English Pre-Raphaelites and J. M. W. Turner

Figure 6 *(left)*
*Clarence Cook*, c. 1864. Photogravure after an unlocated drawing by Thomas Charles Farrer published in Louisa W. Cook, ed., *Poems by Clarence Cook* (New York: 1902).

Figure 7 *(right)*
*James Jackson Jarves*. Photograph. Sterling Library, Yale University, New Haven, Connecticut.

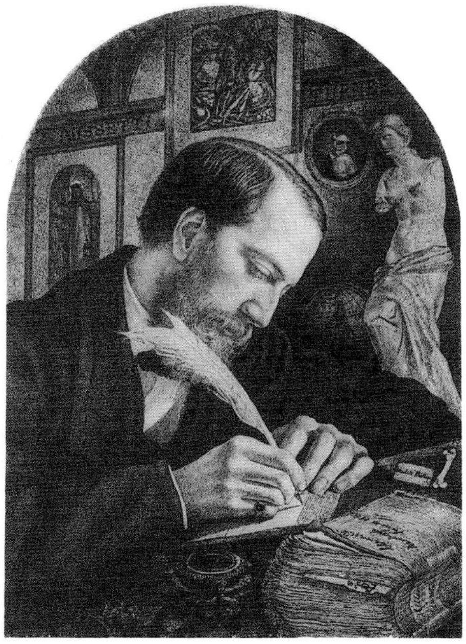

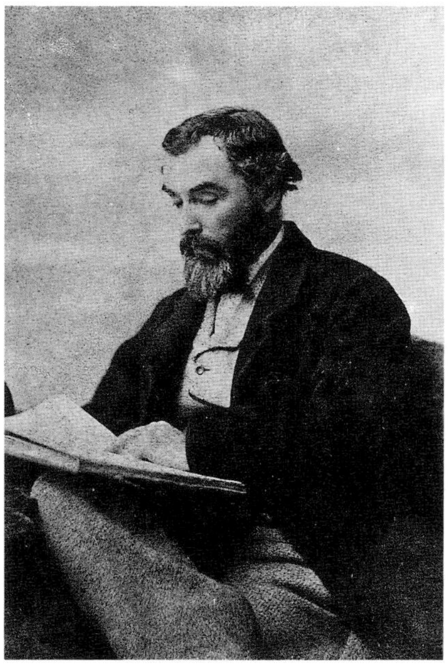

(1775–1851)—but both were highly critical of contemporary mainstream American landscape painting, the so-called Hudson River School. As will be seen, both came to reject the premises of Bierstadt's large panoramic landscapes, questioning the nature of their popular appeal and the artist's role in their presentation and promotion. Both would also attack Bierstadt's early and steadfast embrace of the landscape style of the Düsseldorf school.

Bierstadt's mature style had developed rapidly during his stay in Germany. Unlike his mentor and studio-mate, Whittredge, who greatly modified his own Düsseldorf manner over the years, Bierstadt's vision, once set, varied little during the course of a long career. Despite his immediate success when he returned from Germany in 1857, the popularity of the Düsseldorf style was already on the wane, diminished by growing criticism of what was perceived as an emphasis upon technique at the expense of imaginative content.[31] The pace of decline accelerated after the Civil War, with the growing impact of other European schools on American art. Lamenting Düsseldorf's still widespread influence in America in 1864, Jarves wrote, "The Düsseldorf school is a millstone around our necks." While Jarves recognized Bierstadt's debt to the German style in *The Rocky Mountains, Lander's Peak*, he did commend the young artist for mastering its strengths while avoiding "the conventional lifelessness of the mechanical Düsseldorf school." Confessing that his personal taste had "but transient sympathy with [the] hard-featured rationalism" of the painting, Jarves nevertheless admired "its executive qualities." Bierstadt, he wrote, "seeks to depict the absolute qualities and forms of things. The botanist and geologist can find work in his rocks and vegetation. . . ." Jarves also recognized those particular skills, honed by years of plein air study, that still stand among Bierstadt's greatest strengths as a landscape painter: "In the quality of American light, clear, transparent, and sharp in outlines, he is unsurpassed."[32]

Although Jarves marveled at the skilled and meticulous rendering of geological and botanical details in *The Rocky Mountains, Lander's Peak*, Cook found it wanting. This ardent Ruskinian—leader of the American Pre-Raphaelite radicals—dismissed all of Germany as "an arid waste, where Art lives only as the expression of a rigorous science without life, without sentiment."[33] Düsseldorf detail was not Pre-Raphaelite detail. "It would have been all well enough," Cook wrote of Bierstadt's technique, "if the marks of the brush had, by dexterous handling, been made to stand for scarp and fissure, crag and cranny, but, as it is, we have only too little geology and too much bristle."[34]

Despite his severe reservations about the Düsseldorf influence ("It infected Bierstadt, but he is recovering"), Cook cautiously praised Bierstadt's picture in a long and thoughtful discussion that got at the heart of the painting's popular appeal. He recognized that the primary experience for the viewer of *The Rocky Mountains, Lander's Peak* was theatrical rather than aesthetic: a vicarious journey through space and time, recapitulating the difficult and risky artist's pilgrimage that was itself the subject of repeated accounts in the press. He also acknowledged that the very remoteness of the subject, in combination with the sheer scale of presentation, was a primary source of the landscape's power. "So great a charm have mere grandeur of landscape . . . [and] the word 'the West'—to the mass of our people, especially to the young," he wrote, "that this picture must inevitably have been run after and praised. . . ." Cook would later attack Bierstadt's open promotion of these dramatic attractions; meanwhile, his final opinion of the painting itself was qualified: "But when the best has been said, we must still regard this work as immature, and on too pretentious a scale. The ambition of our young artists is leading them to attempt impossibilities."[35]

In 1864, then, the two influential critics Jarves and Cook, despite reservations, saw Bierstadt as a landscape painter of power and promise. Both hoped Bierstadt's potential to overcome the Düsseldorf "infection" and to forge a more personal vision would be realized in future work. Instead, by the end of the decade, Bierstadt's landscapes had become, for Jarves, Cook, and other critics as well, the epitome of an outmoded style. Bierstadt's German origins reinforced his association in the public's mind with Düsseldorf. His substantial contribution as an artist was repeatedly diminished by the wholesale dismissal of the Düsseldorf manner as devoid of imaginative or emotional content, "a style that can be learned as an apprentice learns a trade."[36] While Bierstadt's popular appeal remained high, the critical censure grew stronger as each successive large work demonstrated his continuing fidelity to his early manner. "Sordello" (Eugene Benson), writing in the New York *Post*, rejected *Looking Down Yosemite Valley, California* (No. 42), despite its eminently American subject, as foreign and as "vulgar, scenic art," claiming that "Germany has a dozen painters . . . capable of just such work."[37] In 1866 *Watson's Weekly Art Journal*, a Ruskin-influenced publication often critical of Bierstadt's work, wrote of *Storm in the Rocky Mountains, Mt. Rosalie* (No. 45) that the artist had "attempted more and effected less than in any previous effort. We do not deny to this artist the possession of brilliant power in the treatment of large masses; but he has not the imagination equal to grandeur of design, . . . preferring as he does, to captivate admirers by clap-trap expedients."[38] With reference to *The Domes of the Yosemite* (Fig. 58), one basically sympathetic reviewer wrote that Bierstadt's "pictures should be judged for what they *are*, instead of what they are *not*. They do not appeal to the highest faculties of the mind; that is, they do not confront one's poetic, devout, spiritual moods. . . . They satisfy the common and universal hunger with which all healthy minds crave breezy, bracing, and striking panoramic effects in Nature. . . ." The writer continued: "[Bierstadt] did not create a great picture, he simply transcribed a grand scene. Much ability . . . and much skill were needed in such a task; but not much genius."[39] "Imagination" and "genius" were terms largely reserved for Church in the frequent comparisons of his paintings with Bierstadt's: if Church's work was imaginative poetry, Bierstadt's was literal prose.

Six years after the debut of *The Rocky Mountains, Lander's Peak*, Jarves concluded that Bierstadt's early painting had not, after all, been a promise of greater things to come but was, in fact, actually "superior" to the artist's "subsequent work." In his book *Art Thoughts* (1869), Jarves assessed what he saw as the "salutary lesson" of the Paris Exposition Universelle of 1867 for what he termed "American artist insularity and self satisfaction." There Bierstadt's picture, with Church's *Niagara* and a selection of other American paintings, had been exhibited in an international context, "in direct comparison with the European, thereby proving [in Jarves's view] our actual mediocrity." By the end of the decade, Bierstadt's painting represented for Jarves the failure of the "lauded" American landscape school. The painting "looked cold and untruthful." "His more recent work," the critic wrote, "is no less illusive and spectacular, thinner in color and may be compared to mere rhetorical oratory." Jarves thought that Bierstadt had, after all, fallen irrevocably into the trap of the Düsseldorf manner. "Bierstadt gives scenic combinations . . . on a large scale, disenfranchised of sentiment and imagination."[40] Jarves's commentary of 1869 reflects the tone of most Bierstadt criticism in the following decades.

By then, Cook's long-standing disparagement of the American art establishment was notorious. It had begun in 1863 with his first editorial in the Pre-Raphaelite magazine, the *New Path*, where he dismissed these artists completely: "Our business is only to bid them 'Farewell.' "[41] Whittredge later identified him as the "savage critic" who had invented "Hudson River School" as a term of derision for the New York landscape painters.[42] Cook's strident negative criticism is said to have prompted an artists' delegation of protest to *Tribune* editor Horace Greeley.[43] According to Christopher Cranch, writing in 1867, Cook set a journalistic fashion for "the slashing and scalping style" of art criticism and focused upon Bierstadt as one of the "ringleaders of bad art."[44] His disappointment in the development of Bierstadt's work and his disapproval of the artist's businesslike approach to marketing his paintings had escalated into a campaign conducted in the pages of his newspaper. In 1866 Cook interpreted *Storm in the Rocky Mountains, Mt. Rosalie* not as an advance, but as "a sign of failing power" despite the painting's effectiveness as "a means of collecting cash."[45] Cook's crusade against Bierstadt culminated in two scathing reviews: an 1867 editorial feature in the *Tribune* decimating *The Domes of the Yosemite* and an 1868 piece on *Mount Vesuvius at Midnight*, 1868, a painting now unlocated (see chromolithograph, Fig. 91). "Mr. Bierstadt is entirely dead to all sense of what is properly termed color," wrote Cook of *The Domes of the Yosemite*. "He paints with ashes, with clay, with brimstone, but never with light. . . . [He] has but little accurate knowledge of nature."[46] Of *Vesuvius* he wrote: "Mr. Bierstadt's latest performance will avail but little to revive his fast-waning reputation. . . . We wish we could see any reason to hope that the failure of Mr. Bierstadt, the chief representative of the sensation or scene-painting school in this country, might debar others from entering upon so evil a course."[47]

The vituperative force and personal nature of Cook's censure did not go without challenge. His attack on *The Domes of the Yosemite* sparked a lively exchange in the New York press. "Next to the Civil War," wrote the *Independent*, "the fiercest conflict of modern times is the controversy now raging among the art-critics of New York. . . . Just now it is the fashion, on the one hand, to extol Mr. Bierstadt as one of the best of masters; and, on the other hand, to defame him as one of the worst of pretenders. . . . To see him abused as *The Tribune* abuses him is altogether shocking to our sense of justice. . . . We put ourselves frankly among Mr. Bierstadt's critics; but we cannot justly join the company of his detractors."[48] The German-American critic Sylvester R. Köhler, surveying Bierstadt's career for *Der deutsche Pionier*, went so far as to suggest that Cook's fierce diatribes against the school of Düsseldorf had contributed to Emanuel Leutze's premature demise in 1868. The critic, he lamented, was now "killing" Bierstadt "with the same stick." "Terrible Fate!" mourned Köhler. "Poor Bierstadt."[49]

There can be little doubt that Cook's relentless criticism contributed to the decline of Bierstadt's American reputation. However, Bierstadt's very public and seemingly sudden fall was, in truth, symptomatic of major changes in American taste and attitudes that were affecting an entire generation of artists. As will be seen later in this essay, by the 1870s American taste had largely turned from the descriptive realism and clear, defining light of midcentury toward a more painterly, intimate landscape vision influenced by French sources. Bierstadt and his contemporaries of the Hudson River School (for Bierstadt, too, painted the scenery of the Northeast; see, for

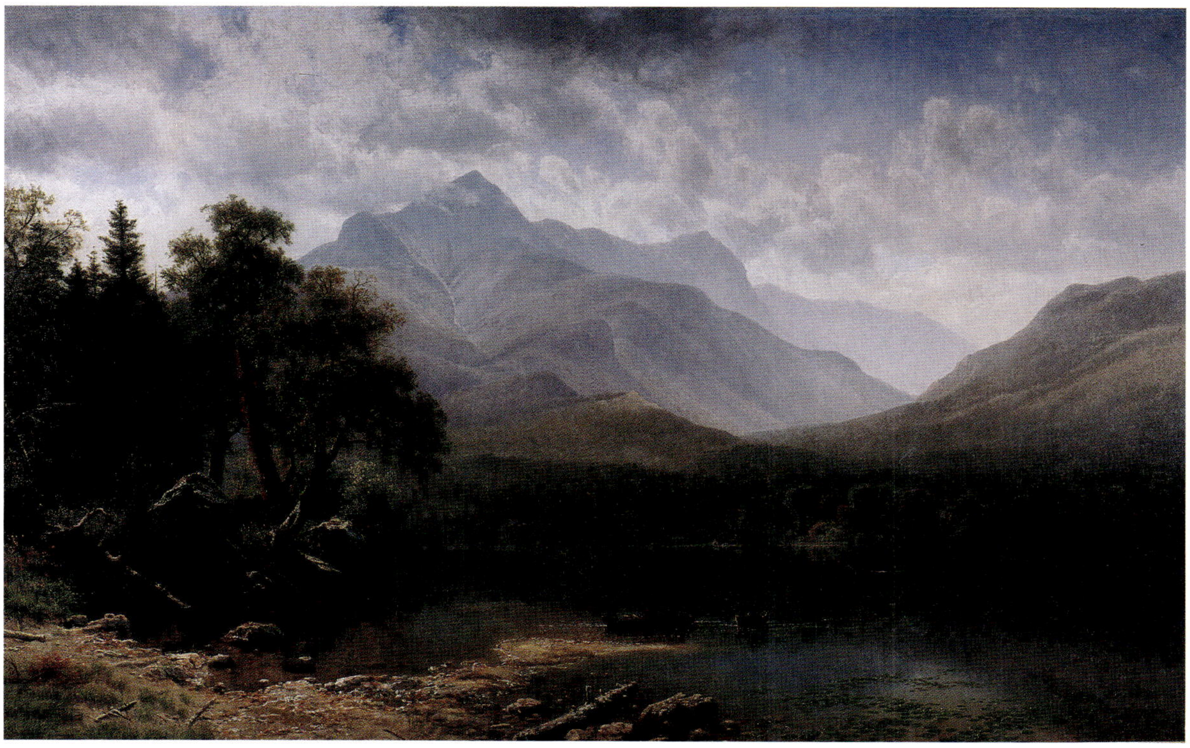

Figure 8
Albert Bierstadt. *Mount Washington*, 1862. Oil on canvas, 36 × 58 in. (91.4 × 147.3 cm).
Collection of William Nathaniel Banks.

example, Fig. 8), steeped in meticulous depictions of native scenery based upon earlier English and German landscape models, were undermined by the growing cosmopolitanism of American taste. Implicit in this stylistic shift was a fundamental change in the meaning of American landscape painting from a vehicle for national and religious messages to a medium of private poetry and the subjective interpretation of nature.

## The Artist: Priest or Showman?

The vigorous promotion of Bierstadt's large panoramic works as "Great Pictures," with frank appeal to popular taste and commercial gain, attracted at least as much fire from his critics as did his style. While Cook expressed qualified praise in 1864 for *The Rocky Mountains, Lander's Peak* as a landscape painting, he strenuously objected to the means by which it was being popularized. In keeping with the "Great Picture" scenario, the painting, Cook complained, "is at present going through the ceremonies of exhibition and puffery preparatory to being engraved. . . . [The] upholsterer has done his work, the tin lorgnettes and the magnifying glass have been duly provided, the puff-disinterested has been written, printed on the sheet of letter-paper that etiquette prescribes, and distributed, and the gentleman-in-waiting stands ready, at all hours, to enter in his subscription-book the names of those who desire to add this combined result of Mr. Bierstadt's genius and Mr. Smillie's [the engraver's] talent, to their plethoric portfolios." Cook disliked what he saw as the corrupting influence of the "Great Picture" phenomenon: "the assistance of well-adjusted draperies, innumerable tin tubes [for viewing], [and] nicely printed critical-descriptive sheets of letter-paper." Cook went on to denounce the "vast machinery of advertisement and puffery," the "devices to rouse and stimulate public curiosity," and the "artist connivance in this system." He concluded, "We call upon all artists who wish to elevate their profession above that of the showman, to help us abate it."[50]

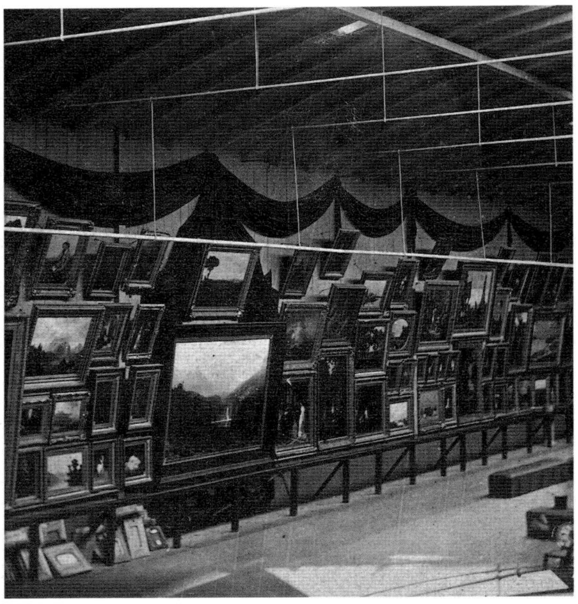

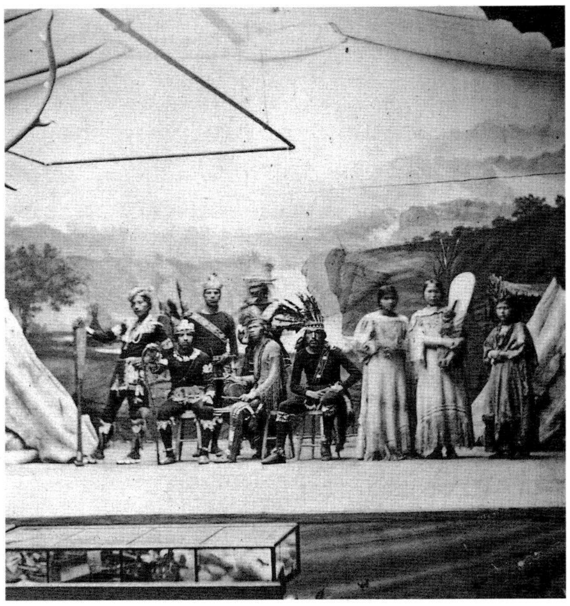

While hardly the inventor of the system, Bierstadt was a truly masterful promoter. Far from shunning such "artist connivance," he had, at the time of Cook's article, temporarily assumed the role of showman at the Metropolitan Fair, which was held to raise funds for the United States Sanitary Commission and opened in New York on 1 April 1864. Bierstadt's participation was not limited to serving on the Art Committee and to lending *The Rocky Mountains, Lander's Peak* to the Art Department (Fig. 9); he also initiated and managed the fair's Indian Department, a popular attraction where several hundred "curiosities," a "Monster Wigwam," and some eighteen or nineteen Indians were on display (Fig. 10). Anticipating Wild West shows to come, Bierstadt's Indian troupe performed dances before a painted backdrop, gave "other illustrations of Indian life," and, of course, helped to stimulate interest in his own painting on exhibition close by in the fair's Picture Gallery, where it hung opposite Church's *Heart of the Andes* (Fig. 11).[51]

While Bierstadt was commended in the press for the "public spirit" of his novel contribution to the fair, such endeavors, like the "Great Picture" exhibitions themselves, were incompatible with certain conventional pieties: cherished notions of the artist as a priestly figure whose life was a quasi-religious vocation free of worldly goals. It was considered unseemly to acknowledge the commercial activity that was a part of the artist's livelihood; rather, these transactions were publicly disparaged. This highly idealized perception, violated by Bierstadt's open conduct of his career in a businesslike manner, permeated nineteenth-century literature and criticism. When William Cullen Bryant quoted Thomas Cole in his 1848 funeral oration before the National Academy of Design, his words resounded like a final exhortation to fellow artists from the grave. Cole, recalled Bryant, "could not bear that his art should be degraded by inferior motives. 'I do not mean,' said he, not long before his death, 'to paint any more pictures with a direct view to profit.' "[52] Asher B. Durand's (1796–1886) nine "Letters on Landscape," published in the *Crayon* in 1855 as a beginner's manual of landscape painting, were even more explicit about the evils of material gain for the artist. "We cannot," he declared, "serve God and Mammon." "It is better to make shoes, or dig potatoes," Durand wrote in Letter IV, "than seek the pursuit of Art for the sake of gain. . . . This is one of the principal causes operating to the degradation of Art, perverting it to the servility of a mere trade."[53] Durand's pulpit resonance and his high-minded ideas reflect a close reading of Ruskin and strongly echo the English critic's recoil from the mercantile values of an industrial society. In a long article of 1858, the writer Henry Tuckerman articulated the same concerns, just as Bierstadt was launching his American career: "Where trade and politics, material luxury, and

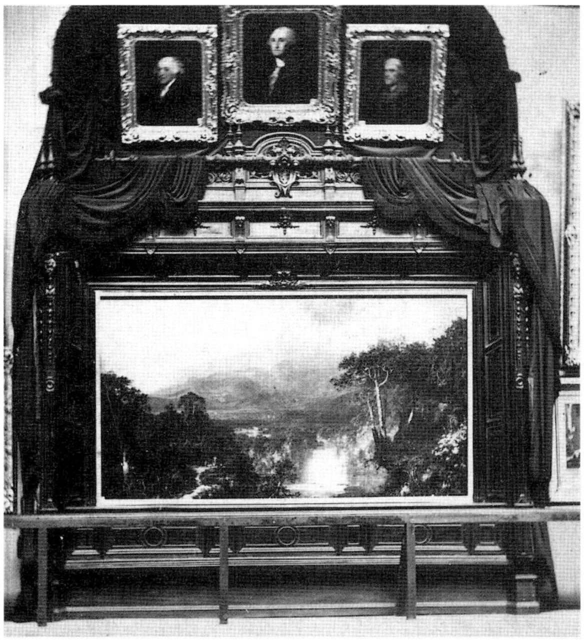

Figure 9 *(facing page, left)*

J. Gurney & Son, New York. *"The Rocky Mountains, Lander's Peak" on exhibition at the Metropolitan Fair, New York,* 1864. Stereograph. Collection of Leonard A. Walle.

Figure 10 *(facing page, right)*

J. Gurney & Son, New York. *View in the Wigwam* (Metropolitan Fair, New York), 1864. Photograph published in *A Record of the Metropolitan Fair* (New York: 1867).

Figure 11 *(left)*

*Frederic Church's "Heart of the Andes" on exhibition at the Metropolitan Fair, New York,* 1864. Photograph. Collection of Leonard A. Walle.

utilitarian habitudes, overlay finer instincts—where there is so much struggle, such devotion to the immediate, such faith in enterprise and assertion of self-hood—[only] small range is allowed for . . . the refined sense, the delicate feeling, the keen insight, which characterize the genuine artist. . . ."[54]

In 1864 Jarves was also very uneasy, but not entirely pessimistic, about the profit motive in art. "The speculating blood infuses itself into art," he wrote. "Within proper limits, the zest of gain is healthful; but if pushed to excess, it will reduce art to the level of trade." Jarves saw the perfect example of both the rewards and the liabilities of this delicate balance—between the energies of "democratic vulgarity" and necessary standards of "refinement, elegance and finish"—in contemporary American landscape painting, particularly the work of Church and Bierstadt: "The prominent characteristics of the American landscape school are its realism, vigor, enterprise, and freshness. . . . Partaking of the enterprise of commerce, it sends its sons to Brazil, to the Amazon, to the Andes, beyond the Rocky Mountains; it orders them in pursuit of icebergs off frozen Labrador; it pauses at no difficulties, distance, expense, or hardship in its search of the new and striking." Jarves was uncertain about the long-term value of such works, though he acknowledged the merits of such "speculating blood": "Both [Church and Bierstadt] are as laborious as they are ambitious, regarding neither personal exposure nor expense in their distant fields of study."[55] By the end of the decade, however, Jarves would reject the "sensationalist" landscapes of Bierstadt and Church as commercial successes and aesthetic failures, submitting to the conventional wisdom that these paintings were merely "bold and effective speculations in art on principles of trade, [but] emotionless, and soulless."[56]

Counterarguments were occasionally mounted. In the *Independent*, a spirited defender of Bierstadt asserted the positive influence of that artist's conduct: "Mr. Bierstadt . . . has done a great service to artists by teaching them how to get large prices for their pictures. He has an unusual share of common sense, business shrewdness, and practical tact—qualities as valuable and praiseworthy in a painter or a writer as in a broker. . . ."[57] Indeed, Christopher P. Cranch, who had left the ministry years before to become a poet and painter, suggested in 1867 that many artists chafed at the supposed sanctity of their calling, remarking upon what he saw as an unfortunate double standard for professional conduct: "[The critic] may sneer at your very natural desire to sell

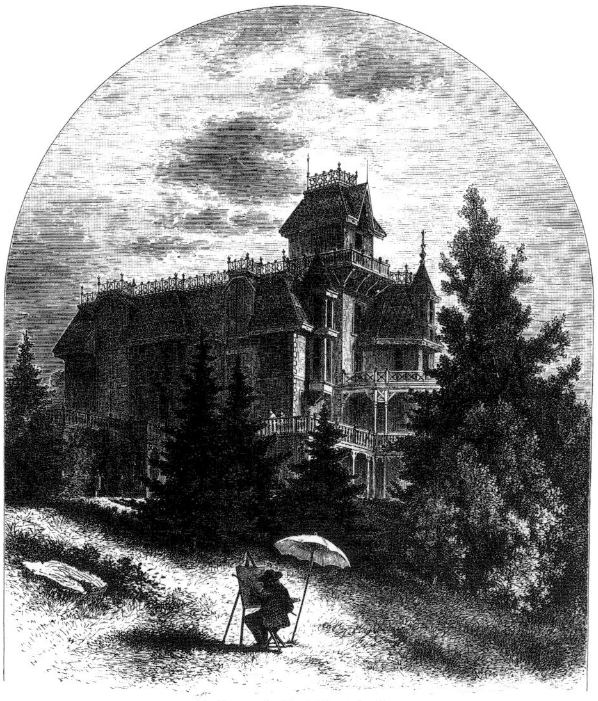

*Residence of Albert Bierstadt, Esq.*

Figure 12

*Residence of Albert Bierstadt, Esq*. Engraving published in Martha Lamb, "The Homes of America," *Art Journal* (1876).

your pictures, and preach you a sermon on the duty of despising dirty dollars and living supremely for art. He may tell you that you should be content to feed on air; . . . that, while journalists and critics may count their columns in greenbacks, you must never touch a canvas with an eye to its market value; that the gentlemen of the press may look sharp after their business, but you must 'scorn delights and live laborious days,' and let the heavens drop miraculous manna in your wilderness."[58]

In marked contrast to such preconceptions of the artist's role, Bierstadt, at the peak of his career in the mid-1860s, was rapidly adopting the style of living enjoyed by his wealthy patrons. In December 1865, a Boston paper reported the following: "It is said that Bierstadt's brush has earned him $120,000 in the last three years. He has the finest team in the Central Park and is building a villa at Irvington, on the Hudson."[59]

## A Château on the Hudson

Bierstadt's great studio house on the Hudson River preceded Frederic Church's Olana by several years. Sometime during the summer of 1865, Bierstadt purchased about five acres in Westchester County, between Irvington and Tarrytown, on a hillside overlooking the Hudson River at the Tappan Zee.[60] Construction must have progressed quickly, for, by late November, it was reported that a "fine studio and dwelling" were near completion. "It is built of gray granite; the studio is 60 feet in length, 30 feet wide, and 34 feet high; and the dwelling-house connected with it, and built of the same material, is of an octagonal form" (Figs. 12, 13).[61] By May 1866, Bierstadt was at Irvington for the summer.[62] The house must have been complete by November, when he married Rosalie Osborne (Fig. 14), recently divorced from Fitz Hugh Ludlow, the artist's western traveling companion in 1863.

While he was sketching along the river, according to the artist's own romantic account, a circling hawk had led him to the site, whose spectacular view inspired him to build there.[63] This tale and the original name of the house, Hawksrest (the mansion later came to be known as Malkasten), both suggest the enactment of an artistic destiny and emphasize the wildness of the spot. There were, however, other attractions at Irvington-on-Hudson, by then a suburban retreat connected to New York City by the railroad, that drew Bierstadt to the "genial and cultivated neighborhood." The village had many distinguished residents. Bierstadt's neighbor down the hill at Lyndhurst was financier Jay Gould. The artist's friend (and patron) John C. Frémont, the western explorer and soldier, and his famous wife, Jessie Benton, had a country seat, Pocaho, in nearby Tarrytown. The region was also rich in historic and literary associations. Washington Irving's picturesque cottage, Sunnyside, designed years before by Bierstadt's former Dissolving Views partner, George Harvey, was close by. Most important, the banks of the Hudson River were long-hallowed sketching grounds for the American landscape school. This careful selection of site immediately linked Bierstadt's name to those illustrious artists who preceded him. "It was because of his conviction that the patient and faithful study of nature is the only adequate school of landscape art that Bierstadt, like Cole and Church, fixed his abode on the banks of the Hudson," wrote Henry Tuckerman shortly after the house was built.[64] In establishing a retreat on the Hudson, Bierstadt, like his distinguished predecessors, could draw landscape inspiration not far from the equally important academy, studio, and market activity of New York City.

While the site may be interpreted as a testament to Bierstadt's wish to affirm his connection with the native landscape school, the scale of the house and the enormous studio were conspicuous evidence of his business talents. While Tuckerman recognized the former, the latter was not lost on Bierstadt's less sympathetic critics. Clarence Cook opened his scathing review of *The Domes of the Yosemite*, which had been painted at Irvington, with a sarcastic quip about the mammoth scale of the artist's grand country studio: "Mr. Bierstadt seems to be under the delusion that the bigger a picture is the finer it is. 'Tis mere village gossip; not worth repeating, that he has built his studio at the point where the Hudson River is widest, in order that he may have room to turn his canvases."[65] *Watson's Weekly Art Journal* had announced both the McHenry sale and the report "that the artist is erecting a huge studio somewhere in the open country" in a similarly tongue-in-cheek vein: "The title of his next picture, it is reported, will be 'All Outdoors.' "[66] Bierstadt apparently encouraged an association of the size of his future works with the scale of the studio. A hometown newspaper had reported earlier, probably on the basis of an interview, that the "large pictures upon which the artist is engaged, and the still larger ones he has commissions to paint, make the erection of this structure almost a necessity."[67]

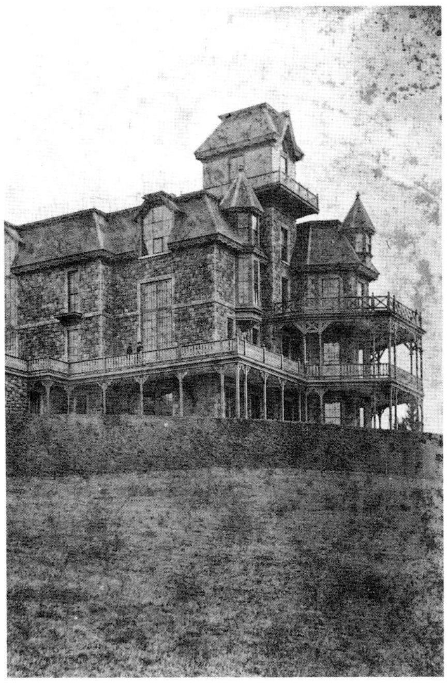

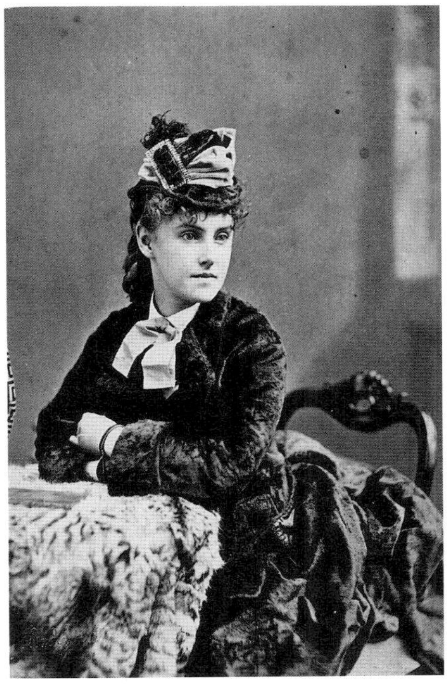

Figure 13 *(left)*

Bierstadt Brothers, New Bedford, Massachusetts. *Malkasten, exterior from the northwest*, c. 1867. Photograph. Collection of Ralph Gosse. The enormous studio windows are visible at the left. Ornamental ironwork was later added on the roof.

Figure 14 *(right)*

Bradley and Rulofson, San Francisco. *Rosalie Bierstadt*, c. 1871–73. Photograph. Collection of James P. Crain.

In marked contrast to the modest residences of Cole (at Catskill) and Church (then at Cozy Cottage near Hudson), Bierstadt's Malkasten was a four-story stone mansion with a tower rising some five hundred feet above the river, said to offer a panoramic view from West Point to Staten Island. The design of Malkasten appears to have been a fruitful collaboration between the artist and the English-born and -trained architect Jacob Wrey Mould.[68] As newly discovered photographs of Malkasten's exterior demonstrate, Mould was then at the top of his form as an avant garde practitioner of a vigorously eclectic style. The animated treatment of major architectural masses, the polychrome facade (contrasting hues of native rough bluestone gneiss with lighter granite trim), and the polychrome tiled mansard crowned with iron grillwork were characteristic elements of Mould's picturesque and bold manner. They also marked Bierstadt as both daring and astute in the selection of his architect. The house immediately became known, because of its scale and "advanced taste," as "one of the most commanding and noticeable on the banks of the Hudson."[69]

Set high on the rocky hillside, less heavily wooded than today, the house was sited and planned to command an unobstructed panorama of the river valley from multiple oriels, bays, balconies, porches, and piazzas that faced north, west, and south. Bierstadt's large painting of 1866, *View of the Hudson Looking Across the Tappan Zee Towards Hook Mountain* (Fig. 16), depicts the panoramic vista from the house looking west and north.[70] The steep grade was accommodated by building the east end of the first story into the hillside. While the principal ground-floor entry at the west was approached from a carriage drive, the second-story exits at the east end of the house gave direct access onto the same drive, as well as onto lawns, gardens, and piazzas.

The great studio was the true heart of the house. "Being an artist," wrote Martha Lamb in *The Homes of America* (1879), "Mr. Bierstadt naturally built his house to paint pictures in, and one half of it is given to studio."[71] The studio setting had been a critical element in maintaining Bierstadt's image even before he built his retreat on the Hudson; his New York studio, filled with exotic paraphernalia from his travels, had been the scene of artists' receptions as well as private entertainments for a wide circle of friends. In the design and decoration of the spectacular studio at Irvington, Bierstadt's natural flair for showmanship and grandeur found powerful architectural expression (Fig. 17). Several views of the studio were published as stereographs by his brother Charles (Figs. 18–20). The eastern two-thirds of the studio wing comprised work space (Figs. 18, 19) in which were distributed "some half-a dozen easels, containing pictures in various stages of progress."[72] Among the most remarkable and remarked-upon features of this room were the three large sliding doors, each some fifteen feet in width, reaching from floor to ceiling, which were placed

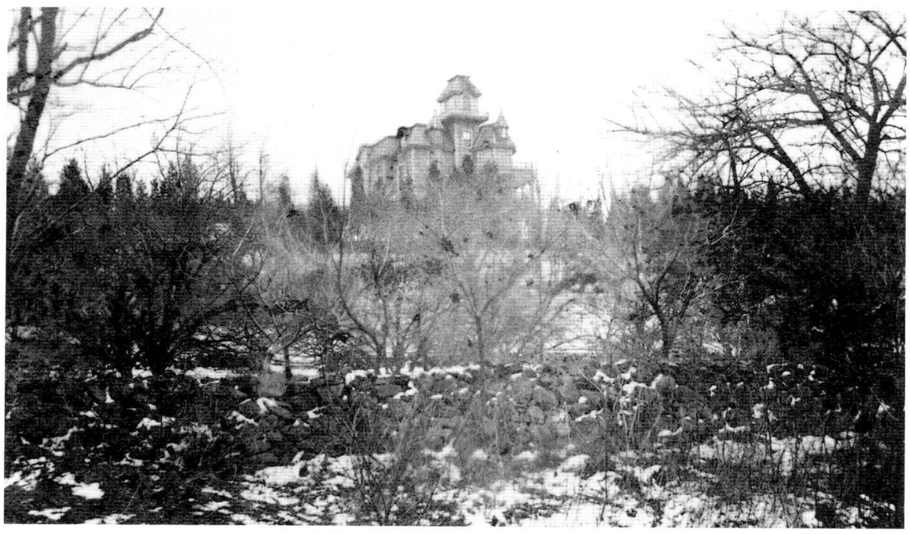

Figure 15
Charles Bierstadt, New Bedford, Massachusetts. *Malkasten, from the west*, c. 1867. Photograph. Collection of Ralph Gosse.

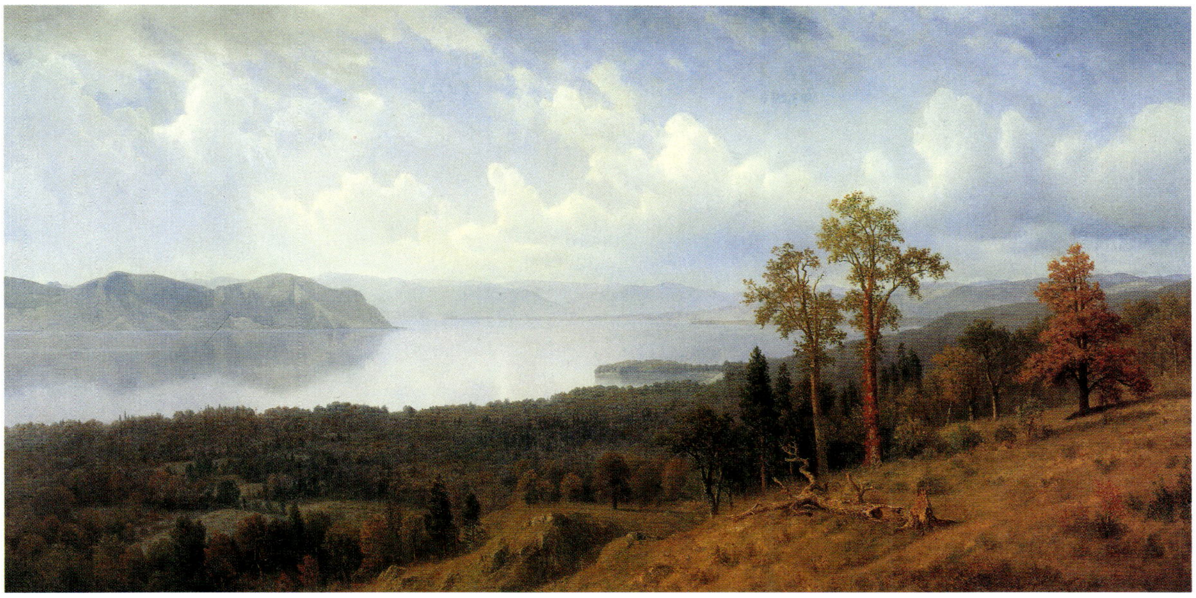

Figure 16
Albert Bierstadt. *View of the Hudson Looking Across the Tappan Zee Towards Hook Mountain*, 1866. Oil on canvas, 36¼ × 71¼ in. (92.1 × 183.5 cm). Private collection.

in the north, east, and south studio walls. "Set into these great doors," wrote author and critic "Barry Gray" (R. B. Coffin) in 1871, "are windows of plate-glass, the light through which can be regulated by shades and screens." These huge portals opened onto the hillside lawns for use "when the artist paints from life a horse, deer, buffalo, or other animal, or an object which it is desirable to see at a greater distance than even his capacious studio will permit." Decorating the walls, "artistically arranged," were objects brought back from western journeys: "numerous curiosities, including weapons of warfare, implements of savage life, and the product of the chase."[73] The last included a mounted buffalo head and, by 1882, an extensive collection of other horned animals. There was ample space for hundreds of Bierstadt's oil studies, and many were displayed, some literally set into the walls (Fig. 18): "For internal decoration, Mr. Bierstadt has had the rare privilege of selecting, from his own studies, pictures which are set in mouldings of black walnut and oak, the effect of which is beautiful and rare."[74]

A similar frieze of studies adorned the western end of the studio wing, designed as a library and music room (Fig. 20), which was divided from the work area by a doorway hung with portieres of striped Algerian stuff. Coffin wrote: "Here are bookcases filled with choice volumes, beneath which are drawers, which sliding out, can be opened, portfolio-like, for viewing engravings. Here, too, is a grand piano; and . . . [a] wide and deep fireplace."[75] The windows in the library, which faced the river, reached to the floor, opening onto the broad piazza that surrounded the house on all four sides. These adjoining studio areas—work space and library—were also designed to function as a theater (surely the artist had a major hand in this), complete with two boxes (Fig. 17), a balcony gallery, great depth of vista, gaslights, and music. This was the ideal setting in which to present Bierstadt's monumental landscapes to best advantage. The gallery, accessible from the third-floor hall of the house, crossed the west (or library) end of the studio at a height of about fifteen feet above the floor. Coffin offered a description of the ambience of this "cozy retreat, half gallery and half balcony" as he recalled viewing Bierstadt's large *Donner Lake from the Summit*, 1873 (Fig. 61), from this vantage point: "The light of the chandelier was there, but very dim it shone; the music . . . rose softly from the floor below; the silken sofa was also there. . . . Nearly seventy-five feet distant from him [the author], on a canvas that extended not quite half way across the apartment, was a picture, not yet finished, on which the artist had but an hour or two before

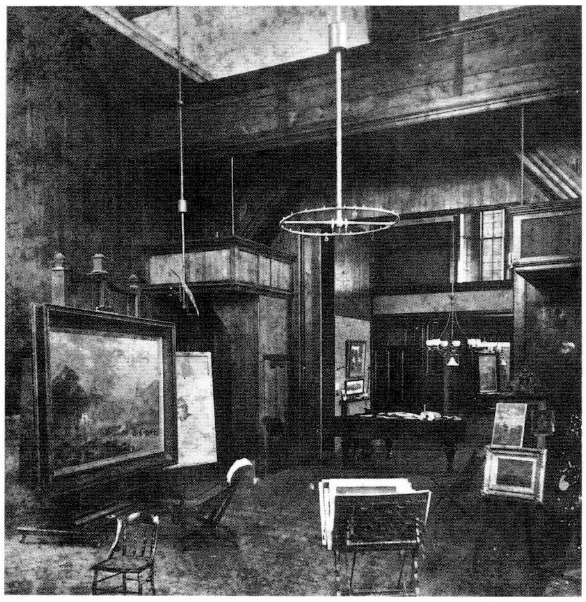

Figure 17

Charles Bierstadt, Niagara Falls, New York. *View of Malkasten studio, looking west,* c. 1867. Photograph. Collection of Wilfred Thompson, courtesy of Leonard A. Walle. *Emigrants Crossing the Plains,* 1867 (National Cowboy Hall of Fame and Western Heritage Center, Oklahoma City), is on the easel.

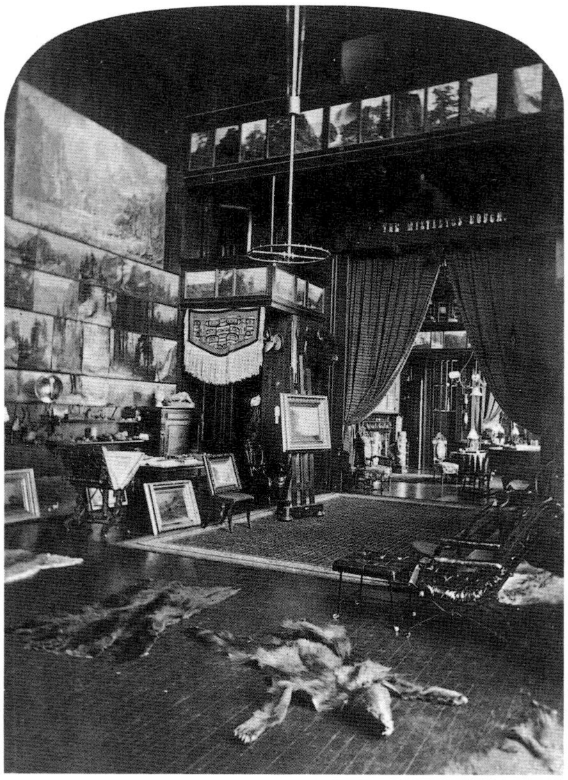

Figure 18

Charles Bierstadt, Niagara Falls, New York. *Malkasten studio, looking west toward the library,* c. 1875. Stereograph. Collection of Joyce Randall Edwards.

been working. . . . The distance from which he viewed, and the full blaze of gas-jets which lighted it up, made it look like another and better picture from what it had appeared in the daylight, and near by."[76] Many a would-be patron, after dinner and billiards, must have warmed to a potential purchase in the carefully contrived atmosphere of Bierstadt's luxurious studio-theater, enjoying what amounted to a private "Great Picture" exhibition.

The south, or residential, wing of the house was an octagon joined to the basic rectangle of the studio wing to the north. On the ground floor were a dining room and a billiard room. Kitchen, butler's pantry, and laundry, all "fitted with the latest . . . improvements and conveniences," were located at the rear. On the second floor were a parlor and two guest chambers, and on the third were Rosalie Bierstadt's boudoir, her library, and more bedrooms. All rooms in the house commanded spectacular views of the river, and most offered direct access to a porch, a balcony, or deep bay windows. Much commented upon was the rich and eclectic decoration of the interior: floors "composed of colored woods, laid in patterns, like mosaic work"; a large fireplace "ornamented with quaint old Dutch tiles"; and imported furnishings "of exquisite design and finish." Many paintings, by Bierstadt and others, were displayed. "Numberless articles of *vertu*," collected by the Bierstadts on their travels, testified to the couple's affluence and cosmopolitan experience.[77]

Bierstadt's establishment included not only the house itself, but barns, stables, and carriage houses, as well as "about an acre" of garden "with its fruit trees and vegetables, its beds of strawberries, and long rows of raspberry and blackberry bushes."[78] Country life at Irvington was conducted on a grand scale, with a staff that included a butler, a footman, a coachman, and a French maid.[79] While Bierstadt maintained his Tenth Street studio, he did not live there after his marriage. He and his wife divided their time between Irvington and an apartment at the Brevoort

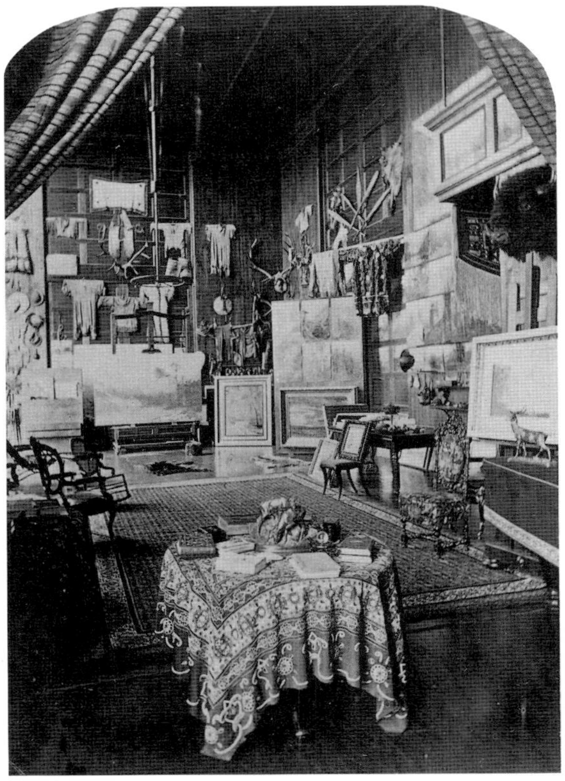

Figure 19
Charles Bierstadt, Niagara Falls, New York. *Malkasten studio, looking east from the library*, c. 1875. Stereograph. Collection of Joyce Randall Edwards.

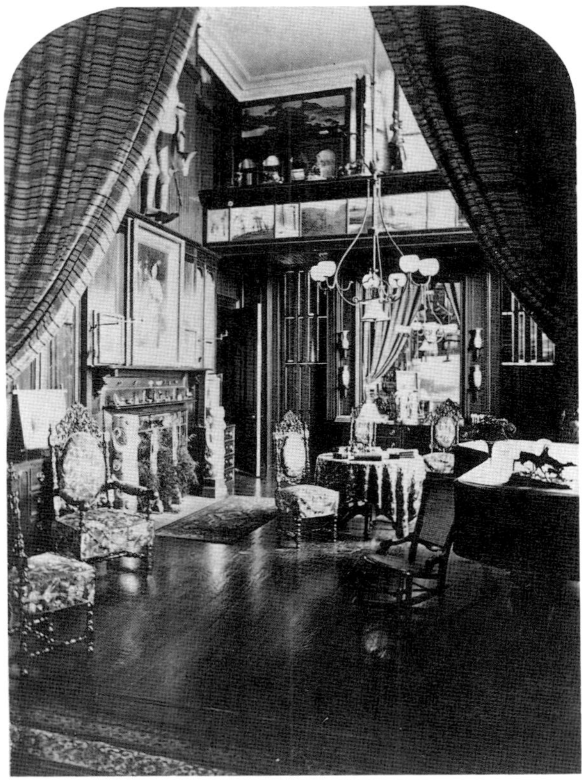

Figure 20
Charles Bierstadt, Niagara Falls, New York. *Malkasten studio, looking into the library alcove*, c. 1875. Stereograph. Collection of Joyce Randall Edwards.

House on lower Fifth Avenue, "a quiet and aristocratic hotel" famous for fine cuisine and a cosmopolitan clientele.[80] The memoirs of Rosalie's younger sister, Esther Osborne, who spent a good deal of time with the Bierstadts in the 1870s, offer glimpses of a very busy social life in New York and at Malkasten among the well-connected American and English circles that provided much of Bierstadt's patronage. "We had a gay life there—in Albert's and Rose's fine house," Esther recalled. "What tales of pleasures it could tell—of bright entertainments, clever people, beautiful women, talented men—artists, authors, poets."[81]

Tragically, Malkasten with most of its contents burned to the ground on 10 November 1882. The disaster consigned to historical oblivion an important architectural monument that not only predated, but rivaled Frederic Church's Olana in site, scale, and ingenuity of design. The fire, "lighting up the midnight sky for miles around," was widely reported in the press, and the artist's loss was estimated to be as much as $200,000.[82] By the time it burned, the house had been rented for a number of years, although the artist's furnishings and studio contents remained. As Rosalie's health declined, the couple stayed more in New York; beginning in 1876, she spent the winters in Nassau. As American demand for Bierstadt's work waned in the 1870s, the artist devoted more time to traveling in search of novel subject matter and new markets. There is ample evidence to suggest that the high cost of maintaining the Irvington house, established at the very peak of Bierstadt's fortunes, soon became a financial burden for the artist. Shortly before the fire, the Tarrytown *Argus* reported signs of neglect at Malkasten and efforts by Bierstadt to sell the property.[83]

Before the leaner times of the 1870s and 1880s, however, Malkasten was a potent and exuberant symbol of the boom years that brought Bierstadt's greatest artistic, social, and material success. It was at the crest of that popularity and lavish private patronage that he began to seek a congressional commission.

Figure 21

Albert Bierstadt. *Discovery of the Hudson River,* 1874. Oil on canvas, 72 × 122 in. (182.9 × 309.9 cm). Architect of the Capitol, Washington, D.C.

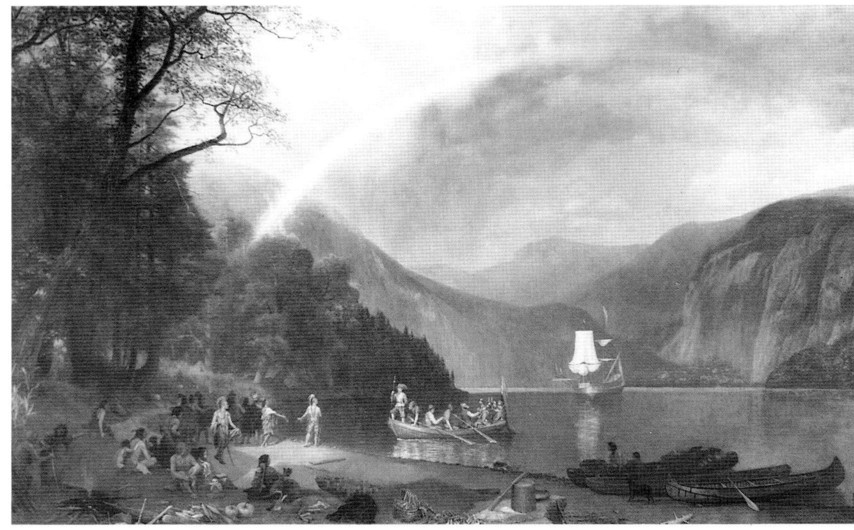

Figure 22

Albert Bierstadt. *Settlement of California, Bay of Monterey, 1770,* 1876. Oil on canvas, 72 × 122 in. (182.9 × 309.9 cm). Architect of the Capitol, Washington, D.C.

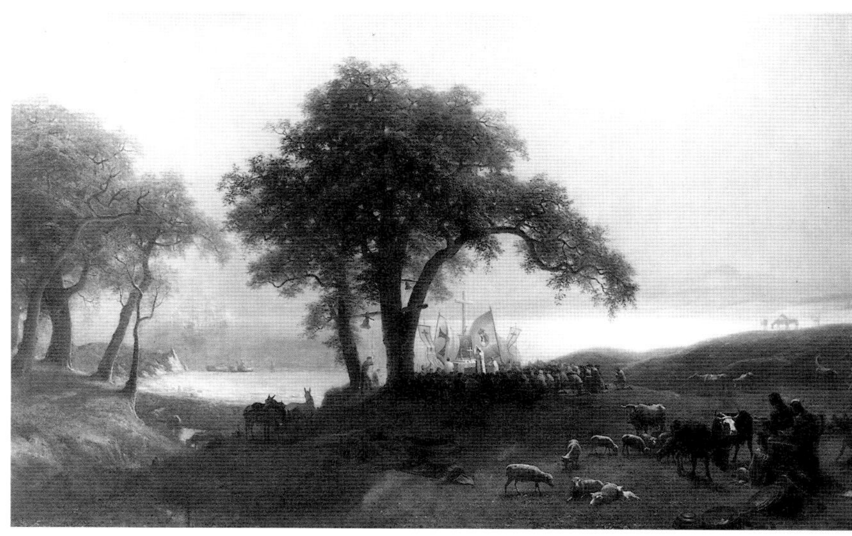

## The Campaign for a National Commission

In November 1866, the New Bedford *Daily Mercury* reported "that the great American landscape-painter, Bierstadt, will be commissioned this winter to paint pictures for two of the panels in the Representatives Hall, in the Capitol."[84] This confident pronouncement in fact marked the beginning of a long saga. Bierstadt completed the congressional commission only after lobbying for over a decade, from 1866 to 1878. Not until 1874 and 1878 did a reluctant Congress purchase the two paintings, for a total that represented only a quarter of Bierstadt's original price. The artist's struggle to place his works in the Capitol demonstrates how important the commission was to him as his reputation declined, despite much-publicized successes with private patrons in the 1860s and 1870s. Ironically, it was Bierstadt's unprecedented price demands that denied him the honor of placing the first landscape paintings in the nation's Capitol. Missing his opportunity at the peak of his fame, he later retreated from his initial proposal for a pair of monumental western subjects to fall back on the conventional formula of two history paintings: old-fashioned costume pieces in generalized landscape settings. The pair of paintings he finally executed for the House Chamber—*Discovery of the Hudson River,* 1874 (Fig. 21), and *Settlement of California, Bay of Monterey, 1770* (formerly known as *Entrance into Monterey*), 1876 (Fig. 22)—are disappointing works, with none of the power of the western panoramas that had made Bierstadt famous in the 1860s.

In the first half of the century, national commissions had been largely the preserve of the history painter. The category of history painting occupied a somewhat ambivalent position in the American canon of subjects. Regard among critics and artists for the traditional academic hierarchy placed history at the summit of artistic achievement. It was deemed the only appropriate vehicle for the required scale and didactic messages of a national art. The general public and private patrons, however, were drawn to the more readily accessible vocabulary of landscape and genre paintings. Bierstadt's rise to fame came at a moment when the climate was ripe for a landscape painter to receive a national commission.

The future of such commissions was a major concern of American artists and critics when Bierstadt returned home from Düsseldorf in 1857. The last Rotunda painting had been completed in 1853 by William Henry Powell (1823–1879); his *Discovery of the Mississippi by De Soto, 1602* was universally judged the worst of what was deemed an undistinguished group of eight Rotunda pictures. In early 1858, the Washington Art Association had organized a National Convention of Artists, which met at the Smithsonian Institution that March to address the issue of national commissions. Bierstadt was a signer of the convention's petition to Congress for the establishment of an art commission to devise a coherent program of decoration for the Capitol and to oversee the selection of artists.[85] His participation in the National Convention suggests an early impulse to engage in national debate, as well as a premonition of his own ambitions in the congressional arena. His premiere at the National Academy of Design that year commanded notice, not least because *Lake Lucerne (Switzerland)* (No. 6) was the largest painting in the exhibition: Bierstadt's scale, if not his subject matter, was already commensurate with that of public art.

The high hopes of Bierstadt and others for a permanent art commission to influence and guide the Capitol's decorative program were to be disappointed, however. By September 1860, Congress had disbanded the commission. Captain Montgomery C. Meigs, who had formerly supervised the Capitol's decorative projects, was soon reinstated.[86]

Bierstadt, by that time settled into the Tenth Street Studio Building in New York, must have been pleased with one of Meigs's first actions. The captain reopened negotiations with Bierstadt's old Düsseldorf friend and neighbor in the Tenth Street Studio Building, Leutze, who had returned to the United States early in 1859. While Bierstadt's own study in Germany had focused on landscape, Düsseldorf was probably best known as a center of modern history painting, and Leutze was one of the most famous exponents of that school. In July 1861, Leutze's commission for a mural in the stairway of the House of Representatives commemorating American westward expansion (Fig. 23)

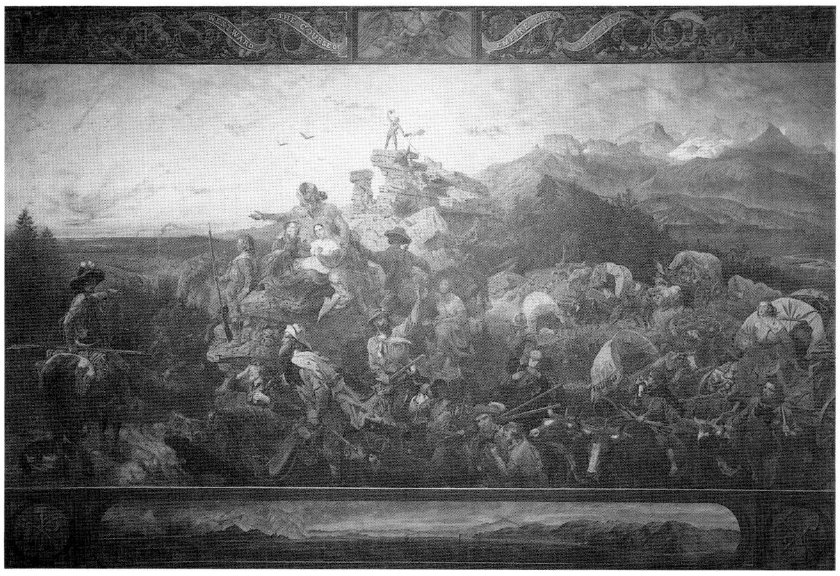

Figure 23

Emanuel Leutze. *Westward the Course of Empire Takes Its Way*, 1862. Stereochromed wall painting, 240 × 360 in. (609.6 × 914.4 cm). Architect of the Capitol, Washington, D.C.

was approved by Congress with an appropriation for $20,000. In August 1861, Leutze traveled to the Rocky Mountains, no doubt with Bierstadt's advice, to make studies for the work. Bierstadt's support and involvement continued with the loan of sketches and western paraphernalia after Leutze began work on the mural in Washington.[87]

Leutze's success in securing a congressional commission for the highest sum yet awarded surely must have served to spur Bierstadt's own ambitions. The strong parallels between their German immigrant backgrounds could not have gone unmarked by the younger man. Bierstadt may well have perceived a personal destiny to answer Leutze's figural interpretation of Manifest Destiny with a painting of his own celebrating the western landscape. He was already at work on *The Rocky Mountains, Lander's Peak*, which was immediately recognized in 1863 as a national subject of compelling interest. *Harper's Weekly* termed it "purely an American scene, and from the faithful and elaborate delineation of the Indian village, a form of life now rapidly disappearing from the earth, may be truly called a historic landscape." Expressing admiration for a painting of Lake George by John F. Kensett (1816–1872), *Harper's* posed a question that must have been on Bierstadt's mind, as well: "Are not these, also, the kind of picture which should adorn the Capitol?"[88]

Several years later, Francis Colburn Adams, reviewing the disappointing history of the commissions to date in a government report titled "Art in the District of Columbia," also lamented "that such artists as Mr. Bierstadt, Mr. Church, and two or three others we might mention, are not represented on the walls of the Capitol." By midcentury, landscape had assumed a commanding importance that rivaled history in the American hierarchy of subjects, and Adams went on to refute any lingering notion that it was "not appropriate to the decoration of great public buildings." Landscapes, he argued, "can be so expressed as to serve a great and good purpose in promoting the interests of a people. That they can be made more useful in interesting and instructing a people than poor and bad figure or historical paintings . . . there cannot be a doubt." He observed that historical painting had not "proved profitable" to Americans: "Hence it is that most of our leading artists have chosen . . . landscape painting."[89] Adams's argument was fueled by the fact that, early in 1865, William Henry Powell had again secured a congressional commission, for a new record price of $25,000. Powell's much-criticized Rotunda painting of 1853 was surely on Adams's mind when he extolled landscape over "bad figure or historical paintings." He also observed that Powell's success in obtaining a $25,000 commission from Congress had brought "a great number of ambitious young painters to Washington in pursuit of similar favors."[90] Albert Bierstadt was among them.

Early in 1865, the artist was about to make his own $25,000 sale, to James McHenry. Bierstadt was still enjoying the popular success of *The Rocky Mountains, Lander's Peak*, which was exhibited in Washington in April, and of another "Great Picture," *Mount Hood, Oregon* (Fig. 55). By February, he had begun work on another in the series of "Great Pictures," *Storm in the Rocky Mountains, Mt. Rosalie* (No. 45). Hailed in the press as the "acknowledged Prince of mountain regions,"[91] Bierstadt may well have determined that the time was right to set about securing the first congressional commission awarded to a landscape painter. His campaign to win recognition among members of Congress may have begun early in 1866, when the Washington *Intelligencer* announced the artist's hopes to premiere the recently completed *Storm in the Rocky Mountains, Mt. Rosalie* in the capital "if a suitable hall can be found."[92] While the painting ultimately made its debut in New York that February, it was seen and admired there by then-Congressman Rutherford B. Hayes, who wrote: "It is very beautiful and wonderful. By gaslight the effect is incomprehensible, such brilliancy and light and shade! Mr. Bierstadt says it is better by daylight. I shall see."[93] That

Figure 24

*Chamber of the House of Representatives, United States Congress, prior to the 1901 renovation*. Photograph. Architect of the Capitol, Washington, D.C. At the far left of the Speaker's platform, *Settlement of California, Bay of Monterey, 1770* (Fig. 22) is visible. *Discovery of the Hudson River* (Fig. 21) is at the extreme right.

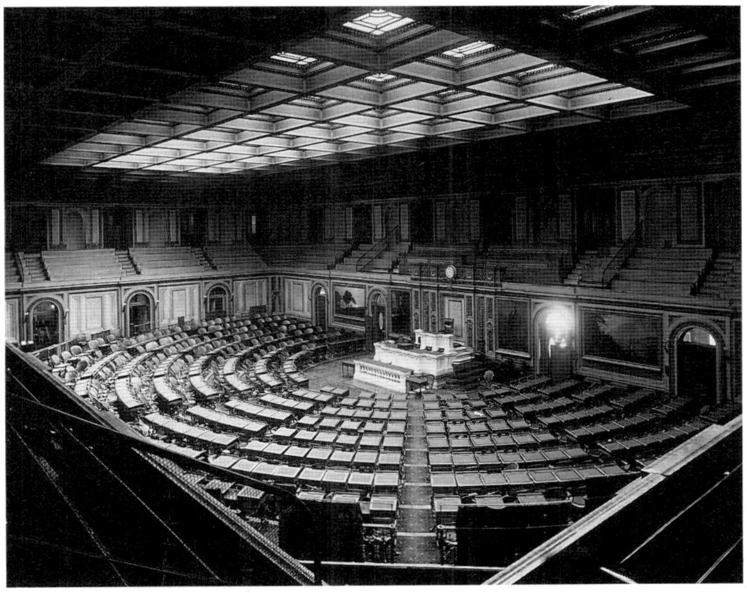

month, Bierstadt paid a call in New York on Schuyler Colfax, Speaker of the House of Representatives.[94] The Speaker and the artist had much in common, for Colfax had recently returned from a trip to the Pacific Coast that had already been, like Bierstadt's own journey, the subject of a published narrative.[95] *Mount Hood, Oregon* was exhibited in Washington in April. Later in the year, Bierstadt sent a small painting to General Nathaniel P. Banks, the congressman from the artist's home state of Massachusetts who soon sponsored the resolution for his commission.[96]

Bierstadt proved himself to be an adept lobbyist. By November newspapers reported that he was to be commissioned to paint not one, but two, works for the House Chamber.[97] The commission was an especially attractive one. The empty panels flanking the Speaker's platform provided a dramatic and conspicuous showcase for any artist's work. In December Bierstadt wrote to a Captain Adams in Washington, outlining his plans: "I would do my best to paint something that would be if possible an ornament to the Capitol and [an] honor [to] myself." He described two programs, indicating his own preference for the first, a pair of western landscapes: "One panel might represent scenery of the Rocky Mts showing in the foreground something of Indian life . . . [and] the other comprising the . . . leading features of the wonderful Yo Semite Valley. Both these subjects it seems to me would be strictly American, and would have the advantage of being in strong contrast to each other. This is my present view of the matter, in case Congress should honor me with such a commission."[98] Yosemite was by then a state park, and Bierstadt was already at work, for Le Grand Lockwood, on *The Domes of the Yosemite* (Fig. 58). He must have envisioned an ideal national commission composed of a spectacular recapitulation of his current Yosemite subject, along with a Rocky Mountain panorama.

Recognizing the novelty of his preferred theme, Bierstadt offered a more conventional alternative. "Some more appropriate subject might be found," he proposed, "where figures would come in to illustrate some event in the history of our country—the discovery, for instance, of the Hudson River which I have in progress." He was less compromising about his price. In response to a query by Captain Adams concerning the appropriation, Bierstadt explained his rationale for insisting upon the enormous sum of $40,000 for each painting—double what Leutze had received in 1861. "My orders from private parties, when viewed in a pecuniary light, are worth more to me," he reasoned, "and the government ought to be willing to pay what private parties give." He did not rule out some discount in the interest of patriotism: "However the honor is worth something, and I would not decline the order for $30,000 each."[99]

On 21 January 1867, General Banks successfully introduced a resolution authorizing the Library Committee to contract with Bierstadt for two paintings "thoroughly American in character, representing some prominent feature of scenery or important event in the discovery or history of America."[100] However, Banks's resolution did not include an appropriation. Perhaps he suspected that Bierstadt's demand would provoke controversy and so left the matter to the determination of the committee, which was instructed to complete the negotiation of the subject and the contract with the artist.

Soon after, Francis Colburn Adams recalled that the Bierstadt commission had been deemed "a movement in the right direction, and was highly commended by the press all over the country." "Mr. Bierstadt then stood at the very head of his profession as a landscape painter. . . . It was felt that he would give us something really good and true in art—something that would be a credit to our national taste, represent fairly the progress we had made in art, and be appreciated by the government and the people."[101] The *New York Times*, getting wind of the pending commission and the price, applauded "the Government giving all legitimate encouragement to art." Nevertheless, the *Times* argued, conditions were not auspicious for such "lavish appropriations for pictures and statuary," stating, "Economy, rigid and universal, is the great patriotic virtue at this day. It is to be hoped, therefore, that Congress will postpone for a year or two, all further appropriations for high art."[102] Bierstadt himself recalled, years later, "how economy and retrenchment was the universal cry."[103] Nevertheless, the artist did not retreat from his demand. On 12 February, the committee requested that Bierstadt submit a formal proposal including his program for the paintings and his price.[104] Absolute confidence must have led the artist to inform the *Mercury* on 15 February that arrangements were complete. Sadly, perhaps in response to committee preference, he had retreated from the more daring suggestion of western landscapes in favor of a pair of historical compositions. "One of the subjects will represent Hendrick Hudson discovering the North River," the *Mercury* reported, "[and] the other will represent the Discovery of the Columbia on the Pacific."[105]

Bierstadt's presumption of imminent success proved unwarranted. At the committee meeting of 13 March, after due consideration of his proposal and price, members voted "to inform Mr. Bierstadt that no appropriation having been made to carry out the purpose of the House resolution respecting the panels in their Hall the Committee deemed it inexpedient in the present state of our finances to recommend an appropriation for the object in question."[106] The measured language of the minutes did not, in fact, convey the committee's outrage at Bierstadt's price. "The committee," Francis Colburn Adams reported, "were disposed to make a liberal contract with him. A letter, however, was placed before the committee from Mr. Bierstadt, demanding $40,000 each—$80,000 for two pictures. This was alike unfortunate for Mr. Bierstadt and the interests of American art, which he professed to represent. The demand seemed to the committee so exorbitant, and so at variance with the spirit of patriotism which should inspire an artist to get one of his works on the walls of the Capitol, that the proposal was promptly rejected."[107] Despite the artist's immediate counteroffer to reduce his price to $30,000 for each painting (he produced the contract for *The Rocky Mountains, Lander's Peak* as evidence of his market value), the project "was not again brought up in the committee."[108]

In what was surely one of the major miscalculations of his career, Bierstadt had assumed, on the basis of recent sales to McHenry, Kennard, and Lockwood, that he could successfully command from Congress, for a single picture, the entire sum that the defunct Art Commission had recommended in 1860 as an adequate budget for eight paintings to fill four panels in the House and four in the Senate Chamber. He reasoned that *The Rocky Mountains, Lander's Peak*, "which was sold for $25,000 . . . is a smaller picture, and less work" than would be expended on such a commission.

Francis Colburn Adams, setting the episode in context, lamented not only Bierstadt's "exorbitant" demand, but also what he interpreted as the pernicious influence of the recent Powell commission: "If Congress could afford to pay Mr. Powell $5,000 more for a picture than it had paid Emmanuel Leutze, Mr. Bierstadt very naturally thought Congress would not object to give him $15,000 more than it had given Mr. Powell for a picture."[109]

There was another very good reason for Bierstadt's demand, which he confided to Captain Adams. "I hope you will sell the pictures," he wrote, "as I am very much in want of money."[110] This complaint was to become a leitmotif sounded repeatedly in correspondence in the years to come. Ensconced in his recently completed mansion at Irvington, with a new bride who shared his social and material ambitions, and about to embark on an extended grand tour, Bierstadt had established a style of life that rapidly became the engine driving his career. The artist chose to interpret the committee's decision as merely a "delay" in what he could hardly have suspected would become a protracted lobbying campaign. Somewhat disingenuously, he continued to claim a congressional commission that had not, in fact, been consummated by the successful negotiation of a contract. Francis Colburn Adams's more accurate account of the episode, published in 1870, was buried in a government report receiving little, if any, public notice, while every biographer from Henry Tuckerman on has repeated the face-saving fiction steadfastly maintained by the artist as he continued to lobby doggedly in Congress over the next decade.[111]

## Seeking Wider Recognition Abroad

Bierstadt suggested that the need to make studies for *Discovery of the Hudson River* took him to Europe in June 1867.[112] In fact, the timing of the trip was probably dictated by the Exposition Universelle, which had opened in April, drawing many Americans to Paris. The mounting challenge to Bierstadt's American standing—*The Domes of the Yosemite* had debuted to the violently mixed reviews noted earlier only a month after the frustrating congressional balk—must have lent fuel to his intentions to gain wider recognition abroad and to develop a market for his work.

Late in 1866, Bierstadt had already begun to make arrangements to show *The Rocky Mountains, Lander's Peak*, by then in London with its new owner, at the Exposition Universelle.[113] Although the eighty-two paintings in the American section of the Fine Arts Department did not make much of an impression on the jury of awards, Frank Leslie dubbed *The Rocky Mountains, Lander's Peak* "the most conspicuous picture in the American gallery" and suggested that the painting had been the popular favorite among "the mass of the lovers and appreciators of art who visited our gallery."[114] The jury deemed otherwise; Bierstadt, especially, must have been disappointed when Church was the only American to win a fine-arts medal, for *Niagara*, at the award ceremonies on 1 July. Sylvester Köhler suggested that Church's native origin had given him the edge over Bierstadt in the eyes of a French jury seeking (it seemed to Köhler) a verifiable artistic product of the New World.[115]

During sojourns in Rome, London, and Paris between 1867 and 1869, Bierstadt concentrated efforts to establish himself and his work in these capitals, setting up studios and collecting commissions and endorsements from both Europeans and visiting Americans. He also made ample use of the device of the "Great Picture." During the course of his two-year stay in Europe, Bierstadt managed various tours (to Paris, London, Berlin, Rome, Brussels, and Munich) for all five of his panoramas of the West. While the Exposition Universelle had not yielded an award, Bierstadt gleaned a gold medal in late 1868 from the Royal Academy in Berlin for *Among the Sierra*

*Nevada Mountains, California* (No. 48). There, his Düsseldorf style and German origin proved, for once, assets rather than liabilities.

Bierstadt's quest for European prizes and official endorsement, echoing his campaign for the Capitol at home, became a central concern in later years. As his American standing faltered, his insistence on the importance of an international reputation escalated. "It is certainly a matter of some importance," he wrote in 1878 regarding his campaign for the remaining House panel, "for a man to have received from almost every European Power the highest recognition they can offer to an American for his works."[116] In the spring of 1869, *Storm in the Rocky Mountains, Mt. Rosalie* was exhibited at the Paris Salon, earning Bierstadt the award he perhaps cherished most: designation by Napoléon III as a chevalier of the Legion of Honor.[117] Samuel P. Avery, a prominent New York dealer and a member of the American Committee for the 1867 Exposition Universelle, claimed that Bierstadt's French decoration was the result of a calculated lobbying effort rather than a simple recognition of merit. Avery wrote to artist William T. Richards: "Bierstadt got his decoration by petition to the Empress—a request that this honor should be conferred on the *greatest* American artist. Signed by all the governors of States, U.S. Representatives, big and other hum-bugs—caught on *their run through* Europe! did you ever?—no I never!!!"[118]

Bierstadt must have held especially high hopes for the London sojourn in 1867–68. Two of his most famous works already belonged to English patrons, and there were long-established cultural, economic, and political ties between England and America.[119] The artist's disappointment at the Exposition Universelle must have been somewhat mollified by a December 1867 invitation from Queen Victoria to accompany his two Rocky Mountain panoramas to Osborne House on the Isle of Wight for a royal audience. Bierstadt reported that Her Majesty "seemed much pleased with my works," while Rosalie noted with satisfaction that "the view from the Queen's Drawing Room is not finer than ours from the [Irvington] Studio."[120]

When the Bierstadts left England for a winter stay in Italy, *The Rocky Mountains, Lander's Peak* and *Storm in the Rocky Mountains, Mt. Rosalie* were on exhibition in London at McLean's Gallery. When the artist returned to London in the spring of 1868, *The Domes of the Yosemite* was the current attraction. Church's paintings had been well known in England since *Niagara* was exhibited in London in 1857, and he, too, had cultivated patronage there. Comparisons of the two painters were inevitable and, in general, paralleled American opinion: "Mr. Bierstadt *is* a great painter. He is not so great a painter as Mr. Church. He is not so daring a colourist. He is not gifted with so lofty an imagination; but he has immense industry—industry not only of production, but of observation and record."[121]

One of Bierstadt's major coups of the 1867–69 European sojourn was the famous and well-publicized Longfellow Dinner he hosted on 9 July 1868 at the Langham Hotel in London, where he was a resident. The elaborate dinner for some eighty distinguished English and American guests was held in tribute to the visiting poet Henry Wadsworth Longfellow, who was on an extended tour of Europe collecting honors and degrees. Hailed as one who "had made himself the poet of the English-speaking race,"[122] Longfellow was just the literary lion with whom Bierstadt could attract powerful and influential figures of both nations. In honor of the occasion, the artist presented the poet with a small painting, *Departure of Hiawatha* (Fig. 25).[123] A carte de visite photograph of Longfellow adorned each souvenir menu.

Among Bierstadt's American guests were Admiral David Farragut; Cyrus W. Field, who had received a Grand Prize at the Exposition Universelle for the Atlantic cable; and Parke Godwin,

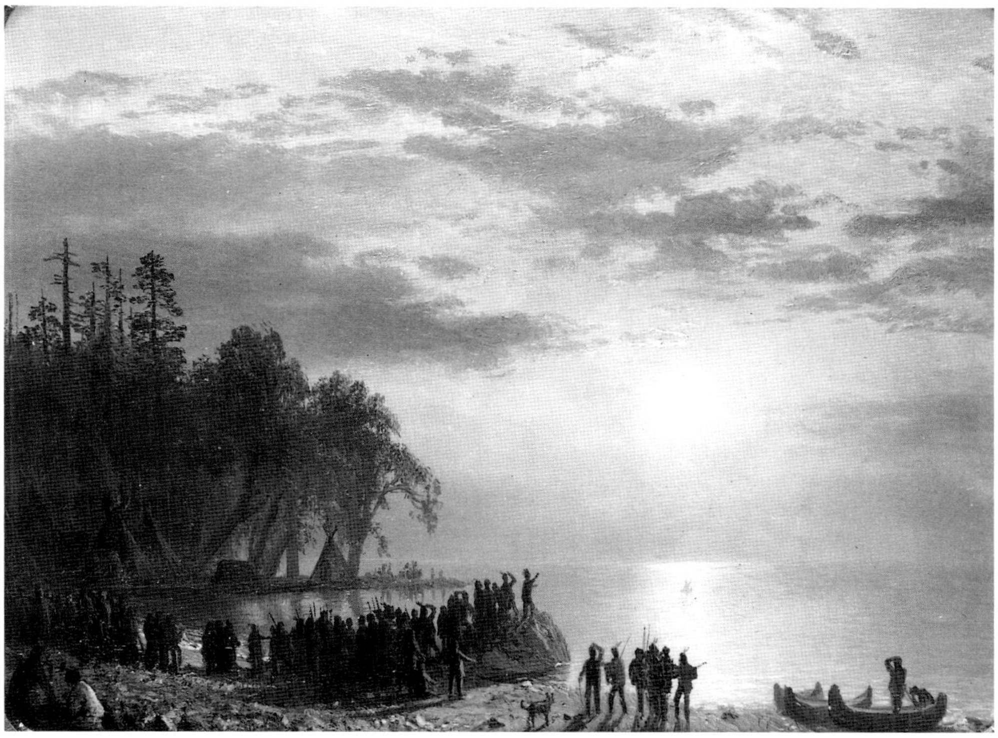

Figure 25
Albert Bierstadt. *Departure of Hiawatha*, c. 1868. Oil on paper, 6⅞ × 8⅛ in. (17.5 × 20.6 cm). National Park Service, Longfellow National Historic Site, Cambridge, Massachusetts.

editor of the New York *Post*. Prominent Englishmen included William E. Gladstone, leader of the Liberal party and soon to be prime minister, and the Duke of Argyll. Church's patron William Watkin was there, as were Robert Browning and Sir Edwin Landseer. It was reported that the dinner was intended as a "private" affair. There were to be none of the customary speeches "according to Mr. Longfellow's express desire, added to that of Mr. Bierstadt."[124] A letter from Bierstadt to Parke Godwin indicates that the artist originally had other intentions, however. Bierstadt informed the journalist that his address "on the Press or Literature of the two countries" would be the seventh of "ten speeches in all." Moreover, he continued, publicity would be international. "Mr. Field tells me that all [via the cable, no doubt] will appear in the New York papers on the following morning."[125] "Private" or otherwise, the dinner received wide coverage in the English and American press. As the host (or, perhaps more accurately, impresario) of this international event, Bierstadt had the immense satisfaction of seeing his name linked in print with those of some of the most distinguished figures (and potential patrons) of the day. Writing to her sister from Rome, sculptor Anne Whitney (1821–1915) passed along what must have been common gossip in the artists' community in which Bierstadt had sojourned the winter before. Acknowledging the Longfellow Dinner as "a master stroke to get [Bierstadt's] name handed around among the English," Whitney nevertheless deplored the event as "largely a subject of comment and sarcasm among critics and other talkers whom we meet. . . . [Bierstadt] is said not to have known any of the people he invited—but to have done it all in the way of business." "A good deal of talk of this kind grows out of the ill-will which success engenders," Whitney admitted, but she also complained "that art becomes more and more of a trade in which the artifices that are used in other trades and professions are brought to bear."[126] Her lament that "real artist feeling is at a low ebb" again reflected the universal conviction that a "real artist" could not also be a businessman—an attitude that rejected the "enterprise of commerce" that Bierstadt had candidly (and successfully) embraced.

## Swimming Against the Tide

Soon after the Bierstadts returned to New York with many orders from England in August 1869,[127] the artist's career suffered setbacks, both critical and financial. Not only did Bierstadt's future competitor Thomas Moran (1837–1926) soar to prominence as a rival interpreter of the western landscape, but—equally important—economic forces ushered in the end of the boom years.

Although Alvin Adams purchased Bierstadt's gold-medal painting, *Among the Sierra Nevada Mountains, California* (No. 48), in late 1869 for the reported sum of $15,000,[128] other of the artist's patrons were not faring well. During the panic that followed Wall Street's Black Friday of September 1869, Le Grand Lockwood, the man who had commissioned the biggest, and one of the most expensive, of Bierstadt's paintings, was ruined. His Norwalk mansion was mortgaged and his firm's railroad interests sold to Cornelius Vanderbilt. A diminished Lockwood and Company resumed business late in 1870, but neither the firm nor its founder ever really recovered. Early in 1872, Lockwood died of pneumonia at the age of fifty-two. In April his painting collection was sold at auction in New York. *The Domes of the Yosemite* (Fig. 58), the acknowledged star of the collection, completed only five years before for a commission of $25,000, brought only $5,100 "amid murmurs of surprise."[129] The first reappearance on the market of one of Bierstadt's "Great Pictures" of the 1860s signaled, in terms of hard cash, that the boom years were over. Bierstadt himself would manage to stay afloat quite handsomely for some time to come, but he was now, like many of his generation of artists, definitely swimming against the tide.

At the time of the Lockwood sale, the artist was far from New York, having once again relocated to greener pastures. The Bierstadts were then in the second year of an extended sojourn in California. Based in the kinder critical climate of San Francisco, the artist made sketching forays for new subject matter into the Sierra Nevada and reaped the patronage of such San Francisco railroad magnates as Collis P. Huntington and Leland Stanford of the Central Pacific Railroad. During this period he also traveled in the Sierra Nevada with Clarence King, head of the United States Geological Exploration of the Fortieth Parallel, which was charged with surveying and mapping the region.

While King seems to have enjoyed Bierstadt's company, the geologist was not at all satisfied with the artist's interpretation of the mountain range he knew so well. A decade earlier, in 1863, King had been a founding member (with Clarence Cook) of the American Pre-Raphaelite Brotherhood. Like others in the American Ruskinian circle, he measured all landscape against the achievement of J. M. W. Turner.[130] Longing for an American Turner to "arise and choose to paint our Sierras as they are," King, like many others of his generation, embraced Ruskin's contradictory but eloquent insistence in *Modern Painters* that the imaginative and painterly license of Turner's Alpine subjects was somehow grounded in an absolute grasp of the science of geology. In his popular book, *Mountaineering in the Sierra Nevada* (1872), King adopted the humorous voice of fictional artist Hank G. Smith to express what were by then widely held reservations about Bierstadt: "It's all Bierstadt and Bierstadt and Bierstadt nowadays! What has he done but twist and skew and distort and discolor and belittle and be-pretty this whole doggonned country? Why, his mountains are too high and too slim; they'd blow over in one of our fall winds. I've herded colts two summers in Yosemite, and honest now, when I stood right up in front of his picture, I didn't know it." King's alter ego concluded, "He hasn't what old Ruskin calls for."[131]

While Bierstadt was in California, an American Turner seemed to have appeared on the scene in the person of Thomas Moran. A Philadelphia landscape painter, Moran had studied in England in 1861 and 1866. There, his admiration of Turner deepened. It was demonstrated by liberal reference in his oil paintings, watercolors, and illustrations to the English master's style. In the summer of 1871, Moran was engaged to accompany Ferdinand V. Hayden, head of the United States Geological and Geographical Survey of the Territories, to Yellowstone. Moran's reputation, like that of Bierstadt before him, was made by the products of that experience: widely published magazine illustrations of the Yellowstone campaign; a series of brilliant watercolors; and a "Great Picture," *The Grand Canyon of the Yellowstone* (Fig. 26), completed early in 1872.[132] The last, surely modeled on Bierstadt's own successes, immediately established Moran as a challenger to the other artist's interpretation of the western landscape. While Bierstadt's vision was based upon the long-problematic Düsseldorf model, Moran's approach to landscape was steeped in a Turnerian idiom. Here was the devotee of Turner whose painted geology had received Hayden's (and, by implication, King's) stamp of approval. Predictably, Moran also received the enthusiastic endorsement of Bierstadt's Ruskinian nemesis, Clarence Cook.[133]

Moran had another advantage over Bierstadt in his practice of the watercolor medium. Extolled by the Ruskinian circle, watercolor was closely associated with Turner and natural to Moran as an extension of his work as an illustrator. Its rising popularity among artists and patrons is signified by the establishment in 1866 of the American Society of Painters in Water Colors. The medium appealed to the more advanced American painters, such as Winslow Homer (1836–1910) and Thomas Eakins (1844–1916), as well as to a number of conservative landscape and marine painters, including Jasper Cropsey (1823–1900), William T. Richards (1833–1905), and Moran himself. For the so-called Hudson River School painters, especially, the intimate scale and delicacy of watercolor offered an attractive way to appeal to an audience increasingly disenchanted with their practice of oil painting. Bierstadt did not respond to this trend, observing to Richards on a visit to that artist's Newport studio that he "liked oil painting better."[134] The intimate scale and freshness of vision characteristic of watercolor remained, for Bierstadt, private phenomena, to be found in the best of his oil sketches, like *Surveyor's Wagon in the Rockies*, c. 1859 (No. 20), and *Wreck of the "Ancon" in Loring Bay, Alaska*, 1889 (No. 72). The public Bierstadt was committed to the increasingly unfashionable studio picture.

## The Capitol Commission Redux

In June 1872, following the designation of Yellowstone as a national park in March, Congress bought Moran's *Grand Canyon of the Yellowstone* for the Senate lobby. The $10,000 purchase, coming only two months after the humiliating resale (for half that price) of *The Domes of the Yosemite*, must have been a very bitter blow to Bierstadt. The event may well have stimulated him to reopen his quest for the Capitol commission with new determination.

Early in 1873, *California Art Gallery* mentioned the project in a long article on Bierstadt, who seems to have suggested a plethora of private commissions as the reason for the six-year delay in executing the works for the Capitol. "He has done nothing, as yet, we believe, on this work," the magazine reported. "In common with half-a-dozen other large orders it has to make way for that which is more in accord with the artist's desire and moods."[135]

Meanwhile, matters grew worse for Bierstadt in Washington. In the summer of 1873, while he was still in San Francisco, Moran had gone west again, this time accompanying John Wesley Powell's United States Geographical and Geological Survey of the Rocky Mountain Region to the Grand Canyon of the Colorado. In July 1874, a second large landscape by Moran, *Chasm of the Colorado*,

Figure 26

Thomas Moran. *The Grand Canyon of the Yellowstone*, 1872. Oil on canvas, 84 × 144¼ in. (213.9 × 266.3 cm). National Museum of American Art, Smithsonian Institution, Washington, D.C., Lent by the U.S. Department of the Interior, Office of the Secretary.

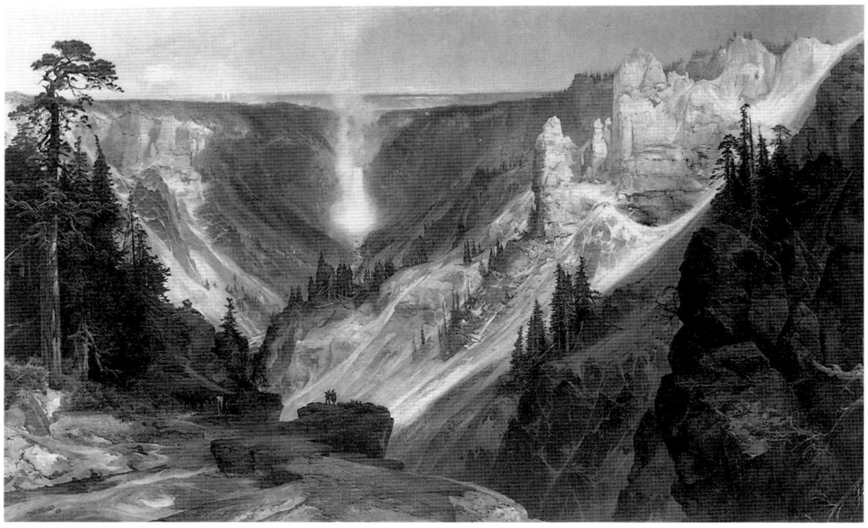

Figure 27

Thomas Moran. *Chasm of the Colorado*, 1873–74. Oil on canvas, 84¾ × 144¾ in. (213.9 × 266.3 cm). National Museum of American Art, Smithsonian Institution, Washington, D.C., Lent by the U.S. Department of the Interior, Office of the Secretary.

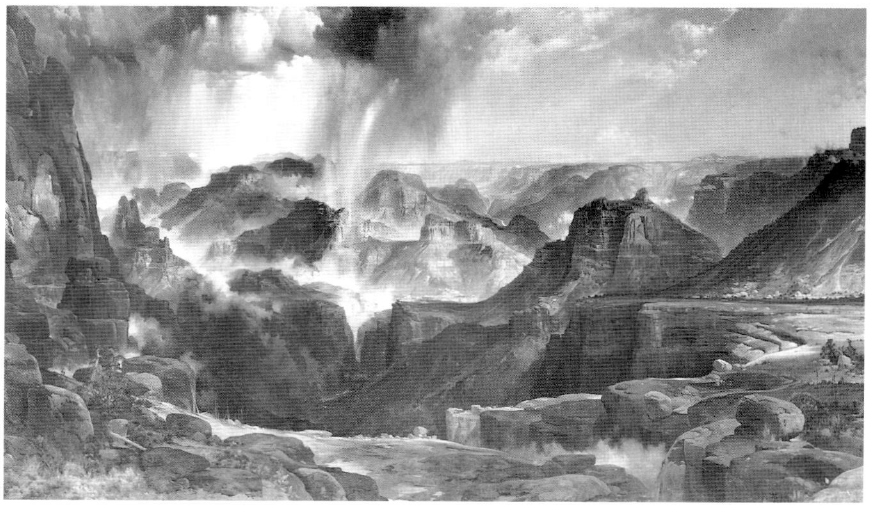

1873–74 (Fig. 27), was purchased for $10,000 by Congress to complement the Yellowstone subject.[136] Bierstadt's dream of pendant western landscapes in the Capitol had been realized by another.

He did not give up, however. In September 1874, back in the East, Bierstadt was reported to be at work on "a field of effort somewhat new to him," a history painting.[137] By October he wrote to George Bancroft, an old friend recently returned to Washington from diplomatic service in Germany, that he was close to completing *Discovery of the Hudson River* (Fig. 21): "I shall send [it] to Washington, and hope to have the pleasure of showing it to you." In the same letter, Bierstadt enlisted Bancroft's aid in presenting a painting of a giant sequoia to the German kaiser; perhaps he hoped the eminent historian and diplomat could be influential in Washington, as well.[138] Plans were already under way to exhibit the history painting, along with a Sierra Nevada mountain subject (Fig. 28), at the Capitol. Bierstadt had not, however, appealed for that privilege to the Library Committee. In August he had written, rather, to Edward Clarke, architect of the Capitol, discussing exhibition arrangements. "I will go in with the pictures myself and put them in position," the artist wrote to Clarke in September. He most certainly intended them to remain permanently, for when Clarke acknowledged receipt of the frames on 23 November, he found it necessary to caution the artist "that, at present, we have no right to cut the walls of the building for the reception of the pictures, but think the pictures might be hung in their places. . . . However, we will try to arrange to suit you when you come on."[139] In December the *New York Times* reported the success of what was seen as an irregular maneuver:

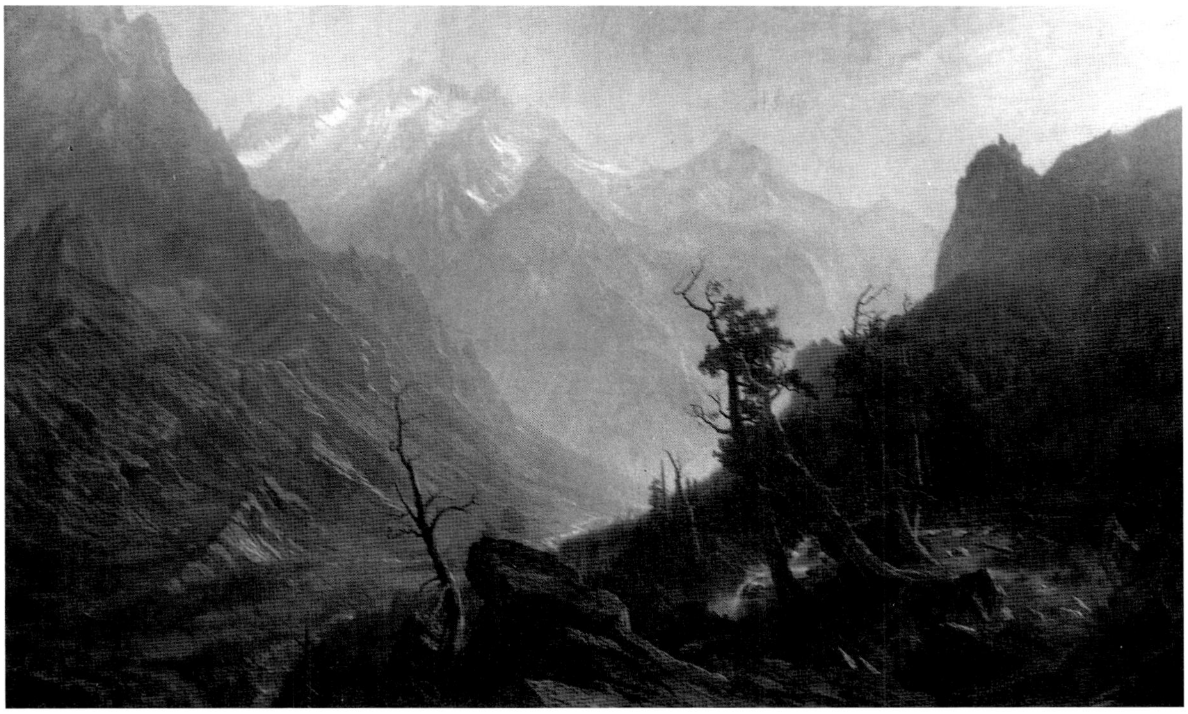

Figure 28
Albert Bierstadt. *Autumn in the Sierras*, 1873. Oil on canvas, 72 × 120 in. (182.9 × 304.8 cm). City of Plainfield, New Jersey.

> Bierstadt . . . has got both of his large pictures . . . hung on two of the House panels. There was no authority for this, as the joint committee on the library declined all responsibility in the matter. A few years ago, on motion of Gen. Banks, a resolution was passed in the House authorizing these pictures, but the Senate declined to agree to it. Subsequently a resolution was adopted declaring it inexpedient to buy them, but Bierstadt went ahead and painted them, and in some way he has got them into the House, and he expects to get $50,000 for them before the session closes.[140]

Bierstadt exhibited the pictures while actually continuing to work on them. "During the past week," one newspaper reported, "two paintings by our great American artist, Alfred [*sic*] Bierstadt, have been placed in the panels on the south side of the Chamber of the House of Representatives. . . . They attract much attention and universally favorable comment. They are not quite finished, and the artist is engaged in giving them their final touches and corrections, so that visitors to the Capitol the past few days have experienced the novelty of seeing in progress two great works of art, which will for centuries to come serve to illustrate our earthly history and perpetuate the fame of their author." Bierstadt's "finishing touches" were, without doubt, superb theater. "I do not understand that they have yet been purchased by the Government," the article continued, "but there is little doubt that they will be." The same account offered yet another explanation, doubtless supplied by the artist, of the long delay in the execution of Bierstadt's commission: "Congress many years ago directed the Library Committee to order or contract with Mr. Bierstadt for two paintings upon national subjects. He declined to sell them in advance, preferring in a very proper spirit, to do his work first and submit it to the judgment of his countrymen. If it should merit a place in the Capitol, he felt sure of its appreciation and acceptance; but if it proved unworthy, he could not afford to let it be purchased by the nation. A little work in the way of finishing, and they will be ready for the final judgment of Congress and the country."[141]

Bierstadt's decision to exhibit a dramatic panorama, *Kings River Canyon* (now known as *Autumn in the Sierras*), 1873 (Fig. 28),[142] depicting an area he had visited with Clarence King, suggests that he still hoped to be represented at the Capitol by a western landscape. Moran's canyon views of the Yellowstone and Colorado river gorges (Figs. 26, 27) may well have influenced Bierstadt's decision to depart from his earlier Rocky Mountain and Yosemite Valley themes. Instead, he depicted a third spectacular chasm that was as closely associated with King as Yellowstone and Colorado were with Hayden and Powell. A Sierra Nevada mountain landscape in tribute to Clarence King, who would soon lead the consolidated United States Geological Survey, was an astute bid for congressional support. Just as Moran had included a figural vignette of Hayden and his associates at the rim of Yellowstone Canyon, Bierstadt placed "a party of explorers" in the foreground of his painting.

Bierstadt's well-orchestrated lobbying effort proved partially successful, for on 3 March 1875 Congress purchased *Discovery of the Hudson River* for $10,000—the price paid to Moran for each of his works—although the artist, characteristically, had hoped for at least $15,000.[143] The Library Committee's choice of *Discovery of the Hudson River*, a *retardataire* costume piece in the tradition of the earlier Rotunda paintings of John Vanderlyn (1775–1852) and Powell, apparently convinced Bierstadt to abandon efforts to place *Kings River Canyon* in the Capitol. He soon began work on another historical subject, this one celebrating the West Coast, *Settlement of California, Bay of Monterey, 1770* (Fig. 22), which he subsequently exhibited at the 1876 Philadelphia Centennial Exposition.[144]

Early in 1877, Bierstadt wrote to Ainsworth R. Spofford, Librarian of Congress, reminding him, in a highly revealing letter, of what was by then a decade of unfinished business. "You remember of course the time when the resolution was passed authorizing the Library Committee to contract with me for two pictures," he began. "I have spoken to you about this matter before and, at the risk of boring you, I do so again. . . . [I write] as I am very anxious for your influence. Two years ago when my Discovery of the Hudson was purchased you know that I received only $10000. for it. I was advised to do this on account of the unsettled state of political affairs and as the picture had been intended for that place I preferred to have it there than elsewhere. . . . [Thus] I sacrificed the picture[.] Now I'm hoping to get enough more for [*Settlement of California*] to make things balance a little." Bierstadt then proceeded to the point of his letter: "The argument has been used that as long as others—one in particular—was willing to take $10000 for a picture of equal size that I ought not to receive any more, but they forgot that our reputations are very different. Mine is European as well as American and I have received practical evidence of the esteem in which I am held there that the gentleman in question never has." Bierstadt went on to cite his familiar list of "stars and crosses": "I have been decorated in France, Russia and Austria. I have received the highest prize (a gold medal) . . . conferred upon a foreigner exhibiting for the first time in Russia. Medals also in Austria and . . . in Germany—and probably no American artist finds as ready a sale for his pictures in England as I do." Once again, the artist invoked his benchmark sale of 1865: "Indeed my picture of the Rocky Mts. by which I first became generally known and which was sold for $25,000. to its present owner has had an offer of $40,000 which has been refused." He concluded with another thinly veiled reference to Moran: "If the Committee is to be guided in their purchase of works of Art by the low rate at which the painters are willing to sell them I could point out men willing to fill all the panels for $500. each."[145]

By January 1878, Bierstadt and Moran were openly competing for the remaining House commission.[146] This time Moran took his cue from Bierstadt, abandoning the geological grandeur of the West for *Ponce de Leon in Florida, 1513*, 1878 (Fig. 29), a pseudohistorical episode set in a lush Florida forest glade and conceived in subject and composition as a pendant to *Discovery of the Hudson River*. Moran made this clear in his petition to the Library Committee: "It seemed to me that a picture commemorative of the first attempt at settlement, and characteristic of the semi-

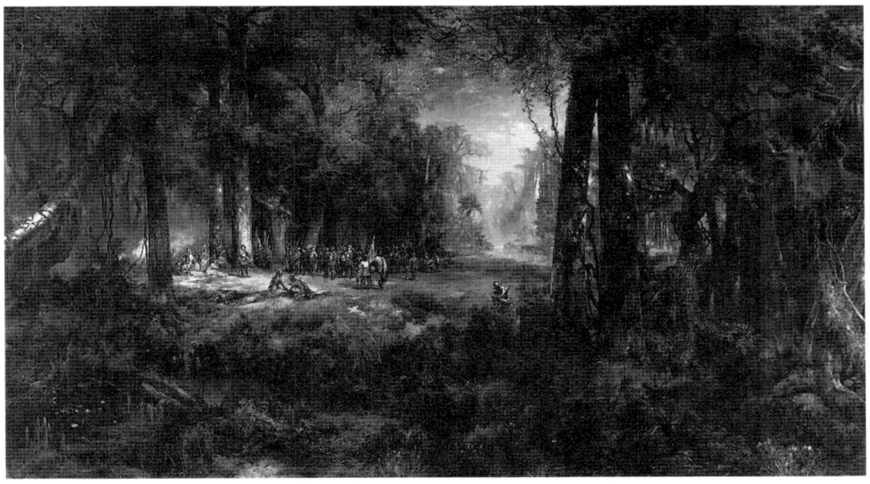

Figure 29

Thomas Moran. *Ponce de Leon in Florida, 1513*, 1878. Oil on canvas, 63½ × 115 in. (161.3 × 292.1 cm). National Cowboy Hall of Fame and Western Heritage Center, Oklahoma City.

tropical part of our country, would be a proper pendant to a picture already purchased representing a later and more northern discovery."[147] By then Bierstadt apparently had achieved the logistical advantage of occupying the disputed panel. Responding to a letter from Ferdinand V. Hayden concerning Moran's bid for yet a third Capitol commission, Bierstadt vigorously defended his own claim: "One of the pictures has been paid for and I do not think the other can be moved without very much trouble. I know that Mr. Moran has attempted and is at work upon this matter. Why he should try & have one removed when there is so much space outside I cannot tell." Bierstadt went on to offer Hayden another version of the events of 1867:

> I could at that time have had the money laid aside for that purpose, but as I could not fill the order for some years I favored the use of the money then in the hands of the library committee to be invested in the Peter Force library which was at that time offered for sale. Selfishness is the motto now and if I had chosen could have had at least 50—or $60,000 laid aside for my works. This fact is not appreciated and as I have an abundance to do I cannot afford to spend my time in Washington for this picture and I do not care to paint any more pictures for U.S. There is no profit in it. . . . I have informed Senator Howe & Edmonds of these facts and I think they will have some regard for my interests.

He recited, somewhat desperately, his credentials: "I have the Cross of the Legion of Honor from France. Two from Russia, the highest awards from Germany, Austria, etc. etc. I only tell you this and this letter like your own is confidential."[148]

In his efforts to consummate the purchase, Bierstadt did not depend on the influence of senators alone. Soon after he wrote to Hayden, the artist was the guest of President and Mrs. Hayes for a week at the White House. As noted earlier, Hayes had admired *Storm in the Rocky Mountains, Mt. Rosalie* in 1866, when he was a congressman. In addition, Bierstadt was on very friendly terms with the President's son, Webb Hayes. We may assume that, in between balls and dinners, the artist alluded to the matter of the House panel. The matter was finally resolved in Bierstadt's favor, probably before the artist sailed for Europe on 20 July. *Settlement of California, Bay of Monterey, 1770*, purchased for $10,000, remained with *Discovery of the Hudson River* in the House Chamber (Fig. 24), while Moran's paintings held sway in the Senate wing.[149] Neither Bierstadt's nor Moran's works have remained in situ. Moran's landscapes were transferred to the Department of the Interior and, finally, to the National Museum of American Art, where they hang today. Bierstadt's paintings were removed from the House Chamber soon after the turn of the century, although they remain in the Capitol. Never among his finest works and now much deteriorated, the paintings are somewhat inaccessible, installed in the stairwells of the members' private stairways in the House wing.

## The Corcoran Affair

At the same time that he was struggling to sell *Settlement of California, Bay of Monterey, 1770* to Congress in 1877, Bierstadt was also conducting the final maneuvers of a three-year campaign to place a painting in the Corcoran Gallery of Art, founded by millionaire Washington banker William Wilson Corcoran. Following the construction of the gallery in 1859, the transfer of the collection in 1869, and long delays caused by the Civil War and Corcoran's political difficulties as a Southern sympathizer, the gallery, housed in a splendid building by James Renwick, finally opened on 19 January 1874. Corcoran's gift to the City of Washington included most of his private holdings of American and European paintings and sculpture, collected over several decades. While Corcoran had acquired works of the American landscape school since the 1850s, Bierstadt was not among the artists represented. On establishing the gallery, Corcoran had relinquished purchasing power to the institution.[150]

Bierstadt wasted no time contacting trustees as well as the curator, a Washington landscape painter named William MacLeod (1811–1892). On 7 January, before the doors opened to the public, Bierstadt wrote to Joseph Henry, secretary of the Smithsonian and a gallery trustee, and arranged to exhibit a large painting, *Mount Adams on the Columbia River, Oregon* (unlocated). Bierstadt offered a deal to Joseph Henry and William T. Walters, another trustee, who was also a collector and Corcoran's own purchasing agent. The painting, he informed them, was worth as much as $15,000, but he would sell it to the gallery for $5,000. The artist reiterated his offer to MacLeod. A month later, apparently having had no response to his proposal, an anxious Bierstadt wrote again: "It has occurred to me that if the Corcoran Art Gallery wishes a work of mine they might prefer a larger one or a different subject from the Mt. Adams. . . . I would take great pleasure in endeavoring to please the Committee, as I would like to be well represented in that gallery." By the end of the year, Bierstadt conceded defeat and recalled the painting.[151] He had not given up in his quest for the gallery's patronage, however.

Bierstadt's pressing desire to be "well represented" in a public collection that already included landscapes by Cole, Kensett, Cropsey, and Church, as well as two paintings by Leutze, is understandable. There were few such collections in America, and Bierstadt had long understood the significance of such recognition. As early as 1858, the Boston Athenaeum had purchased what had quickly become known as a Bierstadt masterwork, *The Arch of Octavius (The Roman Fish Market)*, 1858 (No. 11). Early in 1863, the young artist had presented *The Marina Piccola, Capri*, 1859 (No. 14), as a "free gift" to the newly founded Buffalo Fine Arts Academy "as a sincere expression of my best wishes for the true and abundant success of the Academy." Bierstadt's altruism had paid off handsomely, for the academy purchased the artist's first western panorama, *Base of the Rocky Mountains, Laramie Peak* (see Fig. 3), soon after.[152] Seeking the widest distribution for his works, Bierstadt energetically campaigned throughout his career for the establishment of public galleries in American cities and farther afield as well. Early in 1878, on the occasion of the opening of the Art Association of Montreal's art gallery, Bierstadt, who was a good friend of the governor-general's, made a gift of a California landscape.[153] In every case, he sought to galvanize local citizens with the promise of a painting of his own as a gift or at a substantial discount.

This latter device was of increasing importance to the artist as his market declined in the 1870s. In 1877 he tried, for example, to place *Kings River Canyon* (Fig. 28), rejected by Congress and then on the road as a "Great Picture," as the nucleus of a public collection in Columbus, Ohio. He solicited MacLeod's advice, as well as that of John Sartain at the Pennsylvania Academy of the

Fine Arts in Philadelphia, for "some gentlemen" in Columbus who were inquiring (no doubt with Bierstadt's encouragement) "about starting an Academy of Fine Arts."[154] Earlier, he had tried to interest an unidentified correspondent in Saint Louis, where the same painting was on view, in beginning a local campaign for "a free public gallery." The letter, written in late 1873, gives a vivid glimpse of Bierstadt as a promoter. "I take so much interest in the advancement of Art that I would be glad to contribute a picture for such an enterprise," he began. "If therefore those gentlemen interested in such matters should desire it for such a purpose I would sell them my large picture 'Autumn in the Sierras' . . . at half price." He went on to offer a candid profile of the gallery's prospective benefactor and a plan: "Sometimes men of large fortune whose age and bodily infirmities tell them they are soon to pass away like to leave some memorial behind them. . . . Up to a certain moment they are anxious to accumulate all they can and then it must rapidly be disposed of. Such a man there may be in your City whose thoughts by your suggestion might be turned in this direction." The artist offered his assistance as an agent in "collecting many fine works of Art. Many, too, without cost simply as donations to the gallery. I would give a picture such as I get $2000 or more for and as I said before sell my large one at a very low price." This is vintage Bierstadt; the writer skillfully places his own interests in the benevolent context of a project for the public good.[155]

Meanwhile, the Corcoran's trustees continued to build the gallery collection. In 1876 they purchased a number of European works from the Philadelphia Centennial Exposition,[156] bought two works by Kensett at the William T. Blodgett sale, and acquired Church's *Niagara* for $12,500 at the John Taylor Johnston sale. The last purchase, in particular, may well have motivated Bierstadt to try again. In April 1877, he had exhibited a large landscape composition titled simply *Mountain Lake* (see Fig. 31) at the National Academy of Design, and soon after, this painting, rechristened *Mount Corcoran* (Fig. 32), was in Washington under consideration for purchase by the gallery.[157] The naming of mountains was not a new tactic for Bierstadt. The artist had first adopted such a commemorative device in 1863 with *The Rocky Mountains, Lander's Peak,* whose central painted summit Bierstadt named in memory of the 1859 expedition leader Colonel Frederick W. Lander. The title of his second Rocky Mountain panorama, *Storm in the Rocky Mountains, Mt. Rosalie,* included a similar tribute to Rosalie Ludlow, whom he would later marry. Bierstadt had recently painted the Sierra Nevada peaks already named in honor of the geologists active in the

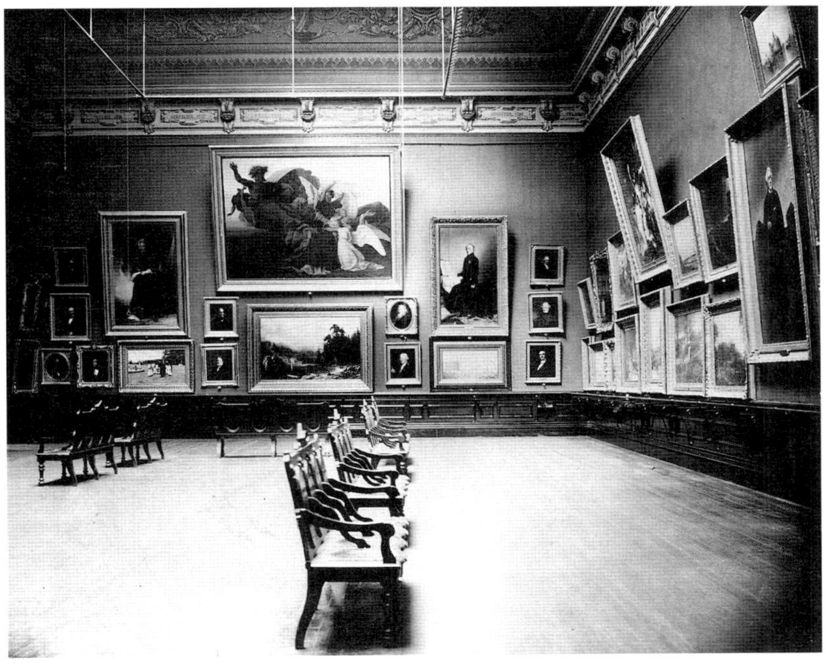

Figure 30

*"Mount Corcoran" hanging in the Grand Salon, Corcoran Art Gallery (now the Renwick Gallery), after 1880*. Photograph. National Museum of American Art, Renwick Gallery, Smithsonian Institution, Washington, D.C.

range, Josiah D. Whitney (see Fig. 66) and William H. Brewer. However, his transformation of what had been, only a few months earlier, a generic mountain composition into the banker's geological namesake can only be construed as a bid for the founder's personal support of an acquisition that the curator and trustees must have been resisting. In December Bierstadt notified MacLeod of plans to remove *Mount Corcoran*, suggesting that the Earl of Dunraven might wish to have it as a companion for his own recently completed commission, *The Rocky Mountains, Longs Peak*, 1877 (Fig. 65). In the same letter, however, the artist reiterated his hope that the painting would be purchased by the gallery. "I cannot give it to the institution," Bierstadt insisted, "although I have the greatest admiration for the man [Corcoran], and think I have done well by him in naming one of our finest mountains after him."[158]

MacLeod's and, one assumes, the trustees' reluctance about the purchase is suggested in a curator's journal entry of 11 January 1878 recording a visit by Powell and Moran. (The latter, like Bierstadt, was in Washington to lobby for the House Chamber panel then under discussion by Congress.) MacLeod must have solicited an opinion about *Mount Corcoran*, for he noted their responses to the painting. Powell, like Clarence King before him, mistrusted Bierstadt's geology: "Maj. Powell thinks Bierstadt's Mt. Corcoran not truthful in form of the mountain—too much of a precipice." Moran, in a generous (or equivocal) comment, thought the painting "the best Bierstadt [the gallery] could buy."[159] By that time, however, the creator of *Mount Corcoran* was about to take the matter into his own hands, boldly calling upon the founder himself. The artist later pronounced himself highly pleased with his reception by the patron, whom he hailed as "worthy of the days of the Medici." Continuing this testimonial and recapitulating what must have been his direct appeal to Corcoran, he wrote to lobbyist and financier Samuel Ward: "I think I speak the minds of all when I say that the greatest living painters would take great pride in being represented in the Corcoran institution by the best work they can produce and at a cost far less than to any private person or dealer for they would refer their friends to that gallery as representing their best efforts. . . . I am happy to have named one of our highest mountains after him, the first to catch the morning sunlight the last to say good night. . . . I painted that picture with a loving hand but when you see the grandeur of the original what a toy it is!" Artistic eloquence and blatant flattery proved effective, for Bierstadt went on to report his triumph: "You will rejoice to hear that feeling as I do upon the subject of the Corcoran Gallery, Mr. Corcoran, its funds being exhausted for the present by late purchases and by its extension, intimated his intention to present his *namesake* to the Institution

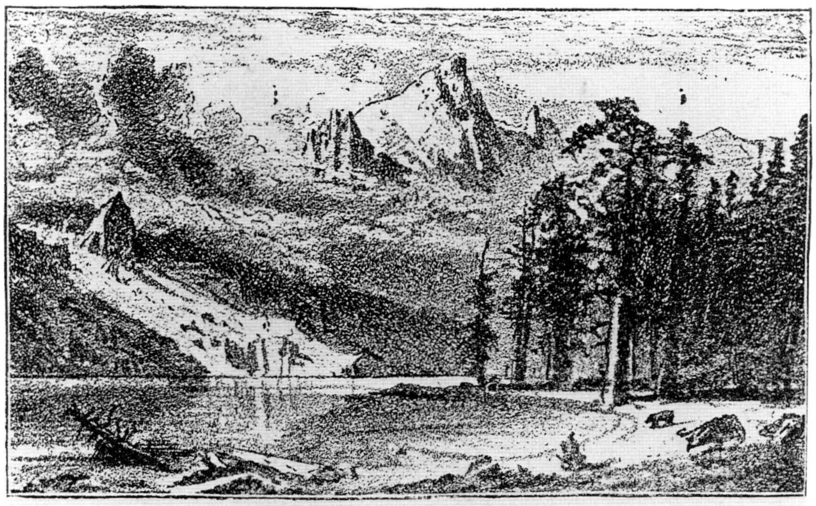

✲ 452—MOUNTAIN LAKE.—60x92.—A. BIERSTADT, N. A.,

Figure 31
After Albert Bierstadt. *Mountain Lake*. Drawing published in *National Academy of Design Illustrated Catalogue of the 52nd Annual Exhibition* (New York: 1877).

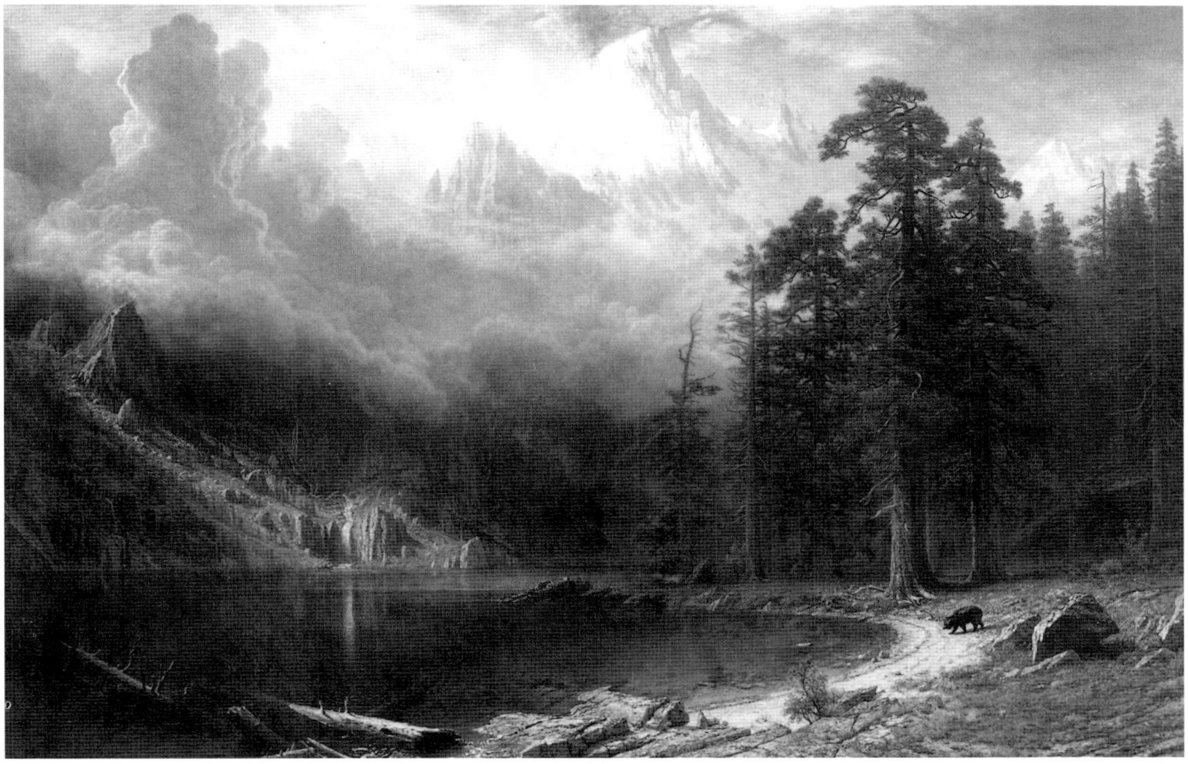

Figure 32
Albert Bierstadt. *Mount Corcoran*, 1877. Oil on canvas, 61 × 96¼ in. (154.9 × 244.4 cm).
The Corcoran Gallery of Art, Washington, D.C.

and that I most cheerfully assented to such a concession [in price] as all my craft would gladly make when treating directly with its munificent Founder."[160]

Bierstadt must have forwarded virtually the same letter to a surprised MacLeod, for the entry of 22 January in the curator's journal contains a revealing exchange between curator and founder: "Letter from Mr. Bierstadt, intimating that the Mt. Corcoran was bought by Mr. Corcoran and expressing his delight that it was to remain here. Showed it to Mr. Corcoran, with a copy of my last letter to Mr. B. and Mr. C. then stated that he *had* bought the picture for $7,000—for *his own house*, but as Bierstadt wrote as if he expected it to be placed in the Gallery, he would let it remain there. The *price* is not to be mentioned."[161] And so, in an unusual gesture, Corcoran in effect overruled his trustees in the case of Bierstadt. Nevertheless, Corcoran's response to MacLeod strongly suggests that he had indeed intended *Mount Corcoran* to be a private purchase. It appears that, by pressing his case directly with the founder and then by artfully "misunderstanding" Corcoran's intentions, Bierstadt had adroitly maneuvered the collector into complying with his desire to be represented at the gallery. No one seemed aware of the fact, or to care, that the work supposedly painted expressly for Corcoran with such a "loving hand" was the selfsame generic *Mountain Landscape* exhibited a year earlier in New York. There was to be, however, in MacLeod's words, "much spiteful comment . . . about the name"[162] and about what was by then recognized as a classic Bierstadt strategy. Corcoran, if not the artist, was to suffer some embarrassment when the episode was recalled in an 1884 article in the New York *Sun* lampooning the founder's overruling of the trustees' committee: "The art committee rejected the picture . . . out of their artistic convictions. Mr. Bierstadt has the gift of invention and telling the art committee to seek a tropic clime, he gayly christened his picture 'Mt. Corcoran.' The amiable banker was delighted at the paternity implied in the title . . . and he could not for the life of him see how the art committee could be so stupid as to hesitate about it for a moment."[163]

## The International Arena

While Bierstadt ultimately prevailed over Thomas Moran in the matter of the congressional purchase and triumphed over the trustees at the Corcoran, the strategies necessary to consummate these transactions demonstrate that, by the mid-1870s, his reputation as a landscape painter was in serious decline. By then, as his insistent letters to Spofford and Hayden indicate, the artist attached an enormous importance to his "European reputation." His disappointments at home undoubtedly fueled his determination to be represented at all costs in every international exposition.

During the first half of the nineteenth century, some American artists developed European patronage through the annual exhibitions at the Royal Academy in London and at the Paris Salon. Other opportunities arose when the world's fair was born in 1851, with the Great Exhibition held in London's Crystal Palace. These international extravaganzas soon began to celebrate cultural achievements with departments of fine arts, offered as "counterpoise" to displays devoted to industry, commerce, agriculture, and science.[164] Competition for access to these fine-art exhibitions, under the control of juries, was intense. The so-called selection committees were composed mostly of artists, with some collectors, dealers, and exposition officials. Reflecting the rapid changes in American taste and styles, the committees were increasingly dominated by younger Munich- and Paris-trained artists. Behind-the-scenes tensions escalated until, finally, at the 1893 Chicago World's Columbian Exposition, a number of older artists, including Bierstadt and Moran, refused to submit paintings for exhibition, convinced that their work could not be judged fairly by a committee of the "new" men.[165]

Beginning with the loan of *The Rocky Mountains, Lander's Peak* (No. 37) to the 1867 Exposition Universelle in Paris, Bierstadt had regularly sought to be included among American exhibitors. Undoubtedly stung by his failure to capture a medal there (and, probably, by Church's success), the artist began his energetic career-long pursuit of European decorations, which he constantly cited as evidence of an international regard that set him apart from other American painters. By the 1870s, Bierstadt was viewed as notorious, not only by critics, but by peers who saw his professional standing compromised by increasing competitiveness as a marketeer. The Legion of Honor award, the Longfellow Dinner, the congressional commission, and the Corcoran affair are among the episodes that brought the artist much-desired public attention and sales but also generated, as we have seen, considerable private criticism. Nowhere was the artist's competitive and determined nature more consistently revealed than in his repeated skirmishes with the selection committees of the expositions, climaxing in the controversy over *The Last of the Buffalo*, 1888 (No. 68), at the 1889 Exposition Universelle in Paris.

Bierstadt's defiance of an American artists' boycott of the 1873 Vienna Exposition did not ingratiate him or his work in American circles. Artists were outraged by the meager space allotted for American production in the fine-arts department. "It is now a settled, unchangeable fact that the United States will send no pictures to the Exhibition at Vienna . . . [because] the Austrian estimation of our artistic efforts is so low," reported the *New York Times*. The article also made note of the single exception: "Mr. Bierstadt, acting independently of the profession, has sent two enormous landscapes [*The Emerald Pool*, 1870, Fig. 33, and the recently completed commission for Collis P. Huntington, *Donner Lake from the Summit*, 1873, Fig. 61], which will very nearly cover the allotted space." "The European world assembled in Vienna," the *Times* charged, "will regard this as the highest effort of American art, and at the next European exhibition, taking counsel from the present, the authorities will probably allot us a still smaller space. . . . And so the vicious circle will complete itself and be perpetuated. . . . We may safely conclude that Europeans will judge us by

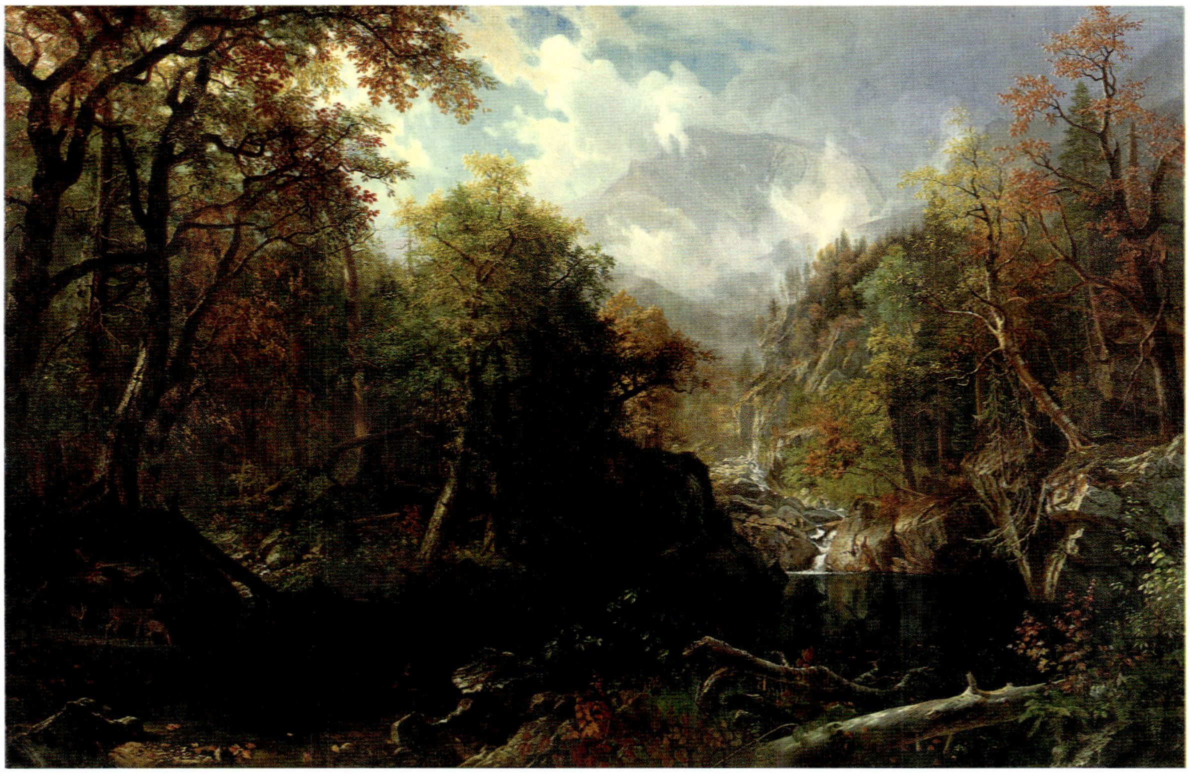

Figure 33
Albert Bierstadt. *The Emerald Pool*, 1870. Oil on canvas, 76½ × 119 in. (194.3 × 302.3 cm).
The Chrysler Museum, Norfolk, Virginia.

Mr. Bierstadt, and will assert that there is no true art in America."[166] The medal Bierstadt collected at Vienna for *The Emerald Pool* must have added insult to injury.

Tempers may still have been warm when Bierstadt again sought to ignore authority at the 1876 Philadelphia Centennial Exposition, deeply offending his fellow artists. Among them was jury member Jervis McEntee (1828–1891), who complained about the arrogance of both Church and Bierstadt: "Bierstadt too persists in not sending his pictures as other artists and expects to get them in by diplomacy over the heads of the Selection Committee."[167]

While Church's entry won a bronze medal (and Moran's a gold), however, Bierstadt's five western subjects received unusually severe criticism in the Centennial's official report. "The earlier works of this artist," wrote John Ferguson Weir (1841–1926), "showed a vigorous, manly style of art that had its undeniable attraction. His pictures exhibited at Philadelphia indicate a lapse into sensational and meretricious effects, and a loss of true artistic aim. They are vast illustrations of scenery, carelessly and crudely executed, and we fail to discover in them the merits which rendered his earlier works conspicuous."[168] The harsh and personal nature of Weir's criticism may well have been at least partly inspired by Bierstadt's attempted circumvention of the jury.

Two years later, when the artist's bid for a place in the American section of the 1878 Paris Exposition was declined by the selection committee, David Maitland Armstrong (1836–1918) saw fit to warn fellow committee member Augustus Saint-Gaudens (1848–1907) about the wily Bierstadt in a confidential letter: "Bierstadt offered a picture here which was declined. He has sent it to Paris & will try to get it in there. This Committee here to head him off passed a resolution that no picture offered here should be considered by the Committee in Paris—Look out for him. He shall not get it in but do not let it be known, as we do not wish to make a Martyr of Bierstadt."[169] Armstrong was politically astute in urging discretion, foreseeing the publicity Bierstadt might wring from such "martyrdom." His intuition would be confirmed in 1889.

Although distaste for Bierstadt's aggressive tactics undoubtedly stimulated a good deal of ill will among fellow artists, their general disaffection was also a result of the rapidly waning power of the midcentury landscape vision embodied in his work. The journal of Philadelphia artist Russell Smith (1812–1896) echoed John Ferguson Weir's disappointment in Bierstadt's Centennial pictures and extended the criticism to Church, the other landscape star of the 1860s: "When Church exhibited his Niagra [*sic*] and 'The Heart of the Andes' and Bierstadt his 'Rocky Mountain Storm' I thought that they were princely painters, and it would be very hard for any one in my day to surpass them. But, from failing powers, wealth and ease, or other cause, they both are much behind in this exhibition. Although the canvases are large, and the subjects grand[,] 'Chimborazo' and others, a Rocky Mountain peak and lake, they are overwrought, heavy and dead. . . . I wish they had both held their rank as formerly."[170]

Those who found something positive to say about Bierstadt's Centennial contribution were careful to separate subject from style. "Edward Strahan" (Earl Shinn) noted of *Western Kansas* (unlocated; see Fig. 107) that "the world of strangers collected here on the Atlantic seaboard should be able to travel . . . on the magic broomstick of one of his colossal brushes, into the heart of the Great West."[171] In a similar vein, a few years later, George W. Sheldon attributed even Bierstadt's much-vaunted international reputation primarily to his choices of subject: "Especially in England have [his western landscapes] been praised and prized, and for the reason, perhaps, among others, that they described to a people, fonder than all others of travel and books of travel, the novel and majestic beauty of our vast Territories."[172] This consistent praise for a visual record of national scenery avoided the issue of style (both authors quickly dismissed Bierstadt as "a typical Düsseldorfian") and became a compromise stance for those who chose to take notice of his work at all. Shinn summarized the artist's position in his lavish survey, *The Art Treasures of America* (1880). Bierstadt and Church, he wrote, embodied "the taste for panoramic art in this country, now gone entirely out of fashion among the lovers of refinement and technique." Shinn qualified his harsh judgment slightly, continuing, "It is only fair to remind ourselves that [Church and Bierstadt] secure for us memoranda of the really great and stupendous scenes of nature. . . . Mr. Bierstadt may be considered as a convenience enabling us to pay a visit to a region we would not take the pains to travel to. . . ." Shinn's remark is poignant evidence that, by 1880, the mighty landscape icons of midcentury—the Rocky Mountains, Yosemite, Yellowstone, Niagara—had been domesticated into tourist sites. Thus, the heroic artist-explorer of the 1860s, risking life and limb, had been diminished to an armchair traveler's "convenience."[173]

## The Demise of the American School

Between the 1860s and the Philadelphia Centennial Exposition of 1876, American art had undergone a radical change. The Centennial was immediately, and subsequently, interpreted as a turning point between what was perceived as a parochial cultural nationalism and a cosmopolitan embrace of international trends. The Centennial Exposition, which inspired a retrospective look at American art, was also seen as the firm dividing line between an art-historical past and present, and Bierstadt and many of his generation found themselves relegated to the defunct "American school." An article of 1880 observed: "The annals of art in America have not been eventful, but the year 1876–7 may be said to mark the beginning of an epoch in them. . . . Before that year, we had what was called, at any rate, an American school of painting; and now the American school of painting seems almost to have disappeared. . . . We are beginning to paint as other people paint."[174] Samuel G. W. Benjamin, author of one of the first systematic surveys of American art, stated a variation of the same theme: "The period when American art finally started in the right way to produce a national school may be set about 1865, gradually increasing in momentum until the Centennial gave it a decided impetus that is destined to continue until the forces now at work result in a genuine national school. . . ."[175] "The worst work on our exhibition walls now rarely comes from the hand of a beginner," echoed critic Mariana Griswold Van Rensselaer in the *Atlantic Monthly*, "but is most often due to some older Academician, or to one of his contemporaries."[176]

By 1880 Bierstadt—although a man of only fifty at the midpoint of his career—was thus cast firmly and irrevocably into the art-historical past, his work of the 1860s now located in some bygone epoch when artist-explorers "dared, discovered, and delineated for us the scenery of which we were hitherto the ignorant possessors." Benjamin, puzzling over the popularity and meaning of *The Rocky Mountains, Lander's Peak* in a way that speaks of both critical and emotional distance from the promise of Manifest Destiny, wrote that the painting "threw the people into an ecstasy of delight, which at this time it is difficult to understand, and [the artist] bounded at one step to celebrity."[177] Dutifully hailed as a pioneer explorer in the official art histories of the last quarter of the nineteenth century, Bierstadt was at the same time consigned to oblivion. His best work was perceived (correctly, for the most part) as long behind him. His current production, primarily formulaic recapitulations of early subjects and compositions, was received as a kind of living fossil.

Benjamin concluded his consideration of Bierstadt with a keen and double-edged insight, astutely suggesting that the change in taste had, after all, not been the only factor in the artist's decline. Praising a work of 1862, *Guerrilla Warfare (Picket Duty in Virginia)* (No. 30), as "fresh, original," he further stated that it "confirms us in the opinion that Mr. Bierstadt is naturally an artist of great ability and large resources, and might easily have obtained and held a reputation as such if he had not grafted on the sensationalism of Düsseldorf a greater ambition for notoriety and money than for success in pure art."[178] There can be little doubt that discomfort (and indignation) at the idea of the artist as a business success colored, and even compromised, certain critical responses to Bierstadt's genuine contribution as a painter. Nevertheless, the pressing need to finance an expensive style of living surely dictated many of Bierstadt's later career choices, driving him in the late 1870s, 1880s, and 1890s to repeat earlier formulas for success rather than allow his "great ability and large resources" as an artist to develop in other directions.

Bierstadt's post-Centennial fall from favor was brought home by the much-publicized Boston auction of Alvin Adams's collection in 1882, when a pair of the artist's most famous early works—*Lake Lucerne (Switzerland)* (No. 6), and *Among the Sierra Nevada Mountains, California*, 1868 (No. 48)—returned to public view. Although the *Boston Transcript* reported that these large paintings had not lost their popular appeal ("The rush to see the Alvin Adams collection . . . is something unparalleled, and the admiring crowds that linger in front of the great Bierstadts never grow small from the opening to the closing of the doors"[179]), popular interest did not translate into spirited bidding. In a stunning disappointment, *Among the Sierra Nevada Mountains, California*, for which Adams had reportedly paid $15,000 and for which the artist had received his Berlin gold medal, "was laboriously urged up to $1400" after an opening bid of $1,000. *Lake Lucerne (Switzerland)* brought only $3,375, after "long and languid" competition.[180] While Bierstadt's paintings commanded some of the higher prices in a generally lackluster sale, such meager sums could hardly have been a comfort to the artist, who was still claiming his record prices of 1865 as a major credential. Even more disturbing must have been the general critical assessment of Adams's collection as one merely of historic interest and containing only a "few pictures that have any real value to-day, and fewer still that will have any a quarter of a century hence."[181] William Howe Downes, writing at the end of the decade, recognized the Adams sale, and the fate of Bierstadt's paintings in particular, as a landmark event in the history of American taste and patronage: "Mr. Adams had paid high prices for two of Bierstadt's large compositions at the time when the Rocky Mountain school was on the flood-tide of popular favor, and the sudden depreciation in value of such works . . . was a startling indication of the change which had come over the public taste."[182]

## The Last of the Buffalo

As Downes was writing his article, Bierstadt was at work on *The Last of the Buffalo* (No. 68). The notorious controversy surrounding this painting's rejection for exhibition at the 1889 Paris Exposition Universelle has been accurately interpreted as the public demise of Bierstadt's faltering career; at the same time, the incident represented his last episode of international celebrity and, possibly, one of his most spectacular marketing coups.

The subject of Bierstadt's work was one of great popular appeal. Aside from the romantic excitement of the hunt imagery, the actual impending extinction of the buffalo was a pressing issue in the late 1880s. Bierstadt's image of vast herds and Indians armed with lances rather than rifles was pure nostalgia: nevertheless, viewers were quick to associate the subject with current events. A long and favorable review of the painting in the New York *World* was immediately followed by a news report on the nearly exterminated herds.[183] Soon after the painting's debut, artist William Sartain (1843–1924), recognizing the commercial potential of Bierstadt's powerful imagery, urged his father, engraver John Sartain, to negotiate with the artist for reproduction rights.[184] Bierstadt would eventually copyright the painting, reproduced as a photogravure (No. 81), himself.

*The Last of the Buffalo* was Bierstadt's sole submission to the American exhibition at the 1889 Paris Exposition, to open on 1 May. Early in March, the press reported that the American exhibition jury, meeting in New York, had rejected the painting. Bierstadt, interviewed by the *World*, affected a neutral stance while pointedly referring to the picture's inclusion in the Paris Salon, where he held exhibition privileges as a chevalier of the Legion of Honor. "It is a matter of indifference to me," he insisted,

> but I cannot understand why they should refuse my picture. . . . I was, of course, anxious to aid the art jury, and designated "The Last of the Buffalo" because it was one of my latest and was considered . . . as among my best efforts. Since then I have heard nothing more about the matter until I read the cable despatch in to-day's World. The picture is now in the Paris Salon, and I hear it has been given an exceedingly good place. Of course, if the American Art Committee don't want my picture it must remain in the Salon. I am, of course, sorry that there has been any trouble, for it is an unpleasant episode; but as my picture has been accepted by the Salon my countrymen visiting the Exposition can see it there. I wish it distinctly understood that I have no feeling in the matter, only that it is unpleasant. Why my picture was rejected I, of course, do not know.[185]

American artists in Paris, interviewed by the *World*, were said to express "indignation" but "asked not to be quoted." Only J. G. Brown (1831–1913), a committee member in New York, spoke for the record, stoutly denying any motives of "jealousy" or "animosity": "There was no hostility to Mr. Bierstadt. . . . We simply did not consider Mr. Bierstadt's picture as doing him justice, so rejected it." Brown insisted that Bierstadt's painting had been rejected "because it was too big and was not truly representative of his style. That is all there is about it. . . ."[186] To be sure, the painting was of "Great Picture" dimensions, but at six by ten feet, it was no larger than other works that were accepted for exhibition. The figural emphasis in the picture, unusual for Bierstadt, might have accounted for jury opinion that the painting "did not represent him as he should be in a national exhibition." Bierstadt himself confessed, "The buffalo is an ugly brute to paint, but I consider my picture one of my very best."[187] Indeed, the painting is the finest large work of Bierstadt's later years.

Whatever the jury's objections were, the Springfield *Republican* quite plausibly suggested that the "proper thing to have done . . . was to communicate with Mr. Bierstadt and invite him to send another painting. At any rate, the arbitrary exclusion of so prominent a painter exposes the committee to unpleasant insinuations."[188] The *World*, a fiercely partisan Bierstadt supporter, saw the decision as an outrage committed by "pigmies of pigment" upon the "distinctly American" Bierstadt by a jury composed of "servile imitators of French fads" who painted "French subjects, handled in French fashion with French brushes and French paint."[189] Some of the seventeen jury members were, indeed, Paris- and Munich-trained. Bierstadt's rejection has long been interpreted as another symbol of the break between the old school and the new men: "Only pictures . . . representing the advance made in American art since [1878] were desired by the committee. . . . Bierstadt as a painter has [not] contributed to the progress of American art for many years. . . ."[190] However, many of the jury members were, in fact, National Academicians, and a closer reading of the episode, especially in the context of earlier incidents, suggests that Bierstadt's exclusion may also have represented a settling of old scores against the artist's energetic self-promotion. Among the jury members who voted "unanimously" against his painting were not only younger men such as Saint-Gaudens (a partner in the cabal that had excluded Bierstadt from the 1878 Exposition), William Merritt Chase (1849–1916), J. Alden Weir (1852–1919), and Frank D. Millet (1846–1912), but also artists of his own generation. These included Hudson River School painters William Hart (1823–1894) and Arthur Parton (1842–1914), sentimental genre painter J. G. Brown, and Bierstadt's old rival, Thomas Moran. His Düsseldorf companion of the 1850s, Worthington Whittredge, was president of the selection committee. While Whittredge would recall the young, industrious Bierstadt vividly and affectionately in his autobiography of 1905, he apparently did not step forward on his colleague's behalf in 1889. While Bierstadt insisted to the press that "they are all my friends,"[191] he never again exhibited in the National Academy's Annual Exhibitions.

Nevertheless, in an era when his works no longer commanded attention, Bierstadt could not himself have arranged for better publicity in the United States or in Paris, where Buffalo Bill Cody's Wild West Show was also a popular attraction, demonstrating the still-potent lure of the American West.[192] Among the many clippings about the 1889 episode preserved in a Bierstadt family scrapbook is one that reports the regular visits of Chief Rocky Bear and fellow Indian performers in the Paris Wild West show to see Bierstadt's painting: "These men of the plains leave their tents in the Cody camp each morning to come and breathe the air—as they put it—of their native soil; and their grunt of satisfaction after a silent half hour of contemplation should be a joy to the painter's soul, for it is a recognition of the truth of the scene and is eloquent to its sentiment and poetry."[193] The story, apocryphal or not, conjures up Bierstadt's own Wild West venture of some twenty-five years before: the artist's famous Indian Department at the Sanitary Fair.

The 1889 Exposition episode provided the artist and his painting with a field day in the press prior to the picture's national tour as a "Great Picture." The subsequent twenty-year history of *The Last of the Buffalo* remains obscure, although it was reported sold to John Thomas North, an English industrialist, for some fifty thousand dollars. One newspaper reported that the purchase price, "without parallel in the annals of American Art, may be regarded as a tribute to the magnificent conception of the artist and as a condemnation of the New York Committee which took upon itself to refuse a place to this truly National masterpiece."[194]

It would seem, then, that the ever-resilient Bierstadt may have ultimately emerged triumphant from his ordeal. His remaining years, however, were spent in relative obscurity and financial distress. His beloved Rosalie died early in 1893 after many years as an invalid. The following year, Bierstadt was quietly married to Mary Hicks Stewart, the wealthy widow of millionaire David Stewart (father of Isabella Stewart Gardner). Although Bierstadt continued to paint, he received little attention. William Howe Downes noted that his sudden death in New York on 18 February 1902 "caused the merest ripple on the surface of the art pool": "I asked an artist, last week, if he had known Bierstadt personally. No. And he added, half jocosely, 'I did not know he was alive until I saw he had died.' The fact is that Bierstadt had done but little work in the past ten or twelve years and what little work he did do during the latter part of his life was, candidly, so inferior that it need not be considered seriously in estimating his true standing as a painter."[195]

Downes went on to offer an accurate and insightful overview of Bierstadt's career and a telling prophesy. "Thirty years ago he was one of the most conspicuous and noted of American painters. . . . Up to the year of the Philadelphia Exhibition, 1876, his reputation was maintained . . . but since that date, approximately, the change in taste, and fashion, the advent of new favorites, and the reaction against an exaggerated renown, have combined to relegate Bierstadt's name and fame to relative obscurity. Yet his pictures are as good today as they ever were; it is not they which have changed. But it is a far cry from Düsseldorf to Barbizon, and a still farther cry from Düsseldorf to Giverny: art history is made so rapidly in these swift times." Noting that "the remarkable vogue of Bierstadt's pictures which prevailed in the sixties and the seventies [was] . . . to some degree due to his enterprise in tackling such immense themes," Downes fairly reasoned that the "enthusiasm" of critics at the "crest" of Bierstadt's "great wave of popularity" should be seen against "the coolness of a later generation of critics, that a golden mean of justice may be struck between the two extremes." He concluded, "This much we may set down as undeniable, in the history of American landscape art the name of Bierstadt will always be entitled to a position of a certain prominence."[196]

Downes's assessment was valid. Bierstadt's work has received a good deal of attention as interest has revived in nineteenth-century American painting during recent decades. Major works have been relocated, and correspondence and other revealing documents discovered. Now, a full century after the 1889 controversy, we are poised to pursue Downes's "golden mean of justice" by reappraising the achievement and contribution of a remarkable career.

# NOTES

1. *Boston Transcript*, 26 Feb. 1902.

2. An obituary noted, "His early opportunities were meager, and he was in the true sense of the word a self-made man" (*Outlook* 1902, p. 507). This success story was narrated repeatedly during his lifetime, as well. Yet another obituary documented his social ascent: "Although . . . by birth [he] was classed as a self-made man of the people, his intimacy with European courts, long residence in London and Paris stamped his demeanor and bearing with the most polished courtliness, enhanced by a presence both commanding and handsome" (*Globe*, Utica, 22 Feb. 1902). The Century Association, one of Bierstadt's many club affiliations, also paid tribute to a somewhat exaggerated "struggle with poverty and privation." These had been overcome "with indomitable resolution, ingenuity, shrewdness and self-command"—personal qualities more commonly ascribed to a Jay Gould, an A. T. Stewart, or a Cornelius Vanderbilt than to a painter of landscapes (Century Association, "Report," 1902, p. 16, Century Association Archives).

3. The term "fortune's favorite" was applied to Church by Worthington Whittredge when comparing his background and advantages to the early struggles of Bierstadt (Whittredge 1969, p. 28; Kelly 1988, p. 1).

4. "Council Minutes," 14 May 1902, NAD Archives. I am grateful to Nanni Kaps for bringing this reference to my attention.

5. Jarves 1960, p. 195.

6. Tuckerman 1967, p. 387.

7. *New Bedford Standard*, 13 May 1851.

8. Ibid., 1 July 1851; *Mercury*, New Bedford, 1, 4 Sept. 1851. For Harvey, see Parker 1943, Shelley 1948a and 1948b.

9. George Henry Hall to the American Art Union, 28 Oct. 1850, New-York Historical Society, quoted in Maurice Bloch, *George Caleb Bingham: The Evolution of an Artist* (Berkeley: University of California Press, 1967), vol. 2, p. 198. For further information on the school of Düsseldorf, see n. 31.

10. Henry Lewis to George Lewis, 1 Nov. 1858, HL Papers.

11. The exhibition opened on 1 July and closed on 7 Aug. 1858 (New Bedford Catalogue 1858). The catalogue included works from collectors and dealers in these major cities, as well as one from Leutze, then still in Europe. Disappointing sales were reported in the New Bedford press (*New Bedford Standard*, 20 July and 2 Aug. 1858; *Mercury*, New Bedford, 6 Aug. 1858).

12. *NY Tribune*, 27 Mar. 1860. For the importance of this site, see Blaugrund 1987.

13. Even before he had traveled west, his first very large landscape painting, a six-by-ten-foot *Lake Lucerne (Switzerland)* (No. 6), had been purchased by wealthy businessman Alvin Adams, founder of the Adams Express Company (*Mercury*, New Bedford, 14 Dec. 1858).

14. The term "Great Picture" is used here as a general reference to the large paintings that were shown to the public in this manner in Europe and America. For example, the pamphlet and engraving prospectus accompanying *The Rocky Mountains, Lander's Peak* introduces "A. Bierstadt's Great Picture." The *Art-Journal* referred to Bierstadt's 1868 one-man London exhibition of *Among the Sierra Nevada Mountains, California*, 1868 (No. 48), *Sunset in the Yosemite Valley*, 1868 (No. 47), and *Mount Vesuvius at Midnight*, 1868, at the Langham Hotel as "Great Pictures By An American Artist" (Aug. 1868, p. 159).

Gerald Carr has noted that the term (and the practice) originated in England and was widely employed in the period. He admirably documents the phenomenon in Carr 1980, 1982, and 1986. Kevin Avery (1986) has discussed in detail the parallels between these large easel paintings and a variety of contemporaneous "optical entertainments." The immense popularity of these tours is amply documented in the nineteenth-century press during and after Bierstadt's heyday: "The Bierstadt pictures of the Yo Semite and of scenes in the Rockies and Sierras, canvasses immense in size and theatric in effect, were taken from town to town and exposed to view in halls and galleries where they were ingeniously lighted, and where the visitor was expected to sit before them in rapt admiration. The press teemed with notices of them wherever they were sent, and they were as much of a sensation as a new play" (*Brooklyn Daily Eagle*, 16 May 1885).

15. Church's work and career are examined in Huntington 1966, Carr 1980, Kelly and Carr 1987, Kelly 1988, and Kelly et al. 1989.

16. "A. Bierstadt's Great Picture. The Rocky Mountains," pamphlet, 186[4], New-York Historical Society; *NY Leader*, 2 Apr. 1864; unidentified clipping [1867], Bierstadt Scrapbook, Edwards Collection.

17. Henry Lewis to George Lewis, 30 July 1863, HL Papers.

18. *NY Times*, 14 May 1868. For Whittredge's western landscapes, see Moure 1973, and Janson 1989, pp. 111–29.

19. Sheldon 1972, p. 148.

20. *National Intelligencer*, Washington, D.C., 15 Apr. 1865.

21. *Mercury*, New Bedford, 14 Dec. 1858; Kelly et al. 1989, p. 164.

22. *NY Tribune*, 4 Apr. 1863; Kelly et al. 1989, p. 164.

23. Carr 1980, p. 88; Carr 1986, p. 61.

24. *Post*, New York, 17 Oct. 1865.

25. Ibid., 28 Mar. 1866. Tuckerman valued the painting in 1867 at $35,000 (Tuckerman 1967, p. 393). It appears that Stewart, who died in 1876, may have tried on more than one occasion to secure one of these early Rocky Mountain subjects, for in 1877 Bierstadt himself noted, "Indeed my picture of the Rocky Mts by which I first became generally known and which was sold for $25,000 to its present owner has had an offer of $40,000. which has been refused" (Bierstadt to Ainsworth R. Spofford, 12 Mar. 1877, Ainsworth R. Spofford Papers, Library of Congress). It was reported in 1884: "A. T. Stewart tried very hard to secure one of those that went to England, and finally offered $40,000 for it, but the owner would not sell" (*Spectator*, New York, 26 Apr. 1884).

26. Jay E. Cantor, "A Monument of Trade: A. T. Stewart and the Rise of the Millionaire's Mansion in New York," *Winterthur Portfolio* 10 (1975): 165; Junius Henry Browne, *The Great Metropolis* (Hartford: American Publishing Co., 1869), p. 289, quoted in Cantor, "A Monument of Trade," p. 171.

27. In 1875 the *Aldine* had reported that Stewart had "no less than three pictures in the gallery: a large landscape of a scene in the Rocky Mountains; a spirited and picturesque view of the 'Seal Rocks, off the Coast of California,' and a new picture called 'Spearing Fish by Torchlight,' a favorite motif with this painter" ("The Stewart Art Gallery," *Aldine* 7 [July 1875]: 370). Three years after Stewart's death, Edward Strahan (Earl Shinn) reported three works by Bierstadt in the collection: *Seal Rock, San Francisco* (private collection, California); *The Rocky Mountains* and *Natural Park and Lake, Southern Colorado* (both unlocated) (Strahan 1880, vol. 2, p. 52). The A. T. Stewart sale in 1887 included the following paintings: *Seal Rock, San Francisco; Natural Park and Lake, Southern California;* and *Emerald Pool, White Mountains*. Apparently, at some point Stewart (or his widow) completed the quest to own one of Bierstadt's monumental landscapes with the acquisition of *The Emerald Pool*, 1870 (Fig. 33).

28. Cantor, "A Monument of Trade," p. 184.

29. *Post*, New York, 26 Nov. 1866, where it was suggested that the picture had been commissioned three years before.

30. For Jarves, see *Dictionary of American Biography*, and Francis Steegmuller, *The Two Lives of James Jackson Jarves* (New Haven: Yale University Press, 1951). His art criticism is discussed in Benjamin Rowland's Introduction to Jarves 1960, pp. xi-xxviii. For Cook, see *Dictionary of American Biography*, and Simoni 1952, pp. 122–347, 433–98. as well as Stein 1968, and Ferber and Gerdts 1985.

31. The influence of the school among American artists and collectors had been aided by the establishment in New York of the Dusseldorf Gallery in 1849. The gallery was composed of the large private collection of a German emigré, John G. Boker. The paintings were for sale. While Boker disposed of his interest in 1857, the Dusseldorf Gallery continued to operate until late in 1862, when the remaining works were sold at auction. Apparently, the paintings unsold at that auction were still on view in New York as late as 1866. Bierstadt had ample opportunity to study the collection on tour in Boston and in New York before and after his own study in Germany. For discussion of the influence of this German school on American artists, see Atkinson 1880a and 1880b; Hoopes 1972; Stehle 1974; Düsseldorf 1976b; Groseclose 1975; Düsseldorf 1979; Annelise Harding and Brucia Witthoft, *American Artists in Dusseldorf, 1840–1865*, exh. cat. (Framingham, Mass.: Danforth Museum, 1982); and Gerdts and Thistlethwaite 1988.

32. Jarves 1960, pp. 143, 192.

33. *NY Tribune*, 16 Apr. 1864.

34. *New Path* 1864a, p. 161. The magazine, edited by Cook, was the voice of the American Pre-Raphaelite movement.

35. Ibid., pp. 161, 162.

36. *NY Times*, 2 May 1867.

37. *Post*, New York, 7 June 1865.

38. "Bierstadt's 'Storm in the Rocky Mountains,'" *Watson's Weekly Art Journal*, 3 Mar. 1866, p. 308.

39. *Independent*, New York, 23 May 1867.

40. Jarves 1869, pp. 298–99. For American artists at the Exposition, see Troyen 1984.

41. Clarence Cook, "Introductory," *New Path* 1 (May 1863): 1.

42. Whittredge 1969, p. 54; Kevin Avery, in Metropolitan Museum 1987, pp. 3–4.

43. Simoni 1952, p. 262.

44. Cranch 1867, pp. 80, 78.

45. *NY Tribune*, 8 Feb. 1866.

46. Ibid., 11 May 1867.

47. Ibid., 3 Dec. 1868.

48. *Independent*, New York, 23 May 1867.

49. Köhler 1871, p. 361.

50. *New Path* 1864a, pp. 160, 161.

51. *NY Herald*, 4 Apr. 1864.

52. William Cullen Bryant, "Funeral Oration on the Death of Thomas Cole before the National Academy of Design, May 4, 1848," in *American Art, 1700–1860: Sources and Documents*, ed. John W. McCoubrey (Englewood Cliffs, N.J.: Prentice-Hall, 1965), p. 97.

53. Durand 1855, p. 97. For Durand and Ruskin, see Ferber and Gerdts 1985, pp. 254–55, and David Lawall, *A. B. Durand, 1796–1886*, exh. cat. (Montclair, N.J.: Montclair Art Museum, 1971), p. 18.

54. Henry T. Tuckerman, "Art in America. Its History, Condition, and Prospects," *Cosmopolitan Art Journal* 3 (Dec. 1858): 5.

55. Jarves 1960, pp. 195, 182, 194–95, 191.

56. Jarves 1869, p. 299.

57. *Independent*, New York, 23 May 1867.

58. Cranch 1867, p. 80.

59. *Boston Transcript*, 26 Dec. 1865.

60. On 10 June, the *Mercury*, New Bedford, mentioned the purchase and noted that "the plans and drawings for the building" were already in Bierstadt's possession. The lot, purchased from Joseph W. Hartley for $18,300, is recorded in a transaction of 7 July 1865 ("Deed Liber," vol. 571, pp. 239–47, Westchester County Clerk's Office, White Plains, N.Y.). Additional property was purchased from Hartley and others on 2 Aug. 1866, 7 Feb. 1871, and 22 May 1874 ("Deed Liber," vol. 601, pp. 42–47; vol. 767, pp. 233–35; vol. 888, pp. 335–40. I am grateful to Andrew Walker for locating these and other documents pertaining to the Irvington property. Published accounts of the cost of building the house ranged from between $40,000 and $50,000 to Bierstadt's own later claim of $100,000 (*Argus*, Tarrytown, N.Y., 29 July 1882; *Post*, New York, 26 Nov. 1866; unidentified clipping [Nov. 1882], Bierstadt Scrapbook, Edwards Collection).

61. *Mercury*, New Bedford, 14 Nov. 1865; "Art Notes: Bierstadt," *Watson's Weekly Art Journal*, 25 Nov. 1865, p. 82.

62. *Round Table*, 19 May 1866, p. 311.

63. Gray 1871.

64. Tuckerman 1967, p. 396.

65. *NY Tribune*, 11 May 1867.

66. "Art Notes," *Watson's Weekly Art Journal*, 21 Oct. 1865, p. 20.

67. *Mercury*, New Bedford, 10 June 1865.

68. Mould is identified as the architect in Lamb 1876, p. 46. For Mould, see Van Zanten 1969.

69. Gray 1871. Martha Lamb declared that "Mr. Bierstadt was five years in selecting the site for his house. . . ." (Lamb 1876, p. 45). We wish to thank Ralph Gosse for bringing these remarkable photographs to our attention.

70. A letter from the artist to a "Mr. Hartley" dated 22 June 1864, Downs Collection, suggests that Joseph W. Hartley, from whom Bierstadt purchased the Irvington property in 1865, had probably commissioned *View of the Hudson Looking Across the Tappan Zee Towards Hook Mountain* (Fig. 16), Bierstadt's painting of the site, a year before. Köhler 1871, p. 363, no. 28, noted that a "Herr Hartley" of Tarrytown owned *The Hudson and the "Highlands,"* 1865–66 (probably Fig. 16, despite a discrepancy in size; Köhler says "4 by 6 feet" and the painting measures 3 by 4 feet). Lamb 1879, p. 151, described this subject at some length as *The Home of Irving*, "a picture subsequently purchased by the gentleman who had formerly owned and improved the site of the artist's villa."

71. Lamb 1879, p. 151. Much of this was published earlier in Lamb 1876.

72. Gray 1871.

73. Ibid.

74. Lamb 1876, p. 46.

75. Gray 1871.

76. Ibid.

77. Ibid.

78. Ibid.

79. Esther Osborne Mayer, "Memoirs," Edwards Collection.

80. Moses King, *King's Handbook of New York City* (Boston: Moses King, 1892), p. 210. I am grateful to Barbara Head Millstein for bringing this reference and other information on the Brevoort House to my attention.

81. Mayer, "Memoirs."

82. Undated clipping, Bierstadt Scrapbook, Edwards Collection; Black 1938, p. 29.

83. *Argus*, Tarrytown, N.Y., 29 July 1882. In 1893, the site was still marked by "a heap of ruins" (*NY Times*, 12 Mar. 1893).

84. *Mercury*, New Bedford, 13 Nov. 1866.

85. Discussions of government patronage and the decoration of the Capitol include F. C. Adams 1870, Hazelton 1914, Fairman 1927, L. Miller 1966, and Gerdts and Thistlethwaite 1988.

86. L. Miller 1966, p. 83.

87. Groseclose 1975, p. 60; Leutze to Bierstadt, undated letter, Turner Collection.

88. "The New Pictures," *Harper's Weekly* 8 (26 Mar. 1864): 194–95.

89. F. C. Adams 1870, p. 747.

90. Ibid., p. 746.

91. Unidentified clipping, 26 Mar. 186[4], Bierstadt Scrapbook, Edwards Collection.

92. *National Intelligencer*, Washington, D.C., 19 Jan. 1866.

93. Hayes to Sardis Birchard, 2 Mar. 1866, quoted in *Diary and Letters of Rutherford Birchard Hayes*, ed. Charles Richard Williams (Columbus, Ohio: 1922–26), vol. 3, p. 19.

94. Colfax to Bierstadt, 2 Feb. 1866, Downs Collection.

95. Colfax's trip was published in Bowles 1865 and A. Richardson 1867. I am grateful to John K. Howat for bringing these references and Colfax's trip to my attention.

96. Bierstadt to Adams, 17 Dec. 1866, Miscellaneous Papers, Manuscript Division, New York Public Library.

97. *Mercury*, New Bedford, 13 Nov. 1866.

98. Bierstadt to Adams, 17 Dec. 1866, Miscellaneous Papers, Manuscript Division, New York Public Library.

99. Ibid.

100. Fairman 1927, p. 270.

101. F. C. Adams 1870, p. 746.

102. *NY Times*, 23 Jan. 1867.

103. Bierstadt to Ainsworth R. Spofford, 12 Mar. 1877, Spofford Papers, Library of Congress.

104. Fairman 1927, p. 270.

105. *Mercury*, New Bedford, 15 Feb. 1867.

106. Fairman 1927, p. 270.

107. F. C. Adams 1870, pp. 746–47.

108. Bierstadt to Adams, 18 Mar. 1867, Eldon Grupp Collection, Mountain View, Calif.; F. C. Adams 1870, p. 747.

109. F. C. Adams 1870, p. 747.

110. Bierstadt to Adams, 18 Mar. 1867, Eldon Grupp Collection.

111. "Having received a Government commission," wrote Tuckerman, "Bierstadt sailed for Europe in June 1867, to make some studies for a picture of the discovery of the North River by Henry Hudson. . . ." (1967, p. 396).

112. Ibid.

113. Count Nieuwerkerke to Thomas McLean, 12 Dec. 1866, Turner Collection. Nieuwerkerke, the "Surintendant des Beaux-Arts," informed both Bierstadt and McLean that the painting would first have to be submitted to the American jury for admission to the United States section of the Fine Arts Department. His letter suggests that the artist was already seeking to bypass the American selection committees, a habit that would persist over the years (Troyen 1984, pp. 3–23 passim).

114. Leslie 1870, vol. 1, p. 12.

115. Köhler 1870, p. 66.

116. Bierstadt to Ferdinand V. Hayden, 31 Jan. 1878, FVH Papers.

117. *Post*, New York, 26 July 1869. A conflicting report stated that Bierstadt received the decoration for *Among the Sierra Nevada Mountains, California* (No. 48) (*Boston Transcript*, 10 Oct. 1869). Köhler recounts that Bierstadt received the award in Paris in June 1869 (1871, p. 327). Since *Storm in the Rocky Mountains, Mt. Rosalie* was then on exhibition at the Salon while *Among the Sierra Nevada Mountains, California* was at the Royal Academy in

London, it seems likely that the former earned the award, although *California Art Gallery* (1873, p. 50) declared that *Among the Sierra Mountains, California* brought the artist both decorations (in Paris and Berlin).

118. Avery to Richards, 11 Sept. 1869, Richards Papers, AAA.

119. See Carr 1980 and 1986.

120. Bierstadt to unidentified correspondent, printed in *Boston Transcript*, 15 Jan. 1868; Rosalie Bierstadt to unknown family member, Dec. 1867 or Jan. 1868, quoted in ROM/MFA Corresp.

121. *Morning Post*, London, 15 Apr. 1868. For Church in England, see Carr 1980 and 1982.

122. James D. McCabe, Jr., *Great Fortunes and How They Were Made* (Cincinnati: E. Hannaford & Company, 1871), p. 563.

123. For the Longfellow Dinner, see Hendricks 1973, pp. 182, 184; Nickerson 1984, pp. 54–55; and Carr 1986, pp. 64–65.

124. Unidentified clippings, London, July, 10 July 1868, Bierstadt Scrapbook, Edwards Collection.

125. Bierstadt to Parke Godwin, 29 June 1868, Bryant-Godwin Papers, Manuscript Division, New York Public Library.

126. Anne Whitney to Sarah Whitney, 17 Oct. 1868, Whitney Papers, Margaret Clapp Library, Wellesley College, Wellesley, Mass. I am grateful to Sara Parrott for this information.

127. *Mercury*, New Bedford, 13 Oct. 1869, reported that the artist, about to settle for the winter at Irvington, "will be kept busy upon orders from England."

128. *Boston Transcript*, 30 Sept. 1869; *Globe*, Boston, 18 Mar. 1882.

129. M. E. Adams 1969, pp. 18–19, 23.

130. For the American Pre-Raphaelites, see Stein 1967, and Ferber and Gerdts 1985. For King, see Wilkins 1988.

131. C. King 1970, pp. 207, 210.

132. Wilkins 1966, pp. 57–71; C. Clark 1980, pp. 9–10, 11–21.

133. In 1874 Cook compared the two artists and praised Moran's blend in *The Grand Canyon of the Yellowstone* (Fig. 26) of the literal and the poetic while condemning Bierstadt's Rocky Mountain and Yosemite paintings as "intolerable" ("Art," *Atlantic Monthly*, Sept. 1874, pp. 375–77).

134. Richards's humorous account of the Bierstadts' visit to his Newport house is worth quoting: "Had a call from the great Alfred [*sic*] Bierstadt and wife. He did not seem much interested in the [watercolor] drawings—'liked oil painting better.' Mrs. B. condescended to think the parlor was a very pretty room, was astonished at the 'neatness' of the studio—, fluttered a moment then sailed away with her big gipsy hat on her little head to La Farge, and I felt thankful I had been carried through that! The big B seemed to be going around like that 'Lion seeking what he may devour'" (Richards to George Whitney, 30 July 1876, Richards Papers, AAA).

135. *California Art Gallery* 1873, p. 50.

136. Wilkins 1966, p. 93.

137. *Bulletin*, San Francisco, 25 Sept. 1874.

138. Bierstadt to George Bancroft, 17 Oct. 1874, Bancroft Papers, Massachusetts Historical Society, Boston.

139. Bierstadt to My Dear Sir [Edward Clarke], 3 Aug. 1874; Bierstadt to Clarke, 16 Sept. 1874; Clarke to Bierstadt, 23 Nov. 1874, Manuscript File, Records of the Architect of the Capitol, Washington, D.C.

140. *NY Times*, 6 Dec. 1874. The Sierra subject was mistakenly identified as "A Scene in the Rocky Mountains."

141. *Inter-Ocean*, Chicago, undated clipping [Dec. 1874], Bierstadt Scrapbook, Edwards Collection.

142. While in San Francisco, Bierstadt had exhibited this painting as *Autumn in the Sierras*, which was described at length in *Bulletin*, San Francisco, 29 May 1873. After his return east, Bierstadt toured the painting for a year to Saint Louis (Bierstadt to unknown correspondent, 20 Nov. 1873, Miscellaneous Bierstadt Papers, New-York Historical Society), Philadelphia (*Philadelphia Daily Evening Bulletin*, 12 Mar. 1874), Boston (*Transcript*, 5 May 1874), and perhaps elsewhere. Deciding to send the painting to the Capitol, Bierstadt must have determined that a change of title would freshen its appeal. At that time, he may also have added the foreground party of surveyors, a detail not mentioned in earlier descriptions. The painting's history afterward is unclear. It was in Bierstadt's New York studio in 1880 (*American Queen*, 6 Mar. 1880) and was among a group of paintings loaned to the White House in 1881 or 1882. Bierstadt hoped they would be purchased. As late as 1893, he was still lobbying for their sale.

143. Fairman 1927, p. 270; Bierstadt to Mr. Gardner, 28 Feb. 1875, John Davis Batchelder Autograph Collection, Vol. 1, Item 146, Library of Congress.

144. As Gerald L. Carr has noted, the painting was exhibited at the Philadelphia Centennial in 1876 as *Settlement of California, Bay of Monterey, 1770* (Metropolitan Museum 1987, pp. 296–97). Hazelton 1914, p. 203, suggested that the subject might be either Viscaino's entry into Monterey in 1601 or Father Junipero Serra's first mass at Monterey in 1769. At some unknown date in this century, the painting was formally retitled, in error, *Expedition under Viscaino Landing at Monterey, 1601* or *Entrance into Monterey*. The artist's title of 1876 confirms the correct subject as the eighteenth-century event.

145. Bierstadt to A. R. Spofford, 12 Mar. 1877, Spofford Papers.

146. Fairman 1927, p. 271.

147. Wilkins 1966, pp. 110–11.

148. Bierstadt to Ferdinand V. Hayden, 31 Jan. 1878, FVH Papers.

149. Taragin 1976, pp. 17–22.

150. See Chronology, 9 July 1878.

151. Bierstadt to Joseph Henry, 7 Jan. 1874; Bierstadt to William T. Walters, 25 Feb. 1874; Bierstadt to My Dear Sir [MacLeod], 15 Nov. 1874, Corcoran Archives.

152. Bierstadt to Henry W. Rogers, 26 Jan. 1863, published in the *Buffalo Courier*, 6 Feb. 1863; Hendricks 1973, p. 95.

153. Pringle 1985, pp. 3–4.

154. *Ohio State Journal*, Columbus, 7 July 1877, where the painting is identified, in error, as depicting the *North Fork of the King's River, Southern California;* Bierstadt to My Dear Sir [MacLeod], 12 July 1877, Corcoran Archives; Bierstadt to John Sartain, July 1877, Archives of the Pennsylvania Academy of the Fine Arts, Philadelphia.

155. Bierstadt to unknown correspondent, 20 Nov. 1873, New-York Historical Society. He mentioned the Pettes and Leathe's Gallery of Saint Louis, thereby placing the unknown correspondent in that city. I am grateful to Nanni Kaps for discovering this information.

156. *Post*, New York, 20 Jan. 1877.

157. Taragin 1976, p. 25.

158. Bierstadt to MacLeod, 28 Dec. 1877, Corcoran Archives.

159. Curator's Journal 5, 11 Jan. 1878, Corcoran Archives.

160. Bierstadt to Samuel Ward, 18 Jan. 1878, William Wilson Corcoran Papers, Library of Congress, Washington, D.C.

161. Curator's Journal 10, 22 Jan. 1878, Corcoran Archives.

162. William MacLeod, "Some Incidents in the Life of the Late Wm. Wilson Corcoran," unpublished manuscript, MacLeod Miscellaneous Papers, Historical Society of Washington, D.C. In this recollection, written after Corcoran's death in 1888, MacLeod sought to ameliorate the episode that had obviously cost him and the collector a good deal of embarrassment. I am grateful to Franklin Kelly for bringing this and other material on Corcoran to my attention, as well as for allowing me to read portions of his unpublished paper on Corcoran as a collector.

163. *Sun*, New York, 28 Dec. 1884, quoted in Candace Nielsen Von Salzen, "William Douglas MacLeod: His Life, Curatorship, and Art," Master's thesis, George Washington University, 1981, p. 129.

164. There is extensive literature on the topic of the international expositions. Among the titles dealing with American contributions are Merle Curti, "America at the World's Fairs, 1851–1893," *American Historical Review* 55 (July 1950): 833–56; Broun 1976; Richard Guy Wilson et al., *The American Renaissance: 1876–1917*, exh. cat. (Brooklyn: The Brooklyn Museum, 1979); David Huntington, *The Quest for Unity: American Art Between the World's Fairs, 1876–1893*, exh. cat. (Detroit: Detroit Institute of Arts, 1983); Troyen 1984; Greenhalgh 1988; Elizabeth Gilmore Holt, ed., *The Expanding World of Art, 1874–1902*, vol. 1: *Universal Expositions and State-Sponsored Fine Arts Exhibitions* (New Haven: Yale University Press, 1988); and Blaugrund et al. 1989.

165. *Sun*, New York, 21 Feb. 1893; *Post*, New York, 23 Feb. 1893; *NY Times*, 24 Feb. 1893; *Transcript*, New York, 25 Feb. 1893.

166. *NY Times*, 26 Apr. 1873.

167. Jervis McEntee Diary, AAA, 31 Mar. 1876. On 9 Apr., McEntee wrote: "Had a talk with Whittredge and John Taylor Johnston. They stick by our committee and if Bierstadt gets ahead of us he will be pretty smart." While Bierstadt did, apparently, submit to the process (3 May 1876), McEntee later noted that

the one painting rejected by the Selection Committee, *California Spring* (p. 228), had been hung anyway by "the Centennial authorities" on 19 June 1876, suggesting that Bierstadt had somehow prevailed after all.

168. Weir 1880, p. 27.

169. Armstrong to Saint-Gaudens, 20 Mar. 1878, Saint-Gaudens Papers, Dartmouth College Library, Hanover, N.H.

170. Quoted in V. E. Lewis 1956, p. 234.

171. Strahan 1876–78, vol. 1, p. 42.

172. Sheldon 1972, p. 147.

173. Strahan 1880, vol. 1, p. 5.

174. Brownell 1880a, p. 1.

175. Benjamin 1887, p. 15.

176. Van Rensselaer 1881, p. 193.

177. Benjamin 1880, p. 97.

178. Ibid., p. 98.

179. *Boston Transcript*, 10 Mar. 1882.

180. *Boston Journal*, 17, 18 Mar. 1882.

181. E. M., "Boston Correspondence," *Art Amateur* 6 (1882): 96.

182. Downes 1888, p. 781.

183. *World*, New York, 10 Mar. 1889.

184. William Sartain to John Sartain, 11 Jan. 1889, Sartain Collection, Historical Society of Pennsylvania, Philadelphia.

185. *World*, New York, undated clipping [Mar. 1889], Bierstadt Scrapbook, Edwards Collection.

186. Ibid.

187. Ibid.

188. *Republican*, Springfield, Mass., 21 June 1889.

189. *World*, New York, 31 Mar. 1889.

190. "Monthly Record of American Art," *Magazine of Art* 12 (July 1889): xxxi, quoted in Blaugrund et al. 1989, p. 20. I am very grateful to Annette Blaugrund for sharing her files on the Bierstadt controversy with me and for allowing me to read her essay, "Behind the Scenes: The Organization of American Paintings," before publication.

191. *World*, New York, undated clipping [1889], Bierstadt Scrapbook, Edwards Collection.

192. Blaugrund et al. 1989, pp. 20, 85–87, 91.

193. Undated clipping [1889], Bierstadt Scrapbook, Edwards Collection.

194. "The family think Uncle Albert has sold some pictures to the enormously wealthy 'Nitrate King' Col. North . . ." (Oscar A. Bierstadt to Anne Turner Bierstadt, 20 July 1891, Turner Collection); unidentified, undated clipping, Bierstadt Scrapbook, Edwards Collection; *Evening Star*, Washington, D.C., 3 June 1890, reported that the picture had been sold for $50,000 but did not identify the buyer.

195. *Boston Transcript*, 26 Feb. 1902.

196. Ibid.

# "Wondrously Full of Invention"

## THE WESTERN LANDSCAPES OF ALBERT BIERSTADT

NANCY K. ANDERSON

DURING A CAREER that spanned the entire second half of the nineteenth century, Albert Bierstadt produced a large and remarkably varied body of work. Arguably, some of his finest paintings date from the early years of his European apprenticeship in the 1850s—including the carefully composed Westphalian farm scenes, several Swiss mountain views, and perhaps his most accomplished genre painting, *The Arch of Octavius (The Roman Fish Market)*, 1858 (No. 11). Twenty years later, drawn to Nassau by his wife's ill health, Bierstadt turned his attention to tropical subjects and produced the marvelously translucent wave at the center of *The Shore of the Turquoise Sea*, 1878 (No. 66). Still later, he traveled to Alaska, where he completed the elegantly spare *Wreck of the "Ancon" in Loring Bay, Alaska*, 1889 (Fig. 75), one of his finest oil studies. Despite the high quality and diverse nature of these works, however, the paintings that brought Bierstadt his greatest success and for which he is still celebrated are the heroic landscapes of the American West.

Though often described as the first major painter to go west, Bierstadt did not see the Rocky Mountains until 1859, a full decade after the siren call of California gold had drawn thousands over the plains, across the Isthmus, and around the Horn. By the time Bierstadt reached South Pass and

Figure 34

Samuel Seymour. *View near the base of the Rocky Mountains,* 1820. Watercolor, 5 × 8 in. (12.7 × 20.3 cm). Beinecke Rare Book and Manuscript Library, W. R. Coe Collection, Yale University, New Haven, Connecticut.

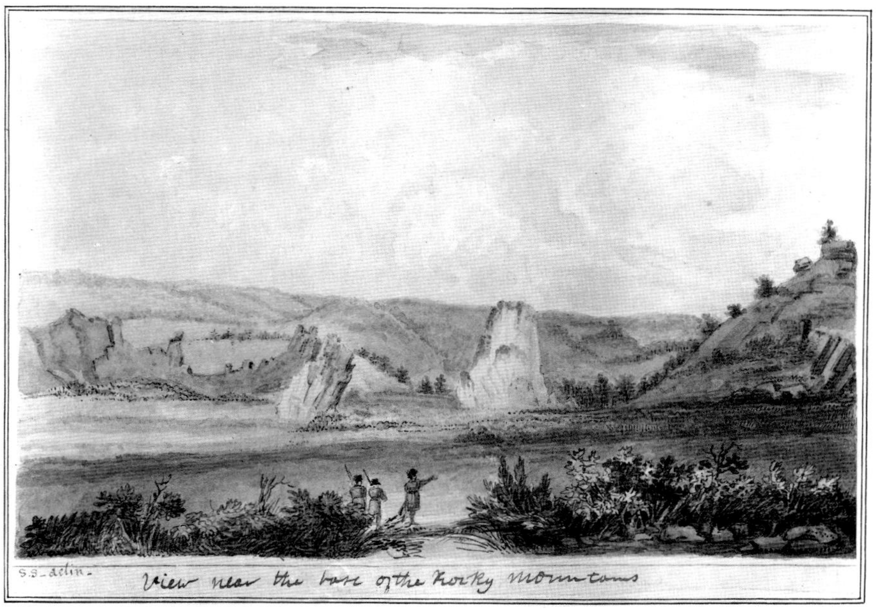

the Continental Divide, the wagon ruts of countless pilgrims already marked the trail. By 1863, when he crossed the Sierra Nevada and entered California for the first time, fifteen years had passed since the discovery of gold at Sutter's Mill had sparked a stampede.

Bierstadt saw neither the Rockies nor California until well after a full corps of writers, journalists, surveyors, and forty-niners had whetted the appetites of both Europeans and Americans for visual confirmation of the alpine peaks, enormous trees, and stunning valleys they had described with all the exclamation words would allow. Ironically, Bierstadt's "late" arrival was perfectly timed, for it allowed him to capitalize on the nation's eagerness to finally see what such accomplished writers as Washington Irving, Richard Henry Dana, Francis Parkman, John C. Frémont, and Bayard Taylor had already described in travel books, histories, survey reports, and countless newspaper columns.[1]

To be sure, Bierstadt was not the first artist to recognize the commercial and aesthetic potential of western subject matter. By the time Bierstadt crossed the Mississippi for the first time, George Catlin (1796–1872) had already completed several extensive expeditions in the Far West and had produced an "Indian Gallery" containing more than six hundred paintings.[2] Well before Bierstadt reached Fort Laramie in Wyoming Territory, Karl Bodmer (1809–1893), Alfred Jacob Miller (1810–1874), and John Mix Stanley (1814–1872) had ventured deep into the American wilderness, emerged relatively unscathed, and completed most, if not all, of the paintings upon which their reputations would rest.[3] Even the Rockies were not fresh to art when Bierstadt saw them for the first time. The earliest known paintings of the snowcapped peaks were completed by Samuel Seymour (active 1796–1823) in 1820, ten years before Bierstadt was born (Fig. 34).[4]

Though a latecomer to the Far West, Bierstadt turned his attention toward the western horizon at exactly the right moment, for by 1859 curiosity about America's distant frontier had reached a fever pitch, thanks in part to the surveyors, journalists, writers, and artists who had begun reporting on the West as early as the 1820s. More important, by 1859 Bierstadt had acquired the personal and professional maturity that would allow him to meet the call for western landscapes grand enough to challenge the European model but distinctive enough to inspire national pride. By the time he departed for the Rockies, he had spent a decade, both at home and abroad, acquiring the requisite skills of his craft. His disciplined application allowed him to travel west with a near-perfect combination of technical expertise, European experience, national enthusiasm, and marketing savvy—everything required to turn the western landscape into an iconic image of national definition.

## "A Different Class of Mountains"

In April 1859, Bierstadt undertook the first of what would become an important series of journeys west when he traveled to Saint Joseph, Missouri, and joined Frederick W. Lander's survey party bound for the Rocky Mountains.[5] Just how Bierstadt and his traveling companion, fellow artist Francis Shedd Frost (1825–1902), obtained permission to travel with the Lander party is not clear.[6] It is possible that Lander, who had a strong interest in the arts and understood well the value of having visual documentation on hand for use in future publications, extended the invitation himself.[7] It is also possible that Bierstadt, recognizing the potential market for paintings of the Far West, approached Lander or another well-placed government figure for permission to travel with the survey party. Whatever the arrangement, the Lander expedition marks the point at which Bierstadt found the subject that would make his career.

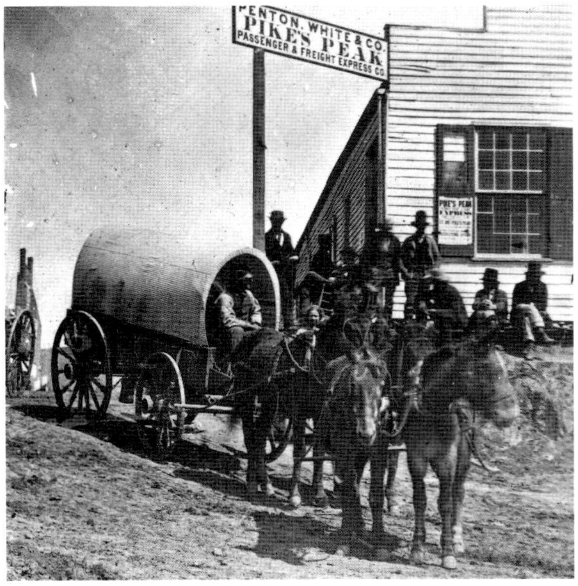


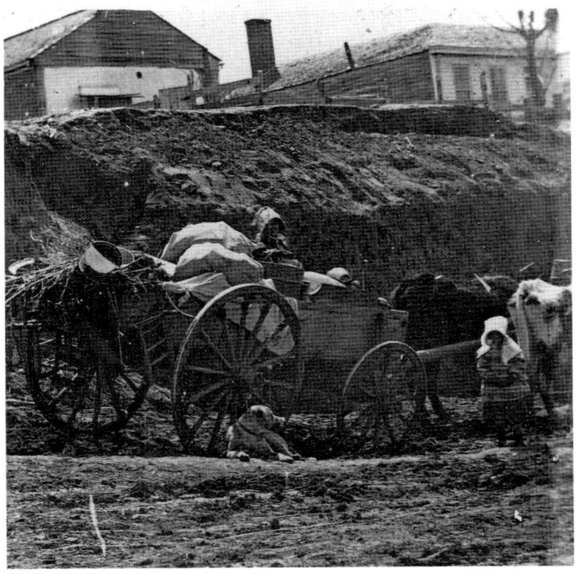

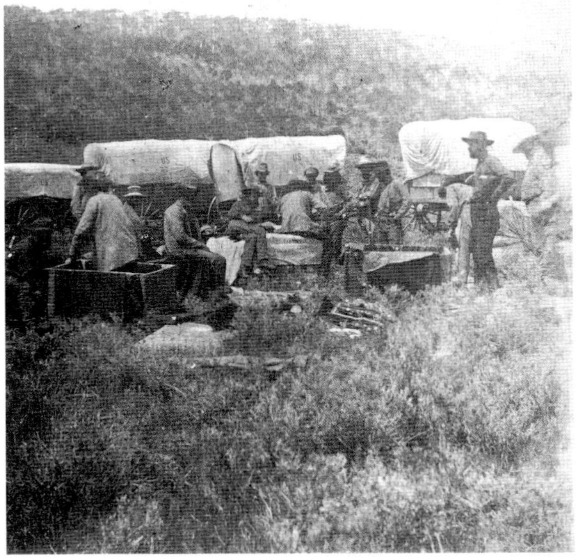

Figure 35 *(above, left)*

Albert Bierstadt. *Pike's Peak Emigrants, Saint Joseph, Missouri*, 1859. Stereograph. Kansas State Historical Society, Topeka.

Figure 36 *(above, right)*

Albert Bierstadt. *Emigrants Waiting for the Ferry, Saint Joseph, Missouri*, 1859. Stereograph. Collection of William L. Schaeffer.

Figure 37 *(left)*

Albert Bierstadt. *Unpacking Goods for the Indians, Nebraska*, 1859. Stereograph. Collection of Wilfred Thompson, courtesy of Leonard A. Walle.

At the time, the Rocky Mountains were the subject of much speculation, for they offered the last real hope that mountain grandeur on a European scale might be found within American borders. Though eager to celebrate the beauty and bounty of the North American continent, Americans had for years joined in a collective lament that the American landscape boasted no alpine peaks. In order to experience the Romantic sublime described so passionately by European poets, Americans were obliged to go abroad. Awed by the grandeur of Swiss Alps, they could only regret that America offered nothing quite so spectacular.

Like many others who had traveled abroad, James Fenimore Cooper expressed disappointment in the rounded hills that passed for American mountains: "Any well delineated view of a high-class Swiss scene must at once convince even the most provincial mind among us that nothing of the sort is to be found in America, east of the Rocky Mountains."[8] Unwilling to yield completely, Cooper held out hope that the Rockies might prove an American match for European Alps. William Cowper Prime, professor of art at Princeton, also declared he would wait to see what the Rockies had to show: "In the Rocky Mountain range, it is possible and even probable, that in time we shall find scenery that will equal anything in Switzerland. But we can have none on this side of the continent for the reason that we have no hills crowned with eternal snow, to pour down their sounding cataracts into vast chasms or smiling valleys. . . . But mountains and lakes we will say nothing more about until we know more what we possess in the Rocky Mountain range."[9]

Intensely curious about the vast plains and rugged mountains on their distant frontier, Americans had invested much national pride in the reported alpine character of the Rocky Mountains. In a letter written in July 1859 and later published in the *Crayon*, Bierstadt offered a reassuring word from the base of the Rockies:

> The mountains are very fine; as seen from the plains, they resemble very much the Bernese Alps, one of the finest ranges of mountains in Europe, if not in the world. They are of granite formation, the same as the Swiss mountains and their jagged summits, covered with snow and mingling with the clouds, present a scene which every lover of landscape would gaze upon in unqualified delight. . . . We see many spots in the scenery that remind us of our New Hampshire and Catskill hills, but when we look up and measure the mighty perpendicular cliffs that rise hundreds of feet aloft, all capped with snow, we then realize that we are among a different class of mountains. . . .[10]

Bierstadt's letter to the *Crayon* was not his only communication from the distant frontier. Clearly aware of the value of publicity in selling paintings, Bierstadt sent letters from various points along the trail to a New Bedford newspaper for publication.[11] Capitalizing on curiosity spurred by the discovery of gold near Pike's Peak, Bierstadt's letters describe, in some detail, life en route to the newest El Dorado. They also contain constant reminders that he traveled west with eyes trained on European models. Upon seeing the Black Hills, for example, he was reminded of Switzerland, and in the foothills of the Rockies he saw "the color of Italy."[12] The letters bear significance beyond the valuable information they contain about the survey party's itinerary, for they mark the appearance of Albert Bierstadt, artist-explorer. This canny bit of self-casting carried with it the promise of future paintings based on firsthand experience—exactly what the market demanded.

While in the field with the Lander party, Bierstadt utilized the working method he had adopted while a student in Düsseldorf. Painting quickly, he completed a large number of plein air oil sketches, which he later used to compose studio pictures. Though not intended for formal exhibition, some of these fresh and often spare studies display a power that belies their size. Among the most compelling examples is *Surveyor's Wagon in the Rockies*, c. 1859 (Fig. 38). Though measuring less than eight by thirteen inches, this extraordinarily delicate painting manages to convey the near-limitless expanse of western space more successfully than some of the artist's later works that

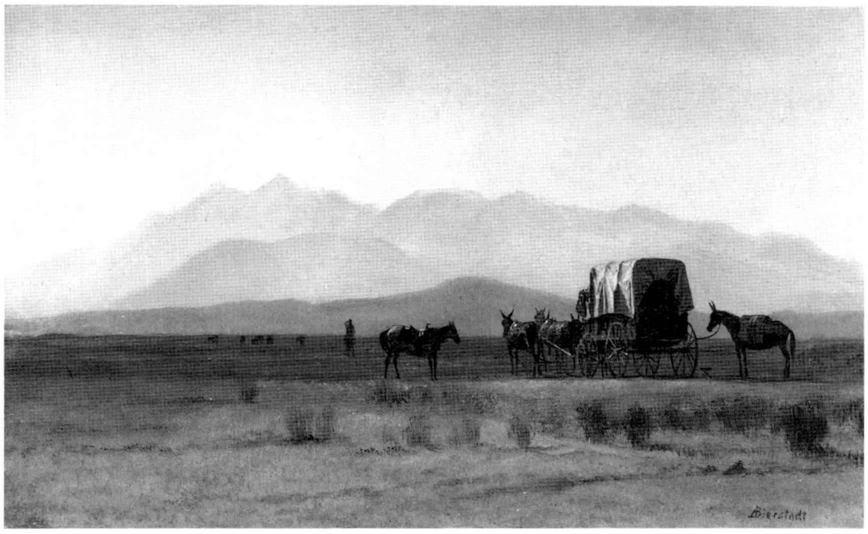

Figure 38
Albert Bierstadt. *Surveyor's Wagon in the Rockies*, c. 1859 (No. 20).

dwarf it in size. Equally remarkable is Bierstadt's subtle comment on the fragility of the expedition enterprise. The lone human figure appears but a specter on the horizon, and the tethered animals stand in isolation on legs rendered with single strokes. As Bierstadt's private rather than public pictures, the sketches stand in marked contrast to the carefully composed and highly structured studio paintings.

## "Purely an American Scene"

In September 1859, Bierstadt returned to New Bedford from his Rocky Mountain reconnaissance with a full complement of sketches, photographs, and Indian artifacts.[13] Recognizing that his skills and ambition required a larger arena, he moved, shortly after his return east, to New York City, the center of the American art market. In the Tenth Street Studio Building, where he had settled by January 1860, he quickly set about turning his studio into a stage set for his Rocky Mountain pictures.[14] Hung with buffalo skins and Indian clothing, Bierstadt's studio made one reporter feel as if he had entered "the depot of a fur trader."[15] Another visitor wrote that the room was "adorned with buffalo robes, blankets, feathers, arrows, moccasins, and all the equipments and paraphernalia of the hunter and the Indian of the Rocky Mountains."[16]

A clever businessman as well as an accomplished artist, Bierstadt shrewdly began to market the adventure of his journey as well as the finished artistic product. Assuming a role not unlike that of the hunters and explorers celebrated in novels and histories, he entertained visitors with tales of adventure on the overland trail. After previewing a work in progress, for example, a writer for the *Boston Evening Transcript* reported what only Bierstadt could have told him: "To obtain the materials of this work, the artist underwent no ordinary privation and fatigue; for weeks, in the vicinity of this very scene, he and his comrades lived upon bread and water—not daring to fire a gun, for fear of betraying their retreat to hostile Indians, tribes of whom had there recently murdered white travelers. The landscape thus achieved, amid the peril and isolation, is not a composition, but a genuine scene drawn from nature. . . ."[17] Clearly Bierstadt could tell a story as well as he could paint a picture.

Bierstadt began exhibiting paintings with Rocky Mountain subjects in January 1860.[18] Like reports from a distant and exotic land, the pictures were greeted with enthusiasm. After viewing one such painting, a writer for the *Crayon* commented: "The scenery of this section of our territory

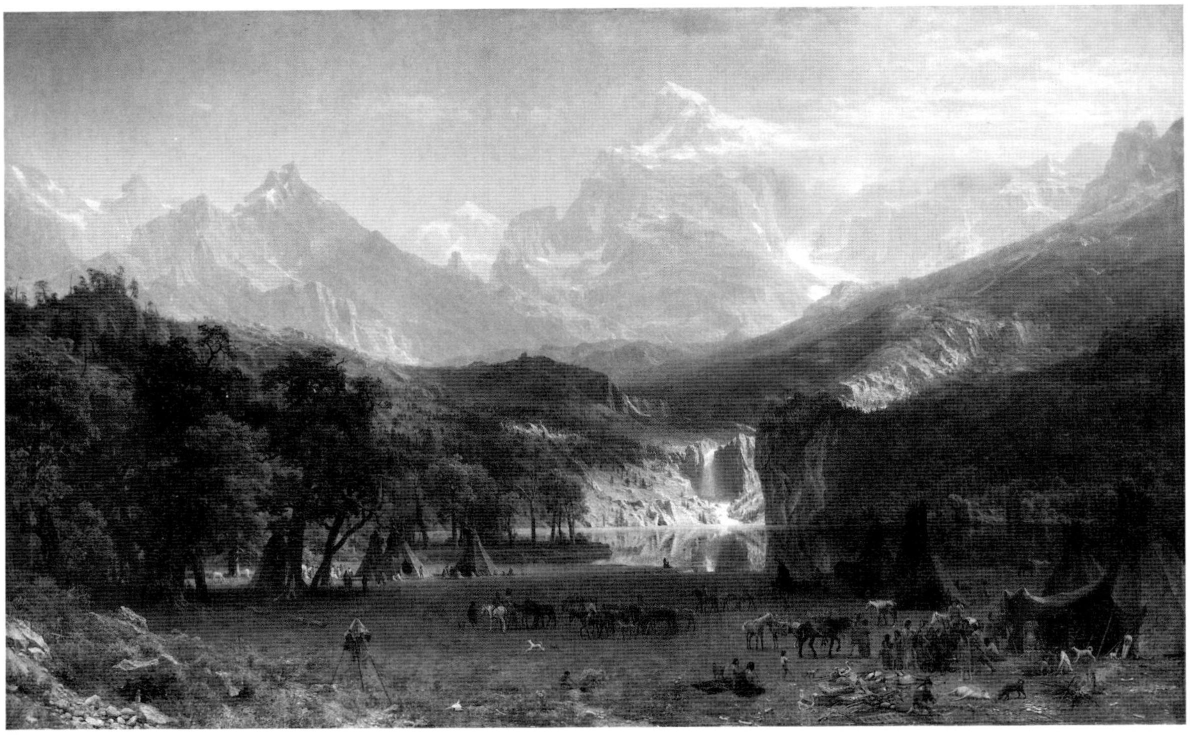

Figure 39
Albert Bierstadt. *The Rocky Mountains, Lander's Peak*, 1863 (No. 37).

has for a long time been a matter of curiosity to lovers of landscape, who have been excited and yet not satisfied by the vague and contradictory reports of explorers. Through the better expression of the brush we can now form some idea of it, Mr. Bierstadt's pencil being too true and too powerful to be questioned."[19]

Perceptive enough to recognize the potential for pictures that answered long-standing questions about the Far West, Bierstadt understood that the idea of the West preceded the mapping and measuring of the physical land and that the idea was born of European models.[20] Bierstadt also understood that while the audible public call was for factual information about a land still relatively unknown, the more subtle expectation was that paintings of the mountainous West would conform with the European ideal of mountain grandeur but would also emerge as distinctly American. With a clear understanding of the mandate, Bierstadt invented the western American landscape by skillfully joining passages of carefully observed and meticulously rendered detail with freely configured compositions that met national needs.

Nowhere is Bierstadt's method more evident than in *The Rocky Mountains, Lander's Peak*, 1863 (Fig. 39), the most important painting to result from the 1859 trip. Measuring six by ten feet, the picture was designed to be exhibited alone, as a showpiece, or "Great Picture." The second of Bierstadt's major western panoramas (*Base of the Rocky Mountains, Laramie Peak*, 1860, now unlocated, was the first), the painting betrays the artist's eagerness to meet the expectations of an audience nursed on the novels of Cooper but also anxious to find an American equivalent for the European sublime.

By no means the first artist to produce pictorial amalgams of fact and fiction, Bierstadt was undoubtedly aware of European precedents. His most important model, however, was much closer to home: while he labored on *The Rocky Mountains, Lander's Peak* in the Tenth Street Studio Building, Frederic Church (1826–1900), America's most successful landscape painter, was at work in the same building.

Shortly after Bierstadt began exhibiting *The Rocky Mountains, Lander's Peak* in New York, James Jackson Jarves, one of the most perceptive critics of the day, commented on similarities in the working methods of Church and Bierstadt: "Each composes his pictures from actual sketches, with the desire to render the general truths and spirit of the localities of their landscapes, though often departing from the literal features of the view. With singular inconsistency of mind they idealize in composition and materialize in execution, so that, though the details of the scenery are substantially correct, the scene as a whole is often false."[21]

Critics were quick to draw other parallels between the two artists' work. In February 1864, the *Round Table* began its review of *The Rocky Mountains, Lander's Peak* by stating, "Mr. Bierstadt's name is now associated with the Rocky Mountains as is that of Mr. Church with the Andes."[22] In fact, however, there are significant differences as well as similarities between *The Rocky Mountains, Lander's Peak* and Church's *Heart of the Andes*, 1859 (Fig. 40). Although both paintings are evocations of the sublime, Bierstadt's picture is far more focused on specific national concerns than Church's broader-ranging composition.

A review of *The Rocky Mountains, Lander's Peak* in *Harper's Weekly* underscores the manner in which the painting met quite specific national needs:

> It is purely an American scene, and from the faithful and elaborate delineation of the Indian village, a form of life now rapidly disappearing from the earth, may be called a historic landscape. It is the curtained continent with its sublime natural forms and its rude savage human life. . . . And unlike Mr. Church's pictures of the equatorial mountain scenery of America, which from their volcanic and tropical character, however luxuriant, yet forbid hope and leave an impression of profound sadness and desolation, this work of Bierstadt's inspires the temperate cheerfulness and promise of the region it depicts and the imagination contemplates it as the possible seat of supreme civilization.[23]

The differences between the two pictures become all the more evident when the text of a flyer published to promote the sale of James Smillie's engraving of *The Rocky Mountains, Lander's Peak*

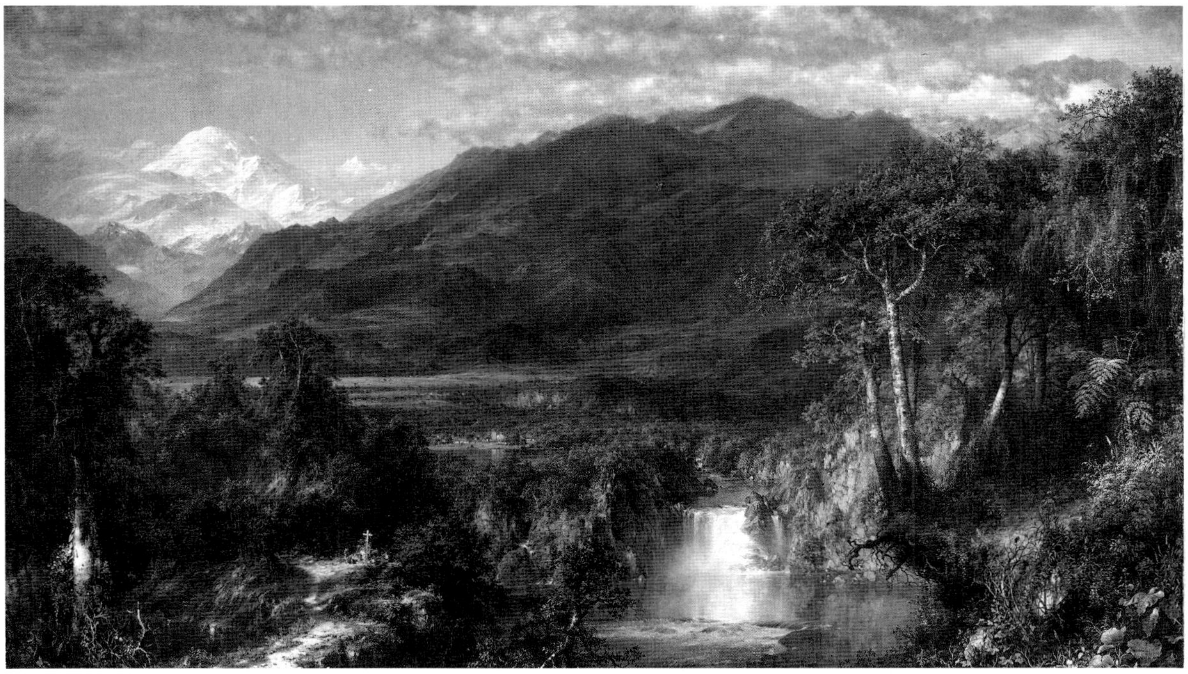

Figure 40

Frederic Edwin Church. *Heart of the Andes*, 1859. Oil on canvas, 66⅛ × 119¼ in. (168 × 302.9 cm). The Metropolitan Museum of Art, New York, Bequest of Mrs. David Dows, 1909.

is compared with Theodore Winthrop's (Fig. 41) more comprehensive explication of Church's painting in *A Companion to "The Heart of the Andes."* Winthrop began his analysis by stating, "In 'Heart of the Andes,' Mr. Church has condensed the condensation of nature. It is not an actual scene, but the subtle essence of many scenes combined into a typical picture."[24] Although *The Rocky Mountains, Lander's Peak* is as much a fictional construct as *Heart of the Andes,* Bierstadt went to great lengths to identify the scene as a specific spot and the Indians as members of a particular tribe. According to the flyer (which was surely approved, if not written, by Bierstadt):

> This picture represents the scenery in the Wind River range of mountains, in Nebraska Territory, being a portion of that great chain known as the Rocky Mountains. . . . The particular portion which the Artist has here depicted lies at a distance of about seven hundred miles northeast of San Francisco, and portrays the western slope of the mountains. The streams which are seen leaping down their sides,—are the headwaters of the Rio Colorado. . . . The principal peak of the group is Mt. Lander. Its summit is covered with perpetual snow, and immense glaciers are formed upon its sides. . . . The Indian encampment in the foreground is known as the Shoshone Village, and the various implements of the chase, warfare, and domestic use, scattered about, are those in general employment by this tribe.[25]

After viewing Bierstadt's Rocky Mountain painting, a reporter praised the artist for correctly representing "a part of our land of which we know comparatively little."[26] Intensely curious about the far reaches of their own continent, Americans looked to Bierstadt for information as they would to a reporter just returned from a distant front. Bierstadt's insistence that the geography of his painting carry specific names and a precise location suggests that he understood and consciously sought to meet the American hunger for factual information about the Far West.

The contrast between the orientations of the two painters is set in clearest opposition in the treatment of the isolated snow peak present in both *Heart of the Andes* and *The Rocky Mountains, Lander's Peak.* For Theodore Winthrop, the snowy peak was the locus and lesson of Church's painting: "In the 'Heart of the Andes' the great snowpeak is master, and its solemn peaceful light the illuminator of the scene."[27] Winthrop went on to state that Church's mountain was a type and not a portrait: "This mountain, dominant at the 'Heart of the Andes,' is not then Cayambe or Chimborazo, or any other peak of the equatorial group. It is each and all of them, and many more than any."[28]

Winthrop defined an isolated snow peak as "the sublimest of material objects" and extolled the "great white thrones of the Almighty" that "demand our worship for their sublimity."[29] The snowy peak that dominates Bierstadt's painting aspires to all the adjectives of sublimity accorded Church's mountain, but to this mix Bierstadt added a strong nationalistic note, giving his mountain a name and particular identity. By labeling his confectionary mountain Lander's Peak, Bierstadt not only established the Americanness of the scene, but also succeeded in linking his snowy peak with a recently martyred war hero.

Frederick W. Lander (Fig. 42), leader of the survey Bierstadt had joined in 1859, had died on 2 March 1862 after a distinguished military career in the Union army. In the fall of 1861, he suffered a severe leg wound in a skirmish near Edward's Ferry. He subsequently participated in the defense of Hancock, Maryland, against the superior forces of General "Stonewall" Jackson and shortly thereafter led another attack, earning a commendation from the secretary of war. His wound, however, had not healed and, coupled with exhaustion and exposure to severe weather, caused his death. The *New York Times,* calling Lander "the fearless soldier, the bravest of the brave," wrote: "There is no officer in the army whose loss could cause more profound and unrivaled sorrow than that of General Lander. He was beloved and trusted in the highest degree by his own

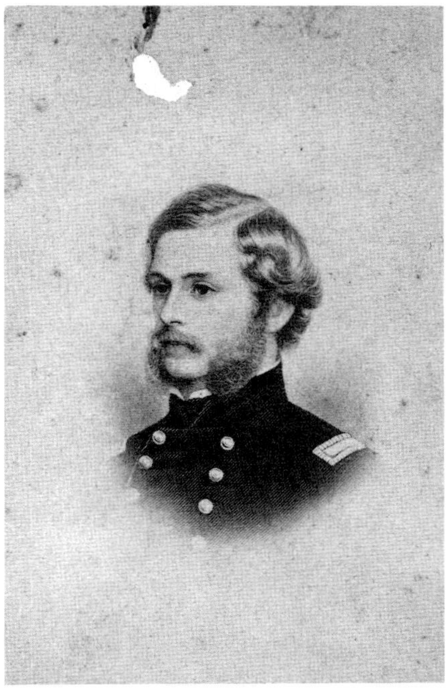

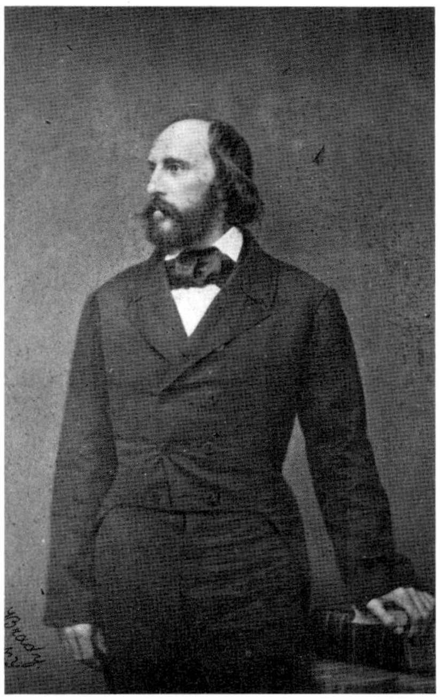

Figure 41 *(far left)*
*Theodore Winthrop*. Carte de visite. Private collection.

Figure 42 *(left)*
Studio of Mathew B. Brady. *Frederick West Lander*. Carte de visite. Private collection.

command; while his character and career, as well as his actions since the war began, led the whole country to look upon him as the very beau ideal of an American soldier, and as a man from whom great and heroic things were to be expected as the war progressed."[30]

Bierstadt exhibited *The Rocky Mountains, Lander's Peak* privately at the Tenth Street Studio Building just eleven months after Lander's death, and the painting began its public tour through New England shortly thereafter.[31] Today the title of the picture is often shortened to read simply *The Rocky Mountains*. Such a title suggests a generalized, or, in the words of Winthrop, "condensed," landscape composition. When exhibited in the 1860s, however, Bierstadt's painting carried insistent references to particulars of geography and Indian culture, and the alpine peak rising in the distance bore the name of a martyred war hero whose exploits and tragic loss were still fresh in the minds of Bierstadt's contemporaries. Thus, although similar in composition to, and perhaps inspired by, Church's *Heart of the Andes*, Bierstadt's painting addressed different issues and was far more national in its focus.

Bierstadt's attempt to balance the call for factual information with the need to produce a compelling image of American alpine grandeur produced a tension within *The Rocky Mountains, Lander's Peak* that Jarves and others noted. For those who came to the painting for information, Bierstadt supplied the facts of flora and fauna; for others, who sought the American sublime, Bierstadt invented mountains to match the Alps.

Celebrated by those who viewed the image as a factual report, *The Rocky Mountains, Lander's Peak* was also cheered by many who recognized the painting as skillfully constructed fiction. A critic for the *Chicago Times* spoke for the latter group: "That he, and no man, ever saw that particular scene of Indian life, matters little, who ever saw Venus or Apollo. . . . Did Dante ever pass through chaos. . . . And yet, although Bierstadt never saw this landscape or witnessed this scene, the picture contains nothing which he had not seen. . . . Deny to the picture, as we assuredly must, poetic suggestiveness, and beauty, and sentiment; yet it remains to be said that it is wondrously full of invention."[32]

For others, even less concerned with the literal accuracy of the subject, the painting became an iconic image of Manifest Destiny. Writing for the *New York Leader*, one critic commented: "I do not reflect, but I feel that this is a glimpse into the heart of the continent towards which civilization is struggling; and the grey peaks, in their massive grandeur, seem to me to be wrapt in a romance new, and fresh, and breezy. It *is* the romance of the *new*. . . . This, to me, is the power of the picture. I know that the nation's future greatness is somehow dimly seen in the great West. This picture is a view into the *penetralia* of destiny as well as nature."[33]

## "A Distant Land of Gold"

The paintings Bierstadt produced following his first trip west in 1859 brought the artist substantial financial rewards. They also allowed him to stake artistic claim to a new subject with great popular appeal—the western American landscape. It is not surprising, therefore, that Bierstadt attempted to return west as early as 1860 and again in 1862. Neither trip materialized. The following year, however, his plans did come to fruition. A far more extensive journey than the first, Bierstadt's expedition to the West Coast in 1863 is the most thoroughly documented of all his western trips, for traveling with the artist was Fitz Hugh Ludlow (Fig. 43), a talented writer and prominent member of New York's literary set.

Bierstadt's choice of traveling companion was brilliant, for in Ludlow he found the ideal publicist. A professional writer who had gained considerable notoriety six years earlier when he published *The Hasheesh Eater*, Ludlow kept interested readers abreast of the overland party's progress in a series of letters written along the trail and published in the New York *Evening Post*.[34] He did the same for California readers in a series of "reminiscences" published in the *Golden Era* early in 1864 (see Appendix B). Once back in New York, he maintained public interest in the western adventure through another series of articles published in the *Atlantic Monthly*.[35] In 1870, seven years after the journey itself, Ludlow published *The Heart of the Continent*, yet another account of the trip, illustrated with woodcuts and engravings after works by Bierstadt. Recast numerous times, Ludlow's recollections of the 1863 overland journey undoubtedly contributed to the market for Bierstadt's paintings.

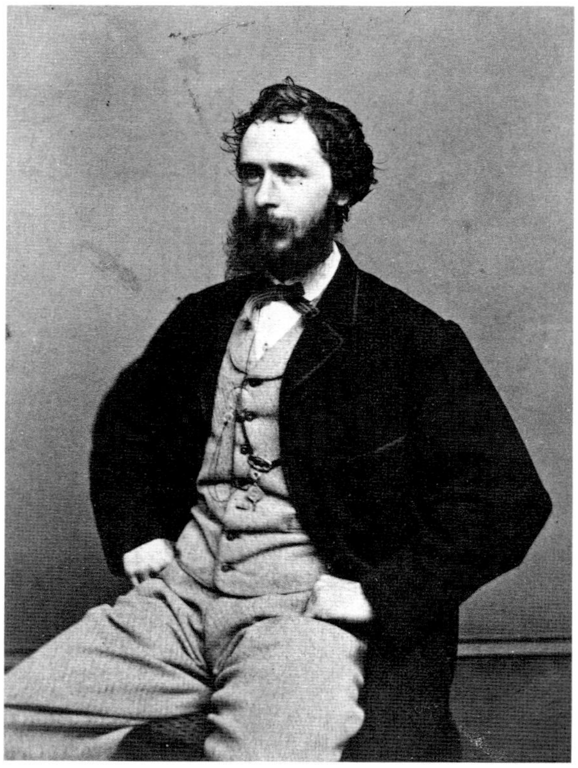

Figure 43 *(left)*

K. W. Beniczky, New York. *Fitz Hugh Ludlow*, inscribed 1863. Carte de visite. Collection of Joyce Randall Edwards.

Figure 44 *(facing page, left)*

Carleton E. Watkins. *Tutucanula—El Capitan*, 1861. Albumen silver print. The Park-McCullough House Association, Inc., North Bennington, Vermont.

Figure 45 *(facing page, right)*

Carleton E. Watkins. *The Sentinel, 3,270 Feet, Yosemite*, 1861. Albumen silver print. The Bancroft Library, University of California, Berkeley.

Surviving documents indicate that although Bierstadt had hoped to travel west in 1860 and 1862, he did not intend to go farther than the Rocky Mountains. By May 1863, however, when he and Ludlow set off on their journey, his plans had grown far more ambitious; California, Oregon, and Canada had been added to the itinerary. Given the flood of information (and misinformation) that had come from the Pacific Coast following the discovery of gold, it is somewhat surprising that Bierstadt had not set his sights on California much earlier. Several factors may have influenced his decision, by early 1863, to travel west to the Pacific shore. Among the most intriguing of these was an exhibition in December 1862 at Goupil's gallery in New York of oversize photographs of California (including views of Yosemite Valley and the Big Trees) by Carleton Watkins (1829–1916) (Figs. 44, 45). The *Post* published a glowing review of the "unequaled" photographs: "The views of lofty mountains, of gigantic trees, of falls of water which seem to descend from heights in the heavens and break into mists before reaching the ground, are indescribably unique and beautiful. Nothing in the way of landscape can be more impressive or picturesque."[36]

By 1863 Yosemite Valley and the Big Trees had been discussed at some length in newspapers and periodicals. Occasionally illustrations (usually woodcuts) accompanied the articles. Additionally, a number of stereographic views of Yosemite and other California wonders taken by Charles Leander Weed (1824–1903), one of California's earliest photographers, had been distributed in the East as early as 1860. These were small images, however, and lacked the impact of Watkins's mammoth prints exhibited at Goupil's. Though Bierstadt was surely aware of published reports extolling California's scenic wonders, he may have discounted as hyperbole the extraordinary claims made for California scenery. It must have been clear, however, to anyone who saw the Watkins photographs that Yosemite was not an exaggeration and that the Mariposa redwoods did, in fact, dwarf every other living thing. Ludlow later confirmed that Bierstadt had seen the Watkins photographs in both New York and San Francisco. In describing preparations for their own expedition to Yosemite Valley, he wrote: "We were going into the vale whose giant domes and battlements had months before thrown their photographic shadow through Watkins's camera across the mysterious wide Continent, causing exclamations of awe at Goupil's window, and ecstasy in Dr. [Oliver Wendell] Holmes's study. At Goupil's counter and in Starr King's drawing-room we had gazed on them by the hour already,—I, let me confess it, half a Thomas-a-Didymus to Nature, unwilling to believe the utmost true of her till I could put my finger in her very prints."[37]

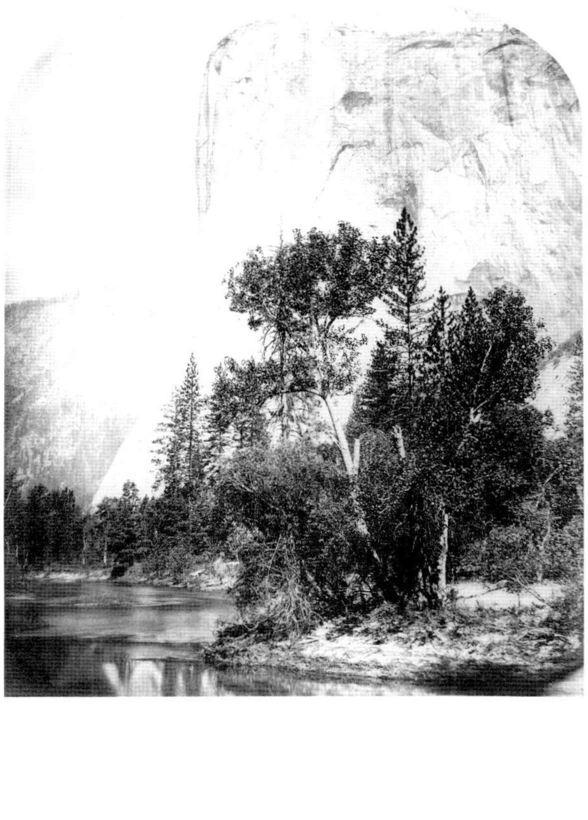

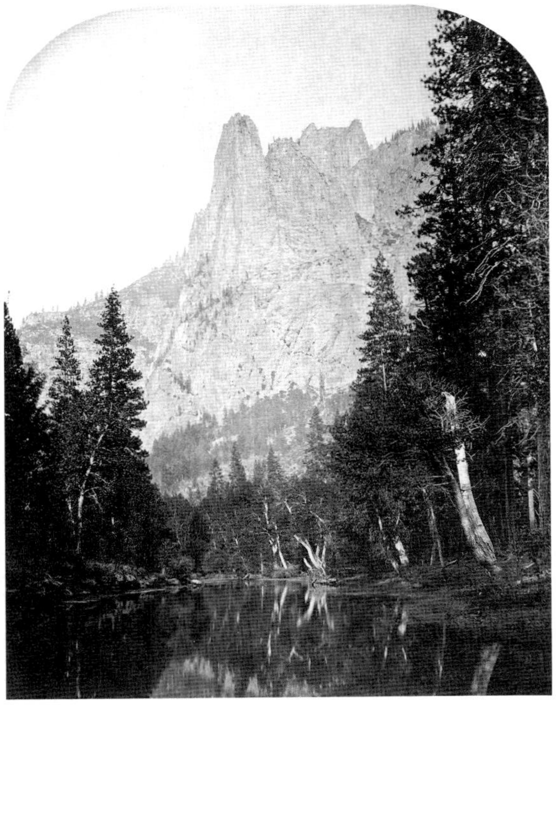

Ludlow's reference to Thomas Starr King (Fig. 46) is also significant, for like Watkins, King had fanned the fires of interest in California scenery. A charismatic preacher who had moved from Boston to San Francisco, King captivated eastern readers with a series of letters in the *Boston Transcript* describing the wonders of California with the passion of a man seeing God's revelation.[38] King had originally planned to accompany Bierstadt and Ludlow to Yosemite, but commitments to war-relief efforts prevented him from making the trip.

Because the paintings that resulted from the 1863 trip invariably offer an idyllic view of a new golden land, it is easy to forget that Bierstadt and Ludlow journeyed west during the darkest days of the Civil War. Two years earlier, during the first months of the war, Bierstadt had visited Union troops camped near the Potomac River.[39] Following this trip, he completed a small painting, *Guerrilla Warfare (Picket Duty in Virginia)*, 1862 (Fig. 47), one of only a handful of pictures by the artist that refer to the war in an overt manner. From a less literal point of view, however, most, if not all, of the paintings Bierstadt completed following his trip to California were war-related, for in the western landscape, and particularly in the mountains and valleys of California, Bierstadt found the perfect visual antidote to war.

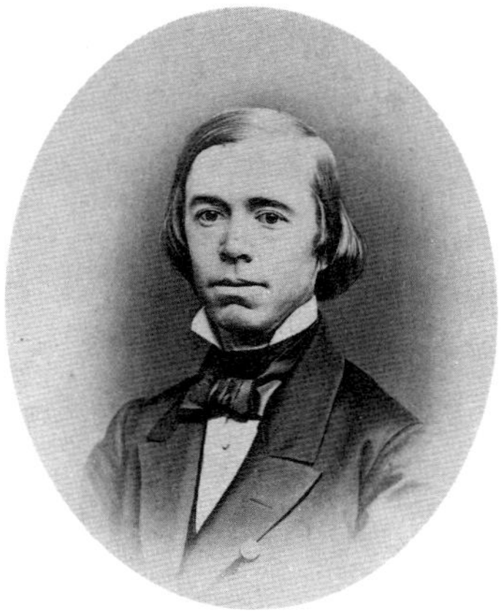

Figure 46 *(above)*
*Thomas Starr King*. Photograph. Bierstadt Album, private collection, Hannover, Germany.

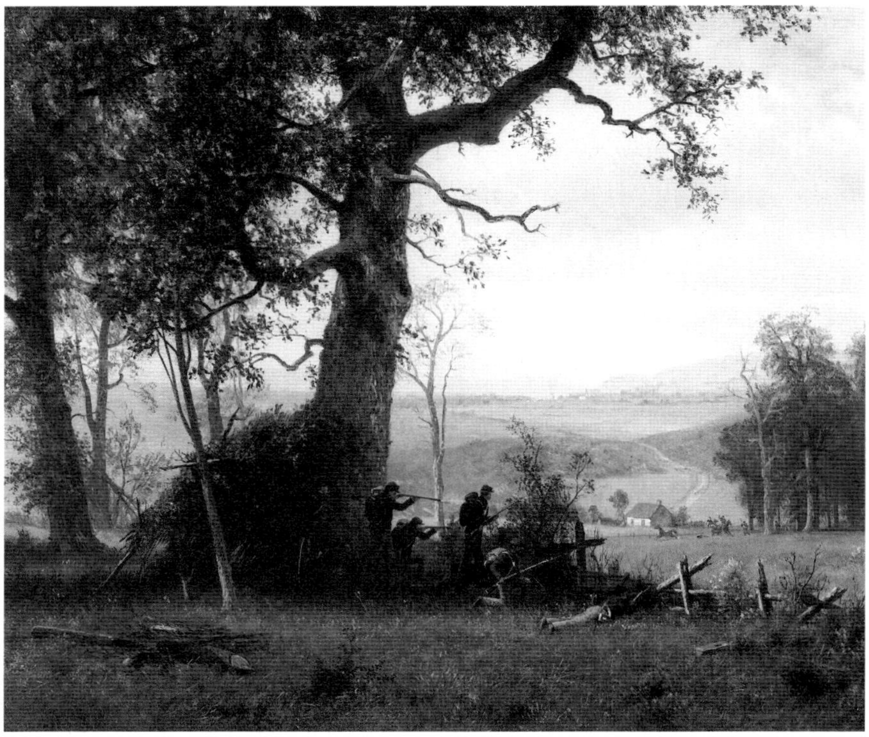

Figure 47 *(right, above)*
Albert Bierstadt. *Guerrilla Warfare (Picket Duty in Virginia)*, 1862 (No. 30).

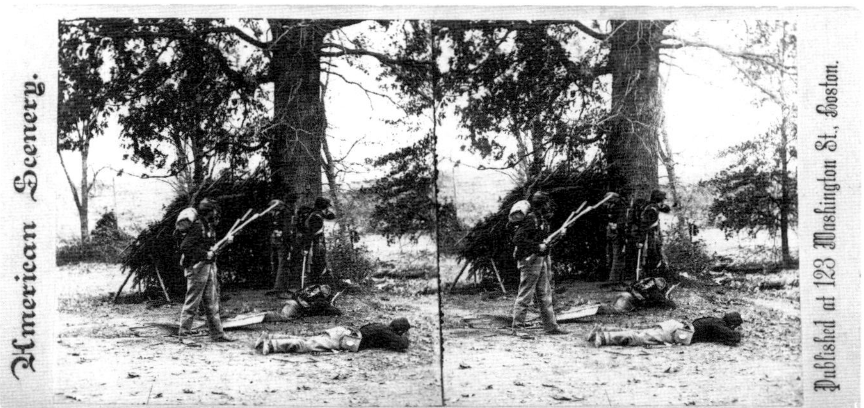


Figure 48 *(right, below)*
Bierstadt Brothers, New Bedford, Massachusetts. *Picket Guard on the alert, near Lewinsville, Va.*, 1861. Stereograph. Division of Photographic History, National Museum of American History, Smithsonian Institution, Washington, D.C.

When the Civil War broke out, blood spilled in Eden. The landscape Americans had used to define themselves was irretrievably changed. Many American landscape painters countered this sober reality with images of nature at peace. In his western paintings, Bierstadt offered something more. Distant plains, rugged mountains, and the valleys of California stood apart, untouched by war. Bierstadt's images of such undefiled wilderness offered hope and held out the promise of a second chance at Eden.

Ironically, a strong art market fueled by war profits provided Bierstadt with a very practical reason for traveling west. Significant financial rewards awaited those whose pictures met market demands. An early decline in sales that had followed the outbreak of war reversed itself as merchants and manufacturers began to make money from the conflict. In April 1863, just prior to Bierstadt's departure for the West, the Tenth Street Studio artists held a "supplementary reception" to take advantage of strong sales. The *Boston Transcript* reported that "a golden shower" had fallen on New York artists.[40] Bierstadt, who was reported to have refused $10,000 for "his Rocky Mountain landscape," undoubtedly recognized an opportunity for substantial gain if he could offer the right images.[41]

Following an overland journey free of mishap, Bierstadt and Ludlow arrived in San Francisco on 17 July 1863. Approximately two weeks later, they were on their way to Yosemite, accompanied by Enoch Wood Perry (1831–1915) and Virgil Williams (1830–1886), two artists living in San Francisco whom Bierstadt had met years earlier in Europe. Expectations were high, for as Ludlow later wrote, "If report was true, we were going to the original site of the Garden of Eden."[42]

We have no account of Bierstadt's first reaction to the view of Yosemite Valley from Inspiration Point, but Ludlow, who had initially described himself as a "doubting Thomas," did record his response: "That name [Inspiration Point] had appeared pedantic, but we found it only the spontaneous expression of our own feelings on the spot. We did not so much seem to be seeing from that crag of vision a new scene on the old familiar globe, as a new heaven and a new earth into which the creative spirit had just been breathed. I hesitate now, as I did then, at the attempt to give my vision utterance. Never were words so beggard for an abridged translation of any Scripture of Nature."[43]

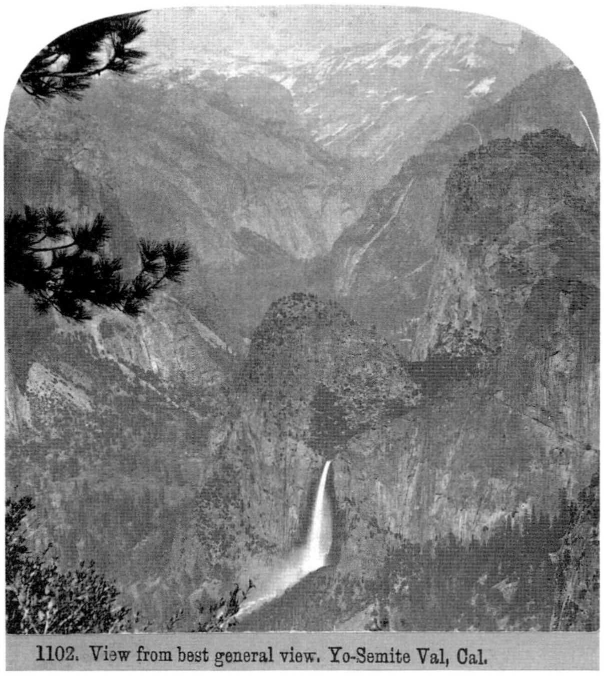


Figure 49

Charles Bierstadt. *View from best general view. Yo-Semite Val, Cal.* Stereograph. Private collection.

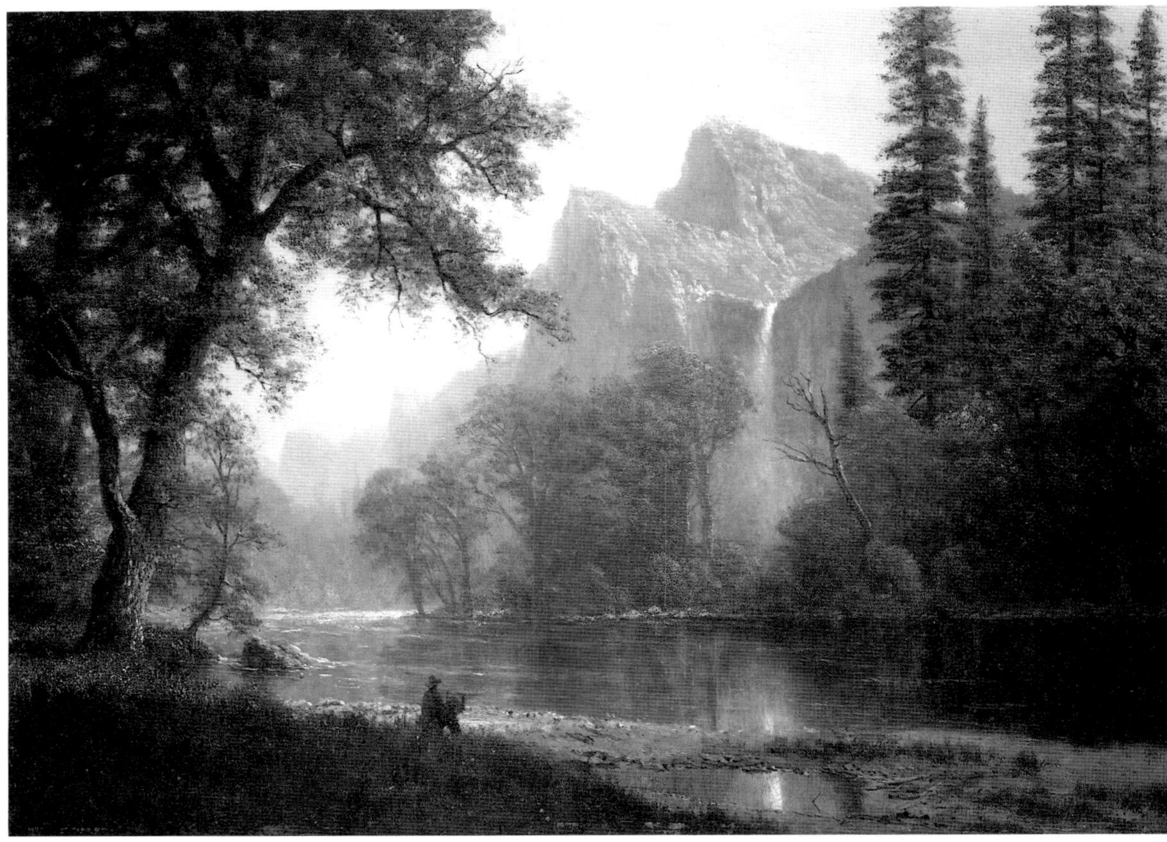

Figure 50
Albert Bierstadt. *The Artist Painting in Yosemite*, c. 1863. Oil on board, 13½ × 19 in. (34.3 × 48.3 cm). Private collection.

Bierstadt and his companions spent several weeks in the valley. According to Ludlow, the artists rose at dawn and shortly thereafter were at work in "their divine workshop," laboring "in that only method which can ever make a true painter or a living landscape,—*color*-studies on the spot."[44] Before sundown, all returned to camp, where half an hour was spent in a "private view" of the sketches completed that day.

By mid-September Bierstadt and Ludlow had returned to San Francisco, where they regrouped before setting off on the second leg of their journey, a trip north into Oregon. Planning to return to San Francisco before traveling east, Bierstadt left behind the sketches he had made on the Yosemite expedition. Ever alert to the value of publicity, he deposited the works at the offices of the *Golden Era*. Predictably, articles describing the sketches followed shortly. A writer for the *Daily Alta* described the sketches as "guides for pictures, which will require months, perhaps years, to complete," while a critic for the *Golden Era* looked forward to the day when Bierstadt's paintings would "introduce" the wonders of California "to the select world of Art."[45]

While the press notices accumulated in San Francisco, Bierstadt and Ludlow made their way north on horseback toward Oregon, passing near Mount Shasta, a snowcapped volcanic peak. Originally, Bierstadt and Ludlow had planned to extend their journey into Canada, but when Ludlow became ill, they were delayed. Enough time remained, however, for a journey up the Columbia River, where Bierstadt secured sketches of another volcanic peak, Mount Hood. Early in November, the two travelers returned to Portland, where they boarded a steamer bound for California. Later that month, they departed San Francisco for Panama, and by mid-December they were back in New York.

Early in January 1864, reporters began to visit Bierstadt's studio for news of his California trip and a preview of works in progress. One visitor noted that "the walls of Bierstadt's studio were covered with the studies made by him during his recent visit to the wilds of California and Oregon."[46] Repeating the practice he had initiated following his first trip west, Bierstadt filled his studio with sketches, photographs, Indian artifacts, and stuffed animal heads secured on his overland journey. Once again, the artfully arranged objects served as an effective backdrop for a remarkable succession of paintings that began to appear almost immediately upon his return.

One of the earliest pictures to result from Bierstadt's California trip was *Cho-looke, The Yosemite Fall*, 1864 (Fig. 52). In June 1864, a reporter for the *Post* described the painting, noting, "In the foreground of the picture, sheltered from the setting sun by massive rocks, a party of travellers, which we may presume was the artist and his friends, is encamped, engaged in preparing the evening meal."[47] The writer's speculation regarding the identity of the figures may be correct, for near a large boulder at the center of the composition an artist's paint box, umbrella, stool, and sketches are visible.

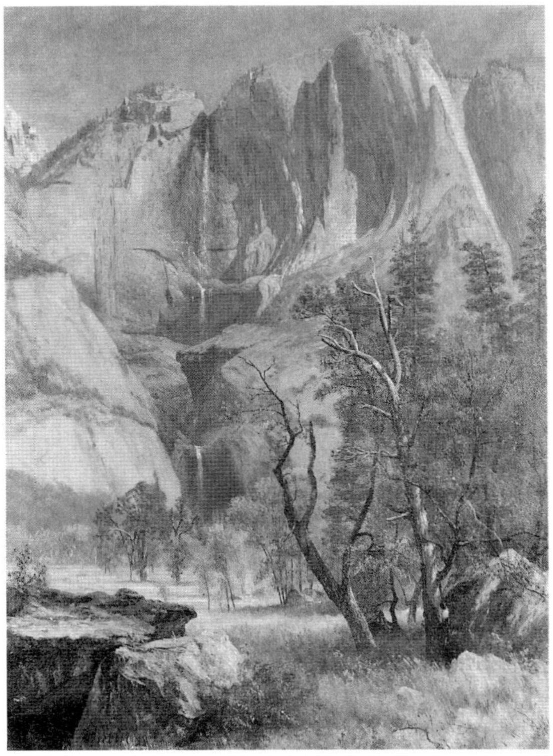

Figure 51 *(left)*

Albert Bierstadt. *View in the Yosemite, California*, c. 1863. Oil on paper mounted on canvas, 25¾ × 18¾ in. (65.4 × 47.6 cm). Collection of Dr. Algernon A. Phillips, Jr.

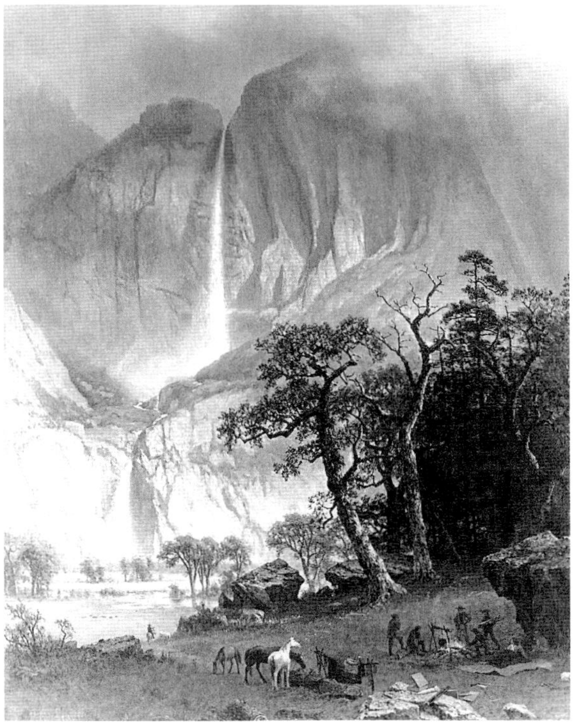

Figure 52 *(above)*

Albert Bierstadt. *Cho-looke, The Yosemite Fall*, 1864 (No. 40).

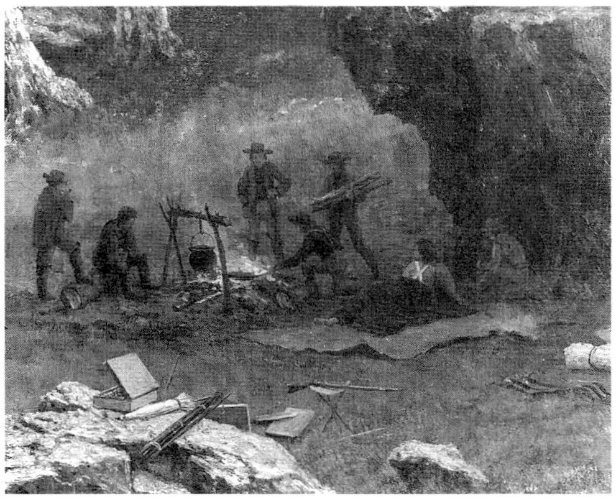

*(left)* Detail.

Figure 53

Timothy H. O'Sullivan. *The Harvest of Death—Gettysburg, July 4, 1863*. Albumen print. International Museum of Photography at George Eastman House, Rochester, New York.

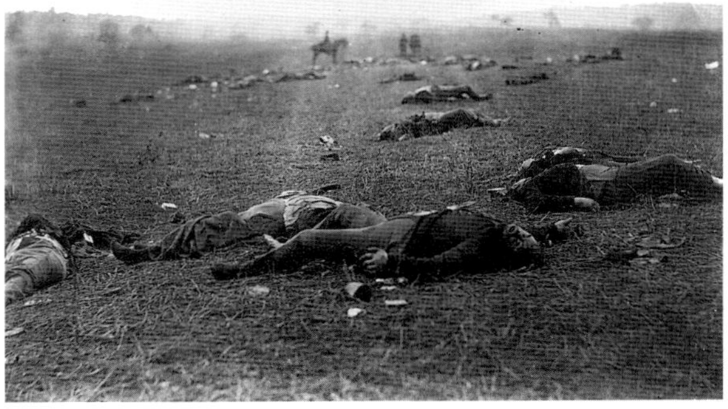

*Cho-looke, The Yosemite Fall* is a western idyll. Bathed in the light of the setting sun, distant Yosemite Falls serves as backdrop for the party of travelers camped in the foreground. Beyond the figures, in the middle distance, the waters of the Merced River are calm and animals graze in verdant wilderness meadows. Not a single threatening note is sounded—no bear lurks in the shadows, no mountain lion stalks the unwary. Compositionally structured to lead the viewer's eye from the height of the falls to the valley below and finally to the shadowed foreground figures, Bierstadt's vertically oriented painting is the very image of peace in the valley. Given the calm that pervades the picture, it is startling to recall that the summer Bierstadt and his companions spent in Yosemite was also the summer of Gettysburg.

From pristine Yosemite Valley and the beauty of dramatically falling water, the distance to the fatally horizontal fields of Gettysburg was at least the width of the continent. An equivalent artistic distance is evident when *Cho-looke, The Yosemite Fall* is juxtaposed with Timothy O'Sullivan's (c. 1840–1882) *Harvest of Death—Gettysburg, July 4, 1863* (Fig. 53). Sprawled awkwardly where they fell, the Confederate dead at Gettysburg share the field with broken caissons and abandoned weapons. It is a grim peace that reigns over this meadow. The stark truth of O'Sullivan's photograph underscores one reason Bierstadt's western paintings enjoyed such popular success during the 1860s. Unlike the allegories of hope and peace offered by other artists, Bierstadt's promise was based on fact. Though distant, Yosemite Valley actually existed. Bierstadt had, after all, been there. Curious before the war began, anxious in its grip, Americans could take comfort from unsullied mountains and valleys that promised an Edenic setting for the new beginning.

Though he clearly recognized the scenic gold mine he had found in Yosemite Valley, Bierstadt turned to another subject for his first major exhibition picture following his return from the Pacific Coast. Choosing Mount Hood, Oregon's volcanic peak, as his subject, Bierstadt may have taken his cue, once again, from Frederic Church, who had begun to exhibit *Cotopaxi*, 1862 (Fig. 54), shortly before Bierstadt's departure for California.

In selecting Mount Hood as his focus, Bierstadt also capitalized on the popularity of a recent best seller by another of the Civil War's young martyrs. Theodore Winthrop, the author of *A Companion to "The Heart of the Andes,"* was killed in a skirmish shortly after the war began. Although he had published little before his death in 1861, he left behind a number of manuscripts, which were published posthumously. One of these, *Canoe and Saddle*, appeared in December 1862, just months before Bierstadt and Ludlow departed for the Pacific Coast. An instant best seller, Winthrop's account of his trip to Oregon Territory in 1853 made such good escape reading that by the end of the war the book had gone through eight editions.

In his essay on *Heart of the Andes,* Winthrop had described the snowcapped peak at the center of Church's painting as an "emblem of permanent and infinite peace."[48] In *Canoe and Saddle,* Winthrop echoed his own prose in a passage related to Mount Hood: "It is only lately in the development of men's comprehensions of nature, that mountains have been recognized as our noblest friends, our most exalting and inspiring comrades, our grandest emblems of divine power and divine peace."[49]

The narrative of wilderness adventure that included such reflective passages undoubtedly had escapist appeal for those caught in a chaotic and horrifying war. In remote western mountains, Winthrop found emblems of "holy calm" and "permanent and infinite peace," powerful symbols during a time of civil unrest.[50] For the modern reader, Winthrop's repeated discussions of the lessons to be learned from the solitary, snowcapped peaks of the Cascades are of equal interest. In such passages, Winthrop addressed several American needs—most obviously the continuing quest for American mountains to match those of Europe. The Rockies had done much to settle that issue, but they could not offer snowcapped volcanic cones to equal those of South America. In the Cascades, however, Winthrop discovered American volcanic peaks. Though inactive, Mount Shasta, Mount Hood, and Mount Rainier still rose above the horizon in splendid isolation.

Bierstadt labored on *Mount Hood, Oregon*, 1865 (Fig. 55), for nearly a year. During that period, a steady stream of newspaper reports kept interested readers abreast of the artist's progress. One month before Bierstadt unveiled his painting, Fitz Hugh Ludlow's article describing the Oregon leg of their journey appeared in the *Atlantic Monthly.* Adding luster to Bierstadt's artist-explorer image, Ludlow described the painter's pursuit of his subject: "After a night's rest, Bierstadt spent nearly the entire morning making studies of Hood from an admirable post of observation at the top of one of the highest foot-hills,—a point several miles southwest of the town, which he reached under guidance of an old Indian interpreter and trapper. His work upon this mountain was in some respects the best he ever accomplished. . . ."[51]

When placed on exhibition in January 1865, *Mount Hood, Oregon* drew favorable reviews, including the comments of a critic for the *Post*, who wrote: "Let us be thankful that Mr. Bierstadt has so successfully reproduced on his canvas the noble form of this king of mountains, and placing it before us, enables us through it to testify to the greatness and power of that Being who created it. That which Coleridge wrote of Mont Blanc may justly be quoted in connection with Mount Hood. . . ."[52] With *Mount Hood, Oregon* Bierstadt brought Americans full circle: poetry inspired by Swiss Alps could now be linked to American mountains.

In paintings like *Mount Hood, Oregon* and *The Rocky Mountains, Lander's Peak*, Bierstadt reconfigured the conventions of nineteenth-century landscape painting to produce an American equivalent for the European sublime. In Yosemite Valley, however, he found a landscape so spectacular, so unique in its grandeur, that he was able to offer what had been desired but not realistically expected: a national landscape for which there was no equivalent.

In a letter published in the *Post* in October 1863, Ludlow hinted at what might be expected from Bierstadt's brush: "Bierstadt, . . . after years spent in making alpine color-studies, asserts that no where in Switzerland, nor indeed throughout all Europe, is there scenery whose grandeur can for one moment be held comparable with that of the Sierra Nevada in the Yosemite district."[53] In view of such comments, it is not surprising that Bierstadt's chief contribution to the exhibition inaugurating the National Academy of Design's new building in April 1865 was *Looking Down Yosemite Valley, California*, 1865 (Fig. 56), a golden view of the landscape Ludlow had described as an American Eden and Bierstadt had found superior to the scenery of Switzerland.

Figure 54

Frederic Edwin Church. *Cotopaxi*, 1862. Oil on canvas, 48 × 85 in. (121.9 × 215.9 cm). The Detroit Institute of Arts, Founders Society Purchase with funds from Mr. and Mrs. Richard A. Manoogian, Robert H. Tannahill Foundation Fund, Gibbs-Williams Fund, Dexter M. Ferry, Jr. Fund, and Beatrice W. Rogers Fund.

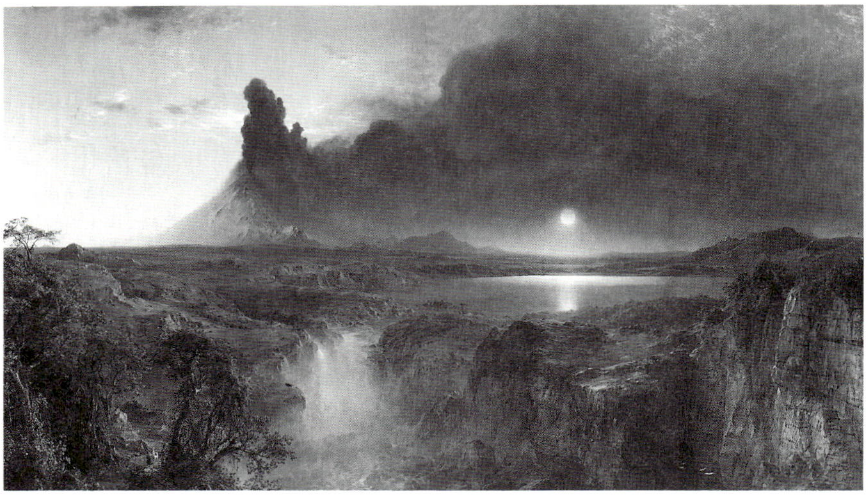

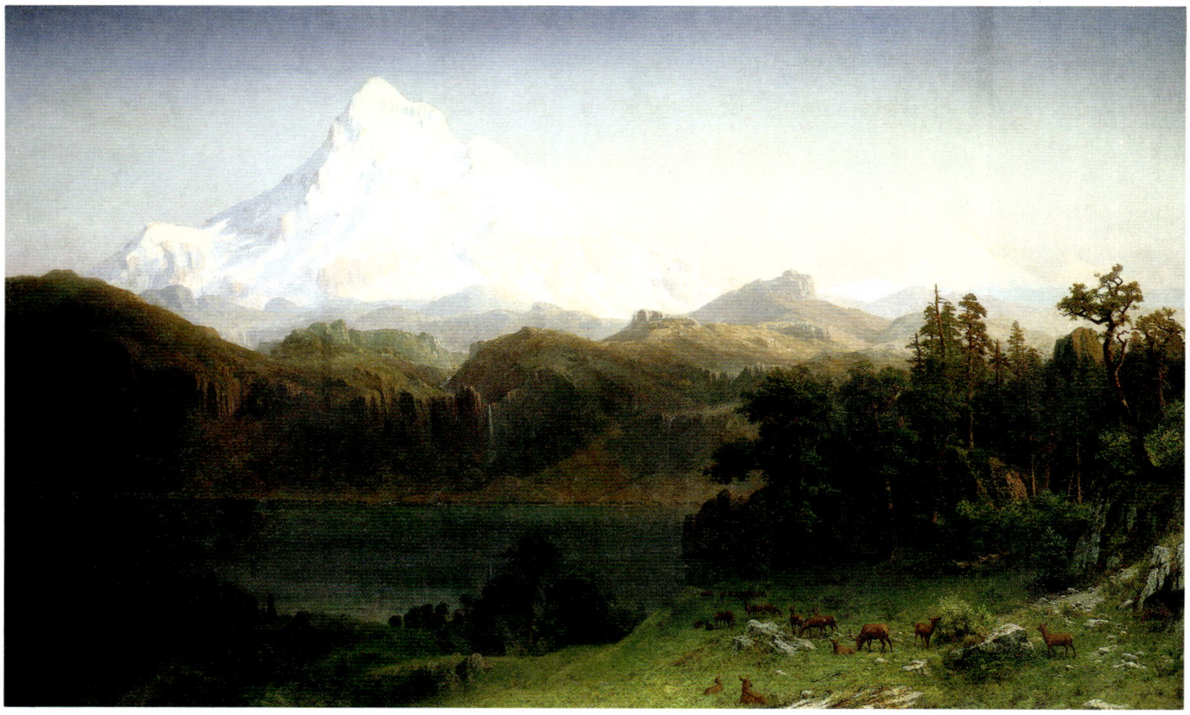

Figure 55

Albert Bierstadt. *Mount Hood, Oregon*, 1865. Oil on canvas, 72 × 120 in. (182.9 × 304.8 cm). Southwest Museum, Los Angeles.

At the National Academy opening, delayed nearly two weeks because of the assassination of President Lincoln, *Looking Down Yosemite Valley, California* was described as occupying "the post of honor."[54] Though some found the subject inadequate for the size of the canvas, others praised the picture "both in regard to its size, quality and subject," describing it as "*the* picture of the collection."[55]

Unlike *The Rocky Mountains, Lander's Peak*, with its foreground frieze of Indians, or *Mount Hood, Oregon*, with its herd of deer, *Looking Down Yosemite Valley, California* contains no human or animal figures. Instead, sculpted walls of granite (El Capitan on the right, Sentinel Rock and Cathedral Spires on the left) and shimmering rays of iridescent light are the players in the natural drama.

In *The Heart of the Continent*, Ludlow wrote that when he and Bierstadt first arrived at Inspiration Point, the gateway to Yosemite, the sun was just about to set. Looking across the chasm,

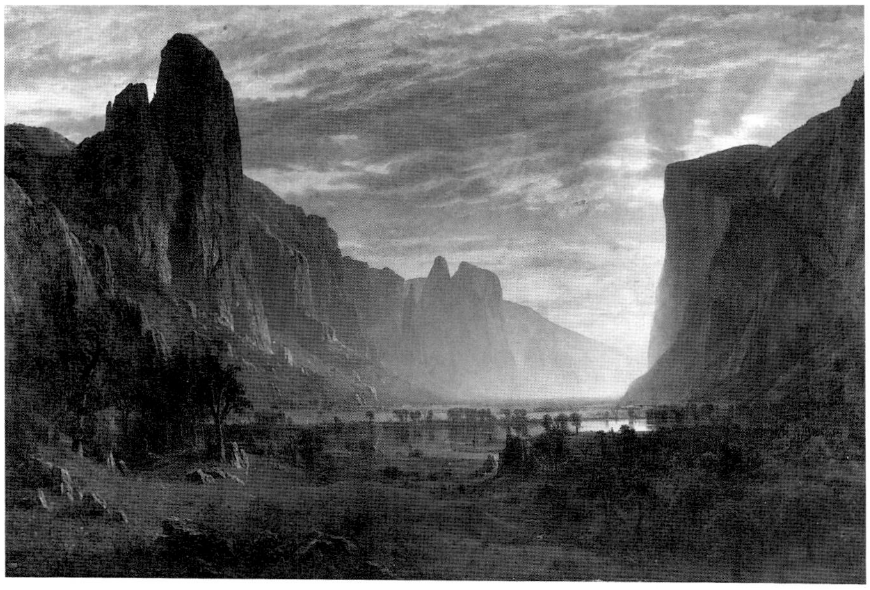

Figure 56
Albert Bierstadt. *Looking Down Yosemite Valley, California*, 1865 (No. 42).

Ludlow saw El Capitan: "Our eyes seemed spellbound to the tremendous precipice which stood smiling, not frowning at us, in all the serene radiance of a snow-white granite Boodh,—broadly burning rather than glistening, in the white-hot, splendors of the setting sun."[56] In Bierstadt's painting the sun sets in deified splendor, speaking of a power and place outside of time. At a moment of wrenching civil conflict, Bierstadt's glowing Yosemite Valley offered sanctuary for the Edenic myth and a glorious refuge from war.

*Looking Down Yosemite Valley, California* received mixed reviews in the East, but Californians offered only praise. Delighted that Bierstadt had introduced California's scenic wonders to an eastern audience, the San Francisco *Evening Bulletin* noted, "Until this picture was painted, the Eastern public had never enjoyed an opportunity to see any views of Yosemite except the small photographs and woodcuts which were so plentifully issued here."[57] In July 1865, the *Golden Era* reported that *Looking Down Yosemite Valley, California* was the most attractive picture in the National Academy of Design exhibition and then supported its claim by quoting the review Californians had been waiting to read:

> Looking down the valley, the view is lost in a sea of golden mist. The shadow of a mighty mountain in the foreground darkens immense forests. We have seen few landscapes since the "Heart of the Andes" that will compare with this. It looks as if it was painted in an Eldorado, in a distant land of gold; heard of in song and story; dreamed of but never seen. Yet it is real. Why should our artists make their pilgrimages to the Alps for mountains, to Italy for skies, or to the Chamouni Valley, when we have the mountains and skies of California, and the valley of Yo-Semite.[58]

California's tourist industry had taken its first tentative steps several years before Bierstadt and Ludlow arrived in San Francisco, but the exhibition of Bierstadt's Yosemite paintings provided the state with its most powerful advertising ploy. So effectively did the pictures promote California as a subject for artists and a mecca for tourists that years later, when it was erroneously reported that one of Bierstadt's large Yosemite paintings had been destroyed in a fire, Ambrose Bierce could write: "It is with grim satisfaction that we record the destruction by fire of Bierstadt's celebrated picture of Yosemite Valley. The painting has been a prolific parent of ten thousand abominations. We have had Yosemite in oils, in watercolor, in crayon, in chalk and charcoal until in our very dreams we imagine ourselves falling from the summit of El Capitan or descending in spray from the Bridal Veil cataract. Besides, that picture has incited more unpleasant people to visit California than all our conspiring hotel keepers could compel to return. . . ."[59]

## "Altogether Too Gorgeous"

In the spring of 1865, just prior to the debut of *Looking Down Yosemite Valley, California* at the National Academy of Design, Bierstadt sold *The Rocky Mountains, Lander's Peak* to James McHenry, a wealthy railroad entrepreneur from England, for the astonishing sum of $25,000; equally astonishing was a follow-up report that two additional pictures (similarly priced) had been "contracted for" by two gentlemen traveling with McHenry.[60] It now seems clear that one of these pictures was *Storm in the Rocky Mountains, Mt. Rosalie* (Fig. 57), which Bierstadt began early in 1865 but did not complete until the following year.

The painting was born of field sketches Bierstadt had completed in the Chicago Lakes region of the Colorado Rockies when he and Ludlow passed through on their way to California in 1863. Ludlow was the first to report on the genesis of the painting when he wrote (in the second of his "Reminiscences of an Overlander"; see Appendix B) that William N. Byers, editor of Denver's *Rocky Mountain News*, was responsible for taking Bierstadt into the mountainous area where he found the subject for his most ambitious Rocky Mountain painting.[61] Ludlow also reported that Bierstadt, "by right of first portrayal," christened the highest peak in the area Monte Rosa in honor

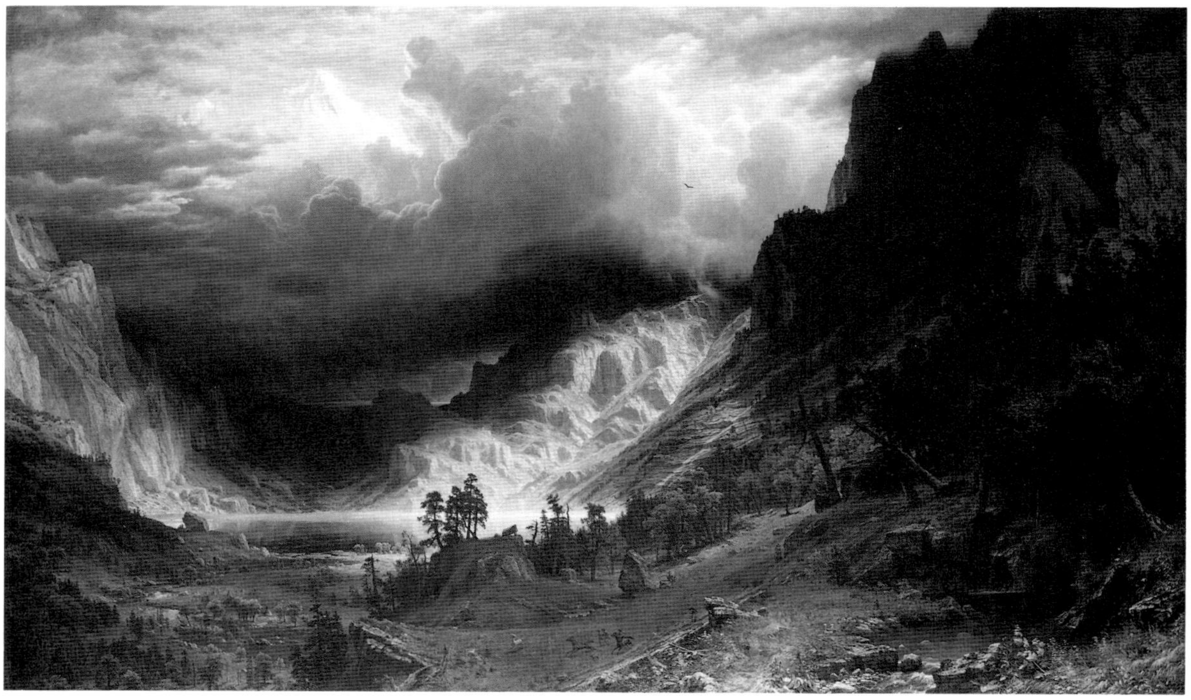

Figure 57 *(above)*

Albert Bierstadt. *Storm in the Rocky Mountains, Mt. Rosalie*, 1866 (No. 45).

*(right)* Details.

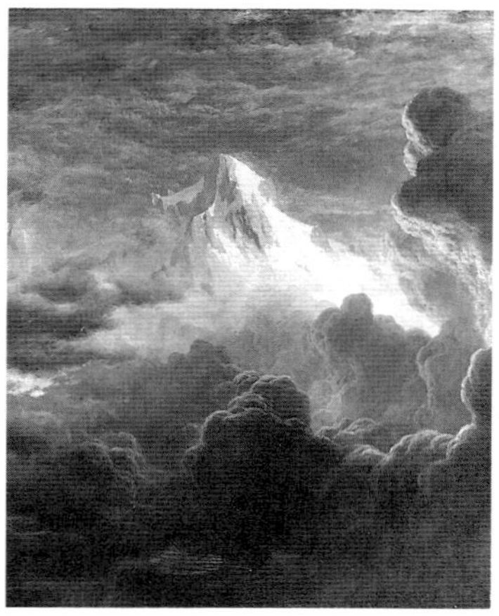

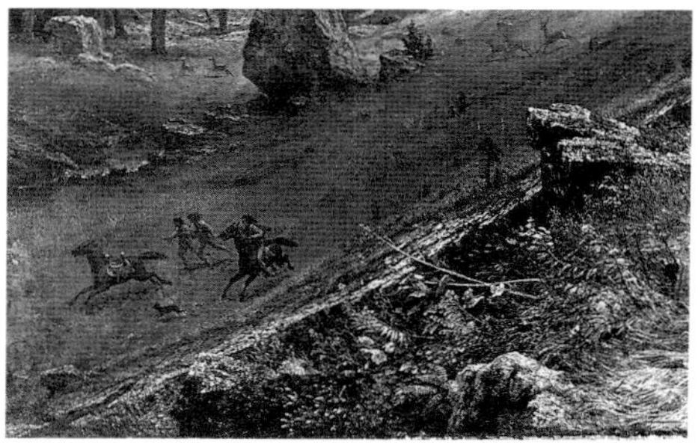

of Rosalie Ludlow (wife of Fitz Hugh Ludlow).[62] Many years later, Byers confirmed the accuracy of Ludlow's initial report and went on to share his recollections of Bierstadt's field technique.

According to Byers, the expedition to the Chicago Lakes area had begun on a day so dismal that, despite reports of spectacular scenery, even Bierstadt's enthusiasm was tempered. Byers offered few words of encouragement en route, hoping to enjoy the artist's "surprise" when they reached the spot he had in mind. As expected, when Bierstadt caught full sight of the chosen view, he was "transformed":

> He said nothing, but his face was a picture of intense life and excitement. Taking in the view for a moment, he slid off his mule, glanced quickly to see where the jack was that carried his paint outfit, walked sideways to it and began fumbling at the lash-ropes, all the time keeping his eyes on the scene up the valley. . . . As he went to work he said, "I must get a study in colors; it will take me fifteen minutes!" He said nothing more. It was indeed a notable, a wonderful view. In addition to the natural topographic features of the scene, storm-clouds were sweeping across the great chasm from north-west to south-east. The north-west wall is serrated—a saw-tooth edge with sharp pinnacles and spires and masses of broken granite—and the clouds were so low that they were being torn and riven by these points. Eddies of wind from the great chasm following up the face of the cliff were again caught in the air-current at its crest and drove the broken clouds in rolling masses through the storm-drift. From the clouds sweeping across the gorge, rain, and large, soft hailstones were falling. Rays of sunlight were breaking through the broken, ragged clouds and lighting up in moving streaks the falling storm. . . . Bierstadt worked as though inspired. Nothing was said by either of us. At length the sketch was finished to his satisfaction. The glorious scene was fading as he packed up his traps. He asked: "There, was I more than fifteen minutes?" I answered: "Yes, you were at work forty-five minutes by the watch!"[63]

Though based on firsthand experience and field studies, *Storm in the Rocky Mountains, Mt. Rosalie* is another of Bierstadt's "wondrous inventions," a deftly manipulated amalgam of mountain scenery, Indian narrative, and orchestrated weather. Clearly intended to be exhibited in isolated splendor, the painting delivers a powerful initial punch. Seen as a whole, the composition pulls the viewer into the landscape through dueling passages of bright sunlight and deep shadow, until, in the far distance, Mount Rosalie emerges from swirling storm clouds, a solitary peak silhouetted against clear blue sky. Upon closer inspection, narrative passages, dwarfed by the far grander celestial drama above, are revealed. An Indian hunting party returning with its spoils has hastily abandoned camp to pursue horses frightened either by the approaching storm or by a faintly discernible bear in the woods at the far right. Left behind, beside a pond painted with characteristic precision, are blankets, bows and arrows, and the carcass of a deer.

*Storm in the Rocky Mountains, Mt. Rosalie* is cast from the same mold as *The Rocky Mountains, Lander's Peak*. As in the earlier painting, the foreground is filled with carefully rendered foliage; an Indian hunting party furnishes the narrative element, a reflective body of water fills the middle distance; and a snowcapped peak towers over all. Unlike *The Rocky Mountains, Lander's Peak*, however, the isolated peak in *Storm in the Rocky Mountains, Mt. Rosalie* carried a personal rather than a national association, for in November 1866, Bierstadt married Rosalie Ludlow, the former wife of Fitz Hugh Ludlow.

*Storm in the Rocky Mountains, Mt. Rosalie* was shown to mixed reviews in New York. The contentious split in critical opinion that had surfaced following the exhibition of earlier paintings, particularly *Looking Down Yosemite Valley, California*, grew more pronounced. While one critic praised the picture as the "best production of American genius," another declared the artist had attempted a "subject much beyond his powers."[64] Predictably, the painting was faulted for overstepping the bounds of literal truth. A writer for *Watson's Weekly Art Journal*, for example, wrote that he doubted Bierstadt retained, "or even sought to retain, those individual details which make up the truth of nature" and went on to declare that "the whole science of geology cries out against him."[65] When exhibited abroad the following year, *Storm in the Rocky Mountains, Mt. Rosalie* drew a far more favorable response.

In 1867, shortly before Bierstadt and his wife departed on a two-year "working honeymoon" in Europe, the artist put the latest of his grand panoramic landscapes, *The Domes of the Yosemite*, 1867 (Fig. 58), on exhibition at the Tenth Street Studio Building.[66] Larger than *Storm in the Rocky Mountains, Mt. Rosalie*, the painting had been commissioned by Le Grand Lockwood, a wealthy financier. Prior to its installation in Lockwood's home, the picture was placed on view at the Tenth Street Studio Building for the benefit of the Ladies' Southern Relief Association. For this exhibition, Bierstadt prepared an elaborate setting, intended to give the viewer the illusion that he was actually standing above Yosemite looking down into the valley. A critic described the arrangements:

> The light is most carefully excluded from that part of the room occupied by the spectators, both by day and night. The walls about the end of the room where the picture is are carefully and gracefully draped with dark stuff, which absorbs most of the light that does not fall directly upon the picture. As the painting represents a view of an extensive valley from a considerable eminence, two galleries have been constructed from which a down view can be obtained, thus heightening the illusion. In the night time this deceptive effect is stronger than can be obtained from a day view, and is not unlike that of a set in a theatre.[67]

The painting itself offers a panoramic view of Yosemite Valley looking east. Although Bierstadt freely manipulated topography for pictorial effect, the major features of the landscape are identifiable. At the left, the cascading water of Upper Yosemite Falls breaks against the rocky outcropping that interrupts its descent to the valley floor. In the middle distance, the Merced River winds toward the cleft that separates Washington Column on the left and Half Dome on the right. In the distance, near the center of the painting and to the left of Washington Column, is North Dome. In the far distance, barely visible, are the jagged peaks of Clouds Rest.

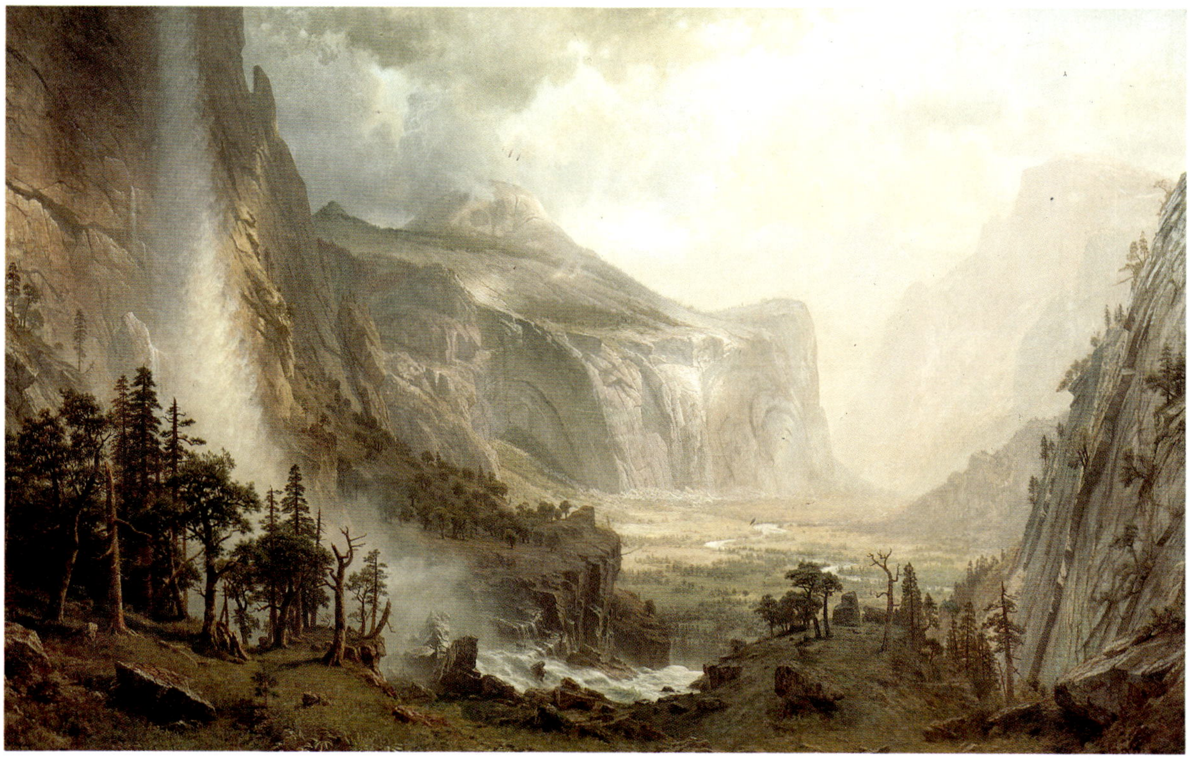

Bierstadt's placement of the major geological features of the valley does not violate the topographical lay of the land. In the foreground, however, Bierstadt freely combined trees, rocks, and foliage to create a "viewing platform," much as he had in *Looking Down Yosemite Valley, California*. From this platform the viewer looks out over a valley free of all reference to man or civilization. Echoing, visually, the descriptions of Fitz Hugh Ludlow and others, Bierstadt offered a landscape that appeared to be fresh from the hand of God.

Although dissonant voices had been heard in reviews of earlier pictures, the exhibition of *The Domes of the Yosemite* sparked a heated battle among critics. Tempers rose to such a point that the *Independent* declared: "Next to the Civil War, the fiercest conflict of modern times is the controversy now raging among the art-critics of New York. To read *The Evening Post* and find a certain picture called admirable, and then to read *The Tribune* and find the same picture called damnable, is quite perplexing to common minds. Just now it is the fashion, on the one hand, to extol Mr. Bierstadt as one of the best masters; and, on the other hand, to defame him as one of the worst pretenders."[68] Critical opinion ran the full range of possibilities. While there were those who judged the painting Bierstadt's "greatest success," others declared the picture a failure.[69]

Recognizing a topic of particular interest to his readers in California, Mark Twain, writing as a special correspondent for San Francisco's *Daily Alta*, reported: "The art critics here abused [*The Domes of the Yosemite*] without stint when its exhibition began, a month ago. They ridiculed it so mercilessly that I thought it surely could not be worth going to see, and so I stayed away. I went to-day, however, and I think it is very well worth going to see. It is very beautiful—considerably more beautiful than the original."[70] Following a detailed description of the painting, Twain summarized each element of the composition, noting, for example, that the "snow-peaks are correct—they look natural; the valley is correct and natural; the pine trees clinging to the bluff on the right and the grove on the left, and the boulders are all like nature."[71] Each pictorial element passed the test of correctness and naturalness except the atmosphere, which for Twain was "altogether too gorgeous": "It is more the atmosphere of Kingdom-Come than of California."[72] No American writer used wit

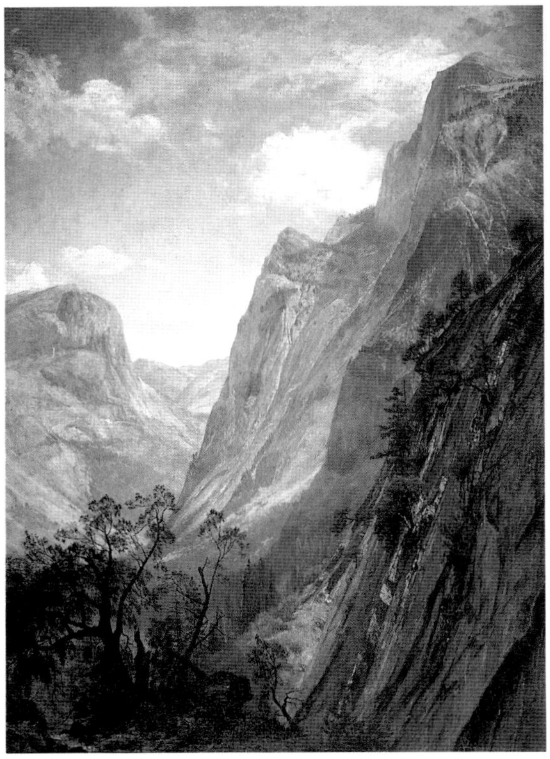

Figure 58 *(facing page)*

Albert Bierstadt. *The Domes of the Yosemite*, 1867. Oil on canvas, 116 × 180 in. (294.6 × 457.2 cm). St. Johnsbury Athenaeum, St. Johnsbury, Vermont.

Figure 59 *(left)*

Albert Bierstadt. *Study for "The Domes of the Yosemite,"* c. 1863. Oil on canvas, 26 × 20 in. (66 × 50.8 cm). Manoogian Collection.

and irony to greater effect than Twain, yet in this instance the ironic twist may be said to have turned on its author, for California as Kingdom-Come, California as the Promised Land, was exactly Bierstadt's subject.

## "A Perfect Type"

Sailing for Europe with his wife in June 1867 and remaining abroad until 1869, Bierstadt was able to leave behind the critical cacophony that had broken out over *The Domes of the Yosemite* and relive, in London and Paris, those halcyon days when the novelty of his subject and the skill of his hand had first captured the public's attention.

Like their American counterparts, most Europeans had read about the American West long before they saw Bierstadt's paintings. The literary works of James Fenimore Cooper and Washington Irving were at least as popular in Europe as they were in America. To be sure, George Catlin had enjoyed considerable success in London and Paris in the 1840s with his "Indian Gallery," but western landscapes on the scale of Bierstadt's showpieces were entirely new. Additionally, the fact that *The Rocky Mountains, Lander's Peak*, Bierstadt's most important early landscape, had been purchased by James McHenry for his London home simply set the stage for the artist's triumphant arrival.

*Storm in the Rocky Mountains, Mt. Rosalie* was already on exhibition at McLean's Gallery in London when Bierstadt arrived late in June 1867. Like American critics several years earlier, the English press was initially struck by the awesome character of the land itself. Writing for the London *Morning Herald*, one reviewer declared that "the picture presents aspects of nature unfamiliar to inhabitants of this part of the world, and on a scale of vastness of which they have no experience."[73] Less concerned with strict topographical accuracy than many American critics, some English reviewers applauded Bierstadt for what they quickly recognized as artifice:

> It strikes you at once as a work of art, not a literal reproduction of nature; indeed, the artifices used are sometimes too evident. But in an age when some hold the theory that art may be dispensed with, and that mere copyism is enough, we welcome a man like Bierstadt, who, though as devoted a lover of the grandest scenes in nature as any painter who ever lived, is at the same time given to plotting and planning for purely artistic ends. He is always trying for luminous gradations and useful oppositions. . . . The excess of his effort after these things may be repugnant to some critics, because it is so obvious, and seems incompatible with the simplicity and self-oblivion of the highest artistic natures. We believe, however, that in art of this kind, where the object is to produce a powerful impression of overwhelming natural grandeur, a painter must employ all the resources possible to him. This may be condemned as scene painting, and we should only be too happy to see more of the same kind. . . . No picture that we have ever seen has more entirely conveyed a sense of natural sublimity.[74]

Six months after his arrival in Europe, in December 1867, Bierstadt was invited to show his two masterworks, *The Rocky Mountains, Lander's Peak* and *Storm in the Rocky Mountains, Mt. Rosalie* to Queen Victoria and the royal family at Osborne House. With the sale of *The Rocky Mountains, Lander's Peak* to James McHenry, and *Storm in the Rocky Mountains, Mt. Rosalie* to his business associate, Thomas William Kennard, Bierstadt had attained a level of patronage matched by few of his contemporaries; the subsequent invitation to exhibit works before the royal family gave the artist a "court painter" status unequaled by any other American painter of his day.

In August 1868, Bierstadt took a studio in Paris and set to work on commissions he had received in London. Following a winter spent in Paris and additional travel to Spain, Bierstadt and his wife returned to New York in the fall of 1869. Abroad for more than two years, Bierstadt returned triumphant from what can fairly be described as a very successful business trip.

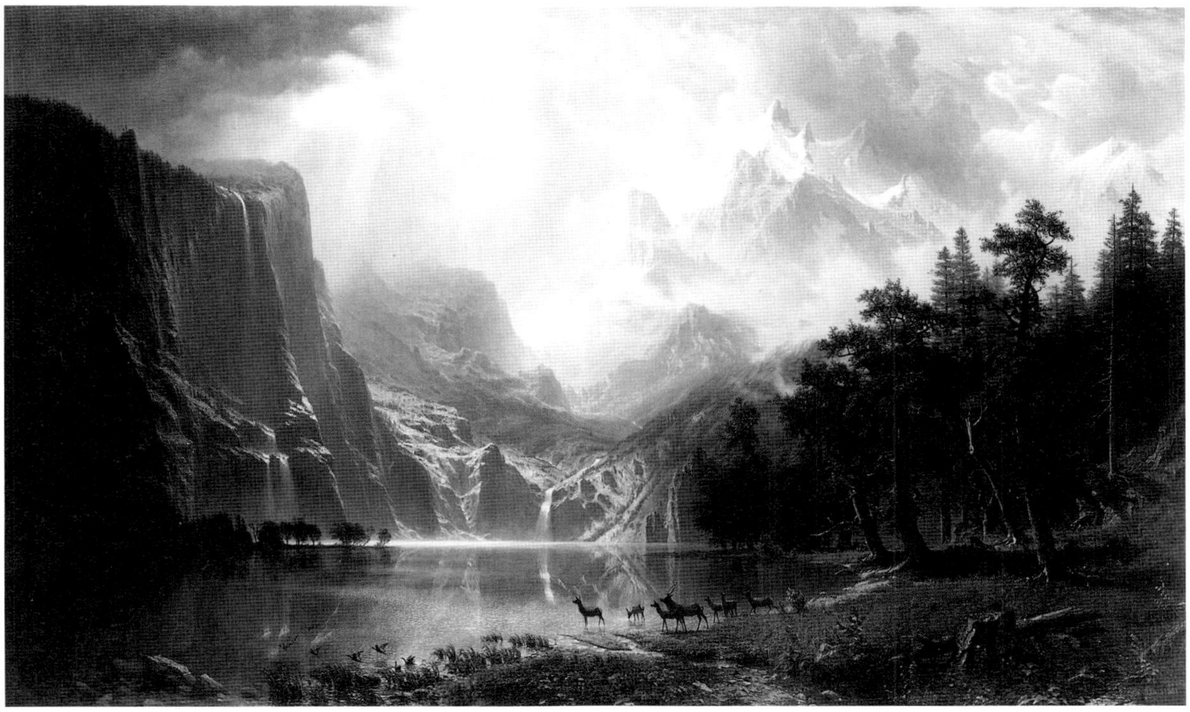

Figure 60
Albert Bierstadt. *Among the Sierra Nevada Mountains, California*, 1868 (No. 48).

When he returned home, Bierstadt brought with him several paintings he had completed and exhibited abroad. One of these, *Among the Sierra Nevada Mountains, California*, 1868 (Fig. 60), may be judged to be among the most important works of his career. Exhibited to much acclaim in Europe (it was awarded a gold medal in Berlin), the painting was placed on exhibition in Boston shortly after the artist's return.[75] Almost immediately, Alvin Adams purchased the picture for his private collection.[76]

Unlike the artist's earlier western landscapes, *Among the Sierra Nevada Mountains, California* carried a nearly generic title. No name was applied to the distant peak, and no claim was made for a specific site. The painting was a construct from start to finish.

Completed in Rome in 1868, *Among the Sierra Nevada Mountains, California* is a composite of elements seen in earlier works. The foreground deer and ducks, for example, had appeared ten years earlier in *Gosnold at Cuttyhunk, 1602*, 1858 (No. 13); the massive cliff at the left is a reconfiguration of Yosemite's El Capitan as it appeared in several paintings, including *Looking Down Yosemite Valley, California;* and the distant snow peak echoes both Mount Lander in *The Rocky Mountains, Lander's Peak* and Mount Rosalie in *Storm in the Rocky Mountains, Mt. Rosalie*.

In *Among the Sierra Nevada Mountains, California*, Bierstadt broke free of the tether that bound him to specific geography. Much closer in conception to Church's *Heart of the Andes* than *The Rocky Mountains, Lander's Peak* had been, *Among the Sierra Nevada Mountains, California* is a type rather than a portrait—a fact that was recognized by Bierstadt's contemporaries. For those who rejected such invention, the painting was "claptrap" and "false."[77] For others, who understood the leap Bierstadt had made, the painting offered evidence "almost for the first time" that the artist possessed "the poetic imagination and feeling, which, as well as or even more than the technical skill of an artist, is necessary to constitute a great landscape painter."[78] One critic praised Bierstadt's "power of combination" and went on to dismiss as unimportant charges that the painting was not a topographically accurate portrait of a specific site.[79] Describing the picture as "an ideal union of the most splendid and characteristic features of our western mountains," he freely acknowledged that "the result is a scene which does not exist, and in fact could hardly exist."[80] Instead, the painting was "a perfect type of the American idea of what our scenery ought to be, if it is not so in reality."[81]

*Among the Sierra Nevada Mountains, California* offers one of the clearest examples of the compositional device—the coupling of minutely rendered detail with panoramic breadth—that lies at the heart of Bierstadt's heroic western landscapes. When the painting was placed on exhibition in London during the summer of 1868, a critic for the *Art-Journal* advised viewers to stand at a distance of thirty feet in order to see the whole of the six-by-ten-foot painting.[82] Although the full magnitude of the panoramic scene may be comprehensible only from a distance, Bierstadt included compositional elements designed to draw viewers close to the surface of the canvas. The artist's ploy, a seductively detailed foreground, was quickly recognized by the *Art-Journal* critic. The extraordinary attention Bierstadt lavished on the rocks, foliage, and shoreline water at the lower edge demanded inspection. For the especially observant viewer, the artist offered a technical tour de force—a fish visible beneath the surface of the crystalline mountain water. It was Bierstadt's coupling of the panoramic view with precisely rendered detail that constituted the power of the heroic landscapes. Initially awed by the grandeur of the scene, viewers were inevitably drawn to the surface. Because of the enormous size of the western showpieces, viewers who stepped forward to inspect the foreground were quickly surrounded by the landscape itself. Even without a darkened room and orchestrated lights, stepping close to the canvas was akin to stepping into the scene.

The skill with which Bierstadt could produce this effect was noted by one critic who testified to the power of *The Rocky Mountains, Lander's Peak* to transport the viewer to a distant land. Writing for the *Congregationalist*, Gail Hamilton advised that anyone seeking "an interval of unalloyed happiness" need only "go up a staircase or two, through a passage or two, round a corner or two, into a darkness, into a light—and—you are no longer in the studio-building on Tremont street, you have crossed rivers, lakes, woods and valleys. You have left behind you railroads, and batteries, and Boston and civilization. You have stridden out to the border-lands. . . . You have struck the trail of the Savage."[83]

Because the landscape Bierstadt offered in *Among the Sierra Nevada Mountains, California* was an invention, it was impervious to change. The conjured scene was, therefore, the ideal refuge for the Edenic myth. Painted with a precision that defied disbelief, Bierstadt's grand invention existed outside of time. Visual embodiment of the wilderness myth at the core of America's definition of itself, Bierstadt's painting offered sanctuary to an idea Americans were reluctant to give up despite their headlong rush into an industrial age.

Conversely, landscapes that did exist in time lacked the immutability of myth. Thus even Yosemite Valley, the natural Eden whose spectacular cliffs and waterfalls had come under government protection, could not escape change. When Bierstadt returned to California in 1871, change was everywhere in evidence.

## "The Hard Fact of the Railroad"

In June 1864, less than one year after Bierstadt visited California for the first time, President Lincoln signed the bill setting aside Yosemite Valley and the Mariposa redwoods as a public park to be administered by the state of California. The attempt to save Yosemite Valley from rampant commercial exploitation was born, in part, of the public outcry over the transformation of Niagara Falls from natural wonder (and national symbol) to commercial eyesore. The official certification of

Yosemite's wondrous qualities did not, however, shield the valley from change and commercial growth. On the contrary, tourism burst into full flower as the curious came to see what so many had described and what Congress had formally sanctified. The government's legislative action meant, however, that an attempt would be made to accommodate visitors without destroying the valley's natural state.

The path to California and Yosemite was smoothed considerably when the transcontinental railroad was completed in 1869. Shortly thereafter, those wishing to make the pilgrimage to Yosemite could travel from the Atlantic to the Pacific enjoying the deep-pile comfort of Pullman palace cars. In 1871 Bierstadt and his wife joined the tourist tide to California, arriving in San Francisco on 20 July.[84]

Much had changed since the artist's first visit in 1863. San Francisco had transformed itself from a fire-plagued boomtown into the most cosmopolitan city on the West Coast. Among its residents were entrepreneurs whose real wealth may have exceeded even the dreams of the original forty-niners. The "new" money came not from gold, however, but from railroads and Nevada silver.

Less than a week after his arrival in San Francisco, Bierstadt journeyed north to Donner Pass in the High Sierra in company with Collis P. Huntington, one of the railroad barons who had overseen the laying of the transcontinental line. Huntington had commissioned a picture of the area near Donner Pass where the railroad's engineering and construction crews had faced their greatest challenge. Together, the artist and his patron traveled to the summit, where Huntington reportedly selected the point from which he wished the picture painted.[85]

Although Bierstadt secured preliminary sketches for the painting on this initial trip; the picture itself was not completed until January 1873. As he had done when working on other large paintings, Bierstadt allowed reporters to visit his studio and report on works in progress. In March 1872, D. O. C. Townley described the Donner Pass picture in some detail and reported that in

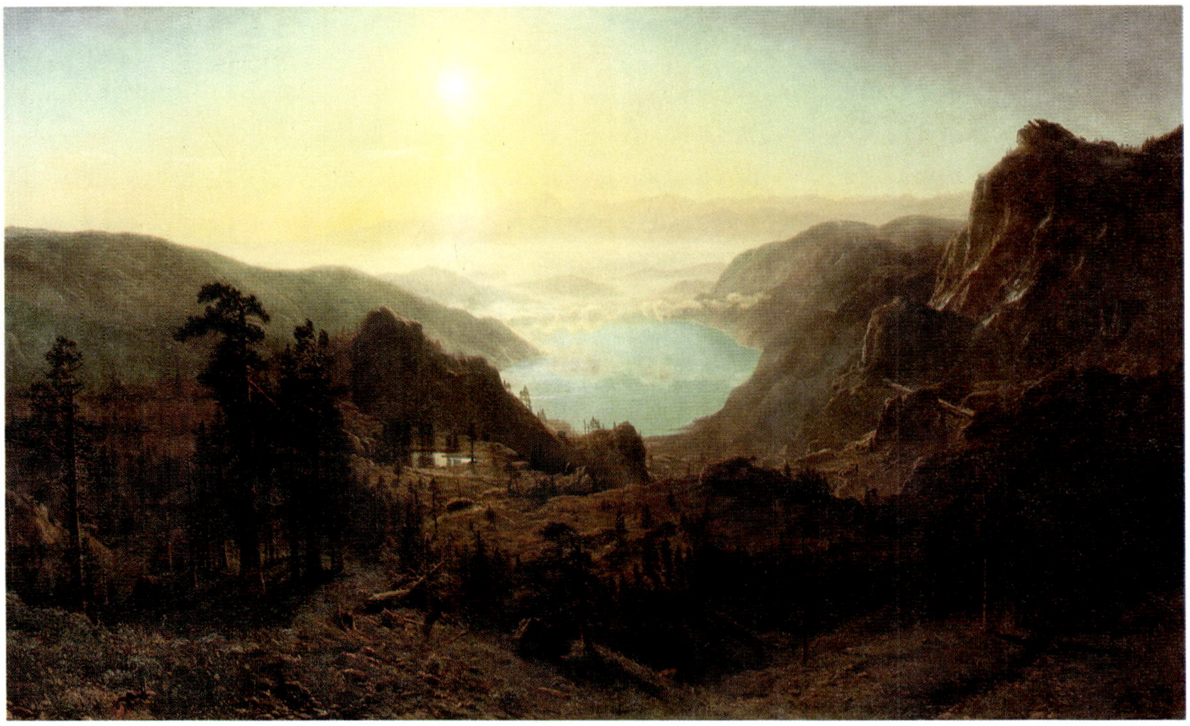

Figure 61

Albert Bierstadt. *Donner Lake from the Summit*, 1873. Oil on canvas, 72 × 120 in. (182.9 × 304.8 cm). The New-York Historical Society.

Figure 62 *(right)*

Charles Bierstadt, Niagara Falls, New York. *Donner Lake*. Stereograph. Private collection.

Figure 63 *(far right)*

*The Donner Party in 1846*. Wood engraving published in Albert D. Richardson, *Beyond the Mississippi: From the Great River to the Great Ocean* (Hartford, Conn.: 1867).

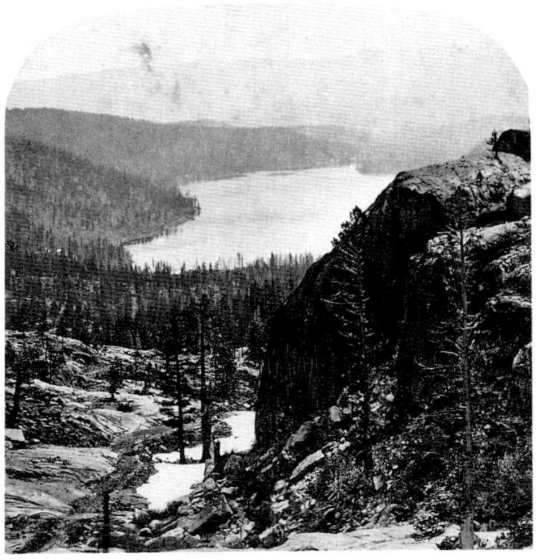

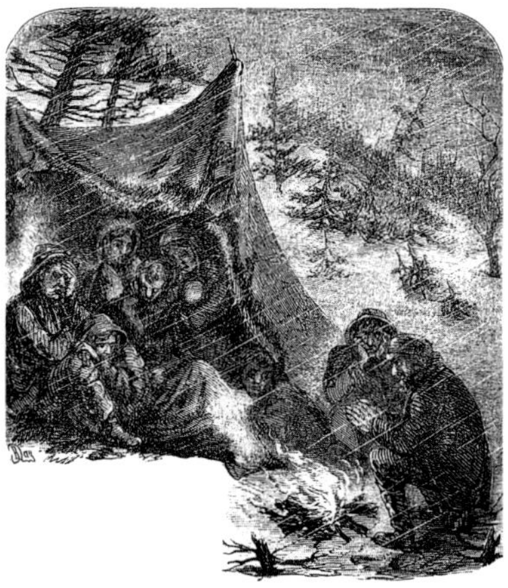

making his studies of the early-morning sun above Donner Lake, "Bierstadt rose morning after morning at four o'clock, until he had secured the desired effect of light and shade and color."[86] Ever aware of the promotional value of the "story behind the picture," Bierstadt worked the press as skillfully in 1872 as he had in 1860.

According to Townley, the Donner Pass picture would be titled "Sunrise on the Sierras." When the painting was exhibited for the first time, however, in January 1873, it bore a very different title, *Donner Lake from the Summit* (Fig. 61).[87] At some point in the interim, Bierstadt had come to appreciate the power of the associations connected with the site. Townley touched on the historical reference when he wrote, "The scene is on the route of the road [Central Pacific Railroad], and the point of view is near the place where, some . . . years ago, a party of emigrants perished within a short distance of the civilization they were seeking, but of the proximity of which they did not know."[88] The "party of emigrants" to which Townley referred was, of course, the Donner party, an ill-guided group of settlers that became trapped in the High Sierra during the winter of 1846–47. Their tale of starvation and cannibalism had become the best known of many stories describing the less romantic reality of California's promise.

*Donner Lake from the Summit* contains no overt reference to the Donner tragedy. The only reference to the historic event is contained in the title. Clearly, Bierstadt knew that the Donner name alone was powerful enough to stir the viewer's imagination. Following the tragedy, few of the many travel books describing various cross-country trips failed to mention what had happened high in the Sierra when a band of emigrants misjudged the season. The memory was still vivid in 1876, thirty years after the event and three years after Bierstadt completed his painting, when Henry T. Williams wrote in *The Pacific Tourist*, "No other tale connected with these early days is so harrowing in its details as this, and no one thinking of Donner Lake turns from its quiet beauty, to think of this tragedy that gave its name, without a shudder."[89] Donner Pass may have been, in fact, the only mountain pass in the Far West capable of eliciting the kind of response Byron and other Romantics experienced when crossing Swiss Alpine passes where history served the Romantic temperament with tales of storms and avalanches.

The power of the allusion to the Donner party was not lost on the citizens of San Francisco, who were the first to line up to see the finished painting. Among the most perceptive of the California observers was the critic for the *Overland Monthly*, who described the point of view as several hundred feet above the Central Pacific Railroad line, at the summit of the Sierra Nevada, and then went on to write:

> This point was chosen at the instance of the gentleman for whom the picture was painted, because right here were overcome the greatest physical difficulties in the construction of the road, while the immediate vicinity was the scene of the most pathetic tragedy in the experience of our pioneer immigration, for it was on the shore of Donner Lake that the Donner party were caught in the winter snows, and suffered horrors worse than the death which overtook so many of them. The two associations of the spot are, therefore, sharply and suggestively antithetical: so much slowness and hardship in the early days, so much rapidity and ease now; great physical obstacles overcome by a triumph of well-directed science and mechanics.[90]

The writer was correct in drawing attention to the antithetical nature of the two "associations" he perceived in the painting. There were, however, additional contradictory elements in the picture, for this was the first and perhaps the only time Bierstadt included the railroad in one of his mythic California landscapes. Here the machine had entered not only the garden, but the landscape of the western sublime. Because of the collaboration between Bierstadt and his patron regarding both the subject of the painting and its precise point of view, *Donner Lake from the Summit* occupies a nearly unique position in Bierstadt's oeuvre. Responding to Huntington's wishes that the picture celebrate the conquest of the Sierra by the railroad, Bierstadt attempted to create a composition that would accommodate both the natural and the technological sublime.

By 1871, when he began *Donner Lake from the Summit*, Bierstadt had brought the "pure" western landscape to its apogee. In paintings like *Looking Down Yosemite Valley, California* and *Among the Sierra Nevada Mountains, California*, he had stripped away all references to man, whether Indian or explorer, and cast as his protagonists towering granite cliffs, spectacular cataracts, and dramatic light. It is not surprising, therefore, that in *Donner Lake from the Summit* the compositional base, to which the historical and technological associations of the Donner party and the railroad were added, is another landscape addressed to the western sublime. All the elements are present. Again Bierstadt provided a minutely detailed foreground so precise in its delineation of flowers and foliage that several reviewers identified the plants by name. The drop to the middle ground is dramatic, as the descent from the Sierra summit to Donner Lake is, in fact, precipitous. In the middle distance, the lake glistens under a newly risen sun, its outline obscured by clouds of rising mist. In the far distance, the peaks of the Sierra Nevada rise above the clouds, and the whole is bathed in the same golden light that gave earlier Yosemite views their mystical quality. Once again, the most active element of the painting is light, which darts from water and treetop to remnants of snow caught in the crevices of granite cliffs. Into this golden view of the Promised Land, however, Bierstadt was obliged, by the terms of his commission, to introduce the railroad.

The forging of the transcontinental railroad through the Sierra Nevada was perhaps the greatest engineering feat of the entire railroad project and one worthy of celebration. Nine tunnels through solid granite were required. Thirty-seven miles of snowsheds were built at a cost of more than two million dollars. Most remarkably, much of the work on the tunnels and snowsheds was completed during the winter of 1866–67, one of the most severe on record. By any measure, the conquest of the Sierra Nevada was a notable achievement.

Bierstadt's solution to the dilemma posed by the need to accommodate both the natural and the technological sublime within the same canvas was masterful, though apparently not one that pleased Huntington, who was reported to have initially rejected the finished painting.[91] Huntington's reservations may have stemmed from the fact that no train appears in the picture. Snowsheds at the far right and a puff of smoke marking the recent passage of a train are the only references to the railroad. If Huntington expected a composition dominated by the railroad, he was undoubtedly disappointed. If, on the other hand, he considered the more subtle message Bierstadt's painting conveyed—namely, that California's spectacular beauty had not been compromised by the construction of the railroad—he should have been pleased.

Bierstadt's decision to minimize references to the railroad was applauded by San Francisco critics. Delighted that the railroad was not more conspicuous, a writer for the *Bulletin* commented: "The railroad, with its enveloping snow-shed, is indicated plainly enough without any obtrusion of its ugliness, the puff of blue smoke that the train left as it plunged into a short tunnel suggesting with a touch of beauty all that is not seen."[92] A critic for the *Overland Monthly* expressed a similar view: "Through a tunnel in this rocky battlement the cars pass; but the hard fact of the railroad is only hinted by a puff of smoke, and by an unobtrusive sketch of the line of snow-sheds."[93] Bierstadt's fictional composition acknowledged the "hard fact" of the railroad—that most conspicuous harbinger of change—at the same time it celebrated the enduring beauty of the land through which it passed.

## "Almost Historic Specimens"

In May 1872, Bierstadt joined the first wave of tourists to enter Yosemite for the summer season. The completion of the railroad and subsequent boom in tourism had brought many changes since he had camped in the valley nine years earlier. The pack mules he and Ludlow had struggled with in 1863 had been replaced by "splendid new six-horse barouches."[94] Bierstadt's paintings had played such a decisive role in publicizing Yosemite scenery that one reporter describing the route of the new carriages remarked, "This line passes over the Mariposa Road, which runs through some of the most enchanting views of the valley, including that of Inspiration Point, rendered world-renowned by the pencil of Bierstadt."[95]

In a large painting titled *Yosemite Valley, Glacier Point Trail*, c. 1873 (Fig. 64), Bierstadt repeated the view seen in *Looking Down Yosemite Valley, California* with one major exception. In place of the elevated foreground from which the viewer looked down into the pristine valley, Bierstadt added a curved section of Glacier Point Trail complete with tourists.

Realizing that Yosemite had been overplayed (one critic confessed to being "sick and weary" of the valley), Bierstadt left the new hotels behind and spent much of the summer and early fall of 1872 traveling to other areas in search of fresh views.[96] With Clarence King he journeyed to Kings River Canyon in the South Sierra, a rugged area that would later become a national park. He also traveled north into Hetch Hetchy Valley, a region resembling Yosemite in its grandeur, but little explored. From San Francisco he journeyed by boat still farther west, to the Farallon Islands, where he painted the distinctive rock islands as well as the resident sea lions and gulls.

Figure 64

Albert Bierstadt. *Yosemite Valley, Glacier Point Trail*, c. 1873. Oil on canvas. 54 × 84¾ inches (137.2 × 215.3 cm). Yale University Art Gallery, New Haven, Connecticut, Gift of Mrs. Vincenzo Ardenghi.

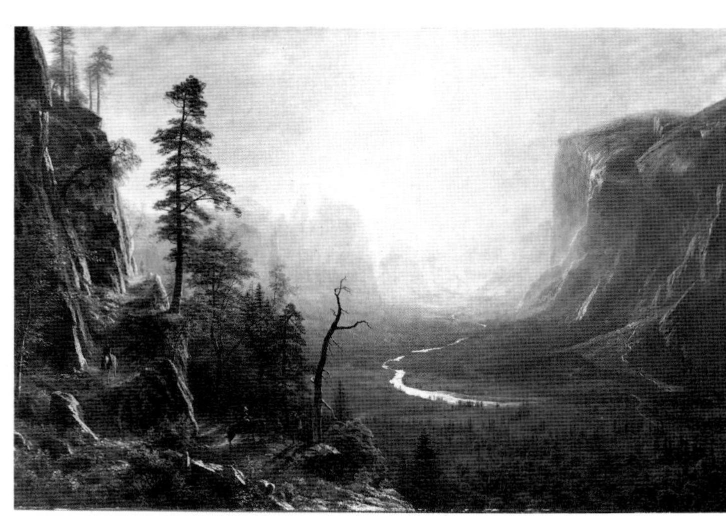

In October 1873, Bierstadt and his wife left San Francisco and returned east. Although he continued to exhibit widely during the 1870s (he contributed six paintings to the Centennial Exposition in 1876) and still sent large exhibition pictures on tour, he was not able to sustain the level of interest and sales he had enjoyed in the 1860s.[97] Increasingly, he courted the rich and powerful, seeking commissions and sales. In 1876, for example, he traveled to Estes Park in Colorado with the Earl of Dunraven, who had purchased land in the area and intended to build a hotel and resort. Together, Dunraven and Bierstadt chose the site for the hotel, and Bierstadt made the sketches he would need to produce *The Rocky Mountains, Longs Peak,* 1877 (Fig. 65), a painting Dunraven had commissioned. The picture was placed on exhibition in several American cities before being sent abroad. While it was on view in Boston, the *Transcript* reported that Dunraven had instructed Bierstadt to paint a literal view of the site, as the landscape was too beautiful to require "idealization."[98]

By 1880 the negative chorus that had cried out against Bierstadt's exhibition pictures as early as 1865 grew even louder (see Ferber essay). In an article in *Scribner's Monthly,* Bierstadt and Church were both described as belonging to an older generation that had fallen out of favor. Bierstadt's fame, however, was said to be "more evidently in decadence."[99]

In 1881 Bierstadt was buffeted by another round of negative criticism following the opening of the Annual Exhibition at the National Academy of Design. Bierstadt's contribution, *Sierra Nevada* (currently titled *Mount Whitney*), c. 1877 (Fig. 66), was a variation on the highly praised *Among the Sierra Nevada Mountains, California*. Although far less successful than the earlier painting, *Sierra Nevada* contained the same compositional elements in nearly the same configuration. By 1881, however, the composition had become formulaic, and, more important, American taste in landscape had undergone a major transformation: in place of Bierstadt's large, heroic

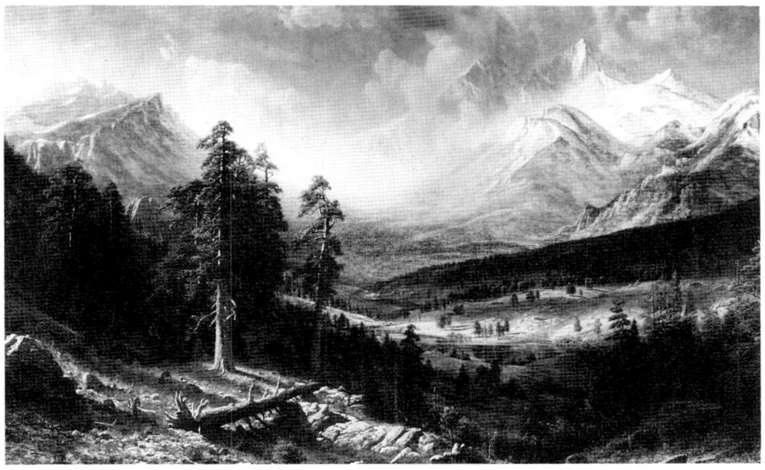

Figure 65

Albert Bierstadt. *The Rocky Mountains, Longs Peak,* 1877. Oil on canvas, 62 × 98 in. (157.5 × 248.9 cm). Denver Public Library, Western History Department.

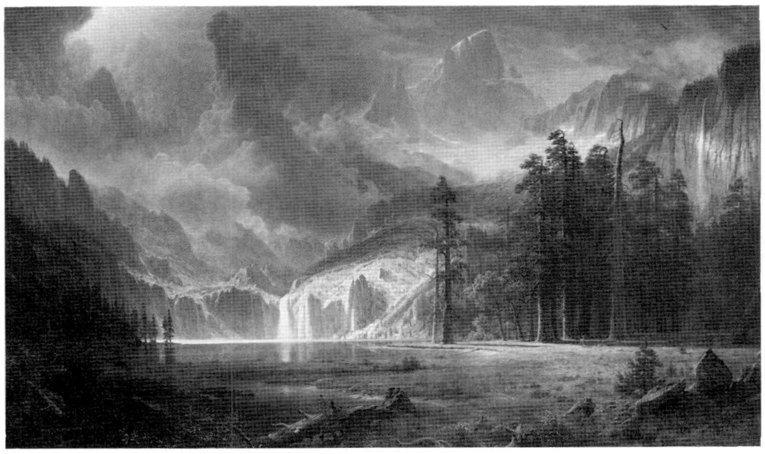

Figure 66

Albert Bierstadt. *Mount Whitney,* c. 1877. Oil on canvas, 68 × 116 in. (172.7 × 294.6 cm). The Rockwell Museum, Corning, New York.

western views that spoke of national destiny, collectors preferred smaller, more intimate and subjective landscapes reflecting French sources. A critic for the *Sun* summarized the prevailing sentiment when he commented on Bierstadt's National Academy contribution:

> Time there was when it had been worth the whole price of admission to see this picture—when extent of superfices and quantity of material were potent factors with the public and people were ready to wonder if they could not admire. Mr. Bierstadt could then play strange fantastic tricks with the Rocky Mountains, exalt their pinnacles, fit them with assorted precipices of thrilling steepness, deck them with waterfalls, and wreath them about with spectral cumuli. In this later day, mere scenery has found its proper place, and pictures of more modest purpose and less ambitious scope possess a deeper and more enduring interest.[100]

A writer for the *Post* described Bierstadt's painting as one that "might have been painted twenty years ago, so like is it to those now almost historic specimens that used to sell for as many thousand dollars."[101] In dismissing the picture, he wrote that American landscape art had "passed its Bierstadt period."[102]

Despite such stinging criticism, Bierstadt continued to paint and exhibit. Increasingly during the 1880s and 1890s, the largest exhibitions of his work were held in cities far from New York—Louisville, Milwaukee, Minneapolis, or abroad.[103] During the last two decades of the century, Bierstadt traveled almost constantly, frequently in Europe. On more than one occasion, he remarked that Europe was still his best market.

## "One Vast Cemetery"

The rejection voiced in the press throughout the 1880s took on literal meaning in 1889 when Bierstadt's last major western painting was refused by the committee selecting works for the American galleries at the Exposition Universelle in Paris. *The Last of the Buffalo*, 1888 (Fig. 67), was rejected, it was later said, because the painting was too large (six by ten feet) and did not

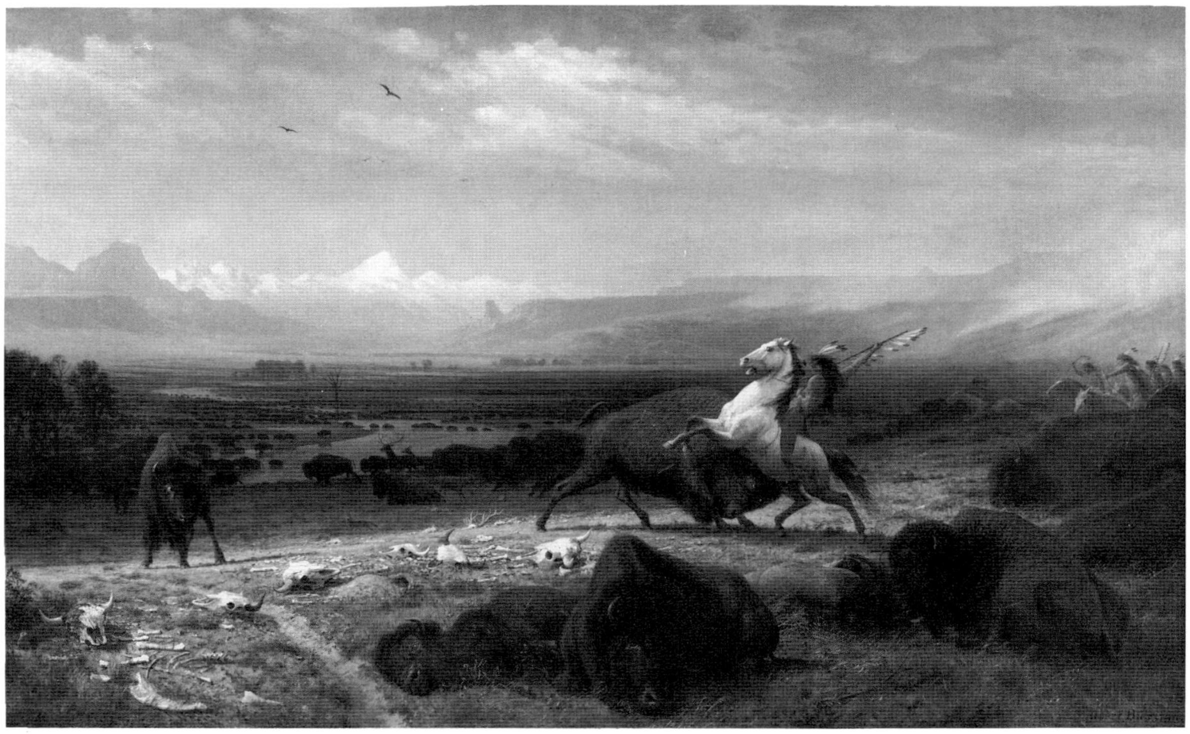

Figure 67
Albert Bierstadt. *The Last of the Buffalo*, 1888 (No. 68).

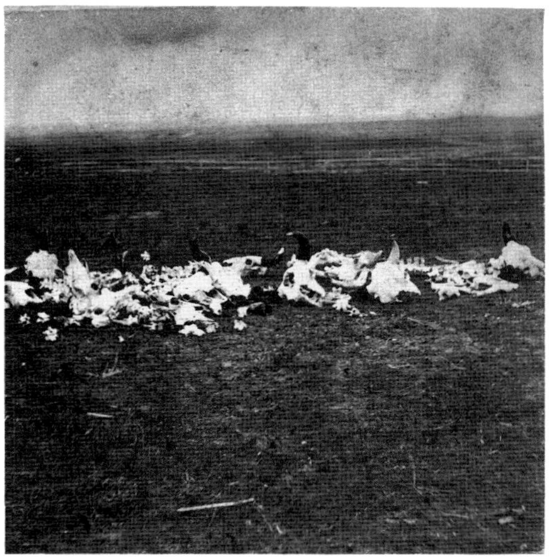

Figure 68 *(left)*

William Henry Jackson. *Buffalo Bones*. Stereograph. Collection of Bill Eloe.

Figure 69 *(below)*

David D. Smith. *The Last of the Buffaloes—A Lesson*. Wood engraving published in *American Field*, 27 Nov. 1886.

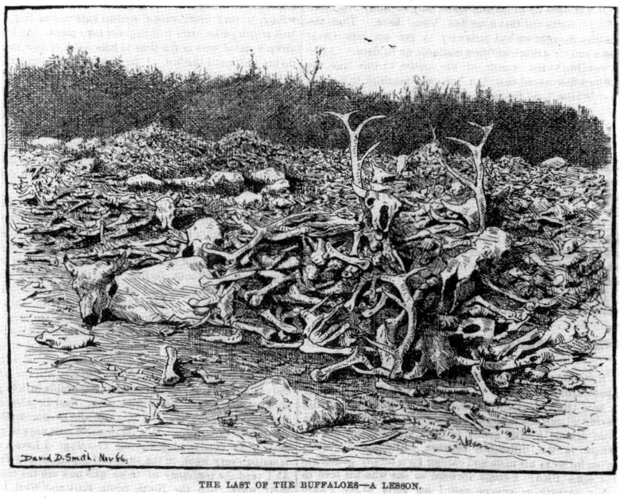


Figure 70 *(below)*

*William T. Hornaday with Buffalo Calf*, c. 1888. Photograph. Smithsonian Archives, Smithsonian Institution, Washington, D.C.

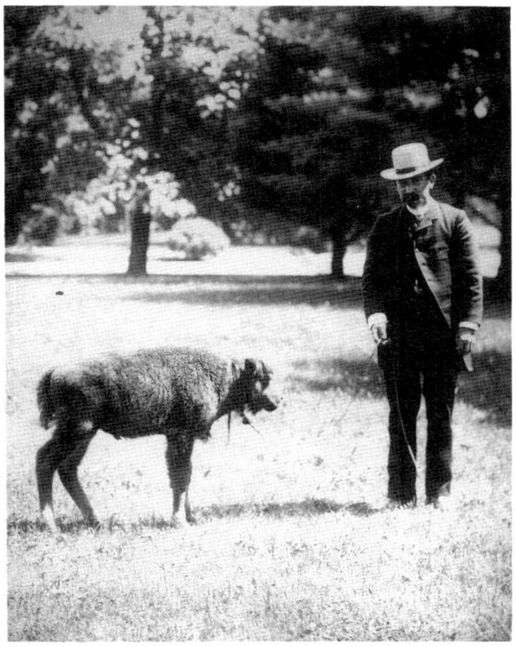

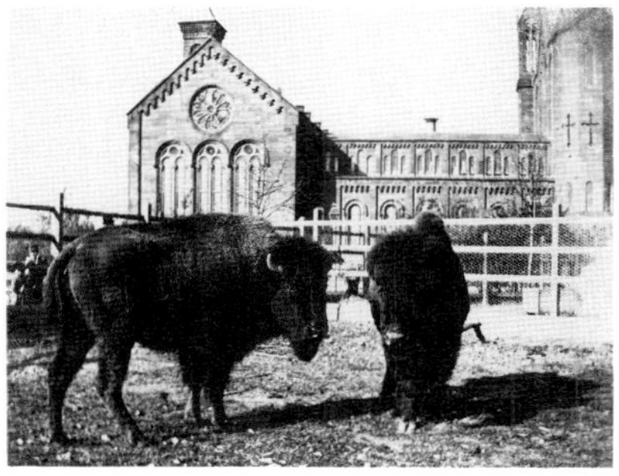

Figure 71

*Buffalo Grazing on the Grounds of the Smithsonian Institution, Washington, D.C.*, c. 1888. Photograph. Smithsonian Archives, Smithsonian Institution, Washington, D.C.

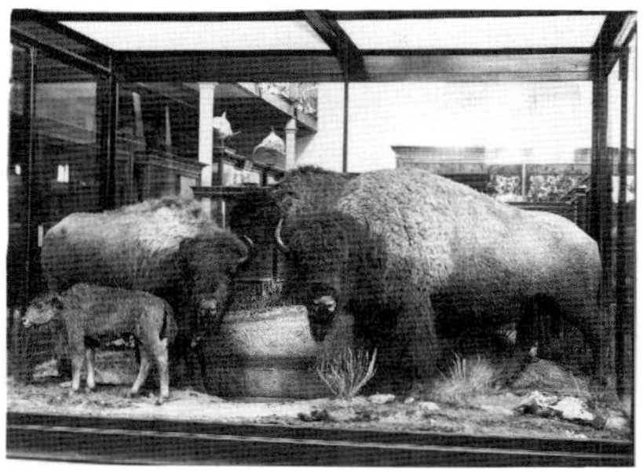

Figure 72

*Buffalo Exhibit, Smithsonian Institution, Washington, D.C.*, 1886–1911. Photograph. Smithsonian Archives, Smithsonian Institution, Washington, D.C.

represent the current state of American art.[104] Whatever the reasons for the decision, *The Last of the Buffalo* is one of Bierstadt's most remarkable paintings, for like the "wondrous inventions" of the 1860s, it is a masterfully conceived fiction that addressed contemporary issues.

Wholesale destruction of the buffalo had begun in the 1870s, when entrepreneurs found a fashionable use for buffalo hide and hunters responded to a boom market. When army officers assigned to control Indians discovered that killing buffalo, the primary food source for the Plains Indians, was a more effective way of subduing hostile bands than doing battle, they too encouraged the slaughter of the buffalo. By the mid-1880s, the number of buffalo still grazing on the plains had been reduced to a few hundred.

The species was in danger of extinction until 1886, when William T. Hornaday, chief taxidermist for the Smithsonian Institution (Fig. 70), went west looking for a few suitable specimens for a museum display. In Montana, Hornaday found thousands of bones strewn over the landscape but only a few living animals. He later confessed that it pained him to admit that he had contributed to the slaughter of the buffalo by killing several animals for their skeletons and hides. Hornaday's experience in Montana transformed him from taxidermist to preservationist.

Shortly after his return east, Hornaday began publishing accounts of his expedition in newspapers and periodicals, hoping to draw public attention to the plight of the buffalo. His now-classic report, "The Extermination of the American Bison," was published in the Smithsonian Institution's Annual Report for the year 1887.[105] In angry prose, he cast the blame for the near-extinction of the buffalo on greed, wanton destructiveness, and improvidence. The report sparked hundreds of articles and editorials calling for wildlife preservation.

It was in this atmosphere that Bierstadt began work on his painting. As early as October 1888, it was reported that the artist's "next important work would be 'The Last of the Buffalo.' "[106] In January 1889, Bierstadt exhibited the painting in an unfinished state at the Union League Club in New York; two months later, he submitted the finished picture to the American selection committee for the Paris Exposition.[107] The announcement that the painting had been rejected set off a fire storm. Despite heated exchanges in the press, the selection committee was not moved, and the painting was not shown in the American gallery at the Exposition.

In 1888, when William T. Hornaday was mounting his campaign to save the buffalo, he commissioned Washington artist James Henry Moser (1854–1913) to paint two mural-size canvases documenting the slaughter of the animal that had long served as a national symbol. The paintings were to be hung in the "extermination exhibition" Hornaday was preparing as part of the Smithsonian Institution's contribution to the Cincinnati Exposition. Painted within months of each other in 1888, Moser's *Still Hunt* and *Where the Millions Have Gone* (Figs. 73, 74) and Bierstadt's *Last of the Buffalo* stand in telling contrast.

In *The Still Hunt*, Moser documented one of the most destructive practices used in hunting buffalo. Because the death of one buffalo did not immediately frighten others, a hunter equipped with a repeating rifle who remained hidden and stationary could kill many animals before alarming the herd. This method of hunting resulted in widespread destruction and was often used by those who removed only the tongue of the slaughtered animal (a delicacy much in demand for a time) and left the rest of the carcass to rot.

*Where the Millions Have Gone* offered a view of the Montana plains littered in every direction with buffalo bones. The scene is one of total devastation; not a single living animal is visible. Moser's view was not an exaggeration. Contemporary reports from those who traveled west in the 1880s, including Bierstadt, are filled with references to bleached bones strewn on the prairie or piled high near railroad stations for shipment east to fertilizer factories. Bierstadt responded to the same reports, but in an entirely different way.

In January 1889, when *The Last of the Buffalo* was placed on exhibition for the first time, Edmund Clarence Stedman, a noted poet and critic, published (undoubtedly with Bierstadt's approval) a short explication of the picture. Stedman's text confirms Bierstadt's awareness of the public outcry that followed Hornaday's disclosure, for he refers to the "scientific expedition" that two years before had "hunted long and determinedly, to procure a few stray specimens."[108]

At first glance, however, Bierstadt's painting does not appear to be about destruction and loss. In place of Moser's bleached bones, Bierstadt conjured up thousands of buffalo. Instead of Moser's vast empty plain, Bierstadt filled his canvas with a stirring Indian hunting scene. Countering Moser's somber palette, Bierstadt created a rich golden land beneath an azure sky. In

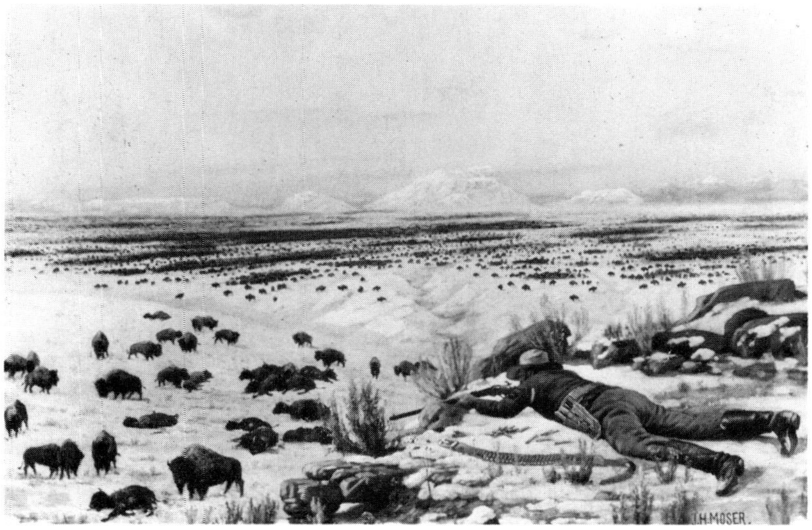

Figure 73

James Henry Moser. *The Still Hunt*, 1888. Oil on canvas, 45¾ × 61½ in. (116.2 × 156.2 cm). Jefferson National Expansion Memorial/National Park Service, Saint Louis.

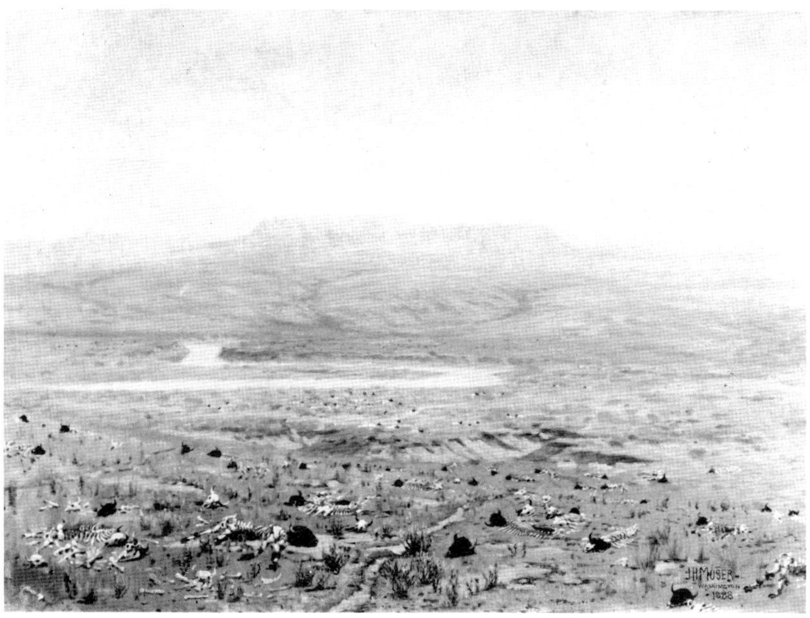

Figure 74

James Henry Moser. *Where the Millions Have Gone*, 1888. Oil on canvas, 45¾ × 61½ in. (116.2 × 156.2 cm). Jefferson National Expansion Memorial/National Park Service, Saint Louis.

place of the stark reality of the present, Bierstadt offered a carefully composed fiction in which equally matched opponents, the Indian and the buffalo, are locked in dramatic combat. Ironically, Bierstadt's painting celebrates what Americans had very nearly destroyed. By 1889, in the name of progress and civilization, the buffalo had been pushed to within a breath of extinction and most of the Indians who had not been killed had been placed on reservations. Even Stedman noted that the "extensive hunting ground" in Bierstadt's painting is "now one vast cemetery."[109]

Bierstadt completed *The Last of the Buffalo* thirty years after his first journey west in 1859. Like *The Rocky Mountains, Lander's Peak*, the most important painting to result from that initial expedition, *The Last of the Buffalo* carried a powerful message for Bierstadt's contemporaries that is easily overlooked today. Unless the question posed by the pointed contradiction between the title and the image—What is the meaning of "Last of the Buffalo" when thousands of buffalo are visible in the picture?—is addressed, the force of the painting is lost. The bitter irony of the answer lies in the fact that, at the time Bierstadt painted his picture, the possibility that the "last of the buffalo" might be those depicted on his canvas was very real.

Bierstadt completed *The Last of the Buffalo* just as large numbers of Plains Indians began to wear "ghost shirts" and perform a "ghost dance" in a desperate attempt to bring back the buffalo, all Indians who had been killed, and a way of life that had been destroyed. Through the power of his

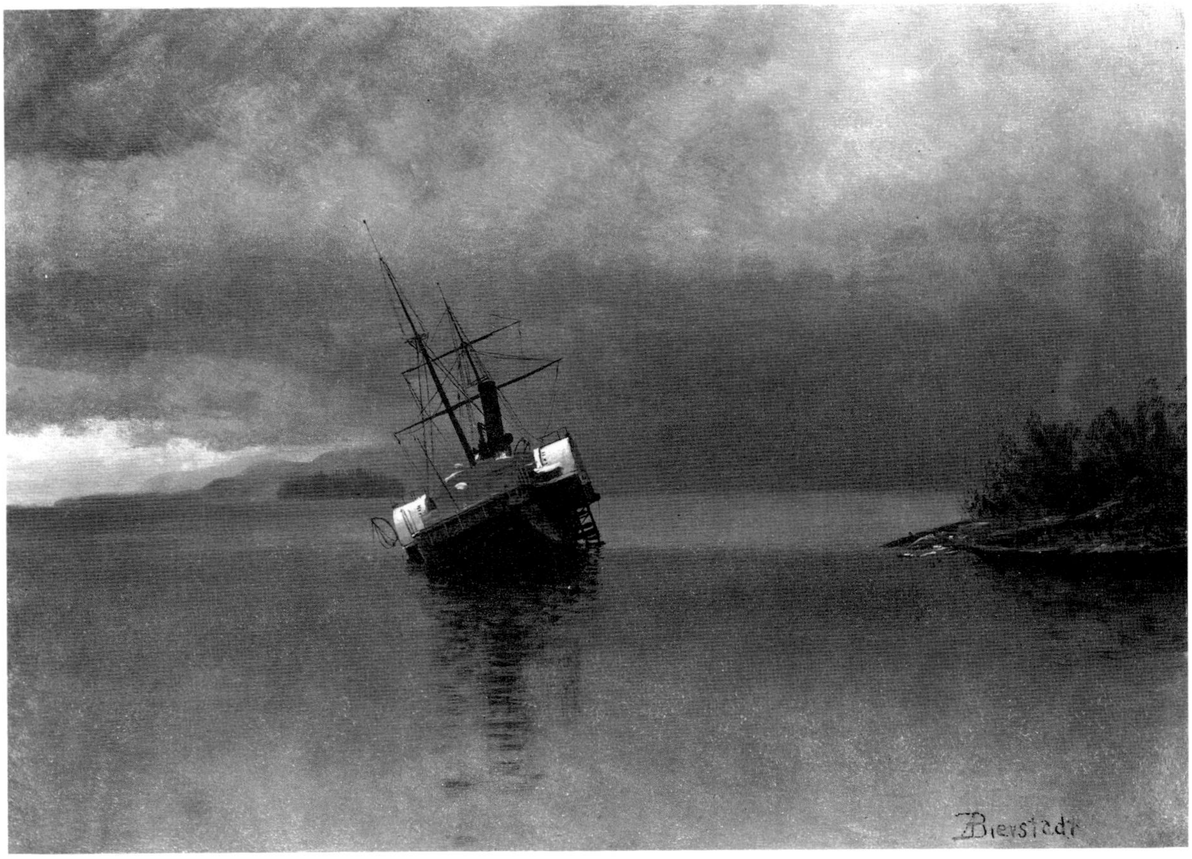

Figure 75
Albert Bierstadt. *Wreck of the "Ancon" in Loring Bay, Alaska*, 1889 (No. 72).

brush, Bierstadt staged a similar resurrection. In a painting with clear ties to European models, Bierstadt placed two of the most potently symbolic figures of the American West at the center of his composition and created an iconic image more closely aligned to memory and myth than history.

In July 1889, just a few months after the controversy regarding *The Last of the Buffalo* had sparked heated debate in New York, Bierstadt traveled across Canada to Puget Sound, where he boarded the steamer *Ancon* bound for Alaska. On 28 August, the *Ancon* went aground on the rocks near Loring Bay, and the passengers and crew were obliged to spend several days in a nearby salmon cannery waiting for a rescue vessel. By his own account, Bierstadt completed sixty "studies in color" while stranded in the Alaskan fishing village.[110] One of these, *Wreck of the "Ancon" in Loring Bay, Alaska* (Fig. 75), offers clear evidence that despite many years of negative reviews and jury rejections, Bierstadt had lost neither his enthusiasm for painting nor his ability to produce powerful images.

A worthy pendant to *Surveyor's Wagon in the Rockies* (Fig. 38), the masterful oil study he had completed thirty years earlier on his first trip west, *Wreck of the "Ancon" in Loring Bay, Alaska* confirms Bierstadt's continued fascination with the subtleties of light. Beneath leaden skies, the *Ancon* flounders in awkward isolation atop unseen rocks while, all around, rain-laden clouds and soft surface mist blur the division between land and sea. Like *Surveyor's Wagon in the Rockies*, *Wreck of the "Ancon" in Loring Bay, Alaska* testifies to the fragile nature of the expedition enterprise and, at this late date, to Bierstadt's continued pursuit of fresh subject matter.

Completed within months of each other, *The Last of the Buffalo* and *Wreck of the "Ancon" in Loring Bay, Alaska* mark the high point of Bierstadt's late career. Each is a summary picture. Responding to the slaughter of the animal he had first sketched in 1859, Bierstadt produced the last of his great fictional constructs. Inventively assembled from studies produced over a period of years, the painting is at once iconic and inextricably linked to contemporary events. *Wreck of the "Ancon" in Loring Bay, Alaska*, by contrast, speaks of Bierstadt's other great strength—his ability to capture, with elegant brevity, the passing moment. Completed on the journey that took him farther west than he had ever been, the small study is filled with reminders that when working in the field, Bierstadt enjoyed the gift of a remarkably quick hand and a superbly focused eye.

## Visual Sanctuary

On 18 February 1902, Bierstadt died suddenly in New York. Witness to a period of astonishing change, he, more than any other artist of his generation, recognized the aesthetic and commercial potential of images of the Far West. From the outset, Bierstadt understood that despite a public call for factual information about the western landscape, the unstated expectation was for mountain grandeur on a European scale. With a clear understanding of the mandate, he skillfully combined fact and fiction to produce images that met national needs. Filled with minutely rendered detail drawn from studies secured on the trail, the earliest paintings provided information about the land and its native people, as well as reassurance that in the Rocky Mountain West, America had found her alps. In later works, particularly the Yosemite pictures, Bierstadt offered a war-torn nation images of a landscape unbloodied and full of promise.

Like other reports from the Pacific shore, Bierstadt's paintings celebrated the bounty of the West as well as its beauty. With the completion of the transcontinental railroad in 1869, that bounty became so accessible that more Americans settled on new land during the last thirty years of the nineteenth century than during the previous three hundred. Inevitably, the result of such an enormous influx was change. Although Bierstadt produced several paintings that acknowledged and even attempted to accommodate change (tourists in Yosemite and the railroad in the Sierra Nevada), he continued to produce panoramic landscapes that betrayed no hint of man.

Early in his career, Bierstadt had been astute enough to recognize in the public call for images of the West a desire to see America's future. In response, he had produced some of the most seductively beautiful landscapes of the nineteenth century. In later years, he demonstrated equal prescience when he correctly perceived that, despite their voracious consumption of western resources and eager pursuit of industrial power, Americans were reluctant to give up the image of America as a pristine land divinely favored. In paintings that became visual sanctuaries (much the way national parks became literal sanctuaries), Bierstadt offered safe haven for the wilderness myth that lay at the heart of America's definition of itself. Disassociated from specific geography, such paintings were fictional constructs resistant to change and therefore ideal preserves of myth.

# NOTES

1. Irving published *A Tour on the Prairies* in 1835, *Astoria* in 1836, and *The Adventures of Captain Bonneville* in 1837; Dana's *Two Years Before the Mast* appeared in 1840; Parkman's *Oregon Trail* was serialized in *Knickerbocker Magazine* in 1847 and published as a book in 1849; Frémont published his *Report of the Exploring Expedition to the Rocky Mountains* (modeled on Irving's *Bonneville*) in 1843; and Taylor's *Eldorado, or Adventures in the Path of Empire* appeared in 1850.

2. George Catlin made his initial trip into Indian territory in 1830 and subsequently completed four additional journeys west before the end of the decade. In 1837 he exhibited his Indian Gallery for the first time in Albany, New York. Following exhibitions in New York, Washington, Philadelphia, and other cities, he took his collection to Europe, where it was shown in London and Paris. In 1855 Catlin journeyed up the Pacific Coast of North America, traveled inland along the Columbia and Snake rivers, and later journeyed through the Southwest.

3. Karl Bodmer traveled west in 1833–34 with Prince Maximilian of Wied Neuwied; Alfred Jacob Miller accompanied William Drummond Stewart west in 1837; and John Mix Stanley traveled widely in the west over a period of two decades beginning in the 1830s.

4. Samuel Seymour painted the Rocky Mountains while traveling with Major Stephen H. Long's survey party in 1819–20.

5. A letter dated 15 Apr. 1859 published in the *Crayon* (May 1859, pp. 161–62) states that Bierstadt and Frost "have just set out" for the Rockies.

6. Francis Shedd Frost had made plans to travel west as early as 7 Mar. 1859 (*Boston Transcript*). Following his journey, he exhibited several paintings with Rocky Mountain subjects, but he never enjoyed Bierstadt's success.

7. Frederick W. Lander, engineer and army officer, was also a poet who delivered a lecture titled "The Aptitude of the American Mind for the Cultivation of the Fine Arts" before the Washington Art Association in 1857. While serving with Isaac I. Stevens's survey of the Northern Pacific Railroad route in 1853, Lander met John Mix Stanley, who was employed as official artist for the survey. Stanley produced drawings, sketches, and photographs, some of which were later used to illustrate the formal survey report. Although Lander was surely aware of the potential value of a visual document of the Honey Road Survey in 1859, the budget contained no allocation for an artist. Bierstadt traveled with the Lander survey as a private citizen. See Jackson 1964, pp. 191–217; Paul W. Glad, "Frederick West Lander and the Pacific Railroad Movement," *Nebraska History* 35 (Sept. 1954): 173–92; and Peter T. Harstad, "The Lander Trail," *Idaho Yesterdays* 12 (Fall 1968): 14–28.

8. James Fenimore Cooper, "American and European Scenery Compared," in *Home Book* 1967, p. 64.

9. William C. Prime, "American vs. European and Asiatic Scenery," *Chicago Tribune*, 11 Oct. 1860.

10. *Crayon*, Sept. 1859, p. 287.

11. See Chronology, 6 May 1859 and following, for references to the letters published by the New Bedford *Mercury*.

12. *Crayon*, Sept. 1859, p. 287.

13. Bierstadt returned to New Bedford on 18 Sept. 1859, according to the *New Bedford Standard*, 20 Sept. 1859. The stereographic photographs that he brought back with him have been the source of much speculation. It now seems clear that Bierstadt, not Frost, took the photographs. Upon his return, Bierstadt turned the stereographs over to his brothers Charles and Edward, who opened a photography studio shortly thereafter. Within months, they published a sales catalogue that included the Lander expedition photographs. See Snell 1958 and 1975, and Lindquist-Cock 1970 and 1977.

14. On 19 Jan. 1860, Bierstadt exhibited *Rocky Mountain Scenery* at the Artists' Reception at the Studio Building. Only resident artists exhibited at the receptions; thus, it is safe to assume that Bierstadt had settled in the Studio Building by mid-January. See Chronology, 19 Jan. 1860.

15. *NY Tribune*, 6 Mar. 1861.

16. *Boston Transcript*, 29 Mar. 1860.

17. Ibid.

18. See Chronology, 19 Jan. 1860.

19. *Crayon*, Mar. 1860, p. 83.

20. European mountain grandeur was a subject explored at great length by artists, poets, and travel writers throughout the nineteenth century. Americans were so familiar with the Alpine mode that, despite innumerable references to Bierstadt's Düsseldorf roots, the European painter with whom he was most often compared was Alexandre Calame (1810–1864), the leading Swiss painter of the day and the acknowledged master of the Alpine view. For Calame, see Anker 1987. For an indication of how closely Bierstadt worked within a European tradition during his early career, compare Calame's *Wetterhorn*, 1840, *Ruines des temples de Paestum*, 1847, and *Chênes dans la campagne genevoise*, 1849–53 (Anker, nos. 27, 34, and 70), with Bierstadt's *Wetterhorn*, 1857 (No. 5), *Ruins of Paestum*, 1858 (p. 123), and *Pioneers of the Woods* (No. 3).

21. Jarves 1960, p. 191.

22. "Bierstadt's Picture of the Rocky Mountains," *Round Table*, 27 Feb. 1864, p. 169.

23. "The New Pictures," *Harper's Weekly* 8 (26 Mar. 1864): 194–95.

24. Winthrop 1859, p. 12.

25. A copy of this document may be found in GH Papers.

26. *Post*, New York, 16 Feb. 1864.

27. Winthrop 1859, p. 14.

28. Ibid., pp. 16–17.

29. Ibid., p. 21.

30. *NY Times*, 3 Mar. 1862.

31. See Chronology, 3 Feb. 1863.

32. *Chicago Times*, 31 May 1865.

33. *NY Leader*, 2 Apr. 1864.

34. Ludlow's "Letters from Sundown" were published on 26 May, 5 June, 24 July, 25 July, 30 July, 24 Oct., and 28 Oct. 1863.

35. Ludlow's articles for the *Atlantic Monthly* appeared in April, June, July, Nov., and Dec. 1864.

36. *Post*, New York, 11 Dec. 1862.

37. Ludlow 1870b, p. 412.

38. King's letters were printed irregularly, beginning 30 Apr. 1860 and concluding 9 Feb. 1861.

39. See Chronology, 15 Oct. 1861.

40. *Boston Transcript*, 14 May 1863.

41. *NY Tribune*, 4 Apr. 1863.

42. Ludlow 1870b, p. 412.

43. Ibid., p. 426.

44. Ibid., p. 434.

45. *Alta*, San Francisco, 25 Sept. 1863; *Golden Era*, San Francisco, 27 Sept. 1863.

46. *Post*, New York, 5 Feb. 1864.

47. Ibid., 9 June 1864.

48. Winthrop 1859, p. 22.

49. Winthrop 1955, p. 29.

50. Ibid., pp. 79–80.

51. Ludlow 1864b, p. 713.

52. *Post*, New York, 17 Feb. 1865.

53. "Letters from Sundown, No. V," *Post*, New York, 24 Oct. 1863.

54. "The Exhibition of the National Academy of Design," *Harper's Weekly* 9 (13 May 1865): 291.

55. "Bierstadt's 'Yosemite,'" *Californian* 3 (19 Aug. 1865): 7.

56. Ludlow 1870b, p. 426.

57. *Bulletin*, San Francisco, 12 June 1865.

58. *Golden Era*, San Francisco, 23 July 1865, p. 5.

59. *San Francisco News Letter and California Advertiser*, 4 Sept. 1869.

60. The sale and price were reported by the *National Intelligencer*, Washington, D.C., 15 Apr. 1865. The New York *Post* noted the additional commissions on 17 Oct. 1865.

61. Ludlow, "Reminiscences of an Overlander," *Golden Era*, 28 Feb. 1864.

62. Ibid.

63. Byers 1890, pp. 237–38.

64. *Rocky Mountain News*, Denver, 27 Feb. 1866; *Watson's Weekly Art Journal*, 3 Mar. 1866.

65. *Watson's Weekly Art Journal*, 3 Mar. 1866.

66. See Chronology, 23 Apr. 1867 and following. The Lockwood commission is discussed in Hendricks 1971, pp. 23–31.

67. *Post*, New York, 7 May 1867.

68. *Independent*, New York, 23 May 1867.

69. *Albion*, 11 May 1867, p. 225.

70. Twain's letter was written 2 June 1867 and published by the *Alta*, San Francisco, 4 Aug. 1867.

71. Ibid.

72. Ibid.

73. *Morning Herald*, London, 13 June 1867.

74. *Saturday Review*, London, 15 June 1867, p. 754.

75. See Ferber essay, n. 117, and Chronology, 1 Oct. 1869 and following.

76. In 1858 Alvin Adams had purchased *Lake Lucerne (Switzerland)* (No. 6), the six-by-ten-foot painting with which Bierstadt had made his exhibition debut at the NAD.

77. *Boston Transcript*, 23 Oct. 1869.

78. *Boston Daily Advertiser*, 2 Oct. 1869.

79. *Boston Morning Post*, 11 Oct. 1869.

80. Ibid.

81. Ibid.

82. *Art-Journal*, London, Aug. 1868, p. 159.

83. Gail Hamilton, "Bierstadt's Picture of the Rocky Mountains," *Congregationalist*, 15 May 1863, p. 1.

84. *Bulletin*, San Francisco, 21 July 1871.

85. *Overland Monthly* 10 (Mar. 1873): 286.

86. Townley 1872, p. 608.

87. On 7 Jan. 1873 the San Francisco *Bulletin* reported that Bierstadt would place *Donner Lake from the Summit* on exhibition briefly before sending the painting east.

88. Townley 1872, p. 608.

89. Williams 1876, p. 228.

90. *Overland Monthly* 10 (Mar. 1873): 286.

91. *Evening Post*, San Francisco, 6 Feb. 1874. Huntington may have accepted the work at a later date (perhaps at a reduced price), for the painting was acquired by the New-York Historical Society from Archer Milton Huntington in 1909. For an extended discussion of the technological sublime, see Marx 1964.

92. *Bulletin*, San Francisco, 11 Jan. 1873.

93. *Overland Monthly* 10 (Mar. 1873): 287.

94. *San Francisco Chronicle*, 3 May 1872.

95. Ibid.

96. *San Francisco News Letter and California Advertiser*, 23 Aug. 1873.

97. See Chronology, 10 May 1876.

98. *Boston Transcript*, 12 Jan. 1878.

99. Brownell 1880b, p. 323.

100. *Sun*, New York, 27 Mar. 1881.

101. *Post*, New York, 16 Apr. 1881.

102. Ibid.

103. Bierstadt exhibited paintings in Louisville during the summer of 1883, in Milwaukee during July and August of 1886, and in Minneapolis in 1886, 1887, and 1890.

104. *Missouri Republican*, Saint Louis, 21 June 1889.

105. Hornaday 1889.

106. *Frank Leslie's Popular Monthly*, Oct. 1888, p. 394.

107. According to the exhibition records of the Union League, Bierstadt exhibited the painting at the club on 10 Jan. 1889.

108. Edmund Clarence Stedman, "The Last of the Buffalo." A copy of this short essay is included in Bierstadt Scrapbook, Edwards Collection.

109. Ibid.

110. See Bierstadt to his wife, 18 Sept. 1889, ROM/MFA Corresp.

# CHRONOLOGY AND COLORPLATES

# 1830–1858

## *New Bedford Youth, European Apprenticeship*

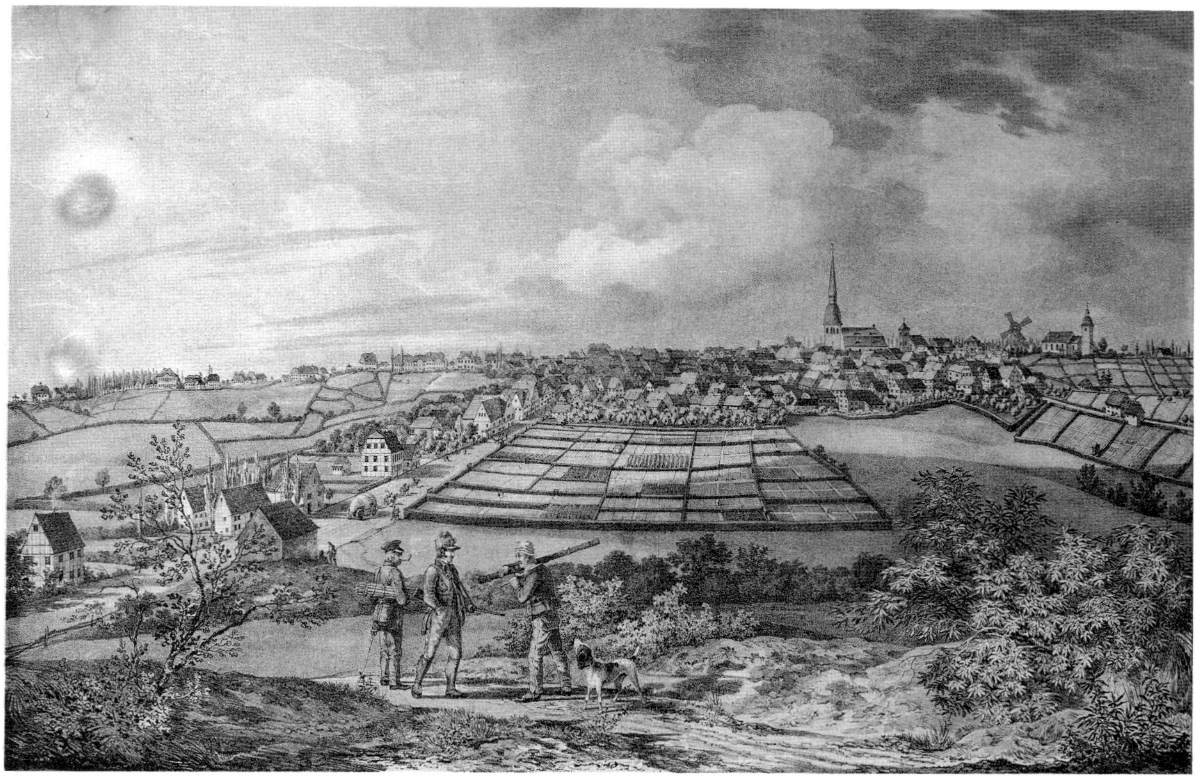

ALBERT BIERSTADT was born 7 January 1830 in Solingen, Prussia, the sixth child of Henry and Christina Bierstadt. Although family documents repeatedly state that the Bierstadts emigrated to the United States in 1832 to avoid military conscription for their sons, hope for a brighter economic future undoubtedly played a role as well. Henry Bierstadt, a cooper by trade, found a secure economic base when he settled, with his family, in New Bedford, Massachusetts, the capital of New England's whaling industry and a city where the demand for skilled coopers was high.

Albert Bierstadt grew to maturity in New Bedford during the halcyon days of Yankee whaling. Little is known about his early years except that he attended local schools and may have "worked the bench" at Shaw's Frame Factory (Chronology, 1848). Although he reportedly showed an early interest in art, no claims of precocious talent were ever made by relatives. On the contrary, despite a reported lack of natural gifts and in the face of family opposition, Bierstadt determined quite early on that he wished to become an artist. Once he had made his decision, he doggedly set about acquiring the requisite mechanical skills. He began by teaching himself the rudiments of drawing and then advertising his services as a drawing instructor in New Bedford, Newport, and Boston. He also spent a summer as an itinerant showman, exhibiting magic-lantern slides in numerous cities up and down the New England coast. After several years of saving the meager profits from such endeavors, he set sail for Düsseldorf, where he hoped to obtain the sponsorship of Johann Peter Hasenclever, a distant relative and prominent member of the Düsseldorf circle of artists.

Fate played against Bierstadt, however, for Hasenclever died shortly before his arrival and the young American was quickly thrown upon his own resources. Rescued by Emanuel Leutze and Worthington Whittredge, two members of the large American colony already established in Düsseldorf, Bierstadt set to work in a corner of Whittredge's studio, taking his "lessons" from American rather than German mentors. Such had not been his intention: according to Whittredge, Bierstadt arrived in Düsseldorf with a group of presentation drawings that he had hoped would persuade Andreas Achenbach, one of the German masters working in Düsseldorf, to take him on as a student (Whittredge 1969, pp. 26–28). Whittredge later recalled that the drawings were so bad that, in an effort to ward off what they felt was certain rejection, he and Leutze lied to Bierstadt, telling him that Achenbach never took students. It was similarly reported that Bierstadt's knowledge of drawing was so poor (despite his teaching career) that his application to the Düsseldorf Academy was rejected (Köhler 1871, p. 323).

Nevertheless, with remarkable singleness of purpose, Bierstadt set out to learn what Düsseldorf had to teach. By all accounts, he was a quick study. Taking notes from the Americans who generously came to his aid, from the German masters whom he came to know through Malkasten, a local artists' club, and from the many works of art on view in Düsseldorf year-round, Bierstadt observed, experimented, and transformed himself with a speed that was so astonishing, one skeptical newspaper reporter in New Bedford questioned whether a painting he sent home to sell was actually by his hand.

In June 1856, Bierstadt left Düsseldorf in the company of Whittredge and several other American artists for a trip up the Rhine and on into Switzerland. Although Whittredge confessed to feeling uncomfortable with the vertical sublime, Bierstadt responded enthusiastically, completing numerous sketches that he later used to compose studio paintings. In Switzerland's Alpine peaks, Bierstadt had unknowingly found ideal prototypes for what he would later see in the Rocky Mountains and the Sierra Nevada.

From Switzerland Bierstadt journeyed to Rome, where he spent the winter of 1856–57. The following spring he traveled to Naples and Capri with Sanford Robinson Gifford, another young American artist seeing Europe for the first time. Along the coast of Italy, Bierstadt again found preparatory models for what he would later see on California's Pacific shore.

In September 1857, Bierstadt returned to New Bedford, after nearly four years abroad. By November he had taken a studio and begun to advertise his willingness (at the request of "numerous citizens") to conduct classes in oil painting (Chronology, 20 Nov. 1857). In April of the following year, amid discussions regarding the establishment of an "art association" in New Bedford, Bierstadt announced his plan to mount a major art exhibition (New Bedford's first) the following summer. Capitalizing on friendships made abroad and other contacts at home, Bierstadt succeeded in gathering in New Bedford a surprisingly broad range of works (see Appendix A), including a major painting by Leutze, works by European masters, including Andreas Achenbach, and several paintings by the founders of the American school (John Vanderlyn, Thomas Cole, Asher B. Durand). To this international mix, Bierstadt added fourteen of his own paintings.

Despite enthusiastic reviews and enviable press coverage, the exhibition was a financial failure. Bierstadt's efforts to establish a local art association also came to naught. Though he had won the support of several loyal patrons in New Bedford, he must have known, by the fall of 1858, that his professional and social ambitions required a larger stage.

Bierstadt did enjoy success in other areas during the year following his return from Europe. In April 1858, he made his exhibition debut at the National Academy of Design and the following month was elected an honorary member. In addition, he began selling paintings for substantial sums. Alvin Adams, a wealthy Boston businessman, paid $925 for *Lake Lucerne (Switzerland)* (No. 6), the large picture Bierstadt had exhibited at the National Academy, and the Boston Athenaeum paid $400 for *The Arch of Octavius (The Roman Fish Market)*, 1858 (No. 11), one of the artist's most accomplished genre paintings. Eighteen months after his return from Europe, Bierstadt had achieved such success that he was able to report to his friend Henry Lewis in Düsseldorf that he had sold "near four thousand dollars worth of pictures" since his return to New Bedford (Chronology, 1 Nov. 1858).

By 1859, less than six years after his departure for Germany, Bierstadt had successfully transformed himself from the "timid, awkward, unpolished specimen of a Yankee" whom Lewis remembered meeting in Düsseldorf into a technically accomplished and socially adept painter (HL Papers, 1 Nov. 1858).

# CHRONOLOGY

1830

**7 Jan.** Albert Bierstadt born, Solingen, Prussia, sixth child, fourth son of Henry Bierstadt (16 July 1785–1 July 1866) and Christina M. Tillmans Bierstadt (14 Aug. 1791–21 Oct. 1864). Older siblings: Charles (28 Nov. 1819–5 June 1903); Helen (7 Dec. 1822–6 Mar. 1905); Edward (19 Sept. 1824–15 June 1906); Anne Wilhelmine (10 Aug. 1826–11 July 1832); John Wilhelm (14 Sept. 1828–Mar. 1829). (Family Bible; Albert Bierstadt's naturalization papers, 15 Sept. 1853, National Archives, Boston Branch, Waltham, Mass.; "Passenger Lists from Miscellaneous Atlantic & Gulf Coast Ports, 1820–1873," National Archives)

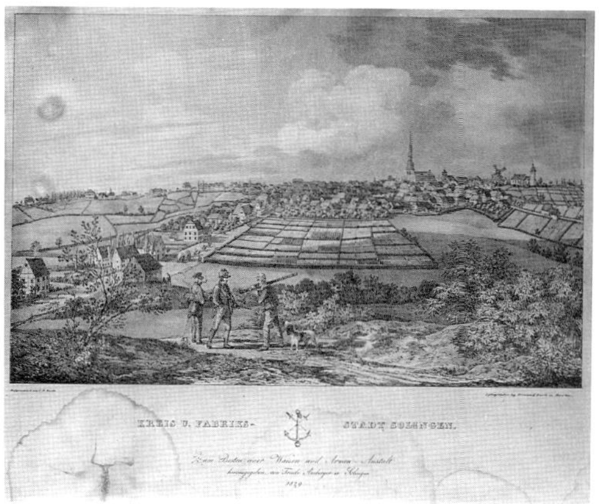

*View of Solingen* (Bierstadt's birthplace), 1829. Lithograph. Collection of Evan Hopkins Turner.

1832

**22 Aug.** Bierstadt family arrives in New Bedford, Mass., aboard brig *Hope* from Rotterdam, Netherlands. Henry Bierstadt listed as "cooper" on passenger roster. (*Daily Advertiser and Patriot*, Boston, 24 Aug. 1832; *Daily Advertiser*, New York, 27 Aug. 1832; "Passenger Lists from Miscellaneous Atlantic & Gulf Coast Ports, 1820–1873," National Archives)

1833

**3 Aug.** Elizabeth (Eliza) Bierstadt born, New Bedford, Mass. (d. 10 June 1896). (Family Bible)

1836

Henry Bierstadt listed as "cooper" with residence at 11 Mill, corner Ray. (New Bedford City Directory, 1836)

1841

Directory listings: Charles Bierstadt, wood turner, works 115 Purchase, boards 11 Mill; Edward Bierstadt, apprentice to John M. Taber, plane maker; Henry Bierstadt, cooper, house 11 Mill. (New Bedford City Directory, 1841)

1842

**12 Nov.** Charles Bierstadt naturalized, Supreme Judicial Court of New Bedford. (Passport Record, 7 Mar. 1873, National Archives)

Family history purports that at age twelve Bierstadt wrote a school composition titled "The Rocky Mountains," principally about a bear hunt. (Repeated in *Scribner's*, Mar. 1872, p. 605)

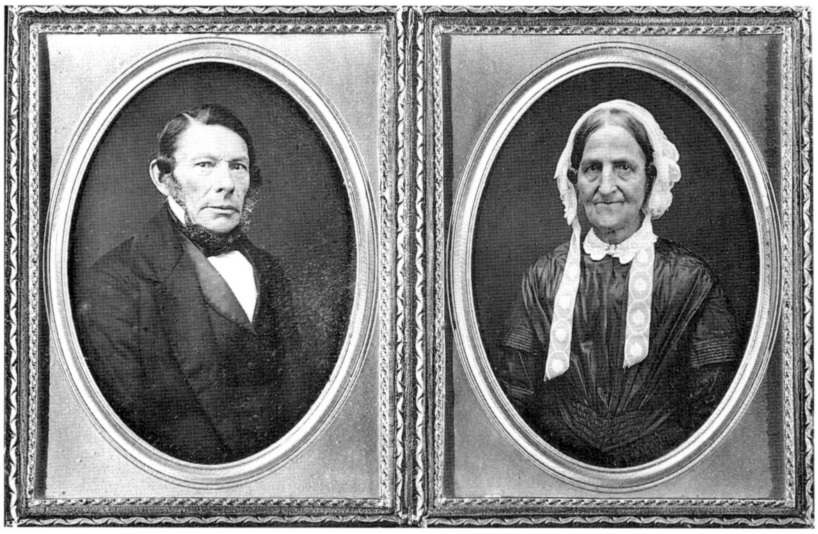

*Henry and Christina Tillmans Bierstadt.* Daguerreotypes. Collection of Evan Hopkins Turner.

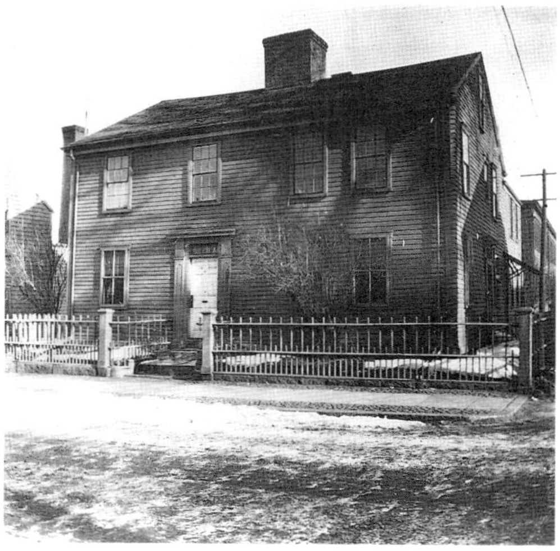

Fred Palmer. *George East House, Acushnet Avenue and Mill Street, New Bedford* (Bierstadt family home), c. 1905. Photograph. The Whaling Museum, New Bedford, Massachusetts.

1847

**9 Nov.** Edward Bierstadt naturalized, Supreme Judicial Court of New Bedford. (Records, Police Court of New Bedford, Year 1847, Petition 221, National Archives, Boston Branch, Waltham, Mass.)

1848

As a young man, Albert Bierstadt is reported to have "worked the bench" at Shaw's Frame Factory, a "Looking Glass and Picture Frame Manufacturer" on Purchase Street in New Bedford. Exact dates of his employment unknown. (*New Bedford Standard*, 19 Feb. 1902)

1850

Directory Listing: "Bierstadt Edward, pattern maker, 8 Wilson Lane, boards 101 Pleasant." (Boston City Directory, 1850)

**13 May** In New Bedford, Bierstadt advertises for the first time that he will give instruction in "monochromatic painting" (a drawing technique); fee "$3 for 24 hours." (*New Bedford Standard*, 13 May 1850)

**6 June** Continuing his advertising campaign, Bierstadt issues a broadside promoting his "improved system of mono-chromatic painting." (Quoted in Trump 1963, p. 23)

**27 Aug.** Seeking a new market, Bierstadt advertises his "improved system of mono-chromatic painting" in Newport, Rhode Island. (*Newport Daily News*, 27 Aug. 1850)

1850–1854

**11–28 Sept.** Exhibits at the Sixth Exhibition of the Massachusetts Charitable Mechanic Association, Faneuil & Quincy Halls, Boston: "207. ALBERT BIERSTADT, New Bedford, Mass. Thirteen Monochromatic Paintings. Mostly copied from prints; one a drawing of the old Mill at Newport." Edward Bierstadt, listed as resident of Boston, exhibits a "case of miniature planes." (Catalogue, Massachusetts Charitable Mechanic Association, 1850, Thomas J. Watson Library, Metropolitan Museum of Art, New York)

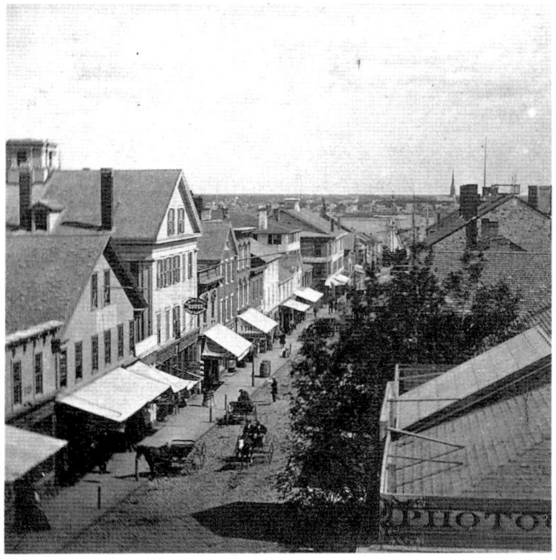

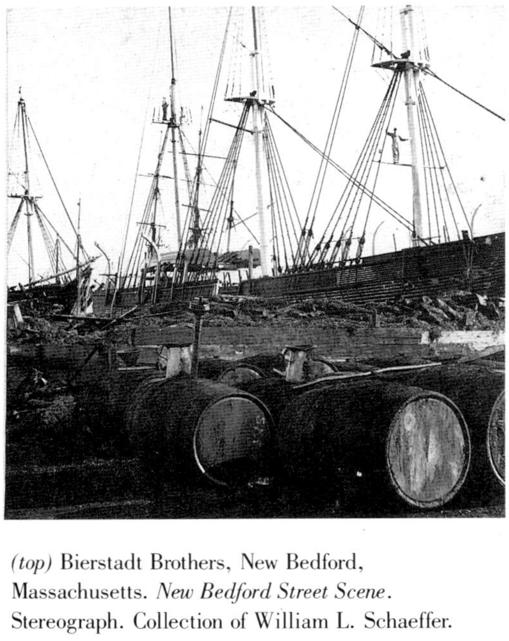

*(top)* Bierstadt Brothers, New Bedford, Massachusetts. *New Bedford Street Scene*. Stereograph. Collection of William L. Schaeffer.

*(above)* Bierstadt Brothers, New Bedford, Massachusetts. *New Bedford Wharf*. Stereograph. Collection of William L. Schaeffer.

**Fall–Winter** Bierstadt moves to Boston, exact date unknown.

1851

Directory Listing: "Bierstadt Albert, monochromatic painting, 265 Washington." (Boston City Directory, 1851)

According to a profile by "Barry Gray" (R. B. Coffin) published in the *NY Leader* (17 Jan. 1863), Bierstadt began painting in oil in 1851. This statement was repeated by Henry Tuckerman (1967, p. 387) and by numerous other writers throughout the artist's career. The date was also noted in obituaries. (*Boston Transcript*, 19 Feb. 1902; *New Bedford Standard*, 19 Feb. 1902; *NY Tribune*, 19 Feb. 1902; *Denver Republican*, 19 Feb. 1902; *Outlook*, 1 Mar. 1902)

On extended exhibition at the New England Art Union, Boston: "No. 76—Landscape,—painted in crayon,—by A. Bierstadt." (*Catalogue of Paintings now on Exhibition in the Free Gallery of the New England Art Union*, 1851, p. 7)

**8 Jan.** In Boston Bierstadt begins to advertise as an instructor of "a new style of drawing, which may be triplicated or quadrupled by a very simple process, being drawn on glass, from which they are transferred to paper. It is valuable for the drawing of flowers, embroidery, or designs where copies are wanted." (*Boston Transcript*, 8 Jan. 1851)

**22 Mar.** American artist George Harvey, recently returned from England, advertises to sell or otherwise dispose of his series of American landscape views painted on glass. (*Boston Transcript*, 22 Mar. 1851)

**7 June** Bierstadt returns to Newport and advertises his lessons in "chromatic painting." "He will be prepared to give instruction in Painting Colored Crayon Heads and Landscapes from nature, or from copies. Also, a new style of sketching from nature which can be acquired in one lesson." (*Newport Daily News*, 7 July 1851, advertisement dated 7 June)

**1 July** Bierstadt announces he has made an arrangement with George Harvey "for the use of his *truly splendid Pictures*, illustrating the progress of our country. Illuminated by the DRUMMOND LIGHT, each Picture measuring 15 by 17 feet." To be exhibited in New Bedford on 3 and 5 July; admission 25 cents. (*New Bedford Standard*, 1 July 1851)

**14 Aug.** William Hathaway, Jr., pays $25 for Bierstadt's *Ruins of Carthage*, "picture and frame." (Receipt, Downs Collection; *New Bedford Standard*, 19 Feb. 1902)

**1 Sept.** In New Bedford, Bierstadt advertises a second exhibition of "Harvey's Illustrations of America." (*Mercury*, New Bedford, 1 Sept. 1851)

**3–9 Sept.** Harvey's "Dissolving Views" exhibited in New Bedford. "The exhibition at Liberty Hall is attracting more and more attention. . . . The dissolving of one picture into another is very magical, for instance we see a view of fishing by torchlight, the sun fires the clouds with its golden hues, until at last the scene is changed into a cedar swamp, where the fire flies are darting about." (*New Bedford Standard*, 8 Sept. 1851)

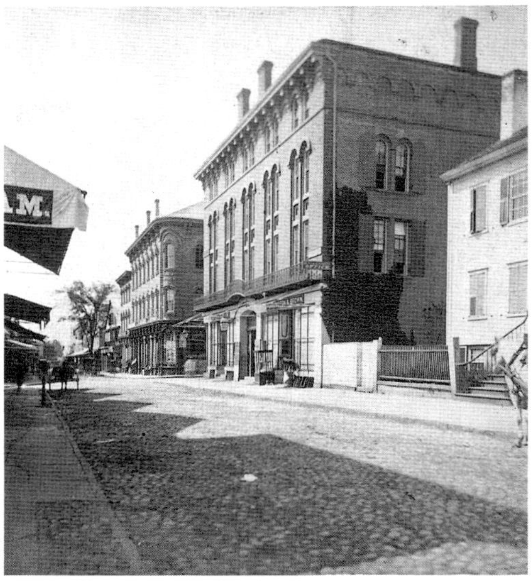

Bierstadt Brothers, New Bedford, Massachusetts. *Liberty Hall, New Bedford* (right foreground). Stereograph. Private collection.

**30 Sept.** Harvey's "Dissolving Views" advertised in Providence, Rhode Island. (*Providence Daily Journal*, 30 Sept. 1851)

**2–8 Oct.** Harvey's "Dissolving Views" shown in Providence. (*Providence Daily Journal*, 1 Oct. 1851)

1852

Directory Listing: "Bierstadt, Albert, monochromatic painting, 265 Washington." (Boston City Directory, 1852)

**Spring** At the New England Art Union Bierstadt exhibits "No. 76.—Landscape,—painted in crayon." (*Catalogue of Paintings now on Exhibition in the Free Gallery of the New England Art Union*, 1852, p. 6)

**31 Mar.** In Boston, Tremont Temple Building burns; many artists' studios are destroyed or damaged. Thomas Thompson loses his art collection in the fire; begins a second collection shortly thereafter; may have purchased a number of Bierstadt's early works. (*Boston Transcript*, 31 Mar. 1852, 8 Dec. 1869; *NY Tribune*, 25 Dec. 1869)

**Apr.–Dec.** Rotating selections from the Dusseldorf Gallery (New York) on exhibition at the Boston Athenaeum. (*Boston Transcript*, 8 Jan., 12 Apr., 11 June, 25 Aug. 1852)

**11 Aug.** Bierstadt at the Summit House on Mount Washington in the White Mountains. (Campbell 1981, p. 14)

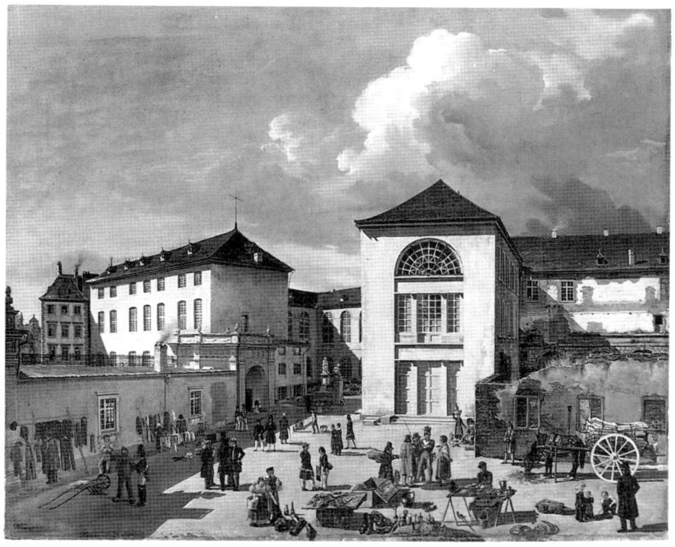

Andreas Achenbach. *The Old Academy in Düsseldorf*, 1831. Oil on canvas. Kunstmuseum Düsseldorf.

## 1853

Directory Listing: "Bierstadt Albert, monochromatic painting, 265 Wash." (Boston City Directory, 1853)

**24 Jan.–1 May** In Boston, at the First Semi-Annual Exhibition of Paintings in the Gallery of the Massachusetts Academy of Fine Arts, Bierstadt exhibits "32. The Old Mill." (Catalogue, First Semi-Annual Exhibition, Massachusetts Academy of Fine Arts, 1853; *Boston Transcript*, 24 Jan. 1853)

**15 Sept.** Albert Bierstadt naturalized, U.S. District Court, Boston. (Naturalization Records, National Archives, Boston Branch, Waltham, Mass.)

**24 Sept.** Bierstadt issued passport no. 2617 by the State of Massachusetts. (Passport Book 2, Office of Secretary of State, Archives Division, Boston)

**Nov.** Sails for Europe. Stops in London a short time before proceeding to Düsseldorf. (*NY Leader*, 17 Jan. 1853; *Ladies Repository*, Jan. 1866, p. 63)

**16 Dec.** Johann Peter Hasenclever, with whom Bierstadt had hoped to study, dies in Düsseldorf. Bierstadt is said to have arrived in Düsseldorf shortly after Hasenclever's death. (Bestvater-Hasenclever 1979, p. 5; Tuckerman 1967, p. 387)

In Düsseldorf, Worthington Whittredge offers to share his studio with Bierstadt. According to Tuckerman, Bierstadt enjoyed "either direct instruction or the personal sympathy of Lessing, Achenbach, Leutze, and Whittredge." (Whittredge 1969, p. 26; Tuckerman 1967, p. 387)

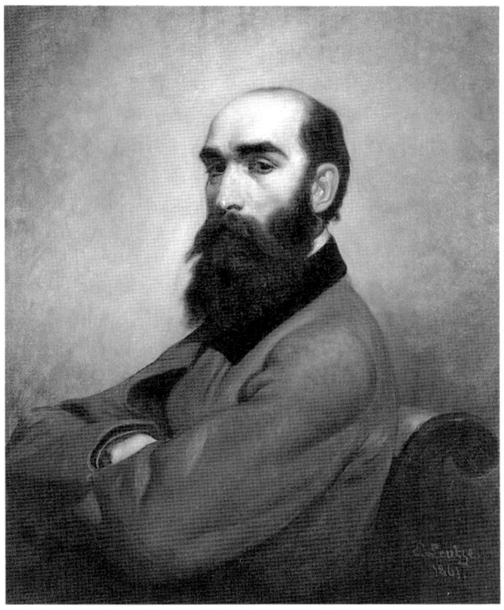

Emanuel Leutze. *Worthington Whittredge*, 1861. Oil on canvas. National Academy of Design, New York.

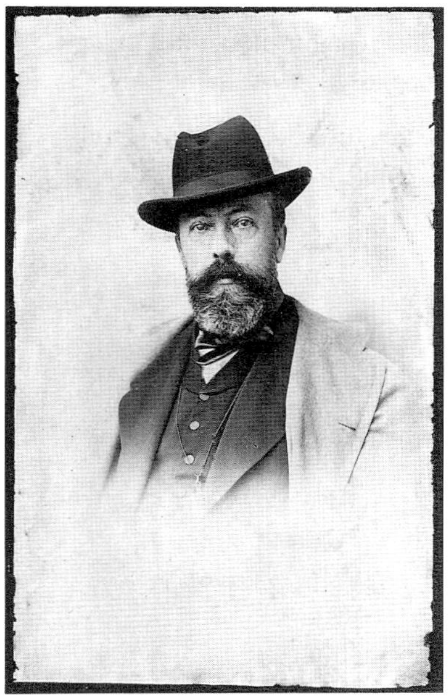

*Andreas Achenbach*. Carte de visite. Bierstadt Album, private collection, Hannover, Germany.

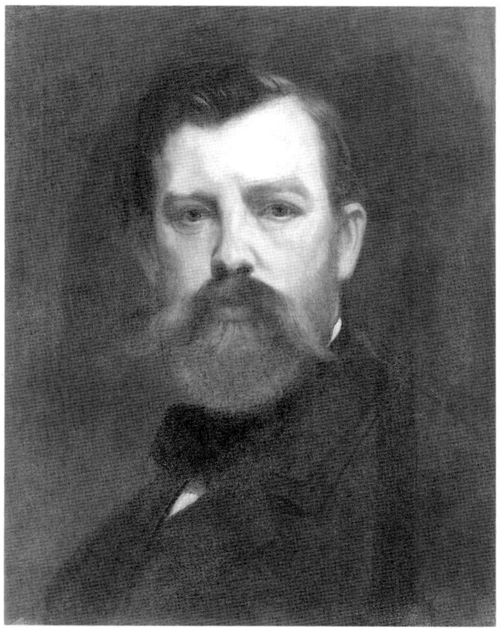

Emanuel Leutze. *Self-Portrait*, c. 1865. Oil on canvas. National Academy of Design, New York.

## 1854

**3 Jan.** Following difficulties in traveling outside Germany with his Massachusetts passport, Bierstadt requests U.S. passport

## 1854–1856

from American Legation, Berlin. (Letter, 5 Jan. 1854, Downs Collection; Letters, 8 Jan., 20 Feb., 27 Mar. 1854, Passport Letters, National Archives)

**29 Mar.** Following numerous letters to Washington and to his brother Edward, Bierstadt is issued U.S. passport no. 4585. (Letter, 27 Mar. 1854, Passport Letters, National Archives)

**Apr.** Bierstadt leaves Düsseldorf on a sketching trip through the Westphalian countryside and remains away until late autumn. (Whittredge 1969, pp. 26–27)

**Fall** Bierstadt returns to Düsseldorf and Whittredge's studio, and quickly begins sending pictures to patrons in New Bedford. (Whittredge 1969, p. 27)

## 1855

**23 Mar.** Bierstadt writes to Mrs. Hathaway, a patron in New Bedford, advising her that he is sending the picture she ordered, a Westphalian landscape, and concludes, "In a few months I shall have some large pictures." (Quoted in Trump 1963, pp. 37–38)

**30 May** Several paintings by Bierstadt completed in Europe are on view in New Bedford at the office of the Commercial Insurance Company. (*New Bedford Standard*, 30 May 1855)

**Summer** Bierstadt on sketching tour through German countryside, accompanied, for undetermined period of time, by American artist Henry Lewis, also a student in Düsseldorf. (Undated letter written after 20 June 1856, HL Papers; *NY Leader*, 17 Jan. 1863; *California Art Gallery* 1873, p. 49)

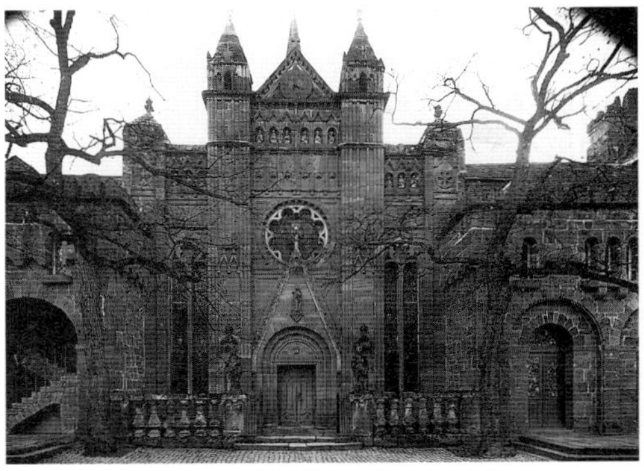

*Chapel façade, Löwenburg, Wilhelmshohe, Kassel, Germany* (subject of Nos. 2, 29, 76). Photograph. Bildarchiv Foto Marburg.

**30 July** Paintings (probably six) by Bierstadt on view at John Hopkins's music store in New Bedford. Titles of four listed: ***A Mill near Altena in Westphalia*, *A View of Cologne on the Drachenfels from Altenberg*, *Farm Scene in Westphalia*, and *View of the Weser near Minden*.** The *Mercury* comments: "Mr. Bierstadt's painting is in the style of the modern German artists, minute and elaborate, but we think these pictures are very free from mannerism." (*New Bedford Standard*, 30 July 1855; *Mercury*, New Bedford, 4 Aug. 1855)

**Fall 1855–56** Responding to charge in a New Bedford newspaper that paintings Bierstadt sent home are not actually by the artist, Leutze writes to Bierstadt's mother that

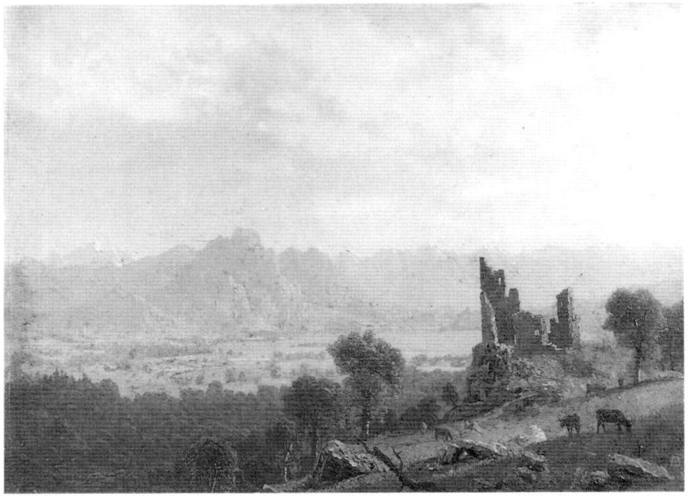

*(left)* Albert Bierstadt. *Scene in the Tyrol*, 1854. Oil on board. Hirshhorn Museum and Sculpture Garden, Smithsonian Institution, Washington, D.C., Gift of Joseph H. Hirshhorn, 1966.

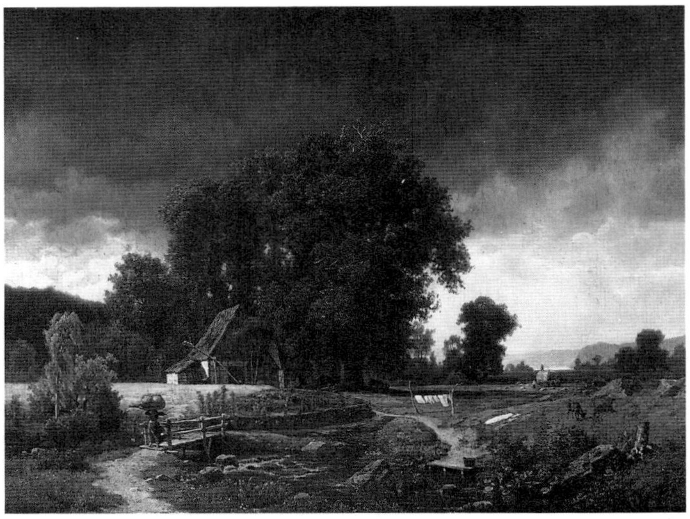

*(left, below)* Albert Bierstadt. *Westphalian Landscape*, 1855. Oil on canvas. Shelburne Museum, Shelburne, Vermont.

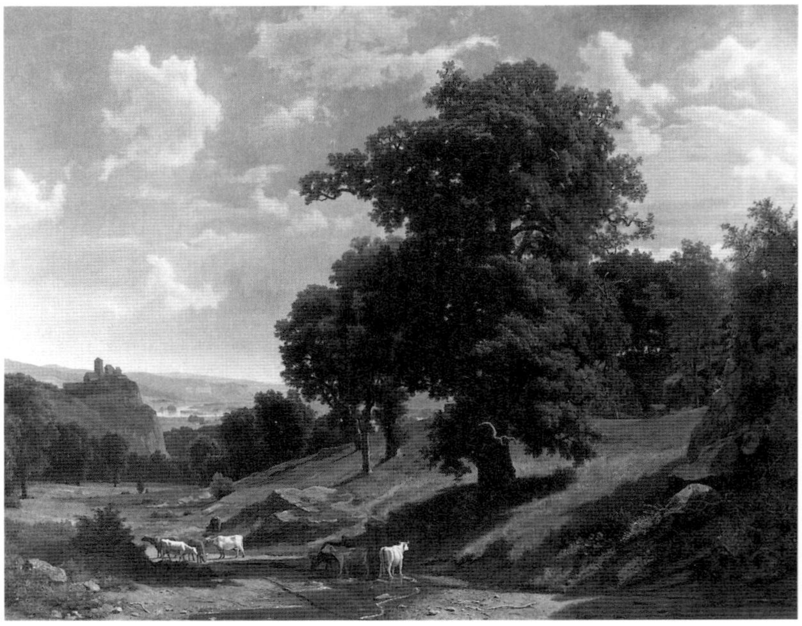

Albert Bierstadt. *A Quiet Valley*, 1855. Oil on canvas. Virginia Museum of Fine Arts, Richmond, The Adolph D. and Wilkins C. Williams Fund.

Bierstadt painted in his Düsseldorf studio and describes Worthington Whittredge as "his teacher." Supporting signatures include Andreas Achenbach, John Beaufain Irving, William Stanley Haseltine. (Letter fragment, Downs Collection; Whittredge 1969, p. 27)

## 1856

**by mid-June** Whittredge, Bierstadt, Lewis, William Henry Furness, Enoch Wood Perry, Haseltine, Irving, and others travel up the Nahe River, a tributary of the Rhine, to sketch near the village of Kirn. Sanford Robinson Gifford, who had intended to join them, decides to travel to Switzerland instead. (Whittredge 1969, p. 30; Plowden 1947, p. 44; SRG Letters, vol. 2, 20 June, 10 Aug. 1856)

**3 July** A group of Bierstadt's New Bedford supporters proposes the subscription purchase of three paintings by the artist (then on exhibit at John Hopkins's store) for the new public library; proceeds to be sent to Bierstadt, who is described as "in need of funds." (*Mercury*, New Bedford, 3 July 1856)

**July** While sketching near the Nahe, Whittredge and Bierstadt both take Kallenfels as their subject. (*View of Kallenfels* by Whittredge inscribed: *July 1856*; Bierstadt painting of same subject, *Kallenfels Among the Hills, Germany*, signed but not dated)

**late July** Whittredge, Haseltine, Bierstadt, and perhaps others descend the Nahe to Bingen and then continue up the Rhine to Switzerland. (Whittredge 1969, p. 31)

**27 July** While walking near Lake Lucerne, Gifford meets Whittredge, Haseltine, and Bierstadt, who intend "to spend several weeks on the lake." (SRG Letters, vol. 2, 10 Aug. 1856)

Few details about these "weeks on the lake" are known. According to Haseltine, he and his companions visited Brunnen on the eastern shore of Lake Lucerne, where they found Alexandre Calame, a Swiss artist noted for his Alpine views, encamped with a group of students. Titles of Bierstadt paintings exhibited shortly after the artist's return from Europe suggest that while touring in the vicinity of Lake Lucerne the Americans also visited Küssnacht, Schwyz, Seelisberg, and

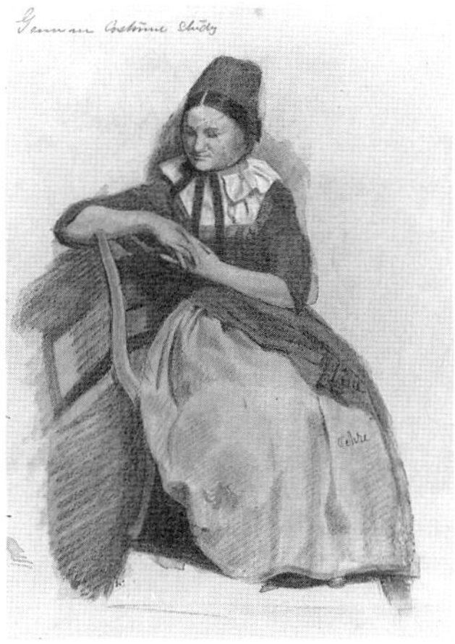

Albert Bierstadt. *German Costume Study*. Crayon, wash, and chalk on paper. Collection of Florence Glickman.

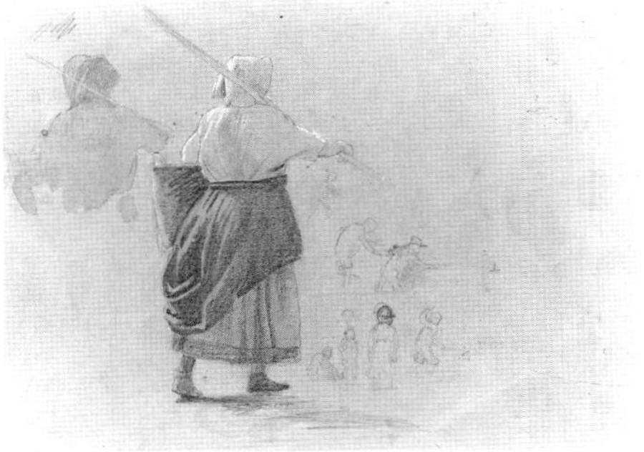

*Figure Studies*. Pencil, crayon, and chalk on paper. Collection of Florence Glickman.

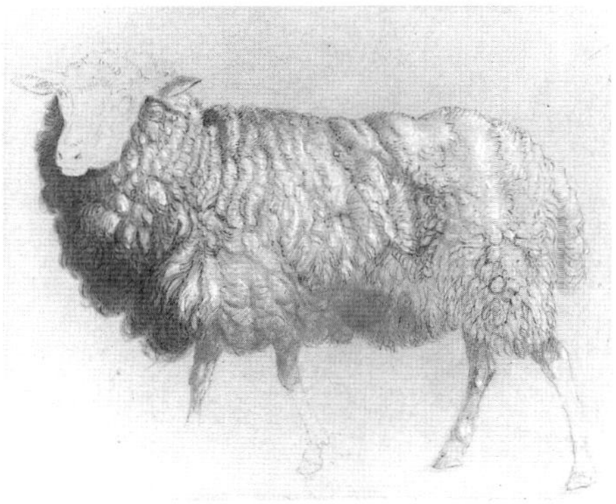

Albert Bierstadt. *Study of a Ewe*. Pencil, crayon, and chalk on paper. The Brooklyn Museum, Purchased with funds given by Mr. and Mrs. Leonard L. Milberg.

(*below, left*) Albert Bierstadt. *Kallenfels Among the Hills, Germany*, c. 1856. Oil on canvas. Shelburne Museum, Shelburne, Vermont.

(*below, right*) Worthington Whittredge. *View of Kallenfels*, 1856. Oil on canvas. Cincinnati Art Museum, Gift of Mary Hanna.

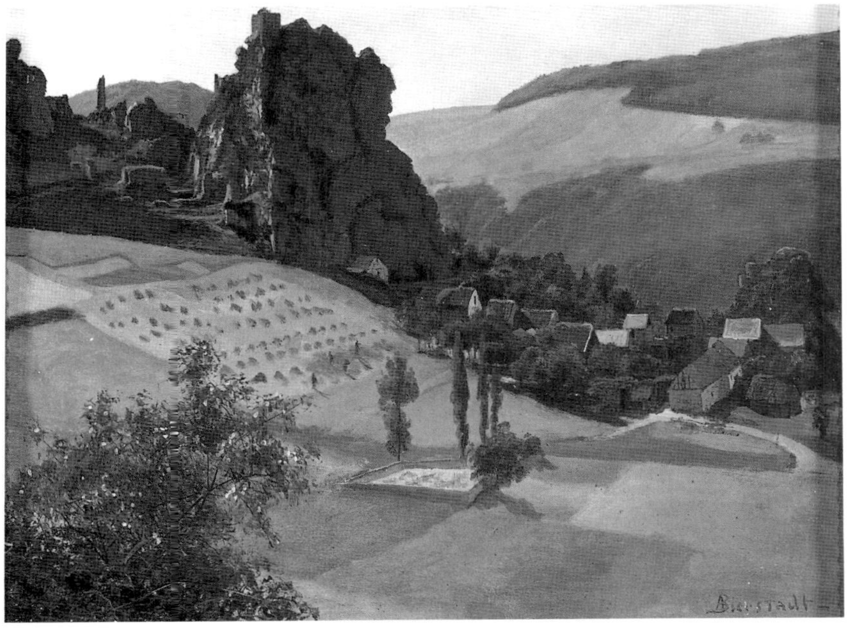


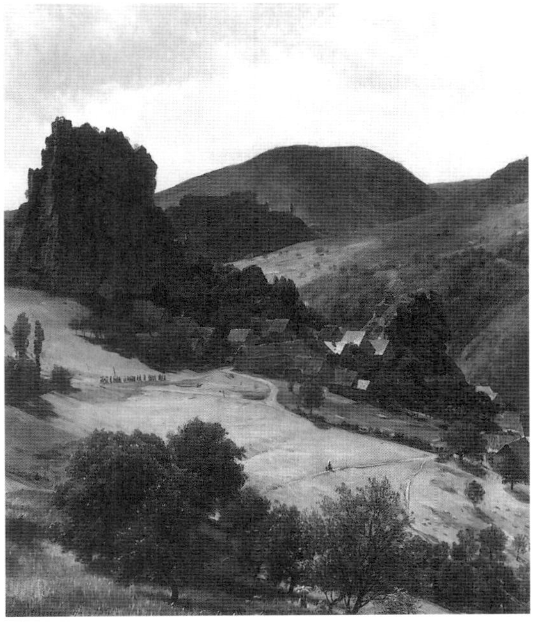

## 1856–1857

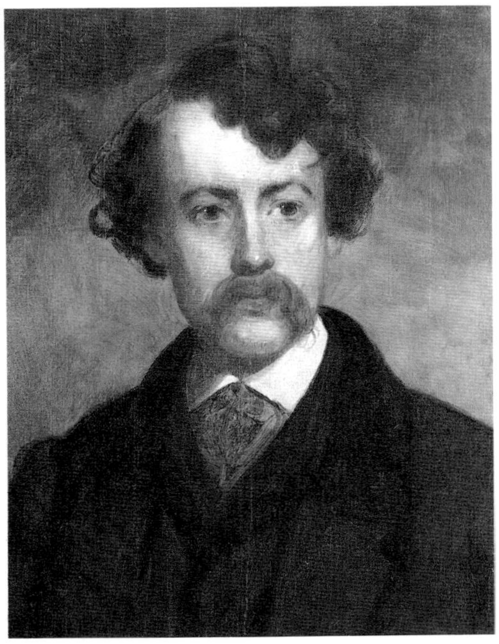

William O. Stone. *William Stanley Haseltine*, c. 1861. Oil on canvas. National Academy of Design, New York.

the Rigi. From the shores of Lake Lucerne, they traveled to Meiringen via the Brünig Pass. (Plowden 1947, pp. 46–49; Whittredge 1969, pp. 31–32)

**Sept.** In Boston, four works by Bierstadt included in the Eighth Exhibition of the Massachusetts Charitable Mechanic Association: "369 . . . Four Oil Paintings. Very good landscapes of the modern German school. Correct in drawing; clear and transparent in tone. The best landscapes exhibited. 'Silver Medal.' " (Catalogue, Massachusetts Charitable Mechanic Association, 1856, p. 137; *Boston Transcript*, 15 Oct. 1856)

**3 Sept.** Staying at a pension in Meiringen catering exclusively to artists, Bierstadt and his companions remain in the valley long enough to climb to the top of Reichenbach Falls and continue on to Rosenlaui glacier and the base of the Faulhorn. Titles of firmly dated paintings indicate that while camped at the foot of the Bernese Alps Bierstadt and the others made sketches of the Wetterhorn, the Jungfrau, Lauterbrunnen, and Staubbach Falls. (Plowden 1947, pp. 47–49)

**Sept.–Oct.** Bierstadt, Haseltine, Whittredge, and possibly others leave Switzerland for northern Italy via Saint Gotthard Pass. (Plowden 1947, pp. 50–51)

**Oct.** Once over the Alps, the Americans visit several northern Italian lakes (Whittredge specifically mentions Lago Maggiore and the "lovely Isola Bella") before traveling south to Genoa, where they board a steamer for Leghorn. From Leghorn they journey to Florence and then (perhaps separately) on to Rome. (Whittredge 1969, pp. 31–35)

## 1857

**3 Jan.** "Several large landscapes with every Dusseldorf merit and fault," sent home by Bierstadt, "who is studying with Leutze," are on exhibit at John Hopkins's music store in New Bedford. (*Home Journal*, 3 Jan. 1857)

**13 Mar.** Gifford, also in Rome for the winter, calls on Bierstadt and his companion Ludwig, "a young painter of western American Indians" (perhaps Heinrich Ludwig [1829–1897], once a student at the Düsseldorf Academy, then living in Rome). (SRG Letters, vol. 2, 14 Apr. 1857)

**17 Mar.** Gifford, Ludwig, Bierstadt, and William H. Beard travel to Monte Mario above Rome for a view of the city and Campagna; they return via the Ponte Molle and the Aqua Cetosa, a mineral spring on the bank of the Tiber. (SRG Letters, vol. 2, 14 Apr. 1857)

**25 Mar.** Bierstadt, Gifford, Virgil Williams, and Beard go to a fair at Grotta Ferrata in the Alban Hills south of Rome and return via the Villa Borghese. Bierstadt, Gifford, Whittredge, and Beard spend the evening together. (SRG Letters, vol. 2, 14 Apr. 1857)

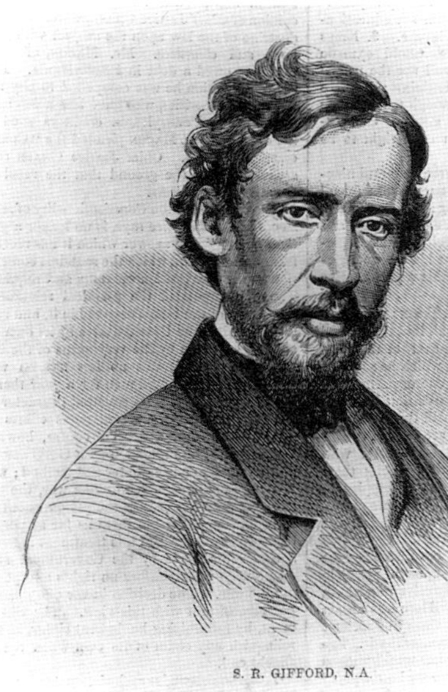


*S. R. Gifford, N.A.* Wood engraving published in *Harper's Weekly*, 13 July 1867.

**29 Mar.** Bierstadt exhibits *The Wetterhorn* (No. 5) at a showing of works by artists of many nations in the Piazza del Popolo in Rome. Gifford calls it "decidedly the best landscape" exhibited. (SRG Letters, vol. 2, 14 Apr. 1857)

**4 Apr.** At Sowle & Ward's, Boston, "the last remaining of Bierstadt's fine Landscapes, and the last that will be received from him prior to his return from Europe the present year, is offered at a price very low considering its real value." (*Boston Transcript*, 4 Apr. 1857)

**12 Apr.** Easter Sunday. Bierstadt calls on Gifford and they go to Saint Peter's to witness the papal benediction. Later they are joined by Beard for a walk in the gardens of the Villa Borghese and along the Tiber. (SRG Letters, vol. 2, 14 Apr. 1857)

**17 Apr.** Bierstadt and Gifford go to the German Artists' Club (Verein Deutscher Künstler) to prepare costumes and props for a pantomime representing the "Siege of Troy" for the upcoming artists' festival at Cervara. (SRG Letters, vol. 2, 2 May 1857)

**18 Apr.** Bierstadt and Gifford visit a horticultural exhibition in the court of Palazzo Doria, sketch buffalo in the Forum, and visit the Colosseum, the Villa Salust, and the Ossuarium under the Church of the Cappuccini. In the evening they go to Saint Peter's to see the dome and colonnade illuminated with hundreds of lanterns. (SRG Letters, vol. 2, 2 May 1857)

**20 Apr.** Bierstadt and Gifford make sketching trip to the Torre di Schiavi several miles out on the Campagna. In the evening they attend a pantomime rehearsal at the German Artists' Club. (SRG Letters, vol. 2, 2 May 1857)

**22 Apr.** Bierstadt and his compatriots perform at the artists' festival at Cervara and then spend the evening at the German Artists' Club. (SRG Letters, vol. 2, 2 May 1857)

**30 Apr.** Bierstadt, Gifford, and Luther Terry go to Thomas Crawford's new residence in the Villa Negroni to see William Page's portrait of Mrs. Crawford. (SRG Letters, vol. 2, 2 May 1857)

**4 May** Bierstadt, Whittredge, Beard, and Gifford call on Peter von Cornelius at his studio in the Palazzo Poli. (SRG Letters, vol. 2, 2 May 1857)

**7 May** Bad weather prevents Bierstadt and Gifford from beginning their trip to Naples; they go instead to the Alban Hills with Peter

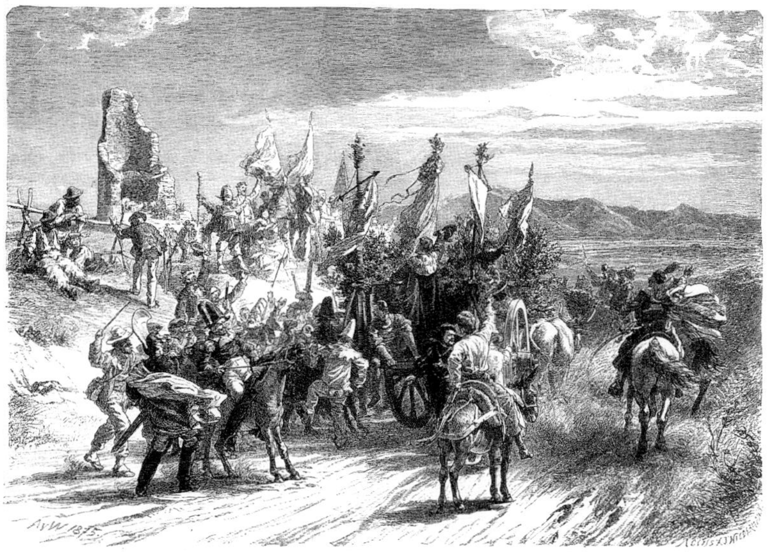

ON THE WAY TO CERVARA. ARTISTS' FESTIVAL IN ROME.

*On the way to Cervara. Artists' Festival in Rome.* Engraving published in Karl Stieler, *Italy from the Alps to Mount Etna* (London: 1877).

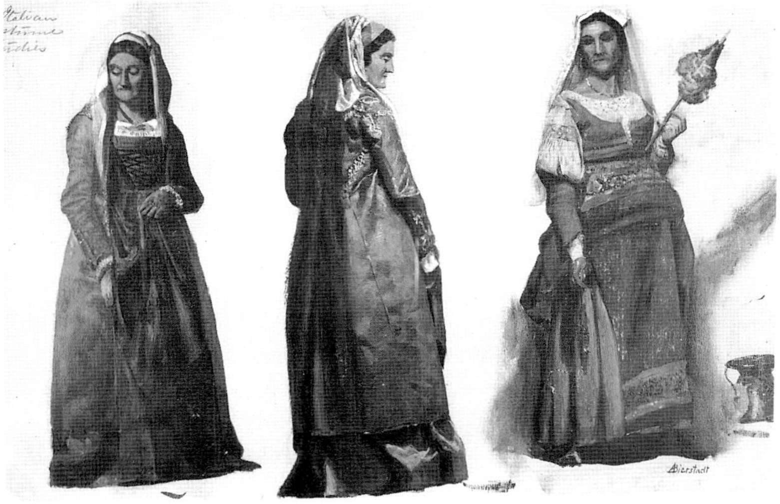

Albert Bierstadt. *Italian Costume Studies*, 1857. Oil on paper. Lyman Allyn Art Museum, New London, Connecticut.

Frederick Rothermel, Whittredge, and Beard. (SRG Letters, vol. 2, 2 May 1857)

**10 May** Bierstadt and Gifford depart for Naples, shouldering knapsacks and walking through the Abruzzi, "the most Italian part of Italy." (SRG Letters, vol. 2, 2 May 1857)

**23 May** Bierstadt and Gifford arrive in Naples; following difficulties with customs officials, they walk along the shore watching fishermen draw in their nets. (SRG Letters, vol. 2, 25 June 1857)

**24 May** Bierstadt and Gifford visit Virgil's Tomb; after dinner they climb to the convent of San Martino for a view of Vesuvius and the Bay of Naples. (SRG Letters, vol. 2, 25 June 1857)

**25 May** Gifford and Bierstadt succeed in retrieving their sketch boxes and guidebooks from customs officials. In the afternoon they outfit their sketch boxes and examine Etruscan vases at the Museo Borbonico. Later they walk on the "Chiaia" and subscribe to the British Library "that we might have something to read while at Capri, where we will stay about a month sketching." (SRG Letters, vol. 2, 25 June 1857)

**26 May** Rain prevents Bierstadt and Gifford's departure from Naples for an excursion to the island of Ischia. (SRG Letters, vol. 2, 25 June 1857)

**27 May** Bierstadt and Gifford travel to the convent of Camaldoli on donkeys; panoramic view "rich in natural beauty and classical associations"; later walk along the shore to the "Sibyl's Cave," which they enter with a guide; take a boat to Ischia and sketch in sunset light; walk to village of Casamicciola, where they spend the night. (SRG Letters, vol. 2, 25 June 1857)

**28–29 May** Bierstadt and Gifford spend morning sketching along the shore and return to Naples aboard a "large open market boat"; late in the afternoon, they board a train for Portici and from there walk to Resina, a village built upon the lava that buried Herculaneum. After dinner and several hours' rest, they engage a guide to take them to Vesuvius's crater; departing at midnight, they reach the crater at 3 A.M. Smoke, fumes, and rumblings produce an "infernal" effect. Bierstadt and Gifford climb to the volcano's peak for a panoramic view at sunrise. Following a quick descent and an hour spent selecting mineral specimens for Bierstadt to send home, they return to Naples. (SRG Letters, vol. 2, 25 June 1857)

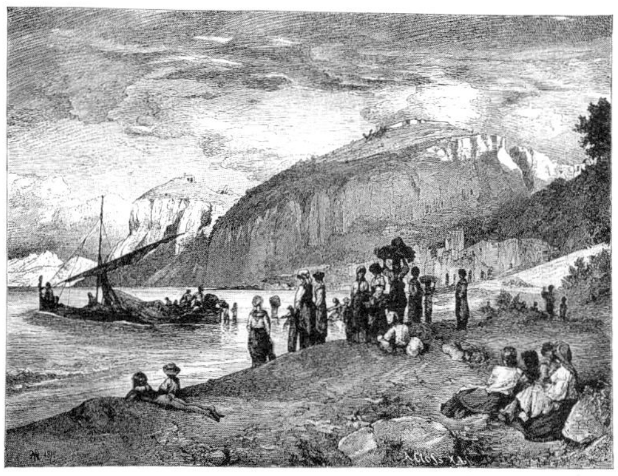

ARRIVAL OF A MARKET BOAT, CAPRI.

*Arrival of a Market Boat, Capri.* Engraving published in Karl Stieler, *Italy from the Alps to Mount Etna* (London: 1877).

**30 May** Bierstadt and Gifford travel in a market boat to Capri; stay at the Hotel Pagano in a room with a view of the sea and the Faraglioni Islands. (SRG Letters, vol. 2, 25 June 1857)

**31 May** Exploring Capri, they visit the ruins of the palace of Tiberius. (SRG Letters, vol. 2, 25 June 1857)

**1 June** Sketch at Marina Piccola, climb to Anacapri, the castle of Barbarossa. (SRG Letters, vol. 2, 25 June 1857)

**2 June** Sketching on this and subsequent days at Marina Piccola. (SRG Letters, vol. 2, 25 June 1857)

**6 June** Bierstadt and Gifford circle Capri by boat; see red, blue, and green grottoes. (SRG Letters, vol. 2, 25 June 1857)

**14 June** *Fishing Boats at Capri* (No. 7) inscribed: *Capri/june 14, 1857*. (Baur 1949, p. 76)

**c. 17–25 June** Sketching on the cliffs on the south side of Capri. (SRG Letters, vol. 2, 25 June 1857)

**26 June** Bierstadt and Gifford leave Capri; plan to sail to Sorrento, walk north along the coast to Castellammare, cross the mountains to Amalfi, walk to Salerno and on to Paestum.

1857–1858

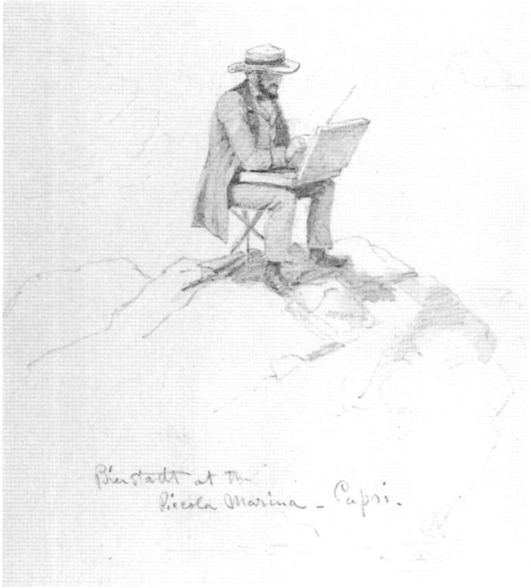


Sanford Robinson Gifford. *Bierstadt at the Piccola Marina, Capri*, June 1857. Pencil on paper. Private collection.

Storm forces them ashore unexpectedly at Massa, and they walk to Sorrento and to Castellammare. From their hotel window they can see "glowing streams of lava" flowing down the sides of Vesuvius. (SRG Letters, vol. 2, July 1857)

**27 June** Bierstadt and Gifford travel to Amalfi on the Gulf of Salerno. (SRG Letters, vol. 2, July 1857)

**28 June** Accompanied by a guide, they climb to Ravello to see ruins dating from the Middle Ages; returning via "the wild and picturesque 'valle dei Molini,'" they witness a fireworks display in honor of Amalfi's patron saint. (SRG Letters, vol. 2, July 1857)

**29 June** Bierstadt and Gifford leave Amalfi, walk along the coast to Salerno, hire a cart, and continue to Paestum, arriving at dusk. Overnight at Capaccio. (SRG Letters, vol. 2, July 1857)

**30 June** They return to Paestum to sketch; from Paestum they reach Silarus before Bierstadt discovers his sketchbook is missing; he walks back to Paestum, locates the sketchbook, rejoins Gifford; they return to Salerno, and by horse continue to La Cava for the night. (SRG Letters, vol. 2, July 1857)

**1 July** They walk to Nocera, noting, "The mountains about here, and this smiling valley were the favorite places of study of Salvator Rosa and Claude. In the mountains we recognized the lines of Salvator's savage landscapes, and in the valley the rich and general character that belongs to Claude." They return to Naples by train; take lodgings at 31 Santa Lucia, on the bay. "Directly in front across the bay rises the isolated mass of Vesuvius. During the day we see only the lazy white cloud that floats over its summit. At night, at intervals of a few minutes, jets of fiery stones burst from the top, illuminating the overhanging cloud." (SRG Letters, vol. 2, July 1857)

**4 July** The two travelers part company; Gifford continues traveling in Italy. If Bierstadt undertook additional European travel before returning to New Bedford, his itinerary is not known. He probably departed Europe from England, where he had sent his trunk following customs difficulties in Italy. (SRG Letters, vol. 2, July 1857)

**by 3 Sept.** Bierstadt is back in New Bedford and "has already been engaged to paint a picture for a gentleman in Boston." (*New Bedford Standard*, 3 Sept. 1857)

**7 Oct.** At John Hopkins's music store, paintings by Bierstadt on exhibition: "There are four new landscapes, a morning in Switzerland . . . a scene on the Roman campagna . . . the 'Upper Glazier of Rosenloni [*sic*], on the Wetterhorm' [*sic*] . . . 'Spearing Fish by torchlight, Lake Lucerne.'" (*Mercury*, New Bedford, 7 Oct. 1857)

**20 Nov.** Bierstadt advertises that "in compliance with the request of numerous citizens [he] is prepared to form a class in Oil Painting." (*Mercury*, New Bedford, 20 Nov. 1857)

**21 Nov.** "Some of Mr. Bierstadt's excellent paintings" are on exhibition in the reading room of the newly opened New Bedford Public Library. (*Mercury*, New Bedford, 21 Nov. 1857)

**25 Nov.** Response to Bierstadt's paintings at the public library: "As an artist who has faithfully studied his favorite art, and has settled among us to prosecute it, Mr. Bierstadt is worthy of the patronage of our citizens and we hope will meet with liberal encouragement." (*New Bedford Standard*, 25 Nov. 1857)

**30 Dec.** "A Beautiful Painting" by Bierstadt commissioned after his return from Europe is on view at Sowle & Ward in Boston. (*Boston Transcript*, 30 Dec. 1857)

## 1858

**22 Jan.** In praising *The Wetterhorn* (No. 5), on exhibition in Boston, the *Daily Courier* declares the picture "does [Bierstadt] credit" and bodes well for future works. (*Daily Courier*, Boston, 22 Jan. 1858)

**17 Mar.** "Mr. Albert Bierstadt, late a student at Dusseldorf, is endeavoring to open an exhibition of pictures in New Bedford." (Letter dated 17 Mar., in *Crayon*, Apr. 1858, p. 117)

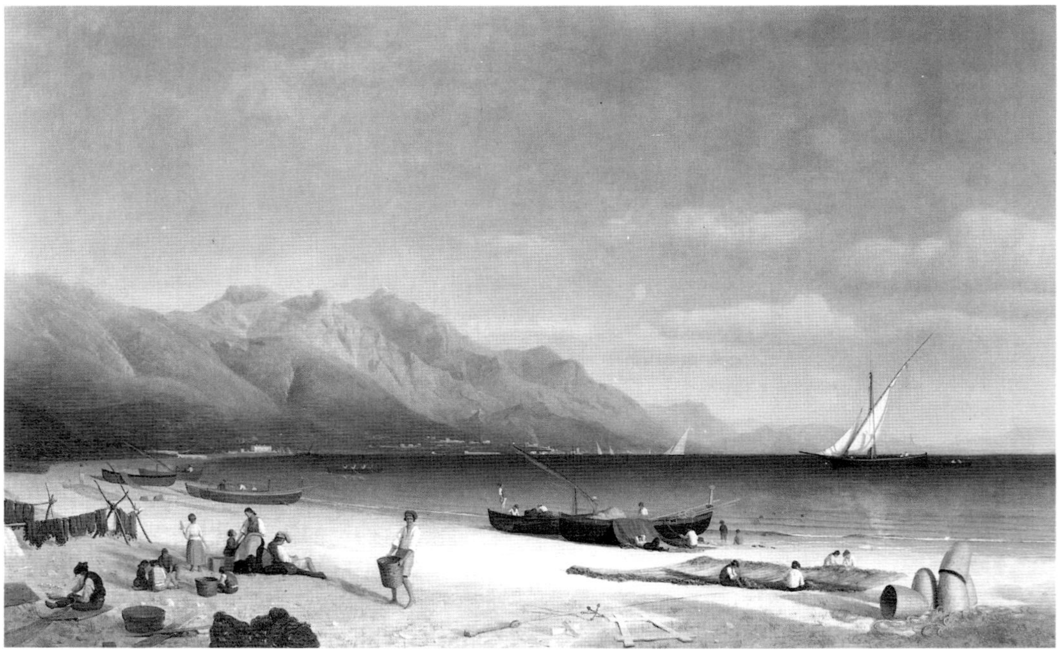

Albert Bierstadt. *Bay of Salerno*, 1858. Oil on canvas. Private collection.

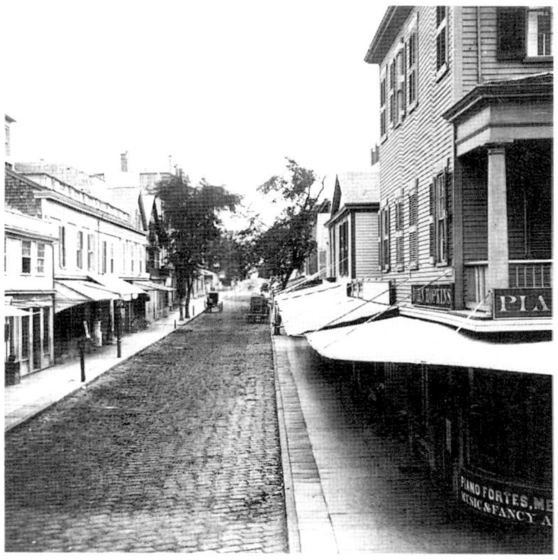

*John Hopkins's Music Store*. Stereograph. International Museum of Photography at George Eastman House, Rochester, New York.

**20–23 Mar.** National Convention of Artists, organized by the Washington Art Association, is held in Washington, D.C., for purpose of recommending that a congressional committee be formed to oversee "the procuring and execution of works of Art for national purposes." Bierstadt's name listed among those supporting the memorial presented to Congress. (*Proceedings of the National Convention of Artists*, Washington. D.C., 1858; *Crayon*, May 1858, p. 148; *Harper's Weekly*, 3 Apr. 1858, p. 2)

**13 Apr.–30 June** Bierstadt debuts in New York, exhibiting *Lake Lucerne (Switzerland)* (No. 6) at the NAD Annual Exhibition. The *Post* describes *Lake Lucerne* as the largest picture in the exhibition (6 × 10 ft.). (Catalogue, NAD, 1858, p. 17; *Post*, New York, 1 May 1858; dimensions from *Home Journal*, 3 Apr. 1858)

"Bierstadt's *Lake Lucerne* invites study; the foreground is indicative of great command of landscape elements. . . . The same ability on a smaller scale, would be more readily appreciated." (*Crayon*, May 1858, p. 147)

**12 May** At the annual meeting of the NAD, Bierstadt is elected an honorary member. (*Crayon*, June 1858, p. 180)

**20 May** In a letter from Düsseldorf, Henry Lewis writes to his brother in the United States, asking him to send two of his pictures to Bierstadt (in New Bedford), who "has started an institution known as the 'New Bedford Art Association.' This society gives their first exhibition this year beginning 1st July and I am solicited to send some of my works there." (HL Papers, 20 May 1858)

**June** The *Crayon* encourages artists to contribute to the upcoming exhibition in New Bedford and lists agents in New York, Philadelphia, and Boston willing to forward works on behalf of artists. (*Crayon*, June 1858, p. 180)

**22 June** A "Special Notice" announces an exhibition of paintings to open July 1 at John Hopkins's music store. "CHOICE WORKS By the most eminent AMERICAN ARTISTS, together with several Pictures by some of the most Celebrated Living European Painters." (*Mercury*, New Bedford, 22 June 1858)

**1 July–7 Aug.** Art exhibition opens in New Bedford. Bierstadt contributes fourteen of his own paintings (see Appendix A). (*Mercury*, *New Bedford Standard*, 1 July 1858; New Bedford Catalogue 1858)

**8 July** Long review of the New Bedford exhibition begins with a discussion of Leutze's *Frederick the Great* and continues with praise for the European pictures, particularly those by Achenbach, Calame, and Landseer. Discussion of American paintings follows, including several contributed by Bierstadt. (*New Bedford Standard*, 8 July 1858)

**20 July** New Bedford exhibition opens with the addition of forty new pictures, including Bierstadt's *Lake Lucerne (Switzerland)*. Early hint of disappointing receipts with announcement that ticket prices have been reduced. (*New Bedford Standard*, 20 July 1858)

**2 Aug.** Still urging local citizens to visit the art exhibition, the *Standard* writes, "We should regret that the exhibition should close without having been visited by all, and still more that the patronage extended to it should be so meagre as to afford little hope that the undertaking will be renewed every season." (*New Bedford Standard*, 2 Aug. 1858)

**1 Sept.** *Lake Lucerne (Switzerland)* and *The Temples of Paestum* (now titled *Ruins of Paestum*) on view at the Boston Athenaeum. (Other works by Bierstadt likely to have been placed on view at the same time: *The Arch of Octavius [The Roman Fish Market]* [No. 11], *On the Weser*, *View From Gaeta*, *The Upper Glacier of Rosenlaui*.) (*Boston Transcript*, 1 Sept. 1858; Perkins and Gavin 1980, p. 20)

**9 Sept.** Bierstadt and William Bradford in Newport for a few weeks of "marine sketching." (*Mercury*, New Bedford, 9 Sept. 1858)

**20 Sept.** In praising *Lake Lucerne (Switzerland)*, on exhibit at the Boston Athenaeum, the *Post* describes the artist as having "arisen up, of a sudden amongst us,—astonishing even our foremost artists with his bold strides." (*Boston Post*, 20 Sept. 1858)

**Fall** Bierstadt travels to New Hampshire, (including possibly the White Mountains); painting titled *Indian Summer, New Hampshire* inscribed: *New Hampshire 1858*. (Hendricks 1973, p. 58)

**c. 20 Oct.** Bierstadt contributes *Brunen—Lake Lucerne* [*sic*] and *Landscape—Autumn—Westphalia* to the Sixth Annual

Albert Bierstadt. *Ruins of Paestum*, 1858. Oil on canvas. The Minneapolis Institute of Arts, The Putnum Dana McMillan Fund.

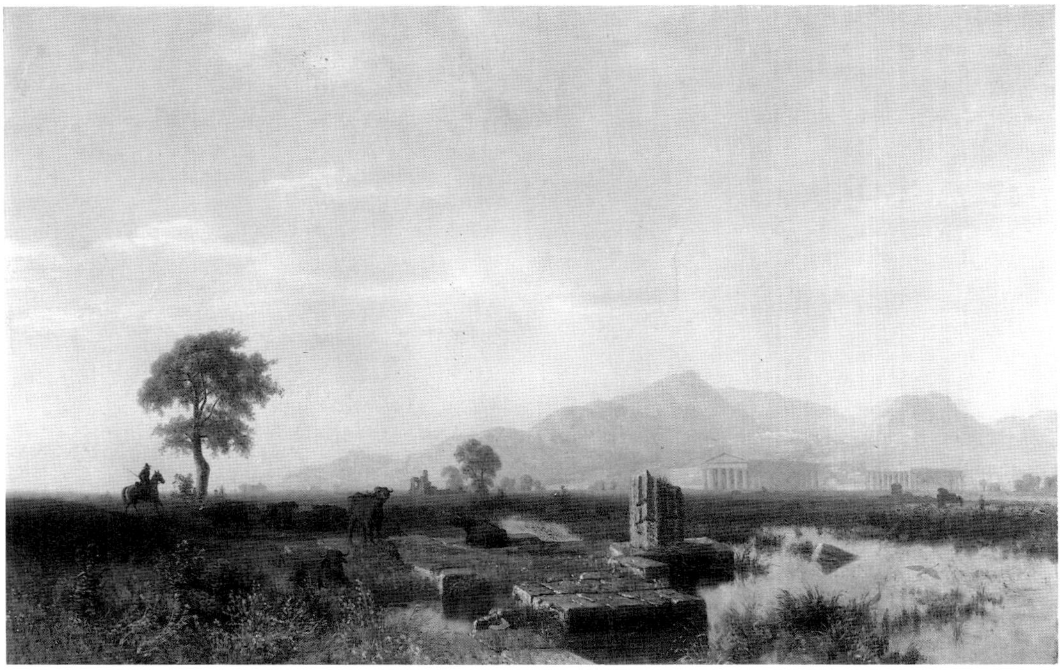

1858

Exhibition of the Maryland Historical Society in Baltimore. (Catalogue, Maryland Historical Society, 1858)

**1 Nov.** In a letter to his brother, Henry Lewis laments his inability to sell paintings and comments: "How different has been the reception of Mr. Bierstadt. He left home and was absent some three years; was the son of a *Cooper* in New Bedford totally ignorant of manners or polite society or literature; and almost equally so of Art. He returns there, is admitted into the best society, everyone seems proud to patronize him, and since his return, some 18 months ago, he writes me he has sold near four thousand dollars worth of pictures." (H. Lewis to G. Lewis, 1 Nov. 1858, HL Papers)

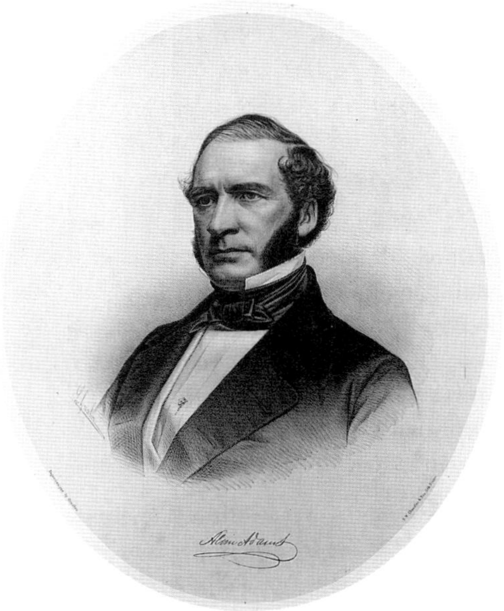

L. Grozelier. *Alvin Adams*, 1854. Lithograph after daguerreotype by Marcus Ormsbee. National Portrait Gallery, Smithsonian Institution, Washington, D.C.

**8 Dec.** A sketch of Newport by Bierstadt on view at Williams & Everett's gallery in Boston. (*Boston Transcript*, 8 Dec. 1858)

**14 Dec.** "Mr. Bierstadt has disposed of his oil painting of 'Lake Lucerne [No. 6],' to a gentleman in Boston [Alvin Adams], for the sum of $925, and his painting of the 'Irish [*sic*] Market' or 'Arch of Octavius' [*The Arch of Octavius (The Roman Fish Market)*, No. 11], to the Boston Athenaeum for $400." (*Mercury*, New Bedford, 14 Dec. 1858)

**15 Dec.** "In a short time Mr. Bierstadt starts for the Rocky Mountains, where he intends to remain a couple of years, making sketches of the scenery, and studying the manners and customs of the Indians, preparatory to painting a series of large pictures." (Letter dated 15 Dec., in *Crayon*, Jan. 1859, p. 26)

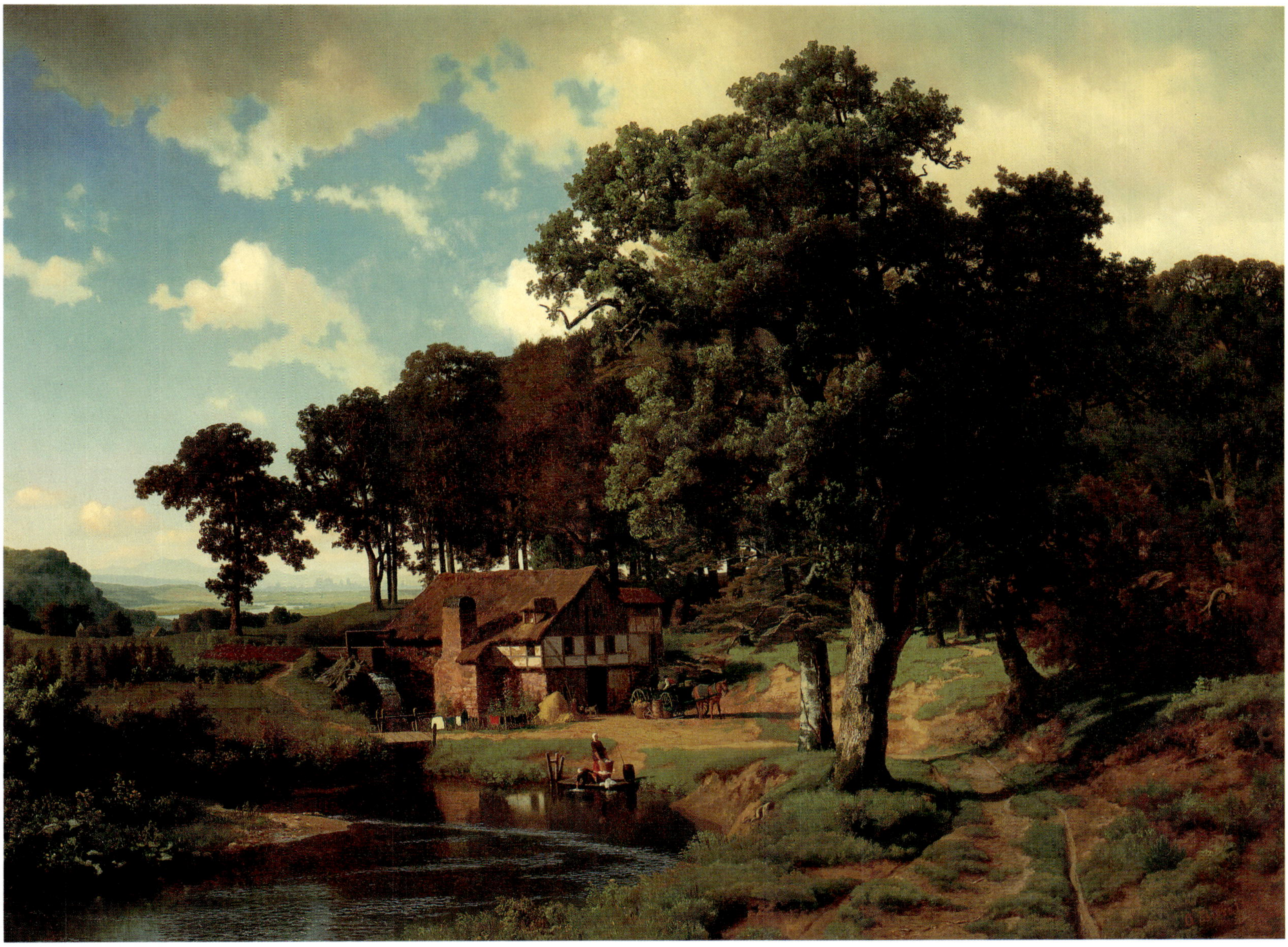

**NO. 1**

*A Rustic Mill,* 1855

Oil on canvas, 43¼ × 58¼ in. (110 × 148 cm)

Signed and dated lower right: *A. Bierstadt/1855*

Private collection

NO. 2

## *Sunlight and Shadow: Study,* 1855

Oil on paper mounted on canvas, 18½ × 13 in. (47 × 33 cm)

Signed lower left: *ABierstadt.*

Inscribed lower right: *Cassel July 1855.*

The Newark Museum, Newark, New Jersey, Gift of Dr. J. Ackerman Coles, 1920

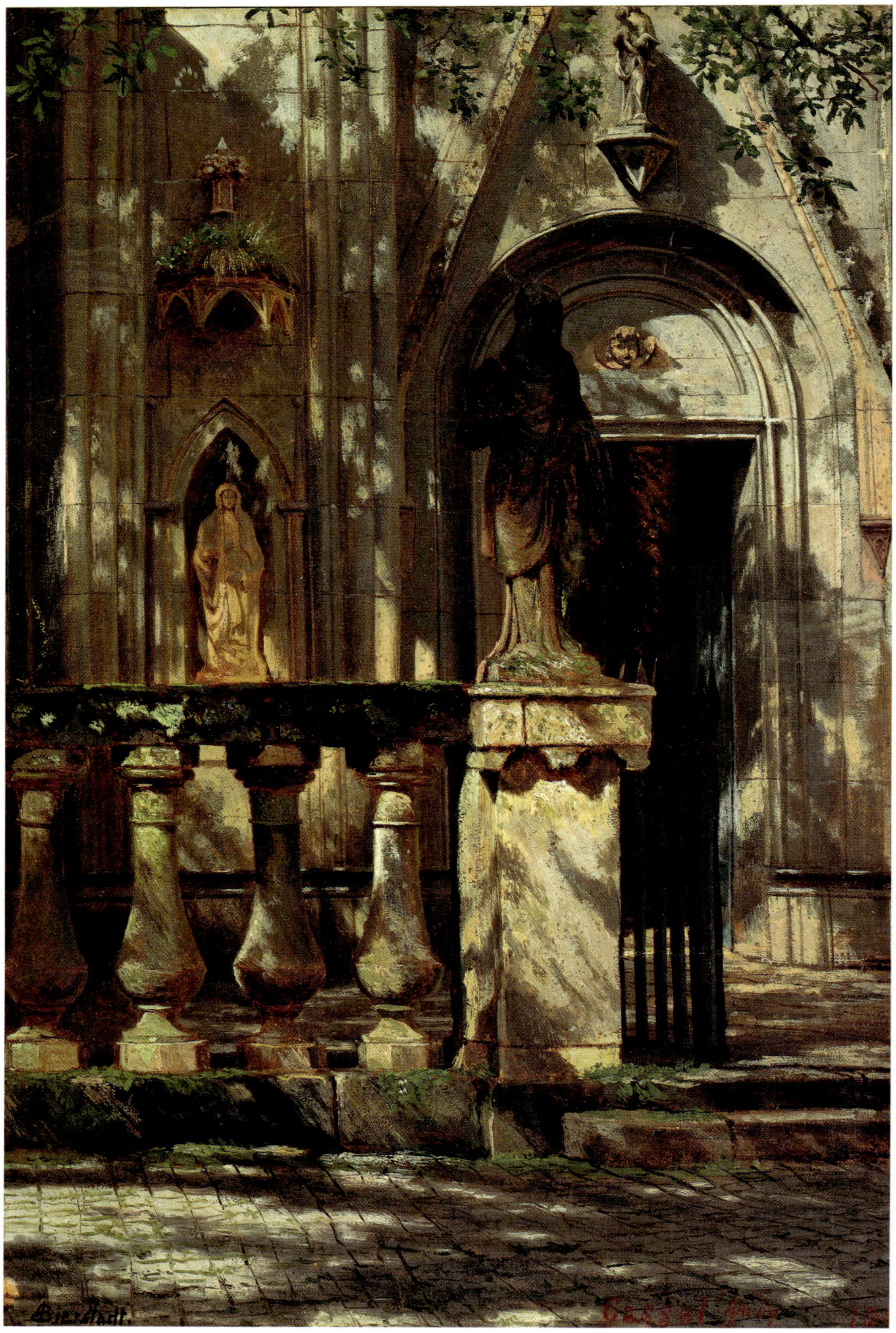

*His next tour, the following year, was through Hesse-Cassel; and, while there, he was much struck, one afternoon, with a beautiful effect of light and shade, on the mossy, massive front and low arched door of a quaint mediaeval church, with a wide-spreading venerable tree beside the wall, and an old woman seated under the gateway. The whole scene was full of mellow, time-hallowed, and consecrated repose. Bierstadt caught, with singular vividness and truth, the details and expression of the scene, so familiar in its materials, yet so eloquent in its "Sunshine and Shadow"—and by this appropriate name which he called the picture which he subsequently elaborated from it, and which first made him generally and favorably known in art. It was so suggestive of the peaceful and picturesque old towns of Europe, that scores of travellers desired to possess it; while the agreeable surprise at so effective and real a picture, whose subject was so unpretending, added to his popularity, and to the merit of the artist as a fond and faithful student of nature.*

Henry T. Tuckerman, *Book of the Artists* (New York: 1867), p. 388

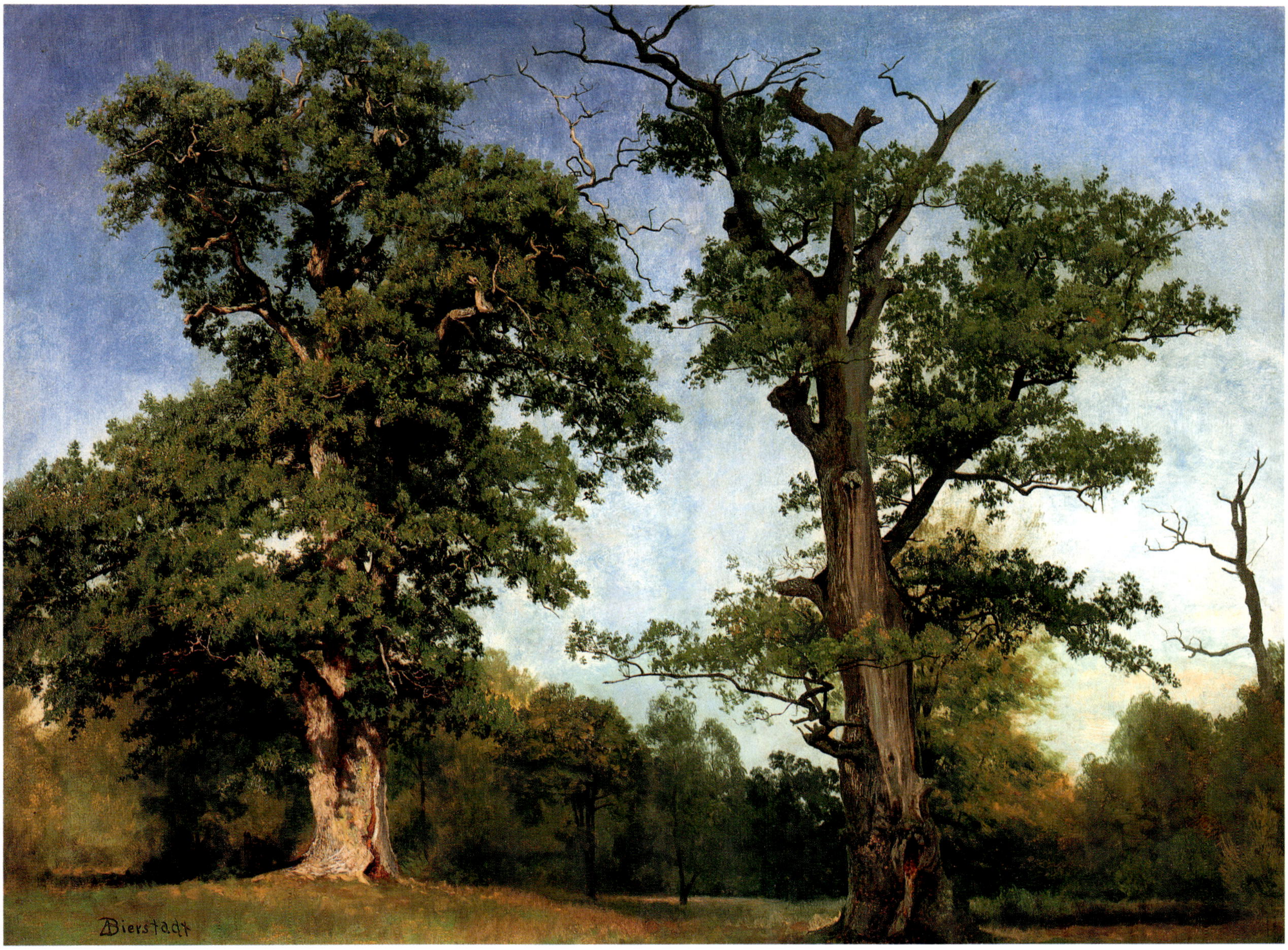

NO. 3

## *Pioneers of the Woods*

Oil on paper mounted on canvas, 19 × 25¾ in. (48.3 × 65.4 cm)

Signed lower left: *ABierstadt*

High Museum of Art, Atlanta, Gift of the Exposition Foundation, Atlanta

*After working in my studio for a few months, copying some of my studies and a few others which he borrowed, he fitted up a paint box, stool and umbrella which he put with a few pieces of clothing into a large knapsack, and shouldering it one cold April morning, he started off to try his luck among the Westphalian peasants where he expected to work. He remained away without a word to us until late autumn when he returned loaded down with innumerable studies of all sorts, oaks, roadsides, meadows, glimpses of water, exteriors of Westphalian cottages, and one very remarkable study of sunlight on the steps of an old church which some years afterwards was turned into a picture that gave him more fame than anything he had ever painted. It was a remarkable summer's work for anybody to do, and for one who had little or no instruction, it was simply marvellous. He set to work in my studio immediately on large canvases composing and putting together parts of studies he had made, and worked with an industry which left no daylight to go to waste.*

Worthington Whittredge, *The Autobiography of Worthington Whittredge* (manuscript completed 1902), ed. John I. H. Baur, in *The Brooklyn Museum Journal* (1942): 26–27

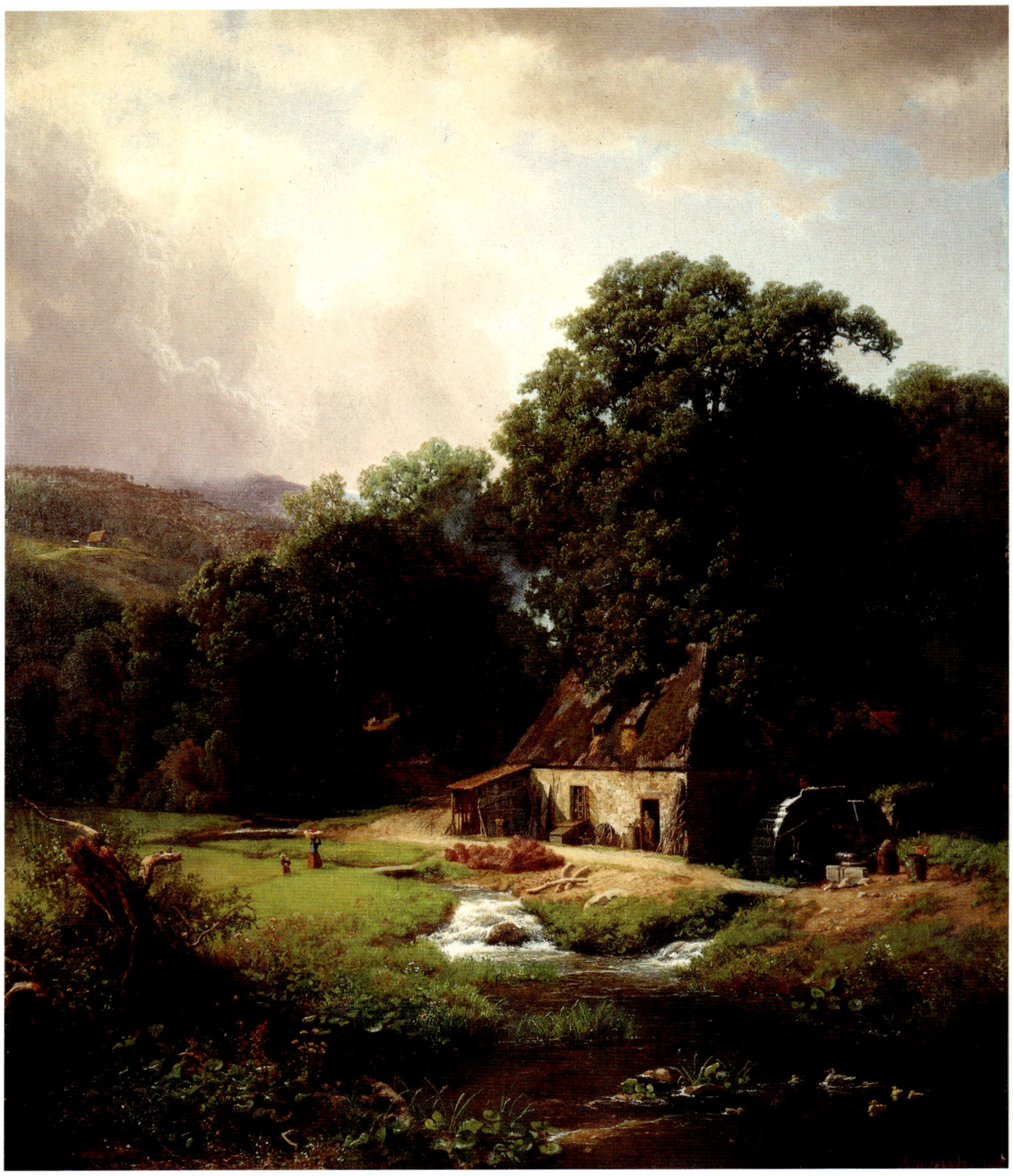

NO. 4

## *The Old Mill*, 1855

Oil on canvas, 43½ × 37¾ in. (110.5 × 95.9 cm)
Signed and dated lower right: *ABierstadt. 1855.*
Private collection

*The work which gives the highest promise of those which Bierstadt executed at this period, is one called "The Old Mill"—which he painted during his first summer, while on a pedestrian tour in Westphalia. It is full of homely truth and rural beauty, and has a rare local fidelity and freshness, and a genial simplicity which remind one of the most naive and candid aspects of life and nature in the Old World.*

Henry T. Tuckerman, *Book of the Artists* (New York: 1867), p. 388

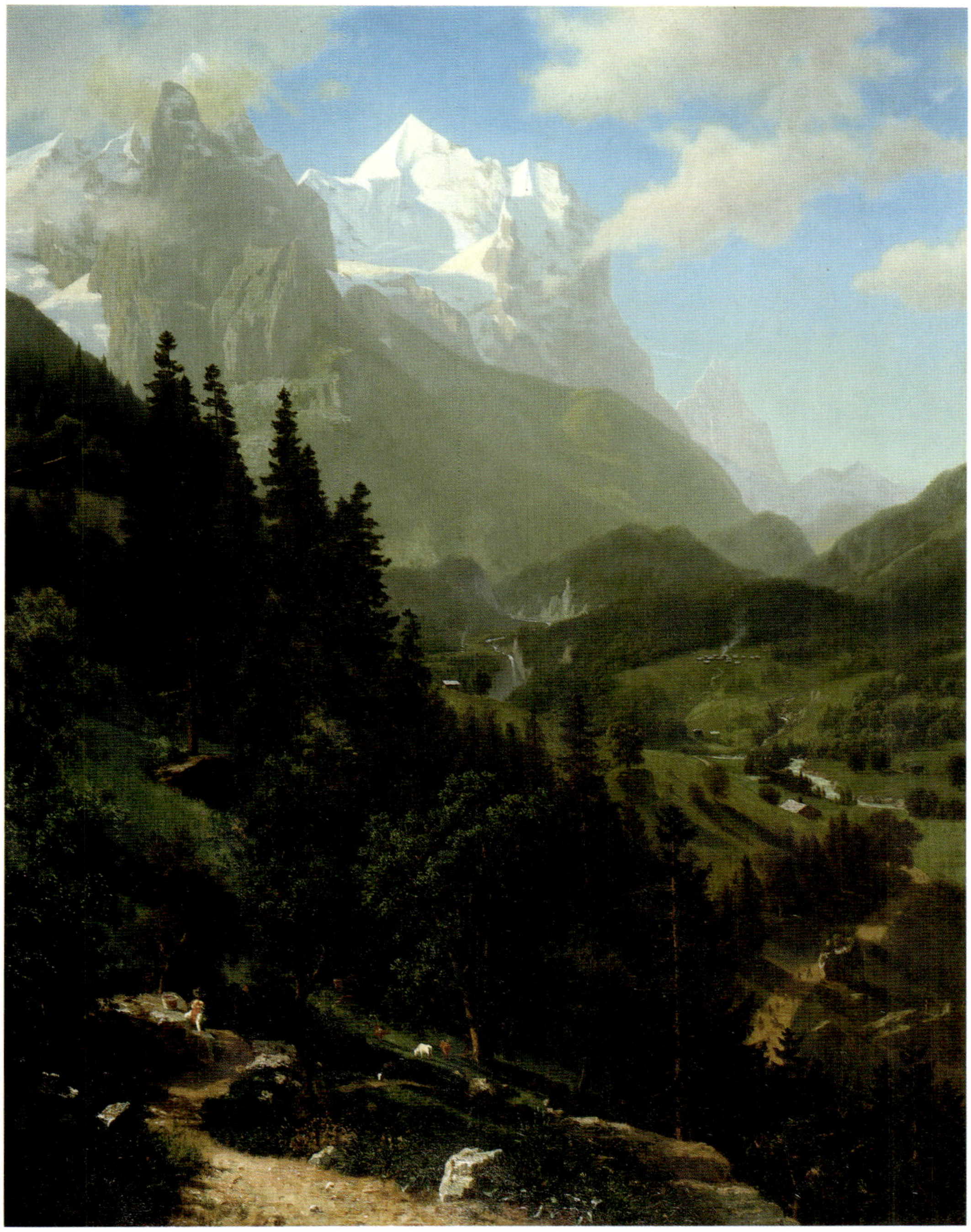

NO. 5

## *The Wetterhorn*, 1857

Oil on canvas, 48⅛ × 38 in. (122.2 × 96.5 cm)
Signed and dated lower left: *A. Bierstadt./1857*
Collection of Dr. Howard P. Diamond

BIERSTADT *(of New Bedford), a young landscapist of fine promise, was also in Switzerland last summer. The principal result of his sojourn there was a very beautiful picture of the "Wetterhorn." It was full of the spirit of Switzerland, and full of the beauty and modesty of nature. This picture was in the "Popolo" exhibition, and was decidedly the finest landscape that appeared there [Rome] during the spring.*

*Crayon*, July 1857, p. 219

*A very pleasing picture has attracted our attention at the establishment of Messrs. Soule, Ward & Co., Summer street. The scene is among the Bernese Alps. . . . The picture is the production, we understand, of Mr. Bierstadt, a young man of American birth, who has pursued the bent of his own genius, and without much formal instruction in the profession he has adopted. The picture does him great credit, and affords a flattering earnest of what he may yet be able to accomplish.*

*Boston Daily Courier*, 22 Jan. 1858

*Mr. Bierstadt, a noble and pleasant young gentleman of indubitable genius, is about to present his claims to the attention of the New York public. He . . . has recently returned from Europe, where he has resided for several years past. While there, he became an intimate friend of Leutze, and spent some time at Dusseldorf. Alpine scenery seems to have concentered much of his interest and toil, as five hundred studies in Switzerland, painted in the open air, sufficiently witness. A view of the Wetterhorn, (upon an upright canvas, three by four feet,) with a splendid distance and a remarkably beautiful foreground, was lately purchased in Boston, and made some sensation among picture-lovers there.*

*Home Journal*, 3 Apr. 1858, p. 7

*The painting which Mr. Bierstadt now offers for exhibition in the Academy of Design, will speak for itself, and, by its quantity and quality of interest, justify its great size—six feet by ten. The spectator stands on a winding road, skirted with rocks, flowers, oaks, and a nooning party of gipsies; to the right is a hamlet, and beneath it flows the river Muotta through a broad and sunny valley, bounded by the village of Brunnen and the turquoise waters of Lake Lucerne; and, beyond the lake, rise the mountains in all their vastness and variety of forest, pasture, precipice, glacier, and peak—heavy-headed Ematten near at hand, then Oberbauen and snowy Uri Rothstok, and finally St. Gotthard, thirty miles off—the fleecy clouds stooping and lifting, trailing and breaking themselves over and among the summits. The infinitude of detailed interest in the nearer mountains, and the fine atmospheric effects which throw off, and mass together, and sublime all the details, are very noticeable. Fifty studies in the open air were made for this picture.*

*Home Journal*, 3 Apr. 1858, p. 7

*We advise you . . . to step as far back as the breadth of the room permits, and taking your place opposite no. 99,* Lake Lucerne, *by Albert Bierstadt, look at it long and earnestly, or you will not compass its exceeding merit. . . . But the water is reached, and skipped over, and we should have beyond it the* sine qua non *of such a view, the majesty and the loveliness of the Alps. For these we look in vain. . . . [I]t seems to us that Mr. Bierstadt therefore has totally failed in conveying the effect of what should be the crowning glory of his picture. His mountain ranges are neither near, nor remote; and for what is called a middle distance they are impracticable, from their overwhelming proportions. He has neither given the boldness and startling effigies of palpable light, nor veiled them in thick curtains of mist. The best thing he can do, after achieving so fine a frame as his foreground, is to repaint his Alpine portions from top to bottom and from end to end. With moderate success in that essential, he would have a very fine work to boast of. At any rate, we are glad to welcome an artist who boldly grapples with difficulties on so large a scale. It is all nonsense to say that the Alps can't be painted. As much used to be said of Niagara; but Mr. Church exposed [that] absurdity. . . .*

*Albion*, 24 Apr. 1858, p. 201

*Bierstadt's* Lake Lucerne *invites study; the foreground is indicative of great command of landscape elements. The trees are admirably drawn, and the road and grass finely painted. The same ability on a smaller scale, would be more readily appreciated.*

*Crayon*, May 1858, p. 147

*The lovers of natural scenery who cannot visit the Alps, will acknowledge themselves somewhat indemnified by a view of Bierstadt's magnificent painting of Swiss scenery, now exhibited at the Athenaeum. The scene is Lake Lucerne and its environs, sketched by the artist from nature, during his residence in Switzerland.*

*In passing through the picture gallery, we observe various paintings by the same artist;—here a Swiss hamlet, and there a pastoral scene; now a beautiful lake, and then an Alpine valley; but in the picture of Lake Lucerne, the broad view of the artist comprehends and groups them all—hill and valley, forest and ravine, pastoral scene and rustic hamlet, limpid lake, towering mountain and misty cloud.*

*Boston Transcript*, 11 Sept. 1858

*The "crack" picture now, is entitled Lake Lucerne; it is by Bierstadt, a young American artist, we are informed, who has arisen up, of a sudden amongst us,—astonishing even our foremost artists with his bold strides. This picture is a magnificent effort, and for a young artist it is immense. We sat gazing upon it until we were nearly lost in its beauties. The pure sweet sky mingling with the soft, dim outlines of distant hills, far, far away as we could think! The giant mountains crested with snow-white clouds; the misty atmosphere that hangs midway over and round about their huge sides; the stately and graceful trees, rich in luxuriant foliage; the sparkling sun-light, so happily dispensed throughout the whole landscape, and so well balanced by the deepening shadows from invisible clouds; the voluptuous foreground, teeming with rich grass, heather, leaves and wild flowers, occasionally relieved with sharp rocks, "Grey with the moss of ages;" all rejoicing and glittering in the garish sun-light that shimmers down upon them in a baptism of golden glory! As we first observed, we came near losing ourself as we gazed upon the rich scene; but as our eye caught sight of the tiny steamer in the distant waters, and finally rested upon the group of gipsies in the middle foreground on the left, we soon came down to our sobermindedness. Ah! "Who from such a dream would wake!"*

*Boston Post*, 20 Sept. 1858

*Mr. Bierstadt's picture of "Lake Lucerne," as might be expected, has attracted much notice at the exhibition now open at the Boston Athenaeum. In fact, it is rated by an intelligent critic in the* Post *of that city, as the "crack" picture, a term rather out of place, but denoting the approbation of the writer.*

*Mercury*, New Bedford, 23 Sept. 1858

*Mr. Bierstadt has disposed of his oil painting of "Lake Lucerne" to a gentleman in Boston for the sum of $925.*

*Mercury*, New Bedford, 14 Dec. 1858

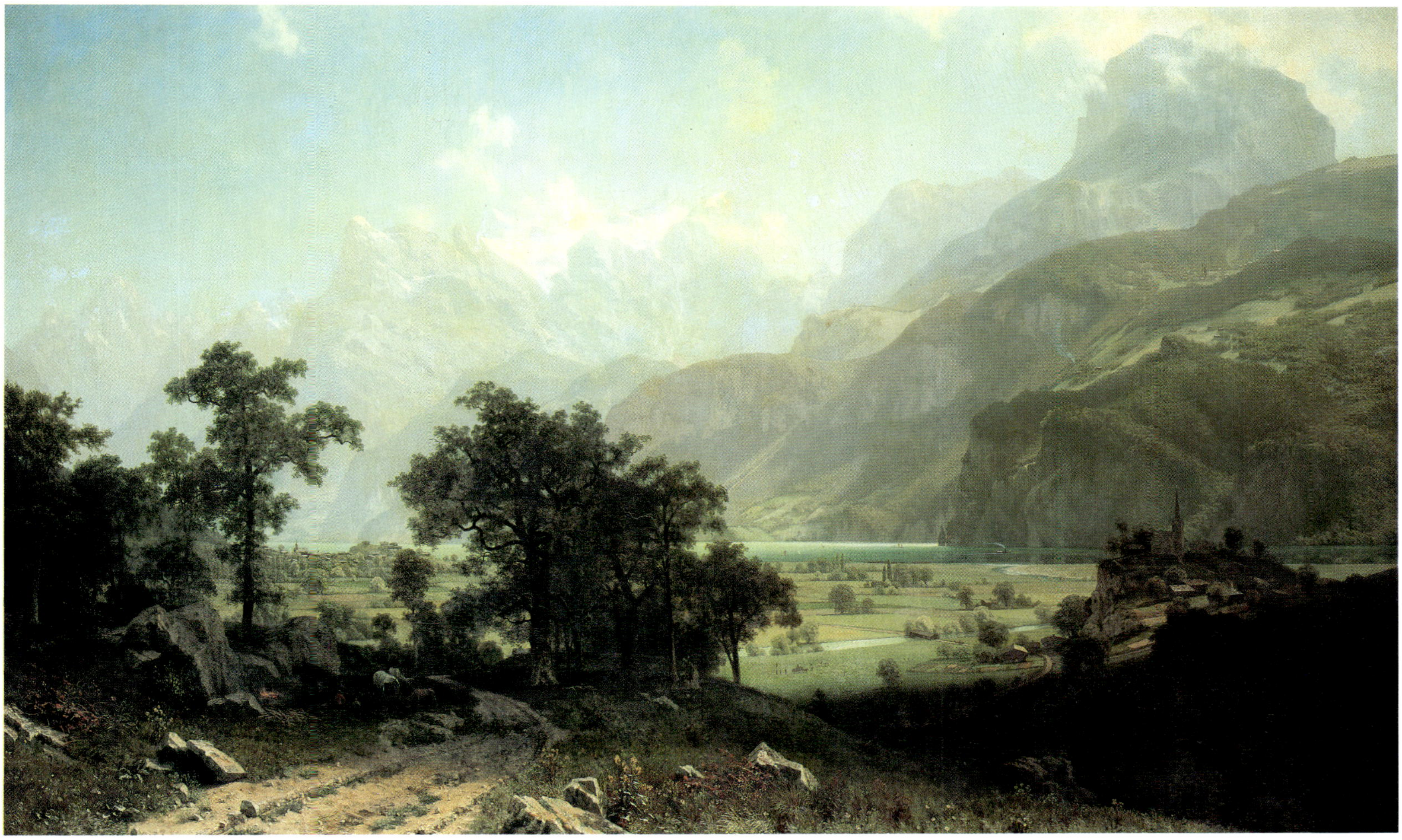

NO. 6

*Lake Lucerne (Switzerland)*, 1858

Oil on canvas, 72 × 120 in. (182.9 × 304.8 cm)

Signed and dated lower right: *ABierstadt/1858*

National Gallery of Art, Washington, D.C.

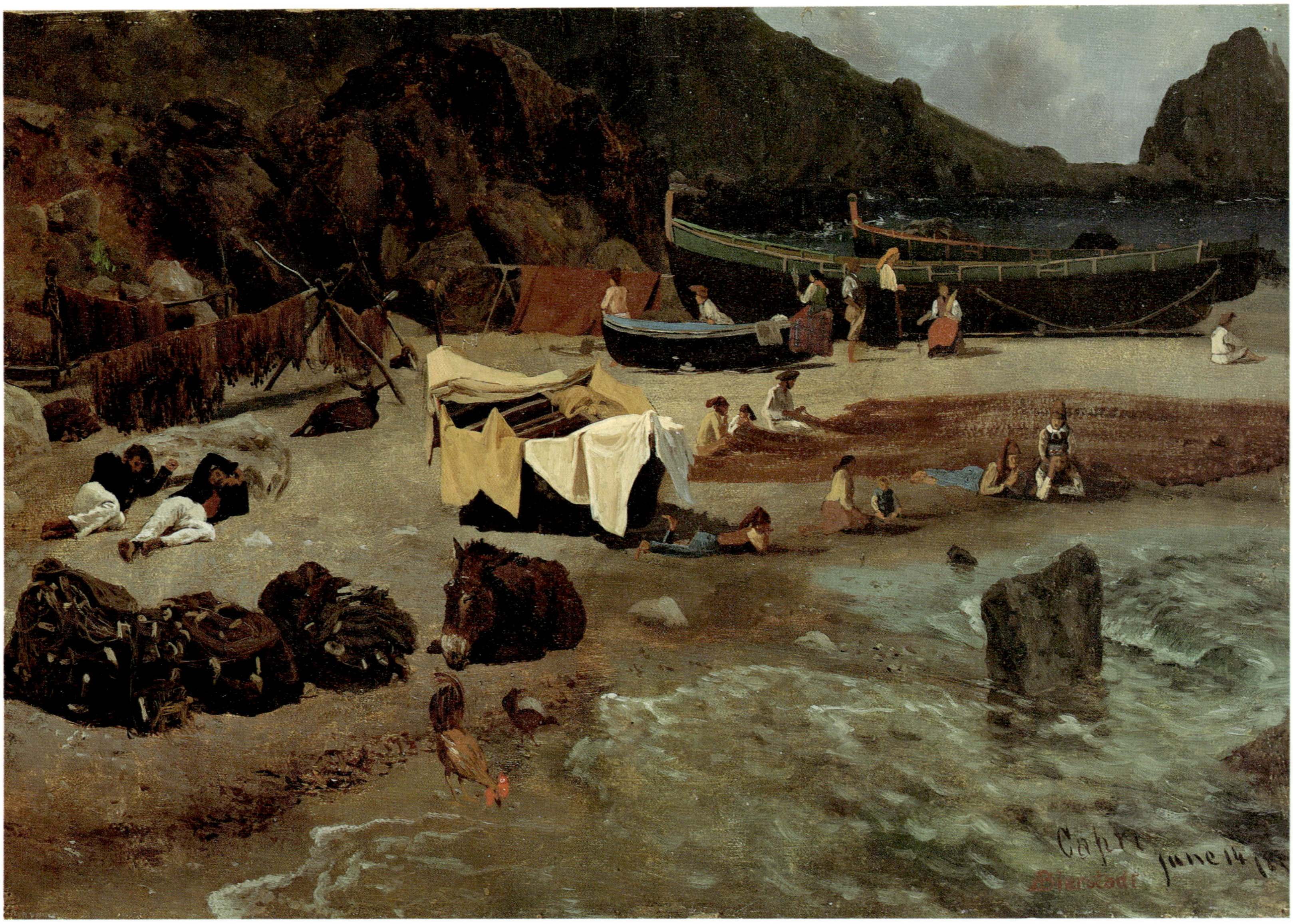

NO. 7

## *Fishing Boats at Capri,* 1857

Oil on paper mounted on canvas, 13½ × 19½ in. (34.3 × 49.5 cm)

Signed and dated lower right: *Capri/june 14, 1857/ABierstadt*

Museum of Fine Arts, Boston, Gift of Martha C. Karolik for the Karolik Collection of American Paintings, 1815–1865

*June First, went down to the Piccola Marina. The Coast is fine from here. The groups of fishermen with their boats and nets on the little beach are very picturesque. Returning, met our fair friends. In the afternoon climbed the cliff to Ana Capri, the castle of Barbarosa, and the telegraph station. Eve[.] wrote Whitridge* [sic]. . . .

*Sketched all day at the "Piccola Marina". We have spent fifteen days sketching there. Since the 15th we have been at the Marina Grande sketching boats, figures etc. We spend the day on the shore. Our lunch is brought down to us every day on the head of a brown girl who has bright eyes and a chubby face. She has a most killing way of saying "addio" when she goes away. We take a bath in the bright sea every day.*

Sanford Robinson Gifford (traveling with Bierstadt) to his mother, 25 June 1857, SRG Letters

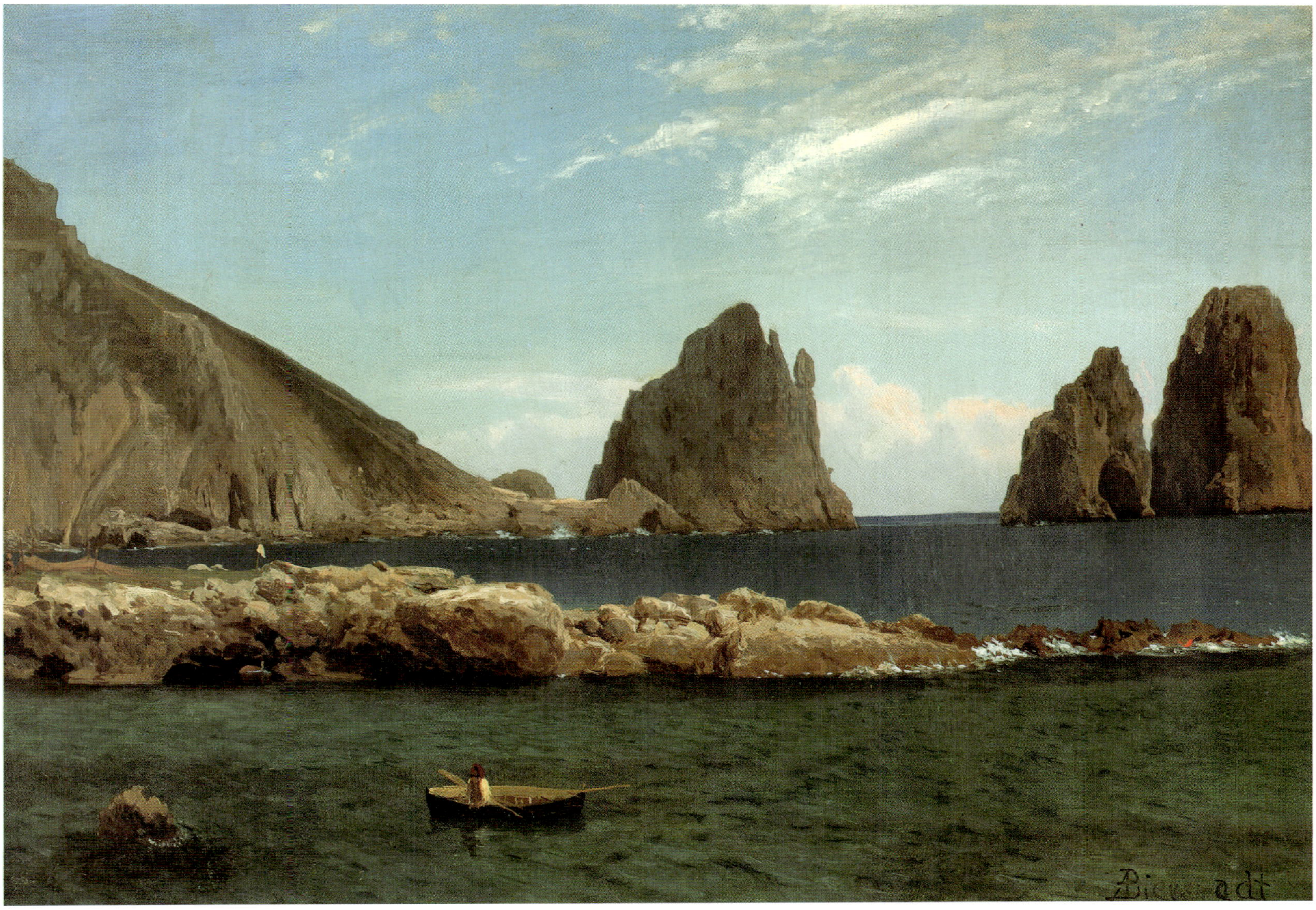


NO. 8

## *Capri*, c. 1857

Oil on paper mounted on masonite, 13¼ × 18¾ in. (33.6 × 47.6 cm)

Signed lower right: *ABierstadt*

Garzoli Gallery, San Rafael, California

*The island [Capri] is about four miles long, and ten around. The shores are very precipitous. There are only two places to land—the Marina Grande on the Naples side, and the Piccola Marina on the other. The village of Capri is on the top of the Ridge between them. Ana Capri is on the high table-land. The only access to it is by 500 or 600 steps cut in the face of the cliff. Took a walk along the wild broken precipice of the south side. The rock is of limestone, and in this part of the island takes the form of "aiguilles". Natural arches and grottos abound. . . . On the south shore, rising out of the sea, are three tall, isolated cliffs called the Faraglioni. Under one of them is a great natural arch, under which boats pass.*

Sanford Robinson Gifford (traveling with Bierstadt) to his mother, 25 June 1857, SRG Letters

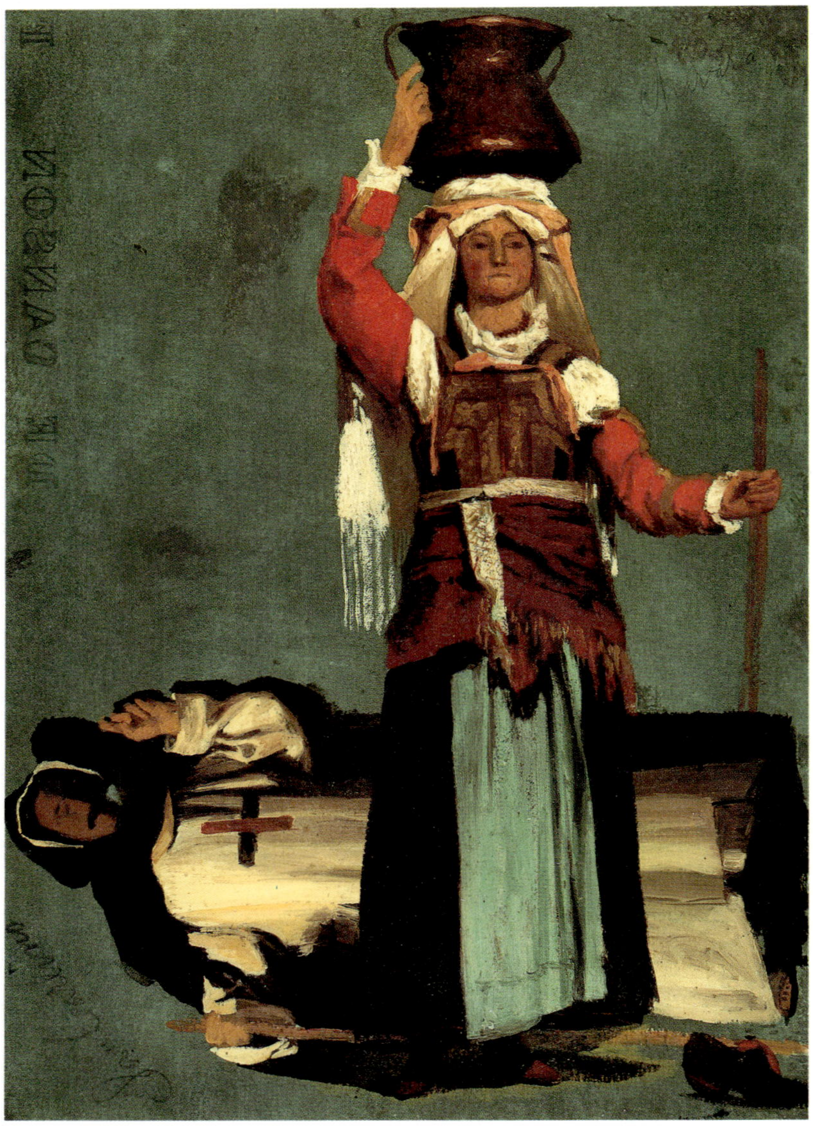

NO. 9

*Italian Costume Studies*

Oil on paper mounted on board, 11¾ × 8½ in. (29.8 × 21.6 cm)

Unsigned

Inscribed lower left: *San Carlino*

Inscribed upper right: *Chavara*

Elliott Galleries, New York

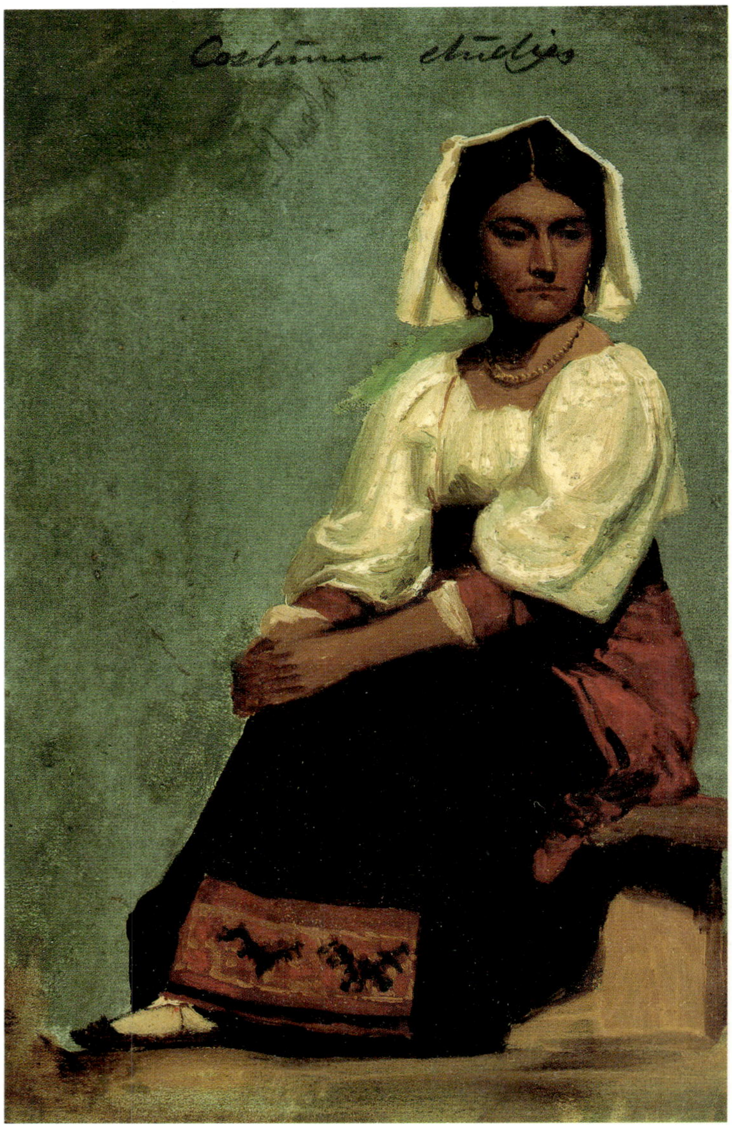

NO. 10

*Costume Study of Seated Woman*

Oil on paper mounted on board, 8¾ × 5¾ in. (22.2 × 14.6 cm)

Unsigned

Inscribed top center: *Costume studies*

Elliott Galleries, New York

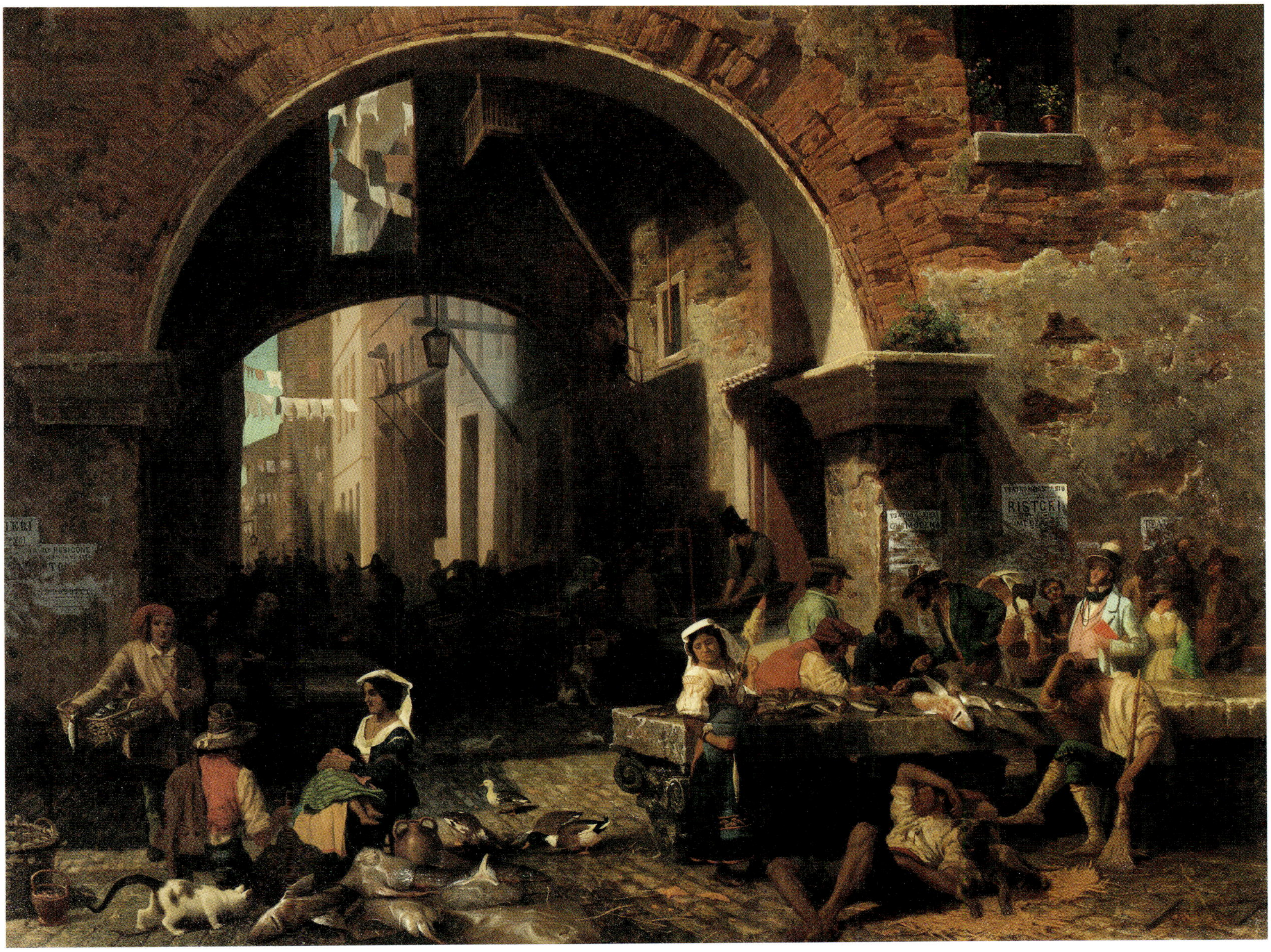

NO. 11

## *The Arch of Octavius (The Roman Fish Market)*, 1858

Oil on canvas, 28½ × 37½ in. (72.4 × 95.2 cm)

Signed lower right: *ABierstadt*

The Fine Arts Museums of San Francisco, Gift of Mr. and Mrs. John D. Rockefeller 3rd

*Roman Fish Market . . . is a picture of great merit. The Octavian Arch is a correct and well finished work. The figures are full of expression, the postures natural, the light well distributed, and the costumes scrupulously preserved. In a word this picture is a little jewel.*

*New Bedford Standard*, 6 Aug. 1858

*Among the works which our artist elaborated from his careful European studies are, a most effective picture of the "Bay of Sorrento," one of "The Arch of Octavian," a "Street Scene in Rome," and "Lake Lucerne;" each of which for accuracy of the local details . . . is an eloquent epitome of its subject, and transports the spectator to the fairest environs of Naples, to the heart of Switzerland, or to the centre of the Eternal City.*

Henry T. Tuckerman, *Book of the Artists* (New York: 1867), p. 388

*Step under this arch and look up that narrow, dirty, but picturesque street on the left—that is the Pescheria. Stone slabs, broken and grappled by iron hooks, stretch out on either side into the street, and usurp it so as to leave no carriageable way between them. If it be market-day you will see them covered with every kind of fishes. Green crusty lobsters, squirming crawfish all alive, heaps of red mullet, baskets of little shining sardines, large spigole, sprawling, deformed cuttlefish—in a word, all the inhabitants of the Mediterranean are there exposed for sale; while the fisherman, standing behind them, slashes [sic] now and then a bucket of water over the benches and cries out his store.*

William Wetmore Story, *Roba di Roma* (London: 1864), p. 312

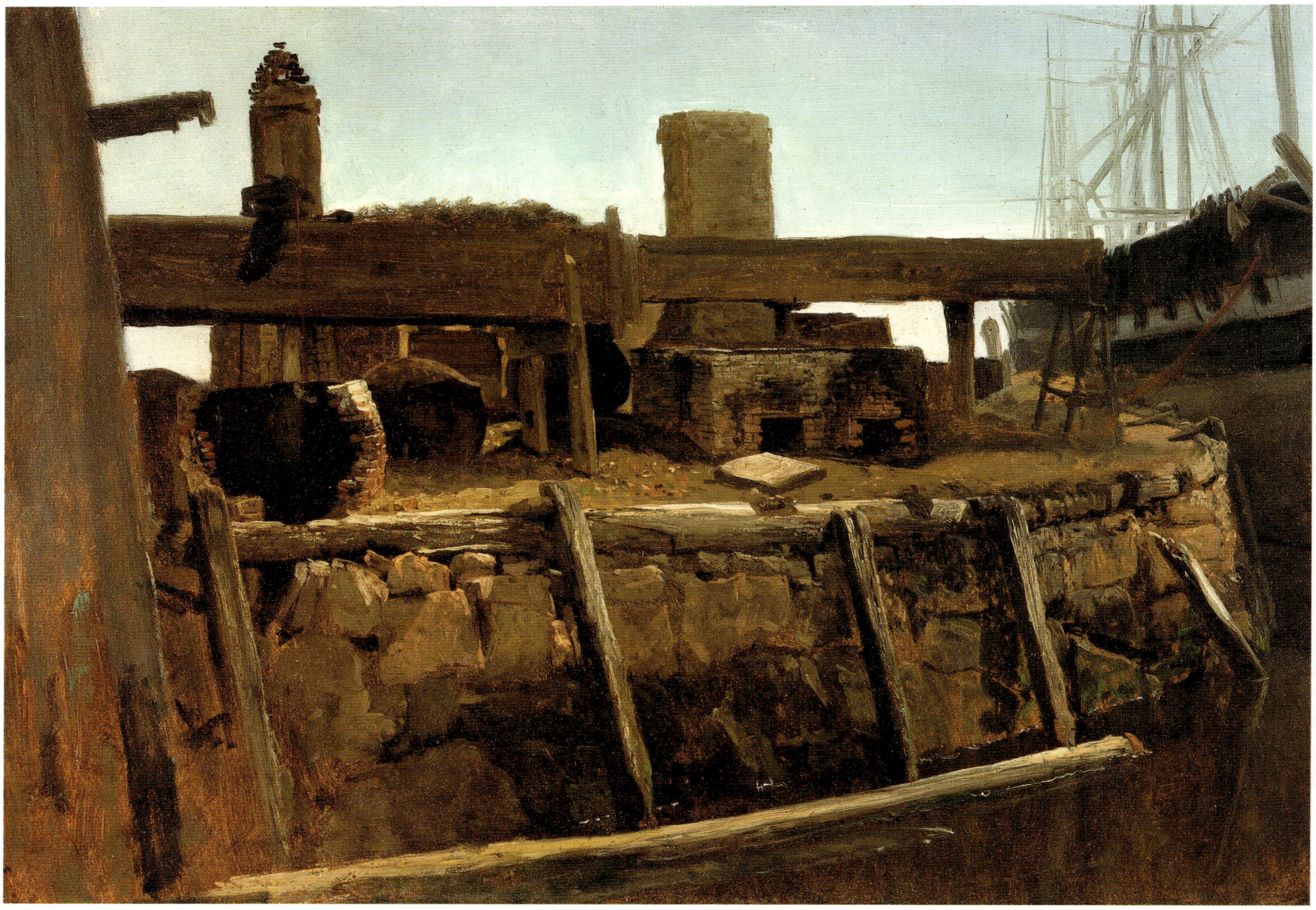

NO. 12

*Wharf Scene with Ship at Dock*

Oil on paper mounted on board, 13¼ × 19¼ in. (33.6 × 48.9 cm)

Unsigned

Elliott Galleries, New York

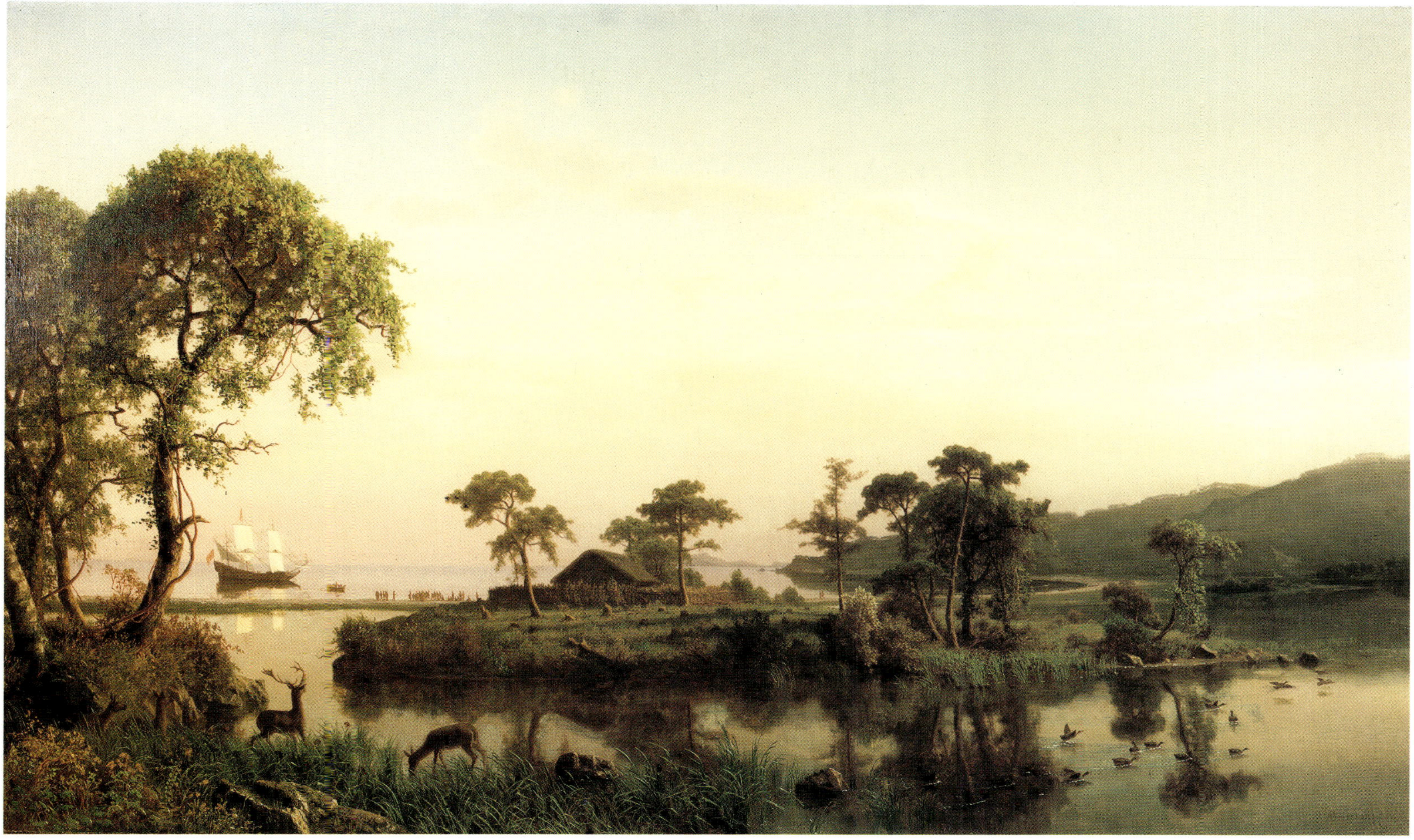

NO. 13

## *Gosnold at Cuttyhunk, 1602,* 1858

Oil on canvas, 30¼ × 50⅝ in. (76.8 × 128.6 cm)

Signed and dated lower right: *ABierstadt/1858*

The Whaling Museum, New Bedford, Massachusetts, Gift of Emma B. Hathaway, 1904

*A Fine Picture—Critics and persons of cultivated and refined tastes, speak very highly of Bierstadt's new picture. . . . The picture represents Gosnold putting off from his ship in a boat to land on the island; the deer then numerous upon the Elizabeth Islands, have come to the pond to drink; a flock of wild fowl are frightened from the shore; a log house rises up . . . ; on the beach are the Indians and their canoes, and beyond is the Vineyard Sound. The picture is very faithful, and abounds in artistic merit, reflecting high credit upon the genius of its painter. It was painted for Thomas Nye, Jr., who owns the locality described.*

*New Bedford Standard*, 1 Jan. 1859

*The picture gallery of the Boston* Athenaeum *was opened on Wednesday. Bierstadt, of this city, has several paintings in it, among them, says the* Bee, *one which attracts unusual attention. "It is a scene representing an event in the early history of New England—a landing of Englishmen and their reception on the sea shore by the Indians. It is like all of this artist's efforts, elaborate, rich, warm and sunny—it is almost tropical—too much so far for a New England scene; but notwithstanding that it is a picture to be admired. The crescent shaped shore of the sea, the ripples creeping up the beach—the island in the middle ground, with its luxuriant grass, the water fowls rising from the water, the stag who sniffs the air, . . . the meeting of the Englishmen in their steeple crowned hats with the Indians in their uncouth habiliments, the ship lying off the land, are all finely produced.*

*New Bedford Standard*, 5 Apr. 1859

# 1859–1862

# *Rocky Mountain Reconnaissance*

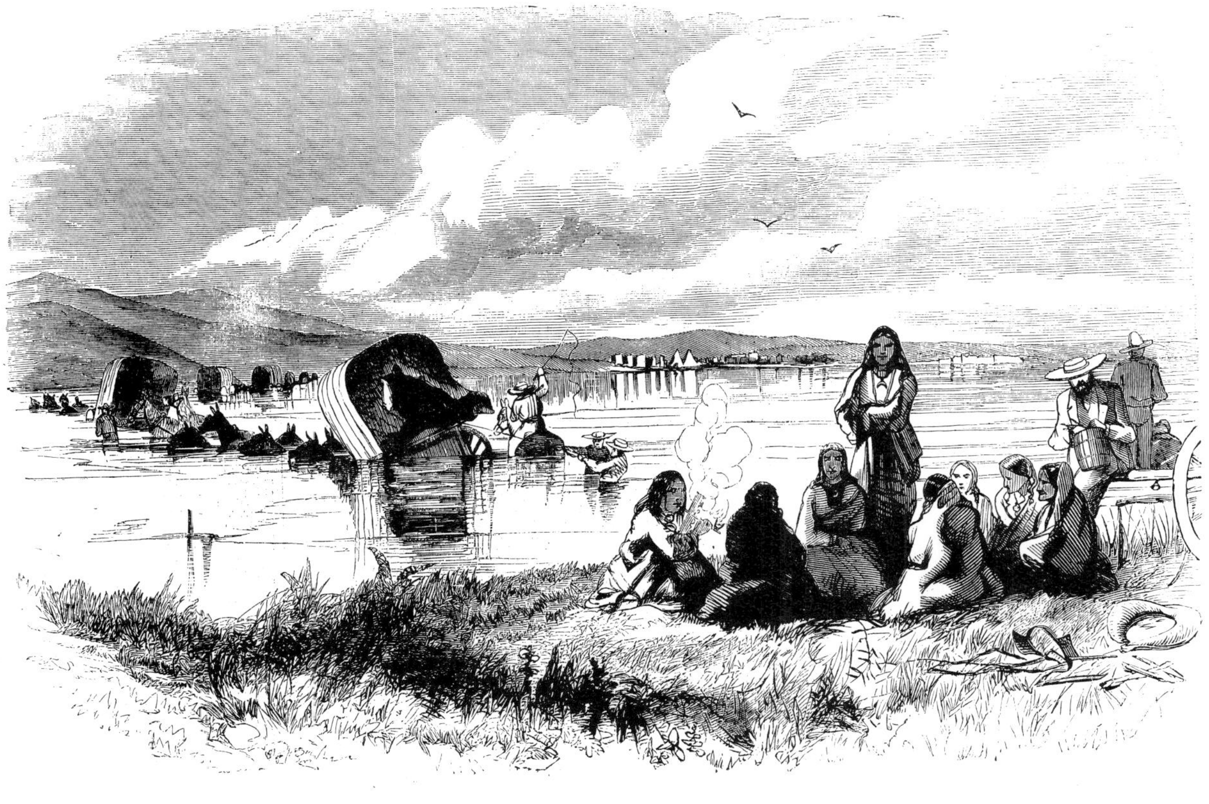

AS EARLY AS December 1858, Bierstadt had made plans to travel west, for the *Crayon* reported that the young artist was leaving shortly for the Rocky Mountains, where he intended "to remain a couple of years, making sketches of the scenery, and studying the manners and customs of the Indians" (Chronology, 15 Dec. 1858). Bierstadt did not actually set out on his journey, however, until April 1859, when he and fellow artist Francis Shedd Frost traveled to Saint Joseph, Missouri, where they joined Frederick W. Lander's survey party bound for the Rocky Mountains. It was this overland journey that changed the course of Bierstadt's career.

On the trail several months, Bierstadt sent letters to a New Bedford newspaper detailing the survey party's day-to-day progress on the road to El Dorado. In addition to keeping friends and family informed, Bierstadt's letters fanned interest in the distant adventures of a fellow townsman. As the young artist undoubtedly knew, such interest could only help future sales.

Although the Lander party traveled as far west as California, Bierstadt and Frost went no farther than South Pass on the Continental Divide. From this Rocky Mountain vantage point, Bierstadt completed a number of studies of the Wind River and Wasatch ranges, as well as the Black Hills. Hoping to avoid the "fall deluge" that annually turned the plains into mud, Bierstadt and Frost turned back sometime early in August. Inexperienced at living off the land, the two greenhorns ran short of rations and were forced to make do with bread and water for several days. An able publicist, Bierstadt later used such tales of peril and deprivation to great advantage, transforming his western sketching trips into romantic adventures.

By 18 September 1859, Bierstadt had returned to New Bedford with a full complement of sketches, photographs, and Indian artifacts. Within three months, however, he had moved to New York and taken a studio in the Tenth Street Studio Building, joining Emanuel Leutze, Worthington Whittredge, Sanford Robinson Gifford, and William Haseltine—all friends from his student days in Düsseldorf. Also working in the Studio Building was Frederic Church, the most celebrated landscape painter of the day. An accomplished businessman as well as a talented artist, Church had already achieved the success to which Bierstadt aspired.

Shortly after his arrival in New York, Bierstadt began exhibiting paintings with Rocky Mountain subjects. The pictures drew considerable attention, for they addressed long-standing questions about the western landscape. Although frequently described by government surveyors, travelers, and writers, the West still awaited its visual historian.

Bierstadt made his bid for that title in March 1860, when he unveiled *Base of the Rocky Mountains, Laramie Peak* (unlocated), his first major Rocky Mountain picture. In April 1860, he contributed the painting to the Annual Exhibition at the National Academy of Design, where it was described by one reviewer as the "*piece de resistance*."

Although he had hoped to travel west again in 1860, Bierstadt's plans did not materialize. Instead, he journeyed to the White Mountains, where he helped his brothers, both photographers, select picturesque views for photographs. Bierstadt remained close to Charles and Edward all of his adult life. It now seems clear that following the destruction of their woodworking shop in 1859, it was Albert who encouraged them to open a photography studio and Albert who turned over the glass-plate stereographs he had secured on the Lander expedition. As photographers and publishers, the Bierstadt brothers went on to distinguish themselves, receiving a number of competitive medals for their work.

In March 1861, Bierstadt contributed four paintings to the Annual Exhibition at the National Academy of Design; all were favorably received. The following month, however, the exhibition was closed early when the academy building was needed for military purposes. The Civil War had begun. Although several of Bierstadt's colleagues in the Studio Building quickly enlisted in the Union army, Bierstadt did not.

Accompanied again by members of his family, Bierstadt returned to the White Mountains in September 1861. That same fall, Edward Bierstadt, recognizing a business opportunity in war-related photographs, obtained permission to set up a temporary photography studio near Washington, D.C. Although early sales of cartes de visite and other photographs to Union soldiers camped nearby were brisk, family matters in New Bedford forced him to close the studio only a few weeks after he began the operation.

In mid-October 1861, perhaps while Edward was still working near Washington, Albert Bierstadt and Emanuel Leutze obtained five-day passes to visit Union troops camped on both sides of the Potomac. Following this tour, Bierstadt produced *Guerrilla Warfare (Picket Duty in Virginia)*, 1862 (No. 30), a small picture that may be based on photographs taken by his brother. It is one of the few paintings in which Bierstadt addressed the war in an overt manner.

The war took a more personal turn for Bierstadt in March 1862, when Frederick W. Lander, with whom he had traveled west in 1859, died of complications from a wound received in battle. Within months of Lander's death, Bierstadt offered his own memorial when he titled his most important early western landscape *The Rocky Mountains, Lander's Peak* (No. 37).

In the spring of 1862, Bierstadt made another attempt to return west when he sought permission to travel under the protection of U.S. government troops. Writing to Senator Charles Sumner, he proposed joining an army regiment already scheduled to journey cross-country to protect emigrants and the mails. In his letter, Bierstadt stated that four students from Harvard University wished to accompany him, as did fellow artist William H. Beard and John Hay, assistant secretary to President Lincoln. Despite Sumner's endorsement, Secretary of War Edwin M. Stanton denied Bierstadt's request. After learning that overland travel without an escort would be too risky because of Indian unrest, Bierstadt explored the possibility of taking a steamer up the Missouri River to Fort Pierce. For reasons that are not presently clear, however, he abandoned all plans to travel west in 1862.

Meanwhile, the war continued unabated, with both sides suffering heavy losses at the Second Battle of Bull Run late in August and again at Antietam in September. The full horror of the conflict became evident when Mathew Brady's photographs of the dead at Antietam were placed on exhibition in New York. Standing in sharp contrast to such grim images were the mammoth plate photographs of California scenery by Carleton Watkins that were placed on view at Goupil's gallery in December 1862. Bierstadt is known to have seen the Watkins photographs at Goupil's. He may, in fact, have recognized in them scenery perfectly suited to his brush, for five months later he departed New York for California.

# CHRONOLOGY

1859

Directory listing: Bierstadt, Albert, artist, room 15 Ricketson Block, boards 13 Mill. (New Bedford City Directory, 1859)

**1 Jan.** Praise for Bierstadt's "new picture," *Gosnold at Cuttyhunk, 1602* (No. 13), painted for Thomas Nye, Jr. (*New Bedford Standard*, 1 Jan. 1859)

**3 Jan.** Washington Art Association exhibition opens in the nation's capital. Bierstadt exhibits *Brunnen*, *Lake Lucerne* and *Autumn, Westphalia*. (Cobb 1963–65, p. 169)

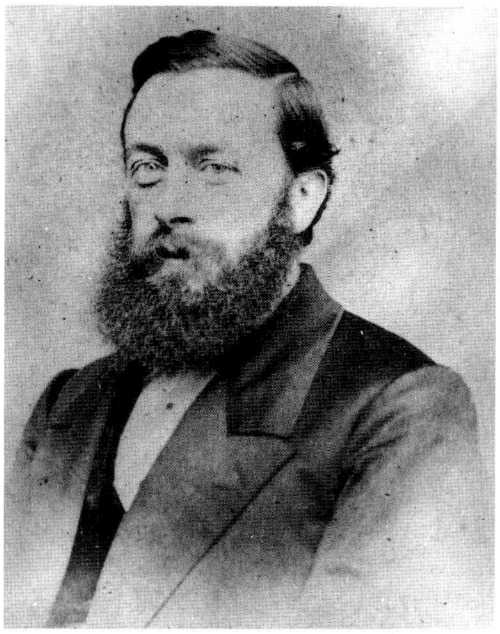

*Albert Bierstadt*, c. 1859. Photograph. The Whaling Museum, New Bedford, Massachusetts.

**6 Jan.** First Artists' Reception held in Boston takes place at Mercantile Hall. The *Home Journal* later reported that Bierstadt "realized hundreds at the first *soiree*." (*Boston Transcript*, 21 Jan. 1859; *Home Journal*, 19 Mar. 1859)

**7 Jan.** It is reported that Bierstadt is about to start for the Rocky Mountains, "to study the scenery of that wild region, and the picturesque facts of Indian life, with reference to a series of large pictures. He expects to remain more than one year. . . ." (*Mercury*, New Bedford, 7 Jan. 1859)

*Gosnold at Cuttyhunk, 1602* is on view at John Hopkins's music store in New Bedford. (*Mercury*, New Bedford, 7 Jan. 1859)

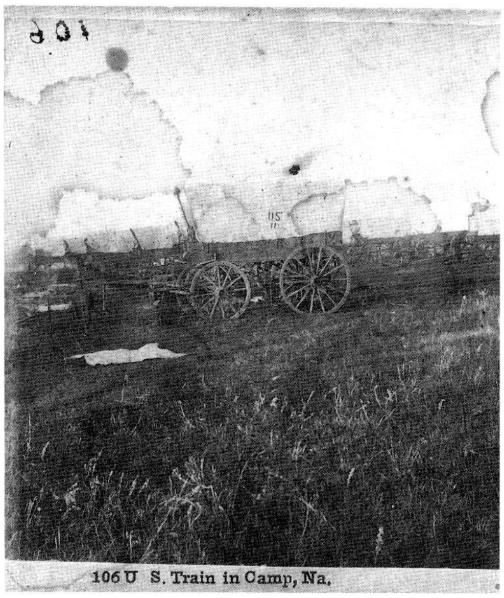


Albert Bierstadt. *U.S. Train in Camp, Na.* [Nebraska], 1859. Stereograph. Collection of Wilfred Thompson, courtesy of Leonard A. Walle.

**19 Mar.** According to the *Home Journal*, Bierstadt, "a rising landscape painter," is active in promoting the establishment of an art school in Boston modeled on the Düsseldorf Academy. "Several wealthy patrons of Art in Boston have offered to erect a studio-building and to give some munificent commissions, particularly to Leutze." The journal reports that "the last two months brought [Bierstadt] thousands in hand and in commission." (*Home Journal*, 19 Mar. 1859)

**8 Apr.** In preparation for his trip west, Bierstadt secures from John B. Floyd, secretary of war, a letter of introduction to "the commanders of such military posts as he may visit" while accompanying Frederick W. Lander's wagon-road survey party. (Photograph of original letter, International Museum of Photography at George Eastman House, Rochester, N.Y.)

**13 Apr.–25 June** NAD Annual Exhibition open to public. Bierstadt exhibits eight works: *View Near Newport; View Near Minden, Westphalia; The Bernese Alps, as Seen Near Kusnach; The Temple of Paestum* (*Ruins of Paestum*, p. 123); *Mt. Washington from Shelburne, N.H.; St. Peters and the Castle of St. Angelo—Sunset; The Arch of Octavius (The Roman Fish Market)* (No. 11); *Capri, Bay of Naples*. (Cummings 1969, pp. 273, 356; Cowdrey 1943, pp. 32–33; Catalogue, NAD, 1859, pp. 26, 31, 35, 40–42)

**15 Apr.** "Messrs. Bierstadt and [Francis Shedd] Frost have just set out for a sketching tour among the Rocky Mountains. They intend to join Colonel Lander's wagon train at St. Louis, and will probably be gone eight or ten months." (Letter dated 15 Apr., in *Crayon*, May 1859, pp. 161–62)

**25 Apr.** *View on the Weser* and a painting of "a fountain in a grove" by Bierstadt are on view at Hopkins's music store. (*Mercury*, New Bedford, 25 Apr. 1859)

Bierstadt exhibits *Lake Lucerne (Switzerland)* (No. 6), *Village of Brunnen*, and *View Near Minden, Westphalia* at the Pennsylvania Academy of the Fine Arts, Philadelphia. (*Philadelphia Daily News*, 26, 28 Apr. 1862; Rutledge 1955, p. 25)

**27 Apr.** From Saint Joseph, Missouri, Bierstadt writes friends in New Bedford: "This place reminds me very much of some Italian towns, so many mules and curious waggons and picturesque dresses. . . . I think in about six months I shall feel like painting pictures again. . . ." (Bierstadt to My Dear Friends, Manuscript Collection, Haverford College Library, Haverford, Pa.)

Frederic Church's *Heart of the Andes* (Fig. 40) completed; exhibited publicly for the first time at Lyric Hall in New York. (Kelly et al. 1989, p. 164)

**29 Apr.–23 May** *Heart of the Andes* on exhibition at the Tenth Street Studio Building; admission charge: 25 cents, receipts often $100 a day. Painting later sold for $10,000 to William T. Blodgett. (Kelly et al. 1989, p. 164; Blaugrund 1987, p. 105)

**6 May** Bierstadt describes the initial stages of the Lander expedition as plagued by rain and mud. He and Frost walk ahead of their mired wagon and spend the night in Troy,

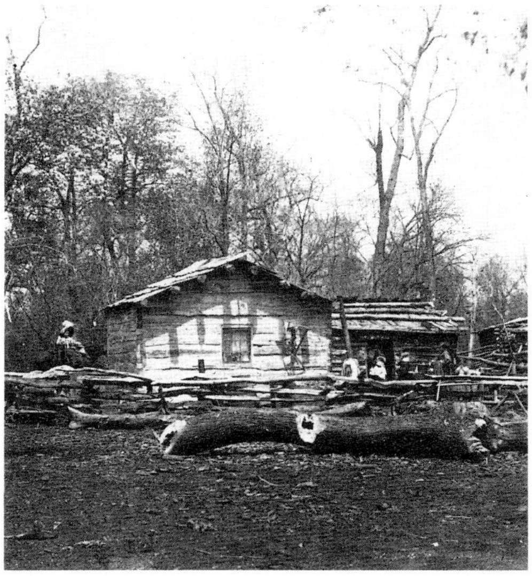

Albert Bierstadt. *Near Troy, Kansas*, 1859. Stereograph. Collection of Wilfred Thompson, courtesy of Leonard A. Walle.

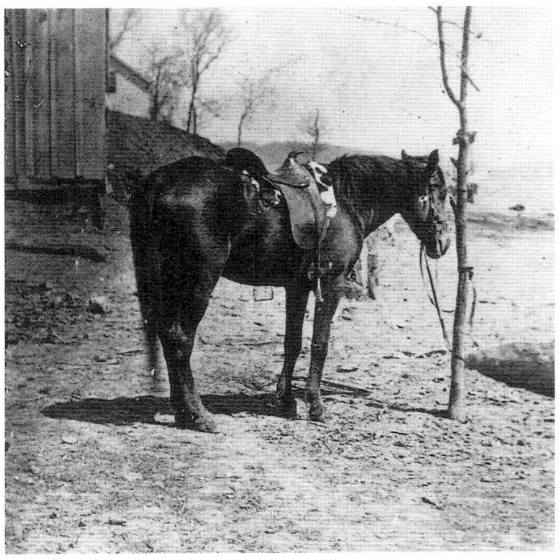

Albert Bierstadt. *Indian Pony, Kansas*, 1859. Stereograph. Kansas State Historical Society, Topeka.

Kansas. (Letter, in *Mercury*, New Bedford, 15 June 1859)

**7 May** Bierstadt and Frost stay in Troy waiting for their wagon to catch up. (Letter, in *Mercury*, New Bedford, 15 June 1859)

**8 May** Following the arrival of the wagon, Bierstadt, Frost, and their companions leave Troy and continue west, traveling about six miles before they camp. (Letter, in *Mercury*, New Bedford, 15 June 1859)

**10 May** Bierstadt and other members of the Lander party ford the Wolf River in

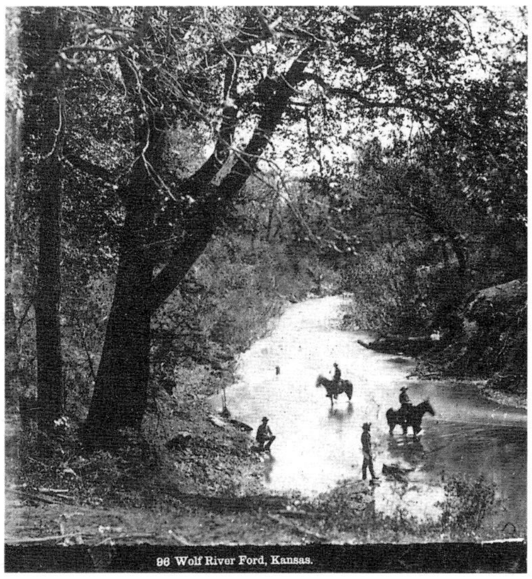


Albert Bierstadt. *Wolf River Ford, Kansas*, 1859. Stereograph. Collection of Wilfred Thompson, courtesy of Leonard A. Walle.

Kansas. (Letter, in *Mercury*, New Bedford, 15 June 1859)

**11 May** After camping for the night, the Lander party is battered by a powerful thunderstorm. (Letter, in *Mercury*, New Bedford, 15 June 1859)

**12 May** Under clear skies, the Lander party makes little progress along a muddy trail. A second thunderstorm follows. (Letter, in *Mercury*, New Bedford, 15 June 1859)

**16 May** After passing a party of discouraged emigrants returning east from Pike's Peak, Bierstadt and his companions camp near Marysville, Kansas, on the Big Blue River. (Letter, in *Mercury*, New Bedford, 15 June 1859)

**17–18 May** Bierstadt and his companions pass a party returning from Pike's Peak containing 150 wagons. They continue to "Patterson's Ranch." (Letter, in *Mercury*, New Bedford, 15 June 1859)

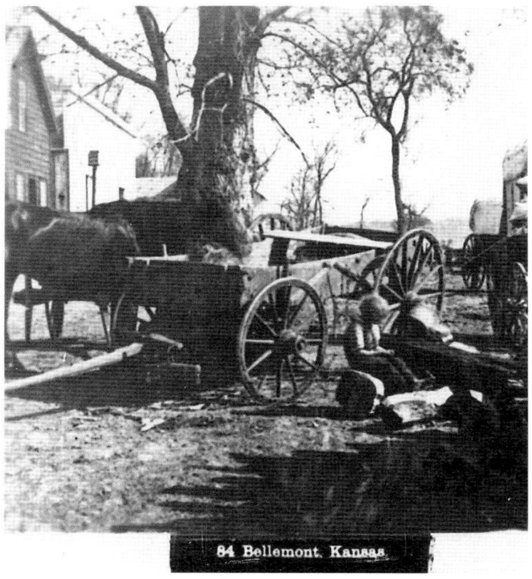


Albert Bierstadt. *Bellemont, Kansas*, 1859. Stereograph. Kansas State Historical Society, Topeka.

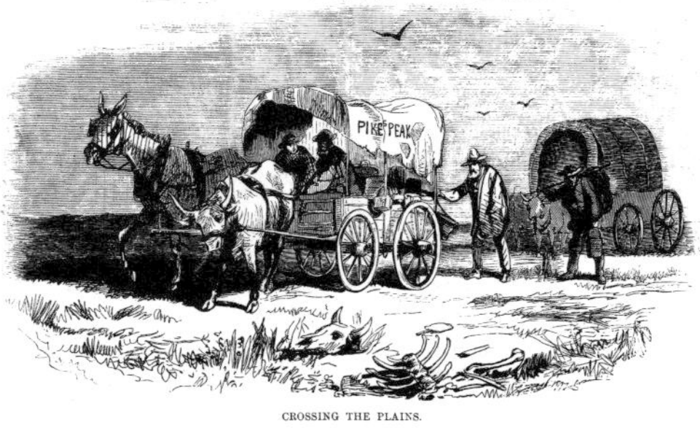


After Albert Bierstadt. *Crossing the Plains*. Wood engraving published in *Harper's Weekly*, 13 Aug. 1859.

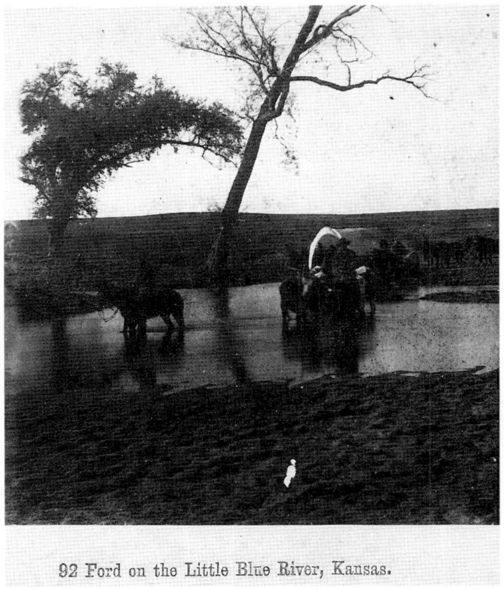


Albert Bierstadt. *Ford on the Little Blue River, Kansas*, 1859. Stereograph. Collection of Wilfred Thompson, courtesy of Leonard A. Walle.

**19 May** Bierstadt and Frost encounter Pawnee Indians begging for gifts. (Letter, in *Mercury*, New Bedford, 15 June 1859)

**20 May** The Lander party reaches the Little Blue River, where game is plentiful and they restock their larder. (Letter, in *Mercury*, New Bedford, 15 June 1859)

**22 May** Several large trains of Mormons bound for Salt Lake City pass the Lander survey party. (Letter, in *Mercury*, New Bedford, 15 June 1859)

**24 May** Bierstadt and Frost reach Fort Kearney, Nebraska, near the Platte River. Describing the landscape as flat and even, Bierstadt anticipates making better progress during the days ahead. (Letter, in *Mercury*, New Bedford, 15 June 1859)

**30 May** Bierstadt and his companions are visited by a party of Indians, including a chief named Dog Belly. Bierstadt obtains stereoscopic portraits of several Indians and completes "some fine studies." (*Mercury*, New Bedford, 18 June 1859)

**31 May** Leaving Fort Kearney, the Lander party crosses the Platte River at Odd Fellows Bluff. (*Mercury*, New Bedford, 18 June 1859)

**1–3 June** Bierstadt, Frost, et al. continue on to Ash Hollow, Nebraska, where they "took a stereoscopic view of some Indian wigwams with Harney's battle ground in the distance." (*Mercury*, New Bedford, 7 July 1859)

**4–6 June** Lander party continues along the Platte River, camping one night near Chimney Rock, Nebraska. (*Mercury*, New Bedford, 7 July 1859)

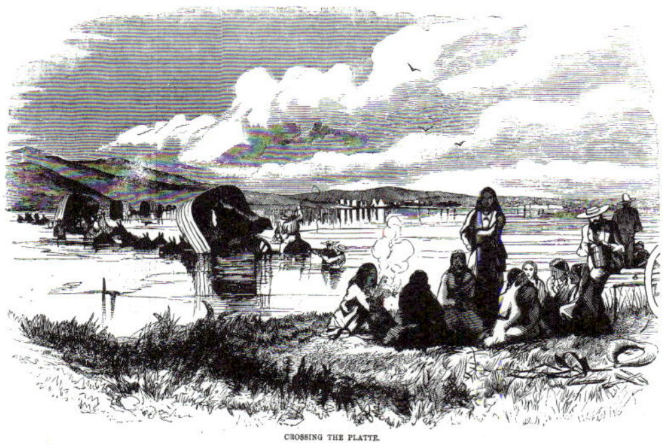

After Albert Bierstadt. *Crossing the Platte*. Wood engraving published in *Harper's Weekly*, 13 Aug. 1859.

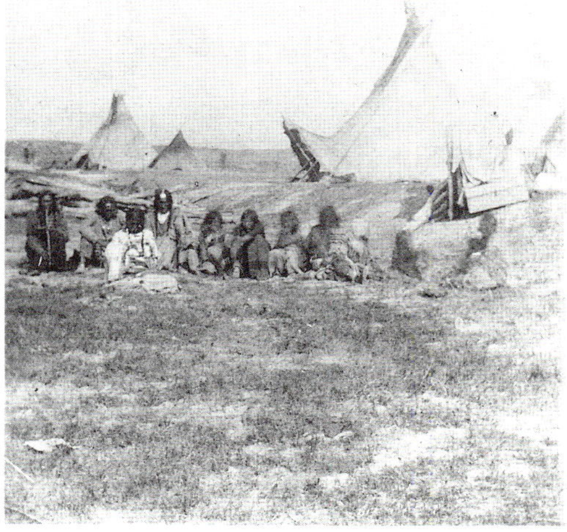

Albert Bierstadt. *Ogalillah Sioux, Horse Creek, Nebraska*, 1859. Stereograph. The New-York Historical Society.

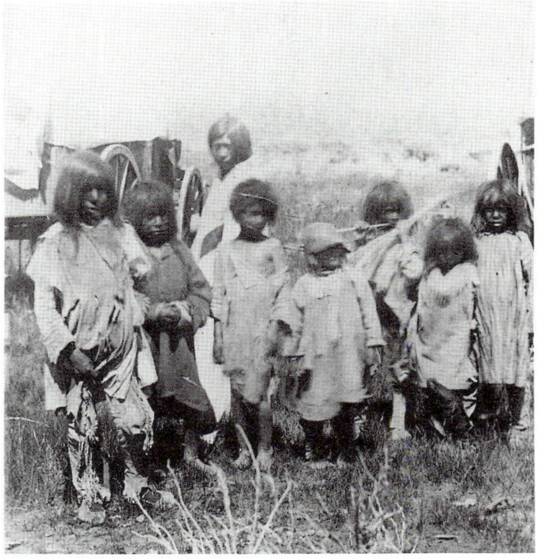

Albert Bierstadt. *Shoshone Children*, 1859. Stereograph. The New-York Historical Society.

**7–9 June** Approaching the Rocky Mountains, Bierstadt writes, "The distant hills remind me of Switzerland." (**Mercury**, New Bedford, 7 July 1859)

**c. 10–12 June** Lander party camps for several days at Fort Laramie. Bierstadt describes the scenery near the fort as "fine" and the dress of some of the Indians as "gorgeous in the extreme." (**Mercury**, New Bedford, 7 July 1859)

**10 July** Bierstadt writes from the "Rocky Mountains": "The mountains are very fine; as seen from the plains, they resemble very much the Bernese Alps. . . . We see many spots in the scenery that remind us of our New Hampshire and Catskill hills, but when we look up and measure the mighty perpendicular cliffs that rise hundreds of feet aloft, all capped with snow, we then realize that we are among a different class of mountains; and especially when we see the antelope stop to look at us, and still more the Indian, his pursuer, who often stands dismayed to see a white man sketching alone in the midst of his hunting grounds. . . .

"We have taken many stereoscopic views, but not so many of mountain scenery as I could wish, owing to various obstacles attached to the process. . . . The color of the mountains and of the plains, and, indeed that of the entire country, reminds one of the color of Italy; in fact, we have here the Italy of America in a primitive condition.

"We are about to turn our faces homeward again . . . to avoid the fall deluge on the plains." (Bierstadt 1859, p. 287)

**13 Aug.** "The Pike's Peak Gold Mines," illustrated with drawings after Bierstadt, is published in *Harper's Weekly*.

**21 Aug.** Bierstadt, Frost, and their animal handler arrive in Button-Wood Springs, Nebraska. (**Mercury**, New Bedford, 14 Sept. 1859)

**24 Aug.** Charles and Edward Bierstadt's woodworking shop burns in New Bedford's worst fire. No insurance. (Ellis 1892, p. 313)

**31 Aug.** Bierstadt and his companions cross the Big Blue River and arrive at Marysville, Kansas. (**Mercury**, New Bedford, 14 Sept. 1859)

**1 Sept.** Bierstadt and his party reach Hiawatha, Kansas, and continue to the Wolf River, where they intend to stay for two weeks sketching. (**Mercury**, New Bedford, 14 Sept. 1859)

**18 Sept.** Bierstadt returns to New Bedford. "His collection of pictures is not as large as he expected, but he has some fine stereoscopic

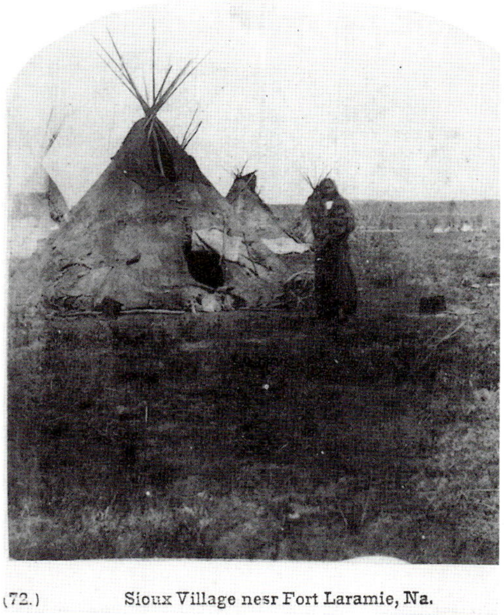


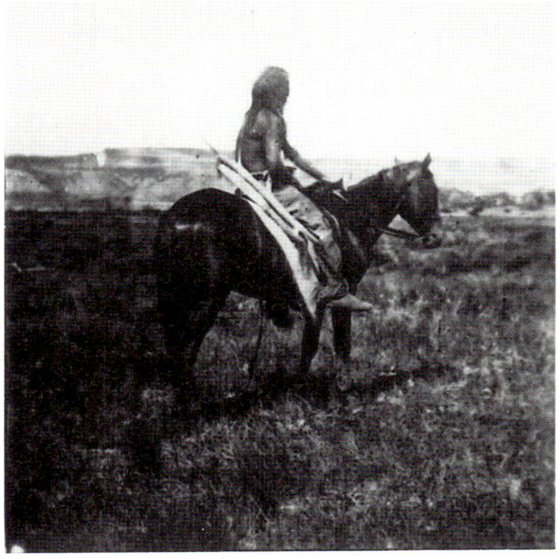

*(top)* Albert Bierstadt. *Sioux Village near Fort Laramie, Na.* [Nebraska], 1859. Stereograph. Miriam and Ira D. Wallach Division of Art, Prints and Photographs, Robert Dennis Collection of Stereoscopic Views, The New York Public Library, Astor, Lenox and Tilden Foundations.

*(above)* Albert Bierstadt. *Shoshone Warrior, Nebraska*, 1859. Stereograph. Kansas State Historical Society, Topeka.

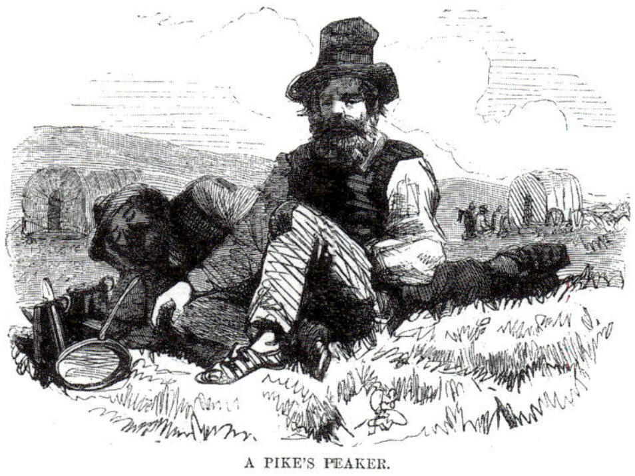


After Albert Bierstadt. *A Pike's Peaker*. Wood engraving published in *Harper's Weekly*, 13 Aug. 1859.

views of scenes which he has visited." (*New Bedford Standard*, 20 Sept. 1859)

**Nov.** "Leutze, Hazeltine [*sic*] and Whitredge [*sic*] have taken studios in the Tenth st. building; Bierstadt, Irving and others are looking out for studios elsewhere, the studio-building being as full as a Broadway omnibus on a rainy day." (*Crayon*, Nov. 1859, p. 349)

**8 Nov.** "We learn that Mr. Bierstadt, the artist, of this city, is about to change his residence to New York, and pursue the practice of his art in that city." (*New Bedford Standard*, 8 Nov. 1859)

**28 Nov.** Charles and Edward Bierstadt "have gone into the business of taking stereoscopic views of objects of interest in this vicinity." (*New Bedford Standard*, 28 Nov. 1859)

**8 Dec.** Bierstadt, Leutze, and Gifford join other artists at Dodworth's Hall in New York in approving a constitution to promote the arts and continue artists' receptions. (*Crayon*, Jan. 1860, p. 25)

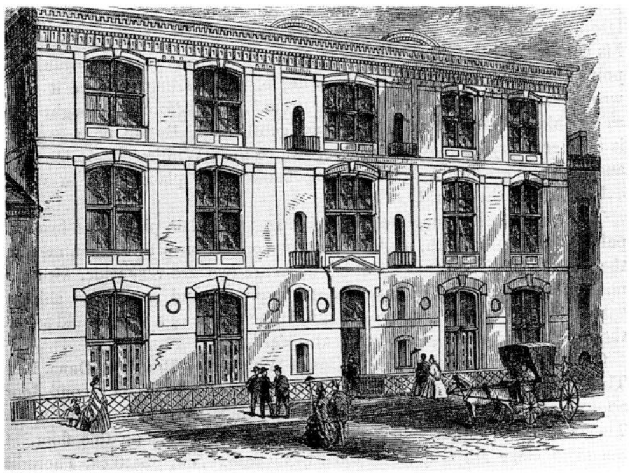

*Tenth Street Studio Building*. Engraving published in *Our Young Folks: An Illustrated Magazine for Boys and Girls*, Sept. 1865.

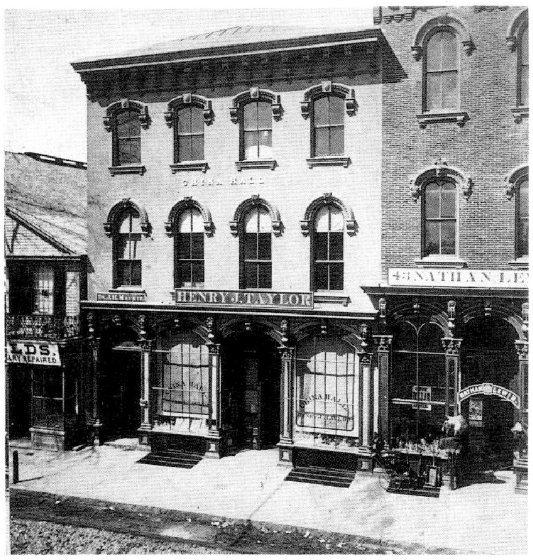


Bierstadt Brothers, New Bedford, Massachusetts. *China Hall, New Bedford, Mass.* (one of the sites of the Bierstadt Brothers photography business). Stereograph. Collection of Leonard A. Walle.

## 1860

**5 Jan.** First Artists' Reception of the season held at Dodworth's Hall. Bierstadt contributes "Rocky Mountain passages." (*Crayon*, Feb. 1860, p. 56; *NY Tribune*, 6 Jan. 1860)

**19 Jan.** First Artists' Reception of the season held at the Tenth Street Studio Building in New York. Bierstadt exhibits *Rocky Mountain Scenery*. "In Bierstadt's room were a good many evidences of his Indian and prairie studies in the shape of buffalo skins and other articles of border life." (*NY Tribune*, 20 Jan. 1860; *Boston Transcript*, 23 Jan. 1860)

**1 Feb.** Third Annual Art Exhibition in Troy, New York, opens to public. Bierstadt contributes *Sioux Village*. (*Crayon*, Feb. 1860, pp. 57–58; Mar. 1860, pp. 85–86; Yarnall and Gerdts 1986, p. 299)

**13 Feb.** Fourth Annual Exhibition of the Washington Art Association opens to the public in Washington, D.C. Bierstadt exhibits "a magnificent landscape, the 'Island of Capri.'" (*Crayon*, Mar. 1860, p. 84)

**29 Feb.** The second Artists' Reception of the season in Boston includes "two scenes from the Rocky Mountains by Bierstadt" and "a Kansas view" by Frost. (Bierstadt to Brewer, 10 Feb. 1860, Massachusetts Historical Society, Boston; *Boston Transcript*, 1 Mar. 1860)

**26 Mar.** At the second and last reception of the season at the Tenth Street Studio Building,

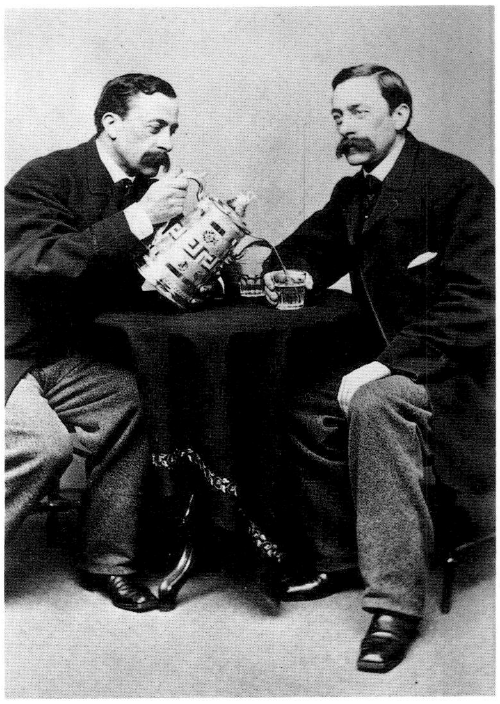

Bierstadt Brothers, New Bedford, Massachusetts. *Albert Bierstadt Pouring Tea for Himself*, 1861. Photograph. Collection of Lloyd Ostendorf.

Bierstadt shows his first monumental western painting, *Base of the Rocky Mountains, Laramie Peak* (unlocated). It receives extensive newspaper coverage. "The light was insufficient for the proper exhibition of such a work, but it made a most favorable impression, notwithstanding. The point of view represented is about seventy miles west of Fort Laramie, on a branch of the Platte; the eye ranges over vast plains, with herds of buffaloes grazing upon them, and the lofty, snow-crowned summits of Mount Laramie and Long's Peak are seen in the distance." (*NY Tribune*, 27 Mar. 1860)

**12 Apr.–16 June** NAD Annual Exhibition open to the public. Bierstadt's *Base of the Rocky Mountains, Laramie Peak* is described as "the *piece de resistance*" of the landscape department. (*NY Tribune*, 12 Apr. 1860; Catalogue, NAD, 1860, p. 35)

The *Herald* notes Bierstadt's contribution to the NAD exhibition: "This is the largest and most elaborate picture in the exhibition, and the artist has treated the subject in a grand manner. . . . The chain of lofty mountains are [*sic*] worthy of Church, and the flora of the valley, display the minute handling of that master." (*NY Herald*, 24 Apr. 1860)

In its review of the NAD exhibition, the *Crayon* notes that *Base of the Rocky Mountains, Laramie Peak* is "the work of a powerful hand. The point of view is well selected, the topographical features are rendered with great accuracy, all the details of trees and table-land, and of the mountains are admirably drawn; the objects that enliven the scene, such as the herds of buffalo and Indian hunters in the foreground, are true in action and character . . . ; the composition is good, and the effects and gradation of atmosphere show fine taste and excellent management. . . . We would make one remark respecting the color of this picture, we should like to see less of the stereotyped Dusseldorf system of color. In every other respect the picture is a remarkable work, indicating resources and feeling which may well be employed upon a higher order of landscape than a faithful view." (*Crayon*, May 1860, pp. 139–40)

The *Home Journal* calls *Base of the Rocky Mountains, Laramie Peak* "strongly, intelligently, faithfully done. . . . The river-bottom, the trees along the stream, the higher broad *plateau* of prairie, the bluffs, with Indians and herds of buffalo, and the purple and icy mountain peaks, fantastic in form—are altogether as typical of the locality as a composition possibly could be; and this we suppose an actual scene." (*Home Journal*, 5 May 1860)

**9 May** At the annual meeting of the NAD, Bierstadt is elected a full Academician. (*Crayon*, June 1860, p. 176)

**14 May** Allston Association in Baltimore holds First Annual Exhibition. Bierstadt contributes *Shoshonee Village*. (*Sun*, Baltimore, 14 May 1860; *Boston Transcript*, 2 June 1860)

**2 July** *Base of the Rocky Mountains, Laramie Peak* is shown at the Boston Athenaeum. (*Boston Transcript*, 8, 12 June 1860; Perkins and Gavin 1980, p. 20)

**6 July** The *Post* reports that Bierstadt, who exhibited *Base of the Rocky Mountains, Laramie Peak* at the NAD "in an unfinished state," has completed the canvas. "The stillness of the piece has been relieved by the introduction of a characteristic buffalo hunt of mounted Indians in the foreground. The enormous ridge, crowned by Mount Long and Laramie Peak . . . have all been retouched. . . ." (*Post*, New York, 6 July 1860)

**Sept.** "Bierstadt . . . has gone into the White Mountain region to sketch, and to experiment photographically, along with his brother, a photographist of eminence. . . . He has laid out another grand Indian Camp scene for his winter's work." (*Cosmopolitan Art Journal*, Sept. 1860, p. 126)

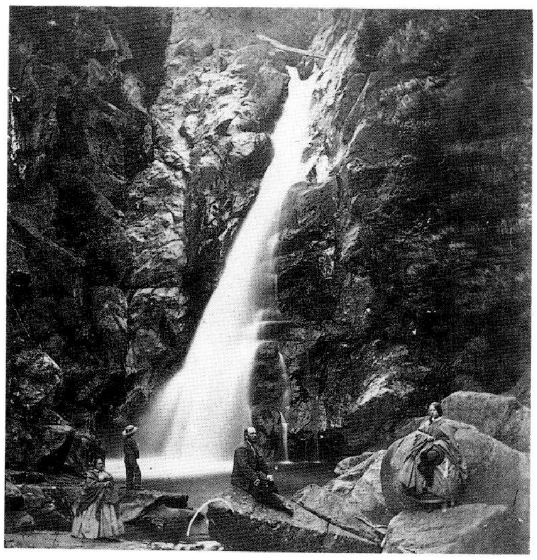

Bierstadt Brothers, New Bedford, Massachusetts. *Glen Ellis Falls, White Mountains, N.H.* Stereograph. Division of Photographic History, National Museum of American History, Smithsonian Institution, Washington, D.C.

## 1861

**Jan.** The *Crayon* addresses "admirers of photographs," calling their attention to "a series of views and studies taken in the White Mountains, published by Bierstadt Brothers, of New Bedford, Mass. The plates are of large size and are remarkably effective. The artistic taste of Mr. Albert Bierstadt, who selected the points of view, is apparent in them. No better photographs have been published in this country." (*Crayon*, Jan. 1861, p. 22)

**12 Feb.** Bierstadt is elected a member of the Artists' Fund Society at the annual meeting. (*Post*, New York, 14, 15 Feb. 1861)

**20 Mar.–25 Apr.** NAD Annual Exhibition open to the public. Bierstadt exhibits *Emigrants Camping*, owned by William Blackler; *Platte River,—Indians Encamped; Recollections of Capri;* and *Echo Lake, Franconia Mts, N.H.*, owned by Henry Tilton. (*Post*, New York, 20 Mar. 1861; Catalogue, NAD, 1861; pp. 20, 26, 28, 31)

In its review of the NAD exhibition, the *Tribune* comments on Bierstadt's *Platte River,—Indians Encamped* and *Emigrants Camping*, which "will recall to the spectator a large picture of the Rocky Mountains by this artist in the exhibition of last year. The whole treatment of the subject shows how earnestly the painter enters into the spirit of this frontier life, and how careful a student he has been of its picturesque phases." (*NY Tribune*, 5 Apr. 1861)

A review of the NAD exhibition focuses on Bierstadt's *Recollections of Capri:* "The 'Grotto of Nymphs,' a remarkable stalactite cave in the Island of Capri, at the south entrance of the Bay of Naples, is the subject. . . . We are in the heart of the cave, and surrounded by a strange gloom. Far in the distance is seen the pale light which marks the entrance, while in one of the fissures on the left the strong red glare of a fire is visible." (*Frank Leslie's Illustrated Newspaper*, 20 Apr. 1861)

**12 Apr.** Confederates fire on Fort Sumter in Charleston Harbor. Civil War begins.

**25 Apr.** The NAD closes its Annual Exhibition early, "the galleries having been given up to a military company." Gifford, Whittredge, David Johnson, and James Hart are reported to "have buckled on the knapsack and are doing the state some service." (*Post*, New York, 30 Apr. 1861)

**29 May** "Upwards of seventy pictures" donated by artists and on view at Goupil's gallery are sold for the aid of families of volunteers (Patriotic Fund). Bierstadt's *South Pass, Rocky Mountains* sells for $50. (*Post*, New York, 29 May 1861; *Home Journal*, 8 June 1861; Catalogue, Patriotic Fund Sale, 1861)

**c. 2 Sept.** Bierstadt, his nephew, sister, and possibly others, begin a trip to the White Mountains lasting about three weeks. (Oscar Albert Bierstadt manuscript, Turner Collection)

**13 Sept.** Bierstadt and his party register at the Crawford House in the White Mountains. (Campbell 1981, p. 18)

**Fall** Edward Bierstadt obtains permission to open a temporary photography studio in the camp of the Army of the Potomac then located on both sides of the Potomac River. He sets up shop at Langley's Tavern, about seven miles above Georgetown on the Virginia side of the river in the camp of the 43rd New York infantry. Until called home by an illness in the family, he does a brisk business in cartes de visite and camp photographs. Albert Bierstadt later used photographs taken at this time to produce *Guerrilla Warfare (Picket Duty in Virginia)* (No. 30). (*New Bedford Standard*, 22 Aug. 1903)

**15 Oct.** Bierstadt and Leutze granted a five-day pass by General Winfield Scott to visit Union troops "on both sides of the Potomac." (Photograph of original document, International Museum of Photography at George Eastman House, Rochester, N.Y.)

## 1861–1862

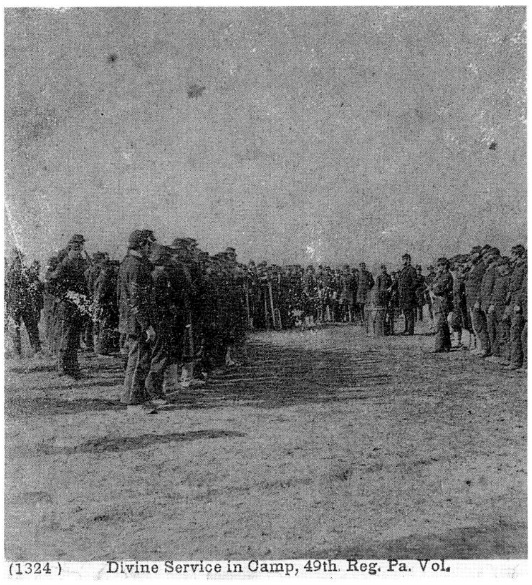


Edward Bierstadt. *Divine Service in Camp, 49th Reg. Pa. Vol.* Stereograph. Collection of William L. Schaeffer.

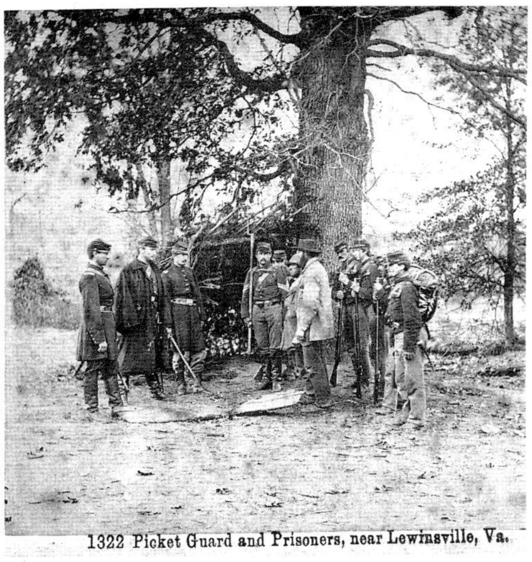


Bierstadt Brothers, New Bedford, Massachusetts. *Picket Guard and Prisoners, near Lewinsville, Va.* Stereograph. Collection of Leonard A. Walle.

**30 Nov.** "Bierstadt has disappeared from the Tenth street Studio Building. Where he has gone we know not." (*Post*, New York, 30 Nov. 1861)

**21 Dec.** Bierstadt's *Trappers' Camp* (No. 27) sold at the Artists' Fund Sale for $65. (*Post*, New York, 23 Dec. 1861)

**24 Dec.** First exhibition of paintings and sculpture sponsored by the Young Men's Association opens in Buffalo. Bierstadt contributes three works: *Indians Traveling near Fort Laramie* (No. 26), *Sun Set—In the Prairies*, and *Bebigio—Scene in Italy*. (Yarnall and Gerdts 1986, pp. 294, 296, 299)

**26 Dec.** Brooklyn Art Association holds first reception of their season at the Academy of Music. Bierstadt exhibits: *Guerrilla Warfare (Picket Duty in Virginia)* (No. 30) and *Dusseldorf*. (*Post*, New York, 27 Dec. 1861; Marlor 1970, p. 123)

## 1862

**4 Jan.** *Base of the Rocky Mountains, Laramie Peak* on exhibit at Tiffany & Co., New York. (*NY Tribune*, 4 Jan. 1862)

**Feb.** *Base of the Rocky Mountains, Laramie Peak* shown at the Fifth Annual Exhibition of the Young Men's Christian Association in Troy, N.Y. (*NY Tribune*, 3 Mar. 1862; Yarnall and Gerdts 1986, pp. 294, 300)

**31 Mar.** Letter from Charles Sumner, senator from Massachusetts, solicits aid for Bierstadt and his "experts" during a proposed trip to the Rocky Mountains. (Sumner to Sir, 31 Mar. 1862, Downs Collection)

**8 Apr.** Bierstadt delivers to Senator Charles Sumner a letter to be forwarded to Secretary of War Edwin M. Stanton in which he asks permission to travel to the Rocky Mountains under the protection of the "regiment about to start across the country for the protection of the mails and emigrants." Bierstadt lists the names of four students of Louis Agassiz ready to accompany him. Also intending to join the party are New York artist William H. Beard, Charles Gould, Jr., of New York, and John Hay, assistant secretary to President Lincoln. Bierstadt writes that he wishes to go west "to study the manners and customs of the Indians as well as the scenery." (Bierstadt to Stanton, 8 Apr. 1862, Letters Received by the Secretary of War, National Archives)

**14 Apr.–23 June** NAD Annual Exhibition open to the public. Bierstadt contributes three works: *Sunlight and Shadow* (No. 29); *Wind River Mountains, Nebraska Territory*; and *View of Dusseldorf, on the Rhine*. (*NY Times*, 14 Apr. 1862; Catalogue, NAD, 1862, pp. 12, 15, 29)

**27 Apr.** Bierstadt writes to Alpheus Hyatt, one of his companions for the proposed Rocky

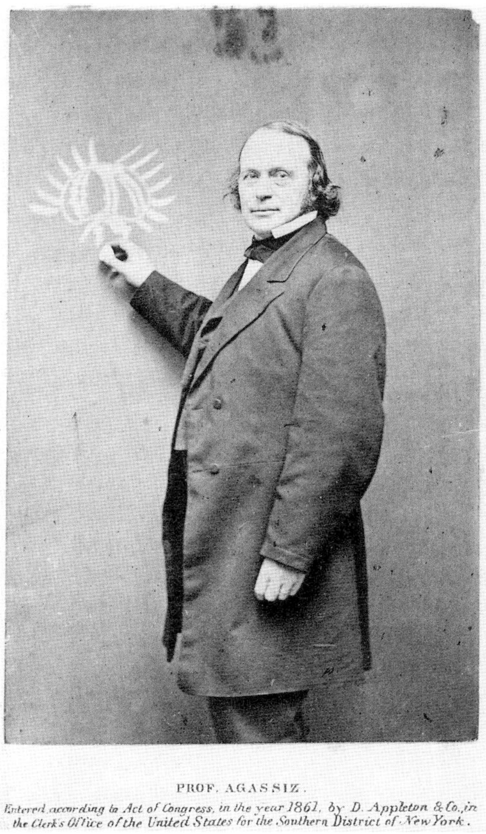


*Louis Agassiz*, 1861. Carte de visite. Bierstadt Album, private collection, Hannover, Germany.

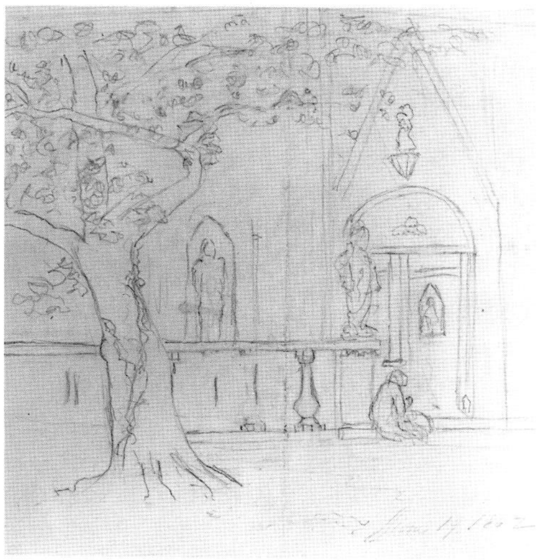

Albert Bierstadt. *Sketch after "Sunlight and Shadow,"* 1862. Pencil on paper. The Whaling Museum, New Bedford, Massachusetts.

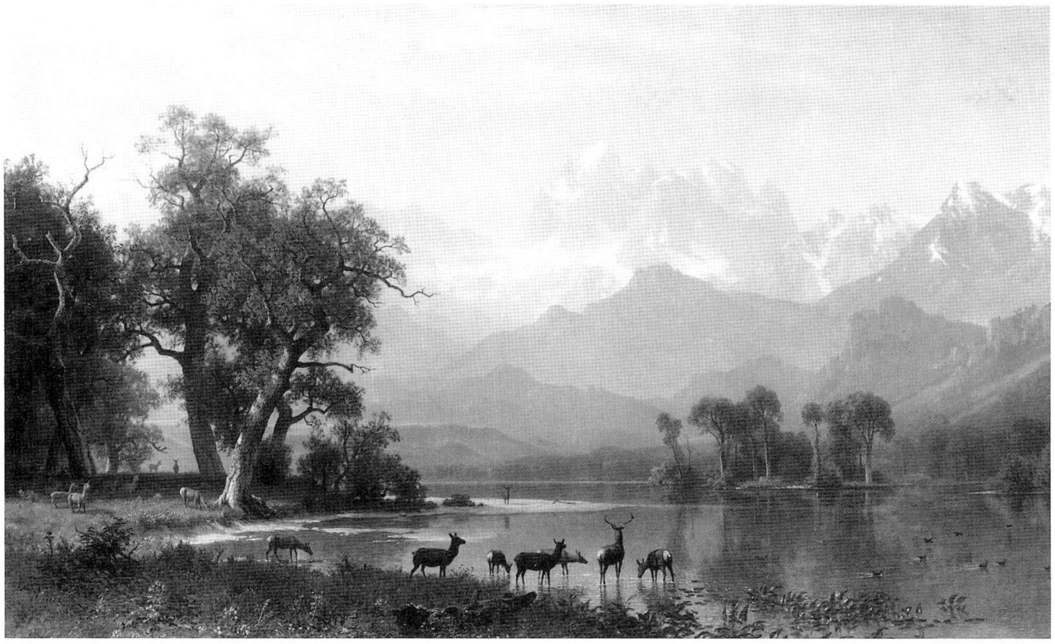

Albert Bierstadt. *Wind River Mountains, Nebraska Territory*, 1862. Oil on canvas. Private collection.

Mountain trip, that he has not been successful in securing permission to travel under the protection of an army regiment. Reports of Indian uprisings suggest that traveling without protection would be too risky. Bierstadt is disappointed and considers taking a steamer up the Missouri River to Fort Pierce. (Bierstadt to Hyatt, 27 Apr. 1862, Metropolitan Museum of Art Library, MS Box II, no. 20)

Bierstadt writes to Caleb Smith, Secretary of the Interior, indicating that he may have to give up his trip to the Rocky Mountains and inquiring if Smith would like to accompany him on a trip to Fort Randall, on the Missouri River. (Bierstadt to Smith, 27 Apr. 1862, Register of Letters, Secretary of the Interior, National Archives)

**5 May** William P. Dole, Commissioner of Indian Affairs, Department of the Interior, responds to a letter from Bierstadt proposing a trip from Saint Louis to Fort Randall. Does not advise against the trip but encourages him to telegraph Chouteau & Company as soon as possible regarding the departure date of their steamer. Bierstadt does not make this trip. (Dole to Bierstadt, 5 May 1862, Outgoing Letters, Department of the Interior, National Archives)

**Summer** Bierstadt reported to have spent much of the summer in the White Mountains. In January 1863, the *Leader* notes that nearly an entire wall of his studio is filled with studies and sketches from his White Mountain sojourn. (*NY Leader*, 17 Jan. 1863)

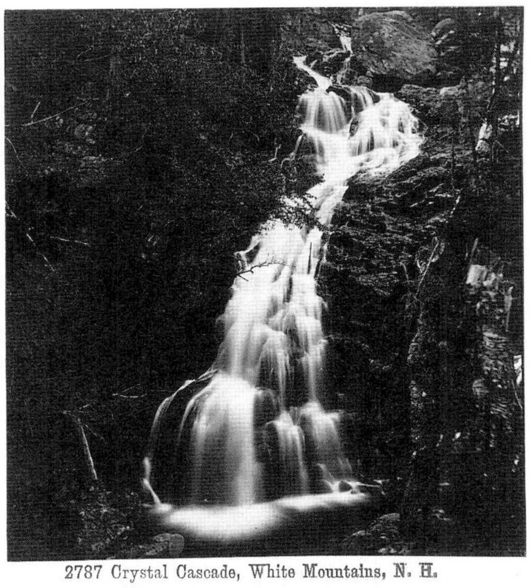


Bierstadt Brothers, New Bedford, Massachusetts. *Crystal Cascade, White Mountains, N.H.* Stereograph. Division of Photographic History, National Museum of American History, Smithsonian Institution, Washington, D.C.

**7 July** A new publication by the Bierstadt brothers incorporates a stereo viewer in the cover of a book containing White Mountain views (*Stereoscopic Views Among the Hills of New Hampshire*). (*New Bedford Standard*, 7 July 1862)

**14 Aug.** Bierstadt is in North Conway, New Hampshire, "where he is making studies of the scenery for a large picture." (*Boston Transcript*, 14 Aug. 1862)

**13 Sept.** Bierstadt registered at Conway House in the White Mountains. (Campbell 1981, p. 18)

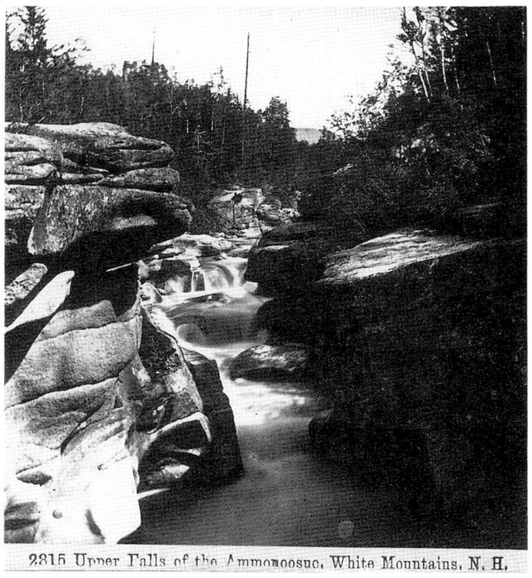


Bierstadt Brothers, New Bedford, Massachusetts. *Upper Falls of the Ammonoosuc, White Mountains, N.H.* Stereograph. Division of Photographic History, National Museum of American History, Smithsonian Institution, Washington, D.C.

**23 Dec.** At the Buffalo Fine Arts Academy Exhibition, Bierstadt contributes *Capri, Bay of Naples; Laramie Peak, Rocky Mountains; The Trappers' Camp—Rocky Mountains;* and *Among the Wind River Mountains.* (Catalogue, Buffalo Fine Arts Academy, 1862)

At the Artists' Fund Sale in New York, Bierstadt's contribution, *Swiss Lake*, sells for $163. (*Post*, New York, 24 Dec. 1862)

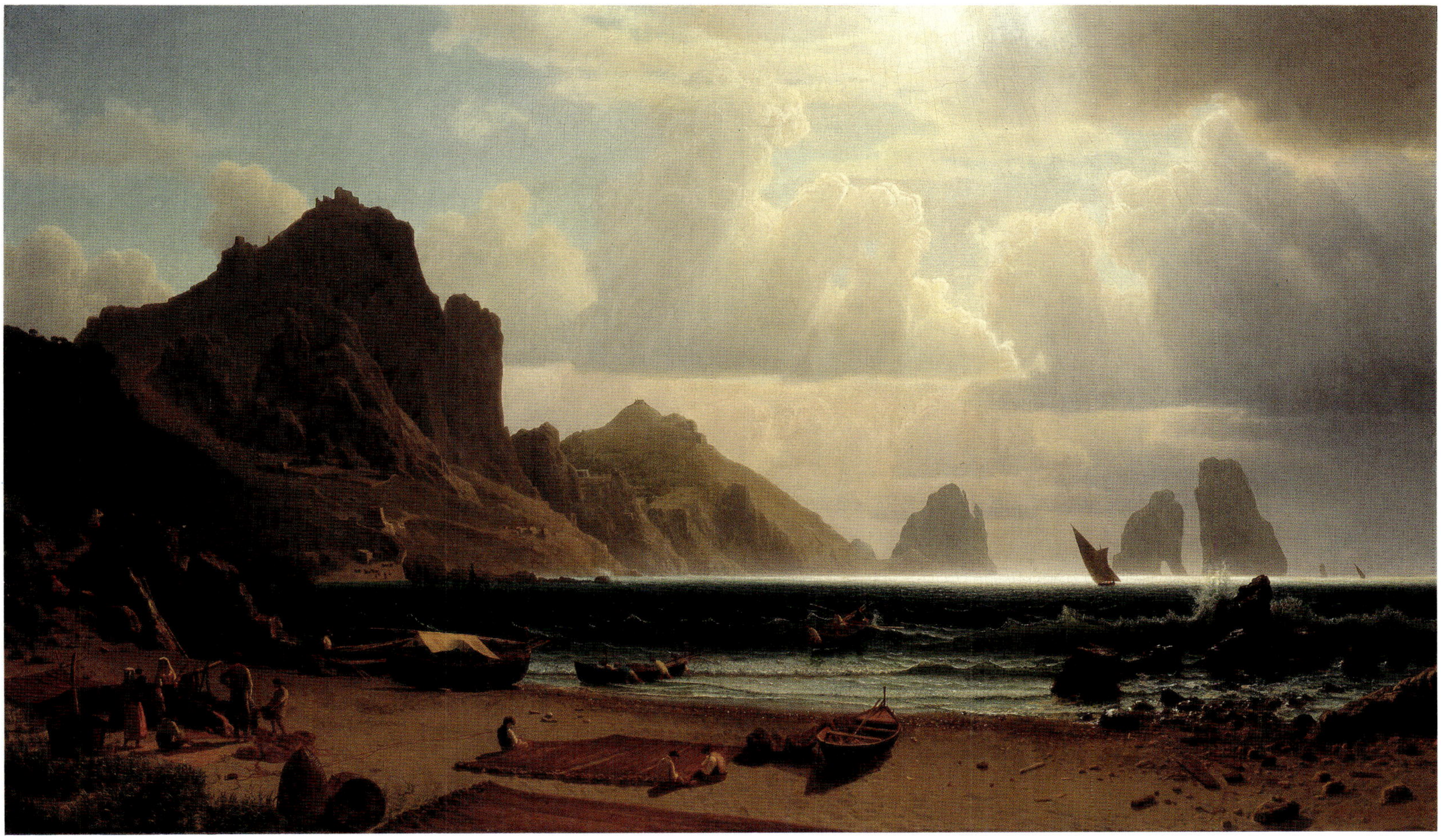

NO. 14

## *The Marina Piccola, Capri,* 1859

Oil on canvas, 42 × 72 in. (106.7 × 182.9 cm)

Signed and dated lower right: *ABierstadt. 1859*

Albright-Knox Art Gallery, Buffalo, Gift of Albert Bierstadt, 1863

*An effective picture, and one that RUSKIN would call great, for it possesses life, feeling, tone and color. Its truthfulness is apparent to every beholder. The luminous quality of the passage of sunlight it would be impossible to excel. MR. BIERSTADT is earning for himself a proud position among his brethren, by whom he is acknowledged as one of the finest and most rising Landscape painters in America. His works are daily increasing in value, and are eagerly sought after by Art connoisseurs. It is not prophesying too much to say that this gentleman, in a very short space of time, will win for himself a high status in the world of Art of Europe as well as of America.*

*The Buffalo Fine Arts Academy Catalogue of American and Foreign Paintings and Sculpture* (Buffalo, N.Y.: 1862), p. 13

*We notice with pleasure Mr. A. Bierstadt has presented to the Academy his beautiful picture "Capri—Bay of Naples" for which we believe he has been offered $1,500. The generous gift was accompanied by the following characteristic note—*

*New York, Jan. 26th 1863*

*Henry W. Rogers, Esq.—My Dear Sir—*
*In accordance with a wish which I have already expressed to yourself, and some others who are interested in the recent art enterprize* [sic] *in your city, I now beg leave to present to the "Buffalo Fine Arts Academy" the picture called Capri, painted by me and now in your possession.*

*And not to encumber a free gift with many words, may I ask you to accept whatever is good in it as a sincere expression of my best wishes for the true and abundant success of the Academy, and as a small payment in account of the large debt which every artist owes to his profession.*

*I remain, dear Sir, yours very truly,*
*ALBERT BIERSTADT*

*Buffalo Daily Courier*, 6 Feb. 1863

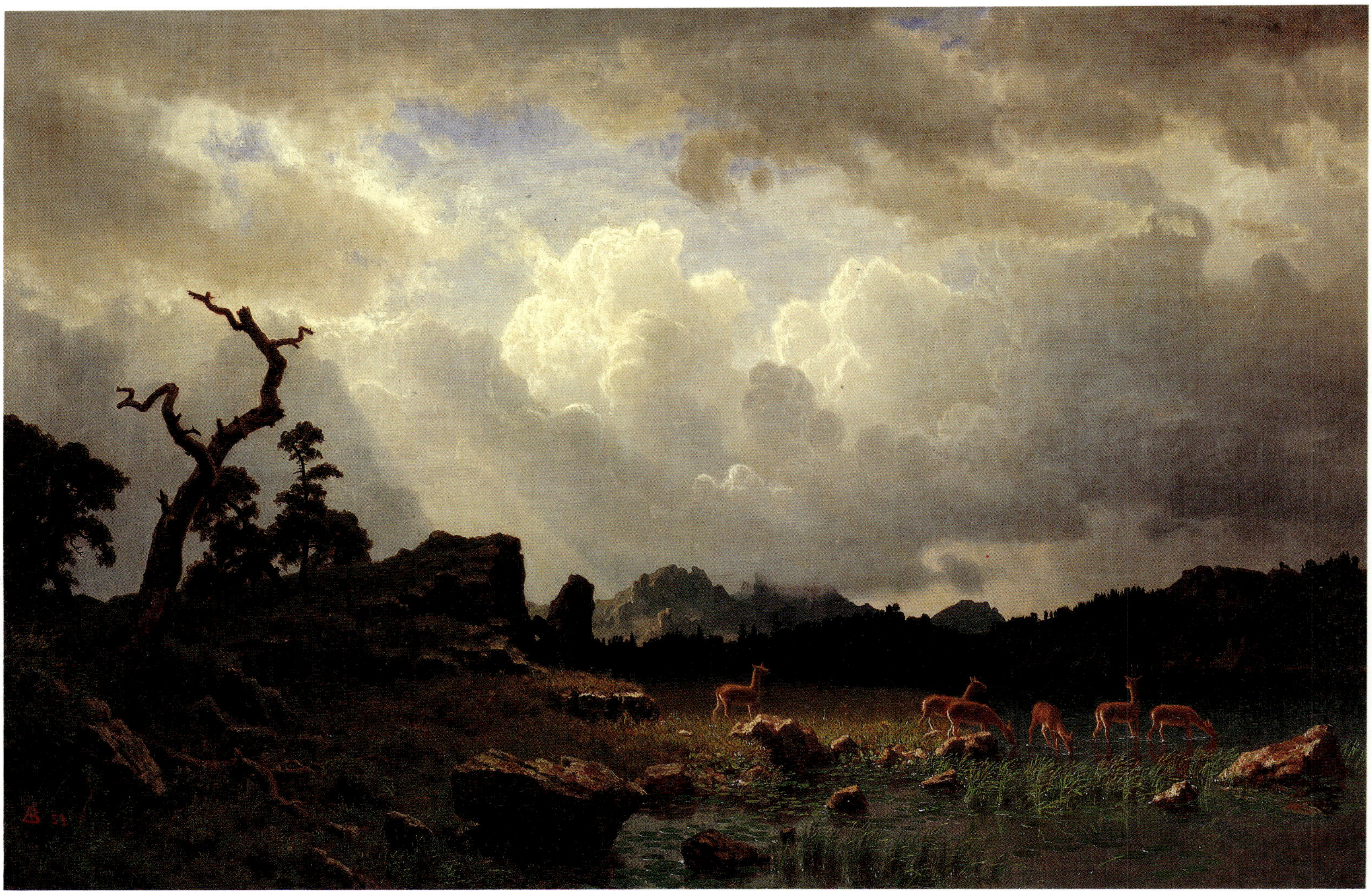

NO. 15

## *Thunderstorm in the Rocky Mountains,* 1859

Oil on canvas, 19 × 29 in. (48.3 × 73.7 cm)

Signed and dated lower left: *AB 59.*

Museum of Fine Arts, Boston, Gift of Mrs. Edward Hale and Mrs. John Carroll Perkins given in memory of their father, Elias T. Milliken

*At night we were overtaken by a tempest. One of our tents was blown down, and it was with difficulty that the others could be retained in their places during the night. The morning, however, dawned brightly upon us. . . . The roads proved bad, and we made little progress during the day; encamping at night under a clear sky, which was soon succeeded by another tempest, accompanied with lightning and thunder. . . .*

Letter from Bierstadt, Fort Kearney, Nebraska, 24 May 1859, in *Mercury*, New Bedford, 15 June 1859

*Between Big Sandy and Comstock's we got our first experience of a thunder-storm on the Plains. . . . The weather had been very warm all day, and we thought likely that this exhibition would prove nothing more than the heat-lightning of our Eastern summer evenings. But about nine o'clock we were undeceived. The sky "meant business." . . . Then . . . the great artillery combat of the heavens commenced in earnest. . . . Then the wind rose to a hurricane; and . . . there followed such a flood of rain as I never saw anywhere, on sea or land. . . . Still the storm did not spend itself in wind and water. The lightning got broader, and its flashes quicker in succession; the thunder surpassed everything I have heard, or read, or dreamed of. . . . One moment we were in utter darkness, . . . the next, . . . earth and heaven illumined with a brightness surpassing the most cloudless noon. . . . If it were only possible to paint such things! But on canvas they would seem even more theatrical than they do in these inadequate words.*

Fitz Hugh Ludlow, *The Heart of the Continent: A Record of Travel Across the Plains and in Oregon, with an Examination of the Mormon Principle* (New York: 1870), pp. 18–21

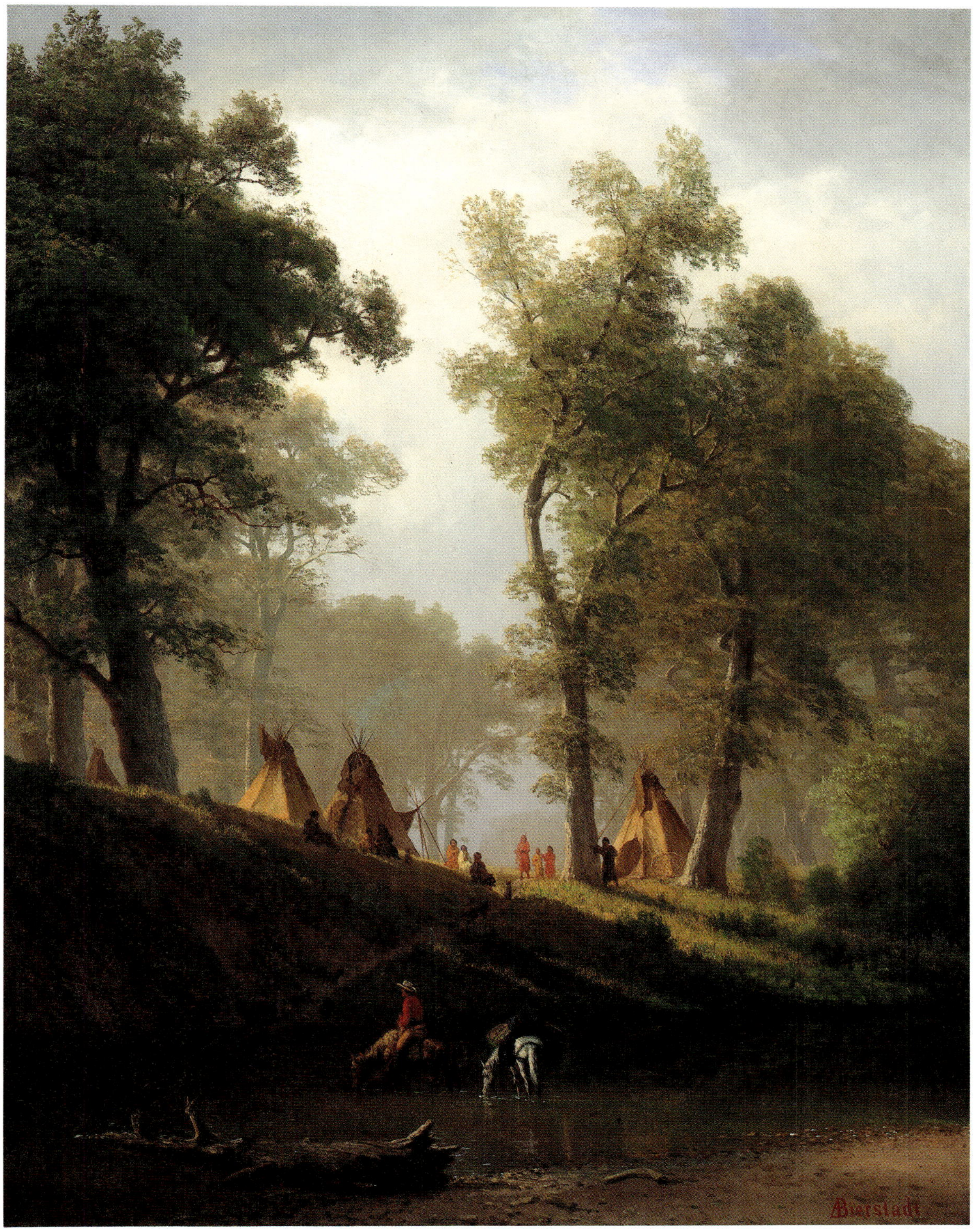


NO. 16

## *The Wolf River, Kansas,* c. 1859

Oil on canvas, 48¼ × 38¼ in. (122.5 × 97.1 cm)

Signed lower right: *ABierstadt*.

The Detroit Institute of Arts, Founders Society Purchase, Dexter M. Ferry, Jr. Fund

*We are now at Wolf River, where we intend stopping some two weeks to sketch—the trees are wonderfully fine, and such beautiful trailing vines, growing in the wildest profusion, forming graceful arches across the river, the wildness and abandon of nature here is very attractive to an artistic eye, and every day nature seems to grow more lovely and beautiful.*

Letter from Bierstadt, Wolf River, Kansas, 3 Sept. 1859, in *Mercury*, New Bedford, 14 Sept. 1859

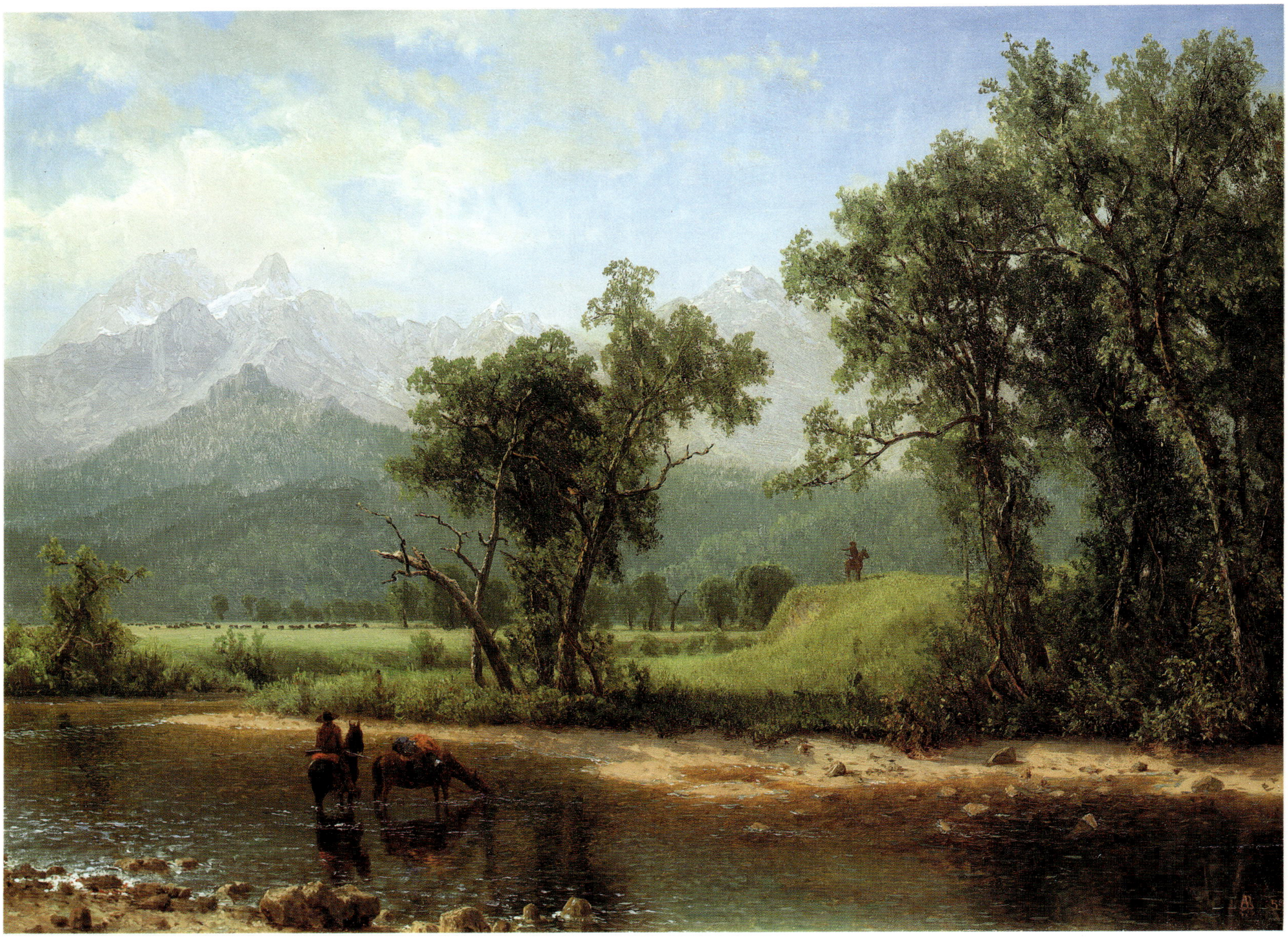

NO. 17

*Sweetwater River, Wind River Mountains, Wyoming Territory*, 1859

Oil on board, 11 × 15¼ in. (27.9 × 38.7 cm)

Signed and dated lower right: *AB 59*

Private collection

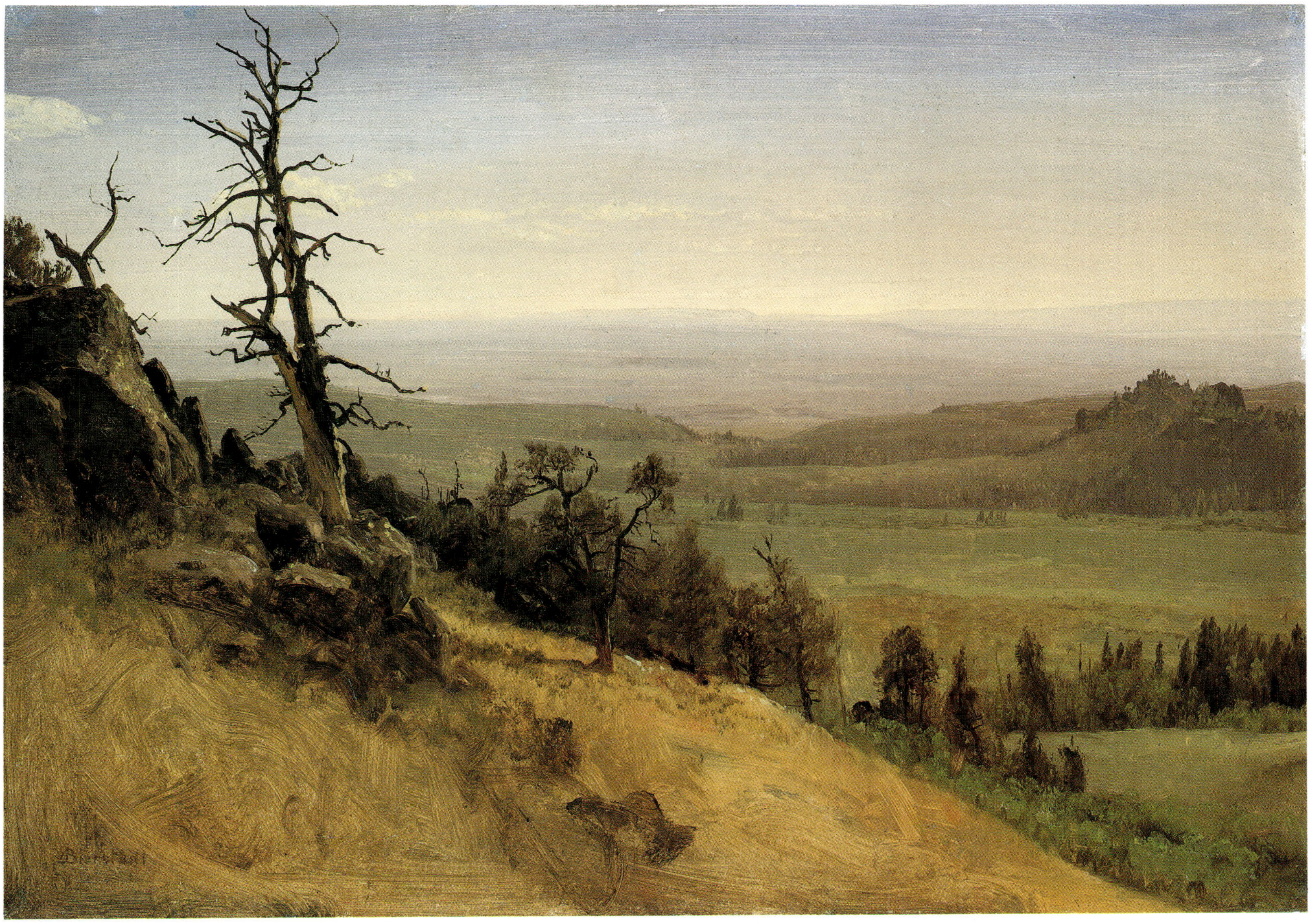

NO. 18

## *Nebraska [Territory]: Wasatch Mountains,* 1859

Oil on paper mounted on board, 13¼ × 19¼ in. (33.7 × 48.9 cm)

Signed lower left: *ABierstadt*

Inscribed verso: *Nebraska: Warcatch* [sic] *Mountains*

The Phelan Collection

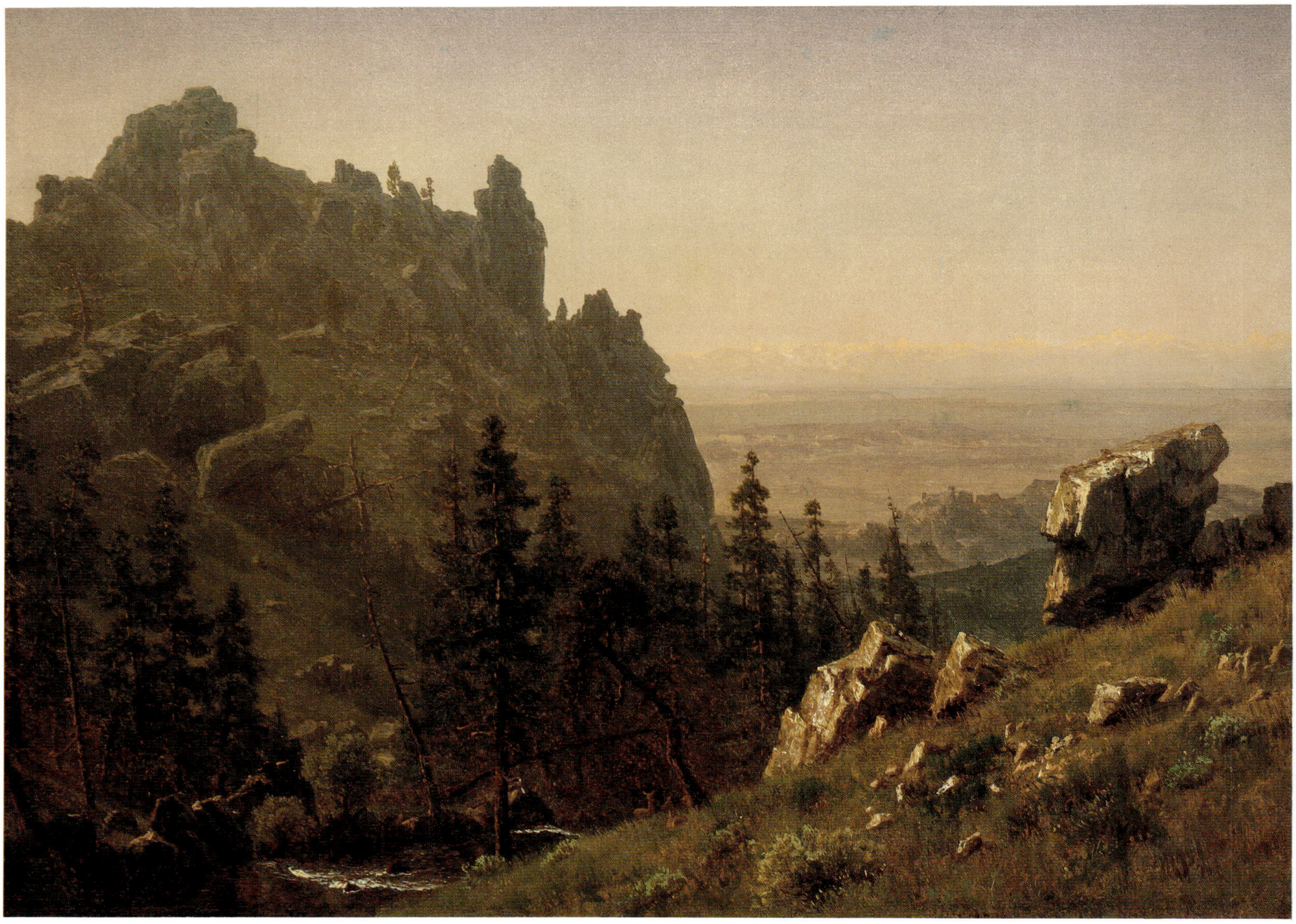

NO. 19

*Wind River Country,* 1859

Oil on paper mounted on board, 13 × 18½ in. (33 × 47 cm)

Signed lower right: *AB '59*

Collection of Edward T. Wilson, Chevy Chase, Maryland

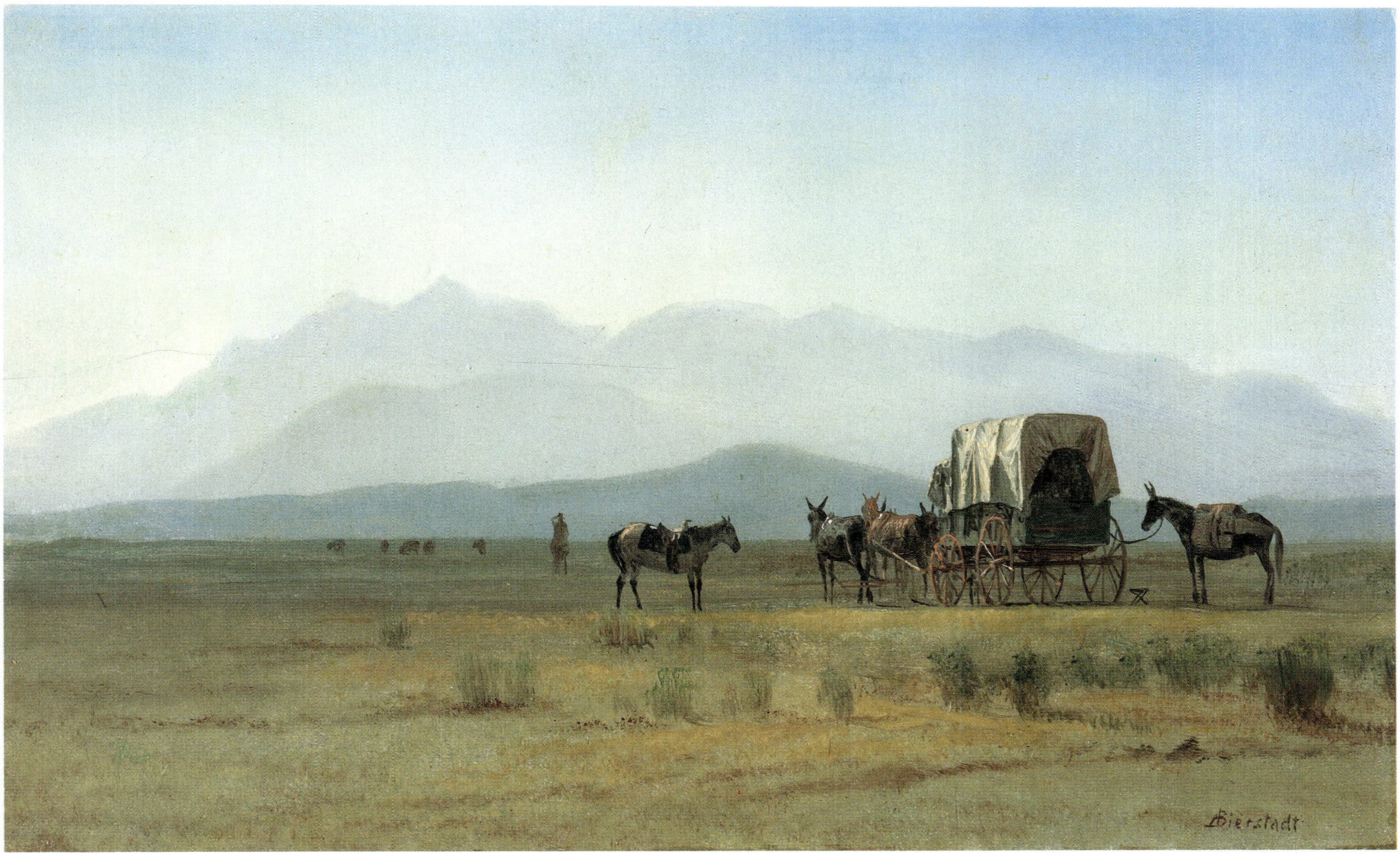


NO. 20

## *Surveyor's Wagon in the Rockies*, c. 1859

Oil on paper mounted on masonite, 7¾ × 12⅞ in. (19.7 × 32.7 cm)

Signed lower right: *ABierstadt*

The Saint Louis Art Museum, Gift of J. Lionberger Davis

*At present, however, our party numbers only three persons; Mr. F——, myself, and a man to take charge of our animals. We have a spring-wagon and six mules, and we go where fancy leads us. I spend most of my time in making journeys in the saddle or on the bare back of an Indian pony. We have plenty of game to eat, such as antelope, mountain grouse, rabbit, sage-hens, wild-ducks, and the like. We have also tea, coffee, dried fruits, beans, a few other luxuries, and a good appetite—we ask for nothing better. I enjoy camp-life exceedingly. This living out of doors, night and day, I find of great benefit. I never felt better in my life. I do not know what some of your Eastern folks would say, who call night air injurious, if they could see us wake up in the morning with the dew on our faces!*

*We are about to turn our faces homeward again, the season being a short one here, and to avoid the fall deluge on the plains, which renders the roads almost impassable.*

Letter from Bierstadt, Rocky Mountains, 10 July 1859, in *Crayon*, Sept. 1859, p. 287

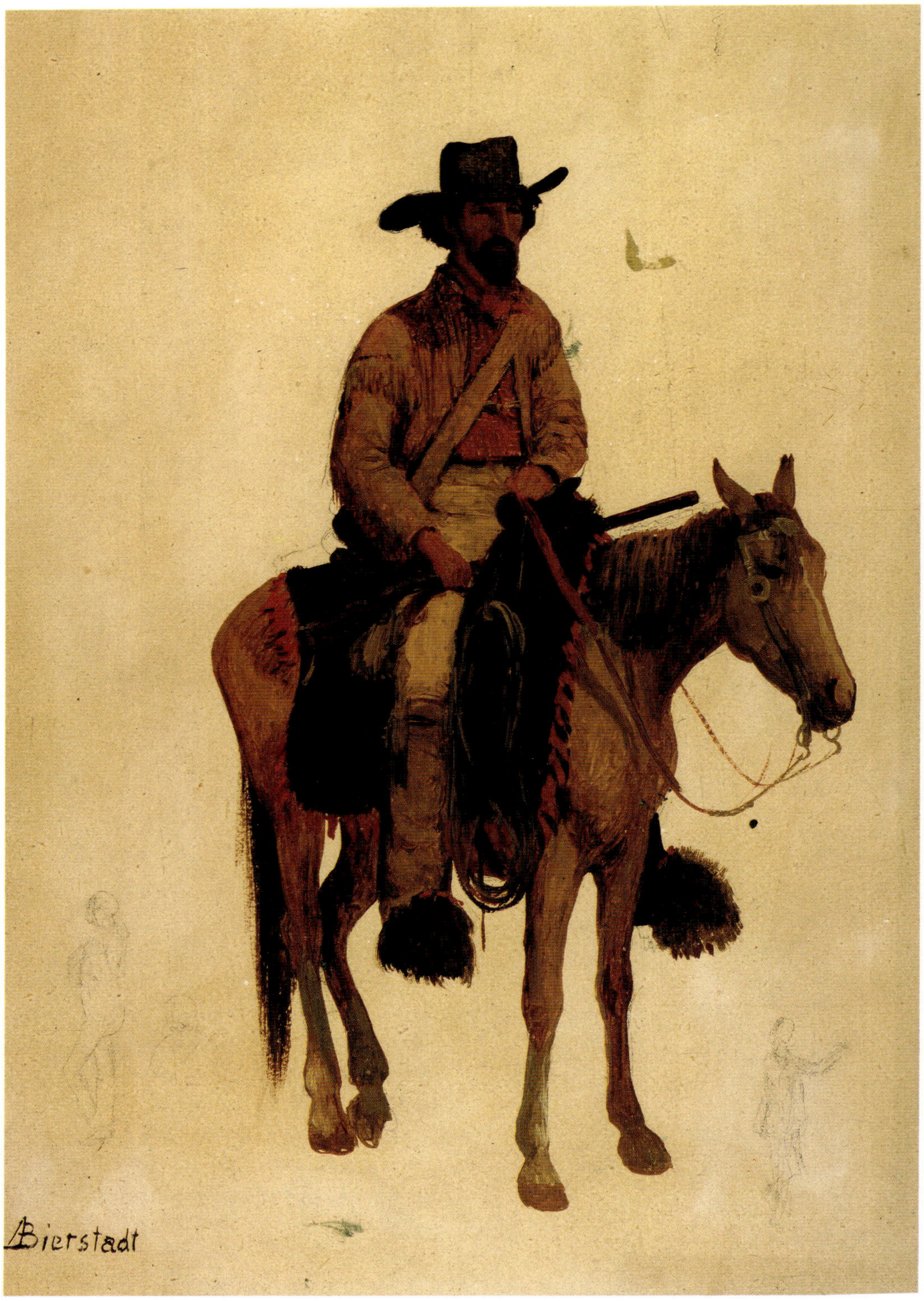


NO. 21

## *Mounted Trapper*

Oil on paper, 12½ × 9 in. (31.8 × 22.9 cm)

Signed lower left: *ABierstadt*

The Thomas Gilcrease Institute of American History and Art, Tulsa, Oklahoma

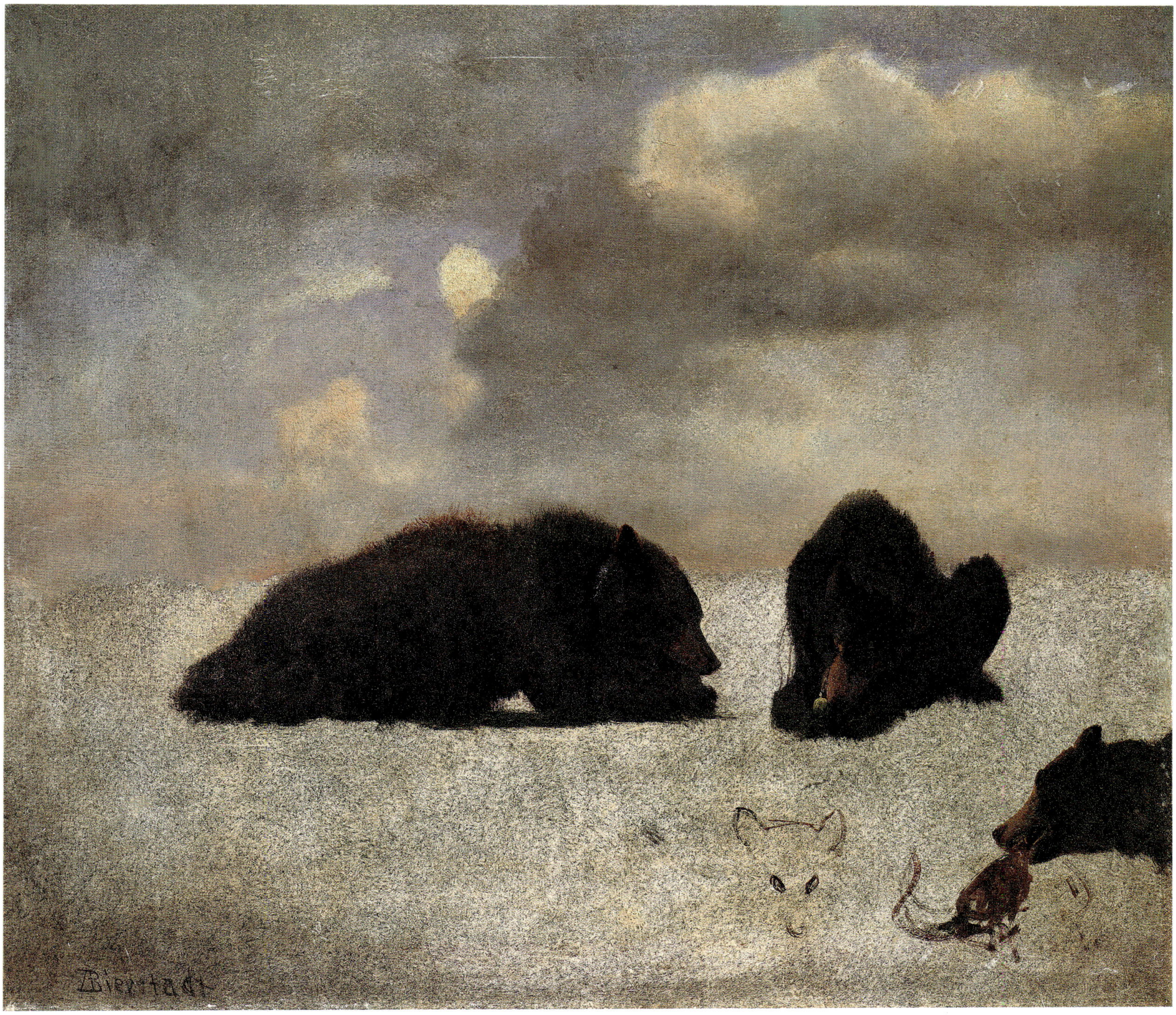


NO. 22

*Grizzly Bears*, c. 1859

Oil on paper mounted on canvas, 14 × 16 in. (35.6 × 40.6 cm)

Signed lower left: *ABierstadt*

Milwaukee Art Museum, Layton Art Collection

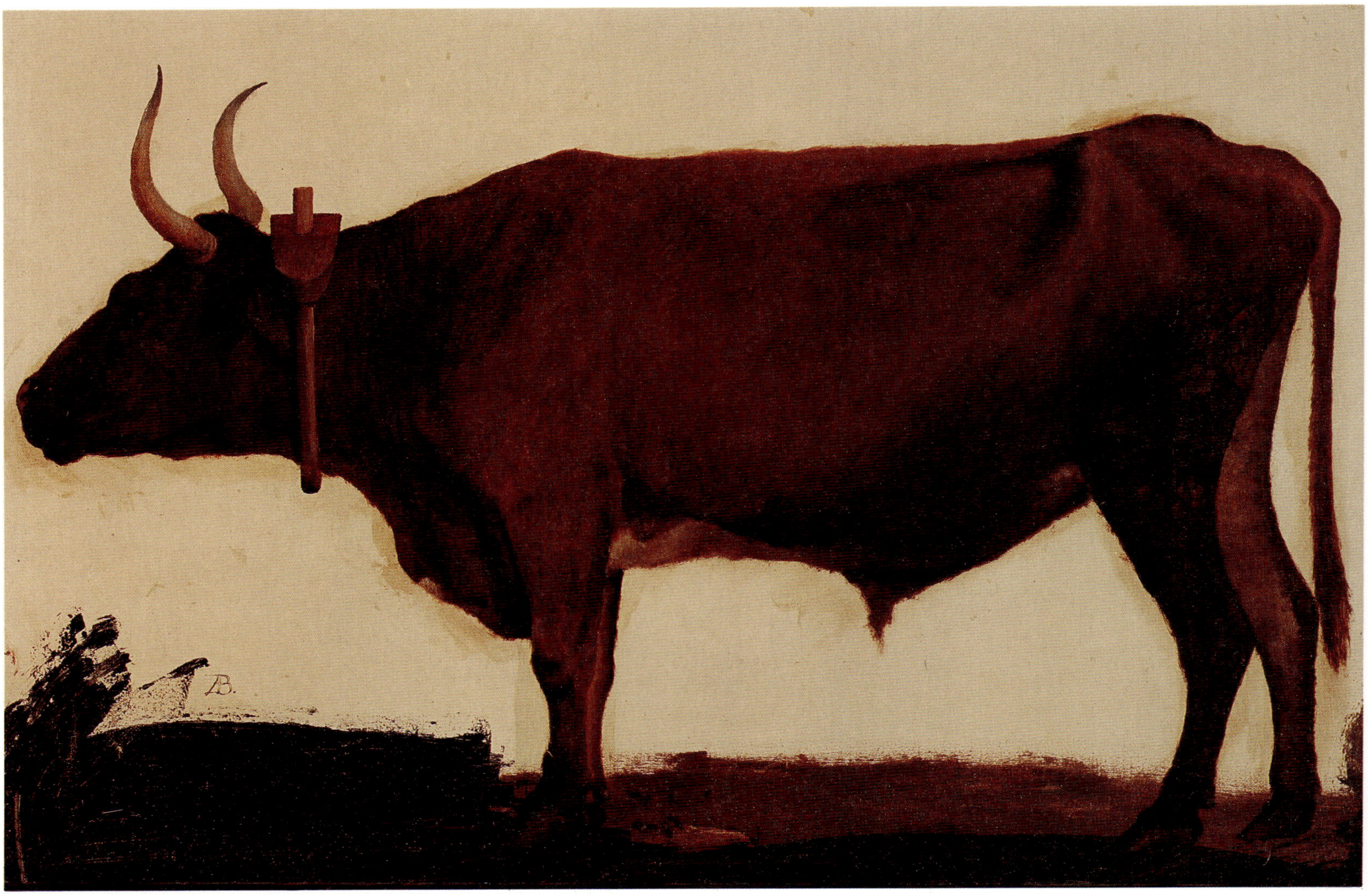

NO. 23

## *Ox*

Oil on cardboard, 12¼ × 19 in. (31.1 × 48.3 cm)
Signed lower left: *AB*.
The Oakland Museum, Kahn Collection

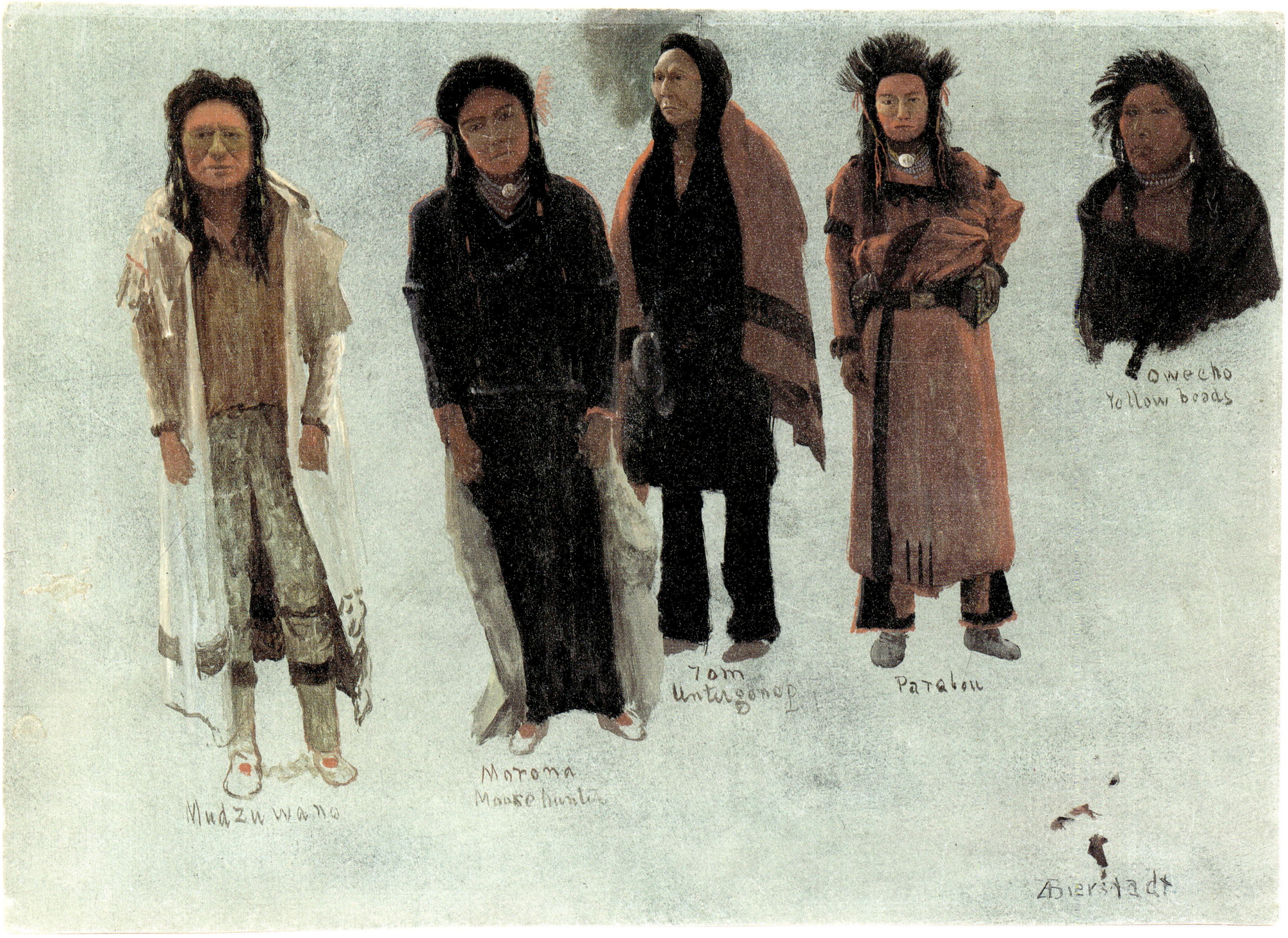


**NO. 24**

*Five Indians*, c. 1859

Oil on paper, 13½ × 18¾ in. (34.3 × 47.6 cm)

Signed lower right: *A. Bierstadt.*

The New-York Historical Society, Gift of Miss Adelaide Milton de Groot, 1941

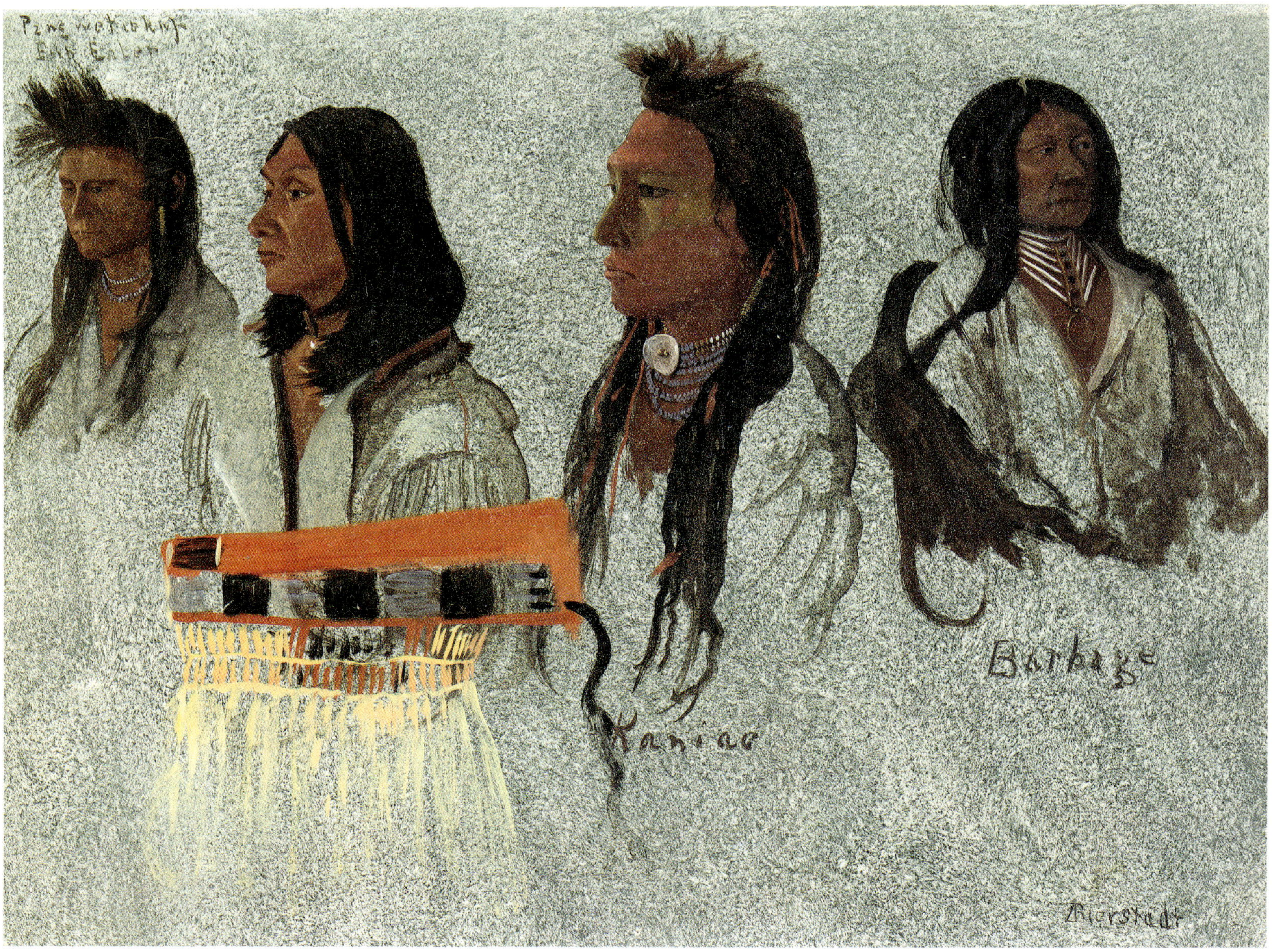


NO. 25

## *Four Indians*, c. 1859

Oil on paper, $13\frac{3}{4} \times 18\frac{7}{8}$ in. ($34.9 \times 47.9$ cm)

Signed lower right: *A. Bierstadt.*

The New-York Historical Society, Gift of Miss Adelaide Milton de Groot, 1941

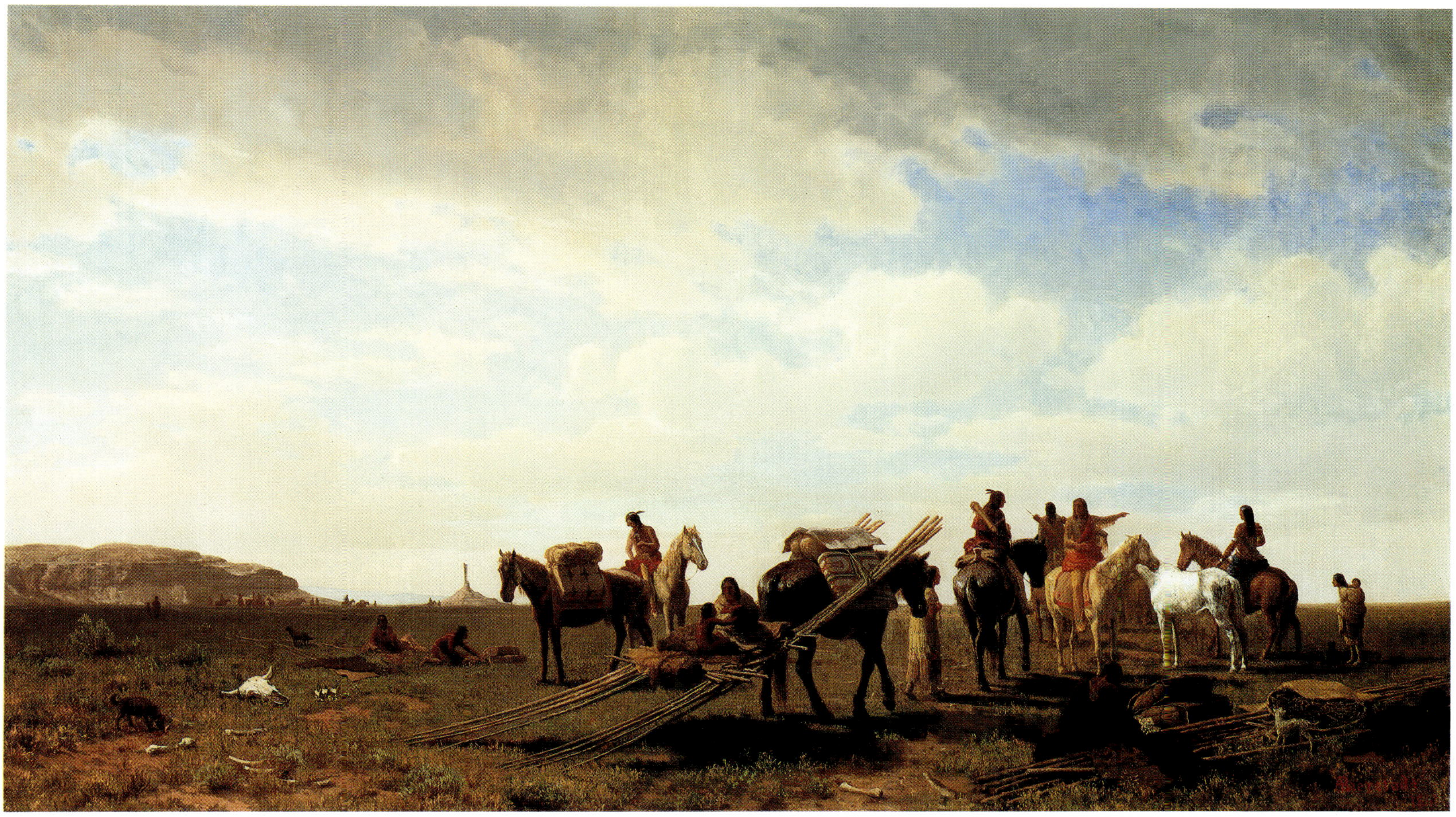

NO. 26

## *Indians Traveling near Fort Laramie,* 1861

Oil on canvas, 23 × 40⅛ in. (58.4 × 102 cm)
Signed and dated lower right: *ABierstadt/1861.*
Manoogian Collection

*Mr. Bierstadt has succeeded in sketching some fine studies including a picturesque group of Indians,—a travelling party, the horses with the tent poles fastened to their sides, one end dragging upon the ground, and seated upon the poles, a squaw and papoose, with blankets and other camp articles.*

Summary of a letter from Bierstadt, Platte River, 31 May 1859, in *Mercury*, New Bedford, 18 June 1859

*One night we encamped near Chimney Rock. Although not very picturesque, yet it is quite various, being composed of sandstone, and stands on a pyramid resembling Bunker Hill Monument. But it is fast wearing away, having lost almost fifty feet of its height during the last ten years. About ten miles from it is another rock resembling a castle, which was produced by the mountains wearing away. Other curious formations are in the vicinity, but less picturesque.*

Letter from Bierstadt, Fort Laramie, 11 June 1859, in *Mercury*, New Bedford, 7 July 1859

*We do not venture a great distance from the camp alone, although tempted to do so by distant objects, which, of course, appear more charming than those near by; also by the figures of the Indians so enticing, travelling about with their long poles trailing along on the ground, and their picturesque dress, that renders them such appropriate adjuncts to the scenery.*

Letter from Bierstadt, Rocky Mountains, 10 July 1859, in *Crayon*, Sept. 1859, p. 287

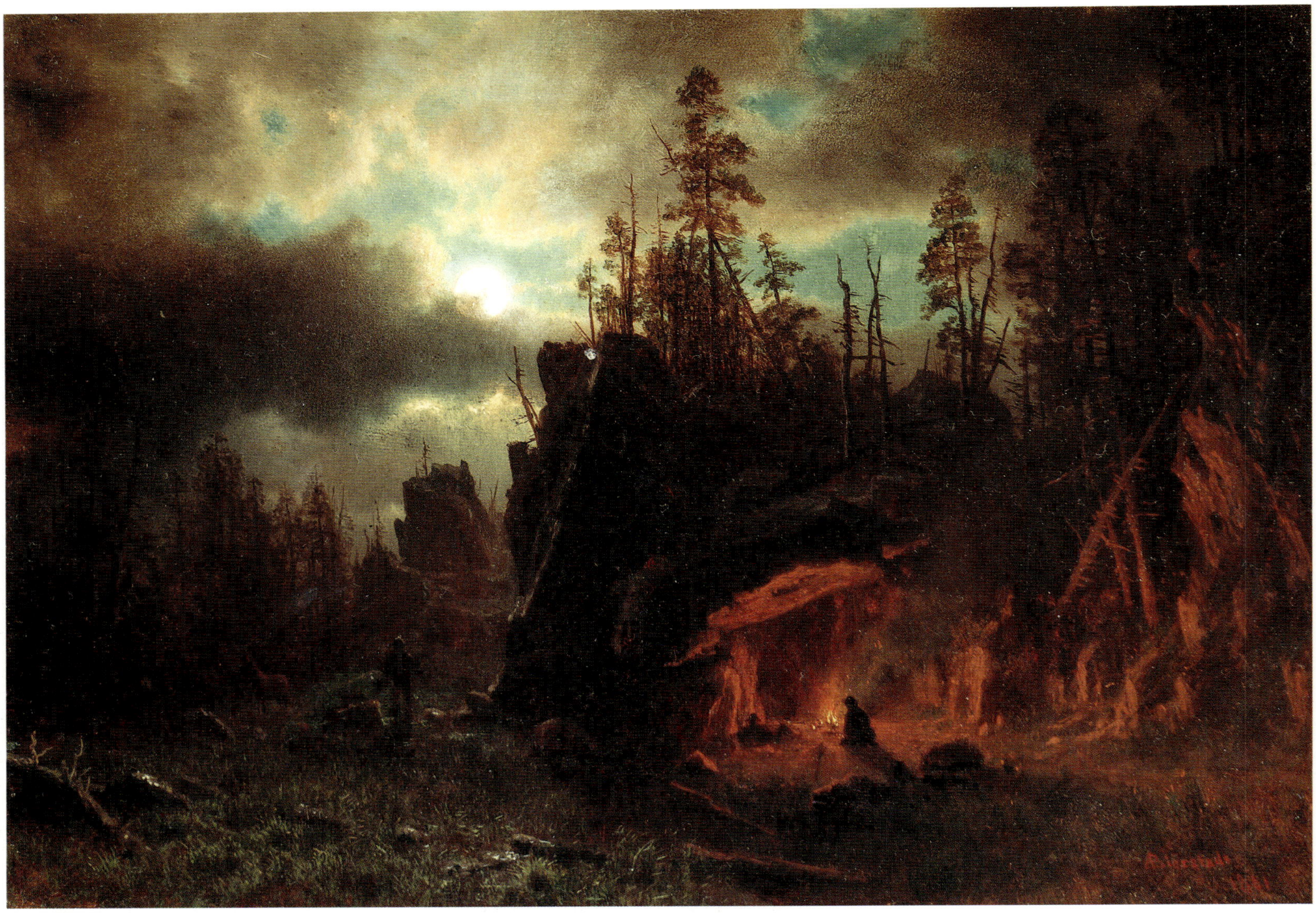

NO. 27

## *The Trappers' Camp*, 1861

Oil on millboard, 13 × 19 in. (33 × 48.3 cm)

Signed and dated lower right: *ABierstadt/1861*

Inscribed verso: *The Trappers' Camp/Rocky Mountains/A. Bierstadt artist/Studio Building/15, 10th St., New York.*

Yale University Art Gallery, New Haven, Connecticut, Whitney Collections of Sporting Art Fund, given in memory of Harry Payne Whitney, B.A. 1894, and Payne Whitney, B.A. 1898, by Francis P. Garvan, B.A. 1897, M.A. (Hon.) 1922

*A. Bierstadt's picture—"The Trappers' Camp"—is one of the results of his visit last season to the Rocky Mountains. It depicts a moonlight scene in that region of country, with the trappers seated about the red blaze of the camp-fire.*

*Home Journal*, 14 Dec. 1861, p. 3

*The Artists' Fund sale at the Studio Building on Saturday evening attracted a large and miscellaneous audience. . . . The most spirited competition was for the works of Durand, Huntington, Casilear, Kensett, Leutze, Gifford, Hubbard, Whittredge and Bierstadt. . . . "The Trappers' Camp," one of Bierstadt's Rocky Mountain Studies, $65. . . .*

*Post*, New York, 23 Dec. 1861

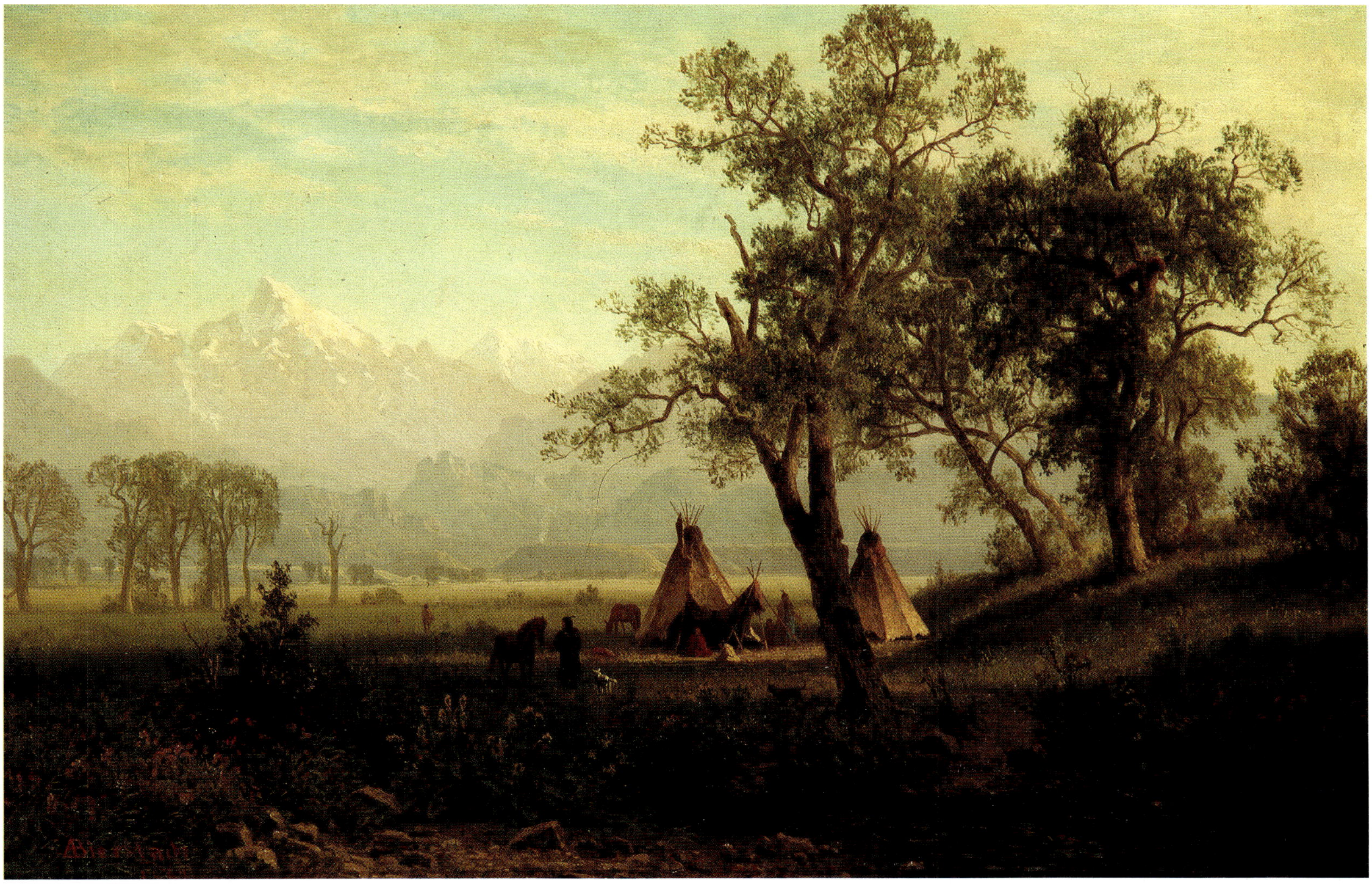

NO. 28

*Wind River Mountains, Nebraska Territory,* 1862

Oil on composition board, 12 × 18½ in. (30.5 × 47 cm)

Signed and dated lower left: *ABierstadt/1862*

Milwaukee Art Museum, Layton Art Collection

*Our route lies for the most of the time by the side of the Platte, as we depend on it for wood and water; but from time to time we make little excursions among the hills. During one of these, I came upon an Indian grave, while wandering through a ravine. They bury their dead in a tree. This was an old cedar about three feet in diameter, and at a distance of about twelve feet from the ground it branched out, and here with raw hides they had bound poles across on a level, on which coarse reeds were laid, and on this the Indian brave, with all he possessed in life. It had the appearance of having been dead five or six years. I climbed into the tree to examine it more closely, and found his buckskin clothes, richly ornamented with porcupine quills, his blanket beautifully wrought with beads, bracelets upon his arms, and his head was bare, with the exception of the scalp-lock. By his side lay the presents from his friends to help him on his way to the "happy hunting grounds," among which I found bullets, coloring material, medicines, etc. I should judge he had been a chief among them. There was something very impressive in the scene before us, and the silence of the little valley, and this the only solitary tree, around which waved the grasses and flowers in wild luxuriance, while beyond in the distance rose the hills covered with cedars.*

Letter from Bierstadt, Wolf River, Kansas, 3 Sept. 1859, in *Mercury*, New Bedford, 14 Sept. 1859

NO. 29

## *Sunlight and Shadow,* 1862

Oil on canvas, 41½ × 35½ in. (105.4 × 90.2 cm)

Signed and dated lower right: *ABierstadt/1862*

The Fine Arts Museums of San Francisco, Gift of Mr. and Mrs. John D. Rockefeller 3rd

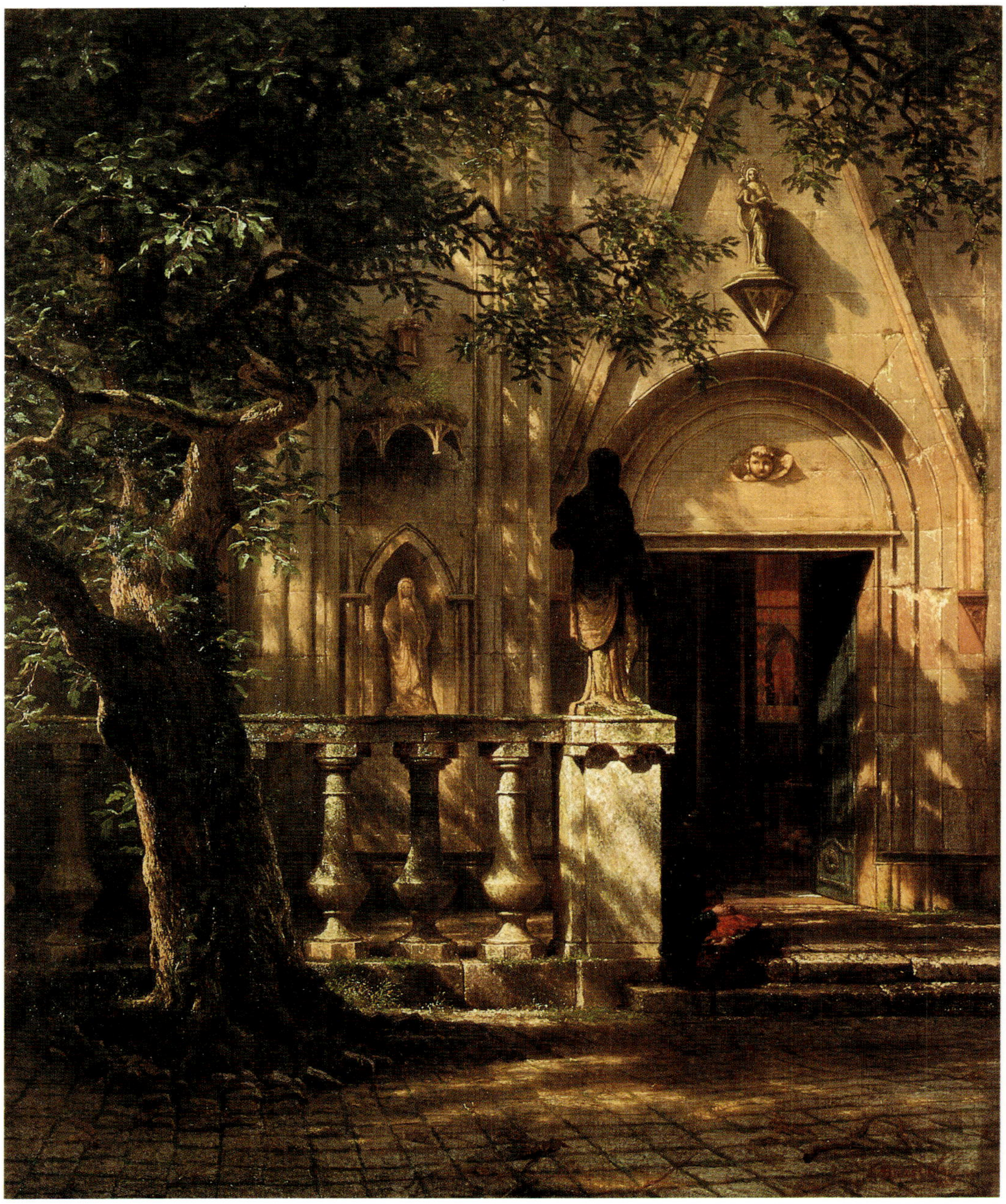

*It is truly a magnificent work, evincing great labor, and a thorough knowledge of the effects of light and shade.*

*Brooklyn Daily Eagle,* 24 Mar. 1862

*The spectator is before the front of an old continental church, through whose portal is seen the bright stained glass of the interior window . . . and on these old statues on the church porch, on the balustrade and on the tesselated* [sic] *pavement before the porch, the sunlight falls, broken in chequered patches by the foliage of an old oak tree which is seen at the left of the picture. The only figure is that of a woman seated on the step of the church, with a sleeping child seated on her lap, and the whole work is one of the happiest delineations of noonday repose which we have ever seen.*

*Post,* New York, 17 Apr. 1862

*Sunlight and Shadow, by A. Bierstadt, . . . is more perfectly painted than any sunshine we ever saw. . . .*

*Harper's Weekly,* 10 May 1862, p. 290

*On looking at your* Cathedral Porch *I found that I had admired the picture in New York without casting a thought on the artist. The effect of sunlight is truly wonderful, and the pretty girl at the exhibition's door told me this picture attracted more attention and comment than any other on the walls. In my opinion, old fellow, you are bound to lead the brotherhood of American Landscape.*

Charles Lanman to Albert Bierstadt, 4 Aug. 1862, Downs Collection

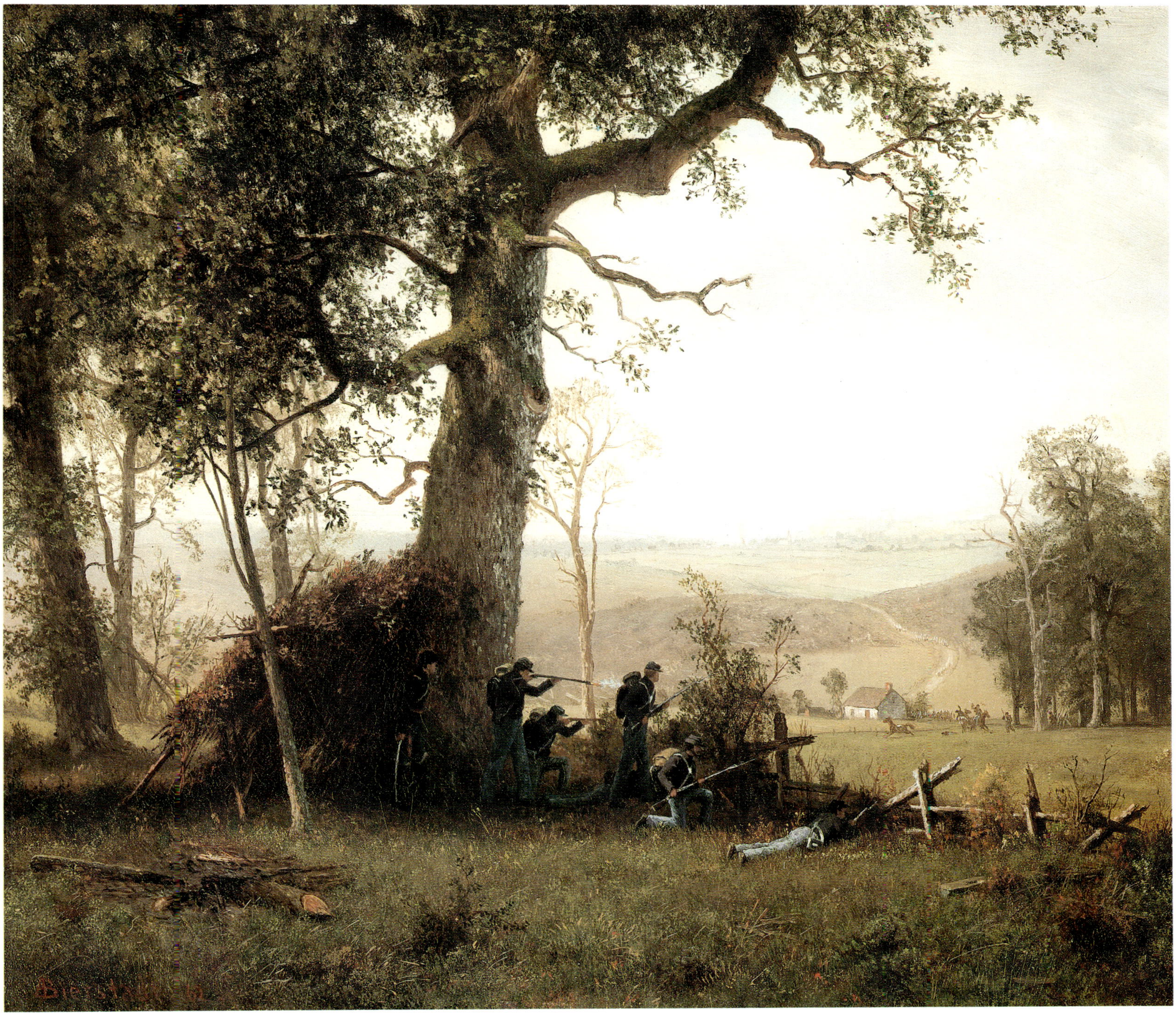

NO. 30

## *Guerrilla Warfare (Picket Duty in Virginia)*, 1862

Oil on panel, 15½ × 18⅝ in. (39.4 × 47.3 cm)

Signed and dated lower left: *ABierstadt 62*

The Century Association, New York

Presented by the artist as his initiation fee, 1862

*Bierstadt gives a good war piece—an effective representation of Picket Duty by the 7th Regiment in Virginia. It is much admired.*

*Brooklyn Daily Eagle*, 27 Dec. 1861

*One of the best compositions we have seen from his easel is a war sketch representing Federal sharp-shooters on the crest of a hill behind some trees. This is an excellent piece of work, fresh, original, and quite free from the Düsseldorf taint, and confirms us in the opinion that Mr. Bierstadt is naturally an artist of great ability and large resources, and might easily have obtained and held a reputation as such if he had not grafted on the sensationalism of Düsseldorf a greater ambition for notoriety and money than for success in pure art.*

S. G. W. Benjamin, "Fifty Years of American Art: 1828–1878," *Harper's New Monthly Magazine* 59 (Oct. 1879): 674

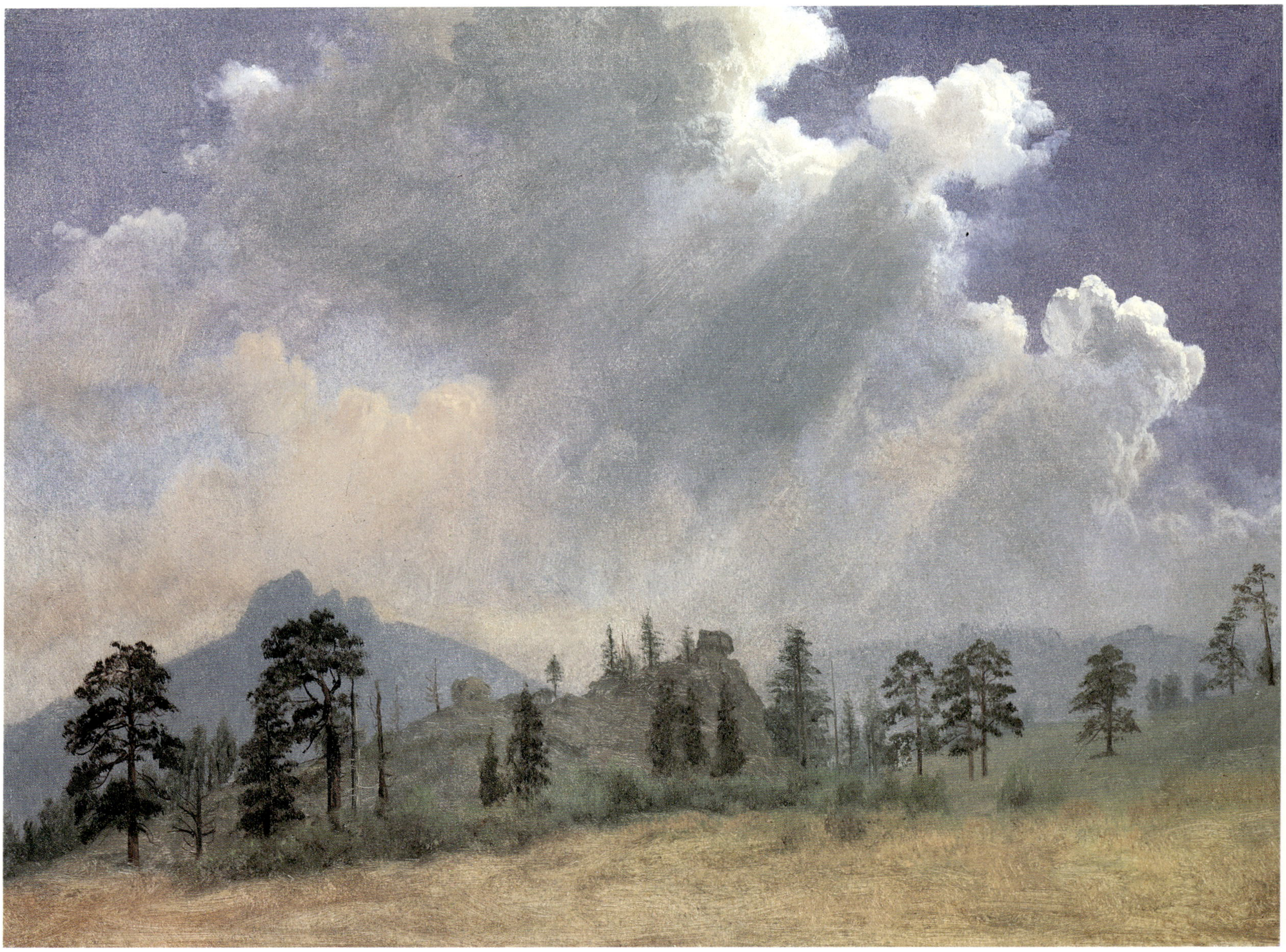

NO. 31

## *Fir Trees and Storm Clouds*

Oil on paper mounted on canvas, 13¾ × 18¾ in. (34.9 × 47.6 cm)

Unsigned

The Cleveland Museum of Art, Mr. and Mrs. William H. Marlatt Fund

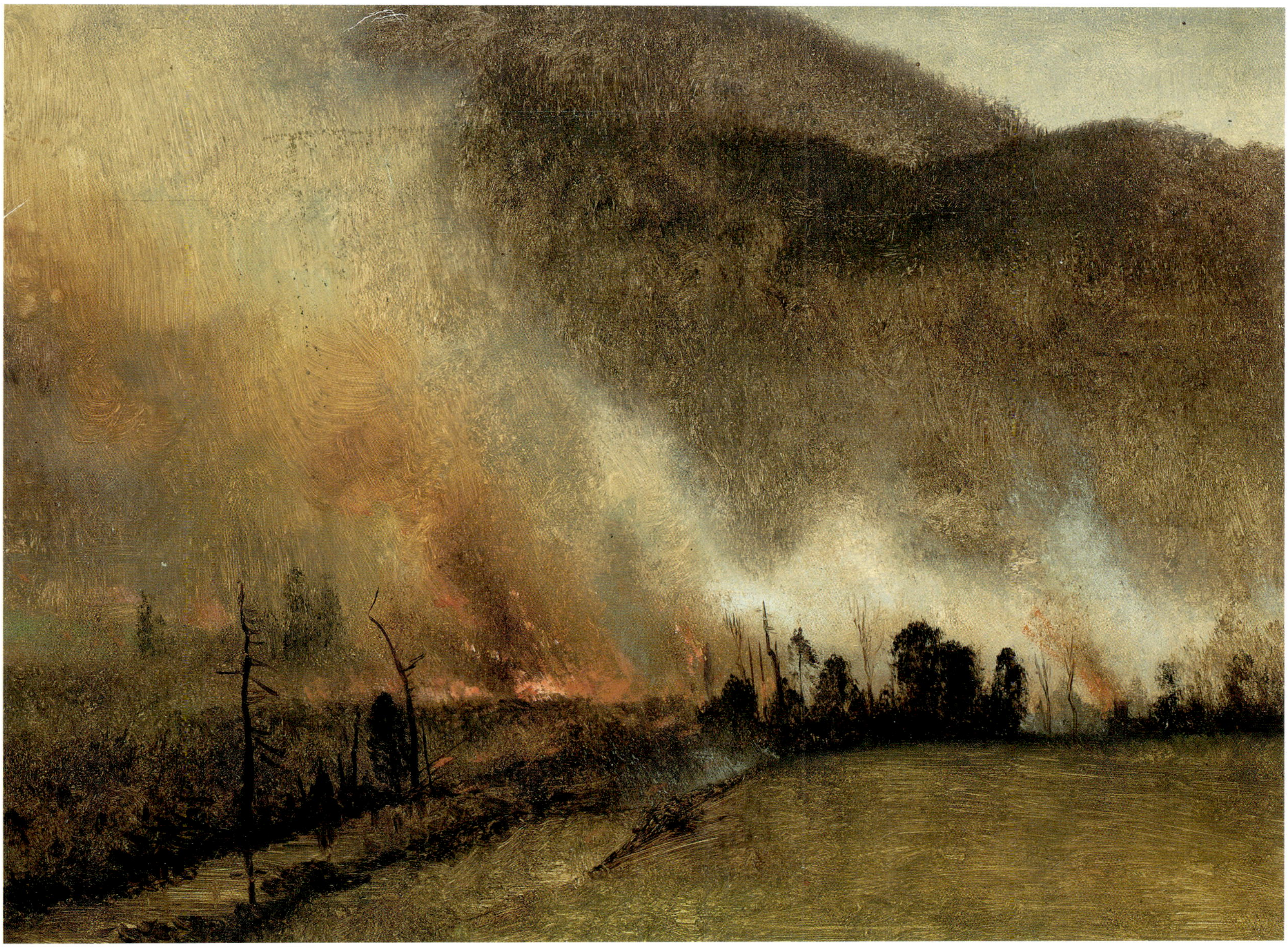

NO. 32

*White Mountains, New Hampshire*

Oil on paper, 11 × 15 in. (27.9 × 38.1 cm)

Unsigned

The Thomas Gilcrease Institute of American History and Art, Tulsa, Oklahoma

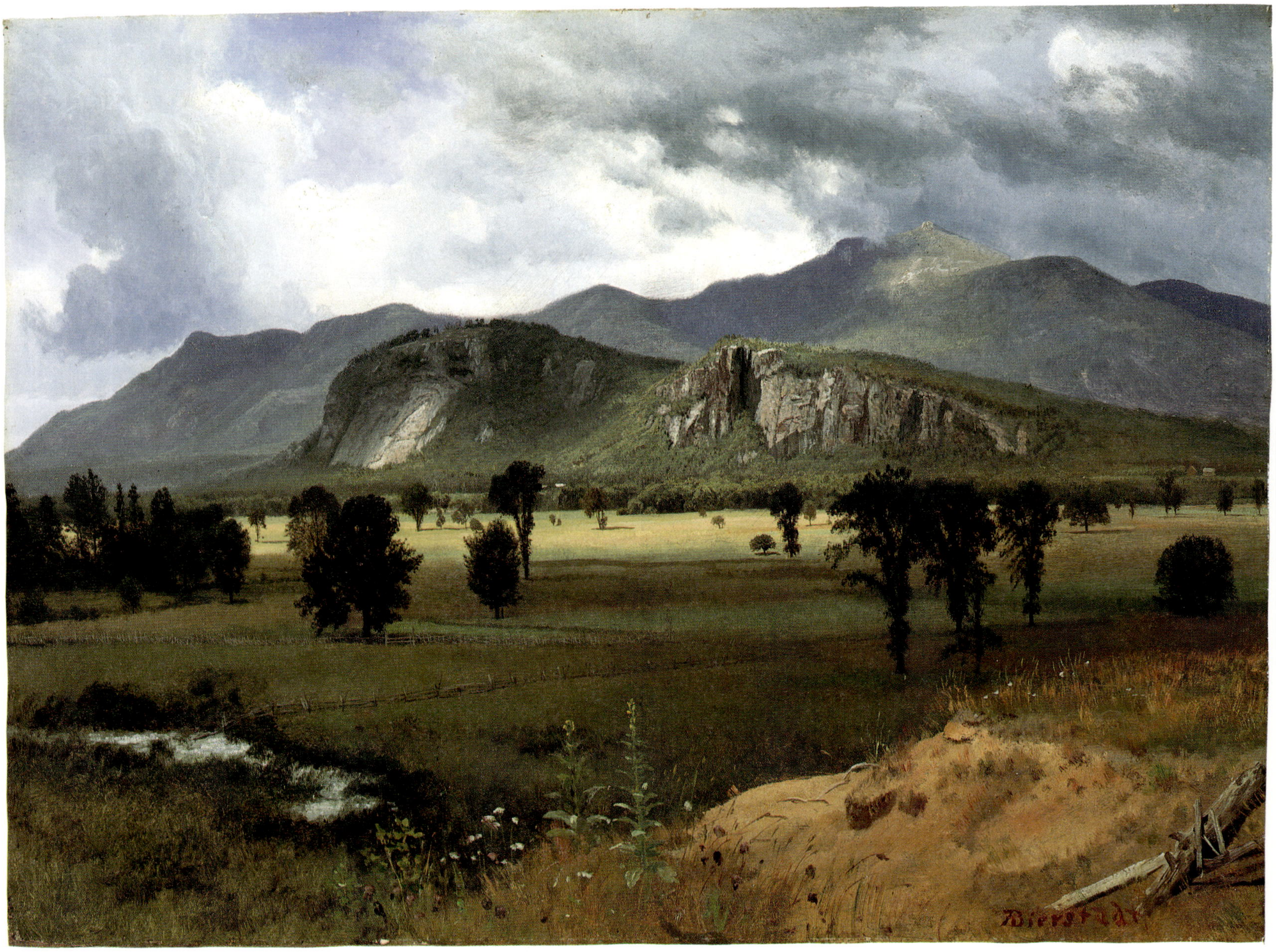

NO. 33

## *Moat Mountain, Intervale, New Hampshire*, c. 1862

Oil on canvas, 19 × 25⅞ in. (48.3 × 65.7 cm)

Signed lower right: *ABierstadt*

The Currier Gallery of Art, Manchester, New Hampshire

*One always finds, we think, on a return to North Conway, that his recollections of its loveliness were inadequate to the reality. Such profuse and calm beauty sometimes reigns over the whole village, that it seems to be a little quotation from Arcadia, or a suburb of Paradise. Who can tell how it is that the trees here seem of more aristocratic elegance,—that the shadows are more delicately pencilled,—that the curves of the brooks are more seductive than elsewhere? Why do the nights seem more tender and less solemn? What has touched the ledgy rocks with a grace that softens the impression of sublimity and age? What has made the "twilight parks" of pine dim with a pensive rather than a melancholy dusk?*

*Certainly, we have seen no other region of New England that is so swathed in dreamy charm. A few years ago, the Mote* [sic] *Mountains were ravaged with fire; and yet their lines give such delight, that few mountains look so attractive in verdure as they in desolation. The atmosphere and the outlines of the hills seem to lull rather than stimulate. There are no crags, no pinnacles, no ramparts of rock, no mountain frown, or savageness brought into contrast, at any point, with the general serene beauty.*

Thomas Starr King, *The White Hills: Their Legends, Landscape, and Poetry* (Boston: 1860), p. 152

# 1863–1870

## *Overland to California, Return to Europe*

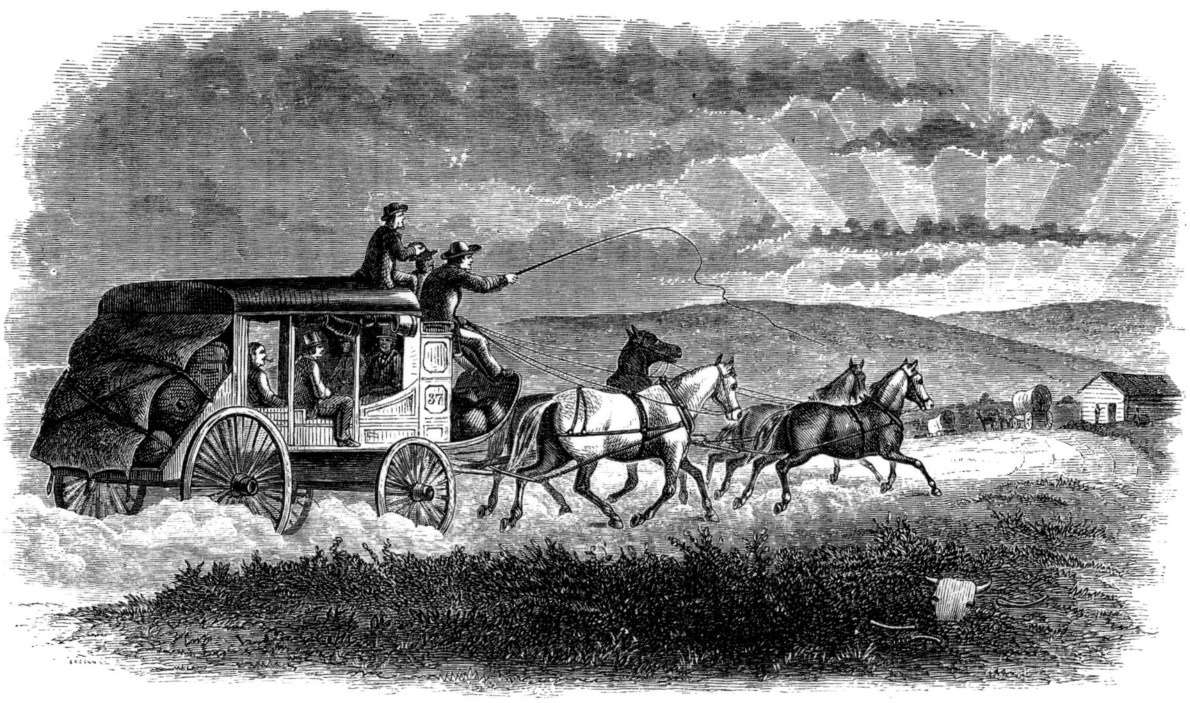

BEFORE SETTING OUT on his second overland journey in the spring of 1863, Bierstadt began exhibiting *The Rocky Mountains, Lander's Peak*, 1863 (No. 37), the most important painting to result from his initial expedition west four years earlier. Shown privately at the Century Club and the Tenth Street Studio Building, the painting attracted much attention and drew favorable reviews. A short time later, it was reported that Bierstadt had refused an offer of $10,000 for the picture (Chronology, 2 Apr. 1863).

Although *The Rocky Mountains, Lander's Peak* was clearly the most important of his recently completed works, Bierstadt chose not to contribute the painting to the Annual Exhibition at the National Academy of Design in the spring of 1863. Instead, he sent the picture to Boston, where it was placed on public exhibition and a twenty-five-cent admission fee was charged. Bierstadt's decision may reflect the artist's growing sophistication in marketing his pictures, as well as his awareness of the success Frederic Church had enjoyed when he exhibited his major paintings in private galleries for a fee.

While *The Rocky Mountains, Lander's Peak* was attracting crowds in Boston, Bierstadt and Fitz Hugh Ludlow, a prominent member of New York's literary circle, were making their way overland to California. Ludlow's letters to the New York *Evening Post* and the San Francisco *Golden Era* (see Appendix B), as well as a later series of articles published in the *Atlantic Monthly* and his book-length account of the journey, *The Heart of the Continent* (1870), mark the 1863 trip as the most thoroughly documented of all Bierstadt's western expeditions.

Following the old Oregon Trail through Nebraska Territory, Bierstadt and Ludlow took the southern route to California and arrived in San Francisco on 17 July 1863. Welcomed as celebrities by the local literati, they spent several days in the city before departing for Yosemite. Accompanied by Virgil Williams and Enoch Wood Perry, two artists working in San Francisco whom Bierstadt had known in Europe, they made their way to Yosemite via the Mariposa Grove of giant sequoias.

For seven weeks Bierstadt, Ludlow, and the others camped and sketched in Yosemite. When they returned to San Francisco in September, Bierstadt learned he had been drafted. Like many others, he paid a $300 commutation fee and was excused from service, but the news must have been a sobering reminder that while he and his companions sojourned in California, the war continued to take its toll.

On 24 September 1863, Bierstadt and Ludlow set off on the second leg of their expedition, a trip north into Oregon Territory. Originally, the artist and writer had planned to continue into Washington Territory and lower Canada, but when Ludlow became ill in Oregon, they cut their journey short at the Columbia River.

Early in November, Bierstadt and Ludlow boarded a steamer in Portland bound for San Francisco and later that month continued to Panama. After crossing the Isthmus, they sailed for New York and by mid-December were home. After spending the holidays in New Bedford, Bierstadt returned to New York, where he set to work on the paintings that would mark the most successful period of his career.

As he had in the past, Bierstadt welcomed journalists to his studio. By mid-February 1864, one such visitor was able to report that the artist was making rapid progress on a painting of Oregon's snowcapped peak Mount Hood. While working on *Mount Hood, Oregon*, 1865 (Fig. 55), Bierstadt continued to garner praise for *The Rocky Mountains, Lander's Peak*, which he had placed on public exhibition in New York. Crowds of people reportedly stood in line to see the painting. Shortly after the painting went on view, Bierstadt announced that he would contribute the picture to the benefit exhibition to be held for the Sanitary Fund (a forerunner of the Red Cross) at the Metropolitan Fair in New York in April. When the fair opened, Bierstadt's large Rocky Mountain picture hung directly across from Frederic Church's *Heart of the Andes*, 1859 (Fig. 40), a circumstance that prompted critical debate regarding the comparative merits of the two paintings.

A showman as well as an artist, Bierstadt also served as proprietor of an "Indian Department" at the Metropolitan Fair. In addition to display cases filled with Indian artifacts that Bierstadt had gathered on his travels, the Indian Department offered live performances by a troupe of Indians. A descendant of George Catlin's tableaux vivants from the 1840s, Bierstadt's Indian Department was also a forerunner of Buffalo Bill's Wild West Shows of the 1880s.

Following the fair, Bierstadt returned to his studio and resumed work on *Mt. Hood, Oregon* and a second major canvas, *Looking Down Yosemite Valley, California*, 1865 (No. 42). Both pictures represent an ambitious attempt to capitalize on new subject matter that Bierstadt rightly perceived would have wide popular appeal.

*Looking Down Yosemite Valley, California* became Bierstadt's major contribution to the Annual Exhibition at the National Academy of Design in 1865. Hung in a place of honor, the picture drew both high praise and stinging criticism. The fourth in Bierstadt's series of panoramic western views, *Looking Down Yosemite Valley, California* was the first of the showpiece pictures that did not include vignettes of Indian or animal life, a fact that was noted by many and criticized by some. The sharp division evident in the critical response to *Looking Down Yosemite Valley, California* was a harbinger of the increasingly strident debate Bierstadt's paintings would engender during the coming decade.

Although the sale of *The Rocky Mountains, Lander's Peak* for an astonishing $25,000 was reported in a Washington, D.C., newspaper as early as April 1865, the news did not appear in New York newspapers until October, when the published price caused a sensation. The sale of the painting to James McHenry, a railroad entrepreneur visiting the United States from England, marked a milestone in Bierstadt's career. Though he continued to produce easel paintings and publish engravings and chromolithographs for a more moderate market, he increasingly pursued the patronage of American entrepreneurs and European aristocrats.

By the time the McHenry sale was announced in New York, Bierstadt was already at work on the next of his showpiece canvases, *Storm in the Rocky Mountains, Mt. Rosalie*, 1866 (No. 45). Even larger than the earlier western panoramas, the painting was purchased by Thomas William Kennard, one of James McHenry's business associates who also resided in England. While working on the picture, Bierstadt was also supervising the construction of an enormous house and studio on the Hudson. Malkasten, as the mansion came to be called, was the home to which Bierstadt brought his bride, Rosalie Osborne Ludlow (former wife of Fitz Hugh Ludlow), following their marriage in November 1866.

In the spring of 1866, James McHenry placed *The Rocky Mountains, Lander's Peak* on public exhibition in London. High praise from English critics paved the way for Bierstadt's triumphant return to Europe the following year. Before his departure, however, Bierstadt placed the largest of his western landscapes, *The Domes of the Yosemite*, 1867 (Fig. 58), on exhibition in New York. Again reviewers split on the merits of the painting, this time so vehemently that one critic called the ensuing brouhaha the most contentious battle since the Civil War.

Meanwhile, Bierstadt had begun lobbying for a congressional commission to paint two pictures for the Capitol building in Washington. Initially he proposed a fee of $40,000 for each painting. Although he later reduced the sum to $30,000, Congress refused to appropriate the funds. Undeterred, Bierstadt continued to press his case. His persistent efforts won the commission, but not without a substantial reduction in the final payment.

In April 1867, Bierstadt made his exhibition debut in Paris when James McHenry agreed to lend *The Rocky Mountains, Lander's Peak* to the Exposition Universelle. Shortly thereafter, *Storm in the Rocky Mountains, Mt. Rosalie* was placed on view in London. Not surprisingly, two months later Bierstadt and his wife set sail for Europe on a combined business trip and honeymoon that lasted more than two years.

The high point of the painter's first year abroad came shortly before Christmas 1867, when he was invited to show his two large Rocky Mountain paintings to Queen Victoria and other members of the royal family at Osborne House on the Isle of Wight. Following his audience with the queen, Bierstadt and his wife traveled to Italy, where they spent the winter months. In Rome Bierstadt completed three major paintings, which he placed on exhibition the following summer at the Langham Hotel in London. Although the first, *Mount Vesuvius at Midnight*, remains unlocated, the other two are known: *Among the Sierra Nevada Mountains, California*, 1868 (No. 48), and *Sunset in the Yosemite Valley*, 1868 (No. 47). *The Domes of the Yosemite* was also on view in London in 1868. Like their American counterparts several years earlier, English viewers were awed by Yosemite's spectacular topography.

Following travel in Germany in August 1868, Bierstadt took a studio in Paris, where he and his wife spent the winter. The following spring, he exhibited *Storm in the Rocky Mountains, Mt. Rosalie* at the Salon. The painting drew critical acclaim from Théophile Gautier, who compared the artist to Alexandre Calame, Europe's premier painter of Alpine views.

While in Paris, Bierstadt, along with several other Americans in residence, drew up a plan for an art museum to be located in New York City. Surviving evidence indicates that they sent their proposal to the president of the Union League Club for discussion. Eventually the Metropolitan Museum of Art was born of these discussions, but the museum apparently evolved in a manner unacceptable to Bierstadt, for he later refused several invitations to participate in its organization.

Early in August 1869, Albert and Rosalie Bierstadt returned to New York. Shortly thereafter, they journeyed to the White Mountains in New Hampshire, where Bierstadt spent several weeks sketching. Before departing, however, he made arrangements for the exhibition in Boston of *Among the Sierra Nevada Mountains, California*, the large painting that had won accolades abroad. The painting drew considerable attention in the press and was quickly purchased by Alvin Adams, the wealthy collector who had also acquired *Lake Lucerne (Switzerland)* (No. 6) a decade earlier.

In December 1869, at the height of his fame, Bierstadt became involved in a controversy that threatened the market value of his paintings. Through statements published in an auction catalogue and additional newspaper reports, his name was linked to the sale of a large collection of paintings from the estate of an eccentric Boston collector, Thomas Thompson, who had purchased a number of Bierstadt's early pictures. As described by the press, the pictures attributed to the artist (probably the juvenilia Whittredge described as without merit) were an embarrassment. By denying authorship of some of the works, Bierstadt embroiled himself in a dispute that was played out in the newspapers. When the sale finally took place in February, some of the paintings attributed to Bierstadt were sold for as little as thirty dollars.

While mired in the Thompson controversy, Bierstadt continued to work on the next of his large exhibition pictures, *The Emerald Pool*, 1870 (Fig. 33). Measuring six by ten feet, the White Mountain forest interior was placed on view for the first time in May 1870. That same month, Fitz Hugh Ludlow published *The Heart of the Continent*, his book-length account of the overland journey he and Bierstadt had undertaken in 1863. As promotion for his paintings, Bierstadt could not have hoped for more engaging publicity.

As early as the fall of 1870, Bierstadt began making plans to return to California. Although he did not actually depart until the spring of 1871, his next visit to the Pacific Coast lasted more than two years.

# CHRONOLOGY

## 1863

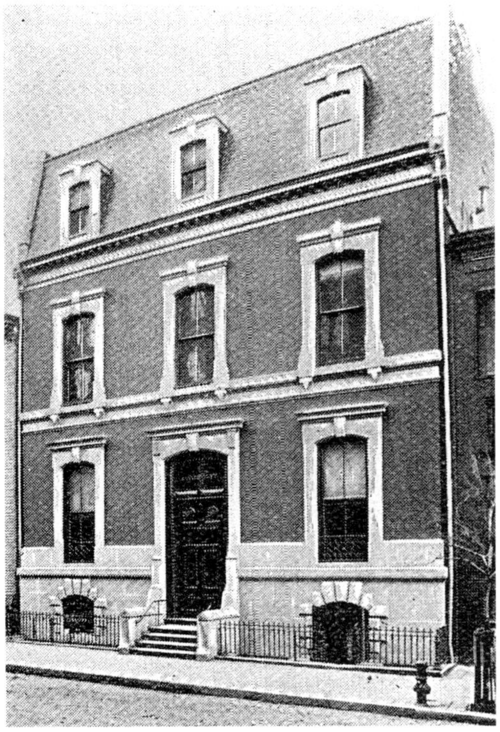

*109 East Fifteenth Street, New York, where the Century Association met from 1857 to 1891*. Photograph published in Moses King, ed., *King's Handbook of New York City* (Boston: 1892), p. 746.

Bierstadt becomes a member of the Century Club in 1863. (Membership Records, Century Association, New York)

**17 Jan.** "Barry Gray" (R. B. Coffin), in a long article on Bierstadt, writes, "Among the younger landscape painters of the day, few occupy a better position in the world of art, than Albert Bierstadt." Claiming to have studied "critically and impartially" nearly every painting by Bierstadt completed during the last four years, Coffin heaps lavish praise on the artist. (*NY Leader*, 17 Jan. 1863)

**19 Jan.** Bierstadt is at work on *The Rocky Mountains, Lander's Peak* (No. 37) and already planning a summer trip "across the continent to San Francisco via the overland mail, then up the Pacific Coast to Vancouver's Island." (Daly 1962, p. 215)

**26 Jan.** Bierstadt gives the Buffalo Fine Arts Academy his painting *Capri—Bay of Naples* (*The Marina Piccola, Capri*, No. 14), then on exhibition at the Academy. (*Buffalo Courier*, 6 Feb. 1863)

**3 Feb.** *The Rocky Mountains, Lander's Peak* exhibited for the first time, at the first Artists' Reception of the season held at Tenth Street Studio Building. (*Post*, New York, 4 Feb. 1863)

**2 Apr.** Tenth Street Studio artists hold "supplementary reception" because the market for pictures is so good. "Mr. Bierstadt . . . is said to have refused $10,000 for his Rocky Mountain landscape [*The Rocky Mountains, Lander's Peak*, No. 37], which goes to Boston for exhibition this month." (*NY Tribune*, 4 Apr. 1863)

**13 Apr.** Bierstadt's *Rocky Mountains, Lander's Peak* placed on public exhibition in Boston. (*Boston Transcript*, 13 Apr. 1863)

**14 Apr.–24 June** NAD Annual Exhibition open in New York. Bierstadt exhibits *The Mountain Brook* (No. 36) and *North Fork of the Platte, Nebraska* (No. 39). (*NY Times*, 14, 24 Apr. 1863; Catalogue, NAD, 1863, pp. 11, 13)

**27 Apr.** *The Rocky Mountains, Lander's Peak* is to be engraved by James Smillie. (*Boston Transcript*, 27, 28 Apr. 1863)

**4 May** "Bierstadt, the artist, departs for the far West this week. He will be accompanied by Fitz Hugh Ludlow, who, it is understood, will make copious notes of the tour, and, on his return home, in the early winter, give to the public the result of the trip in an illustrated volume. . . . Bierstadt proposes to be absent six to eight months, which will, he thinks, give him ample time to . . . make the necessary studies for another large picture." (*Boston Transcript*, 4 May 1863)

**14 May** In an article about the strong market for pictures, Bierstadt is reported to have "refused $6000 for one of his." (*Boston Transcript*, 14 May 1863)

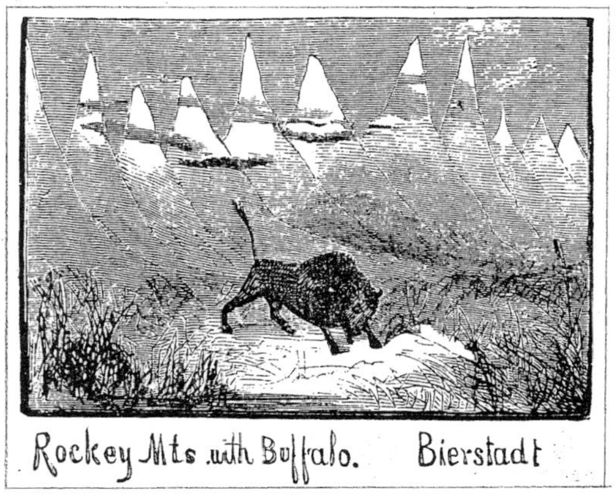


*Rockey* [sic] *Mts. with Buffalo. Bierstadt* (caricature). Wood engraving published in *Harper's New Monthly Magazine*, May 1863.

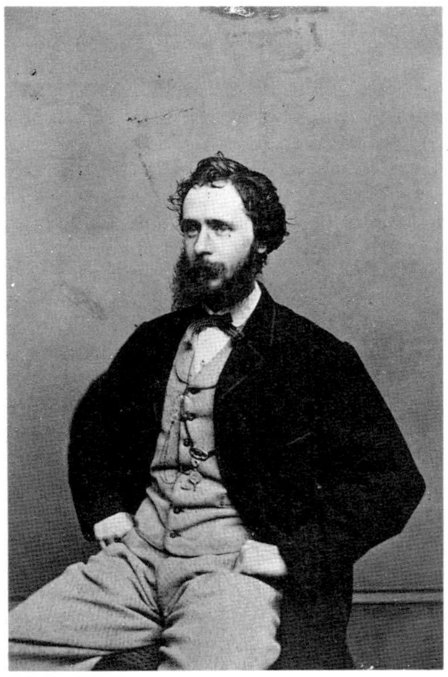

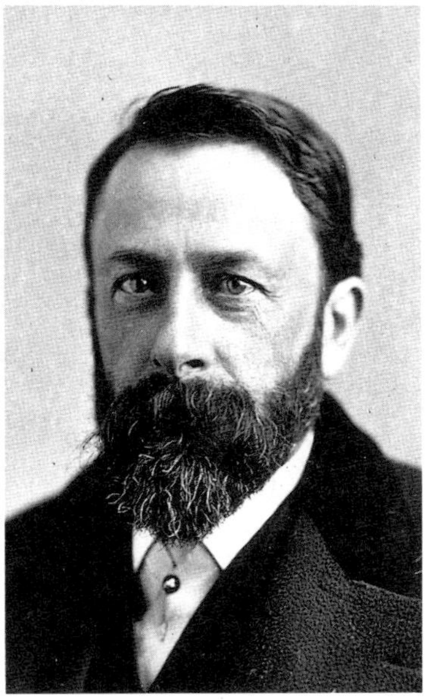

*(far left)* K. W. Beniczky, New York. *Fitz Hugh Ludlow*, c. 1863. Carte de visite. Collection of Joyce Randall Edwards.

*(left)* Napoleon Sarony, New York. *Albert Bierstadt*. Carte de visite. Collection of James P. Crain.

**20 May** Bierstadt and Ludlow depart Saint Joseph, Missouri, and begin their overland journey to California. (*Golden Era*, San Francisco, 22 Nov. 1863)

**26 May** First of Fitz Hugh Ludlow's "Letters from Sundown" published in the *Post*. Bierstadt and Ludlow traveled from Philadelphia to Altoona, Pittsburgh, Cincinnati, Saint Louis, Saint Joseph, and Atchison with free rail passes. In Atchison they boarded the overland stage for California. (*Post*, New York, 26 May 1863)

**3 June** At the sale of the Reverend Henry Ward Beecher's collection, Bierstadt's *Bavarian Farmyard* sells for "the shockingly low figure of $155." (*Brooklyn Daily Eagle*, 4 June 1863)

**5 June** *The Rocky Mountains, Lander's Peak* on exhibition in New Bedford. (*Post*, New York, 5 June 1863)

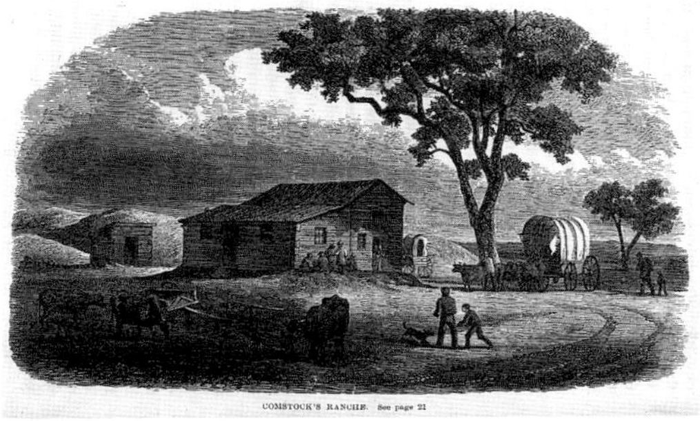

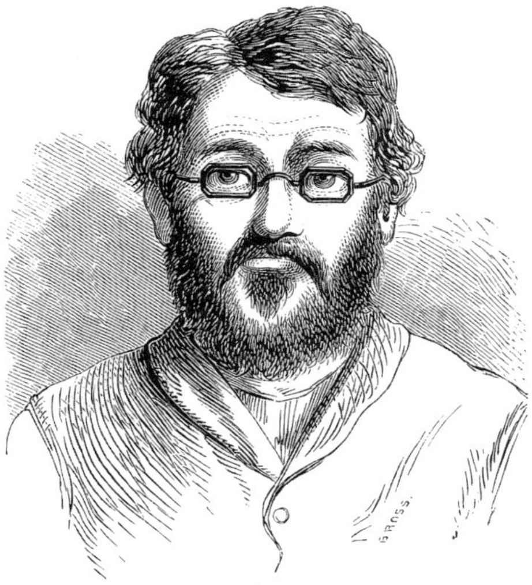

PORTRAIT OF COMSTOCK. See page 24.

*(top)* After Albert Bierstadt. *Comstock's Ranche*. Wood engraving published in Fitz Hugh Ludlow, *The Heart of the Continent* (New York: 1870).

*(above)* After Albert Bierstadt. *Portrait of Comstock*. Wood engraving published in Fitz Hugh Ludlow, *The Heart of the Continent* (New York: 1870).

Second of Fitz Hugh Ludlow's "Letters from Sundown" published by the *Post*. Written at the Comstock Ranch near Oak Grove, Nebraska, the letter describes a buffalo hunt and Bierstadt's plein air studies. (*Post*, New York, 5 June 1863)

**12 June** Engraver James D. Smillie writes to Edward Bierstadt advising him that he will make "a drawing from your brother's painting of the 'Rocky Mts' " in October and have the work completed by November 1." (Smillie to E. Bierstadt, 12 June 1863, private collection)

**July** Review of the NAD exhibition in the *Christian Examiner* describes Church and Bierstadt as rivals "in popular favor" and discusses *The Rocky Mountains, Lander's Peak*. (*Christian Examiner*, July 1863, p. 123)

**13 July–1 Aug.** *The Rocky Mountains, Lander's Peak* on exhibition in Portland, Maine. (*Portland Daily Advertiser*, 13, 15 July 1863)

**17 July** Bierstadt and Ludlow arrive in San Francisco via the overland mail. (*Alta*, San Francisco, 19 July 1863)

**24 July** First half of the third of Ludlow's "Letters from Sundown" published in the *Post;* describes the trip from the Platte River to Denver. (*Post*, New York, 24 July 1863)

**25 July** Second half of Ludlow's third letter published in the *Post;* concerns side trips near Denver, Pike's Peak, and Garden of the Gods. (*Post*, New York, 25 July 1863)

**30 July** Fourth of Ludlow's "Letters from Sundown" published in the *Post*. (*Post*, New York, 30 July 1863)

**by 1 Aug.** Ludlow, Bierstadt, and artists Virgil Williams and Enoch Wood Perry pass through Stockton on their way to Yosemite. (*Alta*, San Francisco, 1 Aug. 1863)

**20 Aug.** Albert Bierstadt drafted for service in the Union army from New York's 15th Ward (see 26 Oct.). (*Post*, New York, 21 Aug. 1863; Records of the Provost Marshall General's Bureau for the 6th Congressional District of New York, National Archives)

**21 Aug.** Bierstadt and his companions sign Register Rock, near Vernal Falls in Yosemite. (Godfrey 1944, p. 50)

**22 Aug.** From Yosemite Valley Bierstadt writes to John Hay that he will not be able to join him on a buffalo hunt in the fall as planned, explaining that the ride on the overland route is "so very tedious and dangerous" that he will take the steamer back to New York. "We are now here in the garden of Eden I call it. The most magnificent place I was ever in, and I employ every moment painting from nature. Two old friends of mine are also here. Mr. Williams and Mr. Perry, both artists. We camp out altogether, get no news, and do not care for any for we are perfectly happy with the fine scenery, trout, ducks, deer, etc. In about ten days Ludlow & myself start for Oregon on horseback going through the Sierra Nevada and returning by the coast range." (Bierstadt to Hay, 22 Aug. 1863, John Hay Collection, John Hay Library, Brown University, Providence, R.I.)

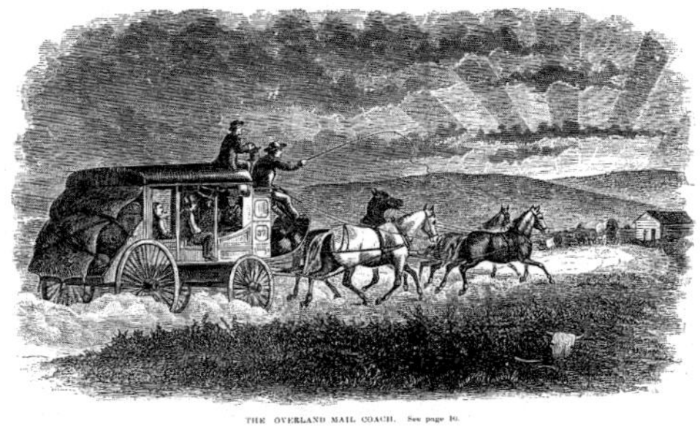

After Albert Bierstadt. *The Overland Mail Coach*. Wood engraving published in Fitz Hugh Ludlow, *The Heart of the Continent* (New York: 1870).

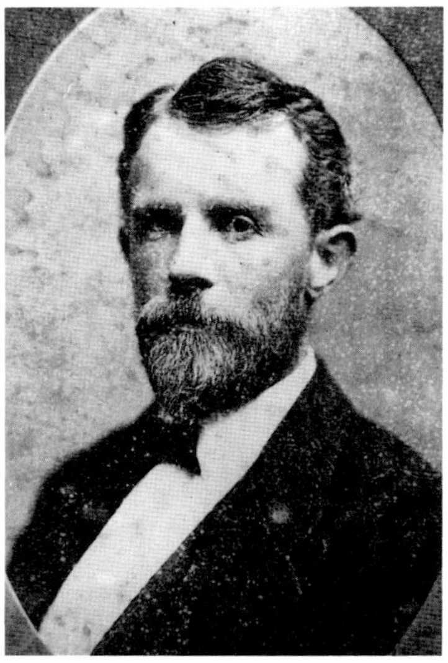

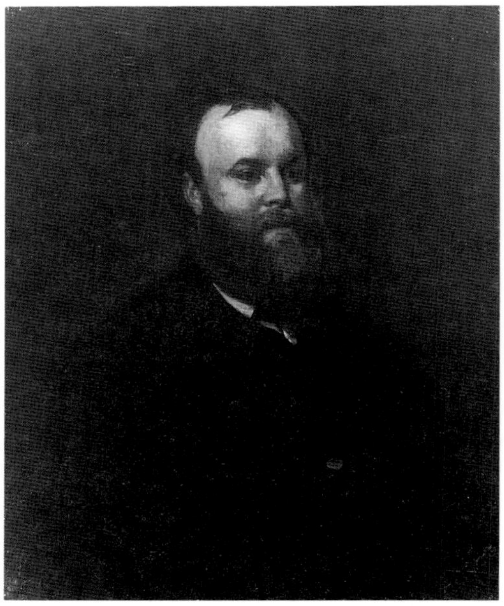

*(top) Virgil Williams*. Photograph. The Silverado Museum, Saint Helena, California.

*(above)* George C. Lambdin. *Enoch Wood Perry*, 1869. Oil on canvas. National Academy of Design, New York.

**7 Sept.** *The Rocky Mountains, Lander's Peak* on exhibition in Boston at Williams & Everett. (*Boston Transcript*, 7, 9, 10 Sept. 1863)

**13 Sept.** The *Golden Era* reports that Fitz Hugh Ludlow has been engaged as a contributor during his sojourn in California and will offer a series of sketches titled "Reminiscences of an Overlander" (see Appendix B). (*Golden Era*, San Francisco, 13 Sept. 1863)

**25 Sept.** "Messrs. Bierstadt and Fitz Hugh Ludlow started yesterday for Oregon on the Sacramento boat. They take their horses by steam to Red Bluff, and thence they will ride past Shasta, through the Klamath, Rogue, Umpqua, and Willamette Valleys. They will ascend the Columbia to the mouth of Snake River, then go down to the Cowlitz, there take to their saddles again, ride across to Puget Sound, and thence come to San Francisco by sea, touching at British Columbia if they have time." (*Alta*, San Francisco, 25 Sept. 1863)

**12 Oct.** Last week of exhibition of Bierstadt's *Rocky Mountains, Lander's Peak* in Boston. (*Boston Transcript*, 12 Oct. 1863)

**24 Oct.** Fifth of Ludlow's "Letters from Sundown" published in the *Post;* reports on the trip to Yosemite. (*Post*, New York, 24 Oct. 1863)

**26 Oct.** Through an agent, Bierstadt pays a commutation fee in New York and is excused from service in the Union army. (Record of Disposition of Drafted Men, 1863–1864, Record Group 110, National Archives)

**28 Oct.** Sixth of Ludlow's "Letters from Sundown" published in the *Post*. (*Post*, New York, 28 Oct. 1863)

**31 Oct.** *The Rocky Mountains, Lander's Peak* brought back to New York "in order to be placed in the hands of Mr. James Smillie, who has contracted to execute a large line engraving of it, which will be ready for delivery, accidents excepted, in about two years." (*NY Tribune*, 31 Oct. 1863)

**5 Nov.** Bierstadt and Ludlow depart Portland aboard the steamer *Pacific*. (*Alta*, San Francisco, 14 Nov. 1863)

**14 Nov.** Bierstadt and Ludlow arrive in San Francisco. (*Alta*, San Francisco, 14 Nov. 1863)

**23 Nov.** Bierstadt and Ludlow depart San Francisco for Panama aboard the steamer *Constitution*. (*Alta*, San Francisco, 22 Nov. 1863)

**16 Dec.** Bierstadt and Ludlow arrive in New York aboard the steamship *Champion* from Aspinwall, Panama. (Passenger Lists of Ships Arriving in New York from Foreign Ports, National Archives)

**21 Dec.** Bierstadt is in Boston and about to leave for a stay in New Bedford before returning to New York, where he will begin "to transfer some of his sketches of the magnificent scenery of California and Oregon." (*Boston Transcript*, 21 Dec. 1863)

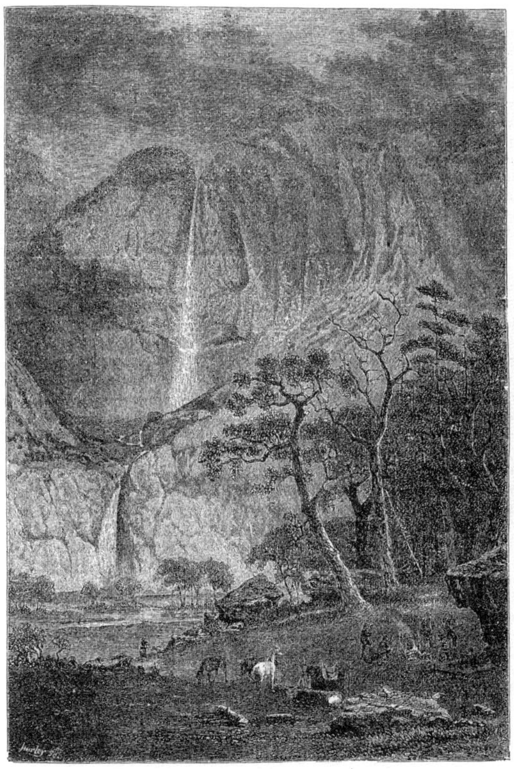

THE YO-SEMITE FALL.

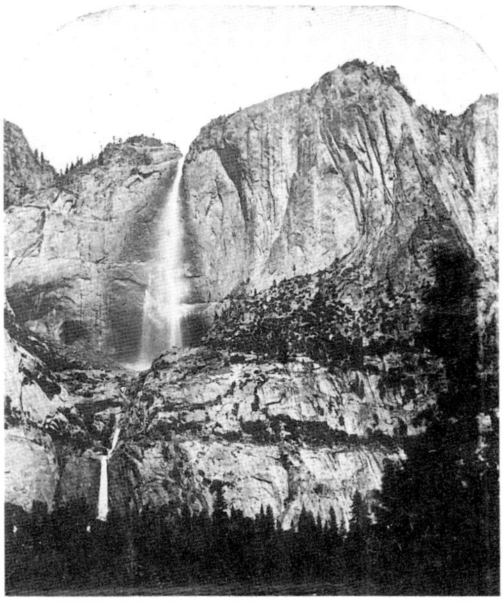

*(top)* After Albert Bierstadt. *The Yo-Semite Fall*. Wood engraving published in *Riverside Magazine for Young People*, Dec. 1869.

*(above)* Charles Bierstadt, Niagara Falls, New York. *Yosemite Falls*. Stereograph. Collection of Leonard A. Walle.

## 1864

**7 Jan.** "In a few weeks [Bierstadt] will begin a large picture, the subject of which will be of the grandest and most imposing character of any of the scenery through which he passed [*Mount Hood, Oregon*, Fig. 55]." (*Post*, New York, 7 Jan. 1864)

**17 Feb.–1 Apr.** *The Rocky Mountains, Lander's Peak* on public exhibition at Seitz's gallery in New York "for a few weeks." (*Post*, New York, 12 Feb. 1864; *NY Times*, 31 Mar. 1864)

**21 Feb.** First of Fitz Hugh Ludlow's "Reminiscences of an Overlander" published in the San Francisco *Golden Era* (see Appendix B).

**25 Feb.** At second Artists' Reception of the season at Dodworth's, Bierstadt exhibits *Mount Adams, Oregon*. (*Post*, New York, 26 Feb. 1864)

**28 Feb.** Second of Ludlow's "Reminiscences of an Overlander" published in the *Golden Era* (see Appendix B).

**29 Feb.** Bierstadt visiting in New Bedford. (*Mercury*, New Bedford, 29 Feb. 1864)

**6 Mar.** Third of Ludlow's "Reminiscences of an Overlander" published in the *Golden Era* (see Appendix B).

**18 Mar.** Bierstadt at work on *Mount Hood, Oregon*. (*Boston Transcript*, 18 Mar. 1864)

**20 Mar.** Fourth of Ludlow's "Reminiscences of an Overlander" published in the *Golden Era* (see Appendix B).

**21 Mar.** George Bancroft commissions Bierstadt to paint a picture for him for $750. (Bancroft to Bierstadt, 21 Mar. 1864, Downs Collection)

**27 Mar.** Fifth of Ludlow's "Reminiscences of an Overlander" published in the *Golden Era* (see Appendix B).

**Apr.** "Among the Mormons," by Fitz Hugh Ludlow, published in the *Atlantic Monthly*.

**1–23 Apr.** Metropolitan Fair for the U.S. Sanitary Commission opens in New York. Bierstadt contributes *The Rocky Mountains, Lander's Peak* to the art gallery and manages an Indian exhibition. In addition to a group of performing Indians, Bierstadt's Indian Department comprises "two or three hundred curiosities, including a large wigwam." (*Post*,

New York, 2 Apr. 1864; Catalogue, Metropolitan Fair 1864, p. 7)

"A New York reporter, describing his visit to Mr. Bierstadt's Wigwam at the Fair, says—'We were treated to a highly spirited rehearsal of Green Cow, Rattlesnake, Racoon, and other dances by the Indians. . . .'" (*Mercury*, New Bedford, 7 Apr. 1864)

**15 Apr.–25 June** NAD Annual Exhibition open. Bierstadt exhibits *Landscape*. (*Post*, New York, 15 Apr., 28 May 1864; Catalogue, NAD, 1864, p. 19)

**16 Apr.** Bierstadt receives permission from the Executive Committee of the Sanitary Commission to extend the engagement of the Indians performing at the fair. (Richard White to Bierstadt, 16 Apr. 1864, Downs Collection)

**17 Apr.** Sixth of Ludlow's "Reminiscences of an Overlander" published in the *Golden Era* (see Appendix B).

**20 Apr.** *Valley of the Yosemite* (No. 41) sold at the Sanitary Fair auction to "Mr. Davis" for $1,600, "the highest price obtained for a single picture." (*Post*, New York, 22 Apr. 1864; Catalogue, Metropolitan Fair Auction, Apr. 1864, p. 13)

**31 May** Bierstadt in New Bedford. (*Mercury*, New Bedford, 31 May 1864)

**June** "Seven Weeks in the Great Yosemite," by Fitz Hugh Ludlow, published in the *Atlantic Monthly*.

**7 June–6 July** Bierstadt's *The Rocky Mountains, Lander's Peak* (No. 37) and *The Wetterhorn* on exhibition at the Great Central Fair for the benefit of the Sanitary Commission in Philadelphia. (*Boston Transcript*, 15 June 1864; Yarnall and Gerdts 1986, pp. 299, 300)

**30 June** President Lincoln signs bill that sets aside Yosemite Valley and the nearby Mariposa redwood grove as a state park (designated a national park in 1890).

**July** "On Horseback into Oregon," by Fitz Hugh Ludlow, published in the *Atlantic Monthly*.

**4 July** "[Bierstadt] is now engaged on two large paintings, for each of which he is to receive $10,000." (*Mercury*, New Bedford, 4 July 1864)

**8 July** *Sunlight and Shadow* (No. 29) is back in Bierstadt's studio "after two years' absence in Europe—where it was sent to be engraved. . . . It has been very successfully chromo-lithographed at Berlin, and copies of it will reach this country in the autumn." (*Post*, New York, 8 July 1864)

**29 July** *The Rocky Mountains, Lander's Peak* on exhibition in Buffalo; after a few weeks it will be sent "to Rochester, Utica, Elmira, Albany, and other inland towns in this state." (*Post*, New York, 29 July 1864)

Bierstadt arrives in New Bedford to remain "a few weeks." (*Mercury*, New Bedford, 30 July 1864)

**13 Aug.** *Sunlight and Shadow* "on free exhibition in New York." (*Mercury*, New Bedford, 13 Aug. 1864)

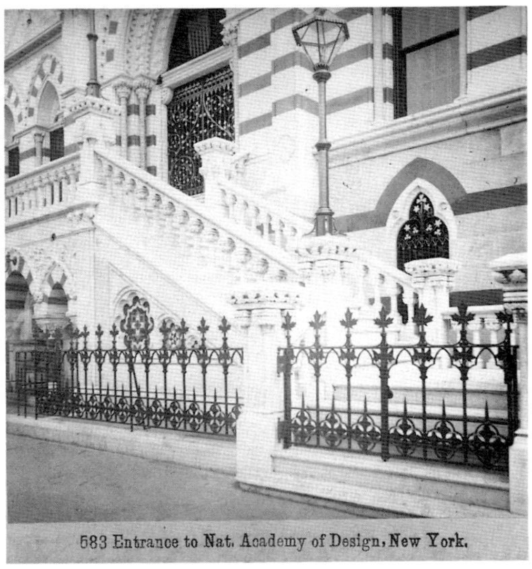


Bierstadt Brothers, New Bedford, Massachusetts. *Entrance to Nat. Academy of Design, New York*. Stereograph. Collection of William L. Schaeffer.

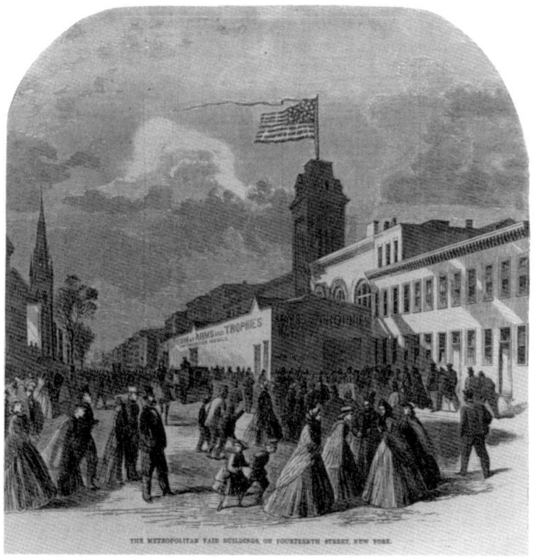

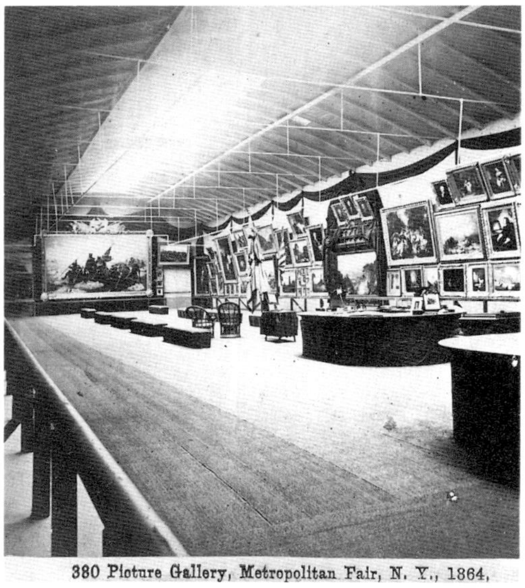


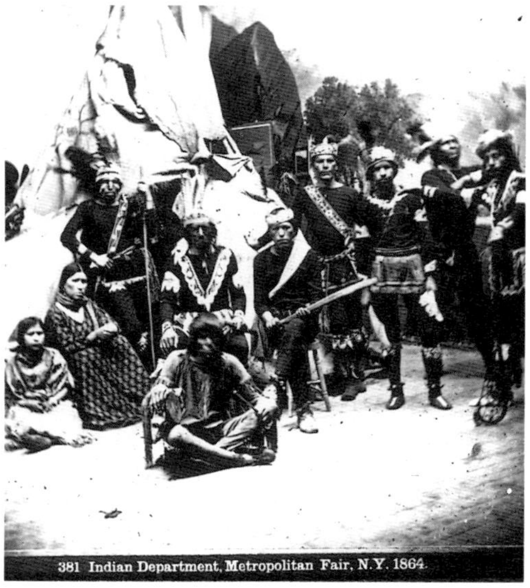


*(above) The Metropolitan Fair Buildings, on Fourteenth Street, New York*. Wood engraving published in *Harper's Weekly*, 9 Apr. 1864.

*(right, above)* Bierstadt Brothers, New Bedford, Massachusetts. *Picture Gallery, Metropolitan Fair, N.Y., 1864*. Stereograph. Collection of Wilfred Thompson, courtesy of Leonard A. Walle.

*(right, below)* Bierstadt Brothers, New Bedford, Massachusetts. *Indian Department, Metropolitan Fair, N.Y. 1864*. Stereograph. Collection of James P. Crain.

**20 Oct.** Chromolithographs (No. 76) of *Sunlight and Shadow* on sale at Seitz's, where the painting remains on view. (*Post*, New York, 20 Oct. 1864)

**21 Oct.** Christina Bierstadt, the artist's mother, dies in New Bedford at age seventy-three. (Register of Deaths, City Clerk's Office, New Bedford, Mass.; *Mercury*, New Bedford, 22 Oct., 4 Nov. 1864)

**31 Oct.** Bierstadt, in New Bedford, painting *Silver Lake*, "a view of a little lake in the Sierra Nevada range, California," for the National Sailors' Fair in Boston. (*Mercury*, New Bedford, 31 Oct. 1864)

**Nov.** "Through-Tickets to San Francisco: A Prophecy," by Fitz Hugh Ludlow, published in the *Atlantic Monthly*.

**1–19 Nov.** *The Rocky Mountains, Lander's Peak* on exhibition at Knight & Son's Gallery in Brooklyn. (*Brooklyn Eagle*, 2 Nov. 1864)

**22 Nov.** *Silver Lake* sold for $975 at auction to Royal E. Robbins for benefit of the Sailors' Fair in Boston. (*Boston Transcript*, 21, 23 Nov. 1864)

## 1865

**9 Jan.** Bierstadt exhibits *Mount Hood, Oregon* (Fig. 55) for the first time (in an unfinished state) at a reception sponsored by the Young Men's Christian Association in New York City. (*Post*, New York, 10 Jan. 1865; *Mercury*, New Bedford, 12 Jan. 1865)

**13 Feb.** Bierstadt is reported to have finished his large painting of Mount Hood. (*New York Weekly Review*, quoted in *Boston Transcript*, 13 Feb. 1865)

**16 Feb.** "Bierstadt has just commenced, on canvas larger than his Rocky Mountains, a storm in the mountains [*Storm in the Rocky Mountains, Mt. Rosalie*, No. 45]." (*Post*, New York, 16 Feb. 1865)

**8 Apr.** John C. Frémont buys painting from Bierstadt (probably *The Golden Gate, California*) for $4,000. (Frémont to Bierstadt, 8 Apr. 1864, Downs Collection)

**9 Apr.** Robert E. Lee surrenders to Ulysses S. Grant at Appomattox, ending the Civil War.

**14 Apr.** *The Rocky Mountains, Lander's Peak* arrives in Washington, D.C., for exhibition. The next day it is reported that the painting, which will be exhibited in Chicago before going to England, has been sold for $25,000. (*Daily National Intelligencer*, Washington, D.C., 15 Apr. 1865)

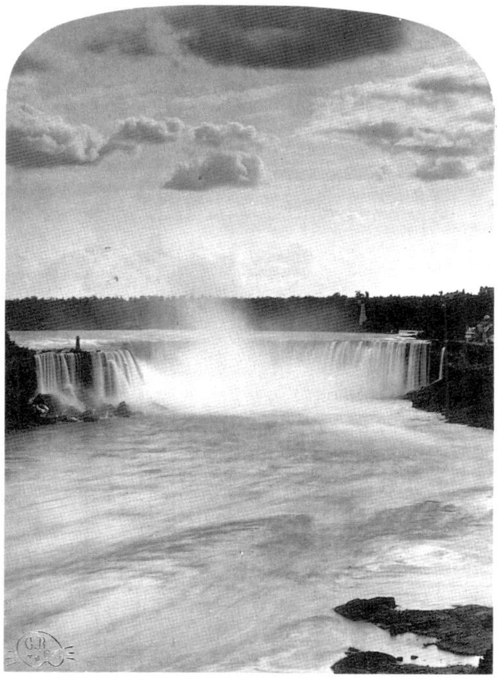

Charles Bierstadt, Niagara Falls, New York. *Horseshoe Falls, Niagara*. Stereograph. Private collection.

**27 Apr.–5 July** Bierstadt contributes two works to the NAD Annual Exhibition: *Looking Down Yosemite Valley, California* (No. 42) and *The Golden Gate, California*. (*NY Times*, 28 Apr. 1865; *World*, New York, 28 Apr. 1865; Catalogue, NAD, 1865, pp. 26, 28)

**2 May** *The Rocky Mountains, Lander's Peak* on view in Washington, D.C. (*Mercury*, New Bedford, 2 May 1865)

**30 May** The Northwestern Sanitary Fair opens in Chicago. "Bierstadt's noble picture, the Rocky Mountains, occupies, as it deserves, the place of honor, being assigned the central portion of the east wall, where the light is the most effective." Bierstadt also contributes *Mt. Chicorua* [sic], *N.H.* and *Conway Meadows, Mohawk River* to be sold at a benefit auction at the conclusion of the fair. (*Post*, New York, 31 May 1865; Yarnall and Gerdts 1986, pp. 293, 298, 299)

**10 June** "[Bierstadt] has recently purchased five acres of land on the Hudson River, between Irvington and Tarrytown, upon which he will erect a fine stone building, the larger portion of which will be devoted to a studio. The spot selected commands some of the finest and most extensive views on the North river." (*Mercury*, New Bedford, 10 June 1865)

**26 Aug.–14 Oct.** *Mount Hood, Oregon* on exhibition in Boston at Williams & Everett. (*Boston Transcript*, 26 Aug. 1865)

**9 Sept.** "Mr. Bierstadt is studying Niagara." (*Round Table*, 9 Sept. 1865, p. 7)

**11 Oct.** "Mr. McHenry, one of the party of English capitalists who have recently made a tour through this country, has purchased Mr. Bierstadt's picture of the Rocky Mountains [*The Rocky Mountains, Lander's Peak*, No. 37], for the sum of $25,000." (*Post*, New York, 11 Oct. 1865)

**17 Oct.** Bierstadt reported to have two more $25,000 commissions "from the English capitalists now on a visit here." (*Post*, New York, 17 Oct. 1865)

**21 Oct.** *Mount Hood, Oregon* on exhibition in New Bedford at John Hopkins's music store. (*Mercury*, New Bedford, 20 Oct. 1865)

**2 Nov.** Plans for an engraving of *Mount Hood, Oregon* announced; subscription book opened at John Hopkins's store, where the painting is on view. (Plans for the engraving were not realized.) (*Mercury*, New Bedford, 2 Nov. 1865)

**3 Nov.** Bierstadt at work on *Storm in the Rocky Mountains, Mt. Rosalie* (No. 45). (*Post*, New York, 3 Nov. 1865)

**12–13 Nov.** Bierstadt visits New Bedford. Construction nearly complete on his "fine studio and dwelling at Irvington." (*Mercury*, New Bedford, 14 Nov. 1865)

**13 Nov.** *Mount Hood, Oregon* on exhibition in Boston. (*Alta*, San Francisco, 13 Nov. 1865)

**26 Dec.** "It is said that Bierstadt's brush has earned him $120,000 in the last three years. He has the finest team in the Central Park, and is building a villa at Irvington, on the Hudson." (*Boston Transcript*, 26 Dec. 1865)

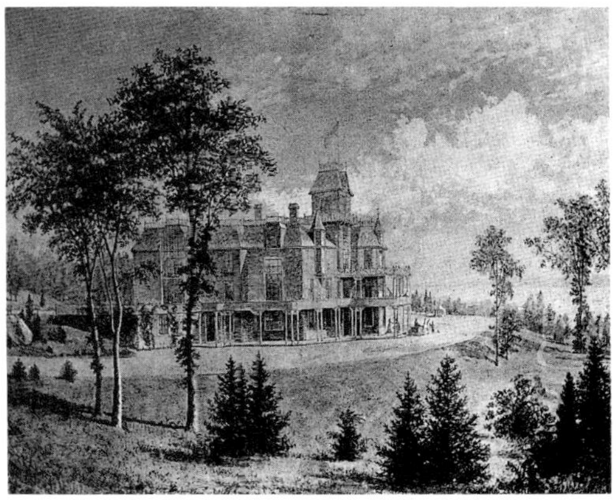

*View of Malkasten*. Artotype. Collection of Joyce Randall Edwards.

## 1866–1867

### 1866

**3 Jan.** Exhibition of *The Rocky Mountains, Lander's Peak* concludes in New York. (*NY Times*, 3 Jan. 1866)

**19 Jan.** Bierstadt reported to have finished *Storm in the Rocky Mountains, Mt. Rosalie* (No. 45). (*Daily National Intelligencer*, Washington, D.C., 19 Jan. 1866)

**6–24 Feb.** *Storm in the Rocky Mountains, Mt. Rosalie* on exhibition at Miner & Somerville Gallery for the benefit of the New York Nursery and Child's Hospital. (*NY Herald*, 2, 7 Feb. 1866)

**26 Feb.** During the last three weeks exhibition receipts for *Storm in the Rocky Mountains, Mt. Rosalie* have totaled more than $2,200, "as much as $250 having been taken in one day." (*NY Herald*, 26 Feb. 1866)

**2 Mar.** Rutherford B. Hayes (then a congressman from Ohio) writes to his uncle from Washington, D.C.: "With a party, Generals Schenck, Crook, Smith, and their ladies, I went to see the picture of 'The Storm in the Rocky Mountains' by Bierstadt. It is very beautiful and wonderful. By gaslight the effect is incomprehensible, such brilliancy and light and shade! Mr. Bierstadt says it is better by daylight. I shall see." (Charles Richard Williams, *Diary and Letters of Rutherford Birchard Hayes* [Columbus, Ohio: 1922–26], vol. 3, p. 19)

**19 Mar.–7 May** *Storm in the Rocky Mountains, Mt. Rosalie* on view in Baltimore. (*Sun*, Baltimore, 15, 27 Mar. 1866)

**28 Mar.** "Mr. Bierstadt has recently sold his 'Rocky Mountains' to an English collector (Mr. McHenry) for $25,000, and his 'Storm in the Rocky Mountains' to another Englishman (Mr. Kinnaird [Kennard] ) for $20,000. After this latter picture had been engaged, the artist was offered $30,000 for it by a New York merchant, but it went to the foreign purchaser." (*Post*, New York, 28 Mar. 1866)

**29 Mar.** Bierstadt's *Platte River, Nebraska* sold at auction for $7,000 in New York. (*Post*, New York, 6 Apr. 1866)

**20 Apr.** *Mount Hood, Oregon* on exhibition in Washington, D.C., for the benefit of St. Ann's Orphan Asylum. (*Daily National Intelligencer*, Washington, D.C., 20, 25 Apr. 1866; *Daily Morning Chronicle*, Washington, D.C., 18 Apr. 1866)

**21 Apr.** In an early review of the NAD exhibition, the *Round Table* notes that Bierstadt sent no "mammoth work. Is he released from his Rocky Mountain engagement, and is he without a theme grand enough to match the colossal proportions of his great fame?" (*Round Table*, 21 Apr. 1866, p. 249)

**7 May** Rosalie Osborne Ludlow granted a divorce from Fitz Hugh Ludlow by the Supreme Court of New York County. (New York County Clerk's Office, Department of Old Records, Supreme Court Equity Judgments, GA 284 [1866])

**17 May** *The Rocky Mountains, Lander's Peak* on exhibition in London at McLean's Gallery. Called the "most important" representation of American scenery ever sent to England. (*Morning Herald*, London, 17 May 1866)

**26 May** *The Yosemite Valley* (*Looking Down Yosemite Valley, California*, No. 42) on exhibition in Philadelphia. (*Round Table*, 26 May 1866, p. 327)

**7 June** Bierstadt arrives in New Bedford for a stay of several days. (*Mercury*, New Bedford, 8 June 1866)

**12 June–25 Aug.** *Storm in the Rocky Mountains, Mt. Rosalie* on exhibition in Boston at Williams & Everett. (*Boston Transcript*, 13 June 1866)

**21 June** Bierstadt has moved to his studio at Irvington. (*Mercury*, New Bedford, 21 June 1866)

**22 June** Advertisement announces that *The Yosemite Valley* (*Looking Down Yosemite Valley, California*) ("valued at $20,000") will be the second premium in the Crosby Opera House lottery to be held in Chicago. (*Chicago Daily Tribune*, 22 June 1866)

**29 June** Henry Bierstadt, Albert's father, is "seriously ill." "Mr. Bierstadt is eighty-one years of age, and until recently has been quite constantly employed, assisting his sons, the Bierstadt Brothers, in their Photographic rooms." (*Mercury*, New Bedford, 29 June 1866)

**1 July** Henry Bierstadt dies in New Bedford, Mass. (*New Bedford Standard*, 2 July 1866; *Mercury*, New Bedford, 2 July 1866)

**20 July** *The Yosemite Valley* (*Looking Down Yosemite Valley, California*, No. 42) goes on exhibition in Milwaukee at Hempsted's Music Store. (*Milwaukee Sentinel*, 20, 21 July 1866)

**13 Aug.** *The Yosemite Valley (Looking Down Yosemite Valley, California)* sent to Cincinnati from Milwaukee for exhibition. (*Milwaukee Sentinel*, 13 Aug. 1866)

**7–30 Sept.** *Storm in the Rocky Mountains, Mt. Rosalie* on exhibition in Chicago at the Crosby Art Gallery. (*Chicago Daily Tribune*, 7 Sept. 1866)

**15 Sept.** A proof of Smillie's engraving of *The Rocky Mountains, Lander's Peak* on view at Goupil's in New York. (*Round Table*, 15 Sept. 1866, p. 108)

**10 Oct.** *Storm in the Rocky Mountains, Mt. Rosalie* goes on exhibition in Saint Louis. (*St. Louis Dispatch*, 10 Oct. 1866)

**31 Oct.** *The Yosemite Valley (Looking Down Yosemite Valley, California)*, second premium in the upcoming Crosby Opera House lottery in Chicago, is on exhibition in Cincinnati. (*Boston Transcript*, 31 Oct. 1866)

**21 Nov.** Bierstadt marries Rosalie Osborne Ludlow (former wife of Fitz Hugh Ludlow) in Waterville, New York. (*Utica Daily Observer*, 23 Nov. 1866; *Utica Herald*, 23 Nov. 1866)

**17 Dec.** Bierstadt seeks commission from U.S. government for paintings to be hung in the Capitol; suggests a Rocky Mountain or Yosemite view or a historical subject such as "the discovery . . . of the Hudson River which I have in progress." (Bierstadt to Captain

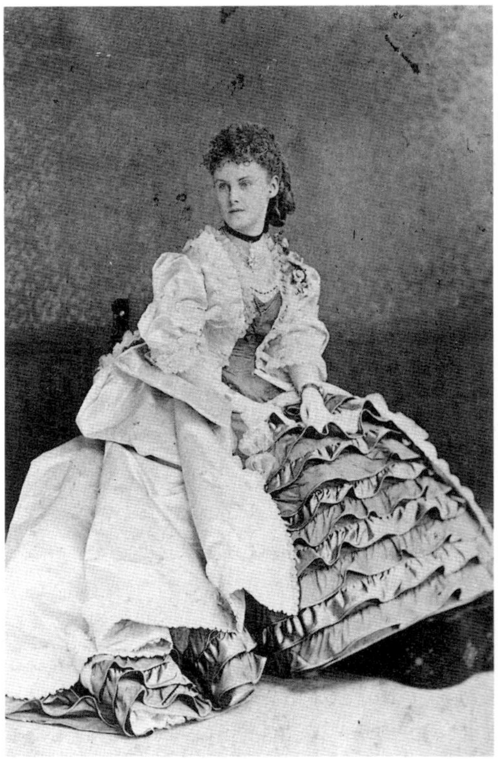

William Kurtz, New York. *Rosalie Bierstadt*. Photograph. Collection of Joyce Randall Edwards.

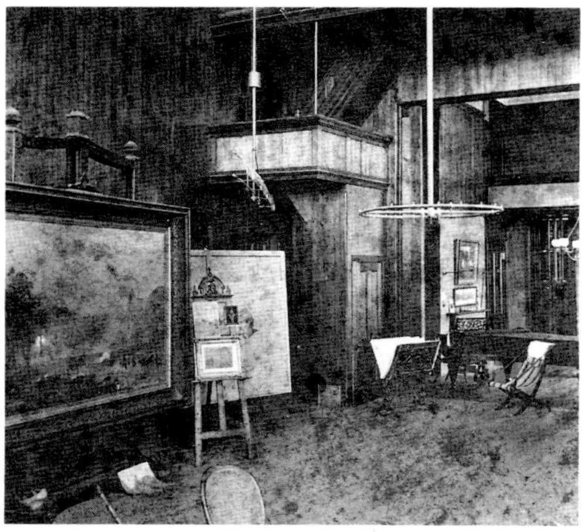

Bierstadt Brothers, New Bedford, Massachusetts. *Interior of Studio, Malkasten*, c. 1867. Photograph. Collection of Ralph Gosse.

Adams, 17 Dec. 1866, Manuscript Division, New York Public Library)

**19 Dec.** *The Yosemite Valley (Looking Down Yosemite Valley, California)*, second premium in the Crosby Opera House lottery, on exhibition in Philadelphia. (*Evening Bulletin*, Philadelphia, 19 Dec. 1866)

**23 Dec.** Exhibition of *Storm in the Rocky Mountains, Mt. Rosalie* closes in Buffalo. Plans announced for painting to be shown in New York before being shipped to Europe. (*Buffalo Express*, 20 Dec. 1866)

**24 Dec.** The engraving (No. 77) of Bierstadt's *Rocky Mountains, Lander's Peak*, "which has been in the hands of the engraver for the past three years, is just completed, and ready to be delivered to subscribers. . . . Knoedler receives subscriptions for this work." (*Post*, New York, 24 Dec. 1866; *Mercury*, New Bedford, 27 Dec. 1866)

**31 Dec.** Bierstadt at work in Irvington on "two large paintings; one representing an emigrant train on its way across the plains [*Emigrants Crossing the Plains*, National Cowboy Hall of Fame and Western Heritage Center, Oklahoma City] for Marshall O. Roberts, of New York; the other, a view in the Yo Semite Valley [*The Domes of the Yosemite*, Fig. 58] for Le Grand Lockwood, of the same city." (*Mercury*, New Bedford, 31 Dec. 1866)

## 1867

**14 Jan.** William Bradford reported to have passed several months with Bierstadt at Irvington and to have just resumed painting in his New York studio. (*Post*, New York, 14 Jan. 1867)

**21 Jan.** Resolution offered in the House of Representatives authorizing a contract with Bierstadt for "two paintings thoroughly American in character, representing some prominent feature of scenery or important event in the discovery or history of America to fill two unoccupied panels in the chamber of the House of Representatives." (Fairman 1927, p. 270)

Crosby lottery held in Chicago; ticket drawn for *The Yosemite Valley (Looking Down Yosemite Valley, California*, No. 42) one of many that remained unsold at the time of the drawing; hence, Mr. Crosby retains ownership of the painting. (*Boston Transcript*, 21, 22 Jan. 1867)

**c. 5 Feb.** Bierstadt returns from a trip "to the western cities, occupying several weeks." (*Post*, New York, 7 Feb. 1867)

**12 Feb.** House of Representatives Joint Committee on the Library requests that Bierstadt submit plans (with prices) for the two paintings commissioned by Congress. (Fairman 1927, p. 270)

**22 Feb.** Engraving of *The Rocky Mountains, Lander's Peak* to be sold only by subscription. "Artists' proofs will cost fifty dollars; proofs before letters, thirty dollars; proofs with letters, twenty dollars; and plain proofs, ten dollars." (*Post*, New York, 22 Feb. 1867)

**13 Mar.** House of Representatives Joint Committee on the Library instructs the Librarian to advise Bierstadt that Congress made no appropriation for paintings for the House Chamber. (Fairman 1927, p. 270)

**18 Mar.** From Irvington, Bierstadt responds to the Library Committee and encloses a copy of the sale contract for *The Rocky Mountains, Lander's Peak* to demonstrate the prices he can command. Reducing his original request for $40,000 per picture, Bierstadt indicates he would take $60,000 for the two paintings. (Bierstadt to Adams, 18 Mar. 1867, Eldon Grupp Collection, Mountain View, Calif.)

**1 Apr.–31 Oct.** Exposition Universelle open in Paris. Bierstadt exhibits *The Rocky Mountains, Lander's Peak*, on loan from James McHenry. (Catalogue, Exposition Universelle, 1867, p. 201)

**15 Apr.** NAD Annual Exhibition opens; Bierstadt does not contribute. (Catalogue, NAD, 15 Apr. 1867; *NY Times*, 16 Apr. 1867)

**26 Apr.–1 June** "Bierstadt's New Picture," *The Domes of the Yosemite*, on exhibition at the Tenth Street Studio Building for the benefit of the Ladies Southern Relief Association. (*NY Times*, 23 Apr. 1867)

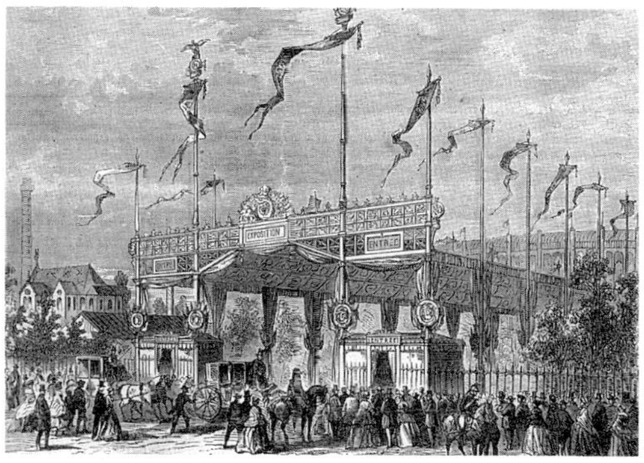

Jules Gaildrau. *Entrée Par La Pont D'Iéna* (of the Exposition Universelle). Wood engraving published in *L'Exposition Universelle de 1867 illustrée* (Paris: 1867). Museum of Fine Arts, Boston.

**May–Aug.** *Storm in the Rocky Mountains, Mt. Rosalie* on exhibition at McLean's Gallery in London. (Carr 1986, p. 64)

**2 May** Mixed review of Bierstadt's *Domes of the Yosemite*: "The painting is executed in . . . the style of Dusseldorf—a style that can be learned as an apprentice learns a trade, and which no disciple of that school ever seems able to unlearn or to forget. All the beauty of his pictures is on the surface. . . . They are always the same, beautiful, full of attractive qualities of composition, form and color, but unimaginative and destitute of sentiment. Yet no American artist is more popular than Bierstadt. His pictures always find ready sale, and of late, we believe he paints only on commission." (*NY Times*, 2 May 1867)

**11 May** The *Tribune* publishes negative review of Bierstadt's *Domes of the Yosemite*: "Mr. Bierstadt's reputation is so out of proportion to any actual achievement of his, has been so easily obtained, and is so difficult to account for, that it was natural to expect it must, some day, be brought face to face with a serious and decisive test." (*NY Tribune*, 11 May 1867)

**27 May** Of the paintings at the Exposition Universelle in Paris, the *Saturday Review* (London) reports: "The American Exhibition is small in quantity, but of high quality, especially in landscape. The 'Niagara' of Church, and the 'Rocky Mountains' of Bierstadt, are at the head of American landscape." (*Boston Transcript*, 27 May 1867)

**5 June** *The Domes of the Yosemite* on exhibition in Philadelphia at the Pennsylvania

## 1867–1868

Academy of the Fine Arts. (*Press*, Philadelphia, 6 June 1867)

**11 June** The San Francisco *Bulletin* describes James Smillie's engraving after *The Rocky Mountains, Lander's Peak* as "one of the very finest reproductions of one of the finest paintings executed in America." (*Bulletin*, San Francisco, 11 June 1867)

**16 June** Bierstadt and his wife sail for Europe. (*Mercury*, New Bedford, 17 June 1867)

**24 June** Long and complimentary article published in London regarding paintings by Bierstadt and William Bradford. In landscape painting, American rather than European artists are said to have taken the lead. Article concludes by noting that Bierstadt has succeeded in commanding prices matched only by J. M. W. Turner among modern masters. (*Daily News*, London, 24 June 1867)

**10 July** Bierstadt contributes *Sunlight and Shadow* (No. 29), *Sierra Nevada Mountains Near Yo Semite Valley*, and *Mirror Lake, Yosemite Valley* to the First Exhibition of the Yale School of Fine Arts. (*College Courant*, Yale, 10 July 1867; Yarnall and Gerdts 1986, pp. 298–99)

*Sunlight and Shadow* described as "undoubtedly the finest picture in the gallery." (*College Courant*, Yale, 11 Sept. 1867)

**2 Aug.–c. 27 Sept.** *The Domes of the Yosemite* on view in Boston at Williams & Everett. (*Boston Transcript*, 1 Aug. 1867)

**by 19 Aug.** Bierstadt and his wife arrive in Paris. (*Post*, New York, 5 Sept. 1867)

**1 Sept.** Bierstadt reported to be at Grindelwald, Switzerland, sketching the Wetterhorn. "From Switzerland Mr. B. purposed going through Holland and Germany; thence to England and France; thence to Rome, where he will probably spend the winter." (*Bulletin*, San Francisco, 19 Oct. 1867)

**3 Sept.–5 Oct.** *Mount Hood, Oregon* (Fig. 55), *Pirate Shenandoah Burning Whalers* (now titled *The Burning Ship*, p. 223), and *View from the Glen House* on exhibition in Providence, Rhode Island, in a benefit for the Society for the Encouragement of Domestic Industry. (Yarnall and Gerdts 1986, pp. 298, 300; Catalogue, Society for the Encouragement of Domestic Industry, 1867, p. 5)

**17 Sept.** Letter dated 17 Sept. 1867 indicates that Bierstadt, traveling in Switzerland, had climbed Faulhorn and painted Devil's Bridge on Saint Gotthard Pass. (Unidentified newspaper clipping, Bierstadt Scrapbook, Edwards Collection)

**by 6 Nov.** Bierstadt and his wife back in London. (Autographed musical score given to Bierstadt inscribed: *Langham Hotel. London. November 6, 1867*, Hannover Album)

**14 Nov.–11 Mar. 1868** Bierstadt's *Mount Hood, Oregon* included in the First Winter Exhibition of the NAD. (Catalogue, NAD, 1867, p. 18; *Putnam's Magazine*, Jan. 1868, pp. 131–33; *NY Times*, 7 Mar. 1868)

**27 Nov.** *Emigrants Crossing the Plains* placed on view at Snow & Roos Art Gallery in San Francisco. (*Bulletin*, San Francisco, 27 Nov. 1867; *Californian*, San Francisco, 30 Nov. 1867)

**late Dec.** Bierstadt exhibits *The Rocky Mountains, Lander's Peak* (No. 37) and *Storm in the Rocky Mountains, Mt. Rosalie* (No. 45) before Queen Victoria and the royal family at Osborne House on the Isle of Wight. (*Morning Post*, London, 25 Dec. 1867)

Bierstadt writes to an unidentified friend: "I was invited to send my pictures to the Royal Palace at Osborne for Her Majesty and the Royal Family to see; I was also desired to accompany them. I did so, and was much pleased with the *very* kind manner in which I was received. Her Majesty is a very charming and agreeable lady, and makes one feel quite at home in her presence. She seemed much pleased with my works. I was then invited to see the Palace, partake of lunch, etc." (*Boston Transcript*, 15 Jan. 1868; paintings identified in letter written by Rosalie Bierstadt, quoted in ROM/MFA Corresp.)

**26 Dec.** In writing to thank the gentleman who "paved the way" for his audience with Queen Victoria (Benjamin Moran, American chargé d'affaires), Bierstadt asks if he may send as a gift "one of the proof engravings of my picture of the Rocky Mountains." (Bierstadt to Moran, 26 Dec. 1867, Bancroft Library, University of California, Berkeley)

## 1868

**13 Jan.** Bierstadt reportedly intends to paint Vesuvius during its current eruption. (*NY Herald*, 13 Jan. 1868)

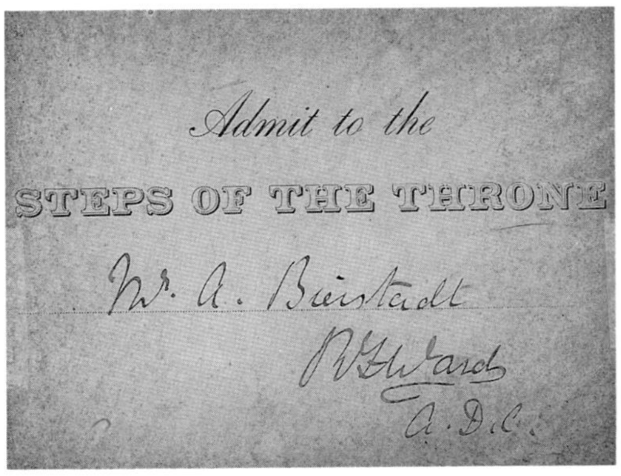


*Bierstadt's admission card for a royal audience.* Collection of Joyce Randall Edwards.

**1 Feb.** *Mount Hood, Oregon* and Church's *Niagara* on exhibition at the NAD. Both are described as the best works by the artists. (*Round Table*, 1 Feb. 1868, pp. 69–70)

**18 Feb.** "Foreign critics" reported to have made negative comments regarding "the business faculty exhibited by Bierstadt and by Bradford . . . in disposing of their pictures at a good round price, without the intervention of middlemen." The same critics have found fault with the large size of several American pictures. (*NY Herald*, 18 Feb. 1868)

**by 18 Feb.–late June** The Bierstadts are in Rome. (Autographed photos from George Peabody and Robert Winthrop inscribed: *18 Feb. 1868;* "The Song of the Camp," a poem by Bayard Taylor dated "Rome, March, 1868"; small pencil sketch inscribed: *H Ludwig Rome April 17, 1868* and autograph from Elihu Vedder also dated 17 Apr.; Sir Morton Peto to Bierstadt, 19 May 1868; all in Hannover Album; letter from Rome dated 1 June, *Post*, New York, 18 June 1868)

**7 Apr.–at least 30 May** *The Domes of the Yosemite* on exhibition at McLean's Gallery in London. A critic for the *Manchester Guardian* writes, "In my judgment it is wanting in all the attributes of high art, being simply an ambitious attempt to give gigantic effects without the least power of bringing conviction to the mind of the on-looker." (*Manchester Guardian*, 7 Apr. 1868)

Long and favorable review of *The Domes of the Yosemite* published in the *Morning Post:* "These Yosemite Mountains are in some respects the most extraordinary in the world; and as this is the first picture of them which has been seen in this country, and as, probably, few English readers have ever heard of them before, we will not apologise for such consumption of time and space as may be necessary to describe them." The article goes on to compare Church and Bierstadt: "Mr. Bierstadt is a great painter. He is not so great a painter as Mr. Church. He is not so daring a colourist. He is not gifted with so lofty an imagination; but he has immense industry—industry not only of production, but of observation and record." (*Morning Post*, London, 15 Apr. 1868)

Writer for the *Saturday Review* comments on *The Domes of the Yosemite:* "He is a servant of nature rather than a master of art; and though this is a noble kind of servitude, there must always be a difference in rank between artists who, like Bierstadt, derive their force from an enthusiasm for natural grandeur and those who are mighty by their own grandeur. When we stand before a picture like this it is not the art which moves us, but the sublimity of the natural objects in such a way as to affect us powerfully by art; but so far as this picture affects us at all it is by a transmitted natural glory only." (*Saturday Review*, London, 30 May 1868, p. 718)

**27 Apr.** The Bierstadts are in Florence. (Two photographs and an autograph from Thomas Ball inscribed: *Florence April 27, 1868*, Hannover Album)

**23 June** A new painting, *Mount Vesuvius at Midnight* (unlocated; see Fig. 91), is on exhibition in London. "It represents Vesuvius in one of the grandest phases of her late volcanic fury, and so real, vivid and startling are the colors that it is difficult to believe it a mere illusion. The scene is at night, and the fiery, dazzling glare of the eruption which crimsons both earth and sky, is blended and softened by silvery moonlight. The effect is wonderful and beautiful and will add vastly to the artist's reputation." (*NY Herald*, 23 June 1868)

**9 July** Elaborate dinner in honor of Henry Wadsworth Longfellow is hosted by Bierstadt at Langham Hotel, London. Approximately eighty prominent English and American gentlemen attend. (Unidentified clipping, Bierstadt Scrapbook, Edwards Collection; *Morning Star*, London, 11 July 1868; *Boston Transcript*, 23 July 1868)

**15 July** The Prince of Wales and Princess Louise grant Bierstadt an interview regarding political issues affecting the two countries. *Mount Vesuvius at Midnight*, *Among the Sierra Nevada Mountains, California* (No. 48), and *Sunset in the Yosemite Valley* (No. 47) on view nearby. (Carr 1986, p. 65; *Art-Journal* [London], Aug. 1868, p. 159)

**early Aug.** The Bierstadts are in Dresden. (*Post*, New York, 26 Aug. 1868)

**by 14 Aug.** "Bierstadt has taken a studio in Paris. While in England he received orders for pictures to the amount of 7000 guineas [approximately $37,000 in 1868 exchange]." (*Mercury*, New Bedford, 14 Aug. 1868)

**30 Aug.** Forty-sixth exhibition of the Royal Academy in Berlin opens; Bierstadt exhibits *Among the Sierra Nevada Mountains, California* (No. 48). (*Art-Journal* [London], Nov. 1868, p. 256; *Boston Transcript*, 10 Dec. 1868)

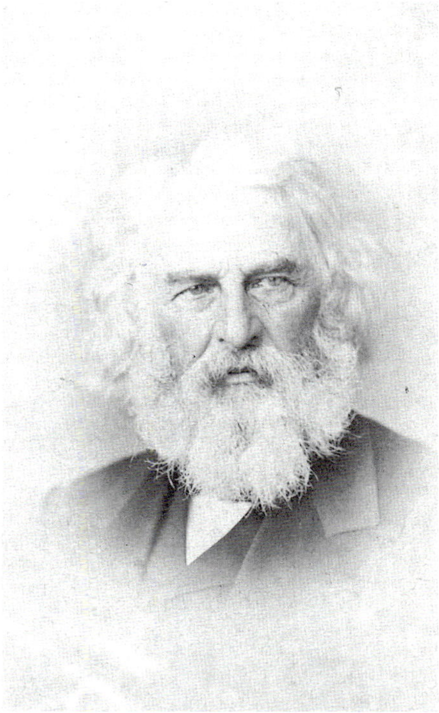

*Henry Wadsworth Longfellow*. Carte de visite. Bierstadt Album, private collection, Hannover, Germany.

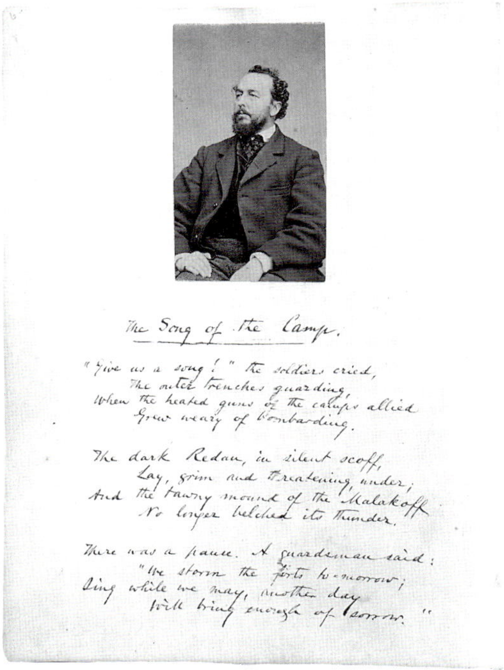


*Carte de visite of Bayard Taylor and autograph copy of "The Song of the Camp."* Bierstadt Album, private collection, Hannover, Germany.

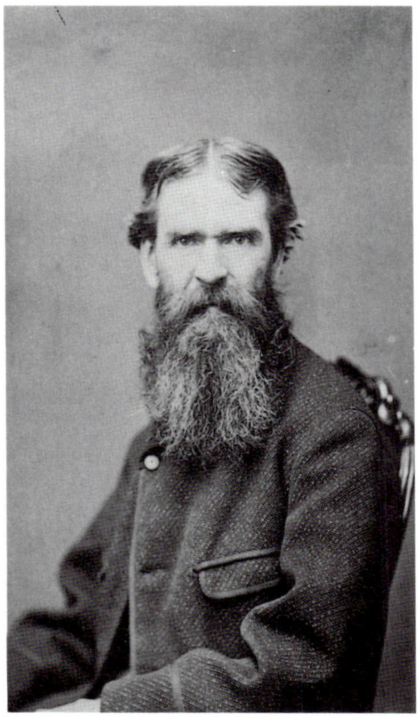

*Thomas Ball*. Carte de visite. Bierstadt Album, private collection, Hannover, Germany.

**7 Sept.** L. Prang & Company announces publication on the 15th of a chromolithograph called *Sunset: California Scenery* (Fig. 86), "after Bierstadt, illustrating California scenery." (*Post*, New York, 7 Sept. 1868)

**16 Sept.** Prang's chromo after Bierstadt reported not quite finished, but it does illustrate "Mr. Prang's skill in the reproduction of strong and brilliant colors." (*Post*, New York, 16 Sept. 1868)

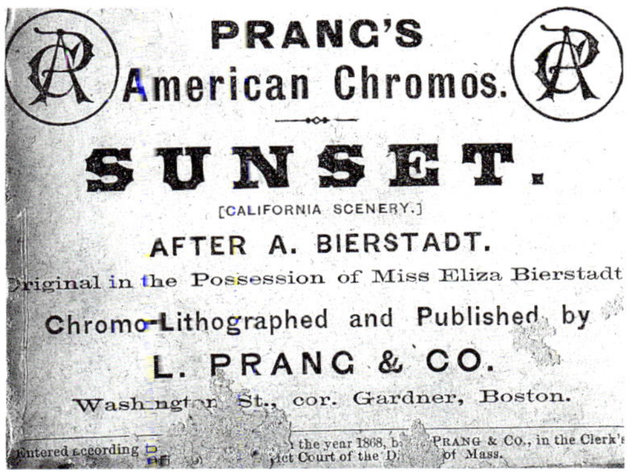


*Advertisement for Prang chromolithograph,* 1868. Private collection.

## 1868–1869

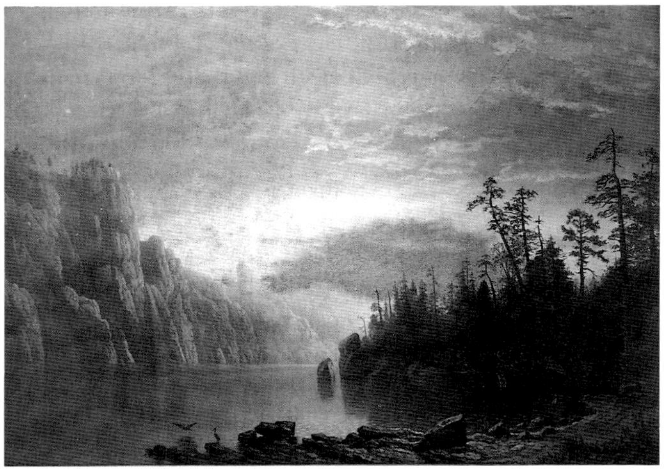

L. Prang & Co., after Albert Bierstadt. *Sunset: California Scenery*, 1868. Chromolithograph. Private collection.

**18 Sept.** Bierstadts in Düsseldorf. (Autographed and dated poem by John Robinson Tait; photograph from Auguste von Wille inscribed: *Dusseldorf* and dated 20 Sept. 1868, both Hannover Album)

**28 Oct.–at least 3 Dec.** Bierstadt's *Mount Vesuvius at Midnight* on exhibition at Putnam's Art Gallery in New York. (*Post*, New York, 28 Oct. 1868; *Albion*, 31 Oct. 1868, p. 525; *Putnam's Magazine*, Dec. 1868, p. 762)

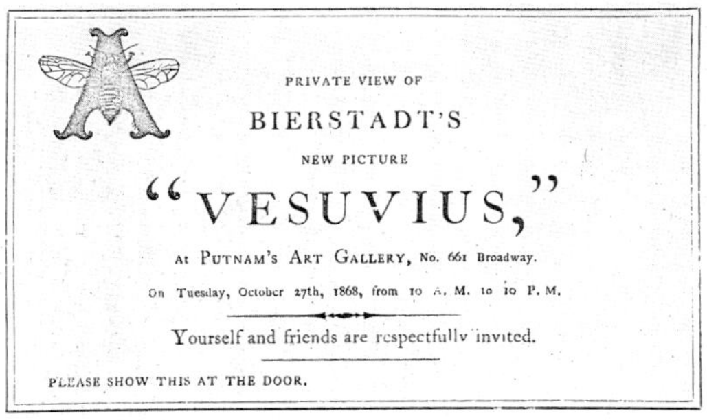

PRIVATE VIEW OF

BIERSTADT'S

NEW PICTURE

"VESUVIUS,"

At PUTNAM'S ART GALLERY, No. 661 Broadway.

On Tuesday, October 27th, 1868, from 10 A. M. to 10 P. M.

Yourself and friends are respectfully invited.

PLEASE SHOW THIS AT THE DOOR.

*Admission ticket*. Photocopy (original unlocated). Gordon Hendricks Papers, Archives of American Art, Smithsonian Institution, Washington, D.C.

The *Times* comments: "There is a great deal of beauty in the foreground, where the snow-covered knolls reflect on one side the glare of the volcano, and on the other the white moonlight; and the ruins of the Hermitage, with the clump of leafless trees, form a very picturesque group. On these details the eye dwell [*sic*] with great pleasure, and finds, indeed, more satisfaction in them than in the painting of the eruption itself, which ought to be the one grand object of interest in the painting. As all of Bierstadt's large pictures previously exhibited had this same defect, we ought not to be surprised to find it in this one." (*NY Times*, 7 Nov. 1868)

In a long and negative review of *Vesuvius*, Clarence Cook refers to the artist's "fast waning reputation." (*NY Tribune*, 3 Dec. 1868)

**4 Nov.** "Bierstadt is in Paris, and will spend most of the winter there." (*Home Journal*, 4 Nov. 1868)

**15 Nov.** Bierstadt sells *Emigrants Crossing the Plains* to Amasa Stone of Cleveland, Ohio, for $15,000. (Bill of Sale dated "Paris Nov 15th 1868," National Cowboy Hall of Fame and Western Heritage Center, Oklahoma City)

**21 Nov.** Bierstadt reported to have refused $10,000 for *Mount Vesuvius at Midnight*. (*Mercury*, New Bedford, 21 Nov. 1868)

**30 Nov.** *Sunset in California* and the Prang chromolithograph after it are hung one above the other at Child's Gallery in Boston. (*Boston Transcript*, 30 Nov. 1868)

**2 Dec.** Bierstadt is in Paris. (Poem by John Savage dated "Paris 2nd December 1868," Hannover Album)

**22 Dec.** *Mount Vesuvius at Midnight* goes on exhibition at John Hopkins's music store in New Bedford. (*Mercury*, New Bedford, 22 Dec. 1868)

**31 Dec.** Frederic Church's family, Mr. and Mrs. Jervis McEntee, Sanford Robinson Gifford and his sister, Albert and Rosalie Bierstadt, Mr. and Mrs. Robert W. Weir, and Launt Thompson have rooms near each other in Rome. (*Post*, New York, 31 Dec. 1868)

## 1869

**20 Jan.** Bierstadt is in Paris. (Poem by W. Cassimati dated "Paris 20th January 1869," Hannover Album)

**23 Jan.** Bierstadt reported to have received a gold medal for *Among the Sierra Nevada Mountains, California* (No. 48) at the Royal Academy in Berlin. (*Boston Transcript*, 23 Jan. 1869)

**24 Feb.** The Bierstadts host "a splendid soiree" in the artist's studio in the Grand Hotel, Paris. French artists Jean-Baptiste Isabey, Adolphe Yvon, and Théodore Gudin attend. *Among the Sierra Nevada Mountains, California*, destined for the Royal Academy in London, is on view at Bowles Brothers' Gallery in Paris. (*Mercury*, New Bedford, 2 Mar. 1869; *Boston Transcript*, 3 Mar. 1869)

**Mar.** The Bierstadts are in Paris. (Ink drawing by Andreas Achenbach inscribed: *Paris 5 März 69*, Hannover Album; Bierstadt to William Henry Riggs, 8 Mar. 1869, Riggs Papers, Library of Congress; inscribed and dated photograph, 31 Mar. 1869, Hannover Album)

**1 Mar.** Chromolithographs of *Storm in the Rocky Mountains, Mt. Rosalie* (No. 45) and *The Rocky Mountains, Lander's Peak* (No. 37) are in progress. (*Art-Journal* [London], 1 Mar. 1869, p. 95)

**1 May–20 June** Salon open in Paris; Bierstadt exhibits *Storm in the Rocky*

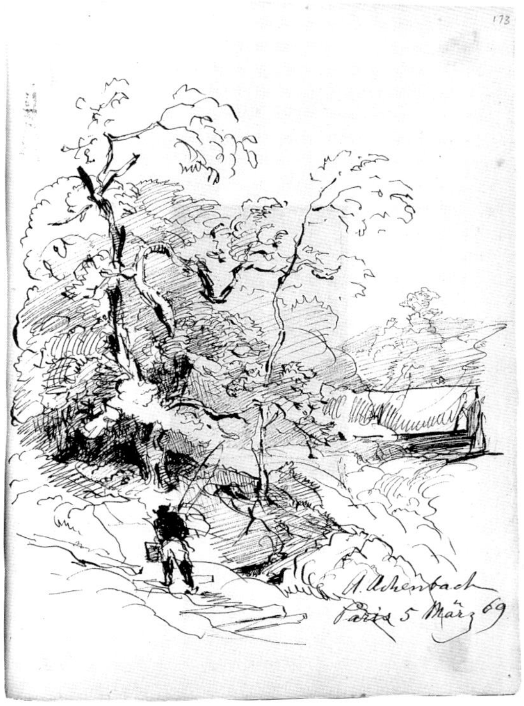


Andreas Achenbach. *Ink drawing*. Bierstadt Album, private collection, Hannover, Germany.

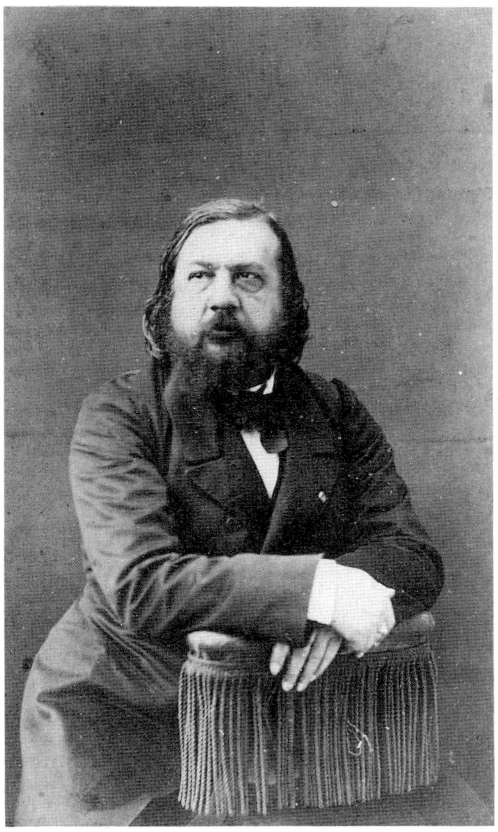

*Théophile Gautier*. Photograph. Bierstadt Album, private collection, Hannover, Germany.

*Mountains, Mt. Rosalie*. (Catalogue, Salon, 1869, p. 32, no. 231, as *Orage dans les montagnes rocheuses d'Amérique*)

**3 May–31 July** Bierstadt exhibits *Among the Sierra Nevada Mountains, California* at the inaugural exhibition in the new Royal Academy building in London. (*Daily News*, London, 1 May 1869; Graves 1905, p. 191)

**10 May** Union Pacific and Central Pacific railroads join at Promontory, Utah, establishing the first transcontinental rail line in the United States.

**22 May** The Bierstadts and their companions arrive in Madrid. Later travel includes trips to Seville, Malaga, Valencia, and Barcelona. (ROM/MFA Corresp.)

**June** The *Aldine Press* publishes illustrated article on Prang's recently completed chromolithograph after Bierstadt's painting *Sunset in California*. (*Aldine Press*, June 1869, p. 51)

**8 June** *Mount Vesuvius at Midnight* on exhibition in Boston. (*Mercury*, New Bedford, 8 June 1869)

**11 June** In noting the sale of a "California Landscape" in San Francisco, the *Bulletin* writes: "Bierstadt's success with Pacific coast subjects has infected several American artists with a desire to come here. . . . The Railroad makes the trip an easy one, and Atlantic and European landscapes have grown rather hackneyed." (*Bulletin*, San Francisco, 11 June 1869)

**1 July–28 Sept.** Exposition Générale des Beaux-Arts open in Brussels. Bierstadt contributes *Mount Hood, Oregon* (Fig. 55). (*Exposition Générale Catalogue Explicatif*, Brussels, 1869)

**1 July** Bierstadt is in Paris. (*Post*, New York, 1 July 1869)

**20 July** Bierstadt is in London. (Photograph of John Lothrop Motley inscribed: *London 20 July/69*, Hannover Album)

**26 July** Louis-Napoléon presents Bierstadt with the cross of the Legion of Honor. (*Post*, New York, 26 July 1869)

**3 Aug.** Albert and Rosalie Bierstadt, accompanied by Rosalie's sister, arrive in New York from Liverpool aboard RMS *Russia*. (Passenger Lists, National Archives; *Post*, New York, 3 Aug. 1869)

**14 Aug.** *Sunset in California* and the Prang chromolithograph after it are on exhibition at Snow & Roos Art Gallery in San Francisco. (*San Francisco News Letter and California Advertiser*, 14 Aug. 1869)

**26 Aug.** New exhibition of paintings opens at Crosby's Opera House in Chicago; *Mount Vesuvius at Midnight* said to be "the most prominent work in the collection." (*Post*, New York, 30 Aug. 1869)

**Fall** Bierstadt, his wife, her sister, and other companions reported to have traveled down the Saint Lawrence River and visited Niagara Falls before spending six weeks in the White Mountains. During a stay in Boston, they are reported to have been houseguests of Mr. and Mrs. Thomas Bailey Aldrich, Thomas Appleton, and the Longfellows. (ROM/MFA Corresp.)

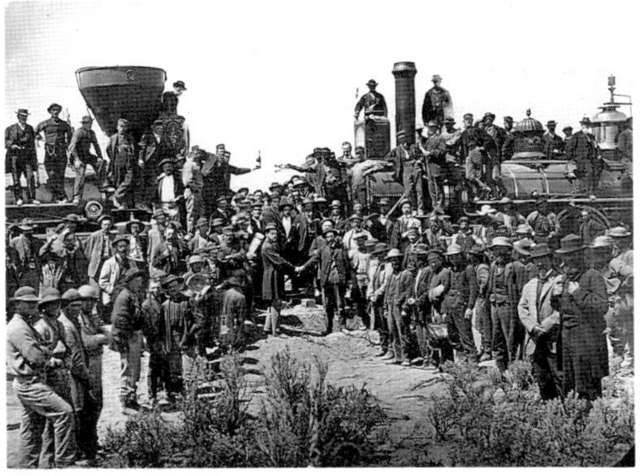

Andrew Joseph Russell. *East and West Shaking Hands at Laying of Last Rail* (joining of transcontinental railroad at Promontory, Utah), 1869. Photograph. History Department, The Oakland Museum.

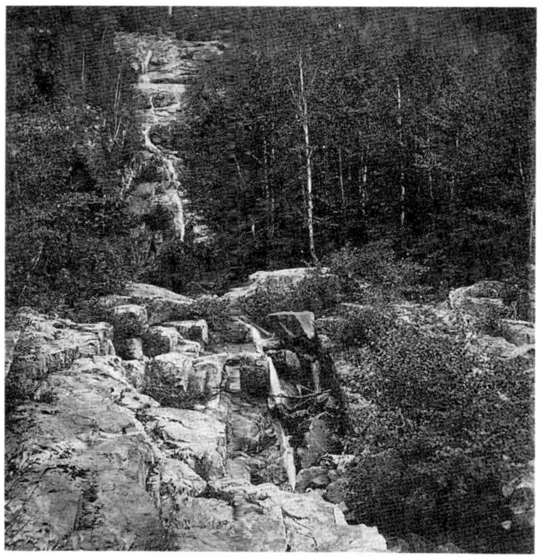

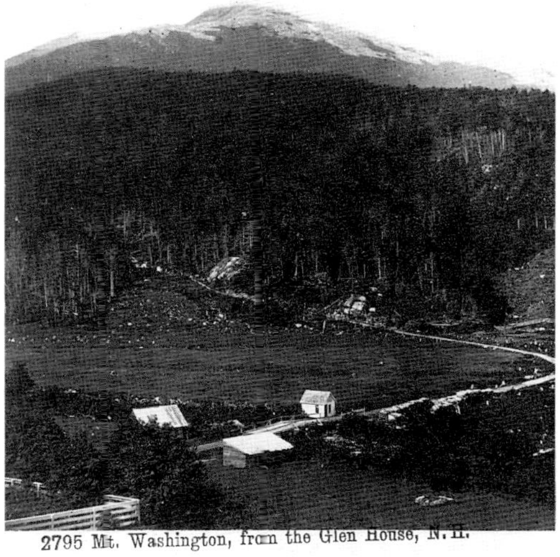


*(top)* Bierstadt Brothers, New Bedford, Massachusetts. *Silver Cascade, White Mountains Notch, N.H.* Stereograph. Private collection.

*(above)* Bierstadt Brothers, New Bedford, Massachusetts. *Mt. Washington, from the Glen House, N.H.* Stereograph. Division of Photographic History, National Museum of American History, Smithsonian Institution, Washington, D.C.

**1 Sept.** Chromolithographs (Nos. 78, 79) of *The Rocky Mountains, Lander's Peak* (No. 37) and *Storm in the Rocky Mountains, Mt. Rosalie* (No. 45) on exhibition at McLean's Gallery in London. (*Art-Journal* [London], 1 Sept. 1869, p. 289)

**4 Sept.** Responding to erroneous news that a large painting of Yosemite by Bierstadt had burned in a fire in Philadelphia, Ambrose Bierce writes that he was pleased, as "the painting has been a prolific parent of ten thousand abominations." He adds: "Besides, that picture has incited more unpleasant people to visit California than all conspiring hotel-keepers could compel to return. . . . We are glad a blow has finally been struck at the root of immigration." (Quoted in Caughey and Caughey 1962, p. 328)

**1 Oct.–26 Nov.** *Among the Sierra Nevada Mountains, California*, owned by Alvin Adams, on exhibition at Child's Gallery in Boston. (*Evening Journal*, Boston, 29 Sept. 1869; *Boston Transcript*, 26 Nov. 1869)

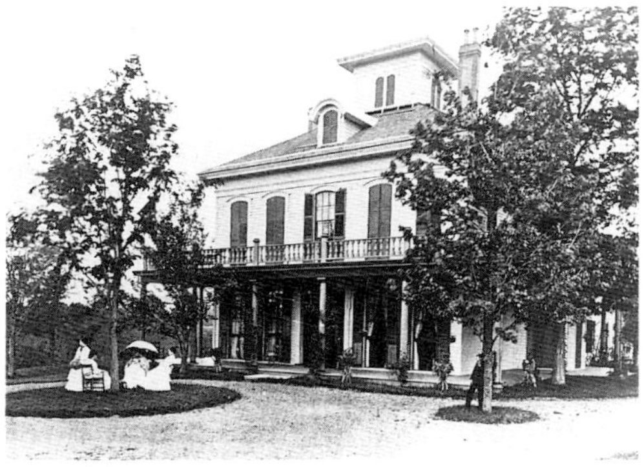

*Alvin Adams's house, Fairlawn (burned 1886).* Photograph. The Watertown Free Public Library, Watertown, New York.

**4 Oct.** Chromolithographs of *The Rocky Mountains, Lander's Peak* and *Storm in the Rocky Mountains, Mt. Rosalie* on exhibition at Goupil's. "[They] are unquestionably the finest examples of the chromolithographic art." (*Post*, New York, 4 Oct. 1869)

**12 Oct.** Bierstadt is in New Bedford and will spend the winter at Irvington. (*Mercury*, New Bedford, 13 Oct. 1869)

**22 Oct.** Bierstadt is in Irvington. (*Post*, New York, 22 Oct. 1869)

**24 Nov.** Bierstadt attends meeting at the Union League Club, during which the establishment of a Metropolitan Museum of Art is discussed. (*Post*, New York, 24 Nov. 1869)

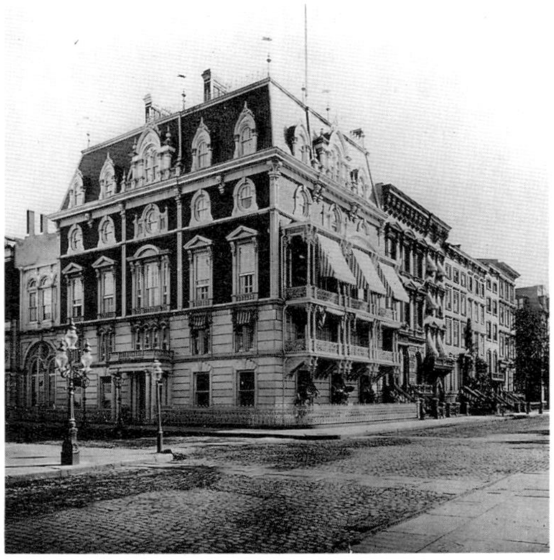

*The Leonard W. Jerome mansion, New York, leased by the Union League Club from 1868 until 1891.* Photograph. The New-York Historical Society.

## 1870

**1 Jan.** *Mount Hood, Oregon* on exhibition at McLean's Gallery in London. (*Art-Journal* [London], 1 Jan. 1870, p. 29)

**27 Jan.** Bierstadt writes to the *Times* protesting the use of his name in the catalogue published for the upcoming sale of the Thomas Thompson collection, claiming some of the paintings attributed to him are not by his hand. "It is true that Mr. Thompson bought a few of my earliest sketches, made before I thought of becoming an artist . . . , but there are others . . . that are falsely attributed to me." (*NY Times*, 29 Jan. 1870)

**29 Jan.** Bierstadt writes to the secretary of the provisional committee organizing the Metropolitan Museum of Art, stating that he does not wish to be connected "with the enterprise at present." (Bierstadt to Theodore Weston, 29 Jan. 1870, Metropolitan Museum of Art)

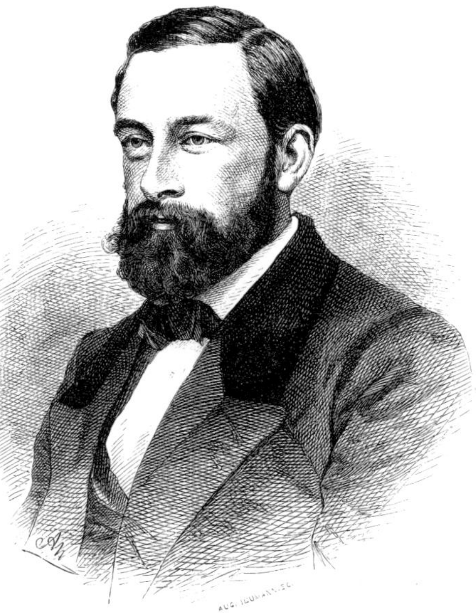

Aug. Neumann. *Albert Bierstadt*. Engraving published in Carl von Lutzow, ed., *Zeitschrift für bildende Kunst* (Leipzig: 1870).

A review of the Thompson collection states: "Here are some forty pieces by Albert Bierstadt, all done in his earliest manner, crude, cold, flat, interesting as examples of beginners' work, but containing no indication of future brilliancy." (*NY Tribune*, 29 Jan. 1870)

Leeds & Miner, auctioneers, and George Rowell, agent for the Thompson estate, respond in the *Times* to Bierstadt's claim of paintings misattributed to him in the Thompson collection. They assert that the artist attempted to exchange two later works for all the paintings attributed to him save four, which he claimed were not his work. The proposed exchange did not take place. (*NY Times*, 31 Jan. 1870)

**7 Feb.** Sale of Thompson collection begins in New York. *A Twilight View of Boston from the Harbor*, by Bierstadt, brings only $30. Later quoted prices range from $33 to $310. (*Post*, New York, 7, 8, 11 Feb. 1870)

**10 Feb.** Artists' Reception at the Opera House in Chicago; Bierstadt represented by two works, one a Sierra Nevada scene, the other unidentified except as being owned by a Mr. Pullman. (*Chicago Daily Tribune*, 11 Feb. 1870)

**1 Apr.** Bierstadt has "almost completed the largest painting he has attempted for many years [*The Emerald Pool*, Fig. 33]. A discriminating knowledge of works of art gains ground so rapidly with us that praise, even for work which implies much technical skill and years of labor, is no longer readily given. We grow fastidious and ask something more than the mastery of technique and industry. We begin to realize that there is that in Nature which is not interpreted simply by the translation of form and color—that there is a soul in things which we have been accustomed to call inanimate. And we begin to feel that the landscape without this is but the body without the spirit. But we ask for both and it remains to be seen when this great canvas of Mr. Bierstadt is brought out into the light, whether or not he gives them to us." (*Aldine*, Apr. 1870, p. 68)

**7 Apr.** Charles Bierstadt arrives in Mariposa, California, on his way to Yosemite Valley, where he intends to take photographs while snow remains on the ground. The *Bulletin* reports he was forced back when he found he was "too early in the season."

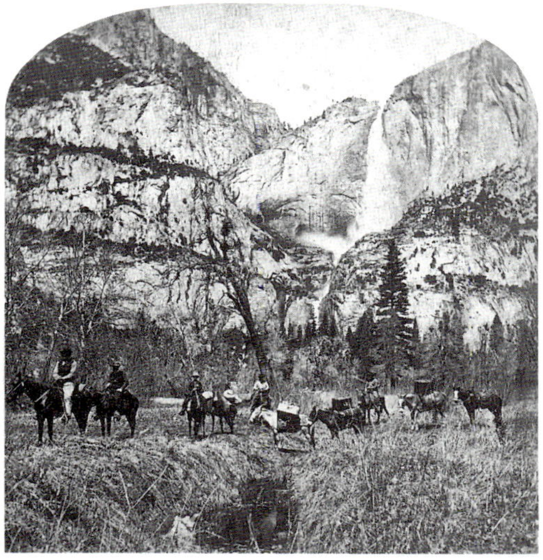

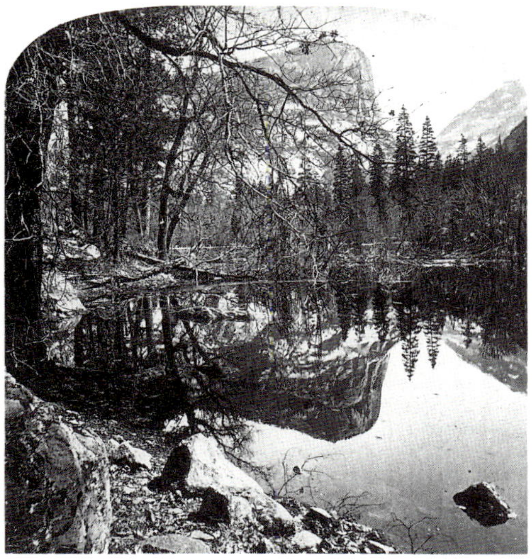

*(top)* Charles Bierstadt, Niagara Falls, New York. *Our Party, Yosemite Valley, Cal.* Stereograph. Private collection.

*(above)* Charles Bierstadt, Niagara Falls, New York. *Mirror Lake, Yosemite Valley, California.* Stereograph. Private collection.

(*Gazette*, Mariposa, 8 Apr. 1870; *Bulletin*, San Francisco, 5 May 1870)

**15 Apr.–25 June** NAD Annual Exhibition open to the public. Bierstadt contributes *Sierra Nevada Mountains, California*, owned by Lewis Roberts. (Catalogue, NAD, 1870, p. 22; *Post*, New York, 14, 15 Apr. 1870)

**May** In a long article on the state of art in America, James Jackson Jarves cites Bierstadt, Church, and Bradford as popular favorites of "the material school." Jarves further describes Bierstadt as a "pretentious realist" whose popularity is based on the admiration of an uneducated public for mechanical skill and novelty. (*Art-Journal* [London], May 1870, pp. 129–32)

**6 May** Publication of Fitz Hugh Ludlow's *Heart of the Continent*, an account of his trip west with Bierstadt in 1863, announced in the *Post*. (*Post*, New York, 6 May 1870)

**23 May** *The Emerald Pool* at the Tenth Street Studio Building; soon to be placed on private view. (*New York Standard*, quoted in *Mercury*, New Bedford, 23 May 1870)

**Summer** Bierstadt in Irvington. Hopes to travel to California in the winter or spring. (He does not go, however, until July 1871.) (Bierstadt to My Dear Russell, 5 June 1870, Manuscript Collection, Library of Congress)

**July** A review of Ludlow's *Heart of the Continent* notes that the journey described took place ten years earlier and that since that time, the West has been "visited by such numbers of travellers that it is wellnigh as stale as the heart of a coquette entering upon her fifth or sixth season of flirtations." (*Atlantic Monthly*, July 1870, pp. 120–21)

**1 July** First summer exhibition at the NAD opens; Bierstadt's *Sierra Nevada Mountains, California* remains on view; additional work, *Landscape*, listed in catalogue. (*Post*, New York, 30 June, 7 July 1870; Catalogue, NAD, Summer 1870, pp. 20, 28)

**Aug.** Bierstadt has on private exhibition in his Tenth Street studio a seven-by-five-foot painting titled *The Headwaters of the Black River, Wind River Mountains, California*, "a masterpiece of composition and of color; but after all rather a dream of fairy land than a translation of any combination of form and color or accident of time and place in Nature." (*Aldine*, Aug. 1870, p. 92)

**c. Aug.–9 Nov.** *The Emerald Pool* on exhibition at Child's Gallery in Boston. "No previous picture by this artist has excited so much comment and so much adverse as well as favorable criticism as the Emerald Pool." (*Boston Transcript*, 12 Aug., 13 Sept. 1870; *Post*, New York, 9 Nov. 1870)

**Sept.** A review of Carleton Watkins's photographs of Yosemite notes that "they bear unexceptionable witness to the fidelity of Mr. Bierstadt's works." (*Art-Journal* [London], Sept. 1870, p. 291)

**7 Sept.** "The landlord of the Glen House, White Mountains, has lately been beset with visitors in search of 'The Emerald Pool,' in the vicinity of that popular hotel. The notoriety given to that romantic and secluded locality by the exhibition of Bierstadt's beautiful painting, at Childs & Co.'s gallery, has excited the curiosity of White Mountain tourists. . . ." (*Boston Transcript*, 27 Sept. 1870)

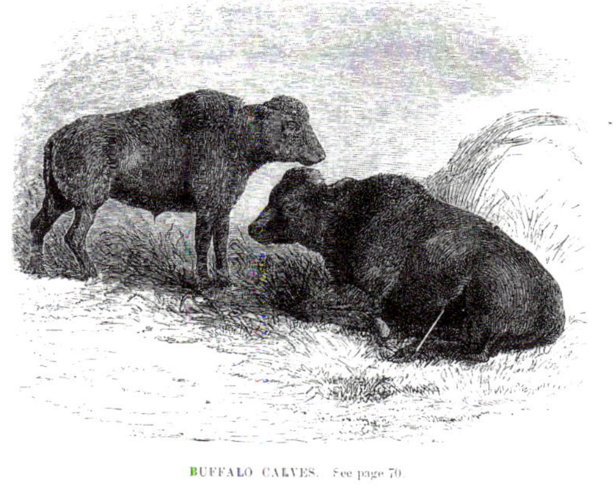


After Albert Bierstadt. *Buffalo Calves.* Wood engraving published in Fitz Hugh Ludlow, *The Heart of the Continent* (New York: 1870).

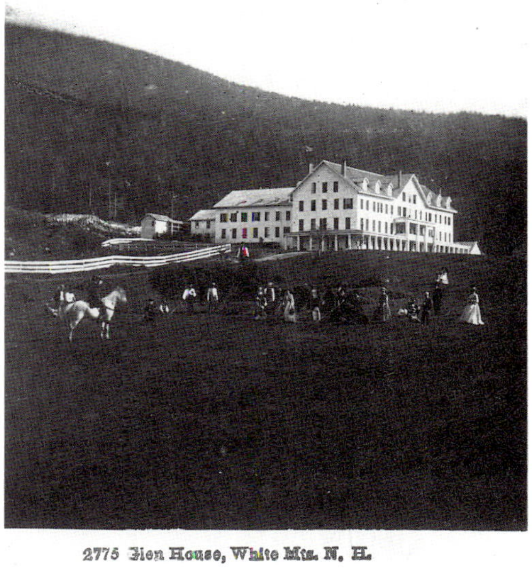


Bierstadt Brothers, New Bedford, Massachusetts. *Glen House, White Mts. N.H.* Stereograph. Division of Photographic History, National Museum of American History, Smithsonian Institution, Washington, D.C.

**13 Sept.** Fitz Hugh Ludlow dies in Geneva, Switzerland. (Osborne Family Bible, private collection; *Post*, New York, 5 Oct. 1870)

**19 Oct.** "A new chromo" (No. 80) after *The Domes of the Yosemite* on exhibition at Sarony & Co. in New York. (*Post*, New York, 19 Oct. 1870)

**21 Nov.** Painting by Bierstadt described as "The Diamond Pool" and later as "Winter Pool" (probably *The Emerald Pool*, Fig. 33) on exhibition at the NAD during the Fourth Winter Exhibition. (*Post*, New York, 21, 22 Nov. 1870; Catalogue, NAD, Winter 1870–71, p. 11)

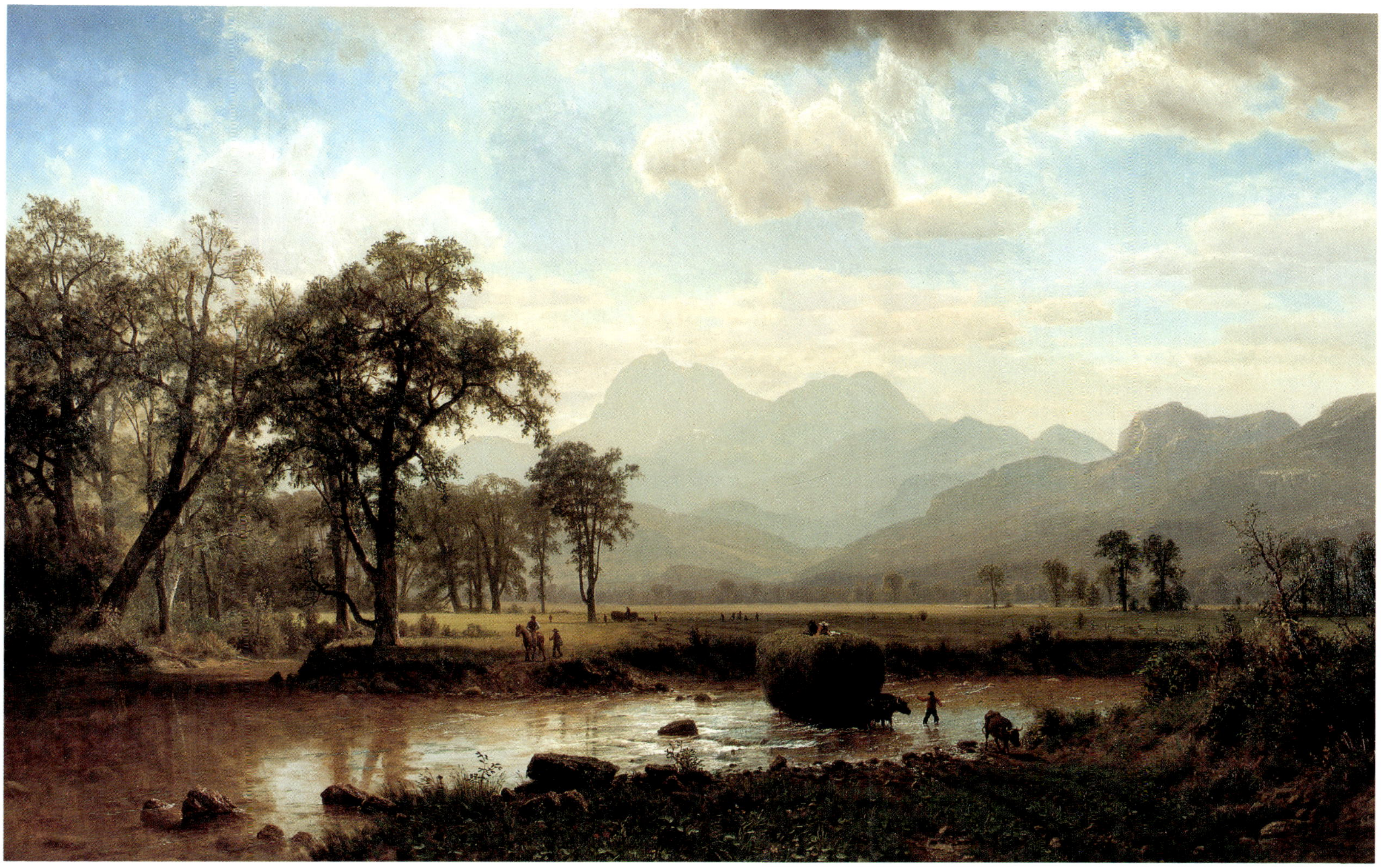

NO. 34

## *Haying, Conway Meadows,* 1864

Oil on canvas, 36 × 58 in. (91.4 × 147.3 cm)
Signed and dated lower right: *ABierstadt/1864*
Private collection

*Now the sun sends mingled light and lengthened shadows over the picturesque labors of the haymakers, in the broad, green, beautiful meadows that spread, a mile wide, waving with grass and grain and patches of glistening corn, clear to the mountain's feet, to the hieroglyphic rocky faces of the curious ledges, that form its outposts in front, and as the winding Saco River, whose course is marked with gracefully overhanging elms and oaks and maples, that also stud the plain in scattered groups, and shade the brooks that ramble, musically gurgling to the river. A lovelier plain was never spread before a poet's feet, to woo the willing thoughts abroad. A scene of plenty, purity, and peace.*

Thomas Starr King, *The White Hills: Their Legends, Landscape, and Poetry* (Boston: 1860), pp. 158–59

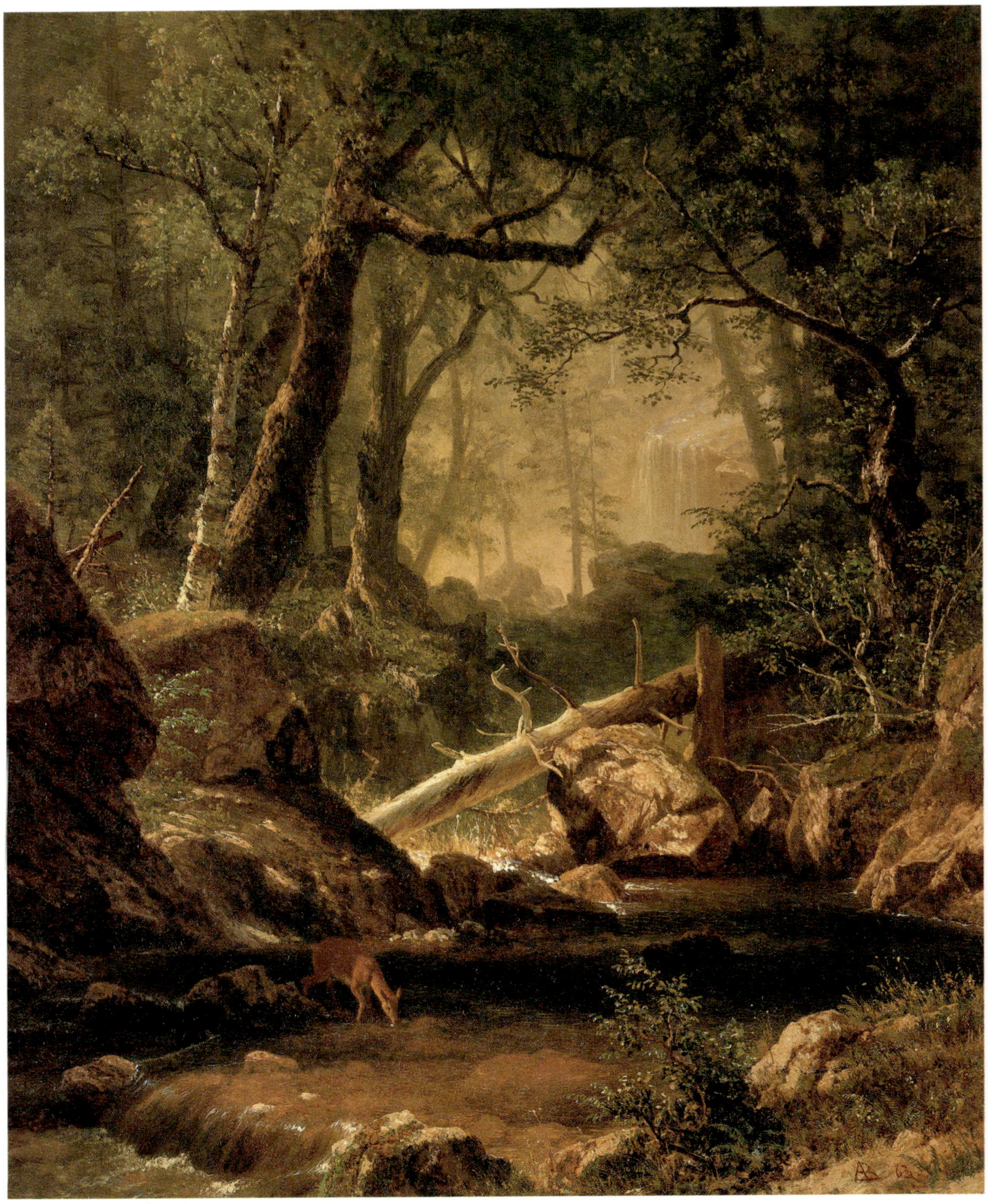

NO. 35

*White Mountains, New Hampshire,* 1863

Oil on board, 18½ × 15 in. (47 × 38.1 cm)

Signed and dated lower right: *AB 63.*

Duke University Museum of Art, Durham, North Carolina, Gift of Mrs. Fred Von Canon

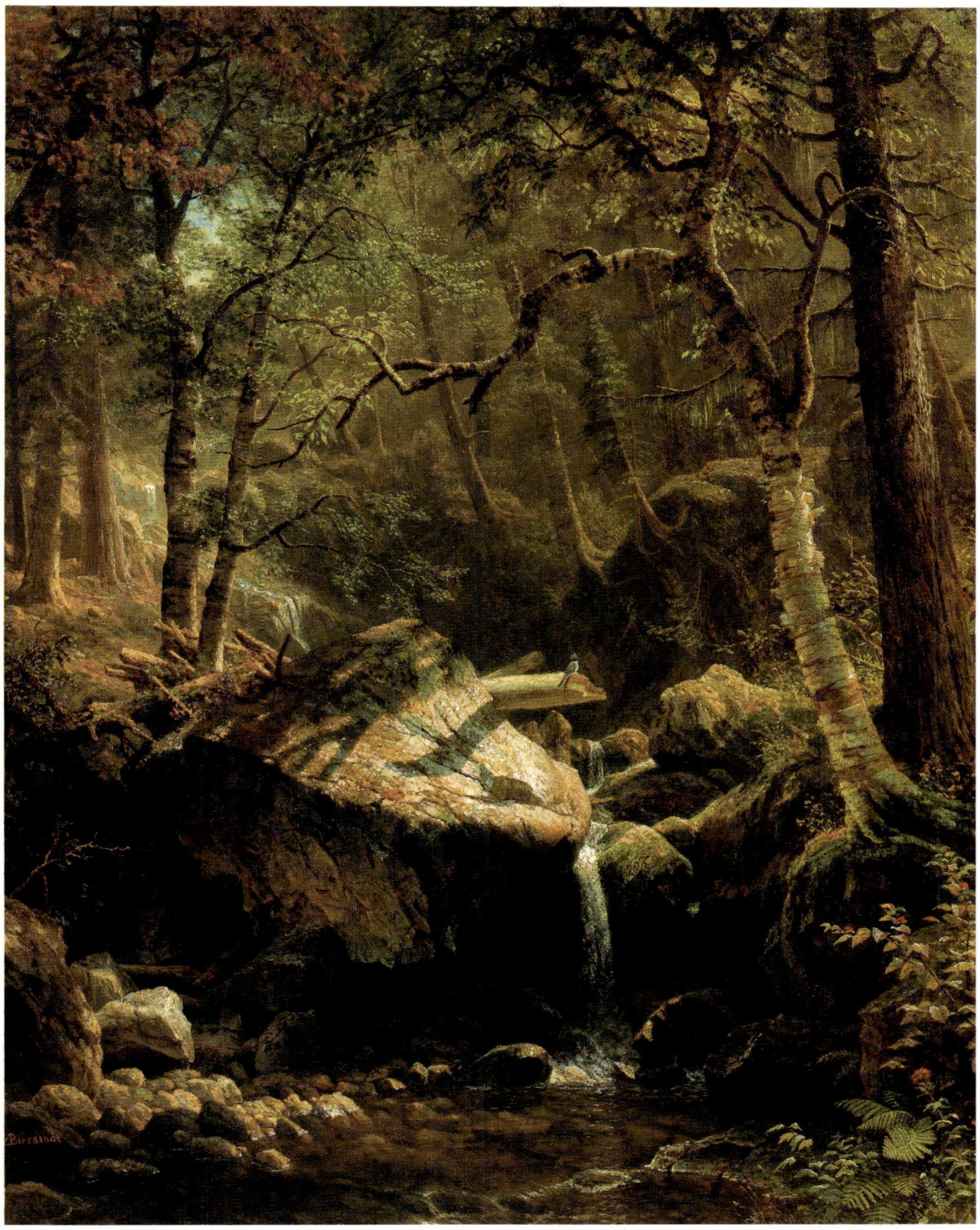

NO. 36

## *The Mountain Brook*, 1863

Oil on canvas, 44 × 36 in. (111.8 × 91.4 cm)
Signed and dated lower left: *ABierstadt/1863*
Collection of Gil Michaels

*In the "Mountain Brook," a picture still on the artist's easel, this realization of sunshine in all its midday splendor is . . . skilfully produced. . . . A white birch seen at the right of the picture . . . is undoubtedly the most truthfully natural tree ever painted by this artist. The trunk, with its peeled and curling bark, its general silvery tone broken and variegated by spots of golden sunlight and sombre shadows, is a finished and exquisite study. . . . This picture is noticeable for several qualities, the most remarkable being its contrasted light and shade, warmth and coolness, strength and tenderness; yet, so skilfully are those contrasts effected, that its harmony is not disturbed, but each quality lends additional interest to its opposite. Mr. Bierstadt has never painted a better picture than this, nor one which will be more gratifyingly received by the public.*

Barry Gray [R. B. Coffin], *NY Leader,* 17 Jan. 1863

*"The Mountain Brook" is an effective rendering of sunlight in the woods, painted in a graphic style and . . . full of good material. It is weak, nay, it is lacking, in all the finer and more delicate realizations of nature, and is without tenderness in touch or color, and may be termed a bold generalization of the subject. We have just enough of the particulars of the subject given to satisfy an ordinary lover of art and a superficial observer of nature. . . . Again, the sense of paint is too strong. The artist has not triumphed over his medium. The large boulder in the centre is not stone-like in texture, but rather like a huge mass of gray paint. . . . It is because Mr. Bierstadt has done better things, that I am thus unrelenting in my comments on "The Mountain Brook."*

*NY Leader,* 18 Apr. 1863

*Bierstadt's Rocky Mountain picture is attracting many lovers of art to the Studio Building. This painting is destined probably to have as great success before the public as Church's* Heart of the Andes. *Ideal or real, the mountains have a grandeur and solidity quite unapproached in any other work, ancient or modern, foreign or American. It is extremely doubtful if in this respect the picture will be excelled in this generation.*

*Boston Transcript*, 22 Apr. 1863

*What a sensation it would produce in the National Gallery [London], if beside the landscapes of Claude and of Turner . . . could be hung for a season Bierstadt's picture of the Rocky Mountains! With the clearest recollection of these and other famous scenes, we have no hesitation in saying that, in our opinion, the work of our own artist is, in grandeur of conception, faithfulness in detail, splendor of color, and harmony of tone, unexcelled by any landscape ever painted.*

*Boston Saturday Evening Gazette*, quoted in *Golden Era*, San Francisco, 29 Nov. 1863

*Mr. Bierstadt's name is now associated with the Rocky Mountains as is that of Mr. Church with the Andes. . . . Mr. Bierstadt's subject, in treatment, is marred in its impression of solitary grandeur by the introduction of an Indian encampment in the foreground. For an incident which is merely one of the accidents of the place, the artist has sacrificed the greatest element of his subject; he has sacrificed sublimity of impression to variety of interest. This is one of the serious esthetical faults of Mr. Bierstadt's treatment of his subject.*

*Round Table*, 27 Feb. 1864, p. 169

*The accuracy with which Mr. Bierstadt has painted the Indian life in all its details, must be evident to those who have had the opportunity of examining the very fine collection of arms, implements, and dresses which he brought with him from the West; or who have, in any way, studied the subject. Indeed, this is by far the best painted portion of the picture; it is plain that the artist is not only thoroughly acquainted with this part of his subject, but very much interested in it.*

*NY Tribune*, 12 Mar. 1864

*Mr. Bierstadt has shown a greater power of filling a large canvas with interesting matter than any man we have yet had. In this respect, he is very far superior to Mr. Church, who never knows what to do with his foreground, and so, generally contrives not to have any. But, as far as the mere mechanical art of laying on color is concerned, Mr. Church is far more dexterous. . . . But, when the best has been said, we must still regard this work as immature, and, on too pretentious a scale. The ambition of our young artists is leading them to attempt impossibilities. . . . Twenty times the study that the artist has given to this picture,—study represented by actual sketches, built upon a previous ten years, at least, of absorbing toil given to various branches of his art, would not have justified him in attempting to fill so large a canvas in such a way that the poet, the naturalist and the geologist might have taken large pleasure from it. And, even if he knew all that Turner knew, he could have put upon a canvas one sixth as large, enough to have brought the world to his doors.*

*New Path* 1 (Apr. 1864): 161

*We have heard it said, that Bierstadt's Rocky Mountains would have been more admirable if he had reproduced nothing but the stillness and majesty of nature. We differ totally from such a view. . . . [We] hold that the scene would have been comparatively voiceless, meaningless, and dead, but for the addition of the wild men of the mountains in their own life and manners.*

George Bancroft, "Nature and Life," *Spirit of the Fair*, 22 Apr. 1864, p. 186

*The next largest, and perhaps in all respects the most conspicuous picture in the American gallery, was Bierstadt's "Rocky Mountains." In arrangement of light and shadow, and in the rendering of the water, its purity and depth, this picture was probably unsurpassed by any in the entire exhibition. And it derived signal advantage from the introduction of an element, too often neglected, even when admissible in a landscape, viz: life in the foreground. The introduction of a camp of explorers, with Indians, etc., is not only effective, but appropriate, and gives a living interest to the picture without detracting from the silent majesty of the natural features which it was the great object of the painter to portray.*

Frank Leslie, "Report on the Fine Arts," in *Reports of the United States Commissioners to the Paris Universal Exposition, 1867*, vol. 1 (Washington, D.C.: 1870), p. 12

*It is Fenimore Cooper upon canvas.*

*Morning Post*, London, 16 Jan. 1868

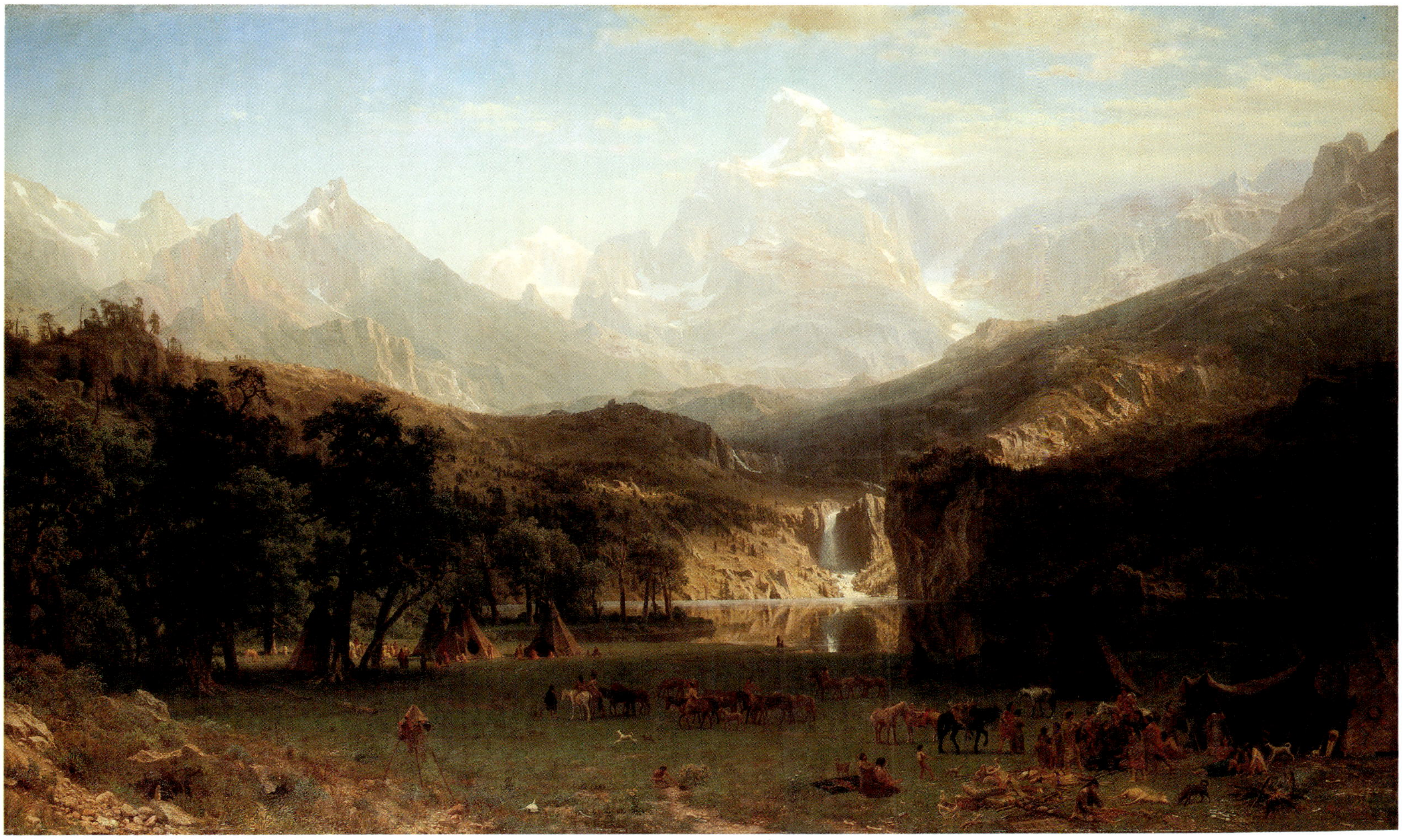

NO. 37

*The Rocky Mountains, Lander's Peak,* 1863

Oil on canvas, 73½ × 120¾ in. (186.7 × 306.7 cm)

Signed and dated lower right: *ABierstadt/1863.*

The Metropolitan Museum of Art, New York, Rogers Fund, 1907

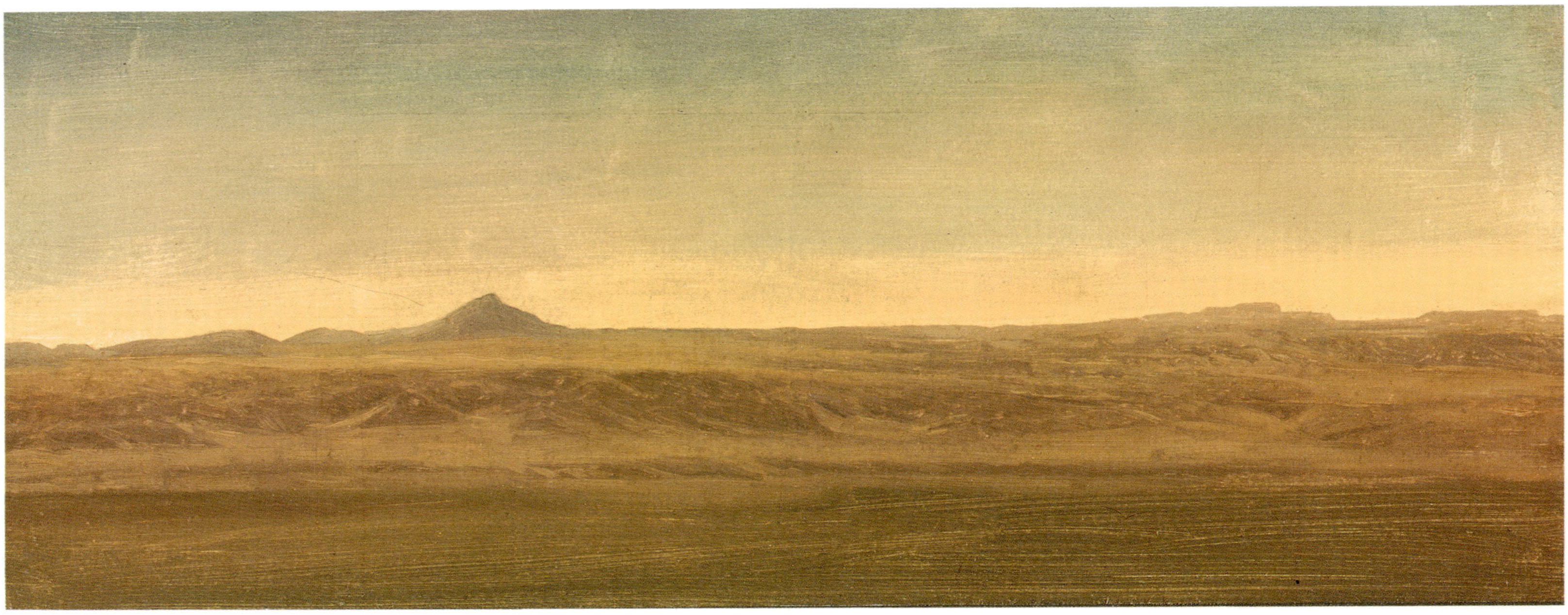

NO. 38

## *On the Plains*, 1863

Oil on paper mounted on board, 7½ × 19 in. (19 × 48.3 cm)

Unsigned

Inscribed verso: *Nebraska/On the Plains, Near Fort Laramie/1863*
*ABierstadt/New York*

Elliott Galleries, New York

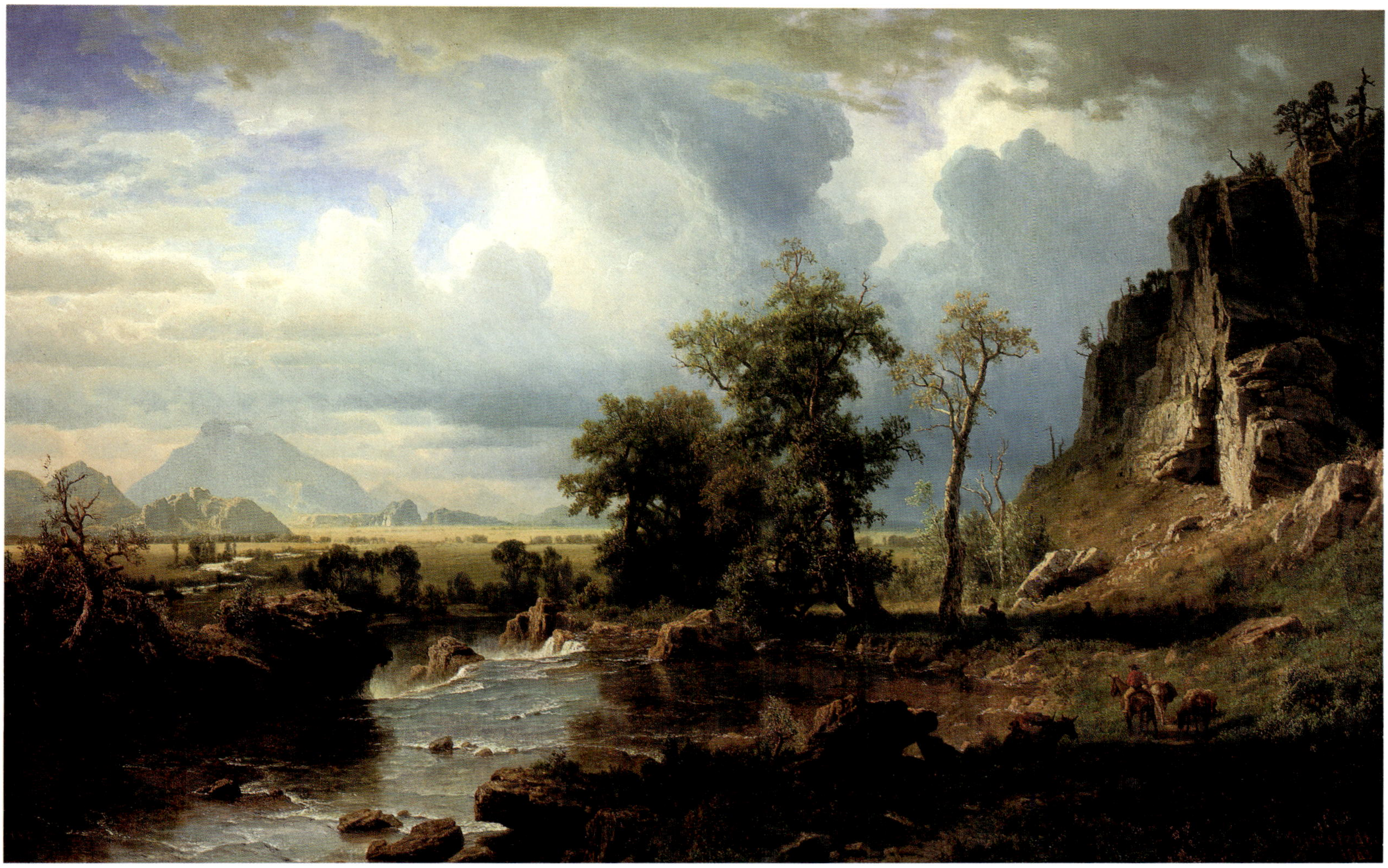

NO. 39

## *North Fork of the Platte, Nebraska*, 1863

Oil on canvas, 36 × 57½ in. (91.4 × 146 cm)
Signed and dated lower right: *ABierstadt./1863*
Manoogian Collection

*Just west of Cottonwood, the Platte River is formed by the junction of its north and south forks. In the neighborhood of the confluence, the land begins rising westward perceptibly. About ten miles from Cottonwood, I got my first sensation of ascent toward the Rocky Mountains. There was a solid, underbraced look in the hills, a firm, resonant quality to the road, which did not belong to alluvial bluffs. I felt as if I were standing on the first fold of the old fire-serpent, who ages ago wriggled himself up under the crust, and protruded his flaming crest in the form of the Rocky Mountain summit.*

Fitz Hugh Ludlow, *The Heart of the Continent: A Record of Travel Across the Plains and in Oregon, with an Examination of the Mormon Principle* (New York: 1870), p. 118

*The "North Fork of the Platte, Nebraska" . . . is a picture of broader lights and distances. Its breadth of light in the background, especially, is indeed admirable. Its rock painting is particularly vigorous. Great tabular masses of limestone, upended and broken into successive ledges—their ruin partly bold and staring, partly veiled under tender foliage—are more picturesque than any remains of British abbeys, and in the symmetry amid destruction give almost a similar suggestion of the work of man. The sky and water of this landscape are pure to the last degree.*

*Post*, New York, 16 May 1863

NO. 40

## *Cho-looke, The Yosemite Fall,* 1864

Oil on canvas, 34½ × 27⅛ in. (87.6 × 68.9 cm)

Signed and dated lower left: *ABierstadt/1864*

Timken Art Gallery, The Putnam Foundation, San Diego

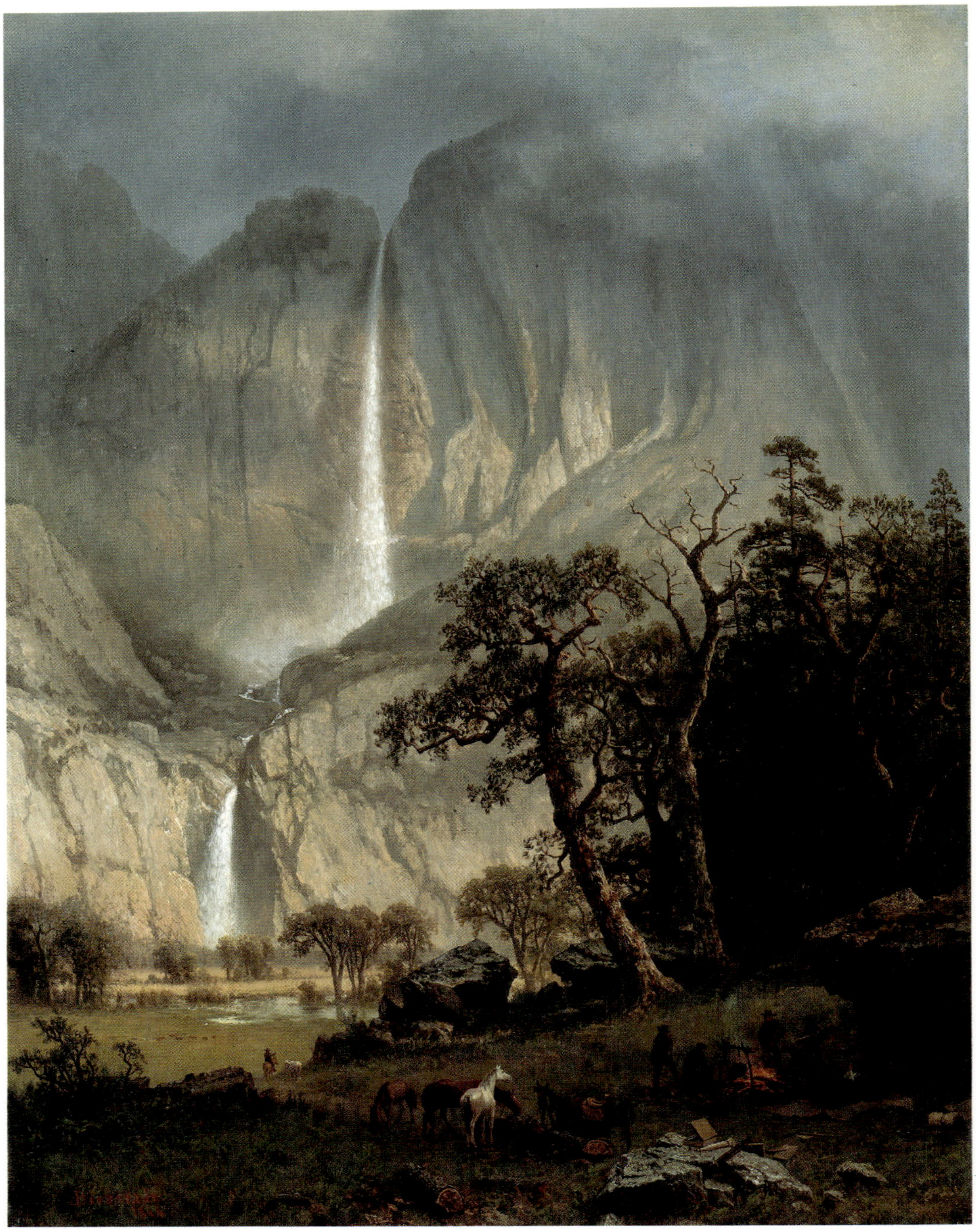

*Bierstadt, who is one of the most indefatigable workers among the artists—for even in mid-June the days are not sufficiently long for his purpose, and he is obliged sometimes to work by gaslight—is engaged, in the moments he spares from his large pictures, in painting an upright of a view of the Yo-Semite valley, including the Great Fall. . . . In the foreground of the picture, sheltered from the setting sun by massive rocks, a party of travellers, which we may presume was the artist and his friends, is encamped, engaged in preparing the evening meal. . . . The picture promises to be one of the artist's best works.*

*Post*, New York, 9 June 1864

*At evening, when the artists returned, half an hour was passed in a "private view" of their day's studies. . . . Our party moved its camp to a position with rich pasture for our animals immediately across the stream, and the loftiest cataract in the world roaring over the bleak precipice opposite. This is the Yo-Semite Fall proper, or, in the Indian, "Cho-Looke." By the most recent geological surveys this fall is credited with the astounding height of twenty-eight hundred feet. . . . In the spring and early summer no more magnificent sight can be imagined than the tourist obtains from a stand-point right in the midst of the spray, driven, as by a wind blowing thirty miles an hour, from the thundering basin of the lower fall. At all seasons Cho-Looke is the grandest mountain-waterfall in the known world.*

Fitz Hugh Ludlow, *The Heart of the Continent: A Record of Travel Across the Plains and in Oregon, with an Examination of the Mormon Principle* (New York: 1870), pp. 436, 438–39

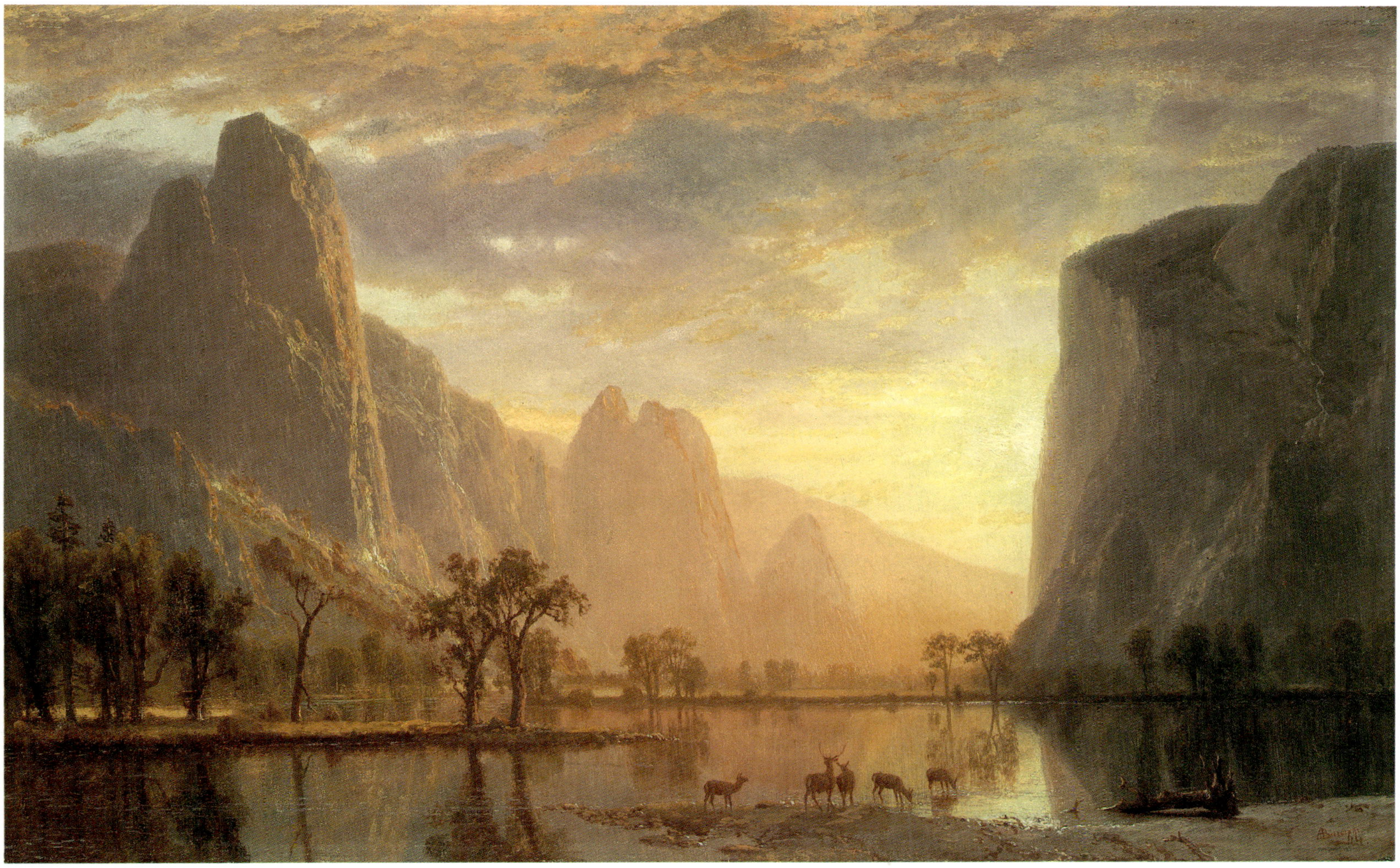

NO. 41

*Valley of the Yosemite*, 1864

Oil on board, 11¾ × 19¼ in. (29.8 × 48.9 cm)

Signed and dated lower right: *ABierstadt./64*

Museum of Fine Arts, Boston, Gift of Martha C. Karolik for the Karolik Collection of American Paintings, 1815–1865

*We are here brought face to face with Nature's living rocks. No composition work are they. A geologist could assign you their place in the world's history. They tower up on either hand, bathed in the golden sunlight. Down through the valley, full towards the beholder, is poured the flood of sunlight. Overhead in the clear air; free from the blue of the sky, float the clouds, a glad company, touched with the same golden glory. Between the lofty escarpments of rock flows the Yo Semite, its waters fondly repeating so much of the magnificence as they receive. Over the rocks, into the light, glitters and falls the tiny cascade. Shadows steal round the peaks and repose in the coverts. Here on the right, a primeval wood, dwarfed by the mountain of rocks behind, hides in obscurity. The picture is full of fine enthusiasm, of a free exultation in the grander forms of nature. . . . The picture, however, is not one of the imagination. The mind is not carried beyond the present glory, is not excited to future expectation, is wrapt in the splendor of the moment. Nor is it, as we have already hinted, one in which a loving study of individual forms is apparent. A closer individualism in the foreground on the left would, we think, have given great additional interest to the picture; amid the bleak vastness of the mountains and the cold brilliance of the sunshine, it would have suggested the interposing hand of a creative nature, taking even these rigid uncompromising rocks to her heart.*

*Watson's Weekly Art Journal*, 20 May 1865, p. 52

*Mr. Bierstadt has painted far better works than this impossible Californian valley, for he has studied nature well and carefully. Whatever he learned thus, however, he ignored at the time of producing this great acre-and-a-half of slovenly and monstrous stage-scenery.*

*If you will take the trouble to compare the height of these mountains with a corresponding length of horizontal measurement on the plain beneath, you will detect at once the grossest exaggeration. No such colossal mountains exist, Mr. Bierstadt, in the world!*

*Still, if the picture were faithfully and artistically painted, I might forgive even this fault; but it is not. The execution reminds me of nothing upon the earth, or in the waters under the earth, or in the heavens above the earth, save the drop-curtain of a minor theatre. It might do credit . . . perhaps, as the background of a melodrama, but it will never do anything for the reputation of the author of "Sunshine and Shadow."*

*NY Leader*, 20 May 1865

To the Editors of the Evening Post:

*In the Academy exhibition Mr. Bierstadt is represented by two large pictures, the chiefest and largest of which occupies a place of honor opposite the main entrance of the large gallery. It is impossible to escape this picture if one enters the main hall. It is a characteristic example of Bierstadt's talent, and has been called his best picture; it certainly is much admired by the public. But we frankly say we do not admire it, for it is vicious, vulgar, scenic art. . . . Mr. Bierstadt's art addresses itself only to the public, and beyond certain scenic characteristics has nothing that claims the attention of the artist. . . .*
*SORDELLO [Eugene Benson].*

*We give place to our correspondent's severe criticism of Mr. Bierstadt's picture, although it does not accord with the estimate we had ourselves formed on the merits of that eminent artist.—EDS. EVENING POST.*

*Post*, New York, 7 June 1865

To the Editors of the Evening Post:

*Will you have the kindness to allow me a few words of reply to the correspondent who signs his name "Sordello"? Although I know full well that Mr. Bierstadt's reputation as an artist, the very foremost in this country, is beyond either his attempts to defame or mine to praise, yet I cannot be silent when this second Daniel in judgment, from his high and lofty pedestal, puts upon all who admire his productions the almost gratuitous insult of being ignorant of nature. . . . Hoping to be enlightened still more, I am very truly yours, "A CHILD OF IGNORANCE."*

*Post*, New York, 9 June 1865

*A New York paper, in noticing the pictures on exhibition in the National Academy of Design, says the largest and most charming landscape in the collection, embracing nearly 700 pictures, is Bierstadt's* Yosemite Valley, California: *"This is one of the series of views taken by the artist during his recent trip over the plains. The view is a long one, a perspective of 20 or 30 miles, down a golden valley flanked on each side by towering crags, thousands of feet high. The scene is soft and delicious steeped in the languid haze of an Indian Summer. This peculiar effect of haziness is generally supposed to be monopolized by New England and the colder regions of the North; but the popular impression on this subject will have to be revised if Bierstadt's painting is to be accepted as correct. In his other pictures of the West, nothing of the kind is observed but a perfectly transparent atmosphere and clear outlines are the rules." The haze that softens California landscapes was well described by Bayard Taylor, in his letters from this state, as the secret of those enchanting colors which characterize our scenery. . . . Bierstadt's Yosemite must be a revelation to the New Yorkers in more respects than this. If the Catskills were suddenly cleft to the level of the Hudson, and the river that pours over them were to be hung in the air for 1,500 feet like a white ribbon, reaching the base of these stupendous walls in spray, the Gothamites would not have a more wonderful spectacle than Bierstadt has pictured for them on canvas from his studies of the actual Yosemite. Until this picture was painted, the Eastern public had never enjoyed an opportunity to see any views of Yosemite except the small photographs and woodcuts which were so plentifully issued here.*

*Bulletin*, San Francisco, 12 June 1865

*Albert Bierstadt's "Looking Down Yo-Semite Valley" is the most attractive picture in this year's exhibition of the N.Y. Academy of Design.—The* N.Y. Day Book *says: "Looking down the valley, the view is lost in a sea of golden mist. The shadow of a mighty mountain in the foreground darkens immense forests. A plain of countless acres spreads out before you. We have seen few*

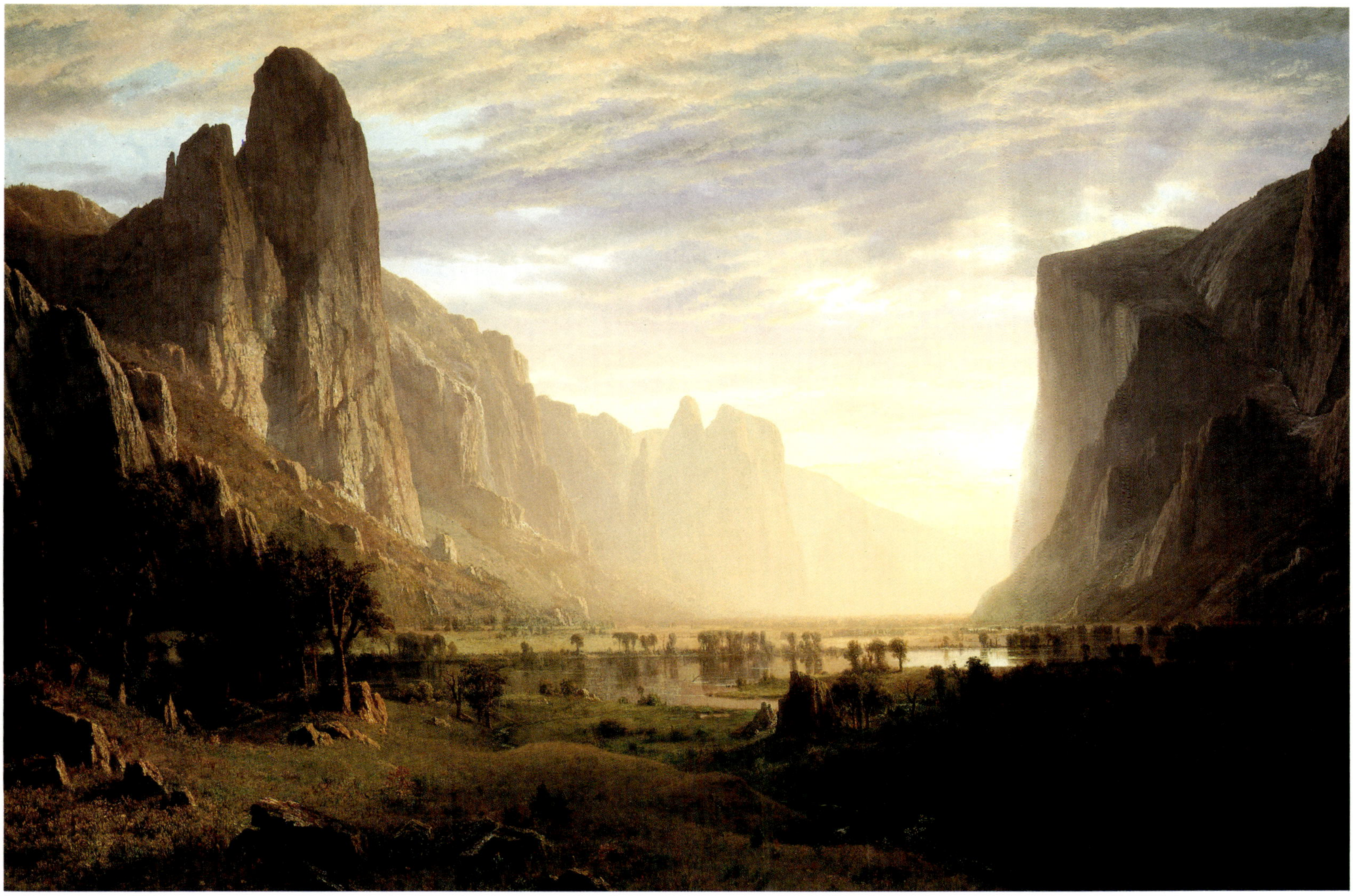

*landscapes since the "Heart of the Andes" that will compare with this. It looks as if it was painted in an Eldorado, in a distant land of gold; heard of in a song and story; dreamed of, but never seen. Yet it is real. Why should our artists make their pilgrimages to the Alps for mountains, to Italy for skies, or to Chamouni Valley, when we have the mountains and skies of California, and the valley of Yo-Semite. . . . Our young landscape painters should not fail to study and understand the principles upon which this fine work is painted. It will be of incalculable benefit to them."*

*Golden Era*, San Francisco, 23 July 1865

*Such pictures as his "Yo-Semite Valley" are mere pieces of scene-painting, gross caricatures of nature, so wanting in all reality and faithfulness, that we know an instance of a person thoroughly familiar with the whole region, and enthusiastically fond of it, who heard that this picture was in the last Exhibition, and went there expressly to see it. Not having a catalogue, he wandered about the rooms looking for it, and at last, on inquiry, found that he had passed and repassed it, and looked at it several times, without suspecting it to be what he was searching for. The truth is that Mr. Bierstadt has been ruined by excessive flattery.*

*Round Table*, 14 Oct. 1865, p. 93

NO. 42

## *Looking Down Yosemite Valley, California*, 1865

Oil on canvas, 64 × 96¼ in. (162.6 × 244.5 cm)

Signed and dated lower left: *ABierstadt/1865*

Birmingham Museum of Art, Birmingham, Alabama

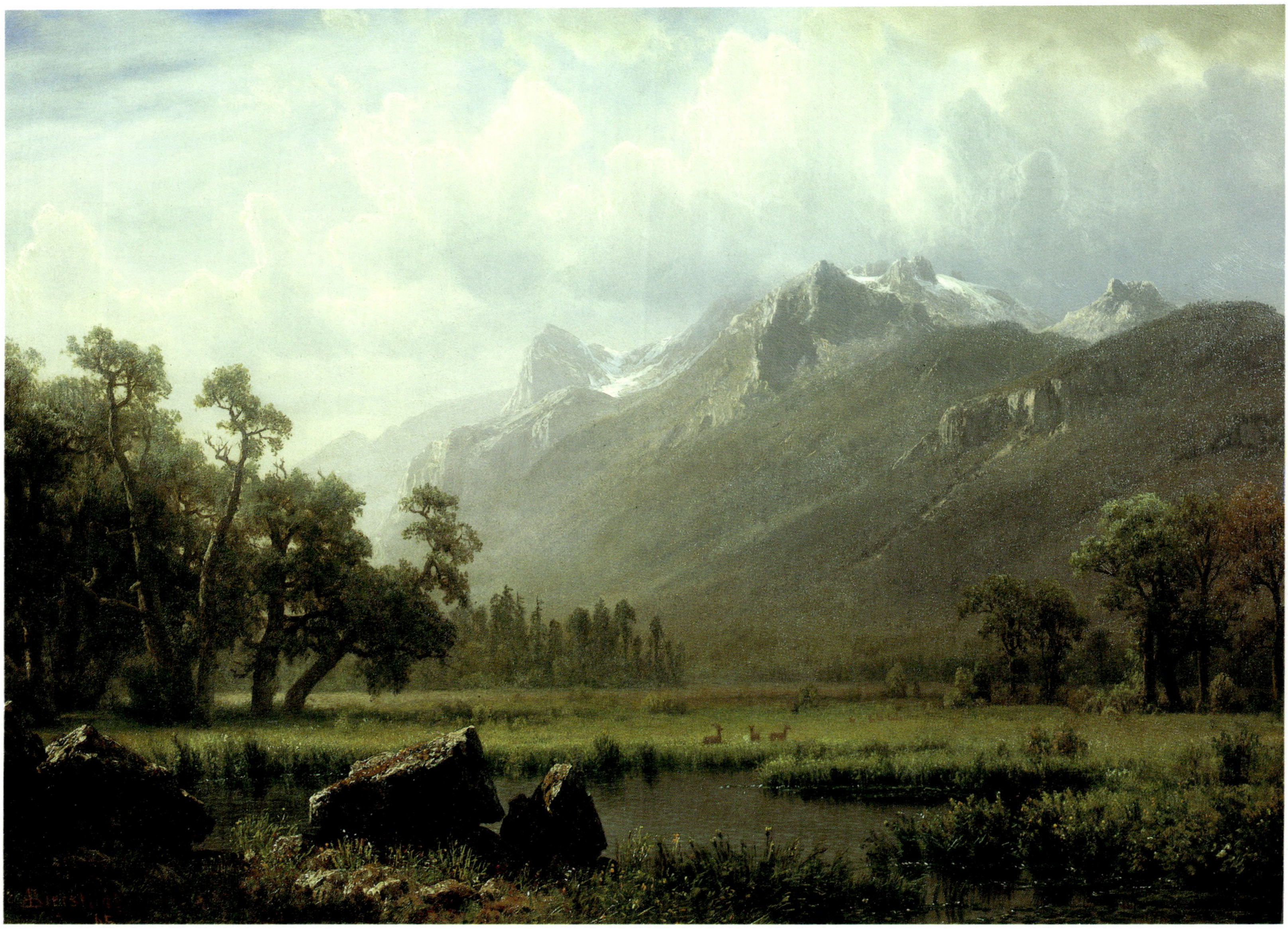

NO. 43

## *The Sierras near Lake Tahoe, California*, 1865

Oil on panel, 15½ × 21 in. (39.4 × 53.3 cm)

Signed and dated lower left: *ABierstadt/65*

Inscribed verso: *Lake Tahoe, California No. 45*

Berry-Hill Galleries, Inc., New York

*Just across the boundary, we sat down on the brink of glorious Lake Tahoe, . . . a crystal sheet of water fresh-distilled from the snow-peaks, its granite bottom visible at the depth of a hundred feet, its banks a celestial garden, lying in a basin thirty-five miles long by ten wide, and nearly seven thousand feet above the Pacific level. Geography has no superior to this glorious sea, this chalice of divine cloud-wine held sublimely up against the very press whence it was wrung. Here, virtually at the end of our overland journey, since our feet pressed the green borders of the Golden state, we sat down to rest, feeling that one short hour, one little league, had translated us out of the infernal world into heaven.*

Fitz Hugh Ludlow, "Among the Mormons," *Atlantic Monthly*, Apr. 1864, pp. 494–95

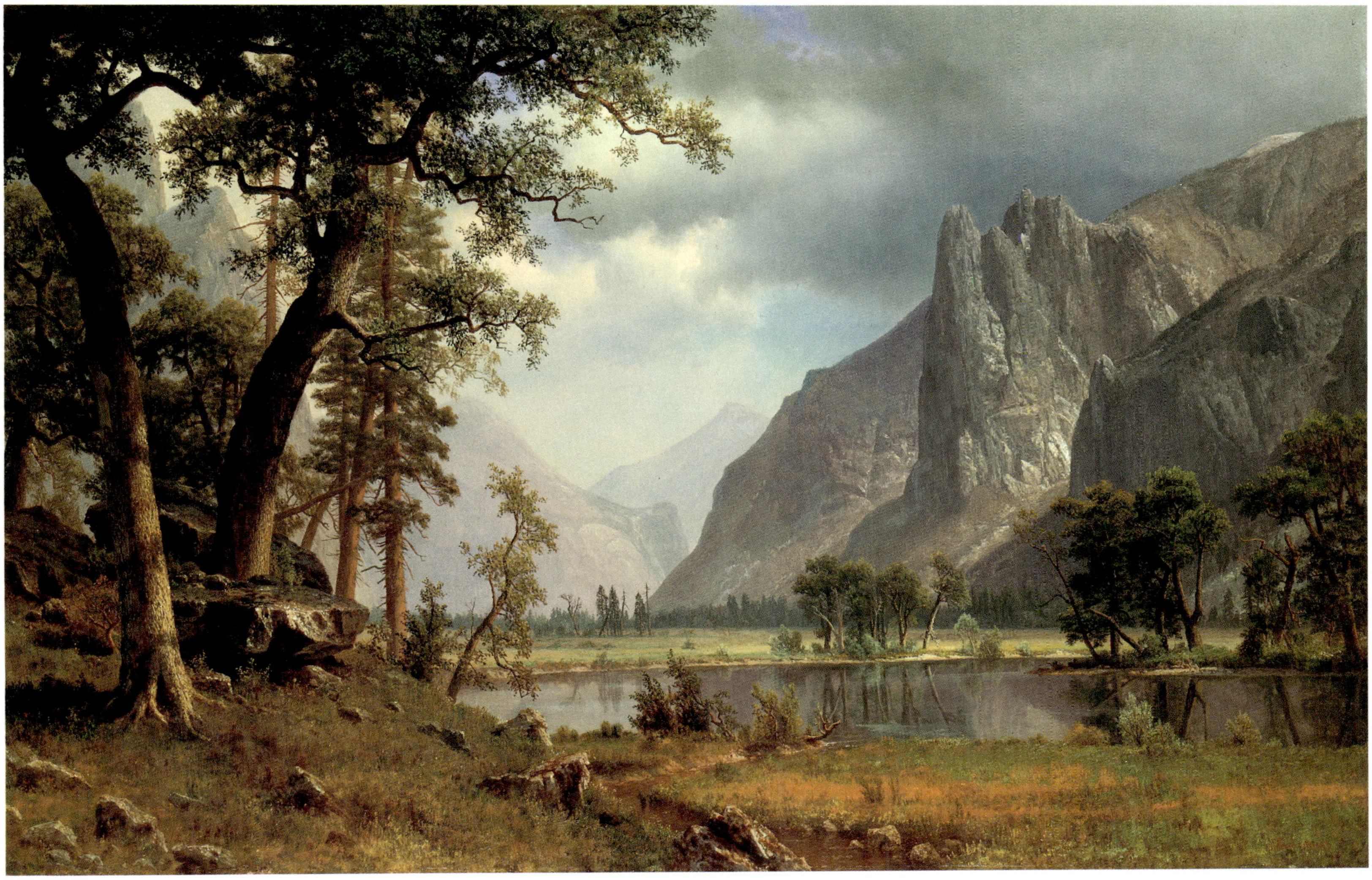

NO. 44

*Yosemite Valley*, 1866

Oil on canvas, 38 × 60 in. (96.5 × 152.4 cm)

Signed and dated lower right: *ABierstadt/66*

Collection of Jo Ann and Julian Ganz, Jr.

*That very deserving charity—the Nursery and Child's Hospital—has been so fortunate as to procure Mr. Bierstadt's last work, "A Storm in the Rocky Mountains," which is now on exhibition at Miner & Somerville's gallery, No. 815 Broadway, for the benefit of this benevolent enterprise. . . . But whatever may be the merits of this picture as a means of collecting cash, its merits as a work of art are inconsiderable; nor have we any doubt that the public will admit that Mr. Bierstadt has taken a subject beyond his power to paint. We have not space to-day to go into details of description. We content ourselves with the assertion that all the defects we have so often pointed out in this artist's work are assembled on this pretentious canvas. All is pretty. Not only are the mountain forms insignificant, frittered and mean; the trees the same stunted and ill-shaped growths with which his former pictures have made us familiar; but, we are pestered with a number of trifling incidents rendered still weaker by the tame and artificial manner in which they are painted. The little pool at the extreme right; the frightened horses in the immediate foreground; the water running over the shelving rock; the gleam of sunlight on the water, help to make up a picture which belongs to the class "drop scene" and has no power to hold the mind captive by its truth to nature, nor to move the spirit of man by the eloquence or subtlety of its interpretation. This work is a sign of failing power; a sign not, indeed, unlooked for, since all the artist's later work has prophesied it, in its disloyalty to the truth; its pandering to the popular love of excitement; its evident want of study; its ever increasing hardness; and its fatal repetitions. Perhaps the omen may yet be averted. But we fear that the long continued draft of flattery and adulation administered by the public and accepted by the artist, has made this consummation almost impossible to hope for. But we are ready to hope whenever he will give us cause.*

*NY Tribune*, 8 Feb. 1866

*Mr. Bierstadt's new picture in some respects is better even than his "Rocky Mountains." It is grander in composition, bolder in treatment, and more interesting in subject.*

*Post*, New York, 23 Feb. 1866

*As a work of art, the picture is almost universally pronounced the best production of American genius. The art critic of the* Tribune *seen* [sic] *fit in his wisdom—or rather want of it—to say some unfavorable things, but in doing so he only displayed his own ignorance. Many people who see it are puzzled at its—to them—peculiarities. They never have seen such a combination of scenery; such clouds and storm, such lights and shadows; hence they are in doubt if such can be, and "that's what's the matter" with the* Tribune *man, only he didn't stop to doubt but decided that they couldn't. Poor fellow. He had better travel and learn, or else 'dry up.'*

*Rocky Mountain News*, Denver, 27 Feb. 1866

*Mr. Bierstadt's new picture, the present exhibition of which closed on the 24th, has, we understand, increased the funds of the charitable society, in behalf of which it was placed on view, by $2,200. The picture has, therefore, in this respect served a very good purpose. We are not certain, however, whether the benefit thus conferred is not greatly overbalanced by the harm done to the public taste. In the course of the exhibition, the work was extensively* noticed *in the daily press; and by* noticed *we mean* puffed. *The press of this country has no conscience in this matter, and very rarely takes the pains to pass a discriminating judgment upon works of art. . . .*

*The truth is, we fear, Mr. Bierstadt has undertaken a subject much beyond his powers. To depict a storm requires imagination; to depict a storm in the Rocky Mountains requires extraordinary intensity of imagination. But Mr. Bierstadt has not displayed, as we think, in any previous picture, with which we are cognizant, certainly he does not display in the present one, the possession in its lowest form of this rare faculty. Mr. Bierstadt is undoubtedly not without great talent of a certain kind; he knows how to bring out on a canvas of large proportions masses of rock, water, and cloud, in such bold and severely defined relief as to impose upon the observer the belief in the actuality of that which is depicted. [However] there is a difference between the actuality and reality. . . .*

*The whole science of geology cries out against him. . . .*

*The law of gravitation leagues itself with geological law against the artist. . . . Now, let him work out a problem in arithmetic: The hills over which he looks are, as we are told, three thousand feet high; right over the hills tower huge masses of cloud which certainly carry the eye up ten to twelve thousand feet higher; above these jut the two "spurs;" what is the height of Mount Rosalie? Answer: Approximately, ten thousand miles or so. Impossible. Then these "spurs" are not affected by nature's law of gravitation, but float up in the air by some artistic license. . . .*

*In fine, in this picture Mr. Bierstadt has attempted more and effected less than in any previous effort. We do not deny to this artist the possession of brilliant power in the treatment of large masses; but he has not the imagination equal to grandeur of design, and is not sincere in his study of nature, preferring, as he does, to captivate admirers by clap-trap expedients.*

*Watson's Weekly Art Journal*, 3 Mar. 1866, pp. 307–8

*In short, Church and Bierstadt have founded a new school—one that has already given pre-eminence to American landscape painting. While contemplating this "Storm in the Rocky Mountains," we felt for the first time a desire to have honest John Ruskin at our side, acting as our guide and interpreter to all its merits. . . . A powerful light is streaking over the rocky gates of the mountain on the left, and radiating down over the lake in the foreground, which it seems to invest with enchantment. Indeed, the light here is handled with such exquisite skill, and is so singularly pure and effective, that many of the spectators fancy it produced by some artificial means behind the canvas.*

*Daily National Intelligencer*, Washington, D.C., 10 Mar. 1866

*This is a true picture, whether it be the portrait of a particular locality and incident, or a composition intended to be representative in its character. Any observing eye, which has ever rested on the scenery of the Rocky Mountains, can see it vividly revived in this noble painting.*

*Daily Missouri Republican*, Saint Louis, 14 Oct. 1866

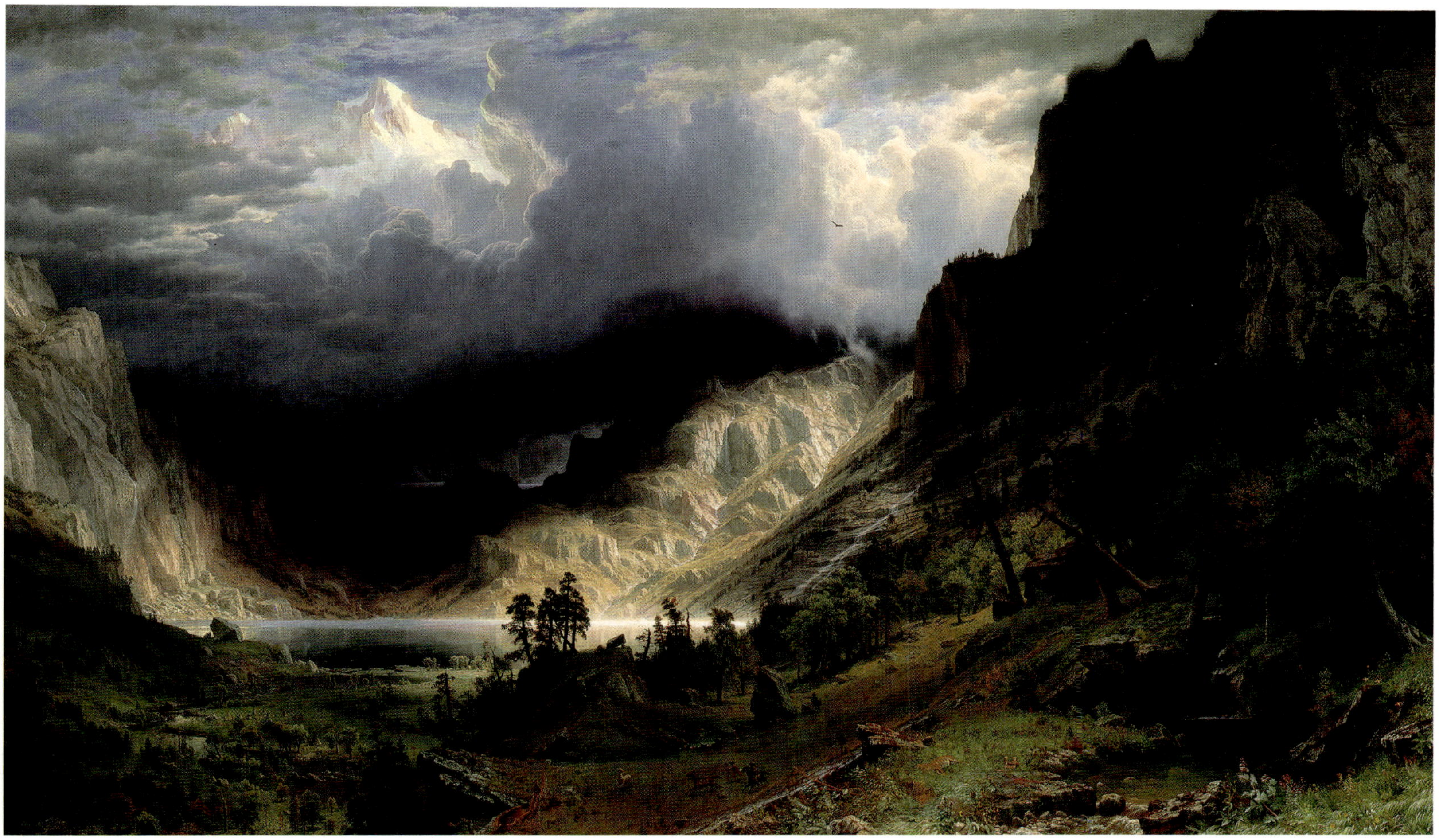

*These works of landscape art are all on the largest scale ever attempted short of panoramic pictures, and in this respect alone they are very remarkable as examples of artistic power and forcible expression of so much that is grand and beautiful in landscape. The large size of these pictures, no doubt, gives them all the imposing effect that belongs to size; but beyond this we find, in Mr. Bierstadt's work especially, a delicacy in the details and brilliancy in the lighting which are not surpassed by some of our best water-colour artists. The stupendous scenery of the Rocky Mountains, and of America generally, has, no doubt, something to do with inspiring such really noble pictures as this "Storm in the Rocky Mountains;" and our small painters may perhaps be allowed something on the score of not living under the same mighty influences of the scenery; but they must hide their diminished heads before these fine landscapes of Mr. Bierstadt.*

*Daily News*, London, 24 June 1867

*Theophile Gautier, the well known art critic, in a recent feuilleton in the* Journal Officiel de l'Empire Francais, *speaking of the pictures at the recent exposition, says:*

*Albert Bierstadt is an American landscape painter who enjoys a high reputation in the New World, and one which he deserves, for he has much talent, as his "Storm in the Rocky Mountain"* [sic] *shows. The size of his canvas is decidedly beyond that which landscape painting generally employs, and we think that the artist has done well to adopt such large dimensions, having to express a nature so gigantic. . . .*

*This picture, which initiates us into a new nature, besides the merit of representing scenery whose character is unknown to us, possesses that of being painted with great skill, and in a manner which recalls the handling of Calame, a painter who was not sufficiently appreciated in France, and who knew how to give Alpine scenes better than all others. Bierstadt may be proud of the resemblance.*

*Alta*, San Francisco, 8 Aug. 1869

NO. 45

## *Storm in the Rocky Mountains, Mt. Rosalie*, 1866

Oil on canvas, $83 \times 142\frac{1}{4}$ in. ($210.8 \times 361.3$ cm)

Signed and dated lower right: *ABierstadt/N.Y. 1866*

The Brooklyn Museum, Dick S. Ramsey Fund, A. Augustus Healy Fund B, Frank L. Babbott Fund, A. Augustus Healy Fund, Ella C. Woodward Memorial Funds, Gift of Daniel M. Kelly, Gift of Charles Simon, Charles Smith Memorial Fund, Caroline Pratt Fund, Frederick Loeser Fund, Augustus Graham School of Design Fund, Bequest of Mrs. William T. Brewster, Gift of Mrs. W. Woodward Phelps, Gift of Seymour Barnard, Charles Stuart Smith Fund, Bequest of Laura L. Barnes, Gift of J. A. H. Bell, John B. Woodward Memorial Fund, Bequest of Mark Finley

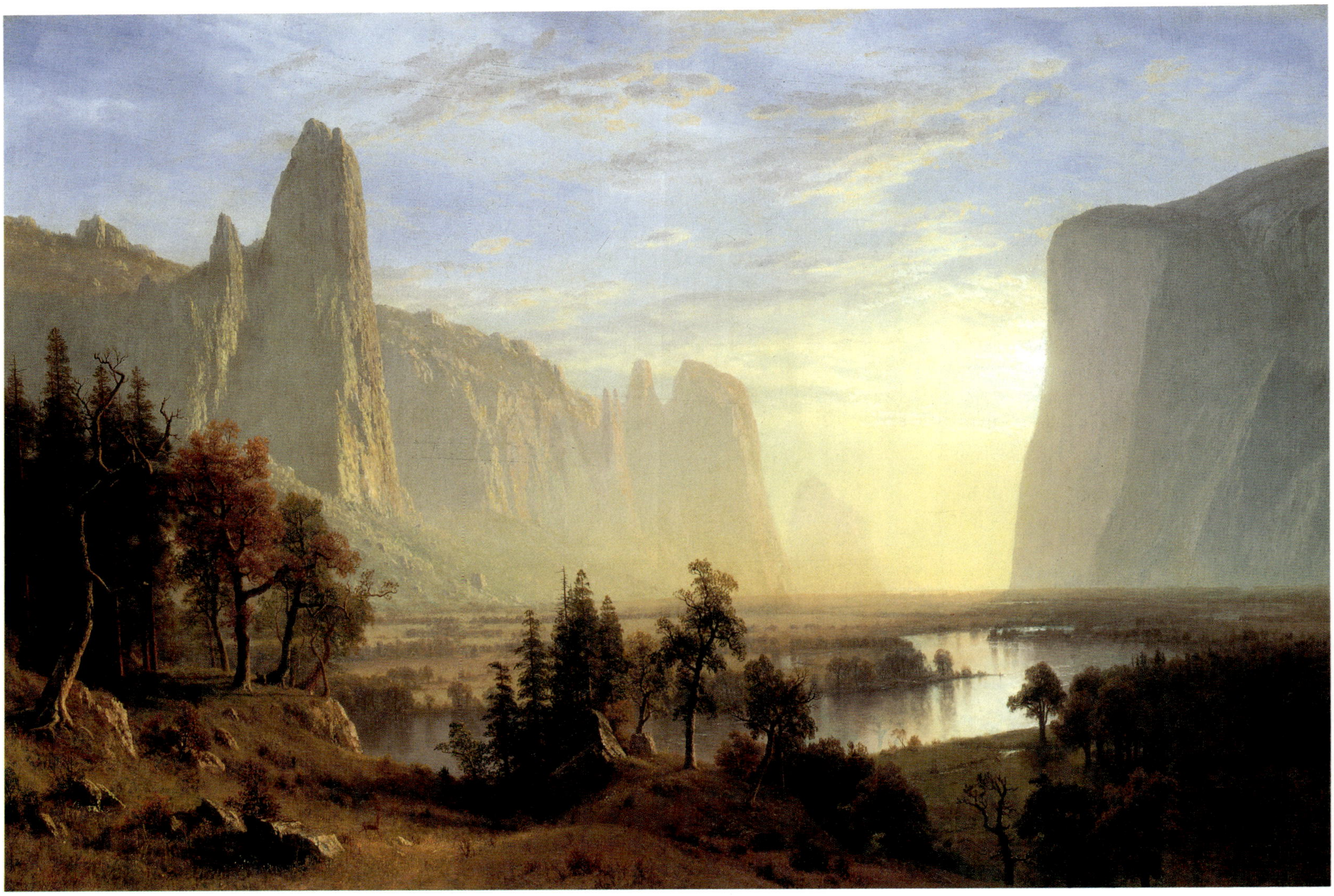

NO. 46

*Yosemite Valley,* 1868

Oil on canvas, 36 × 54 in. (91.4 × 137.2 cm)

Signed and dated lower left: *ABierstadt/1868*

The Oakland Museum, Gift of Miss Marguerite Laird in memory of Mr. and Mrs. P. W. Laird

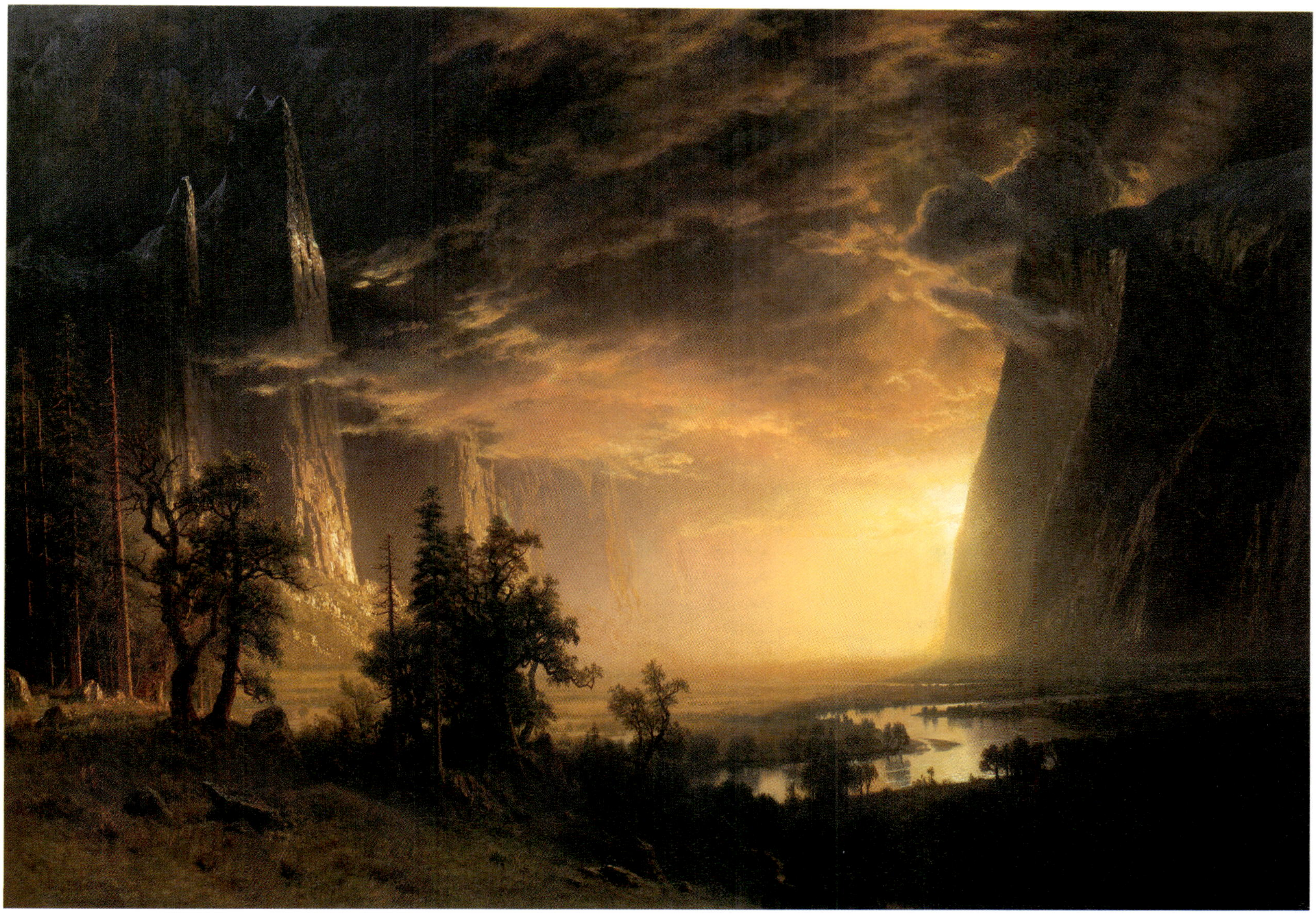

NO. 47

## *Sunset in the Yosemite Valley,* 1868

Oil on canvas, 36¼ × 52¼ in. (92.1 × 132.7 cm)

Signed and dated lower left: *ABierstadt/1868*

Haggin Collection, The Haggin Museum, Stockton, California

*Mr. Bierstadt has also painted a "sunset" on a portion of the same river system, . . . where the golden-haze . . . reminds us of Italy and Italian skies as they lingered on the memory of Claude Lorraine. It is a scenery entirely new to most Englishmen, and the artist who has penetrated these wilds has brought them vividly before the imagination.*

*Art-Journal* (London), Aug. 1868, p. 159

*I found it extremest pleasure to lie there alone on the dizzy brink, . . . watching that slow grand growth of afternoon shadows. Sunset found me there, still disinclined to stir, and repaid my laziness by a glorious spectacle of color. At this hour there is no more splendid contrast of light and shade than one sees upon the western gateway itself,—dark-shadowed Capitan upon one side profiled against the sunset sky, and the yellow mass of Cathedral Rocks rising opposite in full light, while the valley is divided equally between sunshine and shade. . . . The Merced, upon its mirror-like expanses, here reflects deep blue from Capitan, and there the warm Cathedral gold.*

Clarence King, *Mountaineering in the Sierra Nevada* (Boston: 1872), 1970 ed. (Lincoln, Nebr.), p. 144

*In the golden and crimson splendor of the departing day the great valley is sinking to rest under a coverlet of cloud. The incredible magnificence of the western sunset bathes the towering cliffs and the stream that winds its way between them in a glory of color that only the most daring pencil may essay to reproduce. It is as if the auriferous treasures of the earth were fused into the sky in one superb triumph of pigmentary perfection.*

American Art Galleries, *Catalogue of Mr. James H. Stebbins' Private Collection of Modern Paintings* (New York: 1889), p. 48

*The largest of Mr. Bierstadt's pictures, some ten feet by six, is a romantic mountain-landscape in the heart of the Sierra Nevada. . . . At the proper distance of some thirty feet, the whole of this distant landscape assumes the aspect of nature herself. The picture is not only a representation of a scene of romantic grandeur, but a truthful and worthy representation of such a scene. . . . No finer landscape than that representing the Sierra Nevada has, so far as we are aware, been produced in modern times; none in which the merits are so marked, the originality so decided, and the room for adverse criticism so difficult to discover.*

*Art-Journal* (London), Aug. 1868, pp. 159–60

*Mr. Bierstadt's picture is very puzzling. Looking at the size of it, no less than the singular executive skill of the mountain and cloud painting, and the grand natural features of the scene, one is astonished not to feel more impressed. Here seems to be everything to kindle the imagination, yet the imagination is but languidly stirred. Is it that the scale of the work, in itself, impairs its impressiveness, from the impossibility of the mind and eye grasping so much at once? Or does the uniform distribution of care and finish prevent that focussing of attention and interest, which seem necessary conditions for awakening the imagination? Or is it merely the "too much" of the subject, the multiplicity of features and incidents of mountain landscape, which overtaxes the receptive capacity of the mind?*

*Times*, London, 19 May 1869

*We can conscientiously term it a "great work," as it is undoubtedly equal to anything this artist has yet done. . . . Not unfrequently the eye is overpowered by the audacity of the design, and those who are not connoisseurs in art are blinded to defects of detail. This is largely true of the work before us, which is an ideal union of the most splendid and characteristic features of our western mountains. The result is a scene which does not exist, and in fact hardly could exist, but is most imposing and fascinating. It is a perfect type of the American idea of what our scenery ought to be, if it is not so in reality, and if the peaks and snows portrayed by the artist do not exist* "tant le pis pour eux." . . . *Mr. Bierstadt has done himself full justice, and if certain portions of his work do not possess that vitality which belongs to nature, it is hardly to be imputed as a fault that he has failed in any degree in a design so ambitious.*

*Boston Post*, 11 Oct. 1869

*THE SIERRA NEVADA.* Mr. Editor: *Will you permit a few words of comment upon that huge claptrap they call a picture, at Child's Gallery. Without ill-nature, we would say a more false bit of scenic nature has not met our eye. There is no relation in the parts; you can step from the foreground to the farther end of the cliff, or jump on to the mountain top at will. Stiffer trees are not often painted—the artist cannot paint a tree. . . . There is no feeling for distance in the picture. A worse instance of the false American style of landscape, which is simply bombastic, we have not seen. Dioramas, panoramas seen through a darkened hole, are better, for they do not pretend to be other than they are, a pretty illusion. . . . It is a false note from beginning to end, and betrays no feeling for nature in her simplicity and essence. . . . It resembles rhetoric in literature,—all rhetoric and nothing else, hollow, tawdry, sensational, false. E.A.S.*

*Bierstadt's picture is severely criticized on the first page by one of the most exacting of our Art critics. We allow the writer to present his views, which our readers will perceive differ from those of a highly commendatory character that have appeared in our columns.—EDS.*

*Boston Transcript*, 23 Oct. 1869

*"AMONG THE SIERRA NEVADA MOUNTAINS." The public is particularly fortunate in the opportunity to view this beautiful painting—now exhibiting at Childs & Co.'s gallery—which has attracted so much attention in Europe. . . . The picture fully sustains the high reputation acquired by Mr. Bierstadt from his former productions, and certainly no one can gaze upon the scenes of beauty and sublimity depicted upon those few feet of canvas without experiencing a lively sensation of pleasure. . . . It has been suggested, and perhaps with some degree of truth, that the whole picture is somewhat idealized; that the reflection of the light is too beautiful for reality, or that the mountains are too abrupt and sharp; but we must allow the artist as well as the poet a little liberty in clothing his subjects with a pleasing and harmonious effect. THEO.*

*Boston Transcript*, 13 Nov. 1869

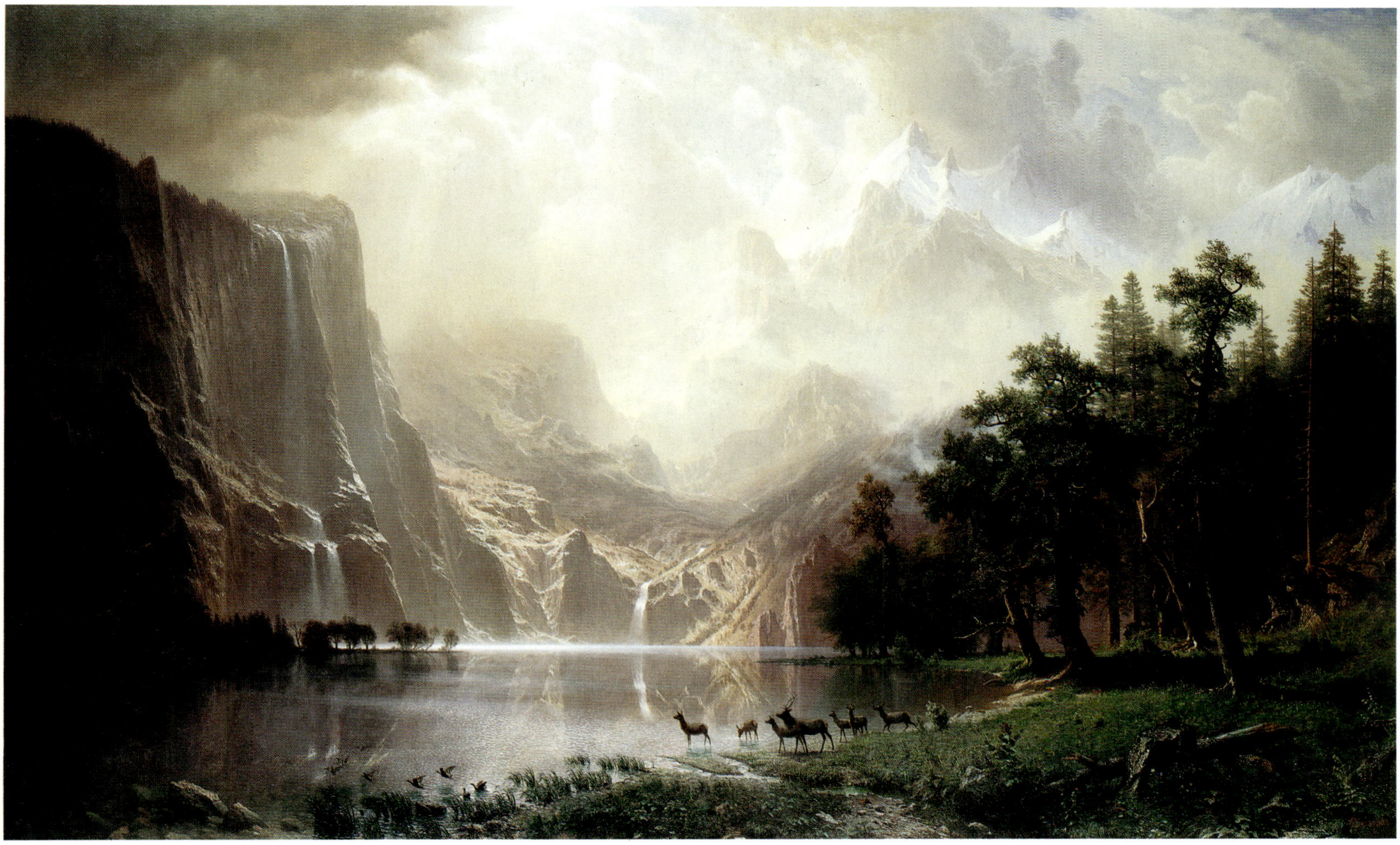

NO. 48

*Among the Sierra Nevada Mountains, California*, 1868

Oil on canvas, 72 × 120 in. (182.9 × 304.8 cm)

Signed and dated lower right: *ABierstadt/68*

National Museum of American Art, Smithsonian Institution, Washington, D.C., Bequest of Helen Huntington Hull

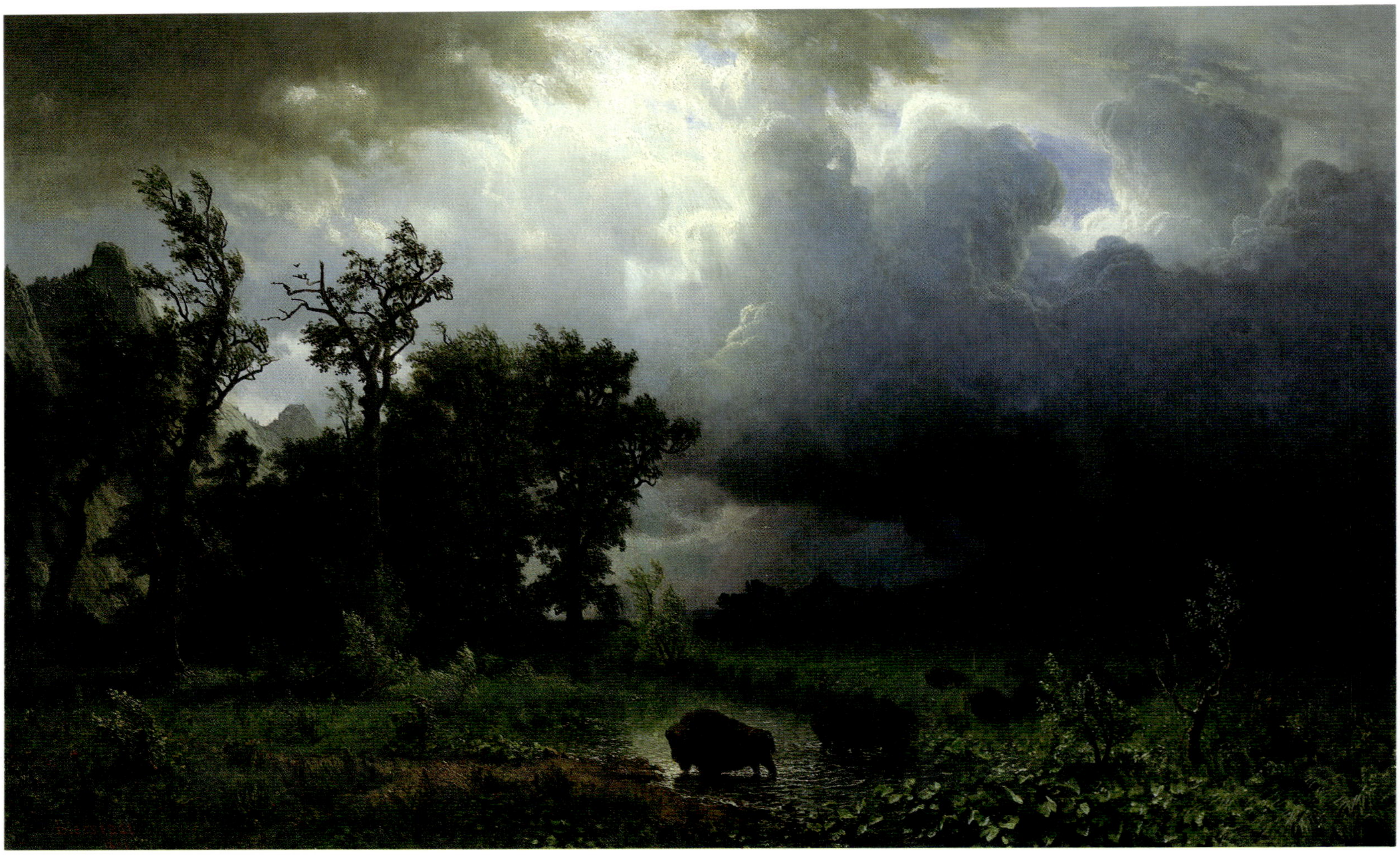

NO. 49

## *Buffalo Trail: The Impending Storm,* 1869

Oil on canvas, 29½ × 49½ in. (74.9 × 125.7 cm)

Signed and dated lower left: *ABierstadt/1869.*

The Corcoran Gallery of Art, Washington, D.C., Gift of Mr. and Mrs. Lansdell K. Christie, 1960

*We find here plenty of buffalo. One morning we saw a noble looking animal crossing the river near us, and I alighted from my ambulance and took a position behind a bluff, in order to give him a reception. As he came splashing through the water, I felt half inclined to lay down my rifle and take up my sketchbook, but I was so wrapped in admiration and study I could do neither for a few moments. My companions soon fired at him, which roused me from my study, when I too sent a ball from my rifle, as he galloped away, and was soon out of sight, leaving between us a cloud of dust.*

Letter from Bierstadt, 3 Sept. 1859, in *Mercury*, New Bedford, 14 Sept. 1859

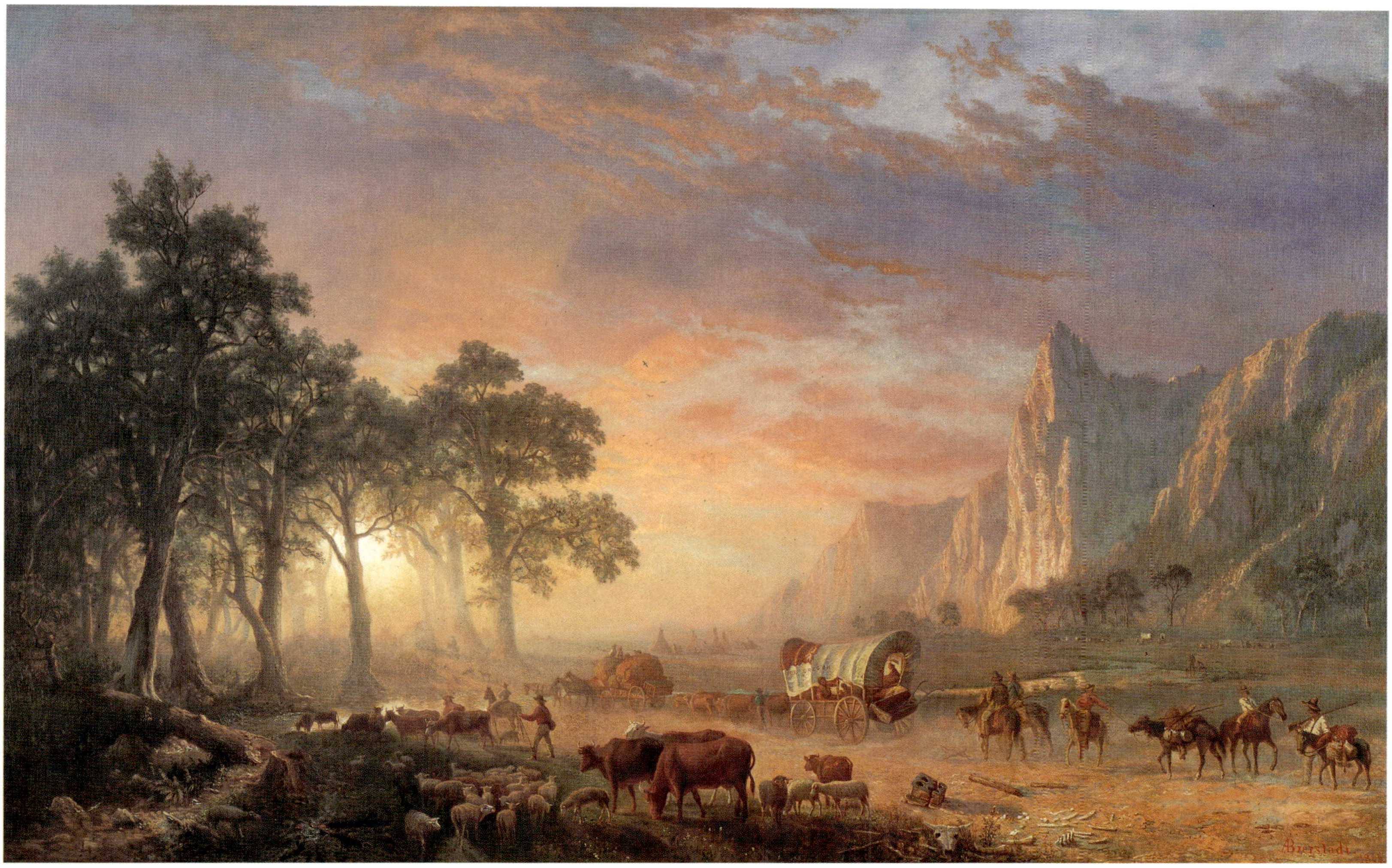

NO. 50

## *The Oregon Trail*, 1869

Oil on canvas, 31×49 in. (78.7×125.7 cm)

Signed and dated lower left: *ABierstadt./1869*

The Butler Institute of American Art, Youngstown, Ohio

*The public has been stimulated to great expectations of Bierstadt's painting [1867 version, National Cowboy Hall of Fame and Western Heritage Center, Oklahoma City], during the past few weeks, by sundry announcements and contradictions of its advent and exhibition. Yesterday, however, the painting was actually on view at the rooms of Snow & Roos, and there it will be found by the lover of art who may desire to feast his eyes upon one of the finest landscapes of one of the first American landscape painters. The picture has never been exhibited in New York, but was sent here from the easel of the artist, who was naturally desirous that his darling production of his genius should first be seen by the people of California, who can appreciate its truthfulness better than those who have never looked upon such a scene as he has here depicted.*

*Alta*, San Francisco, 28 Nov. 1867

*The picture under consideration [1867 version] represents, on a large canvas, an emigrant train drawing up at the close of a hot day's journey. The red rays of the setting sun are slanting through the sultry, dusty air, tinting the whole scene with extraordinary brilliancy, and gorgeously illuminating the long range of high bluffs stretching away in the distance on the right of the picture. . . .*

*On the whole it is a work that no lover of art should omit to see, and one of which Bierstadt, with his excellent reputation, may well be proud; though one, we judge, insufficient to fully justify the exalted position in art claimed for him by his warmest admirers.*

*Californian*, San Francisco, 30 Nov. 1867

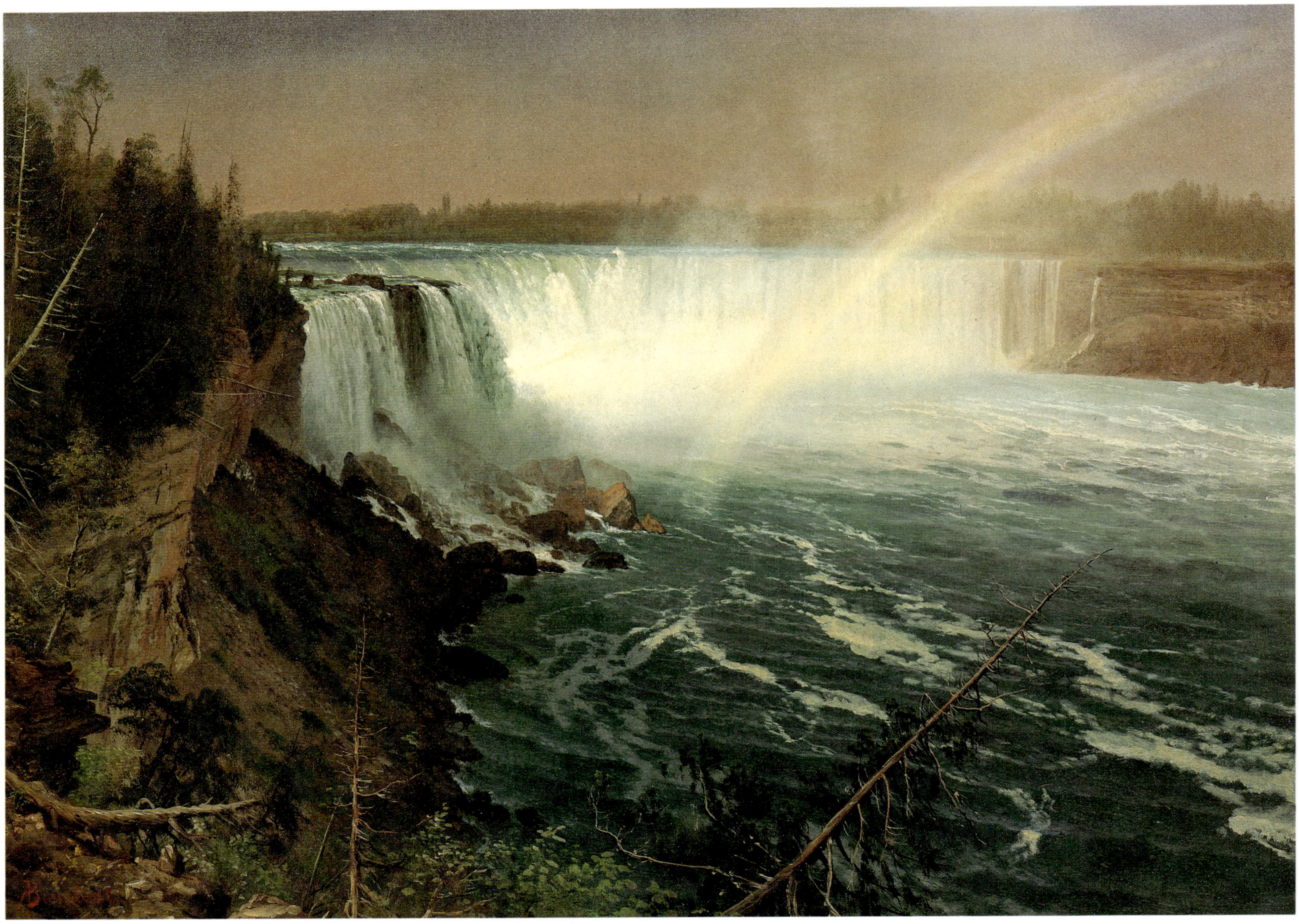

NO. 51

*Niagara*, c. 1869

Oil on paper mounted on canvas, 19 × 27 in. (48.3 × 68.6 cm)

Signed lower left: *ABierstadt*.

Private collection

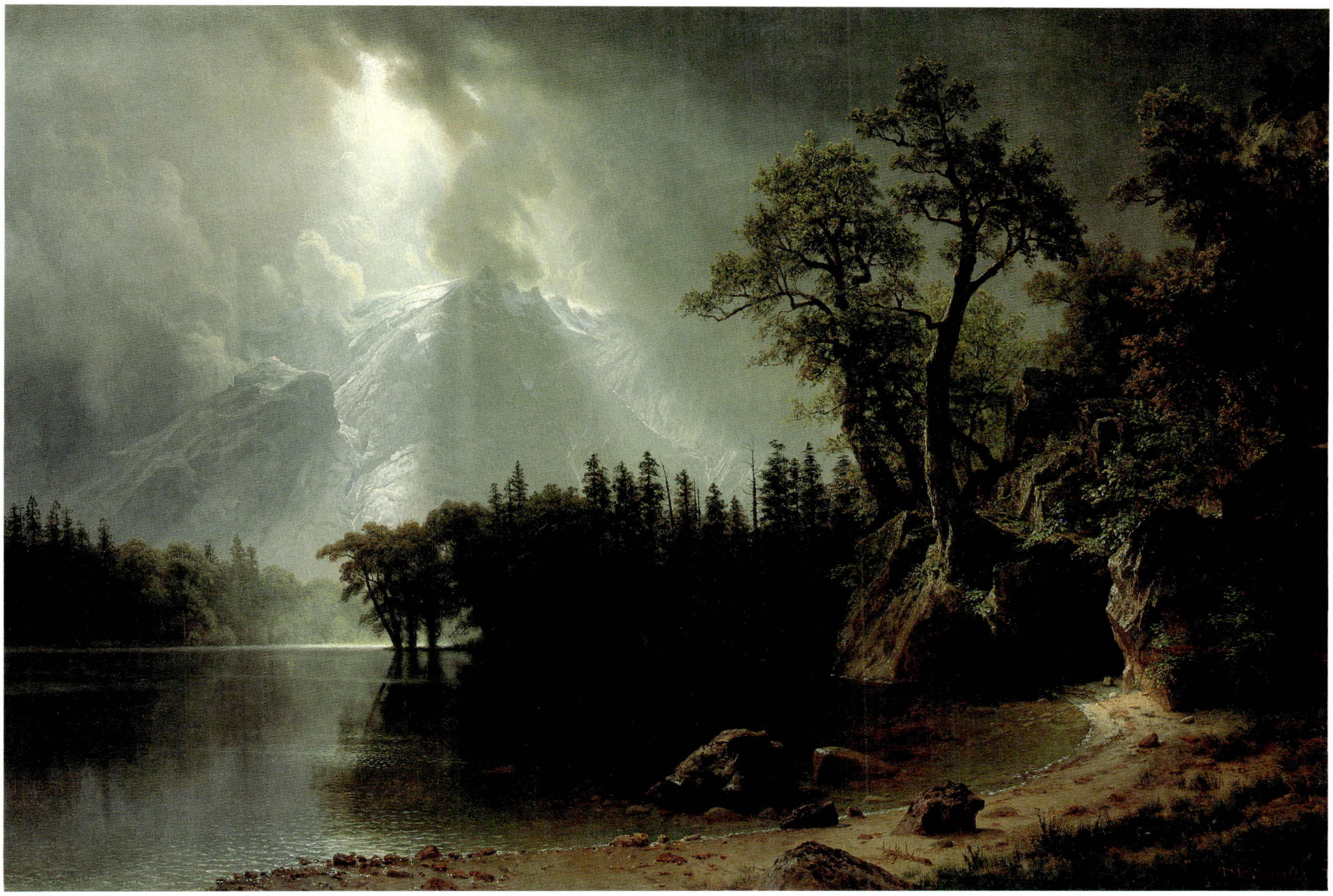

NO. 52

*Passing Storm over the Sierra Nevada,* 1870

Oil on canvas, 36 × 54½ in. (91.4 × 138.4 cm)

Signed and dated lower right: *ABierstadt 70*

The San Antonio Museum Association, Gift of the Robert J. Kleberg, Jr. and Helen C. Kleberg Foundation

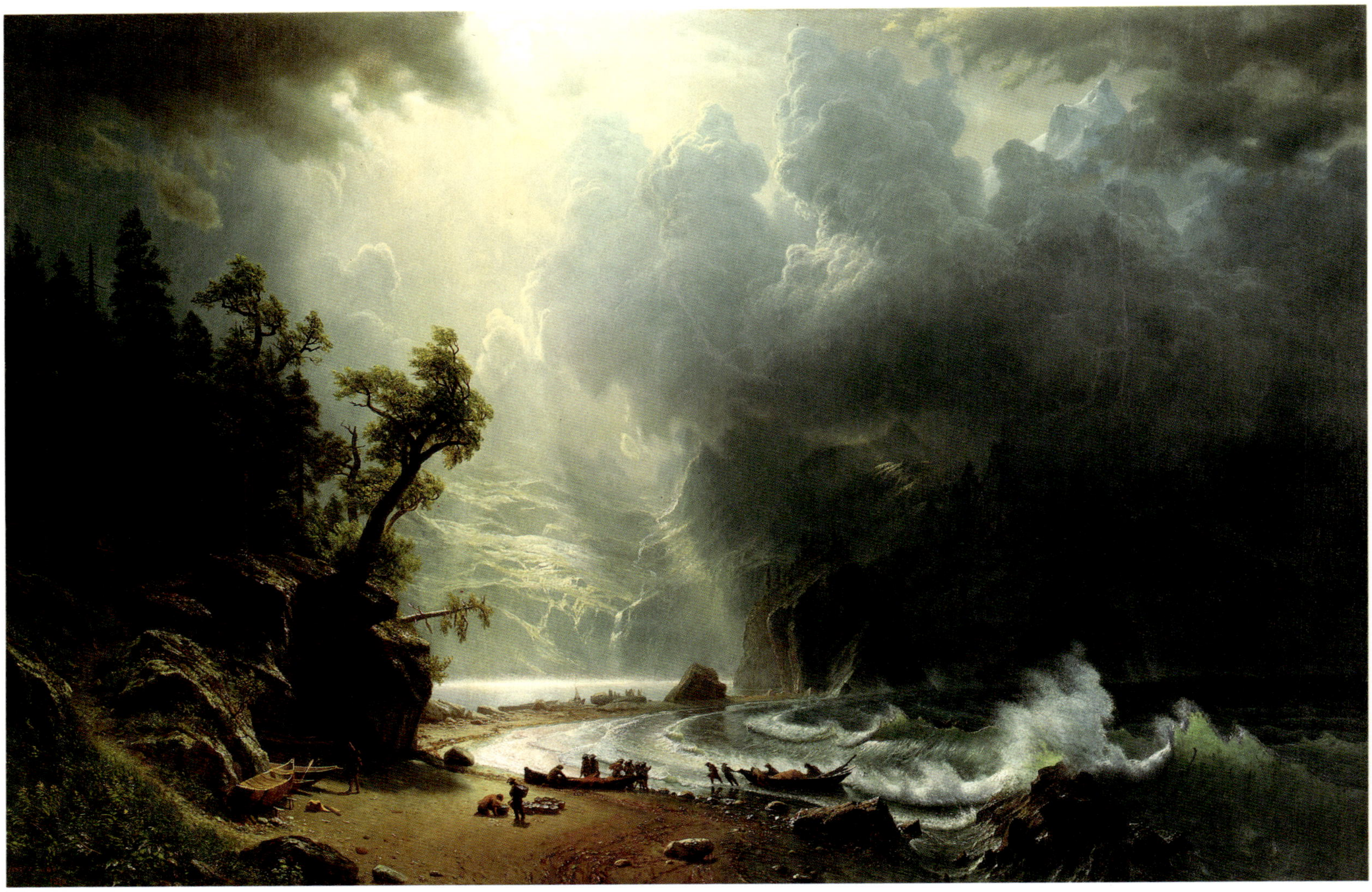

NO. 53

## *Puget Sound, on the Pacific Coast*, 1870

Oil on canvas, 52½ × 82 in. (133.4 × 208.3 cm)
Signed and dated lower left: *ABierstadt/1870*
Private collection

*This is a large canvas and one, to say the least of it, of great interest. It is, we are told, in all essential features, a portrait of the place depicted, and we need this assurance to satisfy us that it is not a superb vision of that dreamland into which our much admired painter has made at least as many visits as he has made among the material wonders of the West. . . . The scene before us is of the rocks and beach and mountains that bound an inlet of Puget's Sound. In the immediate foreground of the picture and to our left, is the nearer stretch of beach, upon which Indians are seen landing from a fishing boat, which, with the aid of a now receding breaker, they have run well up upon the strand. . . . In the middle distance we have the waters of the Sound, and beyond this we plunge into the world of shadowy forms . . . which give its distinctive character to the work. This cloud and mountain painting is dramatic in the highest degree. . . . The eye searches in vain for . . . the limit of the earth, the beginning of the cloudland. To the right, the mountain forms are clearly marked, for here the Sound is narrow, and at these huge upheavals we have the base of Mount Olympia, the summit of which is seen or suggested rather through a reft in the heavier clouds and descending mists which wrap this portion of the view.*

*New York Evening Mail*, 24 Oct. 1870

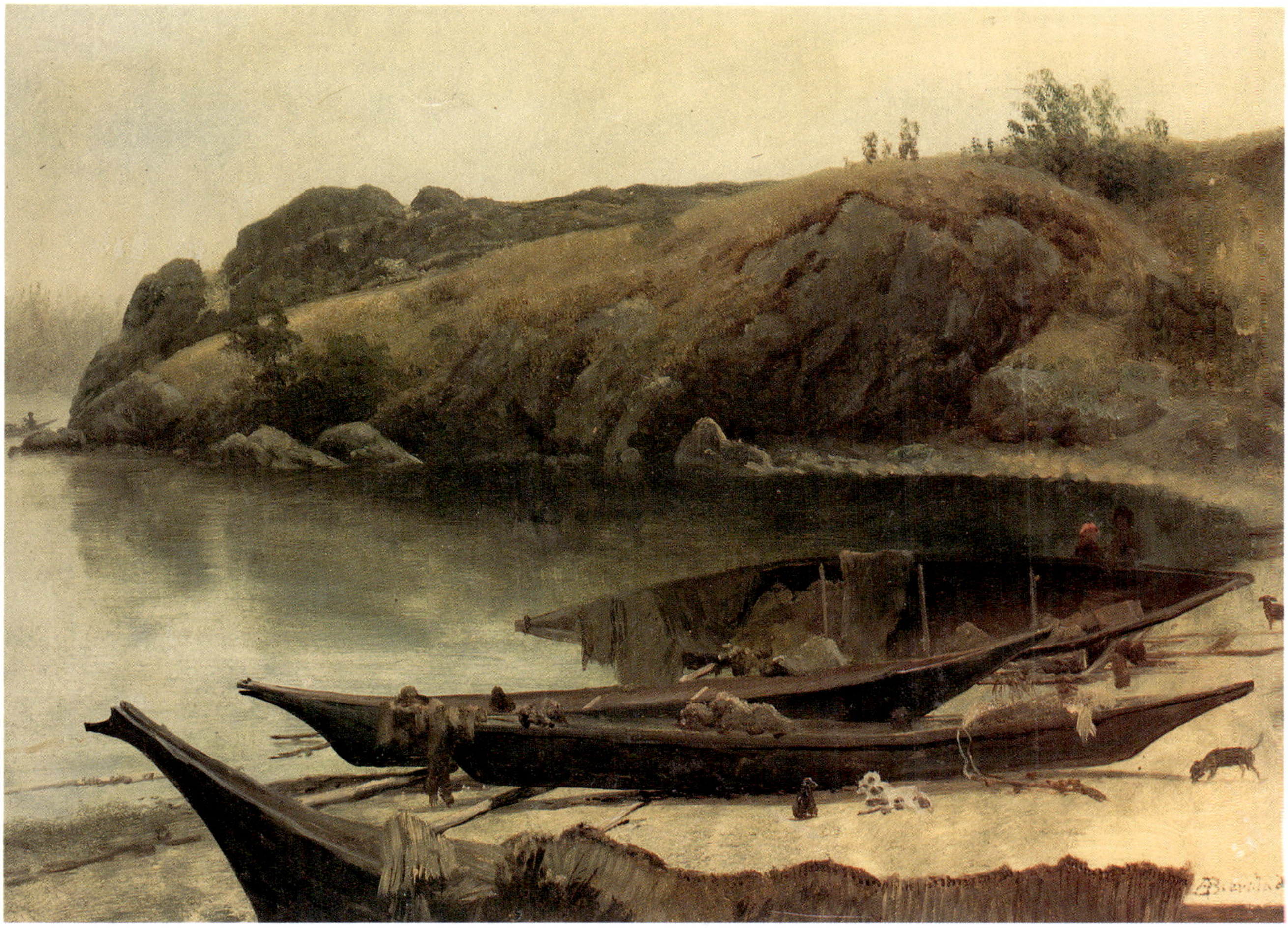

NO. 54

## *Canoes*

Oil on paper, 13 × 18½ in. (33 × 47 cm)

Signed lower right: *ABierstadt*

The Thomas Gilcrease Institute of American History and Art, Tulsa, Oklahoma

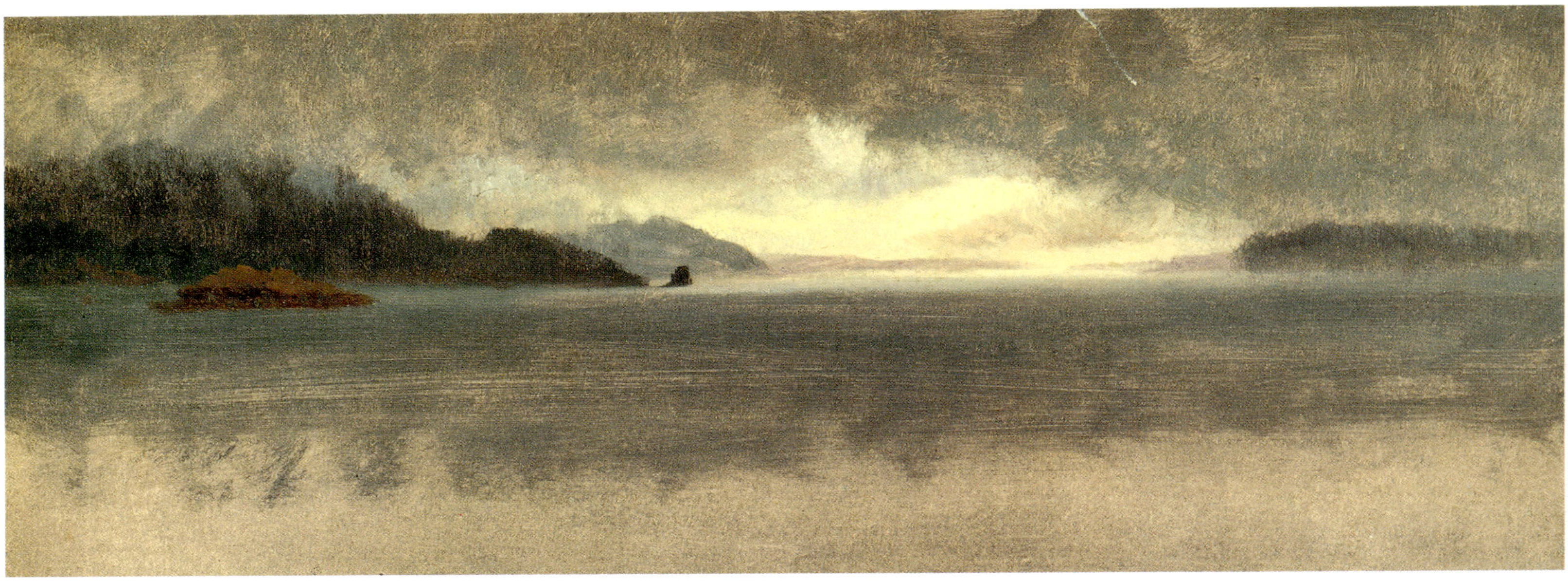

NO. 55

*Stormy Lake Scene (Pacific Northwest)*

Oil on paper mounted on board, 7¼ × 19¼ in. (18.4 × 48.9 cm)

Unsigned

Elliott Galleries, New York

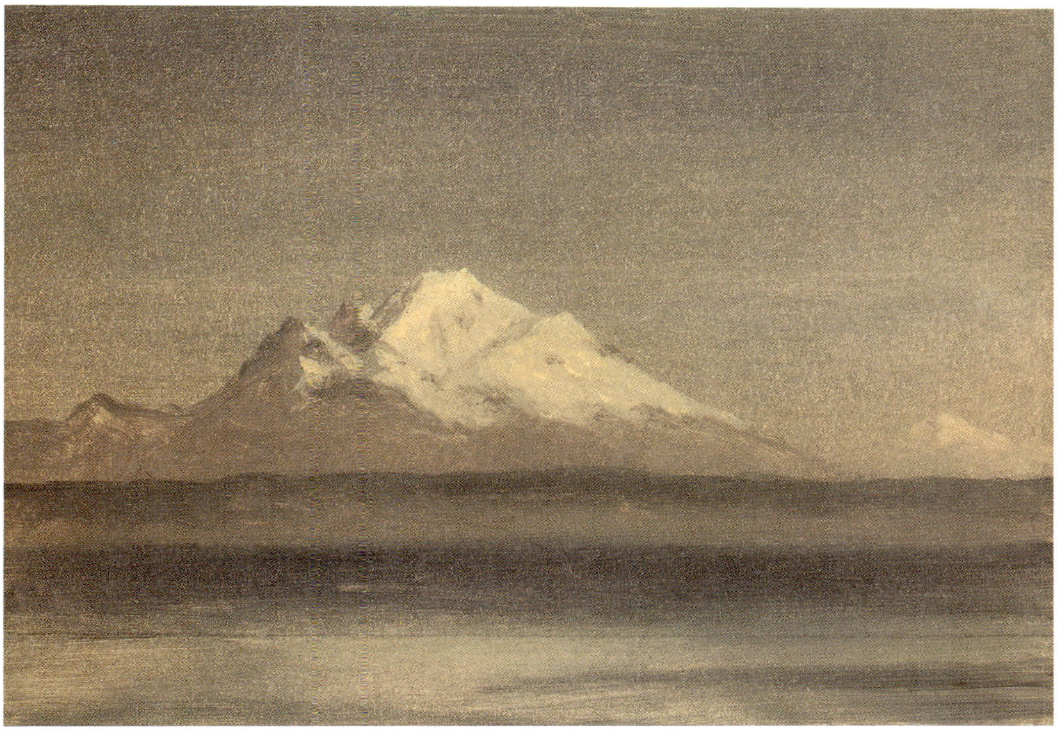

NO. 56

## *Snowcapped Mountains (Pacific Northwest)*

Oil on paper mounted on board, 7⅛ × 9½ in. (18.1 × 24.1 cm)

Unsigned

Elliott Galleries, New York

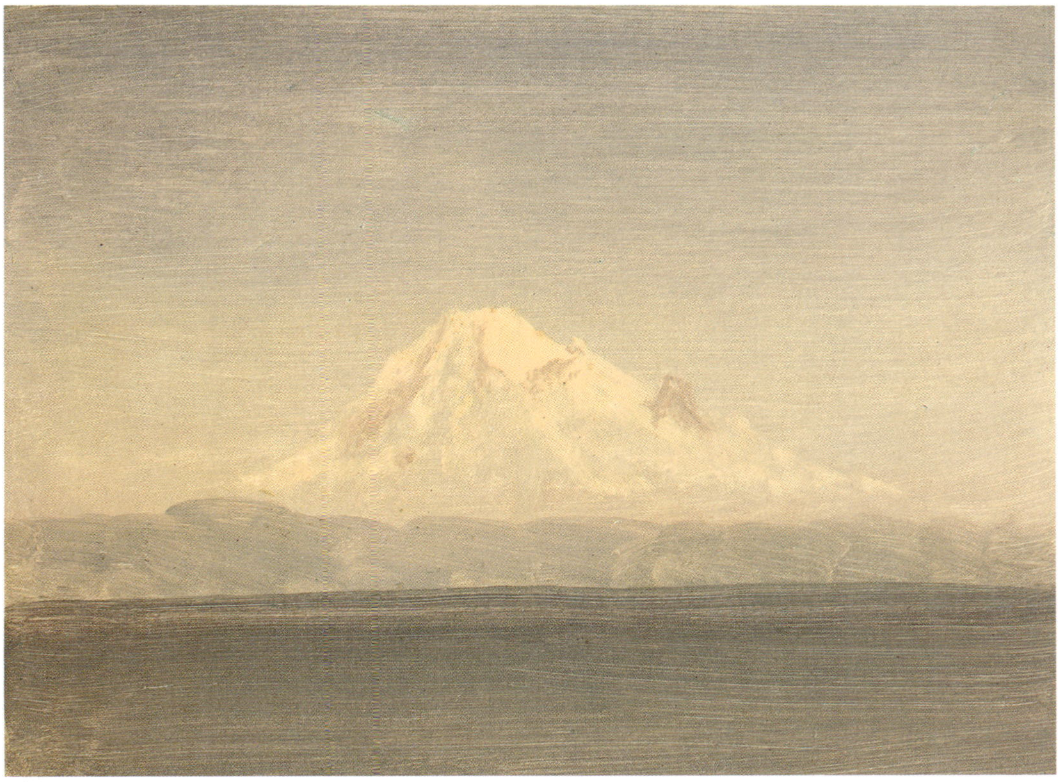

NO. 57

## *Snowcapped Mountains (Pacific Northwest)*

Oil on paper mounted on board, 7 × 10 in. (17.8 × 25.4 cm)

Unsigned

Elliott Galleries, New York

# 1871–1879

## *New Subjects, New Patrons*

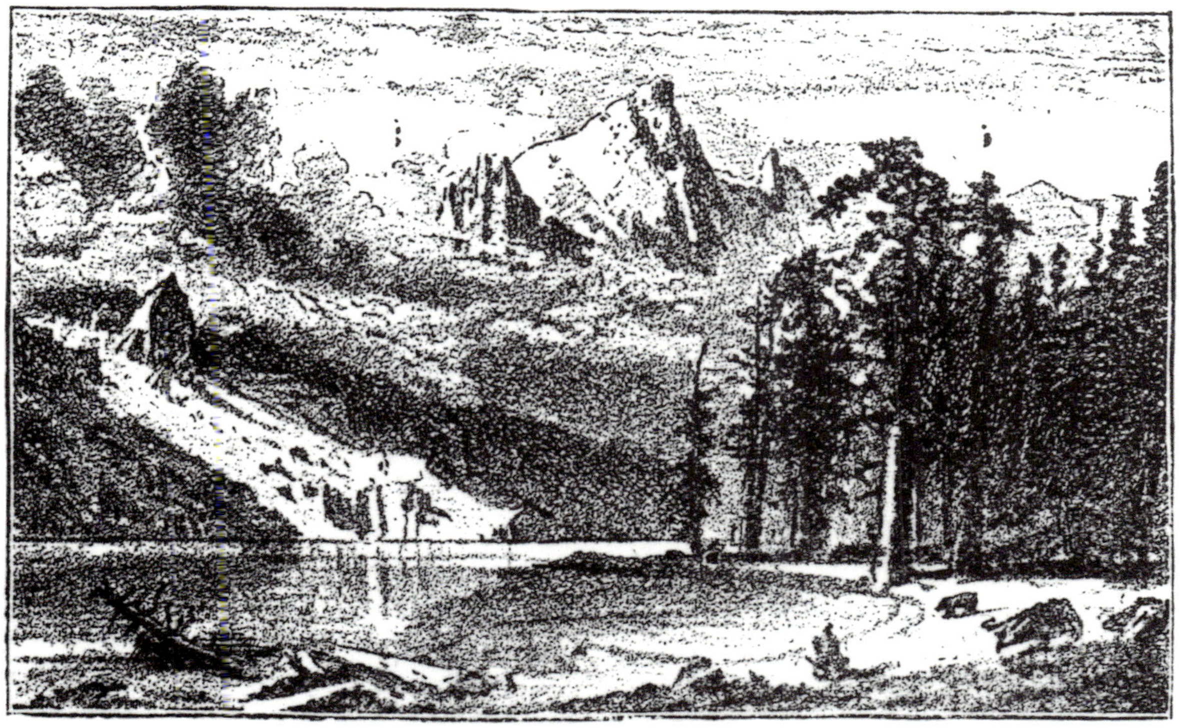

Albert and Rosalie Bierstadt arrived in San Francisco on 20 July 1871, following a cross-country journey aboard the recently completed transcontinental railroad. Almost immediately upon his arrival, Bierstadt retraced his steps as far as Donner Pass in the High Sierra. Accompanied by Collis P. Huntington, one of the "Big Four" railroad barons, Bierstadt returned to the summit to confer with his patron, who had commissioned a painting celebrating the conquest of the granite peaks of the Sierra Nevada, the greatest obstacle in the path of the transcontinental railroad. Bierstadt returned to the site several times to secure additional sketches, particularly of the sun rising over Donner Lake, but because of the frenetic travel schedule he maintained while in California, *Donner Lake from the Summit* (Fig. 61) was not completed until early in 1873.

Less than two months after arriving in California, Bierstadt took advantage of the ease of travel afforded by the railroad and returned to New York to assist with the arrangements for the visit of Alexis, grand duke of Russia. In addition to serving on the executive committee, Bierstadt was instrumental in arranging a buffalo hunt for the duke and his party. Bierstadt's efforts on behalf of the duke did not go unnoticed, for in 1872 the artist was awarded the Order of Saint Stanislaus and, more important, Russian patronage.

Shortly after his return to San Francisco from New York in January 1872, but weeks before the tourist season began, Bierstadt traveled to Yosemite to sketch the valley while snow still covered the ground. From studies gathered during this expedition, he produced several winter views of Yosemite (see No. 61).

In the spring of 1872, while waiting for winter snows to subside sufficiently to allow him access to the high passes of the Sierra Nevada mountains, Bierstadt spent time sketching in and around the San Francisco Bay area, most notably near the Farallon Islands, located twenty-six miles west of San Francisco. In a series of paintings begun shortly after his return from the Farallons, Bierstadt demonstrated his technical expertise in the rendering of translucent waves.

Early in May 1872, Bierstadt returned to Yosemite and the High Sierra, where he spent most of the summer of 1872 exploring valleys and canyons well off the tourist trail. Thanks in part to the popularity of his own paintings and the widespread dissemination of photographs, engravings, and illustrations, Yosemite had become a tourist mecca. In his continuing search for pristine wilderness, Bierstadt was thus forced to travel even deeper into the Sierra Nevada.

In the fall of 1872, he accompanied Clarence King, leader of the U.S. Geological Exploration of the Fortieth Parallel, into Kings River Canyon in the South Sierra, an area so remote that government geologists were just beginning to map and measure the topography. As he had in the past, Bierstadt recognized the market and publicity value of images from a "new country." Just as King and other members of the survey party began reporting on the spectacular peaks and valleys of the South Sierra, Bierstadt began producing paintings of the same terrain. The artist's progress on the first of his South Sierra pictures, begun late in 1872, was thus closely monitored by the San Francisco press. Astutely exploiting such interest, Bierstadt welcomed reporters to his Clay Street studio to view South Sierra and Farallon pictures in various stages of completion.

Late in May 1873, Bierstadt placed *Autumn in the Sierras*, 1873 (Fig. 28), the largest of his Sierra pictures, on exhibition in San Francisco. Accustomed to lavish praise from the local press, he must have been disappointed when the reviews were decidedly mixed.

In June 1873, Bierstadt returned to the Yosemite area, but he spent much of his time sketching in Hetch Hetchy Valley, another relatively unexplored area with scenic wonders rivaling those of Yosemite. Capitalizing again on the novelty of a newly discovered region, Bierstadt produced several paintings based on his initial sketches of Hetch Hetchy.

After more than two years in California, Bierstadt and his wife departed San Francisco early in October 1873. In a remarkable display of stamina and energy, he had spent his time on the Pacific Coast in a nearly constant state of motion. The sketches he had gathered on his travels served as the raw material for a steady stream of paintings that began to appear even before he left California.

Rather than returning to their home on the Hudson, the Bierstadts traveled to Waterville, New York, where Rosalie's father had constructed a special studio for the artist near the Osborne family home. It was here, during the winter months of 1873–74, that Bierstadt set to work composing paintings based on the studies he had completed in California.

In April 1874, he submitted a painting of California's Big Trees to the Annual Exhibition at the National Academy of Design. By the mid-1870s, however, the novelty of Yosemite and the Big Trees had worn thin, and more than one critic declared the subject had been overplayed. Others found Bierstadt's execution "careless" and "not equal to the demands of his reputation" (Chronology, 9 Apr.–6 June 1874). The sharply critical chorus that had begun to find fault with Bierstadt's work in the mid-1860s had lost none of its bite during his absence in California.

Though the quality of his work continued to decline in the eyes of critics, Bierstadt still enjoyed considerable popularity among the gallery-going public. Over a ten-week period during the summer of 1874, more than twelve thousand people visited the gallery in Boston where three of the artist's paintings, including *Autumn in the Sierras*, were on view.

In the fall of 1874, Bierstadt renewed his efforts to secure a congressional commission, and by December he had succeeded in placing *Discovery of the Hudson River*, 1874 (Fig. 21), and a "Rocky Mountain landscape" (actually *Autumn in the Sierras*, retitled *Kings River Canyon* when exhibited at the Capitol) in the chamber of the House of Representatives "on approval" (Chronology, 7 Dec. 1874). A proposal was introduced to buy the paintings. Although Bierstadt had dropped his price to $15,000 each (from the earlier $40,000), the figure under discussion in Congress was $12,500. In March 1875, after considerable debate, Congress finally authorized the purchase of one of the paintings, *Discovery of the Hudson River*, for $10,000.

The following month, Bierstadt contributed four paintings to the Annual Exhibition at the National Academy of Design. Roundly criticized once again, the paintings were described as pretentious, labored, and sure to diminish the artist's reputation.

Undoubtedly adding to Bierstadt's concern at this time were the favorable notices Thomas Moran, the first artist to seriously challenge Bierstadt's monopoly on the panoramic western landscape, continued to receive. Following the sale of his first major canvas, *The Grand Canyon of the Yellowstone* (Fig. 26), to Congress for $10,000 in 1872, Moran produced a pendant in 1874, *Chasm of the Colorado* (Fig. 27), also purchased by Congress for a like sum.

During the summer and early fall of 1875, Bierstadt had on his easel at Irvington the painting that would eventually join *Discovery of the Hudson River* in the Capitol. He undoubtedly hoped that *Settlement of California, Bay of Monterey, 1770*, 1876 (Fig. 22), would be seen as the ideal mate to the painting already in place. The painting was, in fact, later purchased by the government and hung in the House Chamber.

In 1876 Bierstadt devoted much of his time and energy to the preparation of works for the Centennial Exposition in Philadelphia. He contributed six paintings, including a large vertical picture of Grizzly Giant, the most famous of California's Big Trees (*The Great Trees, Mariposa Grove, California*, 1876, No. 65). Although some found merit in the picture, the critic for the *New York Times* singled out the painting as evidence that "Mr. Bierstadt was never equal to his reputation" (*NY Times*, 13 June 1876).

In November 1876, Rosalie Bierstadt made the first of what would become nearly annual trips to Nassau in the Bahamas. Diagnosed as consumptive, she had been advised to spend the winter months in a warm climate. Although in poor health, she soon became a member of Nassau's social elite and a frequent participant in social events.

In December 1876, following his wife's departure for Nassau, Bierstadt traveled to Colorado with the Earl of Dunraven, a member of the Irish nobility who had recently purchased much of Estes Park. Dunraven asked the artist to help him select a site for a hotel and commissioned a large painting of the area (Fig. 65), which Bierstadt completed the following year from sketches made on site.

In March 1877, Bierstadt joined his wife in Nassau. The colors of the Caribbean brought new life to his palette and a fresh subject to his repertoire.

Upon his return to New York, however, Bierstadt was met by another barrage of negative reviews, this time for *Mountain Lake*, 1877 (later titled *Mount Corcoran*, Fig. 32), his contribution to the Annual Exhibition at the National Academy of Design for 1877.

Although Bierstadt supported efforts to establish art associations and galleries in several cities as early as the 1860s and 1870s, his increased support of such activities in the late 1870s reflects a reassessment of his market strength. Banking on a reputation that was still strong in the provinces, Bierstadt contributed increasing numbers of paintings to exhibitions and fairs held at some distance from New York.

A friendship Bierstadt established with Webb Hayes, son of President and Mrs. Rutherford B. Hayes, opened another avenue of patronage. In February 1878, the artist spent several days at the White House, where he attended a formal reception. Sometime later, he placed a number of paintings in the White House "on loan." The pictures eventually became the subject of extended congressional debate as he lobbied for their purchase by the government. In this effort, however, he was not successful.

In the spring of 1878, Bierstadt joined his wife in Nassau, and in July, after returning to New York, the couple set sail for Europe. The Philadelphia *Press* reported that Bierstadt had proposed opening a gallery in London or Paris "composed of the productions of the best American artists" (Chronology, 19 Oct. 1878). Again, the artist seems to have been exploring ways to expand his market, although no evidence has surfaced indicating that any such gallery was established. After several months in London, the Bierstadts settled in Cannes for the winter. By early fall, they had returned to New York, and Rosalie Bierstadt had departed for another winter in Nassau.

# CHRONOLOGY

1871

**30 Jan.** Bierstadt travels to Washington, D.C., hoping to secure clients for a new printing process, the Albertype. (Bierstadt to Nathaniel Banks, Banks Correspondence, Manuscript Division, Library of Congress)

**6 Feb.** Fire and explosion in Edward Bierstadt's photography studio in the basement of the Tenth Street Studio Building. Neither Bierstadt nor his assistant, Albert Ryder, seriously injured. (*Post*, New York, 8 Feb. 1871; *NY Times*, 8, 9 Feb. 1871; *Evening Mail*, New York, 8 Feb. 1871)

**21 Feb.** Bierstadt writes to the Joint Committee on Printing in Washington asking for an extension of the published deadline for presenting bids on a government printing contract. Bierstadt (and probably his brother Edward) are promoting the Albertype process. (Bierstadt Letters, Manuscript Division, Library of Congress)

**5 Apr.** Spencer Baird, assistant secretary of the Smithsonian Institution, writes to Bierstadt regarding the Albertype process and indicates that he is looking forward to receiving a sample shortly. (Baird to Bierstadt, 5 Apr. 1871, Baird Papers, Smithsonian Institution Archives, Washington, D.C.)

**13 Apr.** Bierstadt writes to General John Adams Dix, urging him to join a meeting the following evening during which arrangements for the October visit of Grand Duke Alexis of Russia will be discussed. (Bierstadt to Dix, 13 Apr. 1871, James P. Crain Collection, San Francisco)

**14 Apr.–17 June** NAD Annual Exhibition open to the public. Bierstadt contributes *Burning Whalers off the Island of Ascension* (now titled *The Burning Ship*) and *In the Sierra Nevada Mountains*. (*Post*, New York, 13, 14 Apr. 1871; Catalogue, NAD, 1871, pp. 17, 19)

A reviewer comments on Bierstadt's Sierra picture at the NAD exhibition: "His apparent effort has been to attract by the very novelty of his productions, to startle and captivate the eye by a wilderness of extravagancies. . . . Bierstadt is surely capable of something better than this; wherefore, then, has he descended to the merely sensational?" (*Utica Morning Herald and Daily Gazette*, 24 May 1871)

**May** *Mount Hood, Oregon* on exhibition at McLean's Gallery in London. (*Art-Journal* [London], May 1871, p. 146)

**7 June** A. B. Nettleton, an official of the Northern Pacific Railroad, writes to F. V. Hayden, explorer and leader of the United States Geological and Geographical Survey of the Territories, that Bierstadt may join the survey party to Yellowstone. A week later, he advises Hayden that Thomas Moran will join the party; Bierstadt did not go. (Nettleton to Hayden, 7, 16 June 1871, Hayden Survey Records)

**3 July** In view of his upcoming trip to California, Bierstadt writes to General William T. Sherman asking for letters of introduction to post commanders on the Plains. He also asks for assistance in arranging a buffalo hunt (complete with Indians) for Grand Duke Alexis of Russia. (Bierstadt to Sherman, 3 July 1871, Sherman Papers, Manuscript Division, Library of Congress)

**18 July** Albert and Rosalie Bierstadt pass through Ogden, Utah, and are expected to arrive in San Francisco on 20 July. (*Alta*, San Francisco, 20 July 1871)

**20 July** The Bierstadts arrive in San Francisco and register at the Grand Hotel. (*Bulletin*, San Francisco, 21 July 1871; *Alta*, San Francisco, 21 July 1871)

**by 25 July** Bierstadt leaves Sacramento "for a tour among the mountain lakes to sketch studies for new pictures." (*Bulletin*, San Francisco, 25 July 1871; GH Papers)

**31 July** Reviewing Bierstadt's *Emerald Pool*, on view at Snow & Roos Art Gallery in San Francisco, a writer for the *Alta* questions "whether the artist has ever painted a better picture," noting that "two hundred special studies were made by Bierstadt for the conscientious elaboration of this grand work." (*Alta*, San Francisco, 31 July 1871)

**Aug.** Article in the *Century* on the founding of the Metropolitan Museum of Art states that the idea was initiated by a group of Americans in Paris, including Bierstadt, who wrote to John Jay, secretary of the Union League Club, in 1868 or early 1869 proposing the establishment of an American art museum. Subsequently the art committee at the Union League moved on the recommendation. (*Century*, Aug. 1871, p. 410)

**by 1 Aug.** Bierstadt returns to San Francisco "from his flying trip to the Sierras. In company with Collis P. Huntington, of the Central Pacific Railroad Co., he paid a visit to the camp of Col. Von Schmidt, near Lake Tahoe. . . . We are pleased to learn that Mr. Bierstadt contemplates sojourning for some weeks on the Pacific Coast." (*Alta*, San Francisco, 1 Aug. 1871)

**5 Aug.** At Snow & Roos, Bierstadt answers questions about *The Emerald Pool* from a group of visitors that includes Governor Stanford. (*San Francisco News Letter and California Advertiser*, 5 Aug. 1871)

**7 Aug.** Bierstadt elected first honorary member of the San Francisco Art Association; his letter of thanks is published in the *Alta*. (*Bulletin*, San Francisco, 8 Aug. 1871; *San Francisco Chronicle*, 7 Aug. 1871; *Alta*, San Francisco, 15 Aug. 1871)

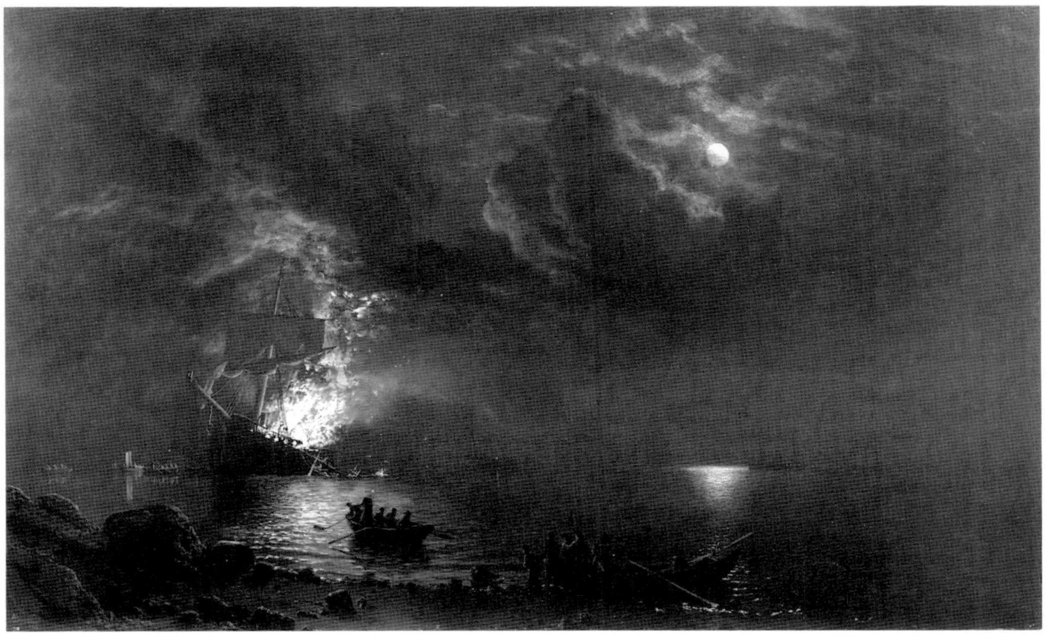

Albert Bierstadt. *The Burning Ship*, 1871. Oil on canvas. Shelburne Museum, Shelburne, Vermont.

## 1871–1872

**8 Sept.** Bierstadt exhibits *The Emerald Pool, Yosemite Valley*, and *Happy Hunting Ground* at the second reception of the San Francisco Art Association. (*Alta*, San Francisco, 9 Sept. 1871)

**17 Sept.** It is reported that "an Eastern gentleman" has purchased *The Emerald Pool* for $20,000. (*Alta*, San Francisco, 17 Sept. 1871)

**18 Sept.** "Albert Bierstadt has gone east for a few weeks. He is one of the Committee appointed to receive the Russian Grand Duke, who will shortly be due at New York. It is understood that Leland Stanford is the fortunate purchaser of the two fine paintings by Mr. Bierstadt which were first exhibited at the late Art Reception in this city." (*Bulletin*, San Francisco, 18 Sept. 1871)

**26 Sept.** Bierstadt is back in New York. (Bierstadt to Mr. Dana, 26 Sept. 1871, Millicent Library, Fairhaven, Mass.)

**8 Oct.** Great Chicago fire. Crosby Opera House is destroyed, but Bierstadt's *Looking Down Yosemite Valley, California* (No. 42) is saved. (*Boston Transcript*, 8 Oct. 1871)

**17 Oct.** NAD notifies Bierstadt that he has been elected to serve on the committee appointed to consider measures to aid the artists of Chicago. (NAD to Bierstadt, Turner Collection)

**18 Oct.** "Some fifty paintings" rescued from the Crosby Opera House during the great fire in Chicago to go on exhibition shortly in Boston. *Looking Down Yosemite Valley, California*, never before shown in Boston, will be included. (*Boston Transcript*, 18 Oct. 1871)

**20 Nov.** Grand Duke Alexis arrives in New York. Bierstadt among the dignitaries greeting his party. (*Post*, New York, 20 Nov. 1871)

**21 Nov.** Benefit auction held for the relief of Chicago artists who suffered losses in the great fire. Bierstadt's *Tuolumne River, California* brings $505. (*Post*, New York, 21 Nov. 1871)

**25 Nov.** General Philip Sheridan writes to Bierstadt offering his services should the grand duke wish to hunt buffalo. (Sheridan to Bierstadt, 25 Nov. 1871, Turner Collection)

**29 Nov.** Reception and ball for Grand Duke Alexis. Bierstadt is a member of the executive committee. (*Post*, New York, 22 Nov. 1871)

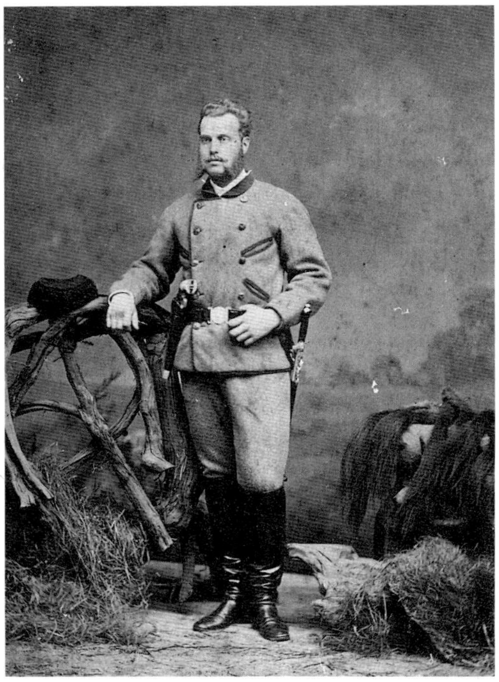

*Grand Duke Alexis*. Photograph. Collection of James P. Crain.

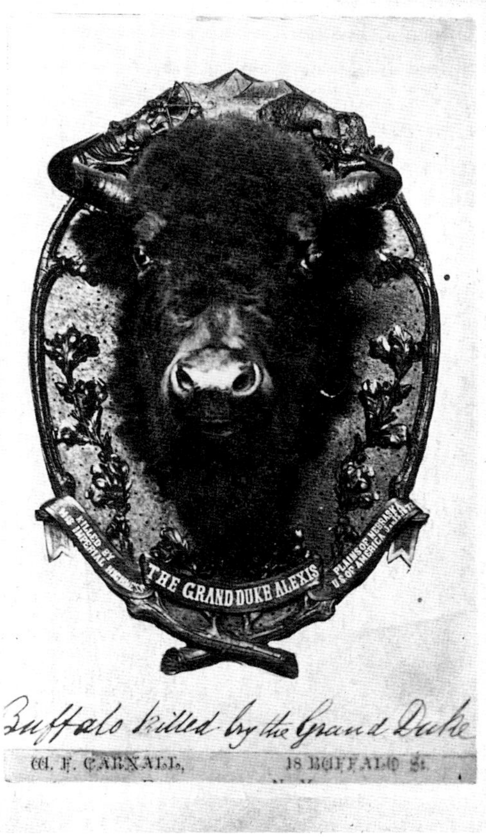


**2 Dec.** Bierstadt is a member of NAD committee that formally presents Grand Duke Alexis with William Page's portrait of Admiral David Farragut at the battle of Mobile Bay. (*Post*, New York, 2 Dec. 1871)

**8 Dec.** Bierstadt writes to a Mr. Hayes indicating that he will "be off for the West early next year," adding, "were it not for my upbringing I would make my permanent home in the West." (Bierstadt to Hayes, 8 Dec. 1871, Loan to Oakland Museum)

## 1872

**by 6 Jan.** Bierstadt returns to San Francisco. (*Bulletin*, San Francisco, 6 Jan. 1872)

**5 Mar.** Bierstadt reported to have entered Yosemite Valley ten days before via Haight's Cove and Merced Canyon: "Albert Bierstadt . . . is first in the field. With characteristic enterprise he has pushed into the Yosemite Valley this early—nearly three months in advance of ordinary tourists—to make sketches of the winter aspects of its unequalled scenery, when the peaks and cliffs are covered deep with snow, and the falls tumble amid icicles and ice-sheeted rocks." (*Bulletin*, San Francisco, 5 Mar. 1872)

**25 Mar.** "Mr. Albert Bierstadt, the painter, recently received the cross of the Order of St. Stanislaus from the Emperor of Russia." The *Times* later reported the medal was presented "in recognition of attentions offered to prince Alexis during his stay here," but

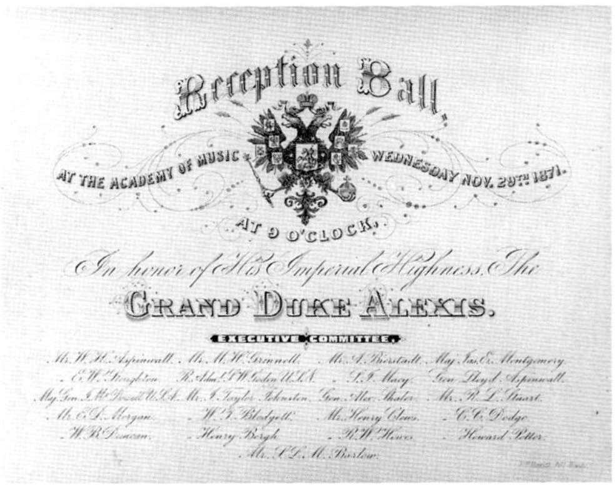


*(above) Invitation to the reception ball in honor of Grand Duke Alexis*, 1871. Collection of Joyce Randall Edwards.

*(left)* W. F. Carnall, New York. *Buffalo Killed by the Grand Duke Alexis*. Photograph. Collection of James P. Crain.

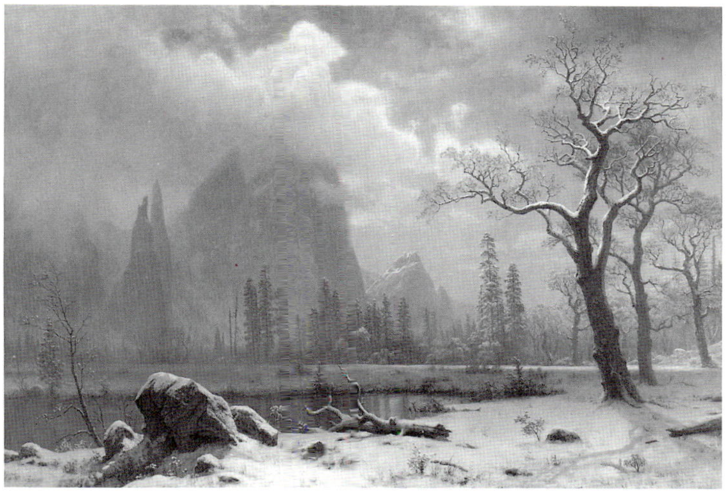

Albert Bierstadt. *Yosemite Winter Scene*, 1872. Oil on canvas. University Art Museum, University of California at Berkeley, Gift of Henry D. Bacon.

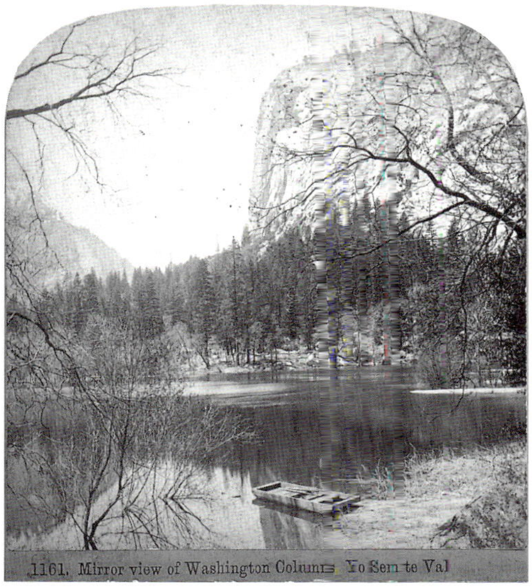


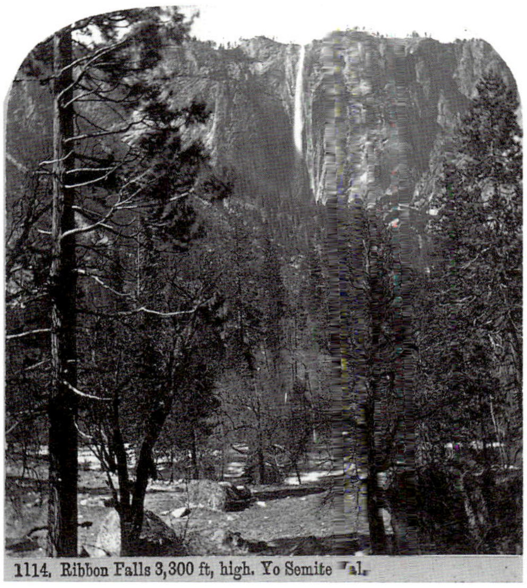


*(above, center)* Charles Bierstadt, Niagara Falls, New York. *Mirror view of Washington Columns. Yo Semite Val*. Stereograph. Private collection.

*(above)* Charles Bierstadt, Niagara Falls, New York. *Ribbon Falls 3,300 ft, high. Yo Semite Val*. Stereograph. Private collection.

William O. Stoddard, representing Bierstadt, subsequently claims in a letter to the *Times* that it was presented "in recognition of his merits as an artist." (*Post*, New York, 25 Mar. 1872; *NY Times*, 7, 14 Apr. 1872)

**7 Apr.** The *Times* reports, "The large landscape by TROYON, belonging to Mr. ALBERT BIERSTADT, exhibited last year in the Academy of Design, was sold in Boston recently, we understand, for $6,000." (*NY Times*, 7 Apr. 1872)

**12 Apr.–6 July** NAD Annual Exhibition open. Bierstadt exhibits *Rainbow in the Sierras*, *View in the Sierras*, and *The Golden Gate*. (Catalogue, NAD, 1872, pp. 16, 25, 27; *Post*, New York, 12 Apr., 6 July 1872)

**14 Apr.** Following Le Grand Lockwood's death, his collection of paintings is on exhibition prior to sale. A reporter for the *Times* finds *The Domes of the Yosemite* "somewhat disappointing" but notes that the picture attracts the most attention of any of the paintings on view. (*NY Times*, 14 Apr. 1872)

**19 Apr.** Second day of Lockwood sale; Bierstadt's *Domes of the Yosemite* is sold to A. S. Hatch for $5,100. (*Post*, New York, 20 Apr. 1872)

**1 May** Bierstadt returns to San Francisco following a sketching trip to the Farallon Islands. (*Bulletin*, San Francisco, 2 May 1872)

**17 May** "Albert Bierstadt was in the Inyo country at last account, 'prospecting' for studies of Mount Whitney, the highest mountain peak in the United States, and the monarch of the highest portion of the Sierra Nevada." (*Bulletin*, San Francisco, 17 May 1872)

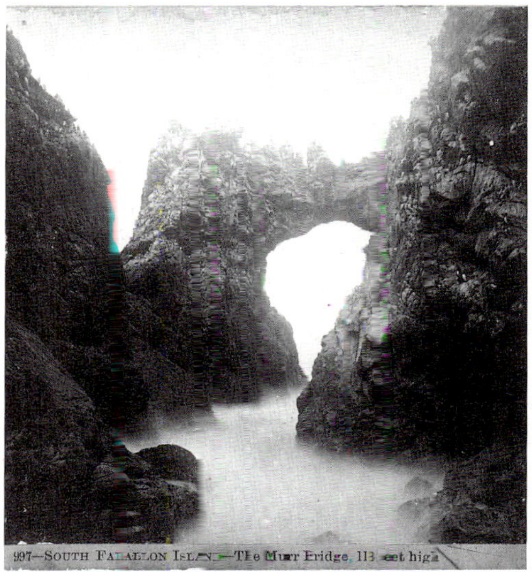


Eadweard Muybridge. *South Farallon Island—The Murr Bridge, 113 feet high*. Stereograph. Collection of Leonard A. Walle.

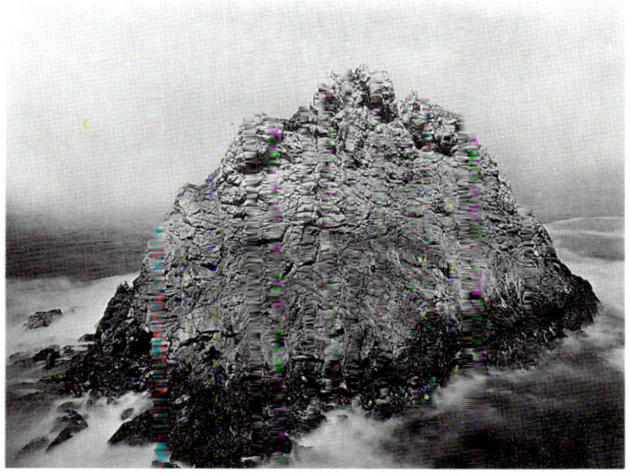

*(above)* Carleton E. Watkins. *Seal Rocks, Cliff House*, c. 1866. Mammoth plate, albumen silver print. Fraenkel Gallery, San Francisco.

*(below) "The Domes of the Yosemite" in the rotunda of the Lockwood Mansion*, c. 1869. Photograph. The Lockwood-Mathews Mansion Museum, Norwalk, Connecticut.

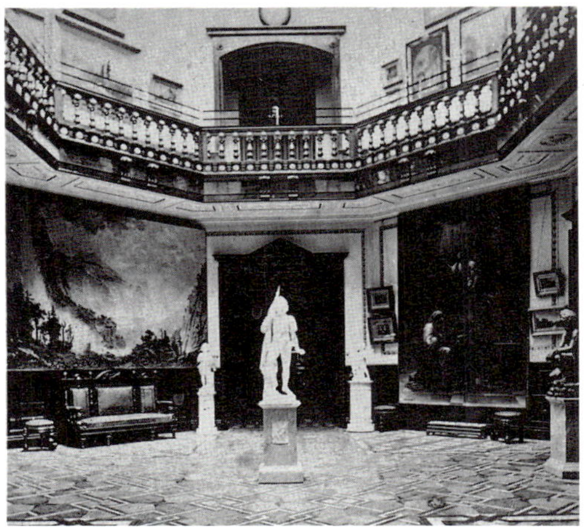

## 1872–1874

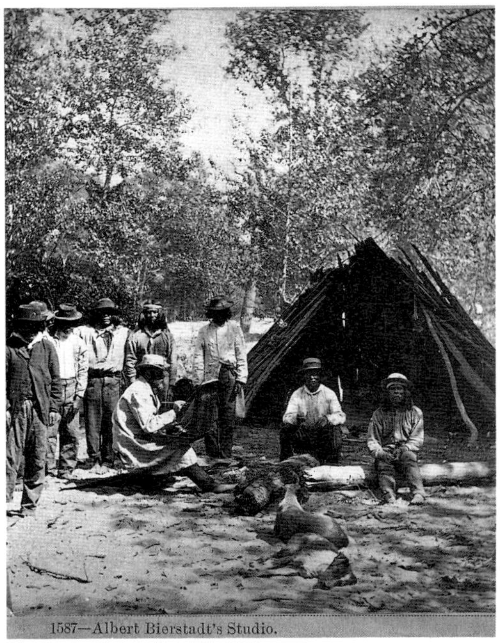


Eadweard Muybridge. *Albert Bierstadt's Studio*, 1872. Stereograph. Collection of Leonard A. Walle.

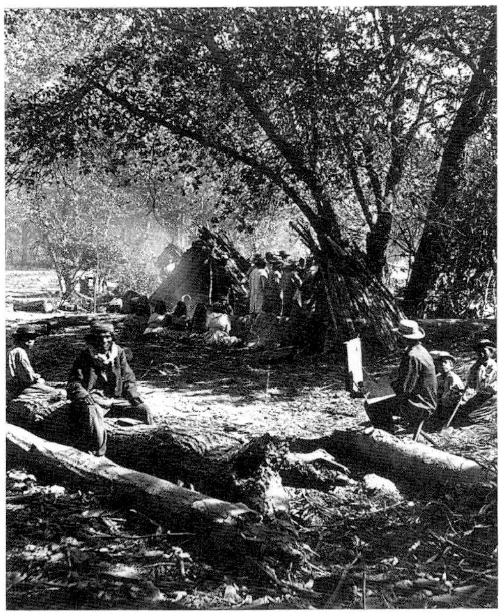

Eadweard Muybridge. *Bierstadt in Mariposa*, 1872. Stereograph. Collection of Leonard A. Walle.

**24 May** Bierstadt registers at Mountain View House in Yosemite. (R. Taylor 1929, p. 72)

**18 June** San Francisco Art Association holds its first Annual Exhibition. Bierstadt represented by *Mount Hood, Oregon* ("recently arrived from Europe") and *Cathedral Rocks in Winter*, owned by D. O. Mills. (*Bulletin*, San Francisco, 18, 19 June 1872; *Morning Call*, San Francisco, 18 June 1872)

**25 June** Paintings by Bierstadt and William Bradford have been refused admittance at the Royal Academy exhibition in London, purportedly because they are too big. (*Boston Transcript*, 25 June 1872)

**20 July** In a letter to William Brewer, fellow geologist Josiah Dwight Whitney writes, "The snow is so deep in the High Sierra yet that Bierstadt cannot get up any where near Mt. Brewer. So he is going via Aurora into Owens Valley." (Whitney to Brewer, 20 July 1872, Whitney Papers, Bancroft Library, University of California, Berkeley)

**24 July** *The Domes of the Yosemite* on exhibition at the Snedecor Gallery in New York. (*Post*, New York, 24 July 1872)

**14 Aug.** Geologist Clarence King writes that Bierstadt has joined the survey party "and will give me liberty to copy any or all of his studies." (C. King to A. Humphreys, 14 Aug. 1872, Letterbook, King Survey, National Archives)

**17 Aug.** Bierstadt traveling and sketching in the South Sierra. (*Inyo Independent*, Independence, Calif., 17 Aug. 1872)

**4 Sept.** "Albert Bierstadt lately returned temporarily to the city from a long field experience in the King's river country, under the shadow of Mount Whitney. He will go back there shortly, and expects to remain in California a year longer. Mr. Bierstadt has been working hard here for many months, making faithful studies of some of our grandest mountain scenery. . . ." (*Bulletin*, San Francisco, 4 Sept. 1872)

**by 13 Sept.** Bierstadt leaves San Francisco for another trip to the High Sierra. (*Bulletin*, San Francisco, 13 Sept. 1872)

**5 Oct.** "Mr. Albert Bierstadt, the artist, and Mr. Clarence King, the explorer and geologist, arrived at the Post, by Sunday morning's stage [29 Sept.], having crossed the Sierra via Yosemite Valley and joined the Northern stage at Adobe Meadows. They left on Tuesday [1 Oct.] for the high Sierras west of camp, intending to sketch and investigate through Onion [Owens] Valley and the Kearsarge trail, afterwards looking up the falls of King's river, and when the storms should drive them out, crossing to the San Joaquin valley. They expect to visit our valley again during the coming winter, to remain longer." (*Inyo Independent*, Independence, Calif., 5 Oct. 1872)

**by 19 Oct.** King and Bierstadt return to San Francisco. (Samuel Franklin Emmons diary, 19 Oct. 1872, Manuscript Division, Library of Congress)

**9 Nov.** "Albert Bierstadt, since his return from the Kern river country, has made two trips to the Sierra in the vicinity of Donner Lake and Lake Tahoe, making studies for important works commissioned by Californians. He has accumulated a great quantity of fine material during his year's residence on this coast, and has exhibited great energy and industry in his pursuit of it among the rugged places of the Sierra Nevada. He will have a studio in this city during the winter." (*Bulletin*, San Francisco, 9 Nov. 1872)

**15 Nov.** Bierstadt is reportedly making studies "for the completion of an important work" (*Donner Lake from the Summit*, Fig. 61) near the summit of the Sierras in the Donner Lake region. (*Bulletin*, San Francisco, 15 Nov. 1872)

**5 Dec.** Bierstadt exhibits *Mount Hood, Oregon* (Fig. 55) at the San Francisco Art Association reception. (*Bulletin*, San Francisco, 6 Dec. 1872)

**28 Dec.** In a letter to W. O. Stoddard, Bierstadt proposes making a gift of his painting of Mount Adams to Jay Cooke, president of the Northern Pacific Railroad, hoping to encourage him to purchase *Mount Hood, Oregon*. Acknowledging receipt of a medal from the czar of Russia, Bierstadt suggests that Stoddard mention the award to Cooke. (Bierstadt to Stoddard, 28 Dec. 1872, Downs Collection)

### 1873

**by 4 Jan.** Bierstadt has built a studio at the top of Clay Street, where he is studying the light effects of sunrise and sunset. (*Grizzly*, San Francisco, 4 Jan. 1873, p. 6)

**7 Jan.** Announcement that Bierstadt will place his painting *Donner Lake from the Summit* (Fig. 61) on exhibition for a few days before sending it and *Mount Hood, Oregon* (Fig. 55) east later in the month. (*Bulletin*, San Francisco, 7 Jan. 1873)

**11 Jan.** *Donner Lake from the Summit* to go on public view 13 January. Collis P. Huntington identified as the patron who commissioned the work. (*Bulletin*, San Francisco, 11 Jan. 1873)

**late Jan.–mid-Feb.** Bierstadt at work on "a large winter view in Yosemite, and . . . a striking study of the seal rocks at the Farallone Islands." (*Bulletin*, San Francisco, 25 Jan., 17 Feb. 1873)

**Mar.** "Bierstadt is engaged on a large picture—exhibition size—which we believe he calls 'A View of the King's River Mountains' [probably *Autumn in the Sierras* Fig. 28]. He has also nearly finished another Yosemite landscape, nearly as large as his 'Donner Lake.'" (*California Art Gallery*, Mar. 1873, p. 36)

**8 Mar.** *Donner Lake from the Summit*, just arrived from California, is on private view in New York. The painting will be sent to Europe, where it will be exhibited with *The Emerald Pool* (Fig. 33; already in Berlin) at the upcoming exposition in Vienna. (*NY Times*, 9 Mar. 1873)

**by 7 Apr.** Bierstadt leaves San Francisco for a sketching trip to Fort Independence in Inyo County. (*Bulletin*, San Francisco, 7 Apr. 1873)

**19 Apr.** Bierstadt arrived at Camp Independence in Inyo County "a few days since." (*Inyo Independent*, Independence, Calif., 19 Apr. 1873)

**26 Apr.** American artists will send no pictures to the Vienna Exposition because the assigned space is too small. "Mr. Bierstadt, acting independently of the profession, has sent two enormous landscapes, which will very nearly cover the allotted space. . . . We may safely conclude that Europeans will judge us by Mr. Bierstadt, and will assert that there is no true art in America. . . ." (*NY Times*, 26 Apr. 1873)

**30 Apr.** Bierstadt returns to San Francisco from the Inyo Mountains. (*Bulletin*, San Francisco, 30 Apr. 1873)

**28 May** Bierstadt's large *Autumn in the Sierras* placed on exhibition at the gallery of the San Francisco Art Association. (*Morning Call*, San Francisco, 29 May 1873; *Bulletin*, San Francisco, 29 May 1873)

"[*Autumn in the Sierras*] has the usual excellencies of his style, but is not a pleasing production. It sometimes happens that a man having reached distinction, grows careless. This may not be the case with Bierstadt, but his later pictures show less study than his earlier ones; a bad effect, whatever be the cause." (*Illustrated Press*, San Francisco, June 1873)

**12 June** From Merced City, Bierstadt writes that he and Mrs. Bierstadt "go to the Yosemite in the morning" and will remain there for a month. (Bierstadt to J. D. Whitney, 12 June 1873, AAA)

**26 July** Bierstadt is in San Francisco. (*Bulletin*, San Francisco, 26 July 1873)

**23 Aug.** The *News Letter* reports that Bierstadt has returned "laden with sketches, from a spot which as yet is almost untrodden soil, the Hetch-hetch-y Valley, twelve miles from Yosemite." Mrs. Bierstadt shared the "pleasures and perils of the trip with him." (*San Francisco News Letter and California Advertiser*, 23 Aug. 1873)

**2 Sept.** Bierstadt has been awarded a medal at the Vienna Exposition for his painting *The Emerald Pool*. (*Post*, New York, 2 Sept. 1873)

**11 Oct.** Albert and Rosalie Bierstadt depart San Francisco for the East. (*Morning Call*, San Francisco, 9, 12 Oct. 1873)

**17 Oct.** "Albert Bierstadt is preparing a studio at Waterville, Oneida county, N.Y. [at his in-laws' home], to spend the winter." (*Post*, New York, 17 Oct. 1873)

**22 Oct.** In an interview, Bierstadt indicates that the two paintings he sent to Vienna will go to England. He also acknowledges painting two works (both forest interiors) for the Duke of Manchester. (*Missouri Republican*, Saint Louis, 22 Oct. 1873)

## 1874

**7 Jan.** From his studio in Waterville, Bierstadt writes to Professor Joseph Henry, secretary of the Smithsonian and a trustee of the Corcoran Gallery of Art, seeking his assistance in placing (and selling, if possible) a seven-foot painting of Mount Adams. Bierstadt's asking price is $5,000. (Bierstadt to Henry, 7 Jan. 1874, Corcoran Archives)

**25 Feb.** From Waterville, Bierstadt writes to William T. Walters of Baltimore, a Corcoran trustee, indicating his willingness to exchange his painting of Mount Adams for another picture. "I would take great pleasure in endeavoring to please the committee, as I would like to be well represented in that gallery." (Bierstadt to Walters, 25 Feb. 1874, Corcoran Archives)

**9 Apr.–6 June** NAD Annual Exhibition open. Bierstadt exhibits *California Forest*, which is listed in the catalogue as being "for sale." (Catalogue, NAD, 1874, p. 21; *Post*, New York, 9 Apr. 1874)

"Mr. Bierstadt must be either very confident of his reputation, or very careless of it, for [*California Forest*] is the most unsatisfactory work of his we have ever seen." (*NY Times*, 13 Apr. 1874)

In a review of the NAD exhibition, the *Post* describes Bierstadt's contribution as "not equal to the demands of his reputation." (*Post*, New York, 25 Apr. 1874)

**by 1 May** *Autumn in the Sierras* (Fig. 28) on view in Philadelphia. (*Boston Transcript*, 1 May 1874)

**5 May** Bierstadt at the Brevoort House in New York for a few weeks. (*Post*, New York, 5 May 1874)

**18 May–at least 24 July** *Autumn in the Sierras* and two other works on exhibition in Boston. By 24 July, more than twelve thousand people have visited the gallery. (*Boston Transcript*, 18 May, 24 July 1874)

**27 May** Bierstadt exhibits *Big Tree of California* at the Royal Academy in London. (*Post*, New York, 27 May 1874; Graves 1905, p. 191)

**23 June** It is reported that Bierstadt will spend the summer sketching in the White Mountain region. (*Post*, New York, 23 June 1874)

**3 Aug., 16 Sept** From Waterville, Bierstadt writes to Edward Clarke, architect of the Capitol, concerning his long-dormant commission. (Bierstadt to E. Clarke, 3 Aug., 16 Sept. 1874, Bierstadt Correspondence, Records of the Architect of the Capitol, Washington, D.C.)

**24 Sept.** *Autumn in the Sierras* on exhibition at the Fifth Annual Cincinnati Exposition. (*Post*, New York, 24 Sept. 1874)

**25 Sept.** Bierstadt reportedly at work on "large historical painting" intended for the Capitol (*Discovery of the Hudson River*,

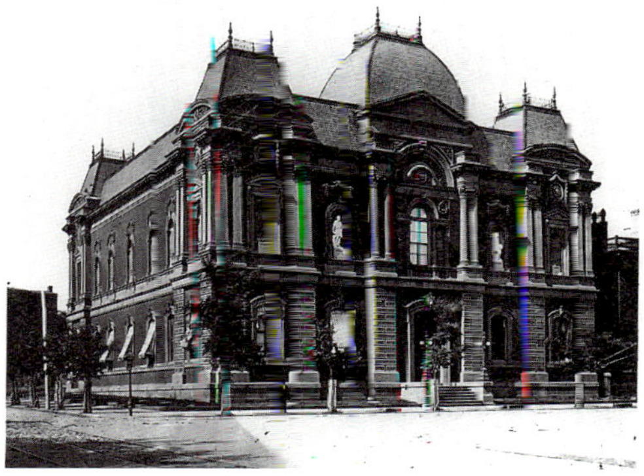

*Corcoran Art Gallery* (now the Renwick Gallery). Photograph. National Museum of American Art, Renwick Gallery, Smithsonian Institution, Washington, D.C.

## 1874–1876

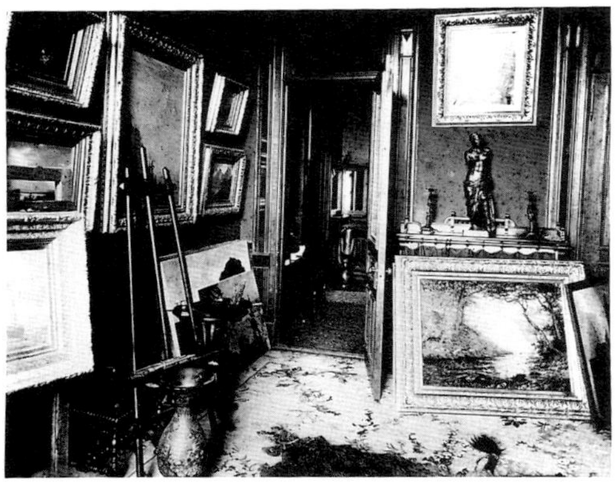

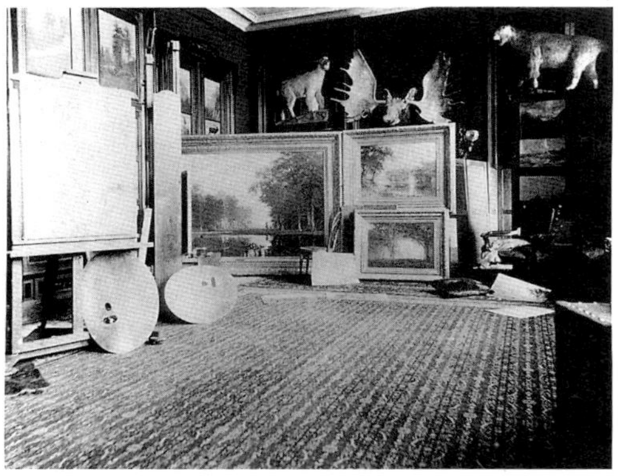

(top) *Interior of Bierstadt's Broadway Studio*. Photograph. Vose Galleries of Boston, Inc.

(above) *Interior of Bierstadt's Broadway Studio*. Photograph. Vose Galleries of Boston, Inc.

Fig. 21) in Waterville. (*Utica Herald*, quoted in *Bulletin*, San Francisco, 25 Sept. 1874)

**17 Oct.** From New York, Bierstadt writes to George Bancroft asking for his assistance in presenting a "study from nature" of the largest tree in California to the German emperor. Bierstadt also writes that he will complete his painting *Discovery of the Hudson River* in a few weeks and hopes to have the pleasure of showing it to Bancroft in Washington. (Bierstadt to Bancroft, 17 Oct. 1874, Massachusetts Historical Society, Boston)

**28 Oct.** Moves studio from 51 West Tenth Street to 1155 Broadway. (*Post*, New York, 28 Oct. 1874)

**24 Nov.** Painting of Kings River Canyon (*Autumn in the Sierras*) on exhibition in New York for the benefit of the Nursery and Child's Hospital. (*Post*, New York, 24 Nov. 1874)

**7 Dec.** "Two of Bierstadt's pictures [*Discovery of the Hudson River* and *Autumn in the Sierras*] . . . are hung in the hall of the House of Representatives, and a proposition is pending to buy them." (*Post*, New York, 7 Dec. 1874)

## 1875

**15 Jan.** "Albert Bierstadt has promised to give the proceeds of the sale of one of his pictures to a proposed art gallery in St. Louis, and to paint and donate to the gallery another large picture. The citizens, it is proposed, shall subscribe half a million dollars for a free gallery and art school." (*Boston Transcript*, 15 Jan. 1875)

**28 Feb.** From New York, Bierstadt writes to Washington regarding the payment Congress is considering for his paintings in the Capitol. Bierstadt had asked $15,000 and the price under discussion is $12,500. (Bierstadt to My Dear Gardner, 28 Feb. 1875, Manuscript Division, Library of Congress)

**3 Mar.** Congress authorizes the Joint Committee on the Library to purchase one of the two paintings by Bierstadt then on exhibition in the Capitol (*Discovery of the Hudson River*, Fig. 21) for a price not to exceed $10,000. (Fairman 1927, p. 270)

**8 Apr.–29 May** NAD Annual Exhibition open. Bierstadt exhibits *Towards the Setting Sun; California Spring*; *Near San Rafael, California*; and *Valley of King's River, California*. (*Post*, New York, 7 Apr. 1875; *NY Times*, 17 Apr. 1875; Catalogue, NAD, 1875, pp. 20, 22, 27; *Boston Transcript*, 2 Apr. 1875)

Negative review of *California Spring* includes comment, "What could have induced an artist of Mr. Bierstadt's taste, knowledge, and experience to imperil his reputation by the exhibition of such a work as this must remain a matter for profound wonder and never-ending speculation." (*NY Times*, 17 Apr. 1875)

A critic, writing in the *Galaxy* about the recently closed exhibition at the NAD, notes that Bierstadt's paintings took up much space on the walls but "little (and even that we grudge them) in our recollections." (*Galaxy*, July 1875, p. 96)

**1 May** Salon in Paris opens to the public. Bierstadt exhibits *Sunset on the Prairies*. (*Boston Transcript*, 18 May 1875; Catalogue, Salon, 1875, p. 30, no. 204, as *Le coucher du soleil, sur les prairies*)

**15 July** From Irvington, Bierstadt writes (probably to Robert L. Stuart, president of the American Museum of Natural History) asking for the measurements of a pair of moose horns. He also inquires about where he could find a live buffalo. (Bierstadt to Stuart[?], 15 July 1875, Archives, American Museum of Natural History, New York)

**7 Sept.** In Irvington, Bierstadt at work on a pendant subject for the Capitol: *Settlement of California, Bay of Monterey, 1770* (formerly titled *Entrance into Monterey*, Fig. 22), "a passage from the history of California, when the western coast was taken possession of by the Spanish." (*Boston Transcript*, 7 Sept. 1875)

**13 Oct.** Seven-hundred-ton bark named after Albert Bierstadt, with an "ornately carved" figurehead of Rosalie Bierstadt, launched at Wiscasset, Maine. The boat was built for William H. Harrison, owner of Valley View Vineyard in Sonoma County, California, who used it for the California coast trade. (*Bulletin*, San Francisco, 2 Nov. 1875)

**3 Nov.** Charles and Edward Bierstadt publish *Gems of American Scenery*, containing

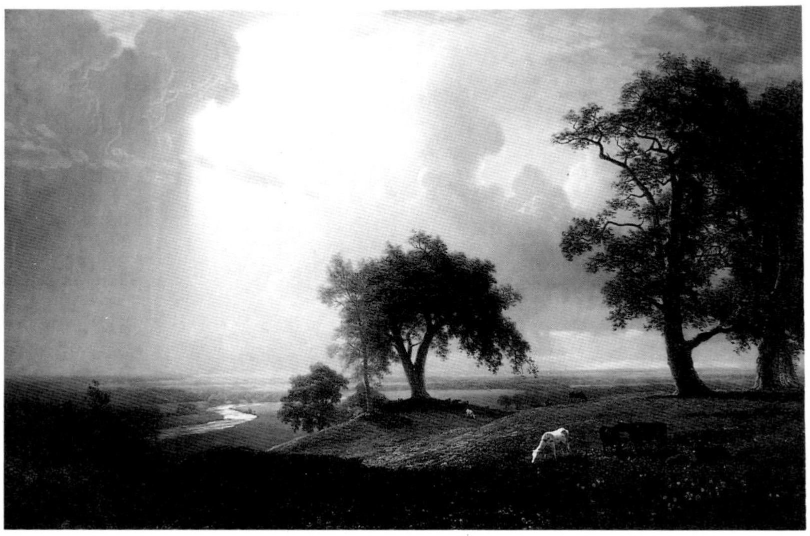

Albert Bierstadt. *California Spring*, 1875. Oil on canvas. The Fine Arts Museums of San Francisco, Presented to the City and County of San Francisco by Gordon Blanding.

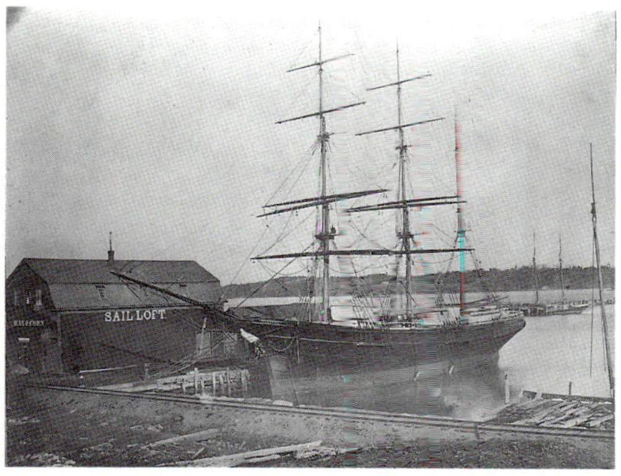

*The bark "Bierstadt," built 1875*. Photograph. Peabody Museum of Salem, Massachusetts.

views of White Mountain scenery and a built-in stereo viewer. (*Niagara Falls Gazette*, 3 Nov. 1875)

**30 Dec.** In his diary, artist Jervis McEntee writes, "Bierstadt had a reception today with a spread from Delmonicos." (McEntee, "Diary," 30 Dec. 1875, quoted in Blaugrund 1987, p. 90)

## 1876

**25 Jan.** Bierstadt entertains the Earl of Dunraven at Brevoort House in New York City. (Bierstadt to Mr. Childs, 20 Jan. 1876, AAA)

**23 Feb.** The Bierstadts attend Grand Ball at Rideau Hall in Ottawa, Canada, as guests of the governor-general, Lord Dufferin. (Unidentified clippings, Bierstadt Scrapbook, Edwards Collection)

**28 Feb.** The Bierstadts attend a ball in Ottawa in celebration of the opening of a new library. (*Times*, Ottawa, 29 Feb. 1876; unidentified clipping, Bierstadt Scrapbook, Edwards Collection)

**28 Mar.** NAD Annual Exhibition opens. Bierstadt does not contribute. (*NY Times*, 28 Mar. 1876)

**7 Apr.** Writes to John Sartain at the Pennsylvania Academy of the Fine Arts to tell him that he is sending *Mount Adams, Oregon* to the Annual Exhibition. Describes the painting as 4½ by 7 feet and for sale for $10,000. (Bierstadt to Sartain, 7 Apr. 1876, Pennsylvania Academy of the Fine Arts Archives, Philadelphia)

**10 May** Centennial Exposition opens in Philadelphia. Bierstadt exhibits *California Spring* (p. 228); *The Great Trees, Mariposa Grove, California* (No. 65); *Mount Hood, Oregon* (Fig. 55); *Settlement of California, Bay of Monterey, 1770* (Fig. 22); *Western Kansas;* and *Yosemite Valley*. (Catalogue, Centennial Exposition, Philadelphia, 1876, pp. 23, 31, 39, 43, 44)

**21 June** August Belmont opens his private gallery for four days as a benefit; Bierstadt's *Burning Ship* (p. 223) on view. (*Post*, New York, 21 June 1876)

*Rosalie Bierstadt in Mary, Queen of Scots costume for Ottawa ball*, 1876. Photograph. Collection of Joyce Randall Edwards.

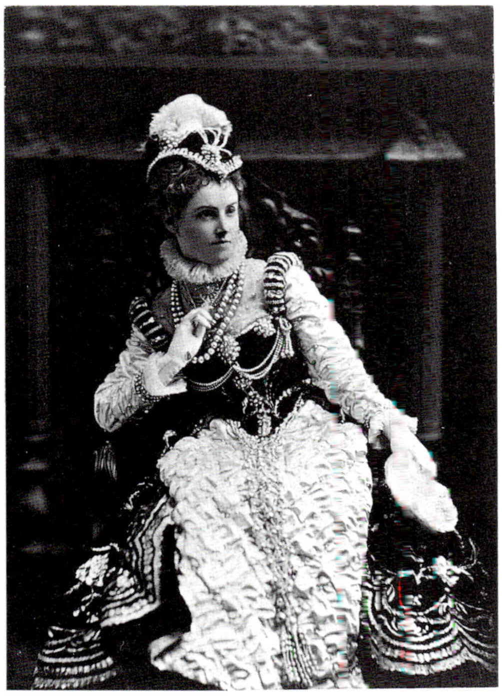

J. Mc. Goffin. *The Art Gallery at the Centennial Exposition, 1876*. Engraving published in Edward Strahan, *Illustrated Catalogue, The Master Pieces of the Centennial International Exhibition, 1876*, vol. 1 (Philadelphia: 1876).

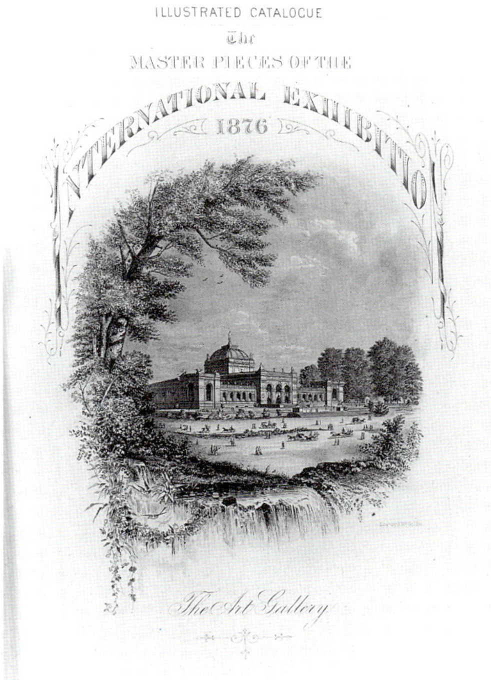


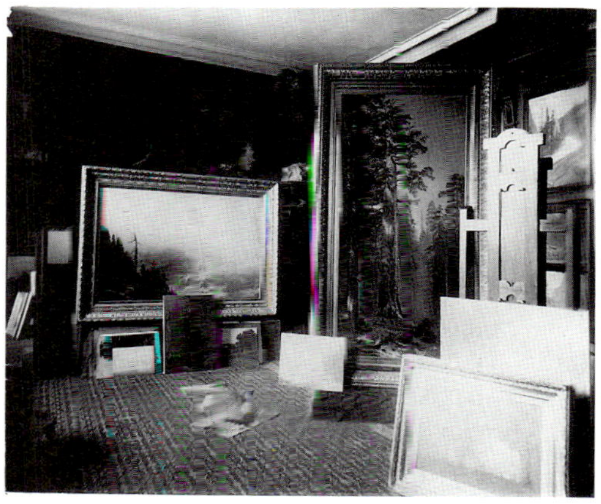

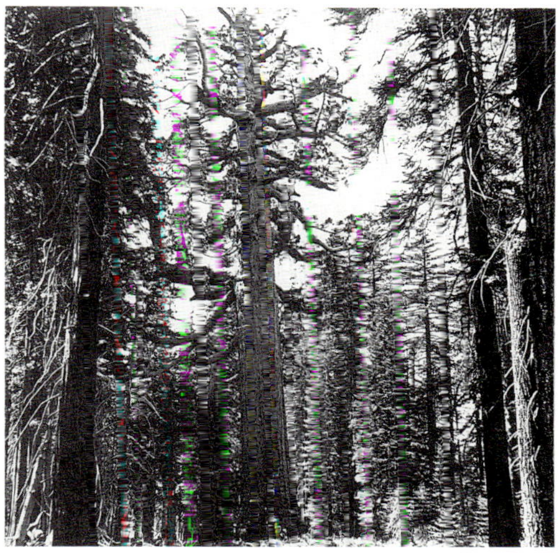

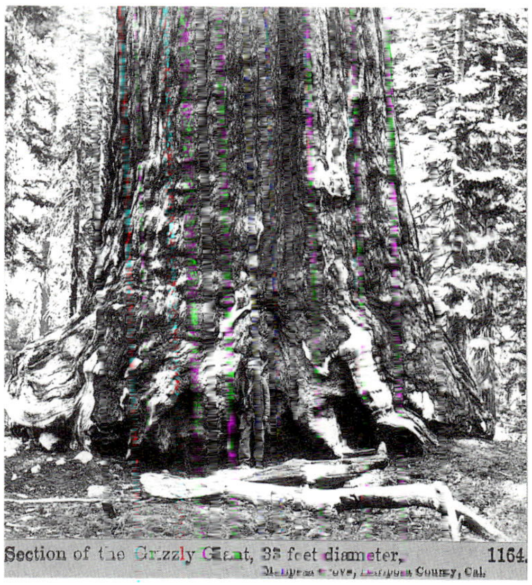


*(top) Interior of Bierstadt's Studio Showing "The Great Trees Mariposa Grove, California."* Photograph. Vose Galleries of Boston, Inc.

*(above, center)* Carleton E. Watkins. *Grizzly Giant*. Stereograph. Collection of Leonard A. Walle.

*(above)* Carleton E. Watkins. *Section of the Grizzly Giant, 33 feet diameter. Mariposa Grove, Mariposa County, Cal*. Stereograph. Collection of Leonard A. Walle.

## 1876–1878

**by 20 July** Bierstadt closes his studio for the summer and goes to Newport. Later in the season, he visits Lake George. (*Post*, New York, 20 July 1876)

**by 12 Oct.** Reopens his studio. (*Post*, New York, 12 Oct. 1876)

**25 Nov.** Rosalie Bierstadt arrives in Nassau and registers at the Royal Victoria Hotel. (*Nassau Guardian*, 29 Nov. 1876)

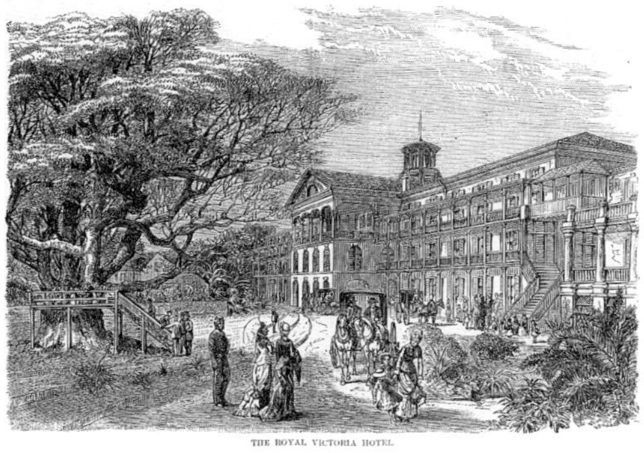

*The Royal Victoria Hotel* (Nassau). Engraving published in William Drysdale, *In Sunny Lands: Out-Door Life in Nassau and Cuba*, Harper's Franklin Square Library (New York: 1885).

**22 Dec.** Bierstadt and Dunraven arrive in Denver aboard the Kansas Pacific train. (*Rocky Mountain News*, Denver, 23 Dec. 1876)

**23 Dec.** Bierstadt and Dunraven go to Estes Park "for the purpose of procuring sketches of winter scenery and effects in the high mountains. . . . The gentlemen named have recently returned from a moose hunt in Canada." (*Rocky Mountain News*, Denver, 23 Dec. 1876)

## 1877

**1 Jan.** "Mr. Albert Bierstadt is painting, to the order of the Earl of Dunraven, a large Rocky Mountain scene, introducing Estes park as viewed from a point in the neighborhood of Long's Peak [Fig. 65]." (*Rocky Mountain News*, Denver, 1 Jan. 1877, quoted in GH Papers)

**2 Jan.** Bierstadt traveling and sketching with Dunraven in Colorado. (*Boston Transcript*, 2 Jan. 1877)

**8 Jan.** Bierstadt returns to Denver from Estes Park; departs the following day for the East. (*Rocky Mountain News*, Denver, 9 Jan. 1877, quoted in GH Papers)

**3 Feb.** Bierstadt lends a watercolor titled *Family of Bears*, by Karl Bodmer, to the Tenth Annual Watercolor Exhibition in New York. (*Post*, New York, 3 Feb. 1877)

**6 Feb.** "Bierstadt's last painting is on exhibition in St. Louis. The canvas on which 'Mt. Brewer' is depicted is of great size—six by ten feet. . . . The Globe-Democrat says that Bierstadt has taken a notion to aid in the establishment of a permanent art gallery in St. Louis. . . . The artist, it is understood, will paint and give to the embryonic gallery a picture for which he would ordinarily charge $10,000, and will part with 'Mt. Brewer' for the same purpose at half the price set upon it, namely, $20,000." (*Boston Transcript*, 6 Feb. 1877)

**1 Mar.** "Ex-Governor Stanford of California has given to Mr. Bierstadt a commission to paint a picture for $20,000." (*Boston Transcript*, 1 Mar. 1877)

**4 Mar.** Bierstadt arrives in Nassau and joins his wife at the Royal Victoria Hotel. (*Nassau Guardian*, 7 Mar. 1877)

**3 Apr.–2 June** NAD Annual Exhibition open to the public. Bierstadt exhibits *Mountain Lake* (now titled *Mount Corcoran*, Fig. 32). (Catalogue, NAD, 1877, pp. 44, 47 (ill.); *Post*, New York, 2 Apr. 1877; *Boston Transcript*, 4 June 1877)

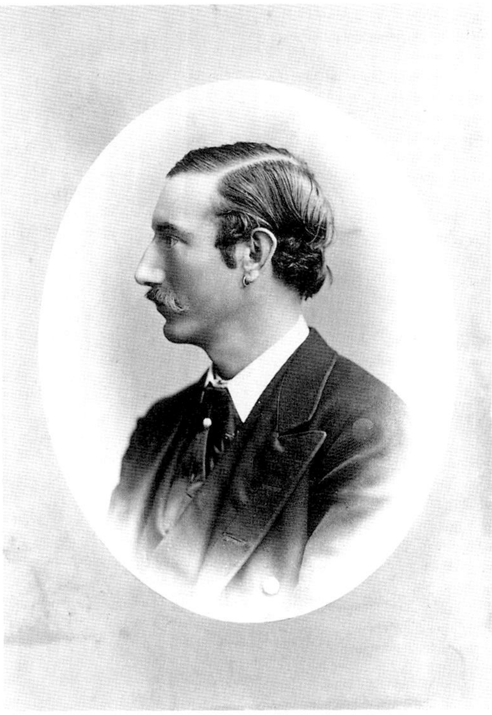

*The Earl of Dunraven*. Photograph. Bierstadt Album, private collection, Hannover, Germany.

Dissatisfaction with the hanging of the NAD exhibition is reported: "Mr. Bierstadt's furious landscape, it is said, is on the line, and in one of the best positions on the line in the South Room, while Mr. Whittredge's artistic landscape in the North Room, full of poetry and peace, is strung up high in dishonor." (*Post*, New York, 10 Apr. 1877)

Bierstadt's contribution to the NAD exhibition is roundly criticized: "The whole picture is a mistake. . . . He possesses skill and talents and fancy; he is industrious and ambitious to excel; he understands the 'popular taste' (Heaven save the mark!) but, he has considerable climbing yet to do before he reaches the top of Pisgah or Parnassus." (*Post*, New York, 21 Apr. 1877)

In an article noting the close of the NAD exhibition and meager sales, it is said that "some of the artists are exceptions to the general rule as regards a demand for their works. Mr. Bierstadt, whose Rocky Mountain scenes have attracted considerable attention in England, has lately received orders from that country for six pictures." (*Boston Transcript*, 4 June 1877)

**24 Apr.** Bierstadt departs Nassau, where he had made sketches of local scenery and worked on the Dunraven commission. (*Nassau Guardian*, 25 Apr. 1877)

**16 June** Bierstadt reportedly planning to spend the summer in the Colorado region. (*Frank Leslie's Illustrated Newspaper*, 16 June 1877)

**20 July** Working to establish an Academy of Fine Arts in Columbus, Ohio. "[Bierstadt] writes to a friend in that city, 'I am certain our Western cities have always been, in proportion to their age and the number of their inhabitants, far more enterprising in art matters than our Eastern towns. Chicago and San Francisco, notably, are examples of this. The latter city, though only a little over 25 years old, already has its academy of fine arts and its life school, and during the gay season, its art receptions.' (*Boston Transcript*, 20 July 1877)

**late July–early Aug.** Bierstadt stays several days with his brother Charles in Niagara. (*Niagara Falls Gazette*, 1 Aug. 1877)

**7 Aug.** Bierstadt is in Newport. (*Boston Transcript*, 7 Aug. 1877)

**c. mid-Aug.** Bierstadt arrives in Colorado. (Bierstadt to General J. G. Mitchell, 10 Aug.

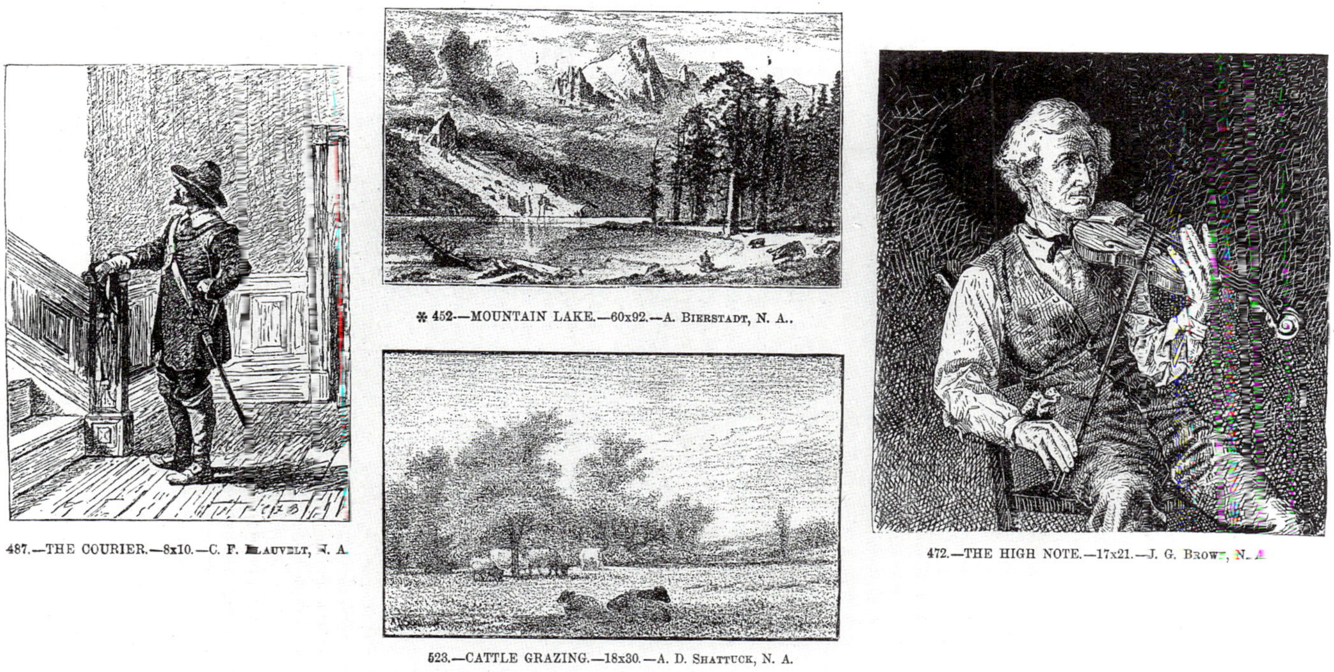


*Illustrated page including "Mountain Lake" (after Bierstadt) from National Academy of Design Illustrated Catalogue of the 52nd Annual Exhibition* (New York: 1877).

1877, Hayes Presidential Center; *Rocky Mountain News*, Denver, 31 Aug. 1877)

**10 Sept.–10 Oct.** At the Saint Louis Exposition Bierstadt exhibits *Landscape; Yosemite Valley; Sunset; Meadow in Westphalia;* and *Misty Morning in Westphalia*. (*Art Catalogue*, Saint Louis Exposition, 1877, p. 213; *Art Journal* [New York], Oct. 1877, p. 320)

**11 Oct.** Rosalie Bierstadt arrives in Nassau. Bierstadt may have joined her later. (*Nassau Guardian*, 13 Oct. 1877; *Boston Transcript*, 5 Oct. 1877)

**28 Dec.** Writing to William MacLeod at the Corcoran Gallery of Art, Bierstadt reports that he has been paid $15,000 by the Earl of Dunraven for *Estes Park, Colorado* (*The Rocky Mountains, Longs Peak*, Fig. 65). He indicates that Dunraven wants a companion picture as well and he might sell the earl *Mount Corcoran* (Fig. 32), although he would prefer the picture to stay in Washington. (Bierstadt to MacLeod, 28 Dec. 1877, Corcoran Archives)

## 1878

**c. late Dec.–c. mid-Jan.** *Estes Park, Colorado* (*The Rocky Mountains, Longs Peak*, Fig. 65) on exhibition in Boston. The painting is described as "an immense canvas, and unlike some of the artist's productions, is said to be a faithful representation of the scene it professes to portray. The view of the valley and the lofty peaks beyond is magnificent, and one can hardly wonder at the taste of the Earl of Dunraven, the owner of the picture, in erecting a summer hotel in one of the most sightly portions of the park. The only element lacking in the picture is strength, and the critic can almost overlook that in the surpassing loveliness of the subject." (*Boston Transcript*, 19 Dec., 2, 12 Jan. 1878)

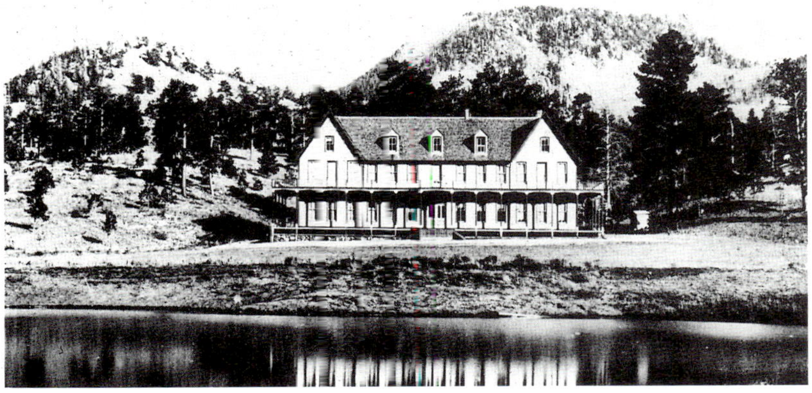

*The Earl of Dunraven's Hotel, Whyte's Lake, Colorado*. Photograph. State Historical Society of Colorado, William H. Jackson Photo-Library, Denver.

**13 Jan.** Bierstadt reported to have nearly finished *On the Coast Near Nassau, Bahamas* (*The Shore of the Turquoise Sea*, No. 66). (*NY Herald*, 13 Jan. 1878)

**31 Jan.** From New York, Bierstadt writes to F. V. Hayden about his pictures in the Capitol, stating that one had been purchased and that seven years earlier a unanimous vote had authorized him to paint two pictures for the Capitol. (Thomas Moran may have requested that one of Bierstadt's paintings be removed.) (Bierstadt to Hayden, 31 Jan. 1878, FVH Papers)

**5 Feb.** Bierstadt travels with Lord Dufferin, President Hayes's son (Webb), and several others to Ottawa aboard Cornelius Vanderbilt's private railroad car. (Webb Hayes to President Hayes, 6 Feb. 1878, Hayes Presidential Center)

**11 Feb.** Bierstadt in Montreal with Lord and Lady Dufferin and Webb Hayes. (*Gazette*, Montreal, 12 Feb. 1878; Bierstadt Scrapbook, Edwards Collection)

**mid-Feb.** Bierstadt promises a painting to the newly founded Art Gallery of Montreal. (*Boston Transcript*, 21 Feb. 1878; *Gazette*, Montreal, 16 Feb. 1878)

**27 Feb.–1 Mar.** Bierstadt stays at the White House. Attends state dinner on 28 Feb. (Invitation list, 28 Feb. 1878, Hayes Presidential Center)

**16 Mar.** Bierstadt not listed among the American artists whose works have been chosen by the selection committee for inclusion in the Exposition Universelle in Paris. (*Post*, New York, 16 Mar. 1878; *Boston Transcript*, 18 Mar. 1878)

**17 Mar.** Bierstadt arrives in Nassau. (*Nassau Guardian*, 20 Mar. 1878)

**20 Mar.** David Maitland Armstrong, head of the American selection committee for the Paris Exposition, writes to Augustus Saint-Gaudens that Bierstadt, whose painting has been rejected, has sent the work to Paris and will try to get it in there. "Look out for him. He shall not get it in but do not let it be known, as we do not want to make a martyr of Bierstadt." (Armstrong to Saint-Gaudens, 20 Mar. 1878, Saint-Gaudens Papers, Dartmouth College Library, Hanover, N.H.)

**28 Mar.** Sale in New York of Milton S. Latham's collection includes two pictures by Bierstadt: *Crossing Green River, California* ($1,350) and *King's River Grove–California* ($600). (Sale Catalogue, Latham Collection, 1878, AAA; *NY Times*, 29 Mar. 1878)

**7 Apr.** In a review of the NAD Annual Exhibition, Bierstadt's absence is noted: "Where is Mr. Bierstadt, with his square miles of California landscape?" (*NY Times*, 7 Apr. 1878)

**24 Apr.** Bierstadt departs Nassau aboard steamship *San Jacinto* bound for New York via Saint Augustine and Savannah. (*Nassau Guardian*, 24 Apr. 1878)

**1 May** Exposition Universelle opens in Paris. (*Post*, New York, 1 May 1878)

**6 May–5 Aug.** *Estes Park, Colorado, U.S. (The Rocky Mountains, Longs Peak*, Fig. 65) among paintings shown at the Royal Academy. (*Times*, London, 4, 11 May, 3 Aug. 1878; Graves 1905, p. 191)

**3 July** Rosalie Bierstadt departs Nassau for New York. (*Nassau Guardian*, 3 July 1878)

**9 July** Apparently aware of a $15,000 appropriation for works of art for the Capitol, Bierstadt writes the Librarian of Congress, urging completion of the purchase of *Settlement of California, Bay of Monterey, 1770* (Fig. 22) before the artist's departure for Europe. He receives $10,000. (Bierstadt to Ainsworth R. Spofford, 9 July 1878, Spofford Papers, Library of Congress; Fairman 1927, p. 271; Hazelton 1914, p. 203)

**20 July** Bierstadt and his wife sail for Europe aboard the *Germanic*. (*NY Times*, 21 July 1878)

**13 Aug.** In London at the Langham Hotel. (Poem by Bret Harte dated "August 13, 1878 Langham Hotel," Hannover Album)

**19 Oct.** Bierstadt "proposes" opening a gallery in London or Paris to show American art. (*Press*, Philadelphia, 19 Oct. 1878)

## 1879

**23 Jan.** Bierstadts at Villa Marie Philippine in Cannes, France. (Bierstadt to unidentified correspondent, 23 Jan. 1879, Manuscript Division, Library of Congress)

**5 May** Reviewer notes absence of Bierstadt's work at NAD Annual Exhibition and comments that he prefers new paintings by Thomas Moran: "We have all . . . been growing away from Mr. Bierstadt. . . ." (*World*, New York, 5 May 1879)

**12 May–22 June** Salon open in Paris. Two works by Bierstadt listed in exhibition catalogue: *Vallée de Hetch-Hetchy (Californie)* (not shown) and *Dans l'Oréjon du Sud (Etats-Unis d'Amérique)*. (Catalogue, Salon, 1879, p. 23, nos. 275, 276; *Boston Transcript*, 6 Feb., 15 May 1879, notes that only one shown)

**6 June** While exhibiting at the Royal Academy, Bierstadt shows *The Grizzly Giant (The Great Trees, Mariposa Grove, California*, No. 65) at "Mr. Agnew's Bond-street Gallery." (*Times*, London, 6 June 1879)

**by 2 Nov.** Bierstadts return to New York. Rosalie Bierstadt sails for Nassau. (*NY Times*, 2 Nov. 1879)

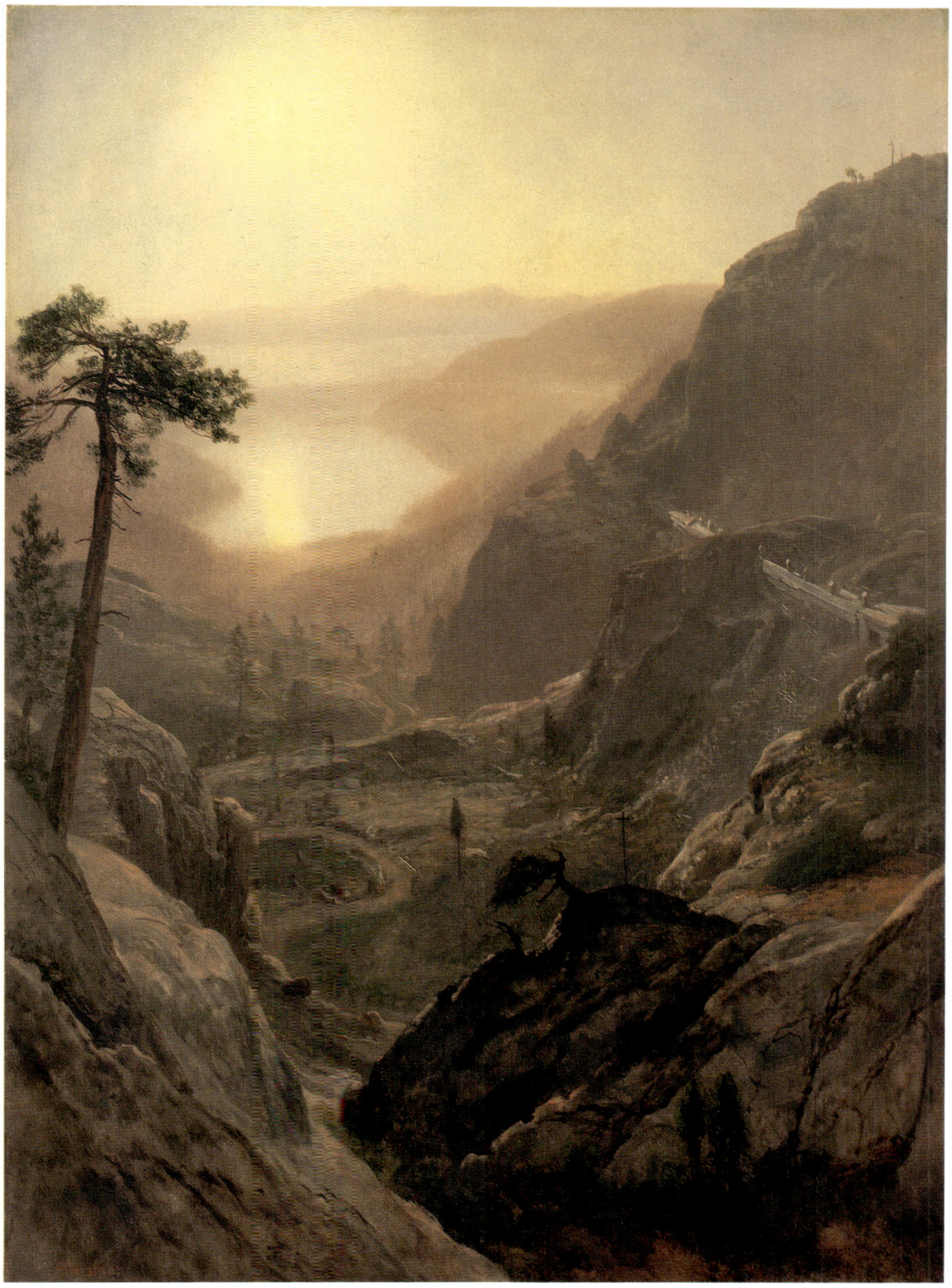

NO. 58

## *View of Donner Lake, California*, 1871–72

Oil on paper, 29¼ × 21⅞ in. (74.3 × 55.6 cm)

Signed lower left: *ABierstadt*

The Fine Arts Museums of San Francisco, Gift of Anna Bennett and Jessie Jonas, in memory of August F. Jonas, Jr.

*Last summer Bierstadt made another trip West, but this time he was carried to and fro at forty miles an hour. For since his previous visit the irresistible engine had eaten its way into the wilderness and laid the forest low before it. This time he made studies for another large painting for which he had received a commission from C. P. Huntington, Esq., President of the Central Pacific Railroad. The scene is on the route of the road, and the point of view is near the place where, some fifteen years ago, a party of emigrants perished within a short distance of the civilization they were seeking, but of the proximity of which they did not know. The rocky summit from which the view is taken is high, and thus a vast extent of mountain, lake, and valley is embraced. The line of the railroad is beheld, a mere thread, where it enters the scene some thirty miles off, and the eye follows it, coming nearer still, along the perilous path cut for it in the trap and granite sides of the great hills which tower above it. In the middle distance is Donner Lake, the central point of interest, and beyond it range after range of hills until the horizon meets them. . . . To make his studies in color for this picture, Bierstadt rose morning after morning at four o'clock, until he had secured the desired effect of light and shade and color.*

D. O. C. Townley, "Living American Artists," *Scribner's Monthly* 3 (Mar. 1872): 608

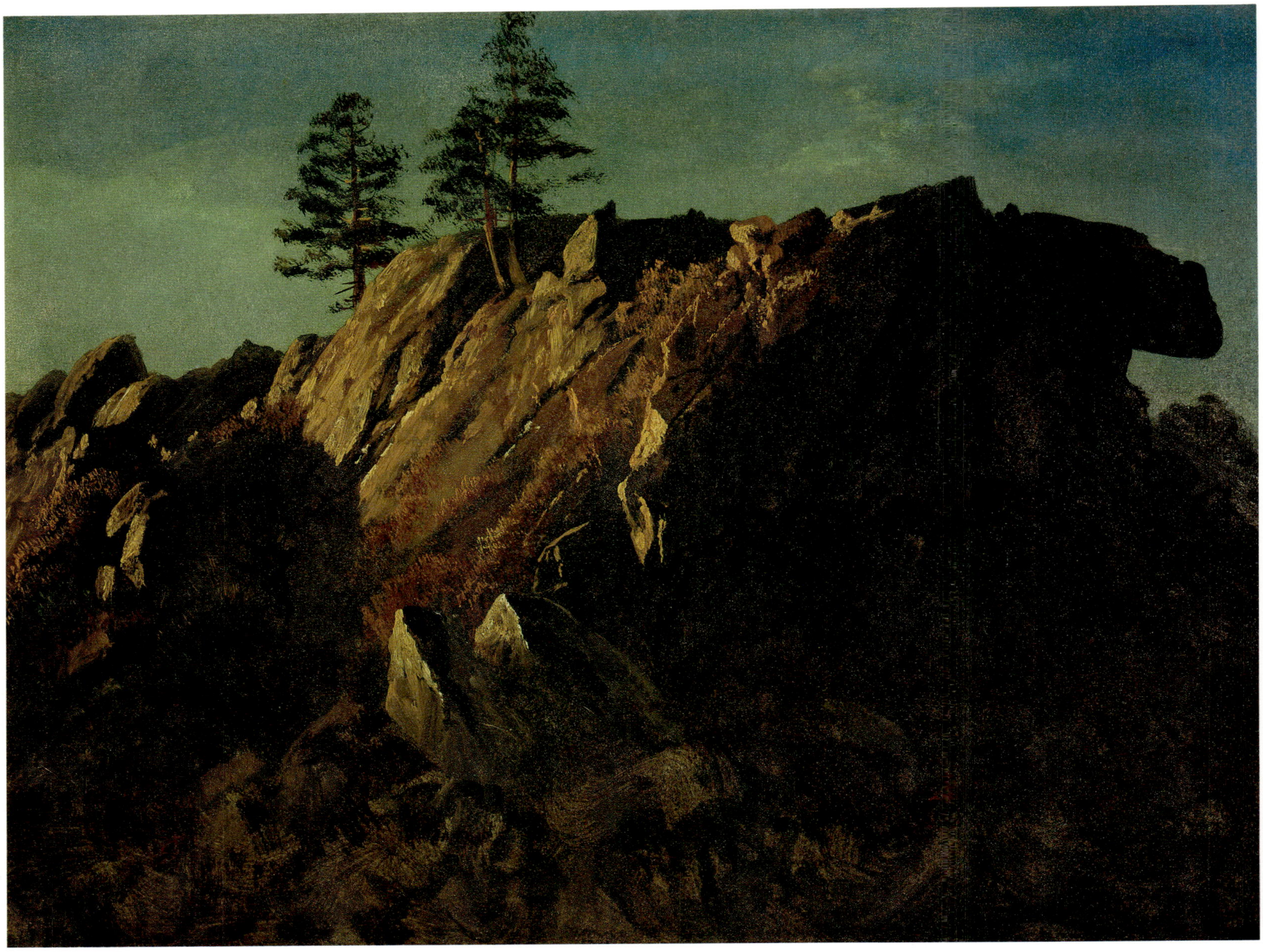

**NO. 59**

## *Mountain Scene*

Oil on cardboard, 13¾ × 19 in. (34.9 × 48.3 cm)

Unsigned

The Oakland Museum, Kahn Collection

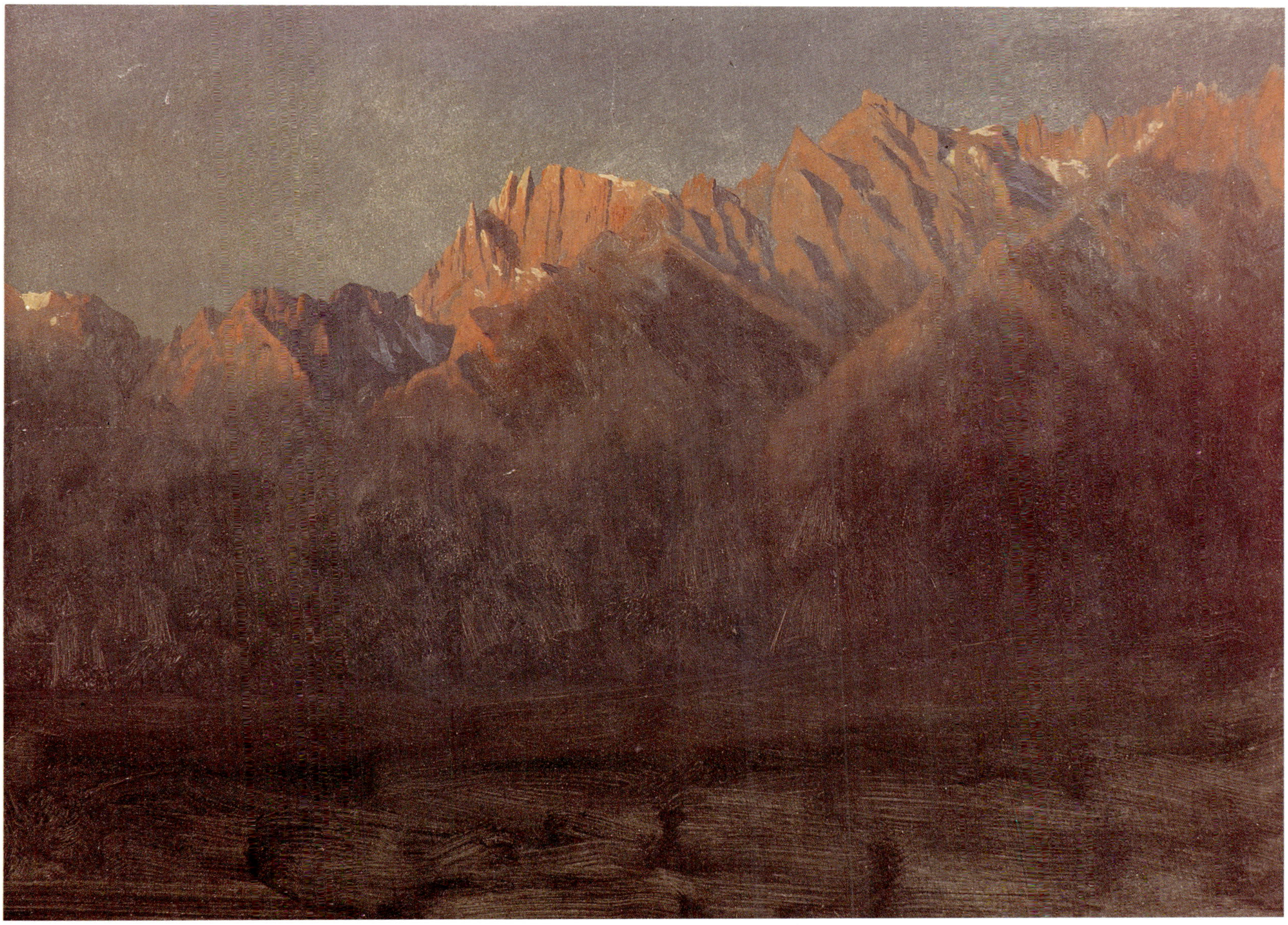

NO. 60

*Sunrise in the Sierras*

Oil on paper mounted on board, 13½ × 18⅞ in. (34.3 × 47.9 cm)

Unsigned

National Museum of American Art, Smithsonian Institution, Washington, D.C., Gift of Orrin Wickersham June

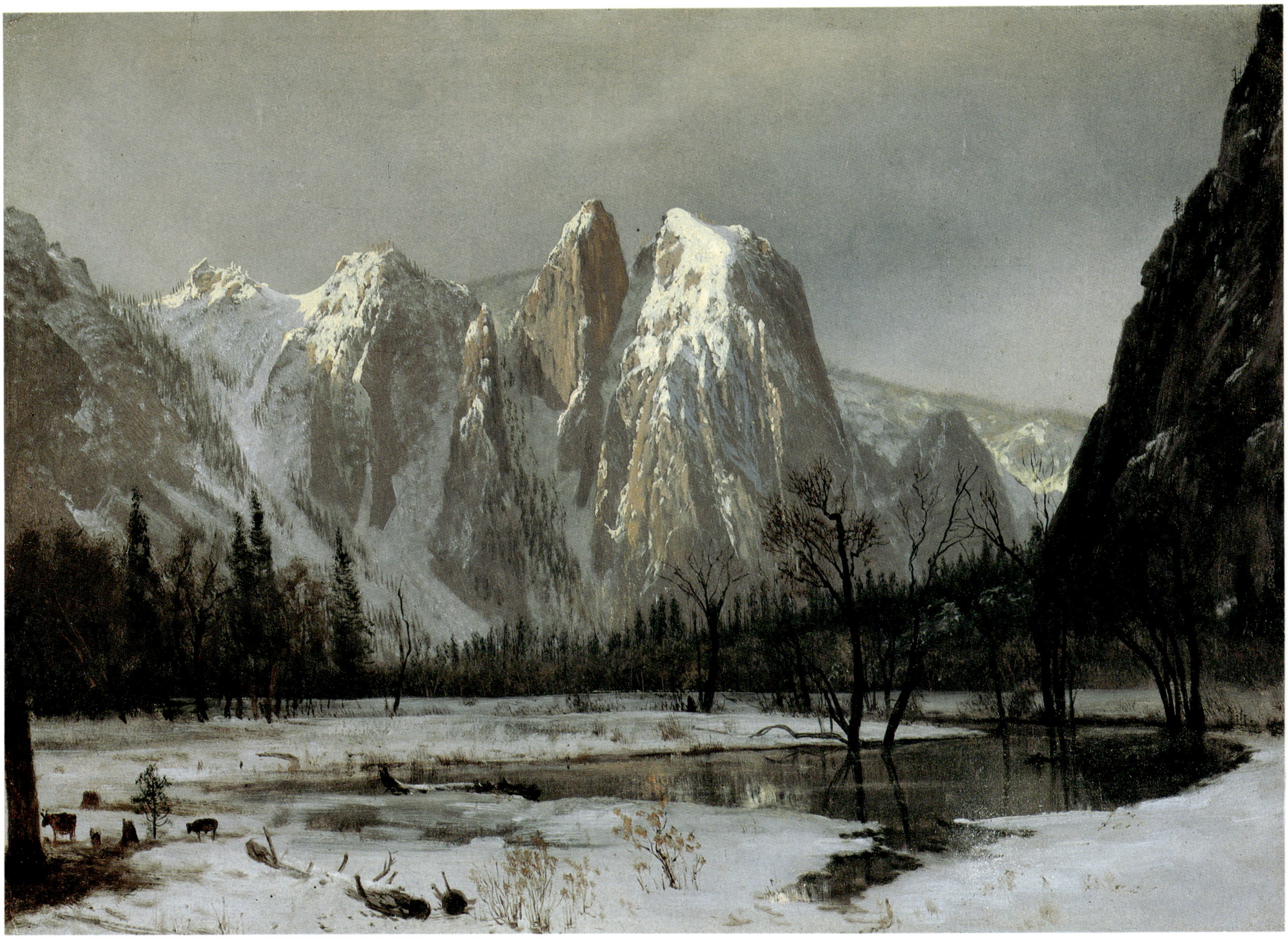

NO. 61

## *Cathedral Rocks, Yosemite Valley, California*, 1872

Oil on paper, 13⅞ × 19⅛ in. (35.2 × 48.6 cm)

Unsigned

Inscribed verso: *Cathedral Rocks, Yosemite Valley, California*

Collection of Ryan M. Cooper

*As the spring advances, and nature in California is putting on her most lovely garniture of verdure and flowers, the artists are preparing for sketching tours. Albert Bierstadt, who has taken up his residence in this State for some months, is the first in the field. With characteristic enterprise he has pushed into the Yosemite Valley this early—nearly three months in advance of ordinary tourists—to make sketches of the winter aspects of its unequalled scenery, when the peaks and cliffs are covered deep with snow, and the falls tumble amid icicles and ice-sheeted rocks. He entered the valley ten days ago, by way of Haight's Cove and the cañon of the Merced river, and will spend considerable time there.*

*Bulletin*, San Francisco, 5 Mar. 1872

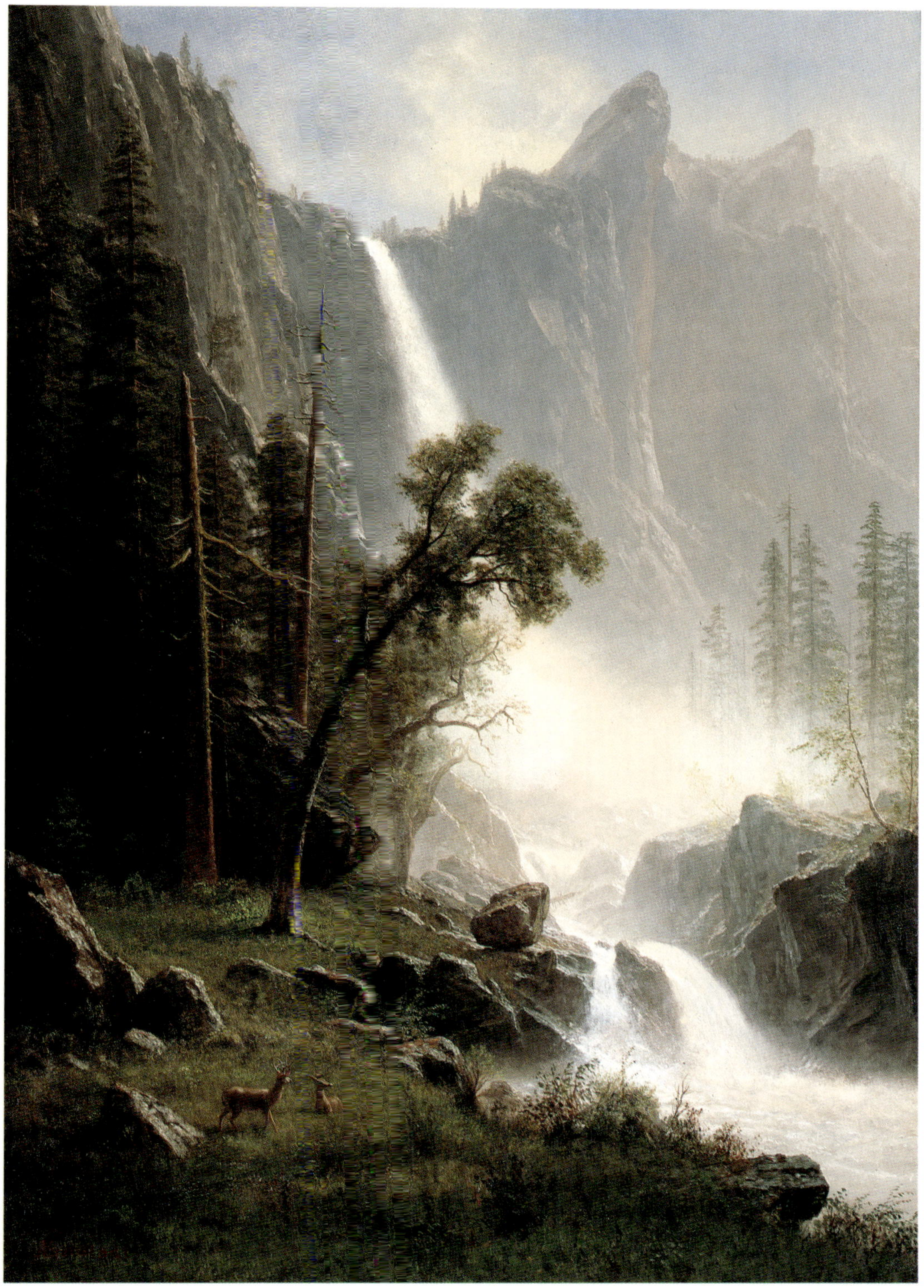

NO. 62

## *Bridal Veil Falls, Yosemite,* c. 1871–73

Oil on canvas, 36⅛ × 26⅜ in. (91.8 × 67 cm)

Signed lower left: *ABierstadt*

North Carolina Museum of Art, Raleigh, Purchased with funds from the North Carolina Art Society (Robert F. Phifer Bequest) and various donors, by exchange

*While I am speaking of waterfalls, let me not omit "Po-ho-nó," or "The Bridal Veil." . . . As Tis-sa-ack was a good, so is Po-ho-nó an evil spirit of the Indian mythology. This tradition is scientifically accounted for, in the fact that many Indians have been carried over the fall by the tremendous current both of wind and water forever rushing down a cañon through which the stream breaks from its feeding-lake twelve or fifteen miles before it falls. The savage lowers his voice to a whisper and crouches trembling past Po-ho-nó; while the very utterance of the name is so dreaded by him that the discoverers of the Valley obtained it with great difficulty. This fall drops on a heap of giant boulders in one unbroken sheet of a thousand feet perpendicular, thus being the next in height among all the Valley cataracts to the Yo-Semite itself, and having a width of fifty feet. Its name of "The Bridal Veil" is one of the few successes in fantastic nomenclature; for, to one viewing it in profile, its snowy sheet, broken into one filmy silver lace of spray, and falling quite free of the brow of the precipice, might well seem the veil worn by the earth at her granite wedding,—no commemorator of any fifty years' bagatelle like the golden one, but crowning the one millionth anniversary of her nuptials.*

Fitz Hugh Ludlow, *The Heart of the Continent: A Record of Travel Across the Plains and in Oregon, with an Examination of the Mormon Principle* (New York 1870), pp. 439–40

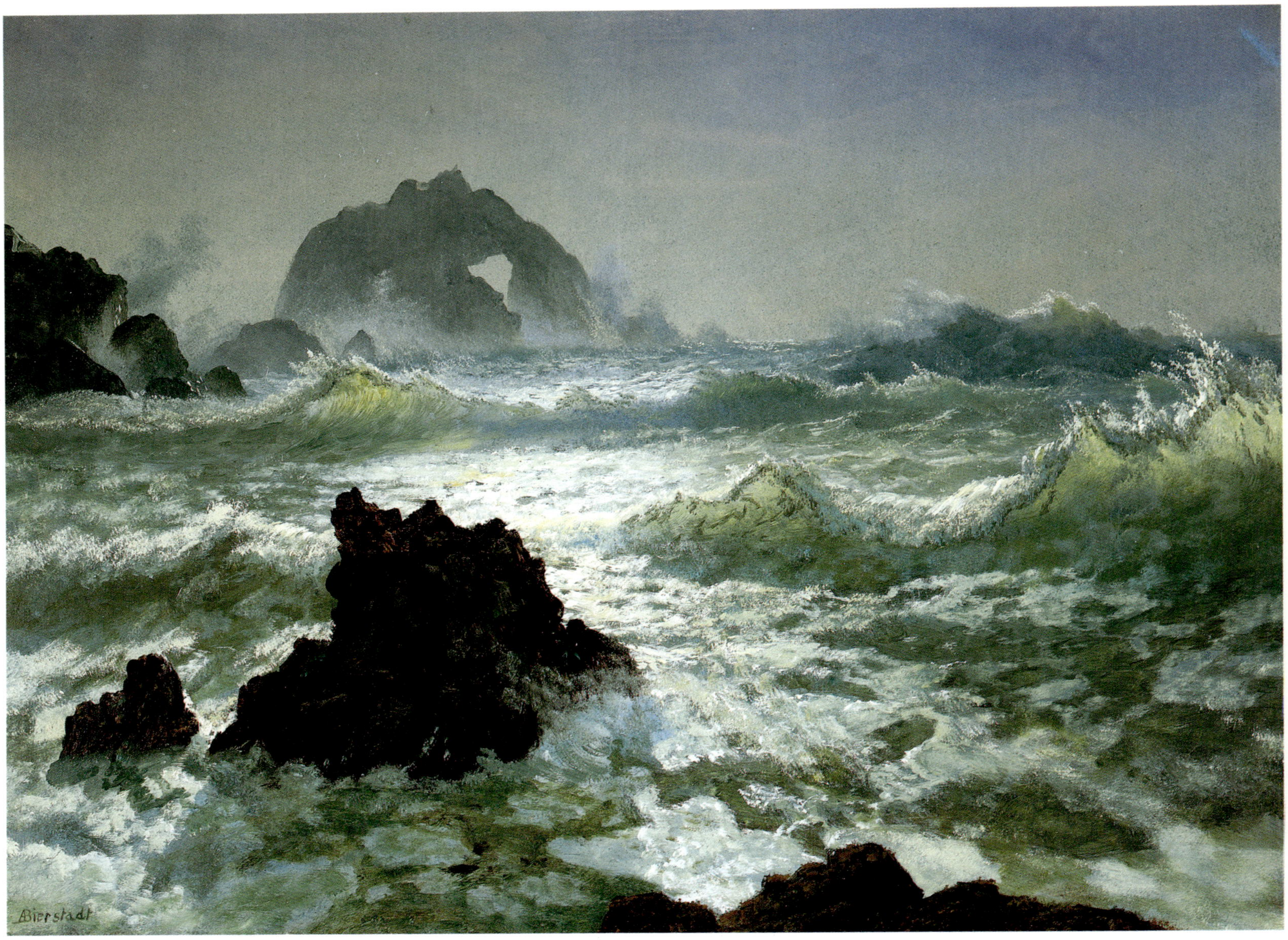


NO. 63

## *Seal Rock, California,* c. 1872

Oil on paper mounted on canvas, 16 × 22 in. (40.6 × 55.9 cm)

Signed lower left: *ABierstadt*

The Warner Collection of Gulf States Paper Corporation, Tuscaloosa, Alabama

*Mr. Bierstadt returned from the Farralones yesterday. He has procured sketches for a marine painting of the Isles, and will doubtless give us a faithful likeness.*

*Bulletin,* San Francisco, 2 May 1872

*If you should approach the harbor of San Francisco from the sea, your first sight of land would be a collection of picturesque rocks known as the Farallones. . . . They are six rugged islets, whose peaks lift up their heads in picturesque masses out of the ocean, twenty-three and a half miles from the Golden Gate, the famous entrance of San Francisco Bay. Farallon is a Spanish word, meaning a small pointed islet in the sea.*

Charles Nordhoff, *California for Health, Pleasure, and Residence: A Book for Travellers and Settlers* (New York: 1882), p. 63

*This is a wild and beautiful scene. The sharp pointed rocks are standing boldly out against the sky, and covered with birds and sea lions. A heavy surf is rolling in, with thundering hoarseness, and as the wild waters break upon the shore, they resemble the low booming sound of distant thunder; while the white spray curls over, and falls with a hissing splash upon the rocks, and then returns again to its native brine. . . .*

*Hutchings' California Magazine,* Aug. 1856, p. 55

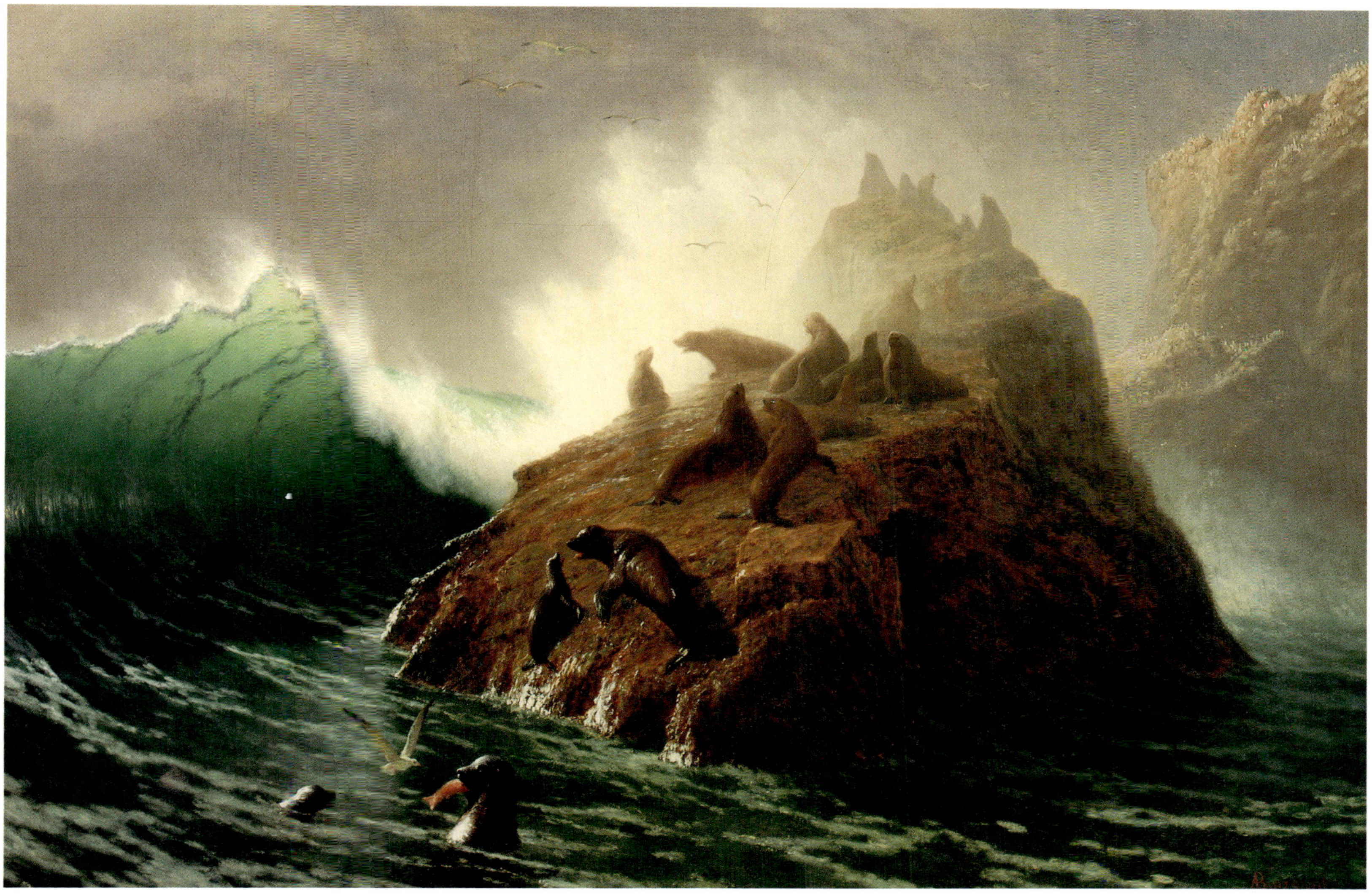

NO. 64

## *Seal Rock*, c. 1872

Oil on canvas, 30 × 44 in. (76.2 × 111.8 cm)

Signed lower right: *ABierstadt*

New Britain Museum of American Art, New Britain, Connecticut, Alix W. Stanley Fund

*It is like one vast menagerie. Upon the rocks adjacent to the sea, repose in easy indifference, thousands—yes, thousands—of* sea lions *(one species of the seal,) that weigh from* two to five thousand pounds each. . . . *On our left, and but a few yards from shore, is an isle, called* Seal Rock, *and where the sea lions have possession, and are waving their lubberly bodies to and fro, upon its very summit; and from whence the echoes of their low howling moans are heard across the sea, long after distance has hidden them from our sight.*

*Hutchings' California Magazine*, Aug. 1856, pp. 52, 57

*But when the vast surf which breaks in mountain waves against the weather side of the Farallones with a force which would in a single sweep dash to pieces the biggest Indiaman—when such a surf, vehemently and with apparently irresistible might, lifts its tall, white head, and with a deadly roar lashes the rocks half-way to their summit—then it is a magnificent sight to see a dozen or half a hundred great sea-lions at play in the very midst and fiercest part of the boiling surge, so completely masters of the situation that they allow themselves to be carried within a foot or two of the rocks, and at the last and imminent moment, with an adroit twist of their bodies, avoid the shock, and, diving, re-appear beyond the breaker.*

Charles Nordhoff, *California for Health, Pleasure, and Residence: A Book for Travellers and Settlers* (New York: 1882), pp. 68–69

*We lingered among them half a day; the artists making color-studies of the most picturesque. . . . Of course our artists neither made nor expected to make anything like a realizing picture of the groves. The marvelous of size does not go into gilt frames. You paint a Big Tree, and it only looks like a common tree in a cramped coffin. To be sure, you can put a live figure against the butt for comparison; but, unless you take a canvas of the size of Haydon's, your picture is quite as likely to resemble Homunculus against an average timber tree as a large man against* Sequoia gigantea. *What our artists did was to get a capital transcript of the Big Trees' color,—a beautifully bright cinnamon-brown. . . .*

Fitz Hugh Ludlow, *The Heart of the Continent: A Record of Travel Across the Plains and in Oregon, with an Examination of the Mormon Principle* (New York: 1870), p. 424

*Mr. Albert Bierstadt has now established himself for winter's work in the gallery of the Tenth street Studio Building, with two great canvases looking Centennialwards. Both of these are under way. One is an upright, whose most salient feature is the Grizzly Giant, which is to say, one of the great trees of Calaveras County, Cal., a cedar, and it is to be presumed in all essential features a portrait, so that the artistic value of the painting will not be the only element of interest in the work.*

*World*, New York, 26 Nov. 1875

*An immense upright picture by Albert Bierstadt, representing the great trees of California, challenges the admiration of the undiscerning, but it will be hard to discover in it any artistic qualities. I am sadly afraid that Mr. Bierstadt never was equal to his reputation, and that he acquired the latter mainly by a judicious system of advertising. . . . And yet the critical foreigners who examine our pictures have been taught to regard him as America's greatest landscape painter.*

*NY Times*, 13 June 1876

*One of the first men to represent to us on an adequate scale the character of the mountain backbone of North America—its gorges, its forests, its fauna, its lakes and waterfalls—was assuredly Mr. Bierstadt; and we have much pleasure in welcoming him back to this country with his pictures of "fresh fields and pastures new." His two grand works of 'The Sierra Nevada Mountains' and 'The Wellingtonia,' or* Segnoia [*sic*] gigantea, *to speak learnedly, are now on view at the galleries of Messrs. Thomas Agnew and Sons. . . . At first glance one would take the tree we have here for a full-length portrait of a fine Scotch fir, or some tree of a kindred genus; but, on looking down the bole to the men at its base, we find that they are the merest pigmies, and it is then that the proportions of the mighty trunk break upon the eye, and we feel that we are in the presence of one of Nature's Titans. These two pictures belong to an order of landscape quite unknown to British practice, and we have no doubt they will attract the keen interest of British artists.*

*Art Journal* (London), July 1879, p. 142

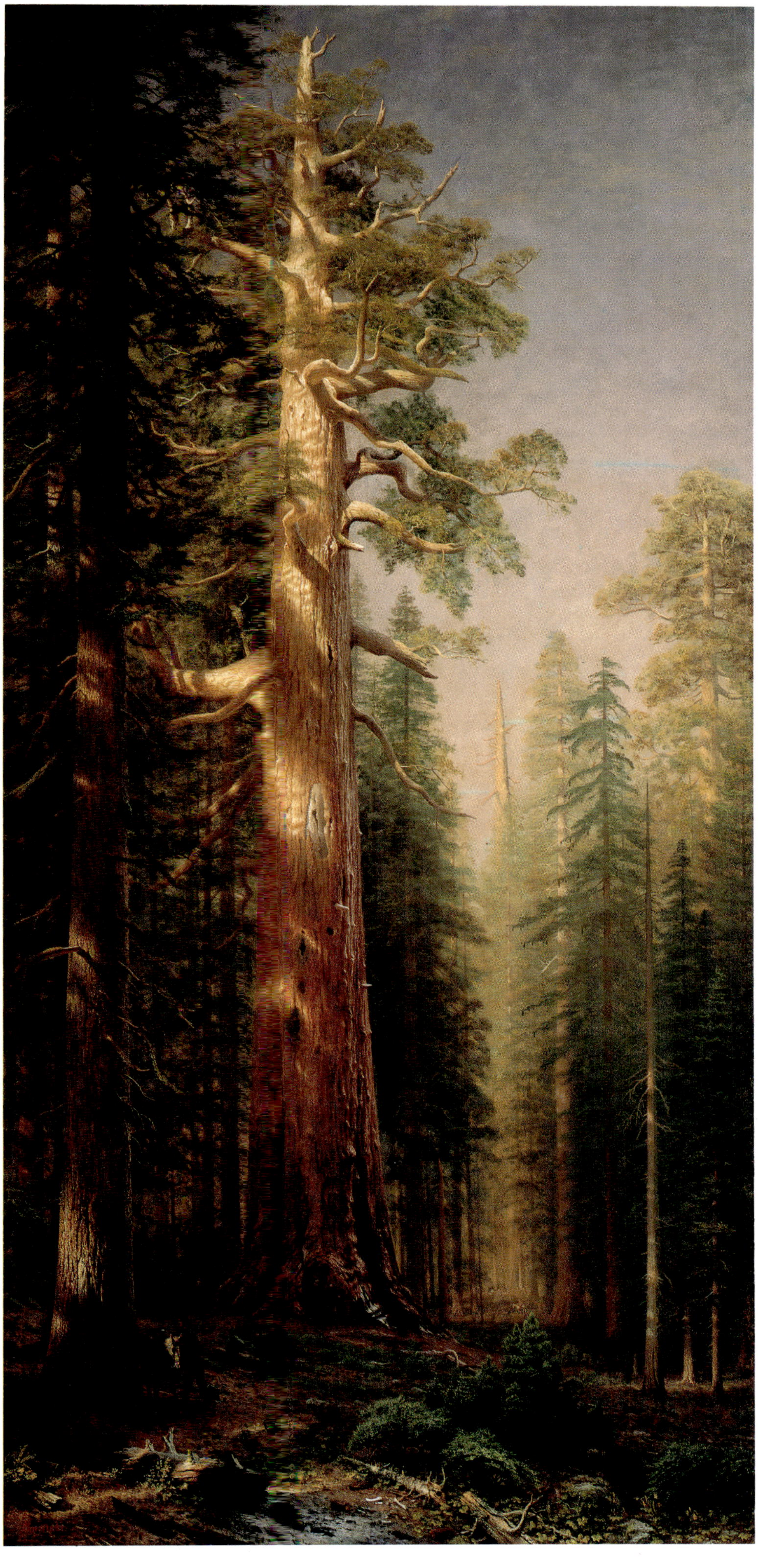

NO. 65

## *The Great Trees, Mariposa Grove, California*, 1876

Oil on canvas, 118⅛ × 59¼ in. (300.1 × 150.5 cm)

Signed lower left: *A Bierstadt*

Private collection

*Bierstadt's new picture of "The Shore of the Turquoise Sea, Bahamas," now on exhibition at Brainard's Art Gallery, is an excellent example of the versatility of his genius, it being, in the strict sense of the term, a marine view, the most prominent objects in which are heavy breakers dashing upon a sandy beach near the town of Nassau, New Providence. These breakers, which rise like a wall in the foreground of the picture, are of that brilliant emerald green peculiar to the salt water of this region; and present a pleasing and striking contrast to the masses of black storm clouds rolling up from the distant horizon. The high, rocky cliff on the left of the picture is powerfully painted, while the little strip of sandy beach in the immediate foreground is remarkable for its realism, its faithful resemblance to nature, indicating much careful study and patient labor. In many respects this is one of the most powerful and satisfactory pictures Mr. Bierstadt has painted in many years. It will remain here but a short time, its destination being the Paris Exposition.*

*Boston Transcript*, 9 Feb. 1878

*Mr. Bierstadt exhibits a marine which is as thin and metallic as ever, but might look well in black and white. Mr. Bierstadt does not want courage; to attempt to paint a tall wave on the scale he has selected, just as the breaker is running along its crest, is no child's play. That Mr. Bierstadt does it well in that sense cannot be denied; given the problem, he does not flinch; but the method of painting, is so inadequate to the task that one longs to see the same thing attempted by a more imaginative and sober painter.*

*NY Times*, 13 Feb. 1880

*[There] hung "The Turquoise Sea" by Mr. Bierstadt, a bright green wave breaking on the shore. The artist's eye has been caught by the tropical color, which is perhaps faithfully depicted, but the water has no life nor motion. It seems made of sugar candy, and a confectioner, with some pistache, could probably produce its counterpart.*

*New York Evening Mail*, 14 Feb. 1880

*Take, for instance, Bierstadt's large picture (No. 334), in the South Room. It represents an alleged incoming surf. There are some toy cliffs on the left, a brown sandy beach that is perfectly dry, a distant view of the sea, seen under a bright blue sky, with a dark, stormy sky in the foreground. There is an enormous incoming breaker, crested with cotton, and there are three or four successive piles of white cotton arranged in rows to the right. . . . Yet in this impossible breaker there is some delicious color. Note the exquisitely transparent emerald green of the upper part of the wave, blending in a cobalt, and from that to an ultramarine and still darker blue, as the water reaches the beach. And yet, beautiful as these colors are in the abstract, has Mr. Bierstadt or any one else ever seen them except in mid-ocean? Certainly they are not to be found on the seashore. But there is every probability that this picture will be looked at and admired, for Mr. Bierstadt encircled his name with a halo when he painted his photographic pictures of the Rocky Mountains and the Yosemite Valley, and there are not many people willing to dissipate the nimbus.*

*New York Evening Express*, 27 Mar. 1880

*This picture by an artist who is nothing, or was nothing if not sensational—for, of late years, Mr. Bierstadt has exhibited but little—affords subject matter for a great deal of talk among the visitors to the gallery, but is in reality not at all a theme for serious criticism. It is, of course, possible that, somewhere on the planet, and perhaps in some well known locality, there may be a sea which breaks upon the shore in the highly colored manner here depicted. But it is, supposing it to be a fact, so unusual and so extravagant a performance on the part of nature that, as we think, it is not the business of art to reproduce it, except it be for scientific purposes, and in that case the artist is bound in his own defense to state where, and when, and under what circumstances, the phenomena here described were met with.*

*NY Tribune*, 18 Apr. 1880

*The South Room is the* ultima Thule *of artistic ambition, for it is in this room that all the finest things are supposed to be put. Here, however, the Hanging Committee have hung Mr. Bierstadt's "Turquoise Sea," and (heaven save the mark!) the South Room must hereafter lose its distinctive characteristic [because of] Mr. Bierstadt's marine eyesore. . . .*

*New York Evening Express*, 8 May 1880

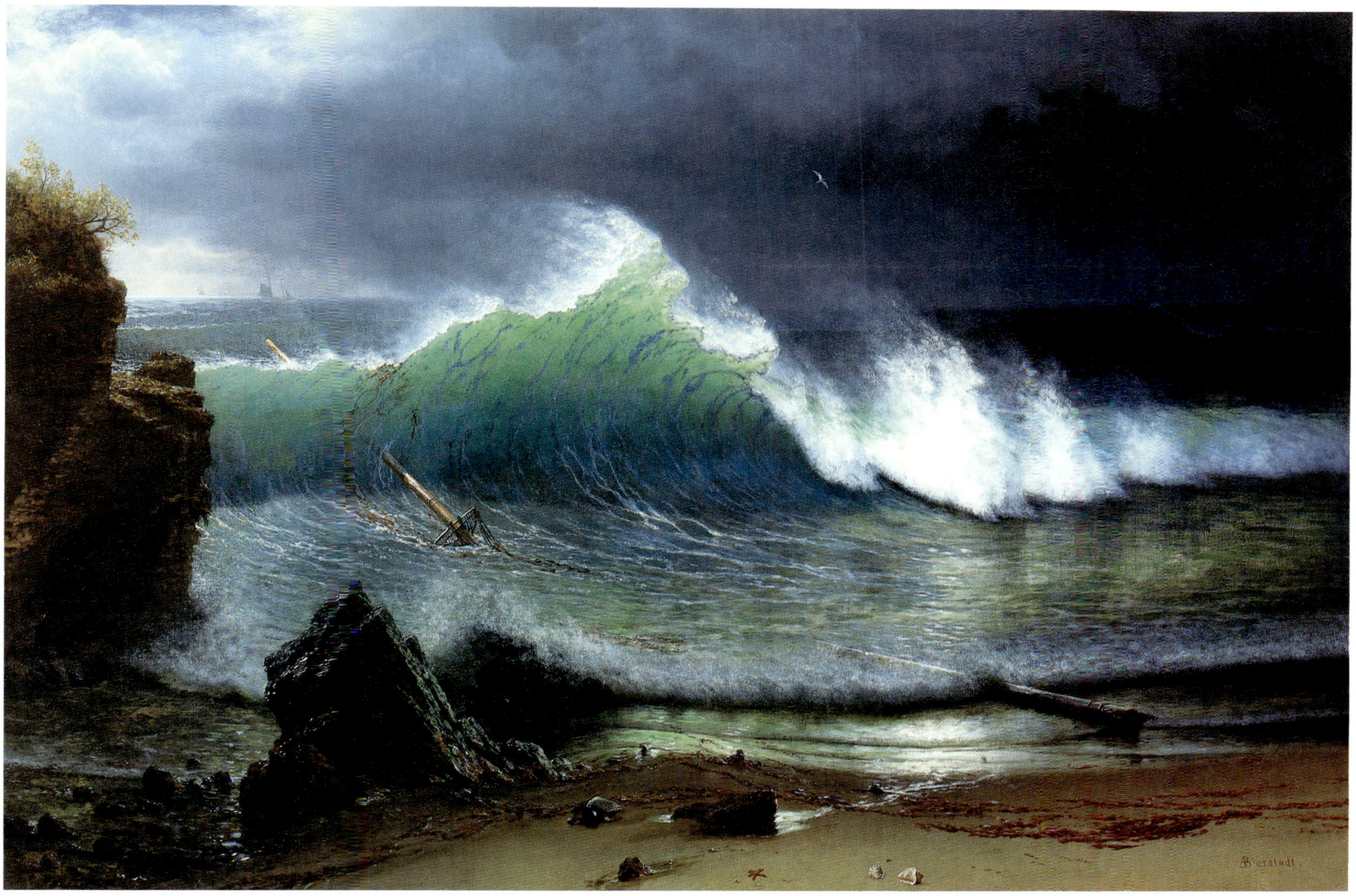

NO. 66

*The Shore of the Turquoise Sea*, 1878

Oil on canvas, 42½ × 64½ in. (108 × 163.8 cm)

Signed lower right: *ABierstadt.*

Manoogian Collection

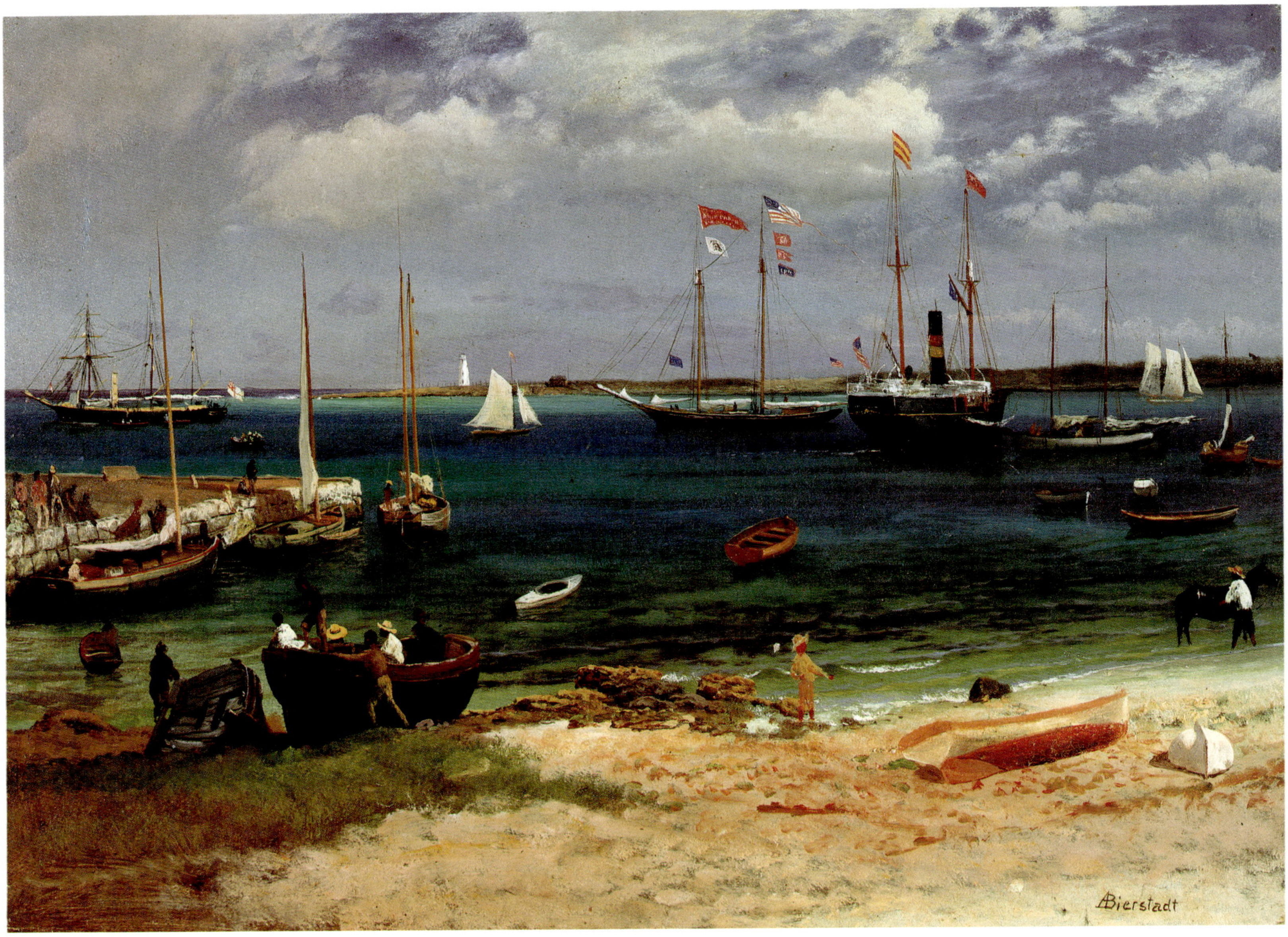


NO. 67

## *Nassau Harbor,* after 1877

Oil on paper mounted on board, 14¾ × 20 in. (37.5 × 50.8 cm)

Signed lower right: *ABierstadt*

The Fine Arts Museums of San Francisco, Mildred Anna Williams Collection

*The city of Nassau is built on the north shore of the island of New Providence. Its harbour is excellent, being protected by a long "Cay"—a name given familiarly to an island in these parts—called Hog Island, which stretches from east to west about half a mile from the shore. The principal entrance to the harbour is at the west end, and is deep enough to admit vessels drawing seventeen feet of water. Within half a mile of the bar the soundings are lost, i.e. they sink suddenly from 15 to 300 fathoms. In an article called "Try the Bahamas," which appeared in the* Fortnightly *for January, 1886, Governor Blake says, speaking of Nassau Harbour:—"The waters, clear as crystal, show ever-varying gradations of colour. No language can describe their tints, and no known pigments can reproduce them." Whilst fully admitting that it requires a much greater command of language than I possess to give an idea of the brilliancy of their tints, I venture to think there are pigments which in hands that know how to use them can reproduce the colouring of Bahamian waters. Bierstadt, for instance, has done it already. . . .*

Louis D. Powles, *The Land of the Pink Pearl, or Recollections of Life in the Bahamas* (London: 1888), pp. 28–29

# 1880–1902

# *Late Years*

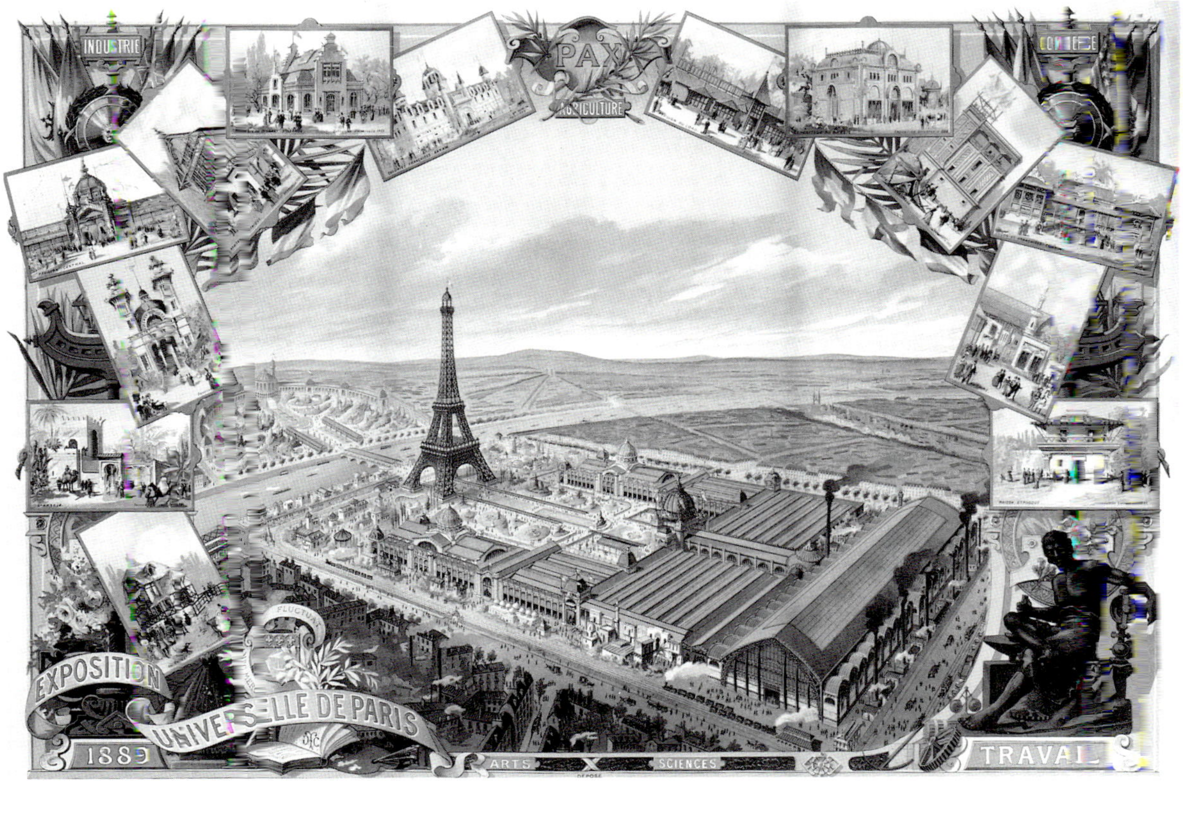

IN JULY 1880, in an article on contemporary American art published in *Scribner's Monthly*, Frederic Church and Albert Bierstadt were described as artists of an older generation whose reputations were in a state of rapid decline (Brownell 1880b, p. 323). As the decade wore on, the perception that a new generation of American artists had come of age and that another was passing into history became a topic of repeated discussion. Invariably, Bierstadt was identified as a member of the older, outmoded generation.

Despite increasingly frequent reviews describing his work as *retardataire*, Bierstadt continued to pursue new subject matter on trips to Canada, Alaska, California, Yellowstone, Nassau, and Europe. He also continued to exhibit at the National Academy of Design, at the monthly meetings of the Century and Union League clubs, and at expositions and fairs in several midwestern and southern cities. Although the market for his work declined in the East, Bierstadt was still accorded celebrity status in more distant cities, where he had greater success selling paintings.

A clear indication of the precipitous drop in the market for Bierstadt's paintings came early in 1882, when the Alvin Adams collection was sold at auction. Adams had purchased two of the artist's most important paintings, *Lake Lucerne (Switzerland)* (No. 6)—the picture with which the artist had made his exhibition debut at the National Academy of Design in 1858—and *Among the Sierra Nevada Mountains, California* (No. 48), a work that had won much acclaim in Europe in 1868 and for which Adams had reportedly paid $15,000. Despite newspaper reports that Bierstadt's paintings attracted more interest than any others during the presale exhibition, *Lake Lucerne (Switzerland)* sold for $3,375 and the Sierra picture for a mere $1,400. Duly reported in the press, such figures further weakened the already declining market for Bierstadt's work.

Not long after the Adams sale, Bierstadt suffered another blow when Malkasten, his lavish home on the Hudson, burned to the ground. Although some paintings were pulled from the house as it burned, many other works (by Bierstadt and other artists), as well as all the furnishings and personal belongings the artist and his wife had collected, were lost.

Early in the 1880s, in what was clearly an effort to reach new markets and expand sales, Bierstadt became involved in a resurrected version of the American Art Union. Until questions were raised regarding its legality, the Art Union sent groups of paintings (for a guaranteed fee if picture sales did not reach a specified level) to fairs and expositions throughout the country. Paintings by artists participating in the union were thus given wide exposure outside the major eastern cities, thereby increasing sales opportunities.

For Bierstadt, picture sales abroad helped counter a slumping market at home. During the 1880s and 1890s, he traveled extensively in Europe, mixing with the social and political elite, who had long been his friends and patrons. By the end of the 1880s, however, enthusiasm for his work had cooled, even in England, where he had sold some of his most important paintings during the 1860s. Perhaps the most telling sign of the shift in Bierstadt's fortunes abroad came in 1887, when none of the twelve pictures he contributed to the American Exhibition in London was sold.

Late in the 1880s, looking to yet another market, Bierstadt turned his attention to Canada, where he hoped to find new subject matter and new patrons among the railroad entrepreneurs. After initial letters of inquiry in which he expressed his interest in painting the natural wonders along the route of the Canadian Pacific Railway, Bierstadt was offered a free pass and unlimited assistance in obtaining the views he wished. His efforts to please the officers of the railroad resulted in a number of paintings of Canadian scenery, but the financial return on his investment of time and energy was disappointing. Several of the large paintings he produced for high-ranking officials were rejected.

In 1888 in preparation for the Exposition Universelle to be held in Paris the following year, Bierstadt undertook what would be the last of his large western showpieces, *The Last of the Buffalo*, 1888 (No. 68). When the picture was rejected later by the American selection committee, considerable controversy arose. Although one of the jurors declared the painting too large (six by ten feet) and not representative of the artist at his best, others suggested that personal ill will and jealousy had played a role. Perhaps the key factor, however, was the change of taste that earlier in the decade had identified Bierstadt as a member of an older, outdated generation. By 1888 his work had come to be seen as representative of America's artistic past, not her future.

Refusing to accede to the judgment of the selection committee, however, Bierstadt exercised his right, as a recipient of the cross of the Legion of Honor, to place any picture he wished on exhibition at the Salon. Thus *The Last of the Buffalo* was on view in Paris during the spring of 1889, but at the Salon rather than at the exposition. Though he maintained a gracious public posture throughout the controversy, Bierstadt was clearly stung by the rejection and did not undertake another panoramic western painting.

Two years later, however, he began making plans for another large picture, which he intended to exhibit at the World's Columbian Exposition in Chicago in 1893. Exercising obvious caution, he chose a subject from history, the landing of Columbus. Contemporary newspapers reported that while in Europe in 1891, Bierstadt had traveled to Spain, Italy, and Portugal to study costumes dating from the time of Columbus. It was similarly reported that while visiting his wife in Nassau in 1892, he had traveled to Watlings Island, where Columbus was believed to have landed in the New World. By June 1892, Bierstadt had completed *The Landing of Columbus*. At the last moment, however, he joined with a number of artists who chose not to submit their pictures to a jury they perceived as biased in favor of a younger generation of artists.

In March 1893, Rosalie Bierstadt died in Nassau. Her death compounded the strain that declining sales, jury rejections, and financial reverses had already placed on the artist.

Late in 1893, in an effort to relieve his financial distress, Bierstadt attempted to revive congressional interest in purchasing the paintings he had deposited at the White House several years earlier. In a serious lapse of judgment (prompted perhaps by an increasingly desperate financial situation), he set a price of $65,000 for the five pictures. When the asking price became known, the press ridiculed the sum, and Congress refused to allocate the funds.

During the last years of his life, Bierstadt attempted to raise money through a number of business ventures unrelated to painting, including a proposal for an expanding railroad car. Having obtained a patent for his design, he attempted to promote the car as a mobile unit that could be turned into a house, a fort, a shop, or even a church. The idea failed to attract investors, however, and was abandoned.

In 1894 Bierstadt married Mary Hicks Stewart, the widow of David Stewart, a wealthy New York banker. Despite the advantageous marriage, Bierstadt's financial condition continued to deteriorate, and in 1895 creditors called in overdue notes. A sheriff's sale was held in the artist's studio. In a complicated legal maneuver, Mary Stewart's brother, Theodore F. Hicks, obtained title to most of the paintings in the studio. With the market for his work already depressed, however, Bierstadt stood little chance of regaining his financial footing.

Following Bierstadt's sudden death on 18 February 1902, obituaries noted the great success the artist had enjoyed during the 1860s and 1870s and the subsequent change of taste that had thrust his work into relative obscurity. Though the author of one obituary wrote that Bierstadt's work was "undervalued," a serious reevaluation of the artist's work did not begin until the 1960s, when a generation schooled in modernism found in Bierstadt's oil sketches an abstraction and economy of stroke they described as "startlingly modern" (Chronology, 1 Mar. 1902; Lewison 1964, p. 33).

# CHRONOLOGY

## 1880

**30 Mar.–29 May** *The Shore of the Turquoise Sea* (No. 66) shown at the NAD Annual Exhibition. (*NY Herald*, 30 Mar. 1880; *American Art Review*, 1880, p. 259; Catalogue, NAD, 1880, p. 21)

**30 Mar.** At the loan exhibition marking the opening of the new Metropolitan Museum of Art building in Central Park, two paintings by Bierstadt are shown: *The Glen*, from the collection of George A. Robbins, and *Sunlight and Shadow* (No. 29), from the collection of Bierstadt's sister Eliza. (Catalogue, Loan Exhibition, Metropolitan Museum of Art, Apr.–Oct. 1880)

**3 Apr.** Bierstadt gives a dinner for the Earl of Dunmore at the Brevoort House in New York City. Guests include Mayor Edward Cooper and Chief Justice Charles P. Daly. (*Boston Transcript*, 5 Apr. 1880)

**10 Apr.** "Albert Bierstadt, while abroad, received an order from the Czar for a picture of Niagara Falls. He expects to have it completed next September." (*Andrews' American Queen*, 10 Apr. 1880, p. 21)

**1 May** Salon in Paris opens to the public. Bierstadt exhibits *Mount Whitney* (Fig. 66). (Catalogue, Salon, 1880, p. 33, as *Le mont Whitney, Californie*)

**13 May** Bierstadt visits the Marquis of Lorne, governor-general of Canada, and Princess Louise in Ottawa. (*Post*, New York, 13 May 1880)

**18 June** Bierstadt writes to James Garfield, candidate for president, asking if his brother Edward and an assistant might come to take photographs of "our next President." (Bierstadt to Garfield, 18 June 1880, Garfield Papers, Library of Congress)

Rosalie Bierstadt departs Nassau for New York. (*Nassau Guardian*, 18 June 1880)

**July** In an article on "The Younger Painters of America," Church and Bierstadt are identified as belonging to an older generation, though "the fame of Mr. Bierstadt is more evidently in decadence than Mr. Church's." (Brownell 1880b, p. 323)

**by 16 July** Bierstadt arrives in San Francisco and immediately leaves for Mount Shasta. (*Bulletin*, San Francisco, 16, 17 July 1880)

**by 2 Aug.** Returns to San Francisco. (*Bulletin*, San Francisco, 2 Aug. 1880)

**14–23 Aug.** Bierstadt is a registered guest at the Hotel Del Monte in Monterey, California. (Accounting ledger, Hotel Del Monte, Pebble Beach Company, Pebble Beach, Calif.)

**24 Aug.** Bierstadt back in San Francisco. (*Bulletin*, San Francisco, 24 Aug. 1880)

**27 Aug.** Leaves San Francisco for New York, having visited Mount Shasta, Clear Lake, and Monterey. (*Bulletin*, San Francisco, 28 Aug. 1880)

**6 Sept.** Bierstadt and his wife en route to Montreal. (ROM/MFA Corresp.)

**9 Oct.** The Bierstadts visit the Citadel, Quebec, as the guests of the governor-general. "Mr. Bierstadt is making some sketches in Quebec. All her friends will be glad to hear that Mrs. Bierstadt's health is much stronger." (*Andrews' American Queen*, 9 Oct. 1880, p. 318)

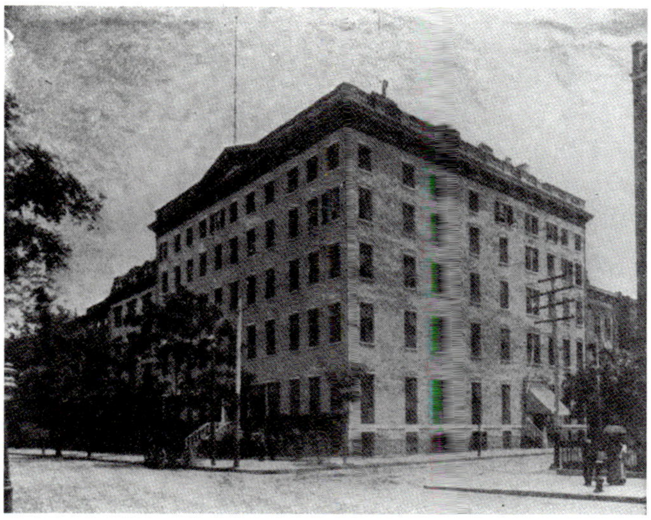

*Brevoort House* (the Bierstadts' New York residence). Photograph published in Henry Collins Brown, *Fifth Avenue Old and New, 1824–1924* (New York: 1924).

**18 Oct.** Bierstadt writes to the editor of the *Times* to say that, contrary to what was printed in the *Express* the preceding week, he is not a Democrat. "Permit me to state that I never voted that ticket; on the contrary, have always been identified with the Republican Party." (*NY Times*, 19 Oct. 1880)

**3 Nov.** Rosalie Bierstadt arrives in Nassau. (*Nassau Guardian*, 3 Nov. 1880)

**26 Dec.** From New York Bierstadt writes his wife of a recent western trip that included Vancouver, Tacoma, San Francisco, Denver, and Chicago. (Bierstadt to Rosalie Bierstadt, 26 Dec. 1880, quoted in ROM/MFA Corresp.)

## 1881

**6 Jan.** Ulysses S. Grant accepts Bierstadt's invitation to join him for dinner at Delmonico's. (Grant to Bierstadt, 6 Jan. 1881, Turner Collection)

**7 Feb.** Bierstadt among those mentioned as a possible candidate for membership in the Royal Academy as an "honorary foreign academician." (*Boston Transcript*, 7 Feb. 1881)

**22 Mar.–14 May** NAD Annual Exhibition open to the public; Bierstadt contributes *Sierra Nevada* (later titled *Mount Whitney*, Fig. 66). (Catalogue, NAD, 1881, p. 24; *Art Amateur*, May 1881, pp. 115, 118; *U.S. Art Directory*, New York, 1882, p. 136)

Negative criticism of Bierstadt's NAD picture includes reference to the fall of his reputation: "Time there was when it had been worth the whole price of admission to see this picture. . . . In this later day, mere scenery has found its proper place, and pictures of more modest purpose and less ambitious scope possess a deeper and more enduring interest." (*Sun*, New York, 27 Mar. 1881)

Describing Bierstadt as "the prince of the sentimentalists at the Academy exhibition," a critic writes of the "huge" *Sierra Nevada:* "American landscape art . . . has passed its Bierstadt period, and at present cares little for the sentimentalism of mere size . . . ; for so-called picturesque effects that are begotten at the expense of sincerity, delicacy and soul. With all his magnitude Mr. Bierstadt never appeals to the sense of grandeur. Even in his bignesses he is pretty and sentimental, not stunning." (*Post*, New York, 16 Apr. 1881)

**28 Mar.** Bierstadt sends Mrs. Rutherford B. Hayes *The Artist's Camp, Lake Tenaya* in thanks for the pleasant memories he has of visits to the White House during the last four

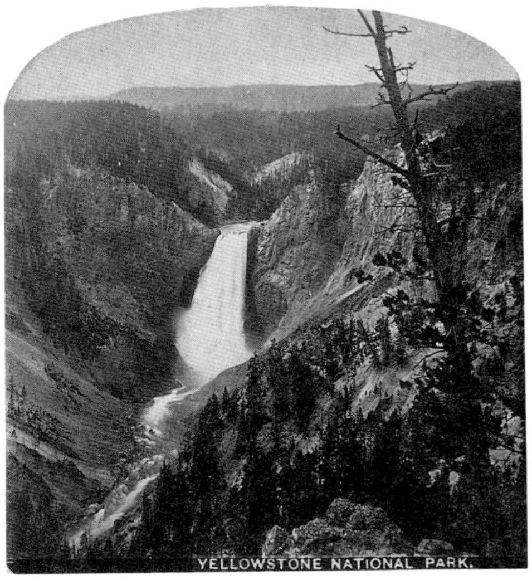


Charles Bierstadt. *Yellowstone National Park*. Stereograph. Private collection.

years. (Bierstadt to Mrs. Hayes, 28 Mar. 1881, Hayes Presidential Center)

**1 May** Bierstadt's New York studio listed at 1271 Broadway, residence at Brevoort House. (New York City Directory, 1881)

**c. 23 June** Bierstadt visits the Citadel in Quebec and goes fishing with the governor-general's party. (ROM/MFA Corresp.)

**c. mid-July** Bierstadt departs for a three-month trip to Yellowstone and the Northwest. (*New York Express*, 28 Oct. 1881; *Missouri Republican*, Saint Louis, 12 Nov. 1881)

**by 4 Oct.** With others, obtains a charter from the state of Illinois to establish an American Art Association in Chicago "for the sale and exhibition of paintings." (*Boston Transcript*, 4 Oct. 1881)

**27 Oct.** Returns to New York following a trip to Yellowstone and the Pacific Northwest. (*New York Express*, 28 Oct. 1881)

**28 Nov.** Rosalie Bierstadt arrives in Nassau and registers at the Royal Victoria Hotel. (Note headed 28 Nov. 1881, GH Papers)

## 1882

Sometime during the year Bierstadt sends President Chester Arthur "three pictures of Yellowstone and two Canadian views" to be hung in the White House. (*Kansas City Times*, 13 Apr. 1884)

**9 Mar.** Collection of paintings to be auctioned from the Alvin Adams estate goes on view at Leonard's in Boston. *Lake Lucerne (Switzerland)* (No. 6) and *Among the Sierra Nevada Mountains, California* (No. 48) included. (*Boston Post*, 11 Mar. 1882)

"The rush to see the Alvin Adams collection of paintings at Leonard's gallery, is something unparalleled, and the admiring crowds that linger in front of the great Bierstadts never grow small from the opening to the closing of the doors." (*Boston Transcript*, 10 Mar. 1882)

*Among the Sierra Nevada Mountains, California*, "for which Mr. Adams is reported to have paid $15,000," sold at the Adams sale for $1,400. (*Globe*, Boston, 17 Mar. 1882; *Boston Post*, 17 Mar. 1882; *Morning Journal*, Boston, 17 Mar. 1882)

*Lake Lucerne (Switzerland)* sold at the Alvin Adams sale for $3,375. (*Boston Transcript*, 18 Mar. 1882; *Boston Post*, 18 Mar. 1882; *Globe*, Boston, 18 Mar. 1882)

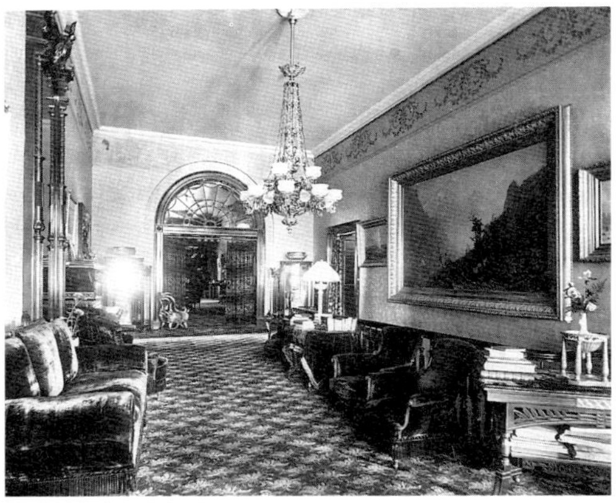

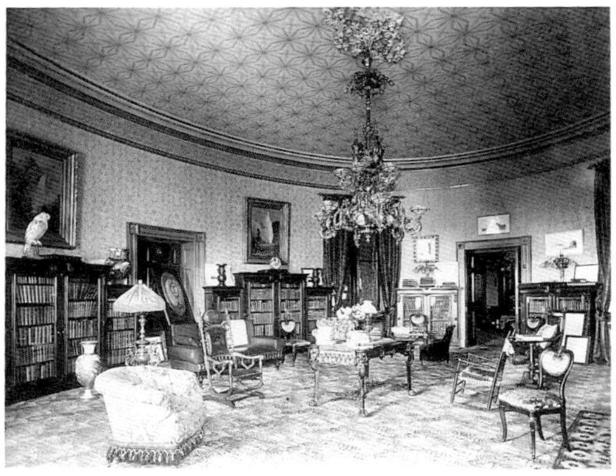

*(top) East Corridor of the White House, with paintings by Bierstadt*, 1890. Photograph. Frances Benjamin Johnston Collection, Library of Congress, Washington, D.C.

*(above) Presidential Library of the White House, with paintings by Bierstadt*, 1890. Photograph. Frances Benjamin Johnston Collection, Library of Congress, Washington, D.C.

**27 Mar.** NAD Annual Exhibition opens; Bierstadt does not contribute. (*Post*, New York, 25 Mar. 1882; Catalogue, NAD, 1882)

**27 Apr.** Rosalie Bierstadt and her sister sail from Nassau for New York. (*Nassau Guardian*, 29 Apr. 1882)

**1 May** Salon in Paris opens to the public. Bierstadt exhibits *Cerfs d'Amérique*. (Catalogue, Salon, 1882, p. 22, no. 251)

**28 June** Bierstadt in Paris. (Bierstadt to Bartlett, Albert Duveen Collection, AAA)

**29 July** Malkasten, Bierstadt's home on the Hudson, reported to be showing signs of neglect. Henry T. Chapman, Jr., currently renting the house. (*Argus*, Tarrytown, N.Y., 29 July 1882)

**5 Sept.** At Niagara Falls, Bierstadt sketches with Princess Louise before she and the Marquis of Lorne depart for the Pacific Coast. (*Buffalo Commercial Advertiser*, 5 Sept. 1882)

**10 Nov.** Malkasten, vacated only the day before by Chapman and his family, burns to the ground. Only a few paintings are saved. Bierstadt states that the loss will be $35,000 to $40,000 above the insurance. (*Post*, New York, 11 Nov. 1882; *NY Herald*, 11 Nov. 1882; *Sun*, New York, 11 Nov. 1882)

## 1883

**1 Jan.** Rosalie Bierstadt arrives in Nassau. (*Nassau Guardian*, 3 Jan. 1883)

**26 Feb.** Bierstadt listed among those favoring bill to be introduced in Congress (27 Feb.) permitting free duty on imported works of art. (*Post*, New York, 26 Feb. 1883; Appendix to the *Congressional Record*, 26 Feb. 1883, p. 133)

**7 Mar.** Bierstadt is in Ottawa. (ROM/MFA Corresp.)

**2 Apr.** NAD Annual Exhibition opens to the public; Bierstadt does not contribute. (*Post*, New York, 2 Apr. 1883; Naylor 1973, p. 59)

**9 Apr.** Bierstadt denies that he has supported a higher duty on works of art. Letter printed from Senator Perry Belmont states that Bierstadt had been vocal in his support of the free-tariff measure. (*NY Herald*, 9 Apr. 1883)

**10 May** Bierstadt is in Ottawa. (Letter, dated 10 May 1883, quoted in ROM/MFA Corresp.)

**11 May** American Art Union incorporated in New York State (Bierstadt a member of the Board of Control). "The organization of the society grew out of the wide spread dissatisfaction with the limited means of bringing the works of American Artists before the public. There was no well-managed permanent gallery for the sale of American pictures, exclusively, in New York City. The general picture dealers handled foreign pictures for exhibition and sale to the almost complete exclusion of the works of American artists." (*Art Union*, Jan. 1884, p. 1)

**2 June** At the Fine Arts Academy in Buffalo, 135 pictures (including Bierstadt's *Storm on Laramie Peak*), selected and sent by the newly established American Art Union, go on exhibition. (*Buffalo Commercial Advertiser*, 2 June 1883)

**15 June** Bierstadt and his wife sail for Liverpool aboard the steamship *Britannic*. (*NY Times*, 15 June 1883; ROM/MFA Corresp.)

**8 July** Bierstadt is described as one of the managers of the American Art Union, which will serve as the chief lender to the Southern Exposition in Louisville. (*Louisville Courier-Journal*, 8 July 1883)

**1 Aug.–10 Nov.** Southern Exposition open in Louisville. Art Gallery not completed until 9 August. (*Louisville Courier-Journal*, 2, 3, 9 Aug., 11 Nov. 1883)

Bierstadt contributes several pictures, including *Mount Whitney*, "which . . . is valued at $25,000." (*Louisville Courier-Journal*, 28 July 1883)

A reviewer of the landscape section of the Art Gallery at the Southern Exposition writes: "The one danger which now besets the American artist is the commercial spirit of gain. This produces the worst form of conventionalism—the copying of one's self. It arrests all development. . . . Its greed has half-way palsied the hand of Bierstadt." (*Louisville Courier-Journal*, 1 Oct. 1883)

**2 Aug.** The Bierstadts are in Paris at Hotel Continental; Albert departs for Berlin. (Oscar Albert Bierstadt Travel Diary, Turner Collection)

**Oct.** Albert and Rosalie Bierstadt sail for New York. (ROM/MFA Corresp.)

**20 Oct.** The Bierstadts arrive in New York. (*NY Times*, 21 Oct. 1883)

**22 Oct.** NAD Annual Exhibition opens to the public; Bierstadt does not contribute. (*Post*, New York, 22 Oct. 1883)

**20 Dec.** At the newly opened American Art Union gallery in New York, Bierstadt exhibits *Nevada Falls*. (*Post*, New York, 20 Dec. 1883)

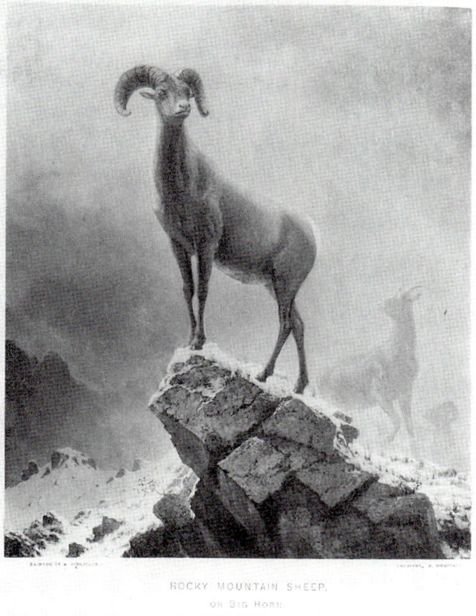


Edward Bierstadt, after Albert Bierstadt. *Rocky Mountain Sheep*. Artotype published in *Art Union*, Apr. 1884. Museum of Fine Arts, Boston.

## 1884

**Jan.** First issue of the *Art Union*, the journal of the newly established American Art Union, published. Bierstadt's *Storm on Laramie Peak* reported sold for $3,500 to a group of citizens in Louisville attempting to establish a permanent art gallery for the city. (*Art Union*, Jan. 1884, pp. 1–2, 6)

**Apr.** April issue of the *Art Union* includes full-page artotype (Fig. 125) after *Rocky Mountain Sheep*. (*Art Union*, Apr. 1884, frontispiece, p. 1)

**5 Apr.–17 May** NAD Annual Exhibition open; Bierstadt exhibits *Near Monterey, California*. (Catalogue, NAD, 1884, p. 26)

**28 May** The Bierstadts sail for England aboard the *Gallia*. (ROM/MFA Corresp.; *NY Times*, 29 May 1884)

**23 June** The Bierstadts leave Paris for Turin, Bellagio, and Lake Como. (ROM/MFA Corresp.)

**12 July** At Lago Maggiore. (ROM/MFA Corresp.)

**13 July** Cross Simplon Pass to Brieg. (ROM/MFA Corresp.)

**16 July** In Paris, en route to Switzerland. (*Post*, New York, 16 July 1884)

**Aug.** In Geneva. (ROM/MFA Corresp.)

**13 Sept.** In Paris. (ROM/MFA Corresp.)

**5 Oct.** Leave for London, whence they continue to New York. (ROM/MFA Corresp.)

**11 Nov.** Rosalie Bierstadt and her sister-in-law arrive in Nassau. (*Nassau Guardian*, 12 Nov. 1884)

## 1885

**6 Apr.–16 May** At the NAD Annual Exhibition, Bierstadt exhibits *Valley of Zermatt, Switzerland*. (Catalogue, NAD, 1885, p. 31; *Boston Transcript*, 16 May 1885)

**11 May** Rosalie Bierstadt sails from Nassau to New York. (*Nassau Guardian*, 13 May 1885)

**Oct.** The Bierstadts are in Waterville. (Unidentified clipping, Bierstadt Scrapbook, Edwards Collection)

**16 Nov.** Rosalie Bierstadt and her sister arrive in Nassau from New York. (*Nassau Guardian*, 18 Nov. 1885)

**1 Dec.** Bierstadt sketches exhibited in Nassau. (*Nassau Guardian*, 2 Dec. 1885)

## 1886

**5 Apr.–15 May** NAD Annual Exhibition open. Bierstadt contributes *On the Saco, New Hampshire* and *California Oaks*. (*Boston Transcript*, 5 Apr. 1886; Catalogue, NAD, 1886, pp. 49, 52)

**May** Colonial and Indian Exhibition opens in London. Bierstadt contributes three paintings with Canadian subjects: *Montmorency Falls, Quebec*; *Quebec Citadel*; and *View from Government House, Ottawa*; as well as *The Rocky Mountains, Lander's Peak* (No. 37); *Storm in the Rocky Mountains, Mt. Rosalie* (No. 45); *After a Norther Off the Bahamas* (*A Wave Breaking on the Bahamas Coast*, Haggin Museum, Stockton, Calif.); and *Estes Park, Long's Peak* (*The Rocky Mountains, Longs Peak*, Fig. 65). (Pringle 1985, p. 7; *NY Times*, 19 Feb. 1902)

**3 May** Rosalie Bierstadt sails from Nassau for New York. (*Nassau Guardian*, 5 May 1886)

**July** Twenty-five paintings by Bierstadt on exhibition in Milwaukee for the benefit of the Milwaukee Art School. (Catalogue, Milwaukee Art Museum, 1886)

**10 Aug.** Bierstadt in Milwaukee. (*Sentinel*, Milwaukee, 10 Aug. 1886)

**11 Aug.** Bierstadt presents the Milwaukee Art School with *The Weeping Oak, California*, valued at $3,000. (*Sentinel*, Milwaukee, 12 Aug. 1886)

## 1886–1889

**23 Aug.** Minneapolis Industrial Exposition opens. Both Bierstadt and William Bradford have "whole rooms hung with the choicest paintings from their studios." In a catalogue published in 1887 for the second Minneapolis Exposition, a commentator wrote that in 1886 Bierstadt "took a special interest in our first grand Exposition and besides bringing in all his unsold pictures borrowed many from owners and showed a large room full of his own brilliant paintings. He was here most of the time, met many of our citizens and sold a dozen or more paintings at good prices." (*Minneapolis Tribune*, 23, 25 Aug. 1886; *Minneapolis and the Great Exposition, Annual 1887*, p. 31)

Describing the paintings at the Minneapolis Exposition, a reporter writes: "Bierstadt's stand at the head in the number and value. His large painting of Mount Whitney, in the Sierra Nevada mountains, comes first in price, the figure being $25,000. Next is the Mariposa grove of big California trees, at $20,000." (*Minneapolis Tribune*, 5 Sept. 1886)

**28 Aug.** At the Southern Exposition in Louisville, Bierstadt exhibits *California Oaks; Capri, Bay of Naples; Laramie Peak, Rocky Mountains; On the Passaic River, New Jersey;* and *Sunrise on the Matterhorn, Switzerland.* (Catalogue, Southern Exposition, Louisville, 1886)

**14 Sept.** Bierstadt is special commissioner for an "American Exhibition" planned for the following year in London, with John Sartain as chief of the department of fine arts. (*Boston Transcript*, 14 Sept. 1886)

**26 Nov.** Bierstadt reported to have received a decoration from the sultan of Turkey. (*Utica Morning Herald*, 26 Nov. 1886)

**13 Dec.** Rosalie Bierstadt, traveling with a nurse, arrives in Nassau and registers at the Royal Victoria Hotel. (*Nassau Guardian*, 15 Dec. 1886)

### 1887

**12 Jan., 8 Feb.** Bierstadt reportedly endeavoring to sell the paintings on loan to the White House for several years. Writing to an unidentified correspondent, he asks for assistance in securing a "lobbyist" to promote the purchase by the government. (*Boston Transcript*, 12 Jan. 1887; Bierstadt to unidentified correspondent, 8 Feb. 1887, AAA)

**9–11 Feb.** Bierstadt's *Sierra Nevada—Morning*, 1879, sold at estate sale of Robert Graves to Judge Henry Hilton for $2,450, the highest price paid for an American picture. (*Art Amateur*, Mar. 1887, p. 75)

**23–25 Mar.** At the sale of the A. T. Stewart Collection, three paintings by Bierstadt sold: *Seal Rock, San Francisco*, 1872 (private collection, California), $2,500; *Natural Park and Lake, Southern California*, $2,500; and *The Emerald Pool* (Fig. 33), $3,100. (Sales Catalogue, Stewart Collection, pp. 51, 72, 81; *Commercial Advertiser*, New York, 24, 25 Mar. 1887)

**1 Apr.** NAD Annual Exhibition opens to the press; Bierstadt does not contribute. (*Commercial Advertiser*, New York, 1 Apr. 1887; Catalogue, NAD, 1887)

**9 May–31 Oct.** American Exhibition open in London. Buffalo Bill's Wild West Show and a gallery of American paintings headline the exhibition. Bierstadt exhibits *Storm in the Rocky Mountains, Mt. Rosalie* (No. 45); *A Geyser of the Yellowstone; Sentinel Rock after a Snow Storm, Yosemite Valley; The Geyser of the Yellowstone; Autumn Woods, Oneida County, State of New York* (New-York Historical Society); *Rain Storm on the Lake; Sunshine and Shade* (*Sunlight and Shadow*, No. 29); *Storm on the Matterhorn* (Joslyn Art Museum, Omaha); *Sunset; Escape from an Indian Attack* (private collection, California); *Washingtonia Gigantia, or Great Trees of California, Mariposa Valley;* and *After a Norther (Bahamas)* (*A Wave Breaking on the Bahamas Coast*). (*Times*, London, 10 May 1887; *American Exhibition: Art Catalogue*, London, 1887, pp. 29–30)

**13 June** From New York Bierstadt writes to Sir George Stephen, president of the Canadian Pacific Railway, asking where he might obtain the "latest maps and photographs" of the scenery through which the railroad passes. (Bierstadt to Stephen, 13 June 1887, CPR Archives)

**24 June** William C. Van Horne, general manager, Canadian Pacific Railway, responds to Bierstadt's letter to Stephen and offers the artist passage on the railroad and letters of introduction. (Bierstadt did not make the trip until 1889.) (Van Horne to Bierstadt, 24 June 1887, CPR Archives)

**27 June** Rosalie Bierstadt departs Nassau for New York. (*Nassau Guardian*, 29 June 1887)

**24 Aug.** The Bierstadts are in Switzerland. (Bierstadt to Van Horne, 24 Aug. 1887, CPR Archives)

**31 Aug.–15 Oct.** Second Annual Minneapolis Exposition open; Bierstadt exhibits *Farrallone Islands*, which is listed for sale at $3,000. (*Minneapolis and the Great Exposition, Annual 1887*, p. 39)

**12 Oct.** From New York Bierstadt writes to John Sartain expressing his regret that none of his pictures at the American Exhibition in London have sold. (Bierstadt to Sartain, 12 Oct. 1887, AAA)

**21 Nov.–17 Dec.** Sixth Annual Autumn Exhibition at the NAD open; Bierstadt represented by *Olevano, Italy*. (*Commercial Advertiser*, New York, 18 Nov. 1887; Catalogue, NAD, 1887, p. 18; *NY Tribune*, 18 Dec. 1887)

### 1888

**Jan.** Regarding the Union League Club exhibition in December, a writer for the *Art Amateur* comments, "Albert Bierstadt's coarse painting of disporting seals on 'Farallon Island' and F. E. Church's gaudy 'Tropical Landscape' were interesting as examples of the dreadful things which were considered good art less than a generation ago." (*Art Amateur*, Jan. 1888, p. 28)

**12 Jan.** Sub-Tropical Exposition opens in Jacksonville, Florida. Bierstadt exhibits *Farrallone Islands off Coast of California;*

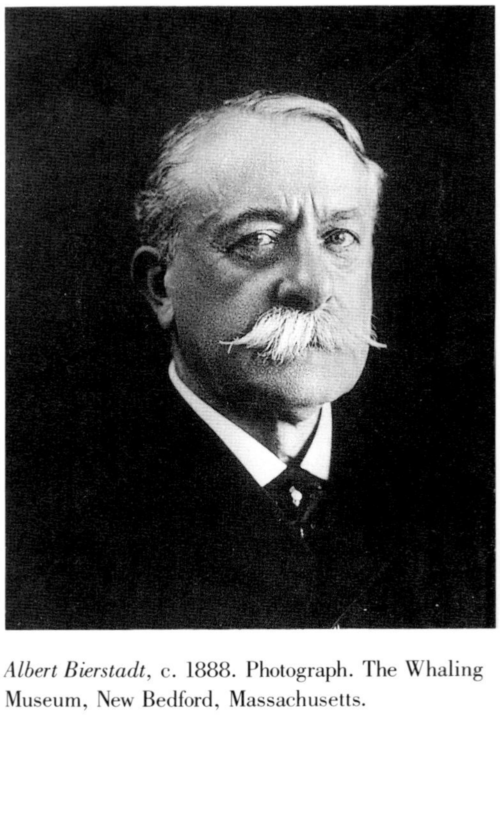

*Albert Bierstadt*, c. 1888. Photograph. The Whaling Museum, New Bedford, Massachusetts.

*Early Snow Lake in Nova Scotia; Niagara Falls; Sunset, Cypress Point, California;* and *A Moose Head*. All are listed as for sale. (*Art Catalogue of Sub-Tropical Exposition*, 1888, pp. 20, 23, 29, 31, 36)

**2 Apr.–12 May** NAD Annual Exhibition open to the public. Bierstadt represented by *Summit Lake, Colorado*, the last work he will contribute to an NAD exhibition. (*Post*, New York, 30 Mar. 1888; Catalogue, NAD, 1888, p. 24; *NY Times*, 11 May 1888)

**June–Nov.** A series of letters from Bierstadt to Colonel Woodworth indicates that the artist's energies are focused on a business venture related to the sale of guns. (Bierstadt to Van Horne, July–Aug. 1888, CPR Archives; Bierstadt to Woodworth, July–Nov. 1888, AAA)

**9 Nov.** Bierstadt continues to lobby for sale of paintings on loan to the White House. (Bierstadt to unidentified correspondent, 9 Nov. 1888, AAA)

## 1889

**10 Jan.** Bierstadt exhibits *The Last of the Buffalo* (No. 68) at the Union League Club in New York. (Exhibition Records, 1889, Union League Club, New York)

**11 Jan.** William Sartain writes to his father, reporting that Bierstadt has asked if the elder Sartain would sketch *The Last of the Buffalo* in preparation for a print after the painting. (William Sartain to John Sartain, 11 Jan. 1889, Sartain Collection, Historical Society of Pennsylvania, Philadelphia)

**17 Jan.** Bierstadt writes to General William T. Sherman, inviting him to his studio to see his "buffalo hunt," which he describes as "nearly completed." (Bierstadt to Sherman, 17 Jan. 1889, Sherman Papers, Library of Congress)

**12 Feb.** At the sale of the James Stebbins collection, a painting of Mount Hood by Bierstadt sells for $400 and *Sunset in the Yosemite Valley* (No. 47) for $1,550. (*NY Herald*, 13 Feb. 1889)

**8 Mar.** In a lengthy article discussing the American representation at the Paris Exposition, *The Last of the Buffalo* is said to have been rejected. (*NY Herald*, 8 Mar. 1889)

**Mar.–May** A storm of controversy surrounds the selection of works for Paris: "It is to MR. BIERSTADT's great credit that the vote in the negative was unanimous. . . . MR. BIERSTADT's great picture was so singularly different from those chosen by the Committee,

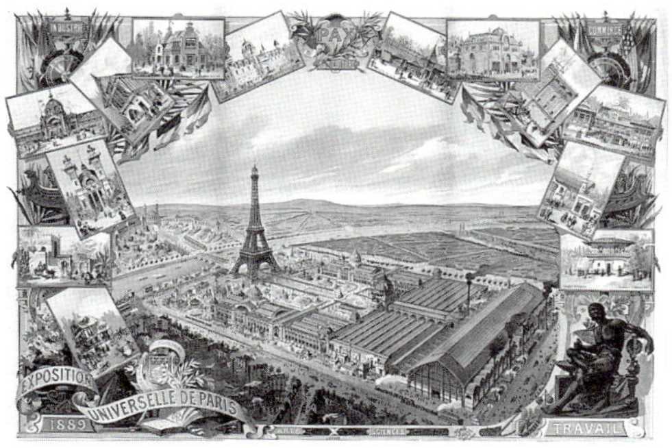


*Exposition Universelle de Paris*, 1889. Poster. Collection of Phillip Dennis Cate and Family.

both in merit and value, that its rejection was imperative—the more urgently because nineteen-twentieths of the exhibit were selected by said Committee from the works of its own members." (*World*, New York, 17 Mar. 1889)

One of the selection committee jurors for the Paris Exposition is quoted as saying that "the Bierstadt was too large, and 'did not represent him as he should be in a national exhibition like this one in Paris.' " The Springfield *Republican* continues: "The proper thing to have done, one would say, was to communicate with Mr. Bierstadt and invite him to send another painting. At any rate, the arbitrary exclusion of so prominent a painter exposes the committee to unpleasant insinuations. Personal rivalry should be excluded in an affair of that sort." (*Republican*, Springfield, Mass., 21 June 1889)

**1 May–15 June** Although rejected by the selection committee for the Exposition Universelle, *The Last of the Buffalo* is on exhibition at the Salon in Paris. (*Boston Transcript*, 31 Jan. 1889; Catalogue, Salon, 1889, p. 20, no. 248, as *Chasse aux bisons*)

**16 July** Bierstadt writes to Van Horne: "I expect to make the trip over your road in about ten days. My wife's ill health will not permit her to go to Europe as we had intended and I hope to see in a few weeks some of the beautiful scenery on the Canadian Pacific." (Bierstadt to Van Horne, 16 July 1889, CPR Archives)

**22 July** Bierstadt writes Van Horne that he expects to arrive in Montreal 30 July and asks him to provide a letter that will allow him to get off and on the train "at some wild places in the mountains." (Bierstadt to Van Horne, 22 July 1889, CPR Archives)

**30 July** Bierstadt leaves Montreal. (Van Horne to John Niblock et al., 30 July 1889, CPR Archives)

**5 Aug** Arrives in Banff, Alberta. Forest fires have filled the air with smoke, obscuring the mountain views. Bierstadt decides to go directly to the coast. He plans to return later, noting that the "scenery is fine" and "will pay me well." (Bierstadt to Rosalie Bierstadt, 5 Aug. 1889, quoted in ROM/MFA Corresp.)

**28 Aug.** The steamer *Ancon*, with Bierstadt aboard, is wrecked in Loring Bay, Alaska. (E. W. Wright, *Lewis and Dryden's Marine History of the Pacific Northwest* [Portland, Oreg.: 1895], p. 371)

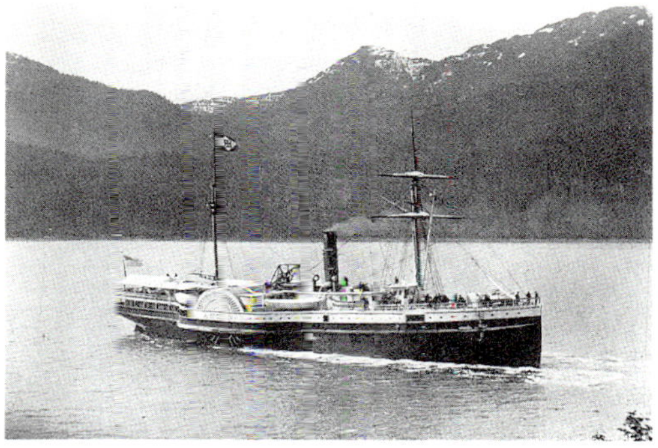

*The Steamship "Ancon."* Photograph published in E. W. Wright, *Lewis and Dryden's Marine History of the Pacific Northwest* (Portland, Oreg.: 1895).

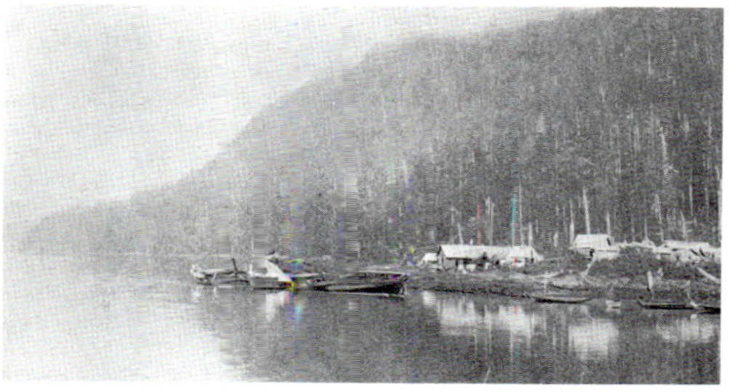

*The Steamship "Ancon" wrecked*. Photograph published in E. W. Wright, *Lewis and Dryden's Marine History of the Pacific Northwest* (Portland, Oreg.: 1895).

**18 Sept.** From Vancouver, British Columbia, Bierstadt writes to Rosalie describing the wreck of the *Ancon* as a "narrow escape" and indicates that he and the other passengers spent five days living in Indian huts and salmon canneries. "I was busy all the time and have 60 studies in color and two books full of drawings of Alaska." He indicates that he has just returned from Portland, Oregon, where he made studies of Mount Hood. (Bierstadt to Rosalie Bierstadt, 18 Sept. 1889, quoted in ROM/MFA Corresp.)

**3 Oct.** Bierstadt in Tacoma, Washington Territory, making sketches of Mount Tacoma (Mount Rainier). (*Utica Morning Herald*, 3 Oct. 1889)

## 1889–1893

**12 Nov.** Bierstadt back in New York. (Bierstadt to Van Horne, 12 Nov. 1889, CPR Archives)

**by 27 Nov.** Rosalie Bierstadt in Nassau for the season. (*Nassau Guardian*, 27 Nov. 1889)

## 1890

**9 Jan.** At the monthly meeting of the Union League Club, Bierstadt exhibits *Mount Sir Donald*. "The half hundred landscapes are led, so far as size is concerned, by a great mountain view by Mr. Albert Bierstadt whose early training in the Rocky Mountain landscape now stands him in stead when the Canadian Pacific has opened up the wonderful formations of Western British America. He has chosen Mount Sir Donald, named from the Canadian who won a knighthood for his service to the Canadian Pacific Railway [Donald Alexander Smith]." (*NY Times*, 12 Jan. 1890)

**27 Feb.** From New York Bierstadt writes to Van Horne that he will keep *Mount Sir Donald* for "[Sir Donald] to look at. Of course if he likes it he would not object to its exhibition at the Royal Academy in London but he might prefer it to be seen in our Academy here. I think they would give it a good place in London and call attention to the beautiful scenery on your road." (Bierstadt to Van Horne, 27 Feb. 1890, CPR Archives)

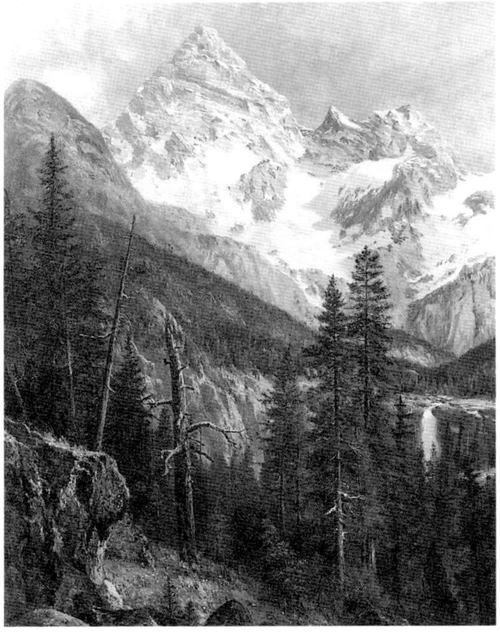

Albert Bierstadt. *Mount Sir Donald*, c. 1889. Oil on canvas. Haggin Collection, The Haggin Museum, Stockton, California.

**7 Apr.** From New York Bierstadt writes to Van Horne, stating that he may have an opportunity to sell *Mount Sir Donald*, which he had offered to Sir Donald for $10,000. Bierstadt goes on to report that he has finished his painting of Lake Louise and has sold a Yosemite winter scene for $15,000. (Bierstadt to Van Horne, 7 Apr. 1890, CPR Archives)

**23 May** Bierstadt arranges to send *The Last of the Buffalo* to Washington for exhibition at the Corcoran Gallery of Art but states that "the picture is not offered for sale." (Bierstadt to Sir, 23 May 1890, Corcoran Archives)

**3 June** In a long review of *The Last of the Buffalo*, on view at the Corcoran Gallery, a writer for the *Evening Star* reports, "The picture has already been sold (for $50,000) and 'published' in France, and will be delivered to the owner at the close of its exhibition here." Price and sale unconfirmed. (*Evening Star*, Washington, D.C., 3 June 1890)

**11 June** From New York Bierstadt writes to Van Horne, stating that Sir Donald did not have time to see *Mount Sir Donald* before he departed for Europe. Bierstadt offers the painting to Sir George Stephen. *Lake Louise* is also offered, at a price of $5,000. "If the Company will give me some stock for the Sir Donald I will think well of it as I would like to be a part owner of some of the finest scenery on this continent." (Bierstadt to Van Horne, 11 June 1890, CPR Archives)

**16 June** Van Horne replies to Bierstadt's letter, indicating that Sir George Stephen "cannot make use of" *Mount Sir Donald* "owing to its size." Van Horne also informs Bierstadt that Sir George is not enthusiastic about the painting of Lake Louise and suggests the artist try a different subject. (Van Horne to Bierstadt, 16 June 1890, CPR Archives)

**21 July** Bierstadt writes to Van Horne suggesting that the title of *Mount Sir Donald* be changed to "a view in the Selkirk Range." "I have thought that Sir Donald had some reluctance in calling to see his namesake and a change in its name might be more acceptable to him. Of course among his friends it would always bear his name. You know him better than I do and to me a beautiful mountain like this is worthy of Sir Donald." (Bierstadt to Van Horne, 21 July 1890, CPR Archives)

**23 Aug.** *Lake Louise* rejected by Sir George Stephen; Van Horne suggests a view of Mount Baker and recommends that Bierstadt use the Canadian Pacific Railway line to make studies of the mountain. (Van Horne to Bierstadt, 23 Aug. 1890, CPR Archives)

**28 Aug.** Bierstadt replies to Van Horne that Mount Baker "will certainly make a fine picture" and says he will go there in about ten days to two weeks. (Bierstadt to Van Horne, 28 Aug. 1890, CPR Archives)

**17 Sept.** *The Last of the Buffalo*, exhibited in the art gallery at the Minneapolis Exposition, described as "one of the great features of the art collection. . . . This picture has the highest value of any in the art gallery. It is listed at $50,000." (*Minneapolis Tribune*, 17 Sept. 1890)

**15 Oct.** Bierstadt departs New York for Montreal. (Telegram, Bierstadt to Van Horne, 15 Oct. 1890, CPR Archives)

**10 Nov.** Rosalie Bierstadt arrives in Nassau and registers at the Royal Victoria Hotel. (*Nassau Guardian*, 12, 26 Nov., 10 Dec. 1890)

## 1891

**7 Mar.** Bierstadt writes to James J. Hill, railroad financier, inviting him to his studio to view a painting of Mount Tacoma, "one of the grandest of mountains" and one located "on the line of your road." (Bierstadt to Hill, 7 Mar. [1891], Hill Library, Saint Paul, Minn.)

**24 Mar.** Van Horne writes to Bierstadt in New York that Sir George Stephen has instructed an agent to send Bierstadt a check for *Mount Baker*. Sir Donald declines to purchase *Mount Sir Donald*. (Van Horne to Bierstadt, 24 Mar. 1891, CPR Archives)

**27 Apr.** Rosalie Bierstadt sails from Nassau for New York. (*Nassau Guardian*, 29 Apr. 1891)

**31 May** Bierstadt continues to press for the purchase of the White House paintings, writing to President Benjamin Harrison directly. (Bierstadt to Harrison, 31 May 1891, Harrison Papers, Library of Congress)

**2 June** Bierstadt is in London. (Bierstadt to Van Horne, 2 June 1891, CPR Archives)

**20 July** Bierstadt's nephew writes to his wife, "The family think Uncle Albert has sold some pictures to the enormously wealthy 'Nitrate King' Col. North. . . ." (Oscar Albert

Bierstadt to his wife, 20 July 1891, Turner Collection)

"Bierstadt's magnificent painting, 'The Last of the Buffalo,' . . . now fills the place of honor in the great picture gallery of the millionaire Col. North, the Nitrate King, who purchased it at a cost of $50,000. As Col. North has been assisted in the selection of the works of art which fill his gallery by Sir Frederick Leighton and other of the most eminent English painters, the choice of Mr. Bierstadt's picture and the fact that the price paid for it is without parallel in the annals of American Art may be regarded as a tribute to the magnificent conception of the artist and as a condemnation of the New York Committee which took upon itself to refuse a place to this magnificent masterpiece." (Unidentified, undated clipping, Bierstadt Scrapbook, Edwards Collection)

**31 July** Bierstadt is in Berlin. (Oscar Albert Bierstadt to his wife, 31 July 1891, Turner Collection)

**early Aug.** Bierstadt travels to Brussels, Cologne, and Berlin. (Oscar Albert Bierstadt to his wife, 4 Aug. 1891, Turner Collection)

**10 Aug.** Bierstadt on the Isle of Wight, visiting the Marquis of Lorne and Princess Louise at Osborne House. (Hendricks 1973, p. 280; GH Papers, 10 Aug. 1891)

**c. mid-Aug.** Bierstadt returns home from Europe, where he has been for several months studying for his picture of. 'The Landing of Columbus,' to be exhibited for the first time at the World's Fair in Chicago [not shown]. He has visited Spain, Italy and Portugal, studying the costumes of the time of Columbus in museums and palaces. . . . In the San Salvador group of islands, some years ago, he made studies for all the flora required in this painting." (Unidentified, undated clipping, Bierstadt Scrapbook, Edwards Collection)

**26 Oct.–24 Dec.** *The Last of the Buffalo* and a number of other paintings on exhibition at the Hanover Gallery in London. The *Magazine of Art* is critical: "These ambitious canvases have no point of contact with art. Their energy is as admirable as the information they convey is useful; but Mr. Bierstadt has sought to paint the unpaintable, and to sacrifice the considerations of dignity and colour to theatrical effect. His style, too, is wholly undistinguished, and, though the untravelled may learn as much from his canvases as from a coloured photograph, the critic turns away from them with relief." (*Times*, London, 26 Oct., 16 Nov. 24 Dec. 1871; *Magazine of Art*, Dec. 1871 p. xi; *Collector*, 1 Nov. 1891, p. 11)

**23 Nov.** Rosalie Bierstadt arrives in Nassau. (*Nassau Guardian*, 25 Nov. 1891)

**29 Nov.** *The Last of the Buffalo, Mount Tacoma*, and *The Rocky Mountains* are among seventy-five pictures by American artists included in the Berlin International Exhibition. "The only American painter not resident abroad was Mr. Albert Bierstadt." (*NY Times*, 29 Nov. 1891)

## 1892

**14 Jan.** Bierstadt elected member of the Union League Club art committee. (*Collector*, 15 Jan. 1892, p. 88)

**18 Jan.** Plans a trip to Nassau, where he hopes to take the private yacht of the governor-general of the Bahamas to Watlings Island to make sketches for the picture he will contribute to the 1893 World's Columbian Exposition. (William E. Curtis to Frederic Ward Putnam, 18 Jan. 1892, Putnam Papers, Harvard University Archives, Cambridge, Mass.)

**15 Feb.** Arrives in Nassau. (*Nassau Guardian*, 17 Feb. 1892)

**20 Feb.** Goes to Watlings Island. (*Nassau Guardian*, 20 Feb. 1892)

**14–15 Apr.** At the sale of the William B. Dinsmore estate, *Among the Sierra Mountains, California* (No. 48) sold for $8,000, "the highest price of the evening," to the son of the former owner. (*NY Herald*, 16 Apr. 1892)

**by 2 Nov.** Rosalie Bierstadt, who "has been recently suffering from a severe illness," arrives in Nassau. (*Nassau Guardian*, 2 Nov. 1892)

## 1893

**21 Feb.** Bierstadt, "whose paintings of the Yosemite are famous and fairly representative of American art," listed among those who will not submit works to the New York selection committee for the World's Columbian Exposition. Discontent with the committee's perceived preference for paintings in the modern "French or German style" is widespread. A clear split between the older and younger artists is seen. "The older artists say they are disappointed in the hope that the exhibit would be fairly representative of what America has done in art and what she is doing." One unidentified older artist is quoted as saying, "They call us the 'Hudson River School,' and lose no opportunity to speak contemptuously of us and our work." (*Sun*, New York, 21 Feb. 1893)

**1 Mar.** Rosalie Bierstadt dies in Nassau after "a prolonged struggle with pulmonary disease . . . Despite her long illness, her death was unexpected, as she had only recently rallied from a dangerous prostration." Her body is to be brought to Waterville for burial. (*Post*, New York, 2 Mar. 1893; *NY Tribune*, 2 Mar. 1893)

**7 Mar.** Financially pressed, Bierstadt revives the issue of the White House paintings, asking if the pictures can be sold or a loan made against them. (Bierstadt to Cooke, 7 Mar. 1893, AAA)

**12 Mar.** Rosalie Bierstadt is buried in Waterville, New York. (Unidentified clipping, Bierstadt Scrapbook, Edwards Collection)

**17 Apr.** Bierstadt listed among the incorporators (with Cornelius Vanderbilt, Andrew Carnegie, J. P. Morgan, and others) of the Historic Art Association, which proposes to exhibit masterpieces from the history of American art in "the large cyclorama building in Chicago" as an expression of discontent with the selection committee for the World's Fair. (*NY Times*, 17 Apr. 1893)

**2 June** Granted a patent for a specially constructed railroad car with side walls and a roof that may be opened outward to form an expanded dwelling. (U.S. Patent Office, Patent No. 559,965; renewed 15 Oct. 1895)

**Oct.** A bill before Congress proposing the purchase of Bierstadt's five White House pictures for $65,000 draws fire: "The bill . . . fairly takes one's breath away. The idea that the Government should encourage American art by buying American paintings is all right, but it is to be hoped that it will show some little discrimination. Think of $65,000 worth of Bierstadts! And at $13,000 each! Really, Mr. Bierstadt, this is carrying a joke too far." (*Art Amateur*, Oct. 1893, p. 104)

**29 Nov.** From New York Bierstadt writes to President Grover Cleveland, strongly advocating the removal of the tariff on works of art. (Bierstadt to Cleveland, 29 Nov. 1893, Cleveland Papers, Library of Congress)

**9 Dec.** Lengthy article on the history of the art-tariff controversy describes the formation of a National Art Association to lobby for the removal of the tariff and lists Bierstadt as one of the vice-presidents of the organization. (*Boston Transcript*, 9 Dec. 1893) interest only were sold in forty paintings, as there was a lien on them for $20,000." (*NY Times*, 18 July 1895)

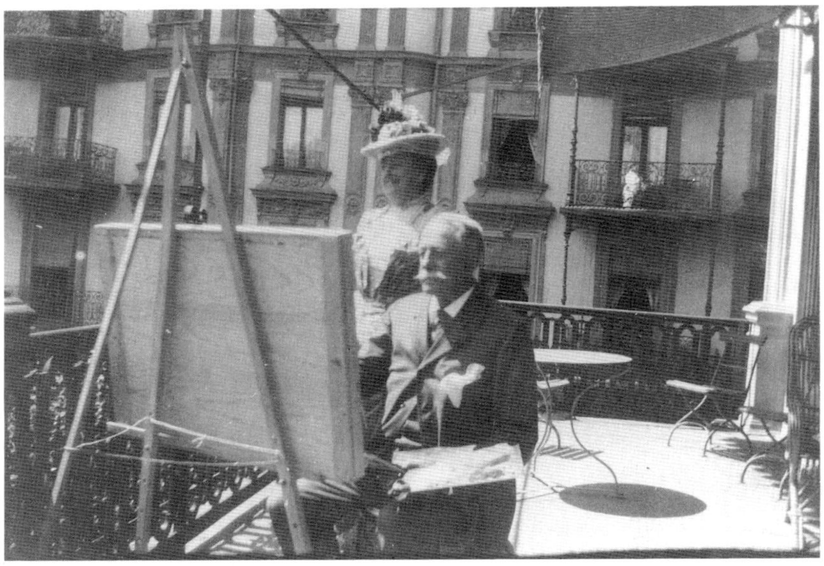

*Albert and Mary Stewart Bierstadt*. Photograph. Collection of Evan Hopkins Turner.

## 1894

**9 Jan.** Bierstadt writes to Van Horne to invite him to his studio to see the model for the railway car he has invented. (Bierstadt to Van Horne, 9 Jan. 1894, CPR Archives)

**7 Mar.** Albert Bierstadt and Mary Hicks Stewart married at the bride's home in New York City by the Reverend J. W. Brown, rector of Saint Thomas's Protestant Episcopal Church. Mary Stewart was the widow of David Stewart (d. 17 July 1891) and the stepmother of Isabella Stewart Gardner. "The wedding was a very quiet one, only members of the immediate families and a few intimate friends being present. . . . Immediately following the ceremony a luncheon was served, after which Mr. and Mrs. Bierstadt left for their wedding tour." (*NY Herald*, 8 Mar. 1894; *Sun*, New York, 8 Mar. 1894)

## 1895

**16 Jan.** The Lincoln National Bank and the National Shoe and Leather Bank (both in New York City) file court claims against Bierstadt for repayment of loans totaling $14,782.53. (Court Records, City of Manhattan, 1895)

**17 Jan.** Bierstadt turns over his property and goods in a trust agreement intended to repay his outstanding debts as his existing resources allow. (Assignment papers, 17 Jan. 1895, Grover Cleveland Papers, Library of Congress; Court Records, City of Manhattan, 1895)

It is reported that, as security for the loan from Lincoln National Bank, Bierstadt turned over "a number of valuable paintings," which the bank put in storage. The *Sun* goes on: "Mr. Bierstadt has been generally regarded as wealthy. In August, 1890, he stated to *Bradstreet's* that he thought he had property [in California, Minnesota, and Irvington] which if properly disposed of, would bring $1,000,000 above all liabilities. . . . Aside from the real estate, he said he had works of art in his studio worth $100,000." (*Sun*, New York, 17 Jan. 1895)

Reporting on Bierstadt's loan default, the *Tribune* writes, "The Sheriff placed a keeper in the studio at No. 1271 Broadway where there are many fine paintings, and Mr. Bierstadt said he would try to arrange a settlement of the claims as soon as possible." (*NY Tribune*, 17 Jan. 1895)

**22 Jan.** Bierstadt makes a settlement of the claims against him in favor of the Lincoln and Shoe and Leather banks. Theodore F. Hicks, his brother-in-law, takes an assignment of the claims from the banks. (*NY Times*, 23 Jan. 1895)

**18 July** While Bierstadt is in Rome, a sheriff's sale is held at his Broadway studio under the direction of Theodore F. Hicks. "It is understood that the sale was made so that Mr. Hicks could get absolute title to the pictures. He bought them all in for about $4,000. They were valued, it is said, at over $50,000. Twelve of the pictures were sold outright. Mr. Bierstadt's right, title, and

## 1896

**12 May** Bierstadt obtains five patents for an expanding railway car. (Patents 559,962 through 559,966, U.S. Patent Office, Washington, D.C.)

Aboard the ship *Majestic* bound for Europe, Bierstadt writes that he intends to go first to London and then to Paris. "Life here is getting to be a burden instead of a pleasure. It is just as bad for the people with money as it is with those who have nothing." (Bierstadt to C. S. Peirce, 12 May 1896, Houghton Library, Harvard University, Cambridge, Mass.)

**21 June** Bierstadt is in Budapest. (Bierstadt to Count d'Anlby, 21 June 1896, Houghton Library, Harvard University, Cambridge, Mass.)

**26 June** Bierstadt is in Lucerne. (Bierstadt to C. S. Peirce, 26 June 1897, Houghton

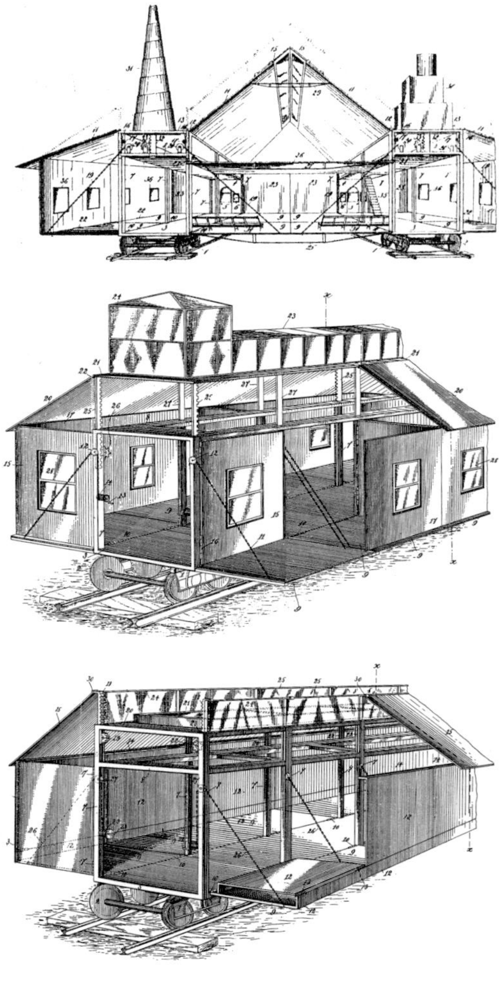

Albert Bierstadt. *Three views of "A Railway Car."* Patent drawings, 12 May 1896. Library of Congress, Washington, D.C.

Library, Harvard University, Cambridge, Mass.)

**18 Aug.** Obtains an additional patent for the expanding railway car. (Patent 566,1[illegible]7, U.S. Patent Office, Washington, D.C.)

**8 Nov.** "Albert Bierstadt, the famous painter, whose invention of the theater-car created such wide interest, has now conceived and patented a novel folding car, which can be utilized as a traveling fort for soldiers." A model is on view at the Patent Office in Washington, D.C. (*Morning Call*, San Francisco, 8 Nov. 1896)

**19 Dec.** Bierstadt is in New York. (Bierstadt to Van Horne, 19 Dec. 1896, CPR Archives)

## 1897

**19 July** Bierstadt in Interlaken, Switzerland. (John A. Porter to Bierstadt, 19 July 1897, McKinley Papers, Library of Congress)

**24 Aug.** In Lucerne, Switzerland. (Van Horne to Bierstadt, 7 Sept. 1897, CPR Archives)

## 1898

**Jan.** Bierstadt is in New York. (Bierstadt to C. S. Peirce, 15 Jan., 7 Apr. 1898, Houghton Library, Harvard University, Cambridge, Mass.)

**26 Jan.** John Adams Porter, secretary to President William McKinley, writes to Bierstadt acknowledging receipt of his letter recommending Colonel Chaille-Long for an appointment in connection with the Paris Exposition in 1900. (Porter to Bierstadt 26 Jan. 1898, McKinley Papers, Library of Congress)

**20 July** Bierstadt is in Maine. (Porter to Bierstadt, 20 July 1898, McKinley Papers, Library of Congress)

**18 Aug.** In New Jersey. (Porter to Bierstadt, 18 Aug. 1898, McKinley Papers, Library of Congress)

## 1899

**Feb.–Mar.** Bierstadt writes to President McKinley and Secretary of State John Hay recommending government purchase of property on the island of Corfu. (Bierstadt to McKinley, 4 Feb. 1899, Massachusetts Historical Society, Boston; Bierstadt to Hay, 20 Feb., 13 Mar. 1899, Library of Congress)

## 1900

**6 Jan.** Bierstadt is in New York. (Bierstadt to General Miles, 6 Jan. 1900, AAA)

**6 May** Bierstadt reportedly goes to Paris. (Whittredge to Helen Plowden [W. S. Haseltine's daughter], 5 May 1900, Haseltine Papers, AAA)

## 1901

**15 Mar.** Bierstadt in New York. (Bierstadt to Mary Harrison, 15 Mar. 1901, Benjamin Harrison Papers, Library of Congress)

**29 Apr.** Bierstadt responds to an invitation to exhibit paintings at the Worcester Art Museum (3 June–14 Oct): "The invitation to send one or two pictures to the Worcester Art Museum has been received. Possibly my two pictures may require more wall room than you can spare. Therefore you can simply ask for one of them. The Destruction of Pompeii & Herculanaeum in the year 79. is a moonlight & fire light effect, and may be called a historical landscape. Great care in making all that is in the picture true to the time in which it occurred has been my study besides I saw the grandest eruption of the last century. The companion picture is the entrance to the Harbor of San Francisco, called the Golden Gate. These two pictures are with frame about 6 feet long and 4½ wide and are valued at seven thousand dollars each." (Bierstadt to Sir, 29 Apr. 1901, Worcester Art Museum, Worcester, Mass.)

**15 May** Edward Bierstadt writes to John Heywood at the Worcester Art Museum, requesting that the paintings by his brother be identified as "not for the 'Prize Competition.'" (E. Bierstadt to J. Heywood, 15 May 1901, Worcester Art Museum, Worcester, Mass.)

**21 Nov.** Bierstadt seeks to exchange a recent picture for *The Arch of Octavius (The Roman Fish Market)* (No. 11). "He asks for it because he has never of late done work equal to this early specimen. This is a question of 20 years standing. More than once he has come to me about it and I have referred him to the Trustees of the Athenaeum." (C. Loring to C. Bolton, 21 Nov. 1901, Letter Book, Boston Athenaeum)

## 1902

**18 Feb.** Albert Bierstadt dies suddenly in New York City, probably of heart disease, at age seventy-two. (Obituaries: *Boston Daily Advertiser; Boston Transcript; Boston Herald; Denver Republican; New Bedford Standard; Commercial Advertiser*, New York; *Post*, New York; *NY Herald; NY Tribune; NY Times; Providence Daily Journal; Evening Bulletin*, Providence; *San Francisco Chronicle*; and *Evening Star*, Washington, D.C., 19 Feb. 1902)

**21 Feb.** Bierstadt's funeral held at Saint Thomas's Protestant Episcopal Church, New York City, 11 A.M. (*NY Times*, 19 Feb. 1902)

**1 Mar.** In a thoughtful assessment of Bierstadt's position in American art, a writer comments: "Forty years ago Mr. Bierstadt was perhaps more popular and more widely known among people at large as a representative of American art than is any American painter of the present generation. The defects of his work are very obvious, and they have been felt so keenly that that work is probably undervalued." (*Outlook*, 1 Mar. 1902, p. 507)

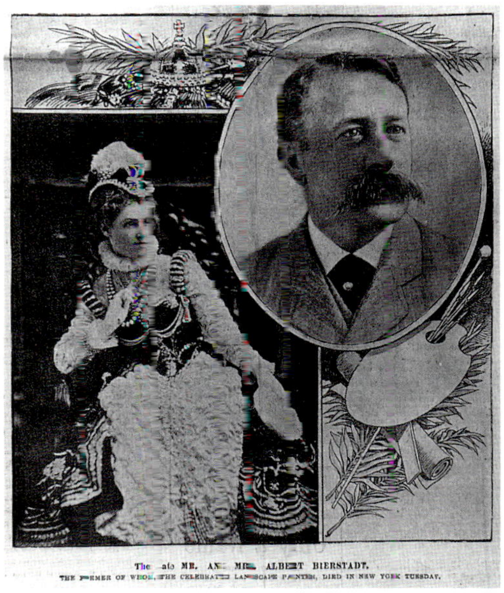

*The Late Mr. and Mrs. Albert Bierstadt.* Photocollage published in *Saturday Globe*, Utica, 22 Feb. 1902. Oneida County Historical Society, Utica, New York.

*The jury of selection has, according to all accounts, acted in a very square way throughout, members even voting openly against each other's works. One picture by Daniel Huntington, the president of the National Academy, was rejected and another secured in its place which the jury thought would represent him better, while a huge buffalo hunting scene by Albert Bierstadt, which is thought decidedly unworthy compared to some things he has done, was among the rejected.*

*NY Herald*, 8 Mar. 1889

AN ENTRANCING VIEW OF BIERSTADT'S GREAT PAINTING

*For two hours last week I sat in Albert Bierstadt's studio entranced. His newest and greatest painting, "The Last of the Buffalo," was before me, and through its huge golden frame, as through a window, I gazed upon such a scene as I myself have witnessed, but upon which no man will gaze again.*

*Who knows better than Bierstadt the grandeur and beauty of the wilderness of the West? Whose brush has transferred to canvas the sublimity of its lifted peaks, the wild rush of its dreams, the crystal clearness of its air, the whiteness of its sunlight, the rich color of its blending of multitudinous blossoms and grasses so well and so lovingly as he?*

*Here stretches the tranquil valley of the Sweetwater, where the river, past its cataracts and white rapids, sweeps in shining curves through the lines of osage and alder and willow and rushes, now rippling over the shallows, now deepening in a broad pool which is blue because it mirrors that sapphire sky.*

*Miles behind rise steeps of the Wind River range of the Rockies, their harsh faces brown, rough hewn and naked of verdure, their summits sharp, shimmering with the virginal radiance of an eternal snow.*

*To the right the slopes of the table land, furrowed and wrinkled by ages of Summer rain, whose sudden rills have fretted their way from the level which is the great plain and pasture.*

*Far up the valley, a butte of columnar trap, like a monument reared to some demigod of the past, its base littered with fragments which vandal frosts and lightnings have struck from its top through centuries of storm.*

*To the left again the gently bosoming hills made velvet by grasses, here and there a sentinel pine, and overall the broad dome of the infinite blue.*

*This is the scene. And the actors? Look upon them! Number them—they are countless. See that dark mass filling ten thousand acres in that expanse between hill and hill—all buffalo. Mark those long lines pushing outward like an army moving by flank—miles of vanguard leading a vaster army's way—all buffalo. Watch those myriads in the broad silver of the stream, not at one ford, but embrowning every pool and bar as far as the eye can reach, floundering, splashing, quick to plunge and quick to clamber [up] the opposite bank, their places in the flood never empty but taken by others—all buffalo. Hear that muffled thunder from the vast slope of the plain above—it is the voice of those billowing dun-colored clouds which you know are dust arising from the trample and rush of ten thousand thousand hoofs—a living cataract pouring down from the table-land to the valley, eager for the grateful coolness of the stream, never ceasing in movement and roar—all buffalo. The very hills are crawling, the pools are seething masses of brown, the broad meadows a swirl and sweep of currents and eddies of life, whose tide sets ever onward and onward—yes, count them if you can—all buffalo. . . .*

*There, to the left, scurry three nimble-footed antelope, fleeter than the wind on whose wings they seem to fly. Before the hour, they will be miles ahead of that clumsy sea whose advance has affrighted them. There trots a coyote, the pauper of the plain, too poor to keep even fleas, too insignificant to fear attack, too cowardly even to dispute with those buzzards which you see overhead their right to the first sickly calf or palsied old bull dropping out from that vast throng to die.*

*And there—see him!—there, fortified behind the mighty skull of a dead king of the herd, fallen last year—that prairie dog, half out of his burrow, yet ready to retreat on the instant—shrilly yelping his surprise and displeasure at the uproar before him—his pigmy shape and impudence unnoticed. . . .*

*A half-dozen Sioux, naked to the waist and painted, have dashed out from behind that knoll upon their ponies and are in the thick of the herd. Hear the sharp twang of the bow and the brief hiss of the shaft—again, and again, and again. . . .*

*See there! Another bull turns upon his pursuer. Well done! With a sudden lowering of the huge head and a lunge, he has impaled the pony, which rears with a scream of anguish. Now you have both, bull, and, if you fail, there stands your wounded brother, ready still for a charge, although two shafts are gnawing his vitals. Now toss them—ah! you were not quick enough!—the yelling murderer raised that lance and shot its yard of thirsty steel downward—your heart is cloven, and horse, Indian and you drop together! . . .*

*A great tragedy is the subject Mr. Bierstadt chose, and in breadth and spirit, in color and exquisite minuteness of detail he has shown the hand of a master.* HENRY GUY CARLETON

*World*, New York, 10 Mar. 1889

AMERICAN ARTISTS IN LUCK

*The Committee of seventeen distinguished artists who were appointed to select pictures for the American exhibit at the Paris Exposition paid a high compliment to* MR. ALBERT BIERSTADT *by rejecting his superb canvas, "The Last of the Buffalo." It is to* MR. BIERSTADT*'s great credit that the vote in the negative was unanimous.*

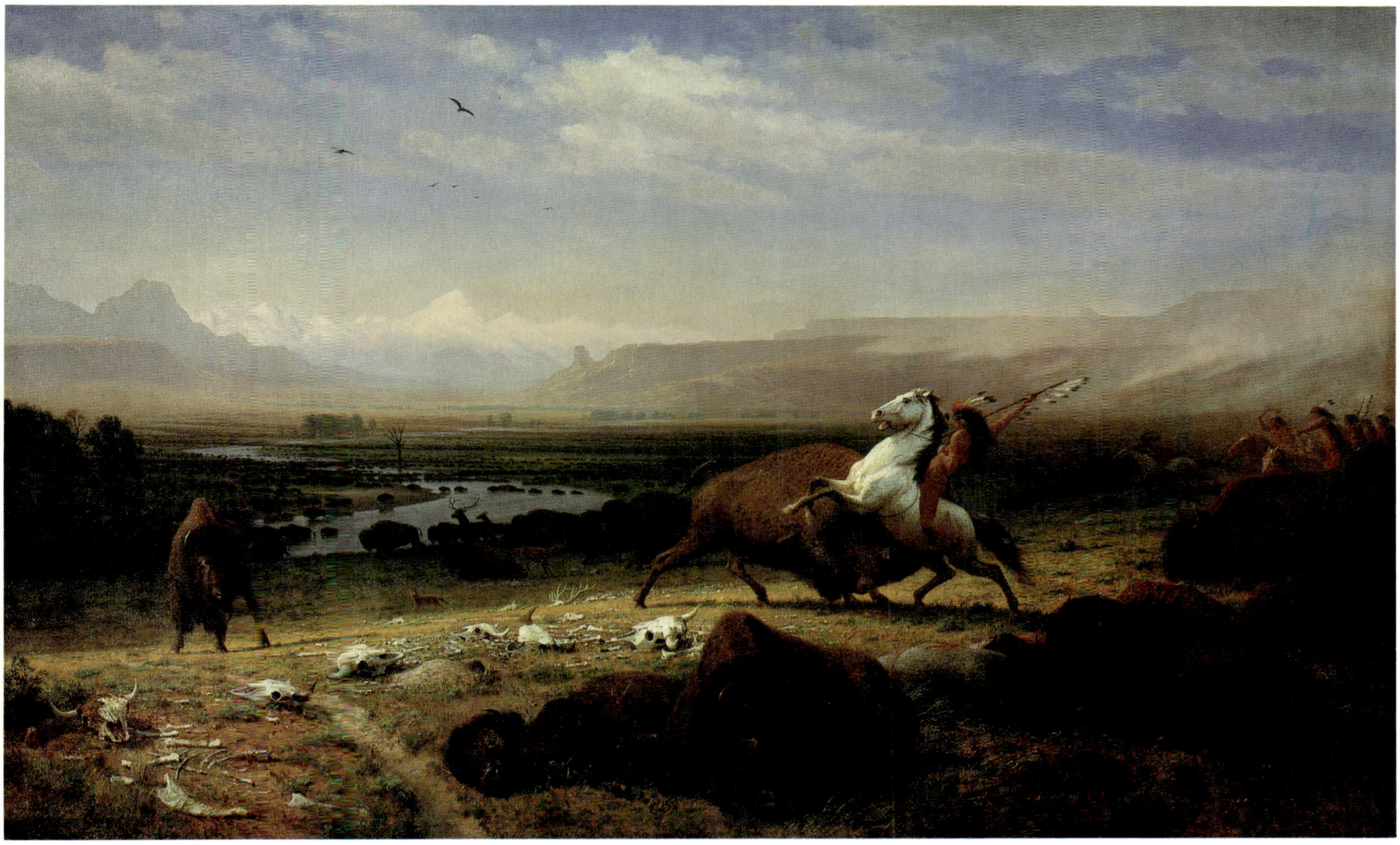

*Those who have seen the collection forwarded by this eminent galaxy can best appreciate the delicate tribute paid the artist in question.* MR. BIERSTADT'*s great picture was so singularly different from those chosen by the Committee, both in merit and value, that its rejection was imperative—the more urgently because nineteen-twentieths of the exhibit were selected by said Committee from the works of its own members. The blasphemy of placing a canvas worth only $25,000 beside works of art worth at least $10 a square yard is so evident that the justification of the Committee in its seemingly ruthless course of discrimination becomes clearly apparent. The only unpleasant feature of the whole matter is that* MR. BIERSTADT, *being a Chevalier of the Legion d'Honneur, a medallist of the French Academy and Knight of half a dozen Royal Orders, has the privilege of sending his magnificent picture to the Exposition—American Art Committee withstanding or not—and has cruelly availed himself thereof.*

*World*, New York, 17 Mar. 1889

NO. 68

## *The Last of the Buffalo*, 1888

Oil on canvas, 71¼ × 119¼ in. (181 × 302.9 cm)

Signed lower right: *Albert Bierstadt*

The Corcoran Gallery of Art, Washington, D.C., Gift of Mary (Mrs. Albert) Bierstadt, 1909

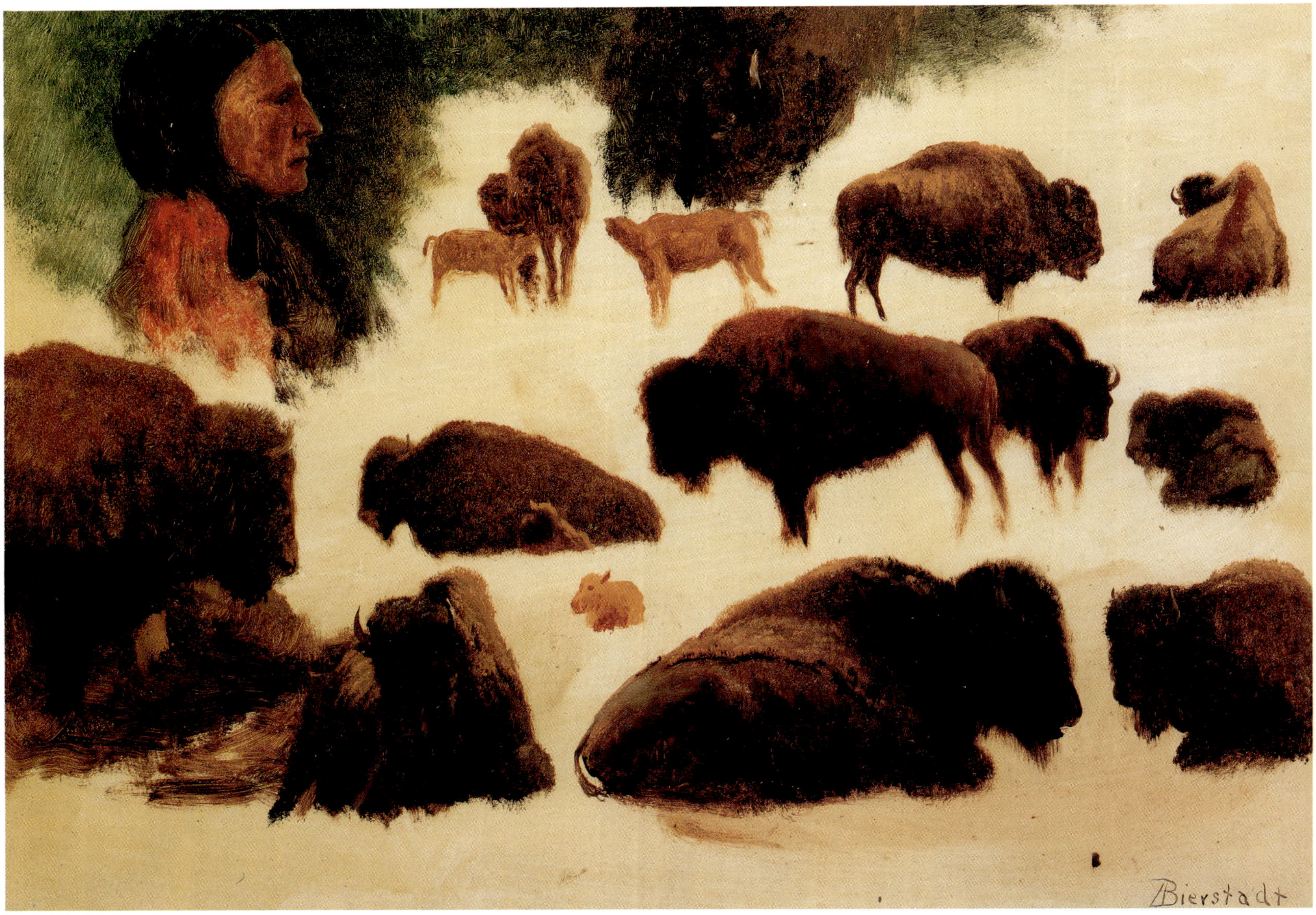


NO. 69

## *Studies of Bison*

Oil on paper, 14 × 19 in. (35.6 × 48.3 cm)

Signed lower right: *ABierstadt*

The Thomas Gilcrease Institute of American History and Art, Tulsa, Oklahoma

*Our artist, though a good shot, and capable of going to market for himself wherever there was any game, as well as most people, had seen enough buffalo-hunting in other expeditions to care little for it now, compared with the artistic opportunities which our battue afforded him for portraits of fine old bulls. He accordingly put his color-box, camp-stool, and sketching-umbrella into the buggy, hitched a team of the wagon-horses to it, and, taking one of our own party in with him, declared his intention of visiting the battle-field solely as "our special artist." . . .*

*[Munger] had ridden upon as big a bull as ever ran the Plains, stopped him with a series of shots . . . , and was holding him at bay . . . for our artist's especial behoof. He, on his part, did not need three words to show him his opportunity. He leapt from the buggy; out came the materials of success following him, and in a trifle over three minutes from his first halt, the big blue umbrella was pointed and pitched, and he sat under it on his camp-stool, with his color-box on his knees, his brush and palette in hand, and a clean board pinned in the cover of his color-box.*

Fitz Hugh Ludlow, *The Heart of the Continent: A Record of Travel Across the Plains and in Oregon, with an Examination of the Mormon Principle* (New York: 1870), pp. 62, 67

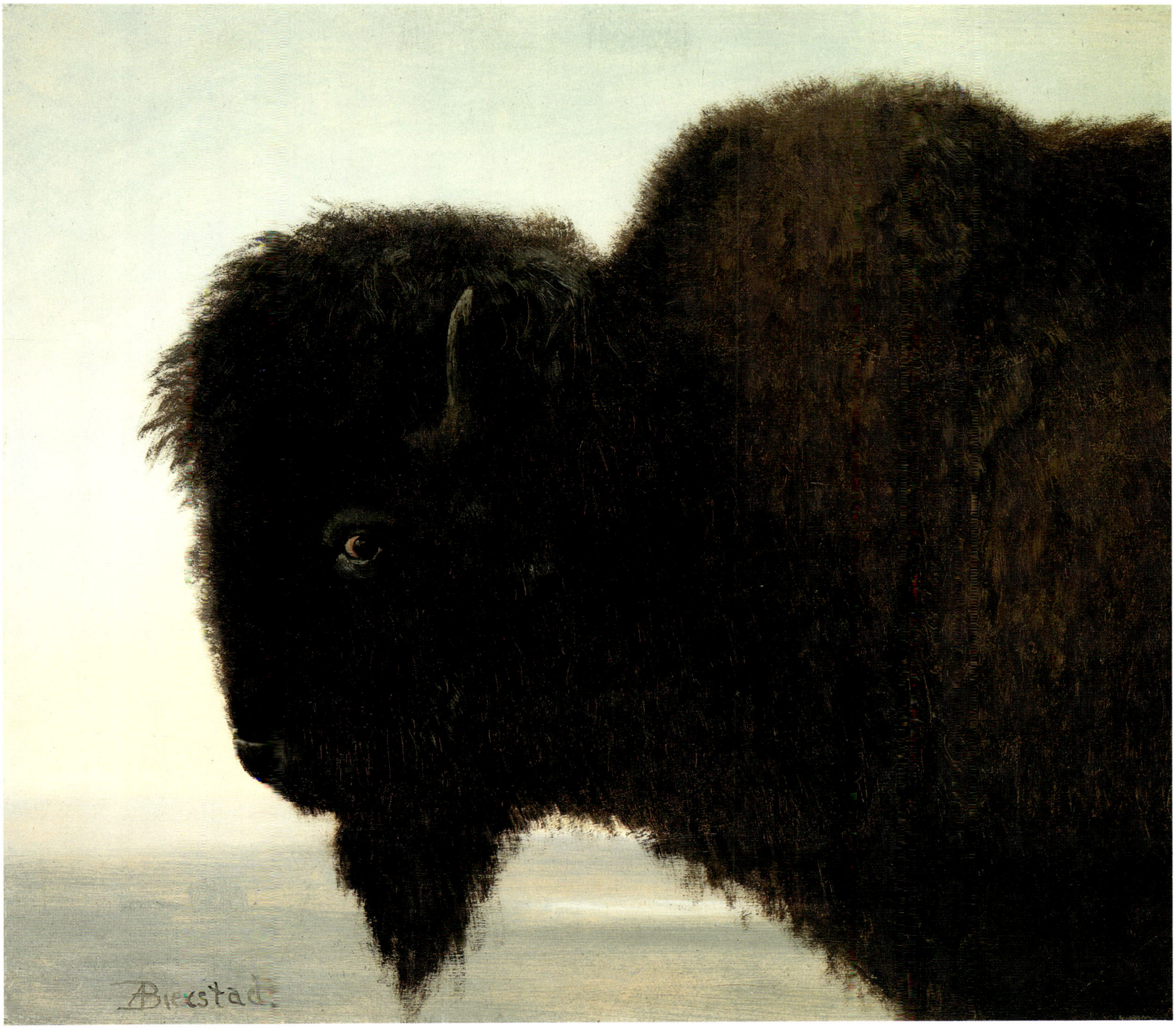

NO. 70

## *Buffalo Head*

Oil on paper mounted on board, 13¼ × 15½ in. (33.6 × 39.4 cm)

Signed lower left: *ABierstadt*

Buffalo Bill Historical Center, Cody, Wyoming

*For the first time I came close enough to a wild native buffalo to examine him minutely, and was obliged to confess that he was one of the noblest specimens of the brute creation.*

Fitz Hugh Ludlow, *The Heart of the Continent: A Record of Travel Across the Plains and in Oregon, with an Examination of the Mormon Principle* (New York: 1870), p. 66

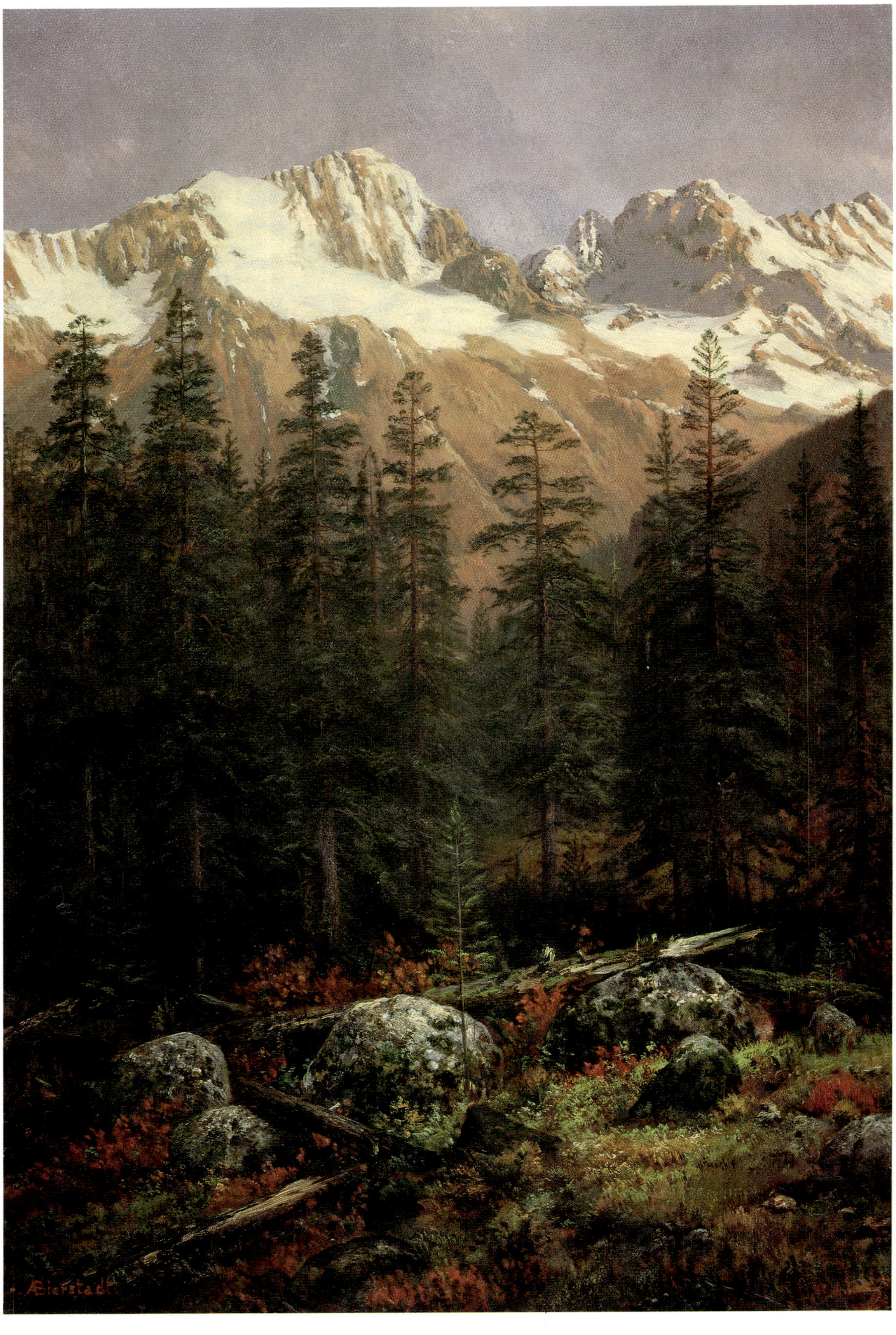

NO. 71

*Canadian Rockies*, c. 1889

Oil on canvas, 27⅞ × 19⅛ in. (70.8 × 48.6 cm)

Signed lower left: *ABierstadt*

Haggin Collection, The Haggin Museum, Stockton, California

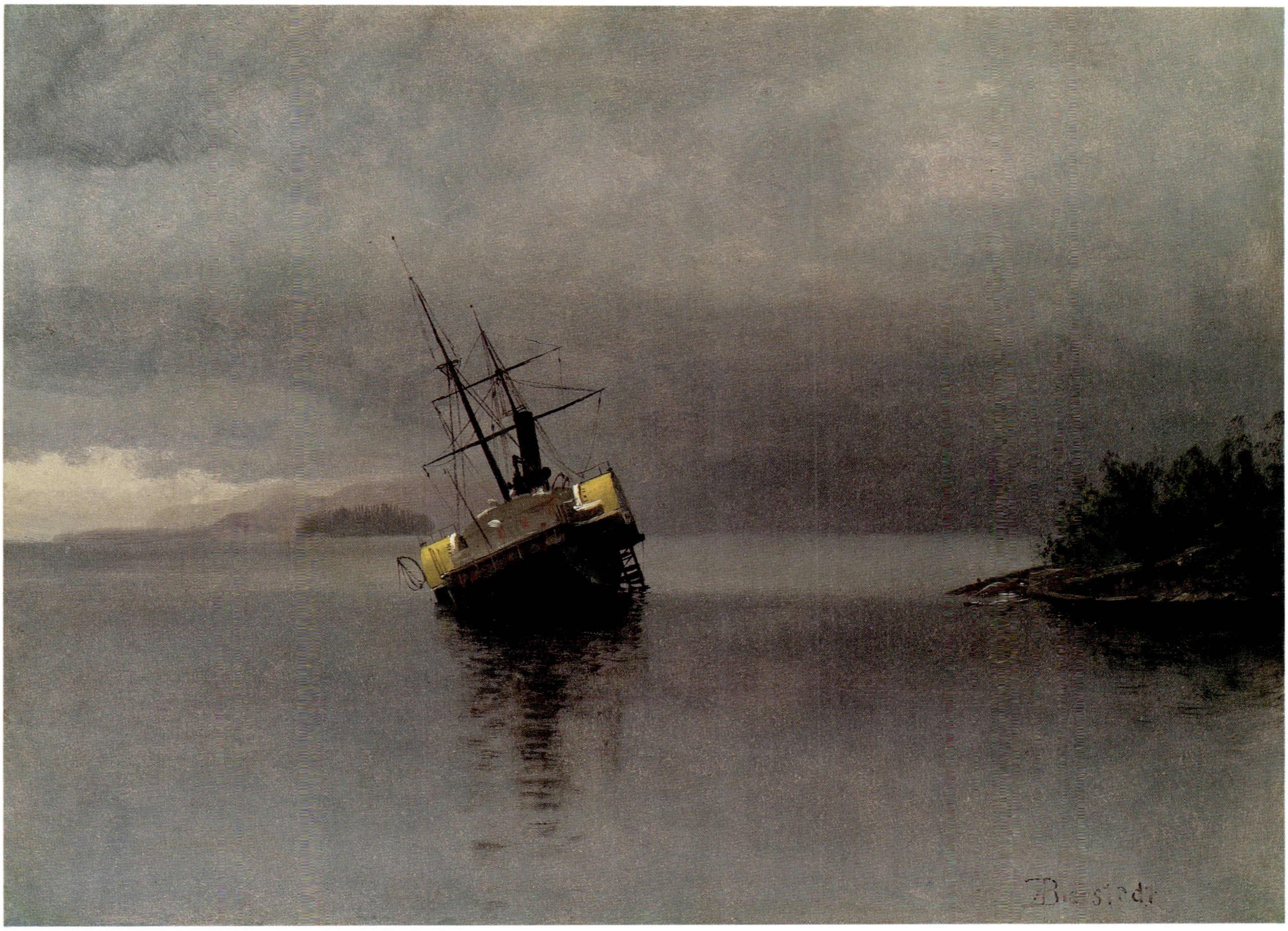

NO. 72

## *Wreck of the "Ancon" in Loring Bay, Alaska*, 1889

Oil on paper mounted on panel, 14 × 19¾ in. (35.6 × 50.2 cm)

Signed lower right: *ABierstadt*

Museum of Fine Arts, Boston, Gift of Martha C. Karolik for the Karolik Collection of American Paintings, 1815–1865

*The Pacific Coast Steamship Company's fine sidewheel steamer Ancon foundered on a rock in Naha Bay, Alaska, on the way from Sitka to Seattle, in the early morning of Wednesday, August 28. . . . The Ancon reached Naha bay at 9 o'clock p.m. Tuesday, August 27, and immediately effected a landing at the cannery wharf at Loring, which is on the bay. Here 2,500 cases of salmon were taken aboard. . . . [I]t was 3 o'clock on the following morning when everything was in readiness to leave. . . . She had just swung clear around, and was running slowly . . . when with a sidelong motion, evidently produced by the tide, . . . she ran upon a reef and was held fast. . . . As daylight dawned the work of transferring the passengers and their baggage ashore began. This was soon accomplished without accident and soon all were snugly housed in the different buildings which constitute the settlement of Loring.*

*Post-Intelligencer*, Seattle, 5 Sept. 1889

*Hotel Vancouver, Vancouver B.C.*
*Sept. 18, 1889*

*Darling Rosa:*

*Yours of Sept. 6 is just at hand. I wrote you of our Ship wreck and sent paper about the poor Ancon, it was a narrow escape. The steamer brought us back after 5 days living in Indian huts and salmon canneries. I was busy all the time and I have 60 studies in color and two books full of drawings of Alaska.*

Bierstadt to Rosalie Bierstadt, 18 Sept. 1889, ROM/MFA Corresp.

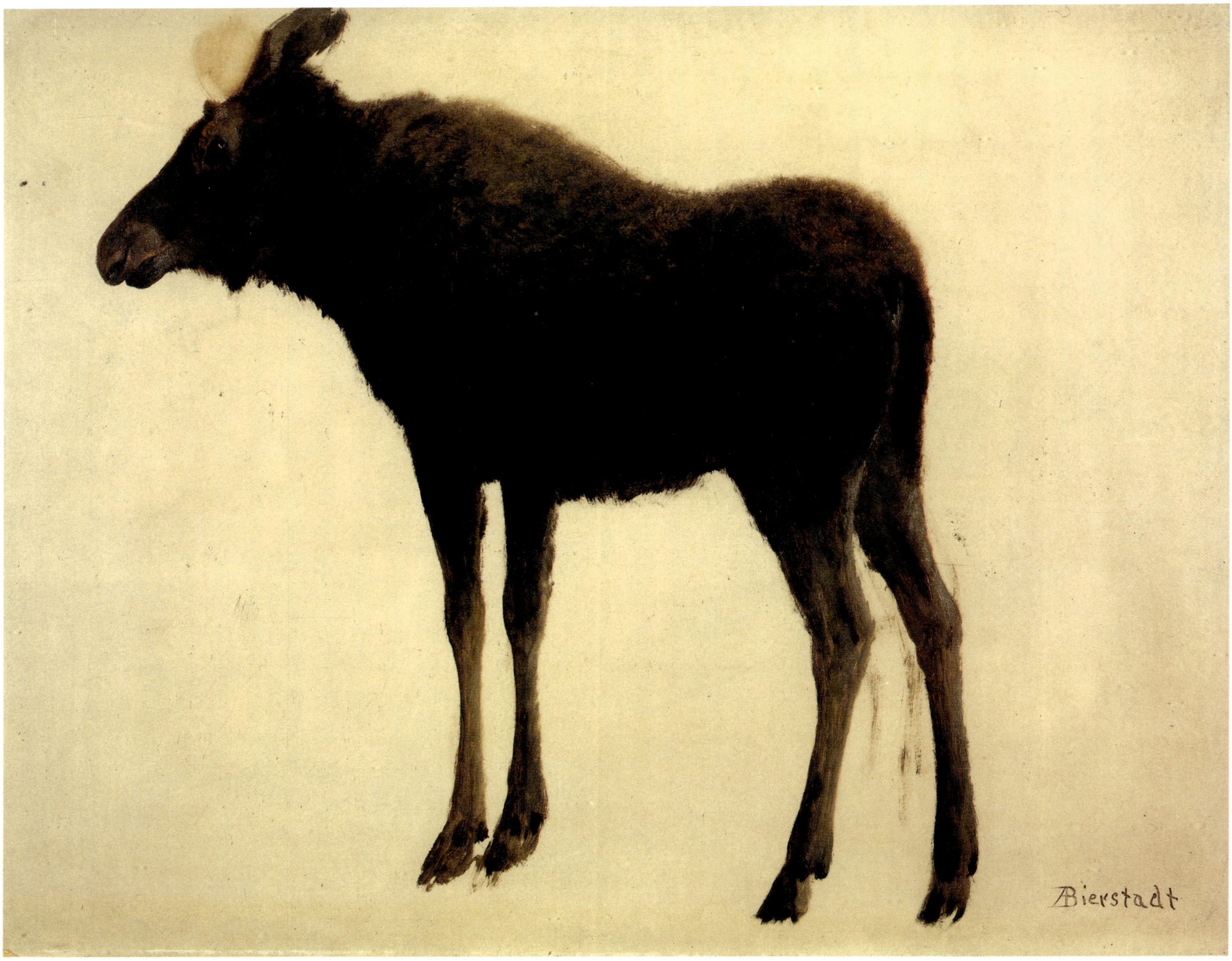


NO. 73

## *Moose*

Oil on cardboard, 14⅜ × 18¾ in. (36.5 × 47.6 cm)
Signed lower right: *ABierstadt*
Collection of Nicholas Wyeth

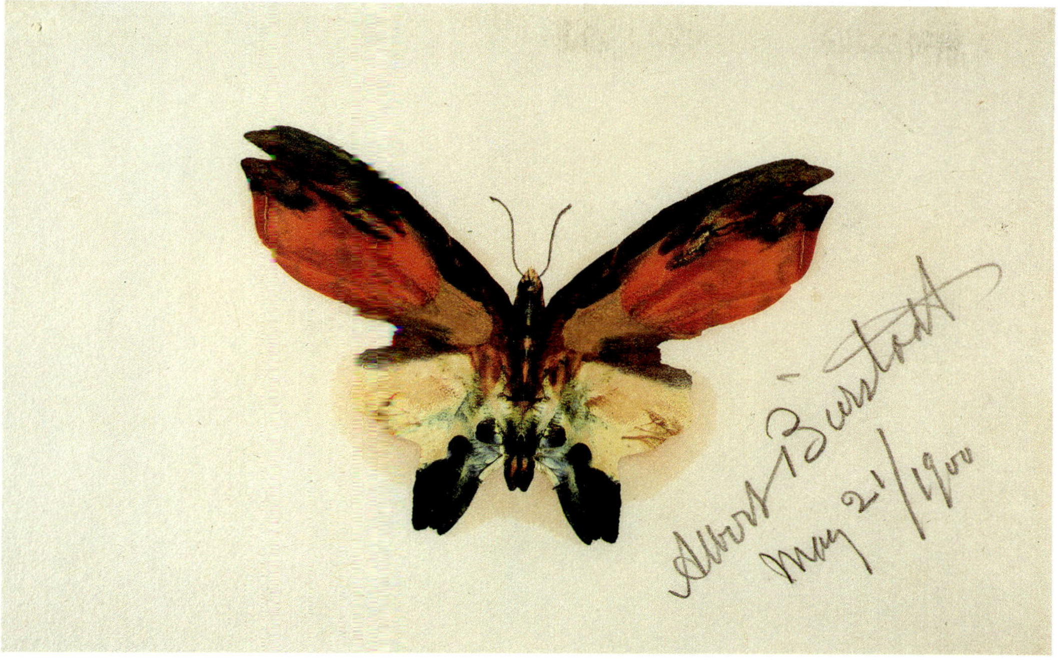


NO. 74

***Butterfly*, 1900**

Oil on paper with graphite pencil, 5 × 8 in. (12.7 × 20.3 cm)

Signed and dated lower right: *Albert Bierstadt/May 21/1900*

Collection of Mr. and Mrs. Leonard L. Milberg

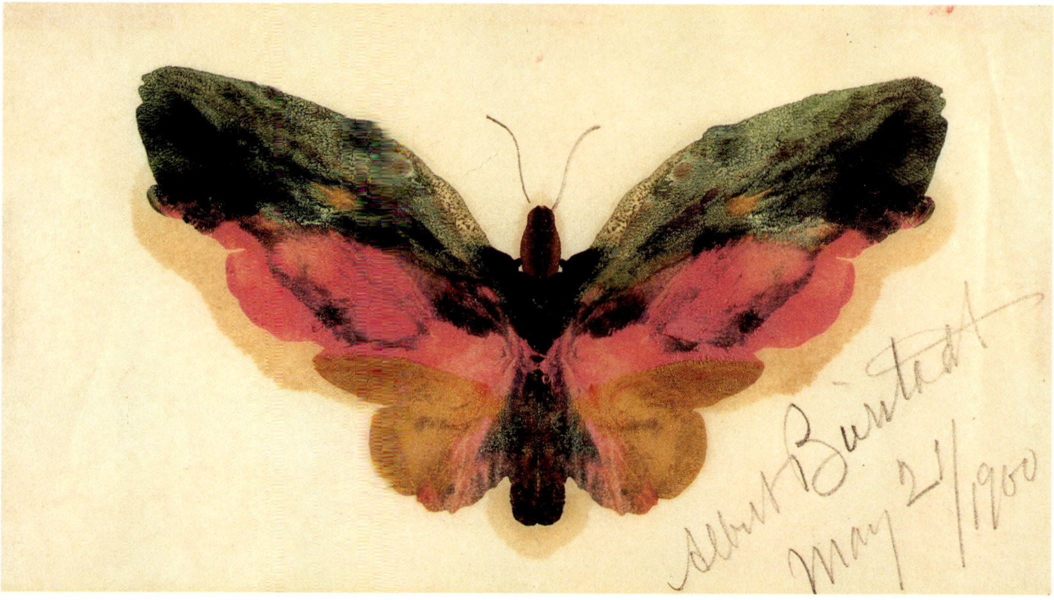


NO. 75

***Butterfly*, 1900**

Oil on paper with graphite pencil, 4¹³⁄₁₆ × 7⅞ in. (12.2 × 20 cm)

Signed and dated lower right: *Albert Bierstadt/May 21/1900*

Private collection

*Please say to Mrs. Hayes that the butterfly Mr. Bierstadt painted for me is now hanging in my home nicely framed. A very valuable souvenir of a very pleasant hour spent in the White House, recently.*

Albert Shaw to President Hayes, 11 Mar. 1878, Hayes Presidential Center

*We women were so glad we were women, that afternoon, for Mr. Bierstadt presented each lady with a souvenir. This is how he made them. We all clustered about the table and he took out a palette, a knife and some large slips of cartridge paper. Two or three daubs of pigment on the paper, a quick fold, and holding it still folded against a pane of glass, he made two or three strokes of that wizard-like palette knife on the outside, and hey, presto, a wonderful Brazilian butterfly or moth, even the veining on the wings complete! A pencil touch added the antennae, the artist's autograph was added in the corner, and now we each of us own a painting by Bierstadt.*

*Detroit Free Press*, 15 May 1892

# *Bierstadt and the Business of Printmaking*

HELENA E. WRIGHT

DURING ALBERT BIERSTADT'S LIFETIME, a series of significant technical innovations in the graphic arts made pictures a part of everyday life. Chromolithography greatly extended the use of printed color. Photography emerged, offering exact replication of life and art. The new photomechanical processes, adding photography's special reproductive powers to traditional media such as engraving and lithography, made it possible to transfer an image to an engraving plate or a lithographic stone for printing in permanent ink. By the 1880s, the perfection of several photomechanical processes had changed pictorial representation forever.

Ever the astute businessman, Bierstadt capitalized on all these changes, and he used a number of reproductive methods in the course of his career. He embraced photography quite early on, beginning with the stereographs he took on the Lander expedition to the Rocky Mountains in 1859.[1] Shortly thereafter, he encouraged his two brothers to start a photographic business in New Bedford, an enterprise he supported with both aesthetic advice and practical assistance. When his brother Edward later became involved with photomechanical printing, the two worked together on a number of projects. Reproducing his own paintings by wood engraving, steel engraving, chromolithography, and the new photomechanical processes of collotype, photoengraving, and photogravure, Bierstadt exercised all the options available to promote his art.

Following the publication of some of his sketches from the Lander expedition as wood engravings in *Harper's Weekly* in 1859, Bierstadt began to produce prints after his more successful paintings. James Smillie's (1807–1885) large steel engraving (No. 78, Fig. 80) after Bierstadt's *Rocky Mountains, Lander's Peak* (No. 37), published in 1866, represents the most elaborate effort of Bierstadt's printed oeuvre.

Bierstadt used the medium of engraving for several prints. With its long tradition conveying a distinct level of aesthetic acceptance, the reproductive engraving was highly valued in the nineteenth century as the finest form in which a painting could be reproduced. To merit an engraving meant that a painting had achieved a certain popularity; this medium permitted distribution of the image to a wide but discerning audience. Having one's work engraved on steel by a fine engraver signaled an artist's arrival to a position of prominence encompassing both quality and permanence. Engraving survived as a healthy and respected practice into the 1870s.[2] At that time, an engraving was imbued with a credibility and association with the artist that today has been lost in common perceptions of a reproductive print. In most instances, artists worked closely with engravers to oversee production of the plate and make corrections at each proof stage. Through most of Bierstadt's working life, engraving remained the most elegant and prestigious means of bringing a painting before a wider audience.

The perfection of printed color in the chromolithograph by midcentury promised remarkable progress in the effort to reproduce paintings. The alternatives of line or color as reproductive choices emerged with the coming of the chromo, and some artists such as Bierstadt and Frederic Church produced both line engravings and chromolithographs after their most famous works. The chromolithograph, however, never achieved the high level of respectability and connoisseurship that the steel engraving had connoted for generations.

Before the 1860s, American artists who reproduced their paintings in color generally chose European lithographers.[3] Louis Prang (1824–1909), who in 1868 published the chromo (Fig. 86) of Bierstadt's *Sunset: California Scenery*, wanted to Americanize the art of reproducing oil paintings. In the years immediately following the Civil War, Prang and other American lithographers worked to improve the quality of the prints offered in "imitation" of oil painting. Art critics in numerous periodicals noted their improvements: "Heretofore we have been compelled to look to England or Germany when wanting a fine chromo but we are rejoiced to find that it need no longer be so. We trust that ere long every American drawing-room may be decorated with American chromos after the originals of American artists. . . ."[4]

When Bierstadt first elected to use the medium, chromolithography enjoyed the praise that often accompanies a technical improvement. The moralizing middle-class press applauded the way that accessible, uplifting pictures could reinforce cultural values. Indeed, Bierstadt's *Sunset* chromo was specifically recommended for inexpensive edification by Catharine Beecher and Harriet Beecher Stowe in *American Woman's Home* (1869): "The educating influence of these works of art can hardly be over-estimated. . . . Children are constantly trained to correctness of taste and refinement of thought, and stimulated—sometimes to efforts at artistic imitation, always to the eager and intelligent inquiry about the scenes, the places, the incidents represented."[5]

The chromo's very success spelled its downfall, however. By so deliberately imitating painting, chromos sometimes fooled the eye. When Prang's chromo was exhibited alongside Bierstadt's painting of *Sunset in California*, gallery visitors sometimes could not distinguish between the two.[6] This confusion, along with the proliferation of poorer-quality examples, led to a rather rapid disillusionment with the process. Increasingly, critics called chromos cheap, superficial copies that detracted from all the good that art was said to effect. Ironically, almost as soon as technical achievements permitted the lithograph to replicate oil paintings successfully, critics rejected the process. The fine-art chromolithograph, reproducing the work of critically received artists, died out almost at birth. Although Louis Prang continued to publish his excellent series of reproductions after some American artists into the 1890s, by the early 1870s Bierstadt and others had backed away from the process because of its increasingly negative reception.[7]

The new direction for reproductive prints entailed the application of photography to pictorial printing. Photography had entered the art market with the development of the collodion negative in the 1850s, which made possible the production of stereographs and larger prints suitable for framing. In the 1860s, the Bierstadt Brothers photographic firm produced stereographs, primarily of landscape subjects, and offered photographic copies "from choice paintings, engravings, &c" in several sizes.[8] Photography's application to the printmaking processes, or photomechanical reproduction, involved the photographic transfer of an image onto a surface that then could be printed with permanent ink. One such process, the collotype, was introduced in the United States by Edward Bierstadt. Albert assisted Edward in establishing a collotype printing business in 1869–70 and worked with him to publish several collotype prints after his paintings.[9] Photogravure, another photomechanical process, produced prints that appeared much like the traditional engravings they replaced, especially as the plates often required a good deal of hand retouching with the burin.[10] Photogravure became the medium of choice for many artists and publishers, and Bierstadt turned to the process in the 1880s to produce his last two major print efforts, *Mount Corcoran* (Fig. 126) and *The Last of the Buffalo* (No. 81, Fig. 130).

Beginning in the 1860s, expanded opportunities for ordinary people to see pictures at public exhibitions and commercial galleries, in conjunction with advances in printmaking techniques and the growth of the print trade, extended the market for art as a commodity. Only one wealthy individual could purchase a canvas, but with the multiple copies that printmaking provided, the viewing public could become a buying public. Enterprising artists like Bierstadt sought to enlarge their circle of patronage through the production of prints after their more successful paintings. Art dealers promoted the works of living artists, offering prints for sale by subscription to anyone who came to look at a painting while it was on tour. Although the primary goal for artists and dealers was to show and sell the painting, sometimes the copyright for the print was sold separately to a publisher. Exhibition entrance fees, copyright sales, and print sales added to the income generated by the sale of the painting and became part of the elaborate marketing scheme promoted by both artists and dealers.[11]

The publication of prints made the fortunes and enhanced the reputations of artists and dealers alike. Taking advantage of his excellent social connections in both Europe and North America, Bierstadt developed networks of patrons, dealers, publishers, engravers, and lithographers. To avail himself of every possible opportunity to further his reputation, he presented his work in numerous formats and diverse media for several audiences. Even after his critical reputation began to decline, Bierstadt found ways to keep his work before the public through reproductions in several graphic media, including prints and popular illustrations.

In the assessment of Bierstadt's contribution as an artist, it is important to look at the printed work in addition to the canvases. Throughout his career, Bierstadt issued prints after his paintings, using all of the available graphic media. He was acutely aware of the latest trends and developments in printing methods; indeed, his choice of reproductive processes mirrors the progress made in the graphic arts during the critical years from 1860 to 1890. His business acumen, combined with his brothers' skills, enabled him to take advantage of these technical developments. His considerable personal involvement in each reproductive effort makes a study of his prints a particularly vital component of this catalogue. The examples that follow provide significant new evidence of Bierstadt's wide-ranging activities in the business of art.

## Checklist of Nineteenth-Century Prints After Paintings by Albert Bierstadt

In this checklist, prints or full-page engraved plates are discussed at greater length than book and magazine illustrations. Full references for author-date citations of books are given in the Selected Bibliography.

### 1859

"Crossing the Plains," "Crossing the Platte," and "A Pike's Peaker" (Figs. 76–78). Wood engravings published in *Harper's Weekly*, 13 Aug. 1859, p. 516.

Bierstadt's first appearance in the mass media came in the form of three sketches printed as wood engravings on a single page of *Harper's Weekly*, all depicting activity he witnessed as part of the Lander expedition. Bierstadt sketched a single "deluded and suffering gold seeker" in "A Pike's Peaker" and recorded the wagons and animals of emigrants, observed by clusters of Ogallala Sioux, in "Crossing the Plains" and "Crossing the Platte." Similar images appeared in his early western stereographs published by Bierstadt Brothers.

### 1864

*Sunlight and Shadow* (No. 76, Fig. 79). Chromolithograph by Storch & Kramer, Berlin, [1864]. (Painting, No. 29, signed and dated 1862.) 22½ × 19½ in. (57 × 49.5 cm) (image). Division of Graphic Arts, National Museum of American History, Smithsonian Institution, Washington, D.C.

On 31 October 1863, the *New York Tribune* reported that *Sunlight and Shadow* had been sent to Berlin to be chromolithographed. The painting represented Bierstadt's first critical and popular success and thus was a natural candidate for reproduction. Alert to the promotional value of such a venture, the artist and his dealer-publisher, Emil Seitz, kept newspapers informed of the painting's travels and the print's publication progress. In the summer of 1864, *Sunlight and Shadow*, recently returned from Europe, was exhibited in New York. By October, the chromolithograph made by Storch & Kramer in Berlin had joined the original at Emil Seitz's Broadway gallery. The chromo represents Bierstadt's first major reproduction, executed on a rather grand scale.

Fine-art chromolithographs such as Bierstadt's maiden effort were printed in opaque oil colors, mounted on canvas, stretched, and varnished to resemble paintings quite deliberately. Such lithographs, as noted by the New York *Evening Post*, "may fairly be regarded . . . as fac-similes of the original picture." The *Post* went on to call Bierstadt's print "the finest specimen of the art yet seen in this country."[12]

The reproduction of *Sunlight and Shadow* as a chromolithograph placed Bierstadt in the vanguard of American artists using this particular medium to expand the market for their art. Before the Civil War, American artists had not yet begun to exploit color lithography, and Bierstadt was among those artists who first realized its potential. The production of most American lithographic houses at this time was centered on commercial rather than artistic printing, employing pale tints and hand coloring. Bierstadt was one of the first American artists to choose a German lithographic firm, one capable of reproducing his work in printed colors.[13] His own training

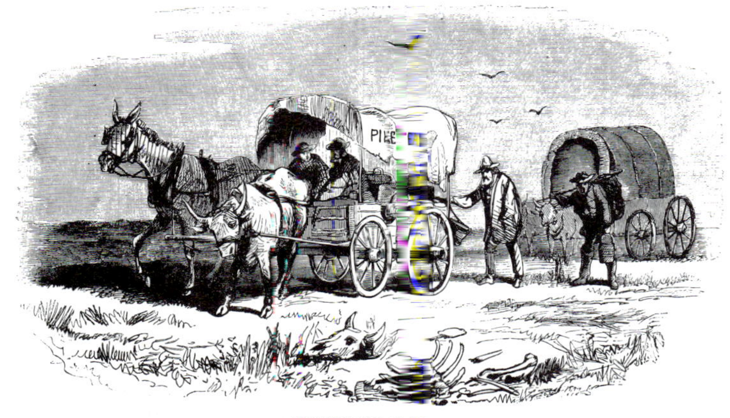


Figure 76

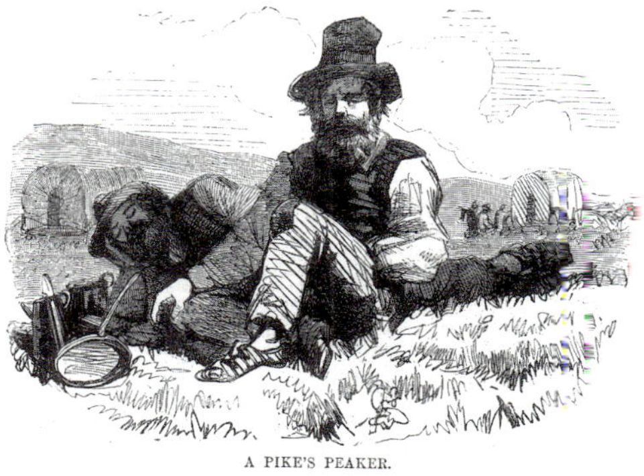


Figure 78

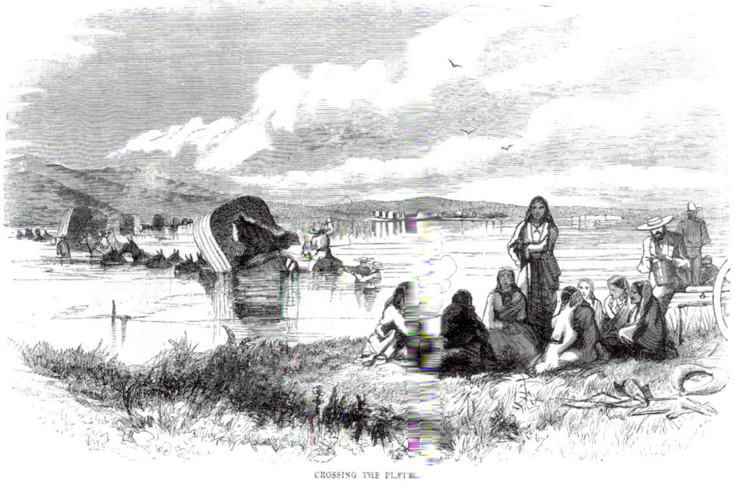


Figure 77

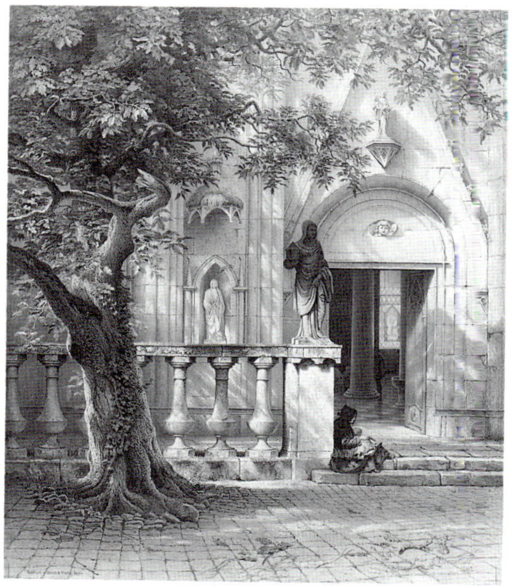

Figure 79

in Düsseldorf or a business connection through Emil Seitz may have provided the impetus for this choice.

## 1866

*The Rocky Mountains, Lander's Peak* (Fig. 80). Steel engraving by James Smillie. Published by Edward Bierstadt, New York, 1866. (Painting, No. 37, completed 1863.) 16¾ × 27¾ in. (43 × 70.5 cm) (image). Division of Graphic Arts, National Museum of American History, Smithsonian Institution, Washington, D.C.

The astonishing critical and popular acclaim for *The Rocky Mountains, Lander's Peak* propelled Bierstadt into the first rank of American artists with remarkable rapidity. To capitalize on that success, he sent the painting on tour, accompanied by a subscription list for ordering an engraving. Even while the chromolithograph of *Sunlight and Shadow* was under way in Berlin, James Smillie, America's premier landscape engraver, was at work on the plate after *The Rocky Mountains, Lander's Peak*.[14] The engraving, although commissioned first, took longer to execute owing to a number of technical problems.

Edward Bierstadt acted as publisher of the print, entering it for copyright protection in 1866. Edward also worked with Smillie and his son, James David Smillie, on Albert's behalf. Drafts of Smillie's letters suggest that James David Smillie agreed to produce a drawing of *The Rocky Mountains, Lander's Peak* suitable for his father to use in engraving the plate. The younger Smillie was to make this drawing from a photograph of the painting to be supplied by Edward Bierstadt, who at the time (1863) operated a photographic studio in New Bedford with his older brother Charles. The more traditional practice was for the engraver to make a reduced drawing by copying directly from the painting, but in this case the painting was not available to be copied, and the Smillies hoped to rely on Edward's photograph.[15]

The first arrangements for making the engraving began early in 1863. Drafts of several letters written by James David Smillie that spring indicate his frustration as he awaited the promised photograph from Edward Bierstadt, who seems to have had difficulty producing it. When the photo did appear, the resulting image was totally unsuitable, without sufficient contrast and detail, and the Smillies were distraught. Albert had left for California, and the painting was on tour.

To complicate matters further, James David Smillie was regularly employed as a bank-note engraver, and because of the unforeseen delay, he had difficulty in arranging time in which to

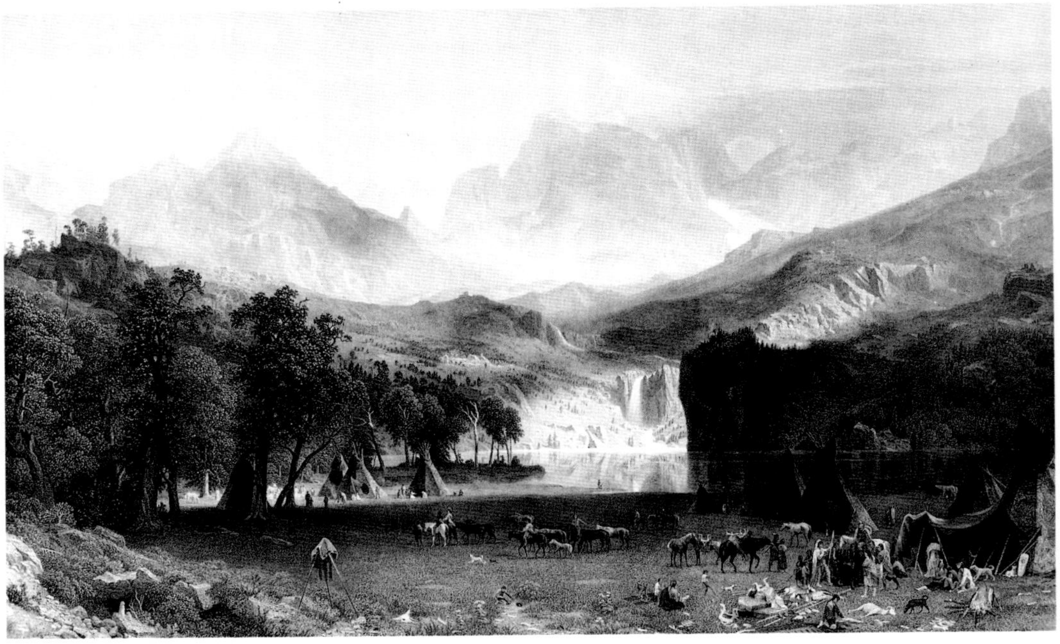

Figure 80

complete the drawing. Moreover, a document dated 6 May 1863 indicates that James David Smillie had contracted separately with Albert Bierstadt to engrave a small plate of another painting, *Forest Glen*, by July. Within a week, in a draft of a letter to an unknown correspondent dated 13 May 1863, Smillie noted that it would be impossible to meet this deadline, but that he had not had the heart to break the bad news to Bierstadt before he went away. No engraving after *Forest Glen* has been located.[16]

Early in 1863, when arrangements were first made with the Smillies, it must have appeared that the engraving of *The Rocky Mountains, Lander's Peak* could be completed in two years' time. An early version of the engraving's prospectus announced that the print would be completed and ready for delivery in the summer of 1865, a line that was deleted from later flyers. The print did not appear until December of 1866; problems with copying the painting were one cause. James D. Smillie's drawing of *The Rocky Mountains, Lander's Peak* was exhibited in New York in March 1864, a date that can be taken as the beginning of the engraving process. More than two years later, well after the contractual deadline, the finished engraving appeared.[17]

While negotiating with the Smillies on the *Rocky Mountains, Lander's Peak* and *Forest Glen* projects, Bierstadt apparently proposed to add another picture, *Mount Hood, Oregon*, 1865 (Fig. 55), to the deal. Taking advantage of his current success with *The Rocky Mountains, Lander's Peak*, Bierstadt also sent *Mount Hood, Oregon* on tour. On 2 November 1865, the New Bedford *Daily Mercury* reported that subscriptions were being taken for an engraving after *Mount Hood, Oregon*. Another account suggested that Bierstadt intended for the senior Smillie to engrave *Mount Hood, Oregon*; as with *Forest Glen*, however, no engraving after this painting has been located.[18]

As demonstrated by the example of his success with *The Rocky Mountains, Lander's Peak*, Bierstadt rather quickly developed the marketing strategy needed to promote his major works. He sent the painting on tour, accompanied by a subscription book and promotional flyers for the engraving. Several versions of this engraving's prospectus survive

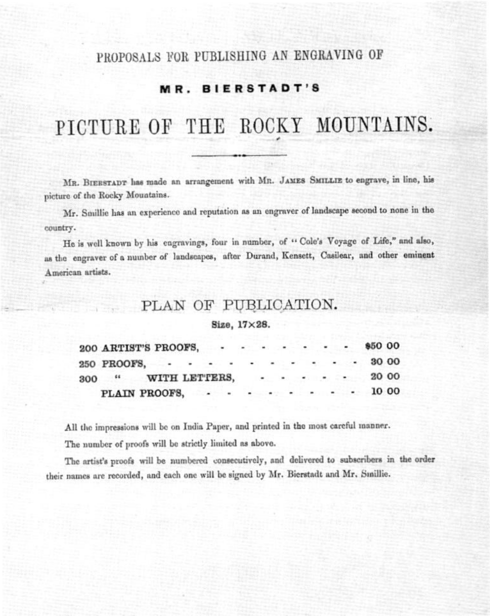

PROPOSALS FOR PUBLISHING AN ENGRAVING OF

MR. BIERSTADT'S

PICTURE OF THE ROCKY MOUNTAINS.

MR. BIERSTADT has made an arrangement with MR. JAMES SMILLIE to engrave, in line, his picture of the Rocky Mountains.

Mr. Smillie has an experience and reputation as an engraver of landscape second to none in the country.

He is well known by his engravings, four in number, of "Cole's Voyage of Life," and also, as the engraver of a number of landscapes, after Durand, Kensett, Casilear, and other eminent American artists.

PLAN OF PUBLICATION.

Size, 17×28.

| | |
|---|---|
| 200 ARTIST'S PROOFS, | $50 00 |
| 250 PROOFS, | 30 00 |
| 300 " WITH LETTERS, | 20 00 |
| PLAIN PROOFS, | 10 00 |

All the impressions will be on India Paper, and printed in the most careful manner.

The number of proofs will be strictly limited as above.

The artist's proofs will be numbered consecutively, and delivered to subscribers in the order their names are recorded, and each one will be signed by Mr. Bierstadt and Mr. Smillie.

Figure 81

Prospectus for engraving of *The Rocky Mountains, Lander's Peak*, n.d. Archives of American Art, Smithsonian Institution, Washington, D.C.

(Fig. 81). Titled variously "Proposals for Publishing an Engraving of Mr. Bierstadt's PICTURE OF THE ROCKY MOUNTAINS," and "A. Bierstadt's Great Picture. THE ROCKY MOUNTAINS. Engraved by James Smillie," these simple printed folders describe the painting in detail and provide particulars about the engraving. The print was to be issued in four states. Two hundred artist's proofs, numbered consecutively and signed by both Bierstadt and Smillie, commanded the highest price, fifty dollars. Two hundred fifty proofs, presumably unnumbered but probably signed, were to be available at thirty dollars. Three hundred proofs with letters (with the title and the names of artist and engraver added to the plate) were sold for twenty dollars. An unlimited number of plain proofs, printed after nearly eight hundred impressions had been taken from the plate, brought ten dollars each; these were noted in the press as being within the reach of almost everyone.

Although the number of impressions taken from the plate is unknown, the prospectus indicates that Bierstadt planned for the edition to reach 750 before plain proofs would be issued. The steel plate would have accommodated an edition several times that size. *The Rocky Mountains, Lander's Peak* has survived in far greater numbers than any of the other prints identified in this checklist, which would suggest a large edition. Surviving examples inscribed by Bierstadt to various dignitaries as late as the 1890s indicate that the artist kept a supply from which he distributed gifts for many years. The impression reproduced here is a proof before letters, signed by the artist in pencil and given by him directly to the Smithsonian's Division of Graphic Arts in 1888.

---

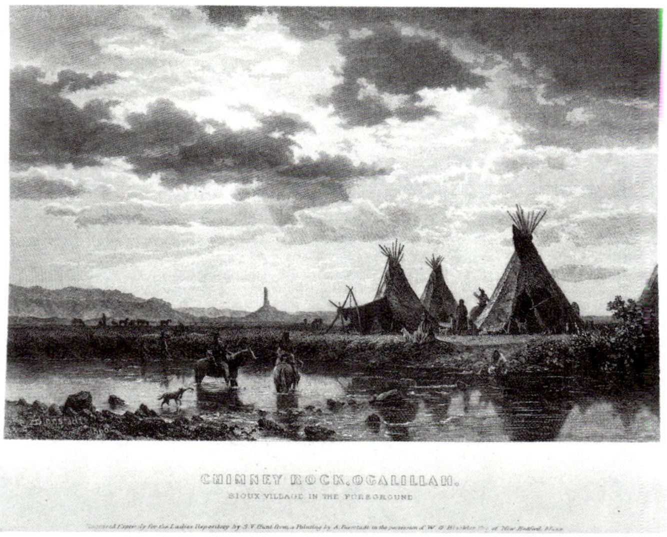


Figure 82

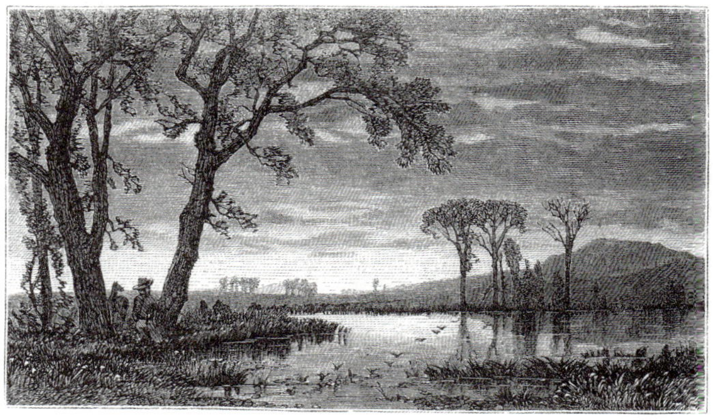

Figure 83

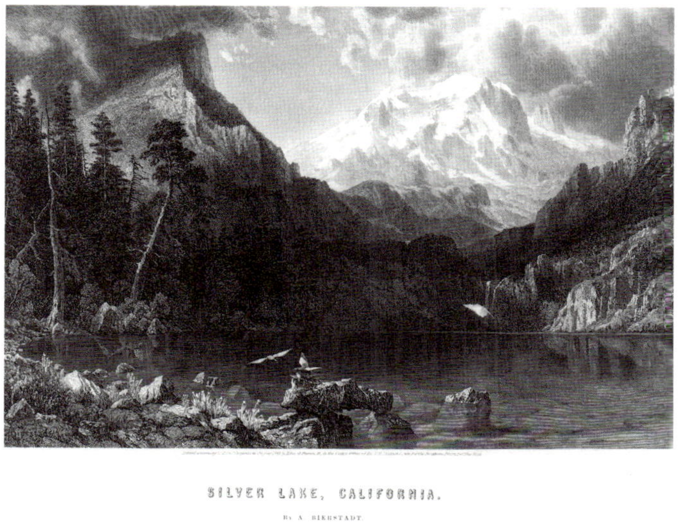


Figure 84

*Chimney Rock, Ogalillah* [sic] *Sioux Village in the Foreground* (Fig. 82). Steel engraving by Samuel Valentine Hunt for the *Ladies Repository*, 1866. 4⅜ × 7⅛ in. (10.5 × 18 cm) (image). Serials, Library of Congress, Washington, D.C. Engraved under title: *Engraved Expressly for the* Ladies Repository *by S. V. Hunt from a Painting by A. Bierstadt in the possession of W. G. Fleckler Esq. of New Bedford, Mass.*

Following the tradition of elaborately illustrated gift books and annuals, periodical s aimed at the growing market of middle-class homes began to include steel engravings by the late 1830s. These periodicals brought art reproductions into many homes around the country at a time when few opportunities existed to see original paintings firsthand. Bierstadt's small but full-page plate after *Chimney Rock* represented his entry into the American drawing room in a more prestigious format than that of the unsigned sketches reproduced in *Harper's* a few years before.

The *Ladies Repository*, published in Cincinnati between 1841 and 1876, offered quality pictures, well reproduced. Each monthly issue presented two steel engravings, usually one portrait and a landscape or genre print after a recognized talent. By the 1860s, the *Repository* had published landscape plates after works by A. D. Shattuck, Asher B. Durand, Sanford R. Gifford, John W. Casilear, and John F. Kensett, among others.

---

"Hunter of the Prairie" (Fig. 83). Wood engraving by Bobbett and Hooper published in *Festival of Song* (New York: 1866).

---

## 1867

*Silver Lake, California* (Fig. 84). Steel engraving [by Samuel Valentine Hunt]. Published by Edward Bierstadt, New York, 1867. 10½ × 16 in. (27 × 41 cm) (image). Prints & Photographs Division, Library of Congress, Washington, D.C.

The engraving after *Silver Lake, California* was the first of Bierstadt's California images to be produced as a print. The painting was exhibited at the National Sailors' Fair, Boston, in 1864 and sold soon thereafter to Royal Robbins.[19] Presumably the new owner allowed the painting to be copied by the engraver, as the finished print was not entered into copyright until 1867. Although the engraver's name does not appear on the print, two sources named Hunt in that capacity.[20]

The marketing effort that accompanied the exhibition and reproduction of *The Rocky Mountains, Lander's Peak* was not repeated in producing the engraving after *Silver Lake, California*. The painting was smaller, the same size as the print, and perhaps owing to its early sale or to Bierstadt's absence abroad, *Silver Lake, California* did not receive the publicity and acclaim of a major work.

While Albert Bierstadt traveled in Europe between 1867 and 1869, his brother Edward acted as his agent in the United States, arranging for the exhibition of pictures and the publication of prints. Edward also began to establish a substantial independent career. By early 1867, Charles and Edward had dissolved their photographic partnership, the New Bedford firm of Bierstadt Brothers. Charles started anew as a photographer in Niagara Falls, and Edward moved to New York, where he set up a darkroom in the basement of the Tenth Street Studio Building. Late in 1869, Edward introduced the new photomechanical process of collotype before a meeting of the photographic section of the American Institute in New York. He acquired the American patent rights to the Albertype process of Joseph Albert, a Munich photographer. With his brother Albert's assistance, Edward established the Photo-Plate Printing Company to print Albertypes; he later developed a related process, the Artotype. Although Edward printed collotypes for numerous clients and publishers, he continued to work closely with Albert on several projects.[21]

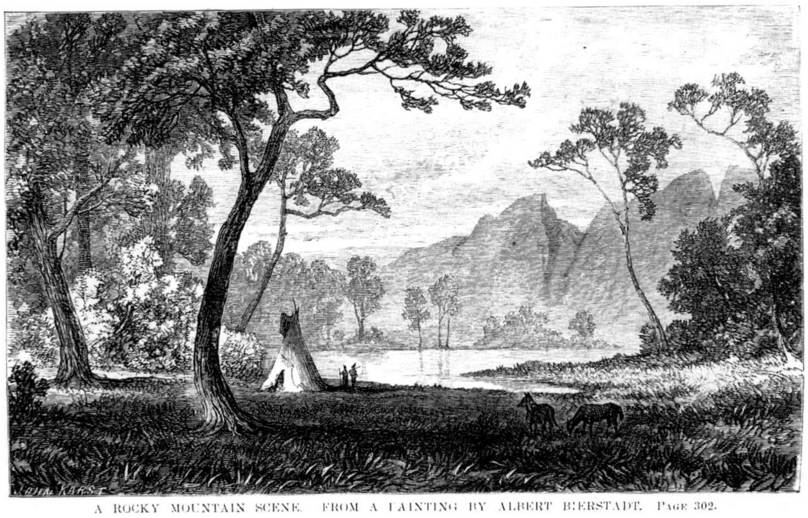
A ROCKY MOUNTAIN SCENE. FROM A PAINTING BY ALBERT BIERSTADT. PAGE 302.

Figure 85

"A Rocky Mountain Scene" (Fig. 85). Wood engraving by John Karst in A. Richardson 1867.

## 1868

*Sunset: California Scenery* (Fig. 86). Chromolithograph by L. Prang & Co., Boston, 1868. 12¼ × 17¾ in. (31.5 × 45.5 cm) (image). Prints & Photographs Division, Library of Congress, Washington, D.C.

Bierstadt was still abroad in the fall of 1868 when his only known American chromolithograph appeared. It seems likely that his brother Edward oversaw its publication, a task simplified by the fact that the painting was owned by their sister Eliza. Prang's price list published in April 1869 indicates that *Sunset: California Scenery* sold for ten dollars. The print was still carried in Prang's 1890 catalogue, but the price had dropped to $2.50, reflecting competition from newer chromos after western images by Thomas Moran and Thomas Hill.[22]

Louis Prang lithographed the works of many artists as part of an ambitious program to provide American chromolithographs of major American paintings. He intended that every American artist of note should be represented in his "Gallery of American Painters" by at least one picture. Originally Bierstadt's entry was to be *Falls of the Yosemite*, but *Sunset* was issued instead.[23]

[Antelopes] (Fig. 87), [Buffalo Charge] (Fig. 88), [Prairie Dogs] (see Fig. 102)]. Wood engravings in the *Riverside Magazine for Young People* 2 (1868).

In 1863 Bierstadt traveled to California with Fitz Hugh Ludlow. A few of the sketches he made on that trip appeared as illustrations in the *Riverside Magazine* in 1868 and 1869. These sketches and more were included when Ludlow's account of their journey was published as *The Heart of a Continent* in 1870 (Ludlow 1870b; see entry for [Mirror Lake], 1870).

## 1869

*The Rocky Mountains, Lander's Peak* (No. 78, Fig. 89). Chromolithograph [drawn by Jacob Lutz; printed by Kell Brothers]. Published by Thomas McLean, London, 1869. (Painting, No. 37, completed 1863.) $21\frac{3}{16} \times 34\frac{9}{16}$ in. (54 × 88 cm, irregular) (image). Amon Carter Museum, Fort Worth.

*Storm in the Rocky Mountains, Mt. Rosalie* (No. 79, Fig. 90). Chromolithograph [drawn by M. H. Long; printed by Kell Brothers]. Published

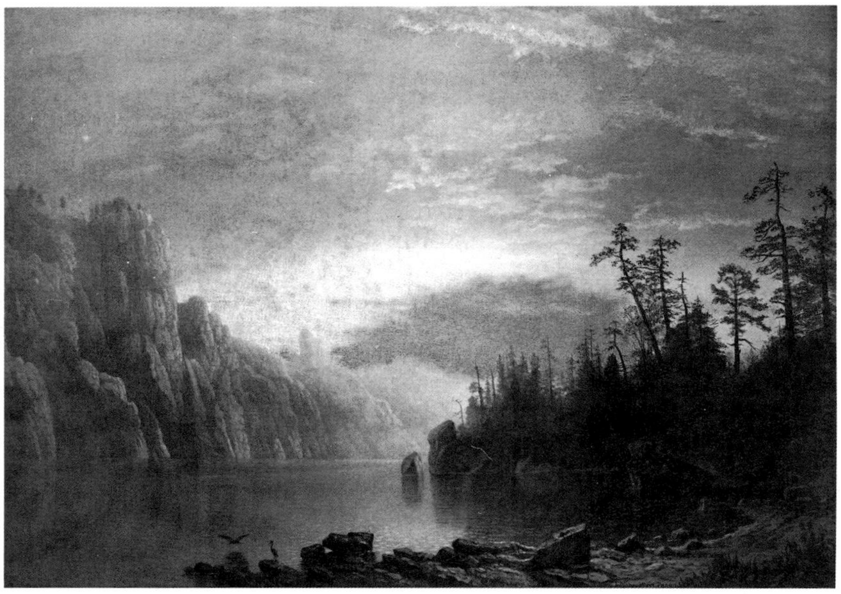

Figure 86

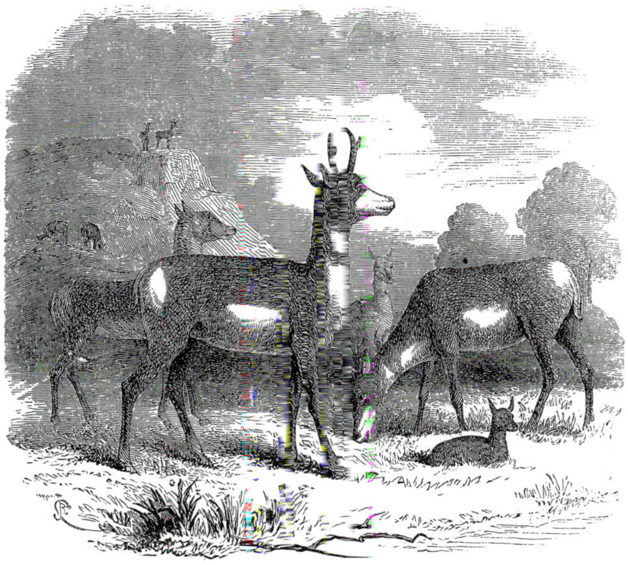

Figure 87

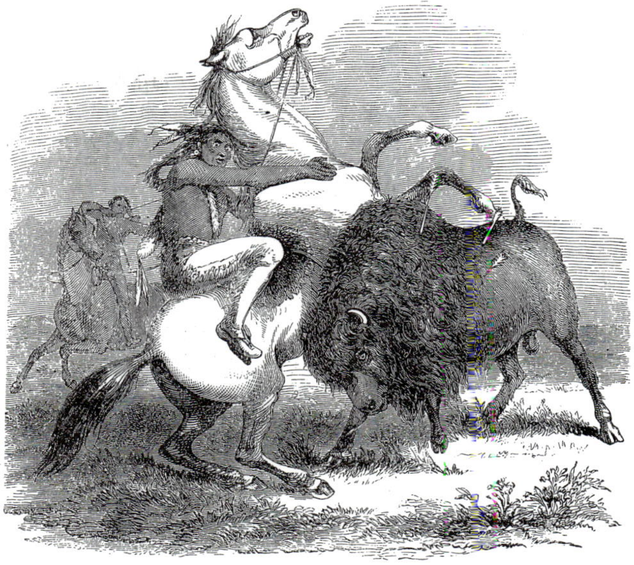

Figure 88

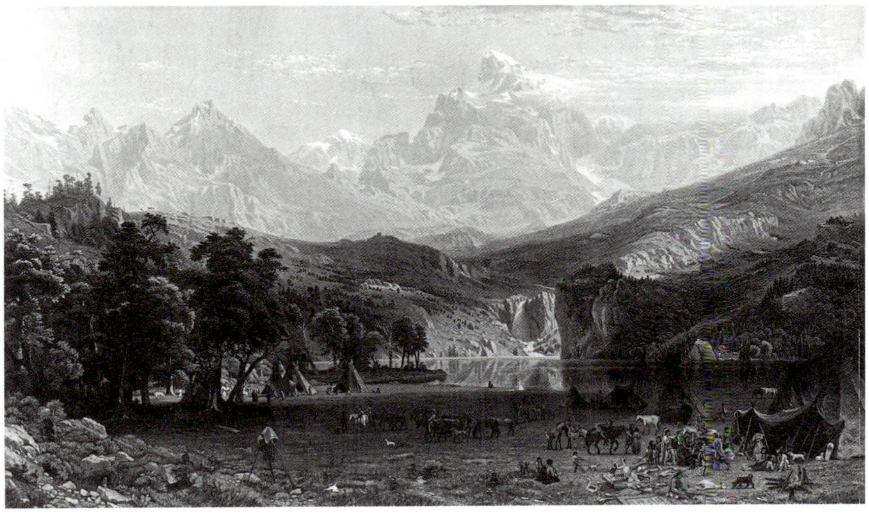

Figure 89

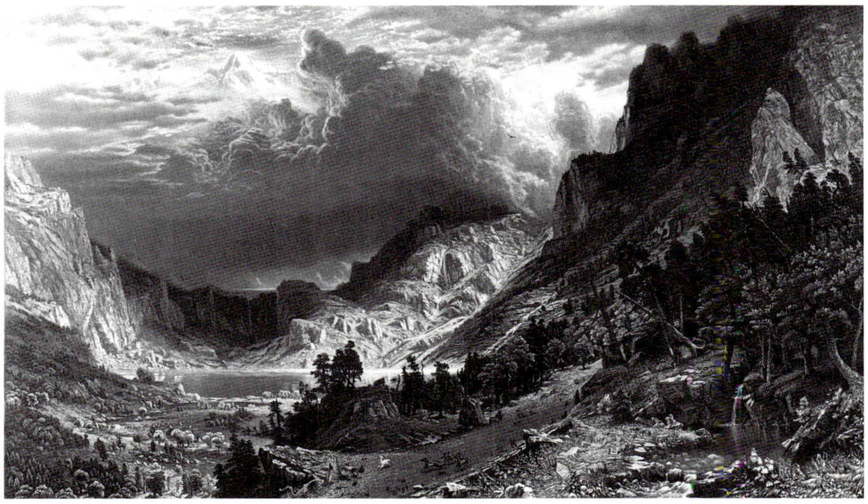

Figure 90

by Thomas McLean, London, 1869. (Painting, No. 45, completed 1866.) 20 7/16 × 34 5/16 in. (52 × 87 cm, irregular) (image). Amon Carter Museum, Fort Worth.

Bierstadt's "Great Picture" *The Rocky Mountains, Lander's Peak* was sold to English railroad magnate James McHenry in 1865. Its popularity prompted a commission from another Briton, Thomas William Bernard, for a similar canvas completed early in 1866: *Storm in the Rocky Mountains, Mt. Rosalie*.[24] Associated as a pair for promotional purposes, the two paintings were sent to England in the spring of 1866, much to the chagrin of engraver James Smillie, who needed access to the original to complete the plate for *The Rocky Mountains, Lander's Peak*. Even though both paintings were privately owned, they were exhibited in the London gallery of print publisher Thomas McLean in connection with his publication of a chromolithograph after each painting.

*The Rocky Mountains, Lander's Peak* was shown at McLean's in the spring of 1866 and then sent to Paris for exhibition in the 1867 Exposition Universelle. *Storm in the Rocky Mountains, Mt. Rosalie* was exhibited at McLean's through the summer of 1867, and then in December Bierstadt took both paintings to Osborne House on the Isle of Wight for a private showing before Queen Victoria. McLean publicized Her Majesty's favorable reaction and hung the two pictures side by side in his gallery in January and February of 1868 to promote the chromos then under way.[25]

The pair of prints was not issued until the fall of 1869, but what slowed their progress is not known. Press reports concerning publication of the chromos began in January 1868. One account stated that they were being printed from twenty separate stones (one for each color or part of the design); another counted thirty stones. There was, however, nothing inherently difficult or unusual about their production to warrant a delay amounting to the better part of two years. Perhaps Bierstadt's travels on the Continent prevented him from returning to London to approve their progress at regular stages.

The prints were heavily embossed to simulate the texture of canvas and mounted on board, suitable for framing. The size of the edition is unknown, but it was clearly large enough to account for sales in the United States into the early 1870s. The prints were distributed by several firms—both Goupil's in New York and Earle's in Philadelphia carried the chromos—but by 1871, Anthony and Company in New York advertised that they had purchased the entire edition.[26]

---

[The Eruption of Vesuvius] (Fig. 91). Chromolithograph. On stone: *Printed by Hangard Mauge, Chromo Lith by [J. E. Henne]*. [Paris, 1869]. (Painting completed 1868.) 17 × 24 in. (43 × 61 cm). Bibliothèque Nationale, Paris.

On 20 September 1869, Albert Bierstadt copyrighted a chromo after his painting *Mount Vesuvius at Midnight*. A few weeks later, the New Bedford *Mercury* of 12 October 1869 announced in less than flattering terms that Bierstadt's "lurid 'Vesuvius in Eruption'" had appeared in chromo. Sylvester R. Köhler noted both painting and print in the list of Bierstadt's oeuvre he prepared for *Der deutsche Pionier* in 1871, and he named the Parisian firm of Hangard Mauge as the lithographer. An impression recently located in the Cabinet des Estampes of the Bibliothèque Nationale in Paris is the only known copy of this lithograph.[27]

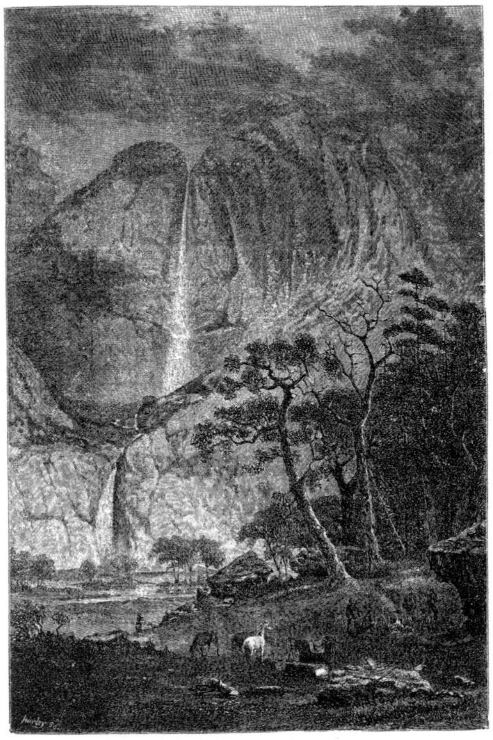
THE YO-SEMITE FALL.

Figure 92

---

"The Yo-Semite Fall" (Fig. 92). Wood engraving in the *Riverside Magazine for Young People* 3 (1869).

This illustration is based on the painting *Cho-looke, The Yo-semite Fall*, 1864 (No. 40). A similar wood engraving, with the same title as the painting, appeared in Ludlow 1870b (see entry for [Mirror Lake], 1870).

---

## 1870

*The Domes of the Yosemite* (No. 80, Fig. 93). Chromolithograph by T. J. Dillman. Printed by Breidenbach & Co., Düsseldorf [1870]. (Painting, Fig. 58, completed 1867.) $22\frac{3}{16} \times 33\frac{3}{16}$ in. (56.5 × 84.5 cm) (image). Amon Carter Museum, Fort Worth.

Bierstadt handled the publication of a print after his large picture *The Domes of the Yosemite* differently from his earlier marketing efforts. The enormous size of the original painting—some nine by fifteen feet—and the fact that it had been painted on commission for Le Grand Lockwood's Connecticut mansion precluded its being sent on an extensive European tour and being lithographed subsequently. It appears, however, that Bierstadt, ever the careful planner, had the foresight to prepare a smaller canvas of *Domes*, which he exhibited at McLean's London gallery during April and May 1868.[28] He then may have sent the smaller version to Düsseldorf to serve as a model for the lithographer, as the chromo printed by Breidenbach was available in New York by the autumn of 1870.[29]

Both Sarony's gallery and E. & H. T. Anthony and Co. in New York advertised the *Domes* chromo. Anthony's, the country's largest dealer in photographic supplies, also carried prints and photographs. Its entire third floor was devoted to picture sales, including many photographs of Yosemite. This print was offered for sale in 1870–71 in Anthony's *Bulletin*, where its price of twenty-five dollars far exceeded that of any other lithograph offered. While *Domes* was a large print, it was listed at twice the price of other large German-made landscape subjects. The *Bulletin* called *Domes* "the grandest effort of this eminent artist."[30]

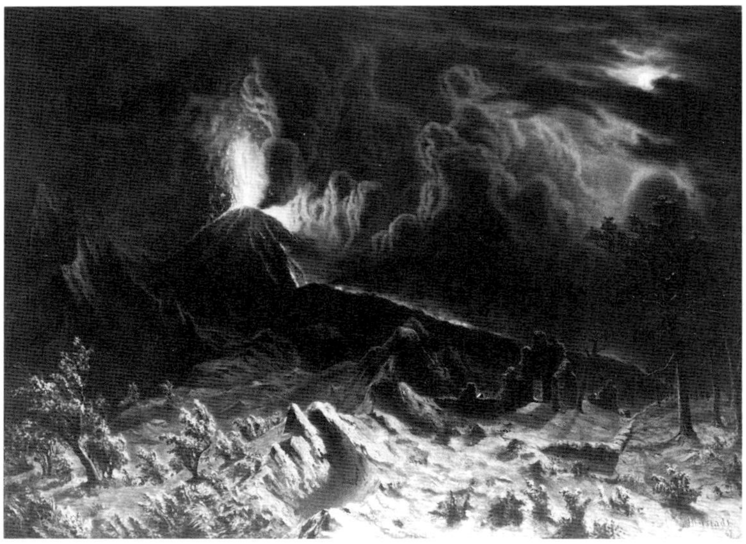
Figure 91

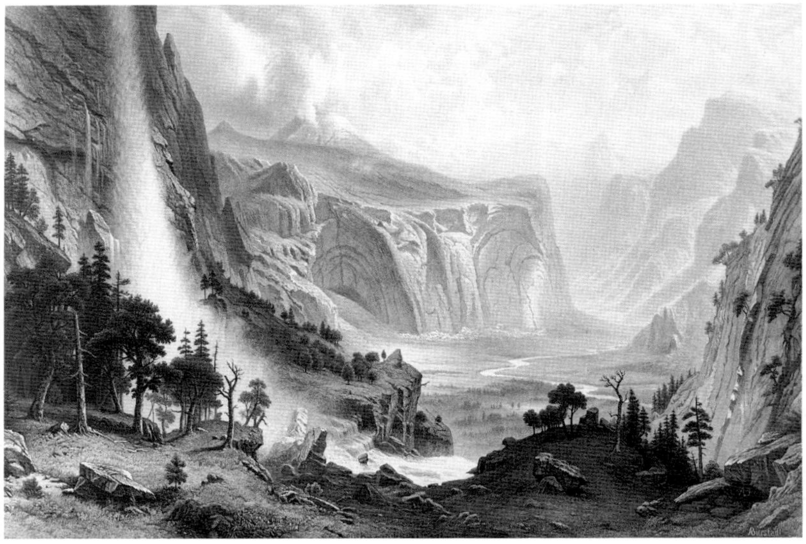
Figure 93

Bierstadt chose a German firm for what was to be his last lithographic print. The exhibition and publication arrangement with McLean had no doubt proved satisfactory for the two paintings owned by British patrons, but the superior quality of German lithography must have been a powerful draw. Perhaps the delay in producing the pair of English lithographs in 1868–69 also led Bierstadt to seek another printer.[31]

---

[Mirror Lake] (Fig. 94). Steel engraving by Vistus Balch. Frontispiece in Ludlow 1870b. 3¾ × 5½ in. (9.5 × 13.5 cm) (image). Engraved below image: *Eng'd by V. Balch from a painting by A. Bierstadt N. York.*

"Antelopes" (see Fig. 87), "Attack of Panther" (Fig. 95), "Buffalo Calves" (Fig. 96), "Buffalo Charge" (see Fig. 88), "Cho-Looke, The Yo-semite Fall" (see Fig. 92), "Comstock's Ranche' [*sic*] (Fig. 97), "Indians on the Move" (Fig. 98), "Jean Baptiste Moncrévié" (Fig. 99), "The Overland Mail Coach" (Fig. 100), "Portrait of Comstock" (Fig. 101), "Prairie Dogs" (Fig. 102), and "Wolves Attacking a Wounded Buffalo" (Fig. 103). Wood engravings in Ludlow 1870b.

Fitz Hugh Ludlow's account of the 1863 California trip he made with Bierstadt was published in 1870 with numerous illustrations after Bierstadt's sketches. The steel-engraved frontispiece, although untitled, resembles the composition of Bierstadt's several paintings of Mirror Lake in California's Yosemite Valley, most particularly *Mirror Lake, Yosemite Valley*, c. 1864 (Santa Barbara Museum of Art). Certain elements also suggest the composition of *Silver Lake, California*. The engraver may have copied a small finished oil study rather than a large named canvas.

An impression of this small print, no doubt removed from a copy of Ludlow's book, is included among the mounted proofs inserted in an extra-illustrated, large-paper edition of Henry Tuckerman's *Book of the Artists* (1867). This special volume, thought to be a unique copy, is now in the Library of the National Museum of American Art, Smithsonian Institution, Washington, D.C. It includes nearly one hundred portraits, views, and other prints representing the work of the artists and engravers discussed in Tuckerman's text.

The wood engravings after Bierstadt's sketches included in Ludlow's book are primarily animal studies, but two illustrations are after fully realized paintings: the engraving after *Cho-looke, The Yosemite Fall*, 1864 (No. 40), and "Indians on the Move," after *Indians Traveling near Fort Laramie* (No. 26). Bierstadt had married Ludlow's former

Figure 94

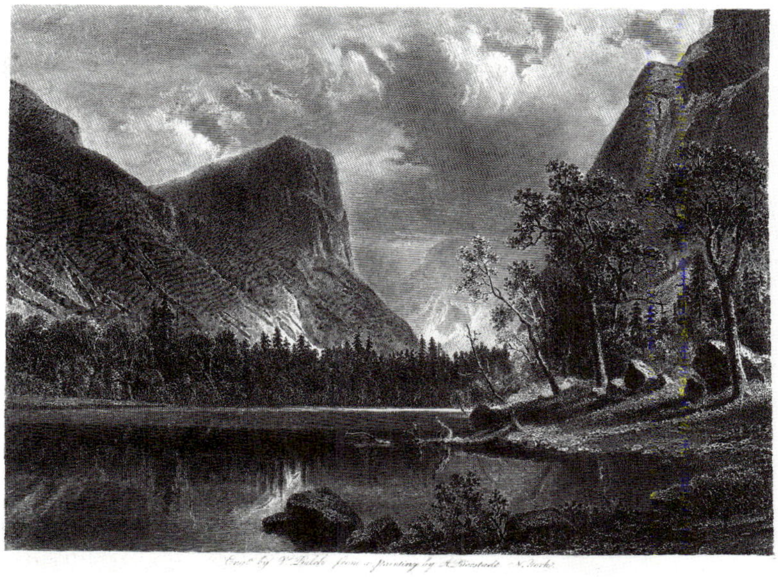

Figure 95

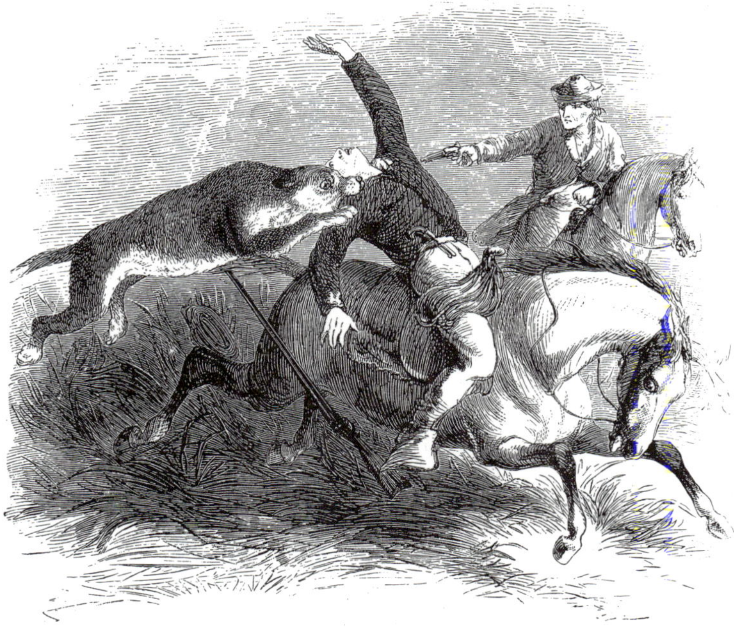

ATTACK OF PANTHER.

Figure 96

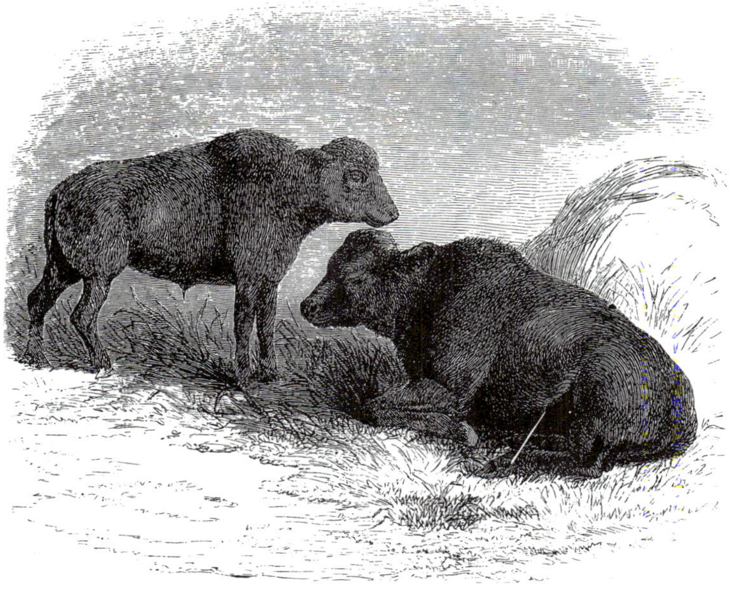

BUFFALO CALVES. See page 70.

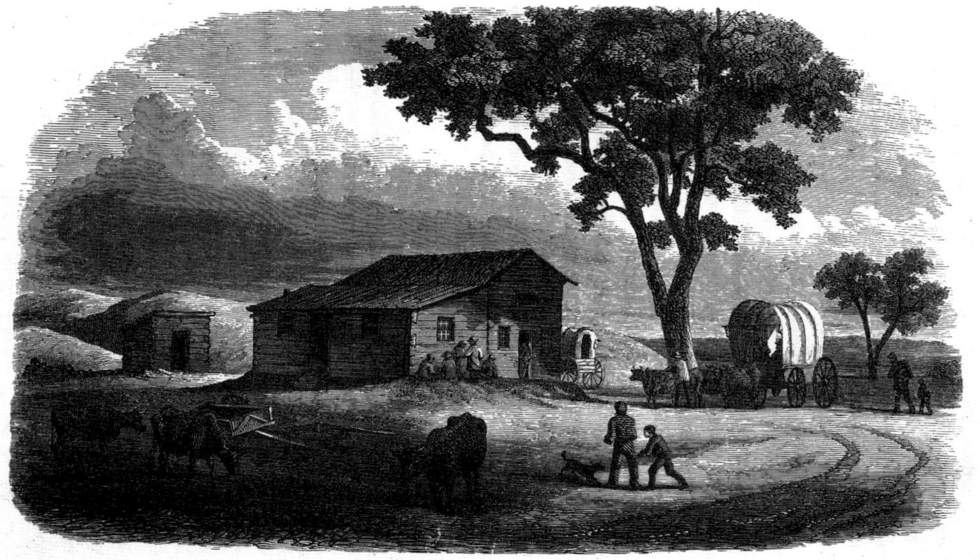

COMSTOCK'S RANCHE. See page 21

Figure 97

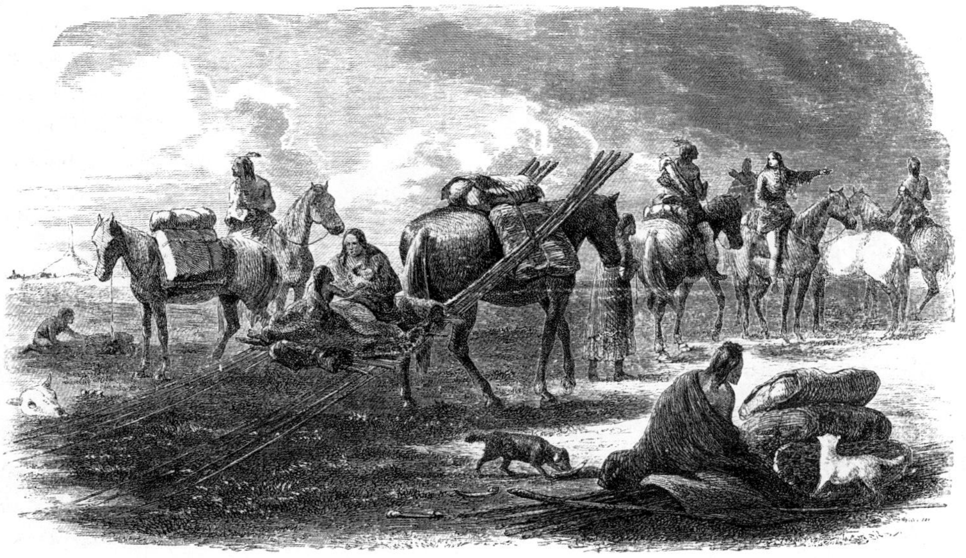

INDIANS ON THE MOVE. See page 195.

Figure 98

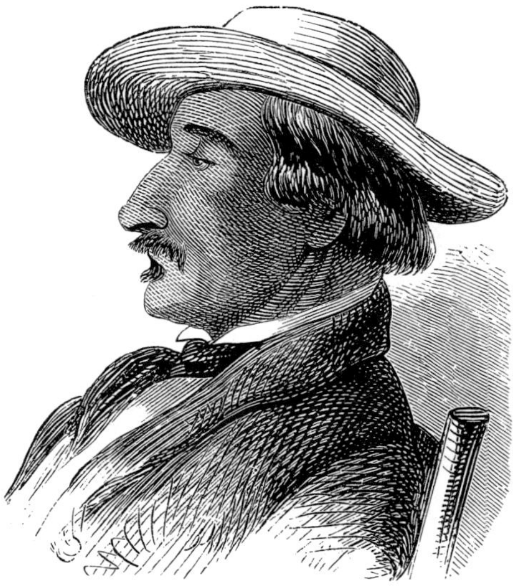

JEAN BAPTISTE MONCREVIÉ. See page 104.

Figure 99

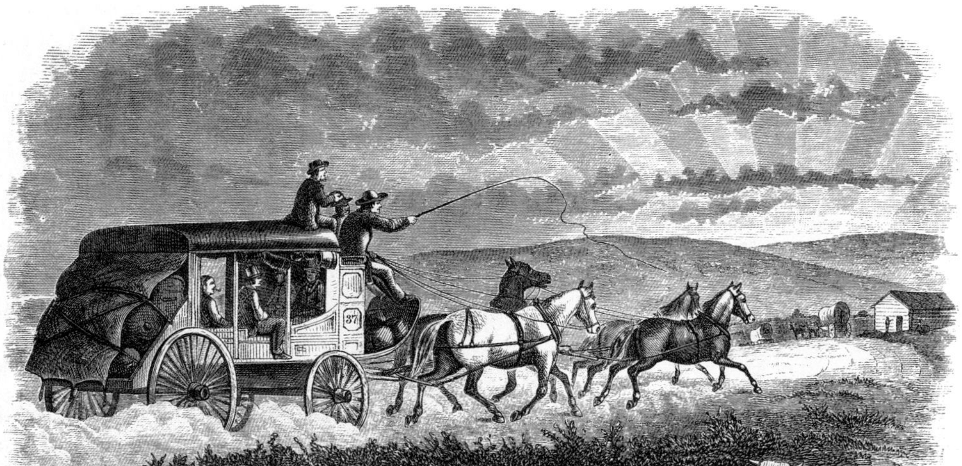

THE OVERLAND MAIL COACH. See page 10.

Figure 100

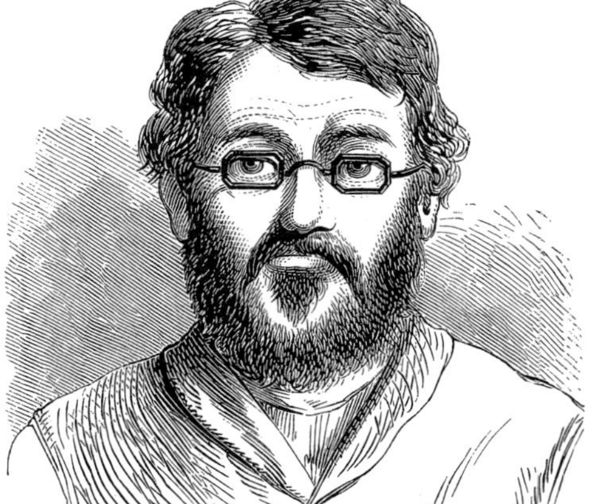

PORTRAIT OF COMSTOCK. See page 24.

Figure 101

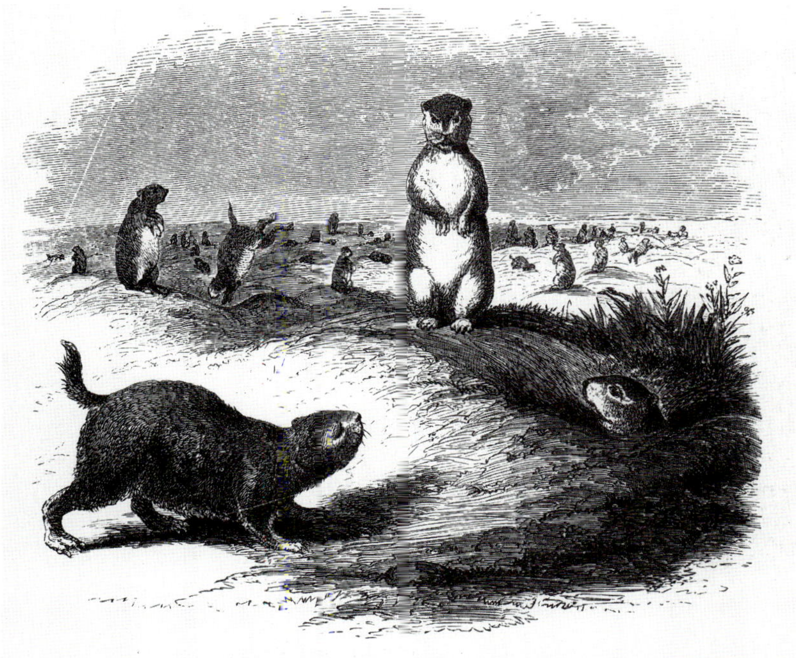

PRAILIE DOGS. See page 46.

Figure 102

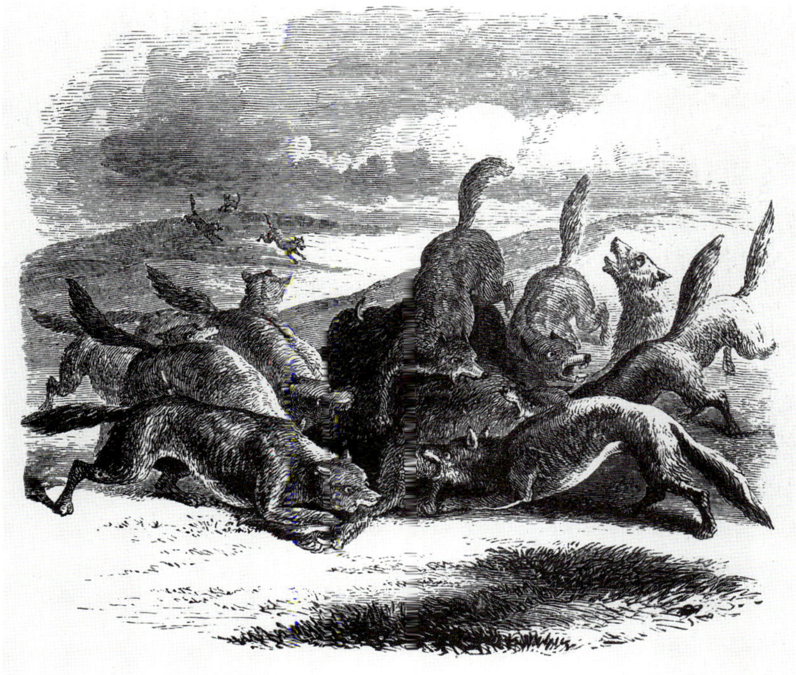

WOLVES ATTACKING A WOUNDED BUFFALO. See page 86.

Figure 103

wife, Rosalie, in 1866 and so, not surprisingly, was not credited as the artist of the sketches illustrating their 1863 journey when Ludlow published his account in 1870.

---

## [1870]

*The Emerald Pool*. "Photograph"/[collotype]. (Painting, Fig. 33, completed 1870.) No impression located.

In 1905 the Anderson Auction Company of New York sold several of Albert Bierstadt's paintings from the collection of his brother Edward. Among the works offered was a rendering of *The Emerald Pool*, identified as a photograph finished in crayon: "The wild scenery of the mountains is caught with the fidelity of the camera, and by enlargement it is prepared for the crayon of the artist. In this case it was finished by one to whom the mountains were well-known, and their wild spirit fully appreciated. The pool mirrors the mountains and the overhanging skies. 56 × 39 in. Heavy plate glass."[32]

While no copies answering this description have been located, the reference presents several interesting possibilities. The print may have been just as described, a photograph with hand-coloring, made as a family memento; or like a photograph of Church's *Niagara from the American Side* touched with pigment, it may have been a working document for the artist's use or for a potential lithograph or engraving.[33]

The 1870 date of the painting also suggests another possibility.[34] The print may have been an early effort in Albertype, the collotype process that Edward Bierstadt began to use late in 1869. When varnished, collotype prints may be easily confused with albumen photographs. Perhaps Edward experimented with a reproduction of Albert's new painting and found the result not quite up to commercial quality. Without a specimen, however, these theories remain only speculations.

---

## 1875

*A Halt in the Yosemite Valley* (Fig. 104). Steel engraving by Arthur Willmore for the *Art Journal* (1875). (Painting completed 1870.) 7⅛ × 9⅞ in. (17.5 × 26 cm) (image). Library, National Museum of American Art, Smithsonian Institution, Washington, D.C.

First published in the London *Art Journal*, Bierstadt's plate also appeared the same year in the new series of that journal begun in New York under the same title and published by D. Appleton and Company. The London plate was issued as "The Halt in A Valley, South America," a mistake that most likely reflects confusion with the South American landscapes of Frederic Church. The English press often garbled accounts of the two artists' oeuvres in reporting on their London exhibitions. The London edition of the journal implied that Bierstadt's works depicted "South American and other scenery," placed the Sierra Nevada range in the Andes, and made other gaffes, which were corrected in the New York edition along with the engraving's title.

In his listing for *Der deutsche Pionier*, Sylvester R. Köhler included a painting and a print engraved after it for the *Art Journal*, but his title was "Sentinel Rock. Landscape with Figures," an appellation that could fit *A Halt in the Yosemite Valley*. Quite possibly the painting was engraved or scheduled for reproduction soon after its completion in 1870. The picture was purchased in 1874 by the Craven family of London, perhaps marking a suitable occasion for its publication in the *Art Journal*.

The plate was reissued in Sheldon 1885–86, a collection of plates from the *Art Journal* also published by D. Appleton and Company.

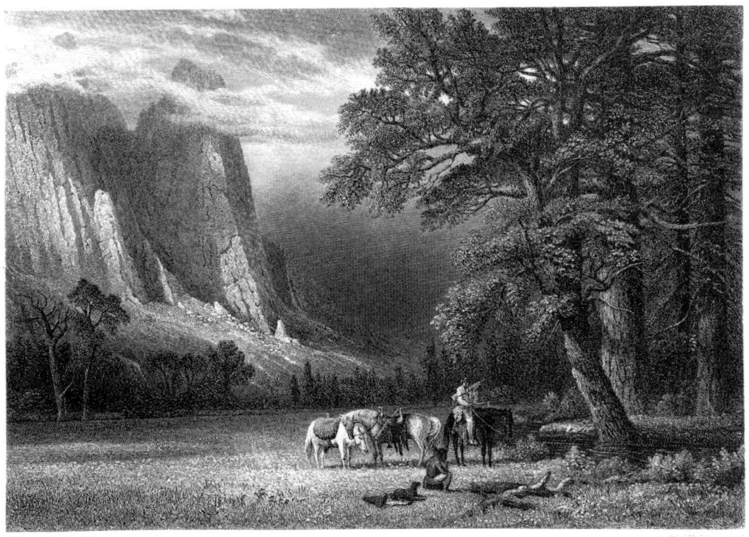

Figure 104

## 1876

*Lake Esther Seirra* [sic] *Nevada Mts. Cal.* (Fig. 105). Steel engraving by Robert Hinshelwood for the *Ladies Repository* (1876). (Painting completed 1870.) 4¾ × 7½ in. (12 × 18.5 cm) (image). Serials, Library of Congress, Washington, D.C. Engraved below title: *Engraved for the* Ladies Repository *(Cincinnati) from the Painting Loaned by R. E. Moore, New York.*

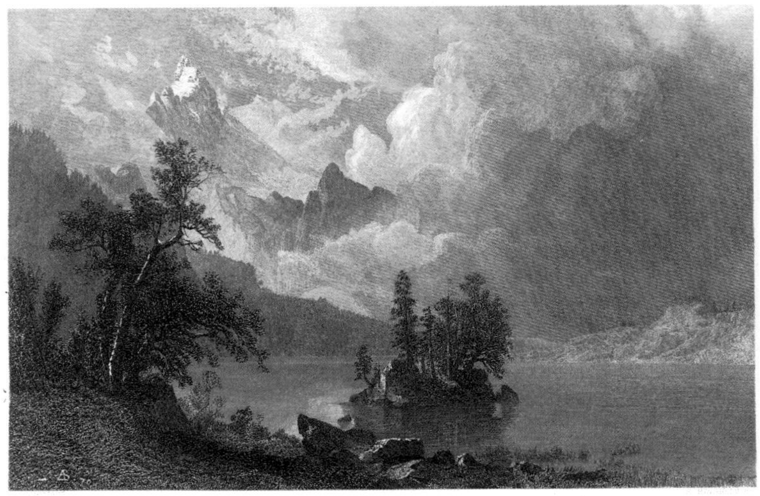

Figure 105

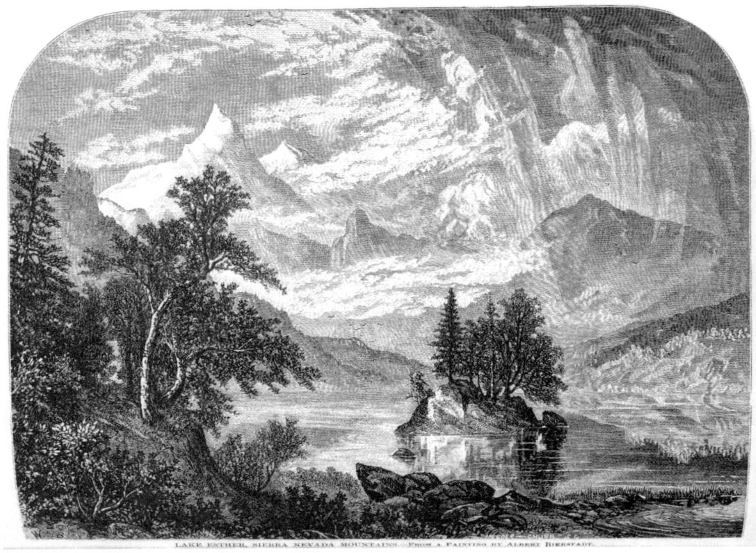

Figure 106

**Bierstadt's second appearance in the *Ladies Repository* came in the periodical's final year. After the Civil War, the publishers had experienced financial difficulties that forced a reduction in the complement of engraved plates, although the magazine remained committed to the coverage of art. During the last two years of publication, the editors returned to the earlier practice of issuing two steel engravings per month, but the expense doomed the publication. Bierstadt's *Lake Esther* had been completed in 1870; the print may have been engraved during the lean years when the number of plates had been reduced. *Lake Esther* represents one of the last two steel engravings known after Bierstadt's work.**

**The same composition also appeared as a wood engraving (Fig. 106) in *The Pacific Tourist*, a railway guidebook published in several editions in the 1870s and 1880s.**

"Western Kansas" (Fig. 107). Steel engraving by Robert Hinshelwood in Strahan 1876–78. (Painting completed 1875.) 5 × 7⅛ in. (12.5 × 18 cm) (image). Library, National Museum of American Art, Smithsonian Institution, Washington, D.C.

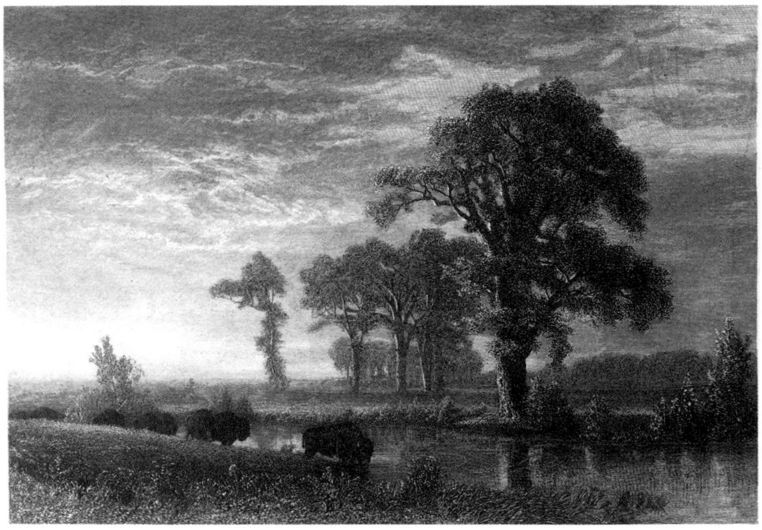

Figure 107

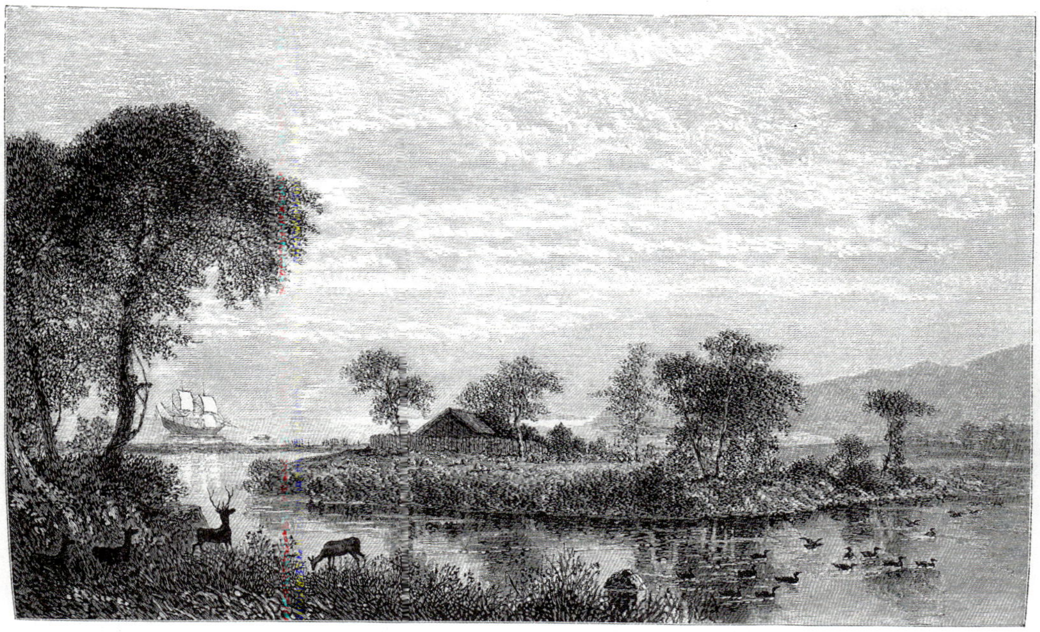

SITE OF GOSNOLD'S FORT.

Figure 108

*Western Kansas*, one of several paintings Bierstadt exhibited at the Centennial Exposition in Philadelphia, merited a full-page plate in Edward Strahan's illustrated account of the great fair. The Centennial offered the opportunity for a number of lavish publications. Other fairs, salons, and exhibitions followed over the next three decades, each of which would engender elaborate books and portfolios of artwork.

In the 1870s, steel engraving, wood engraving, collotype, and lithography all vied for the lucrative market in art reproductions. By the mid-1880s, photogravure had become a serious contender, and plates produced by Goupil in Paris and by Ernest Edwards at his New York Photogravure Company soon led the field. Steel engraving in particular was dealt a mortal blow, and "Western Kansas" represents Bierstadt's last appearance in that traditional medium. Bierstadt earned a place in the burgeoning art-book genre with this engraved plate, which was soon followed by a photogravure of *Mount Corcoran* in the publications inspired by the 1889 Paris Exposition Universelle.

---

"Site of Gosnold's Fort" (Fig. 108). Wood engraving in William Cullen Bryant and Sydney Howard Gay, *A Popular History of the United States*, vol. 1 (New York: 1876).

## 1879

"A Bull Buffalo (Bison Americanus)" (Fig. 110), "The Cathedral Rocks in the Yosemite Valley" (Fig. 111), "The Dead Moose" (Fig. 112), "A Mountain Range, with Black-Tailed Deer" (Fig. 113), "The 'Mountain Sheep' (Ovis Montana)" (Fig. 114), "Prong-Horned Antelope (Antilocapra Americana)" (Fig. 115), "Scene in Estes Park" (Fig. 116), "A Sioux Camp near Laramie Peak" (Fig. 117), "Wapiti Feeding," "Wapiti on the Prairie" (Fig. 118), "A Wapiti Roaring" (Fig. 119), and other unattributed sketches. Wood engravings by R. P. Leitch, R. H. Moore, and others, in Vivian 1879.

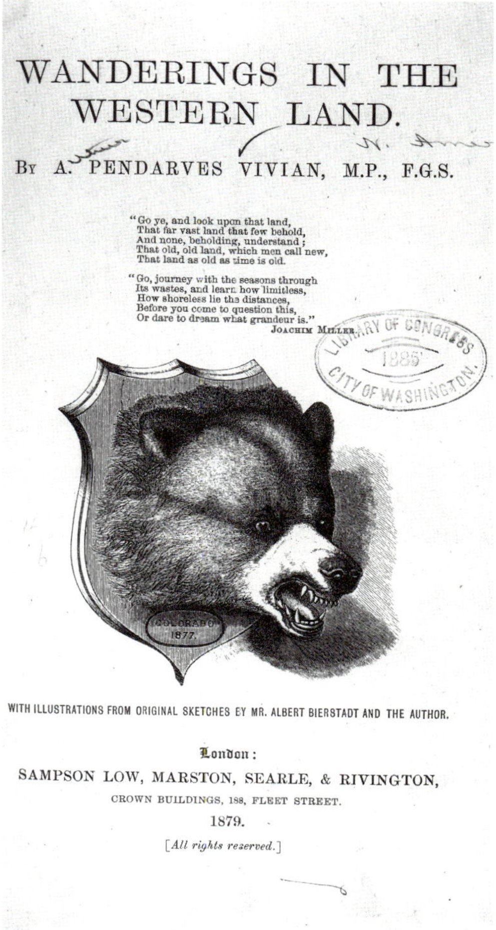

WANDERINGS IN THE WESTERN LAND.

By A. PENDARVES VIVIAN, M.P., F.G.S.

"Go ye, and look upon that land,
That far vast land that few behold,
And none, beholding, understand;
That old, old land, which men call new,
That land as old as time is old.

"Go, journey with the seasons through
Its wastes, and learn how limitless,
How shoreless lie the distances,
Before you come to question this,
Or dare to dream what grandeur is."

JOACHIM MILLER.

LIBRARY OF CONGRESS
1886
CITY OF WASHINGTON.

WITH ILLUSTRATIONS FROM ORIGINAL SKETCHES BY MR. ALBERT BIERSTADT AND THE AUTHOR.

London:
SAMPSON LOW, MARSTON, SEARLE, & RIVINGTON,
CROWN BUILDINGS, 188, FLEET STREET.
1879.

[*All rights reserved.*]

Figure 109

Title page from A. Pendarves Vivian, *Wanderings in the Western Land* (London: 1879), in which Figs. 110–19 were published.

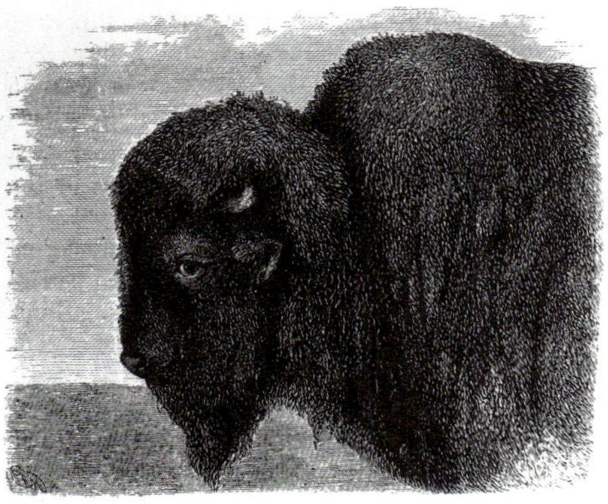

A BULL BUFFALO (*Bison Americanus*).
*From a Sketch by A. Bierstadt.*

Figure 110

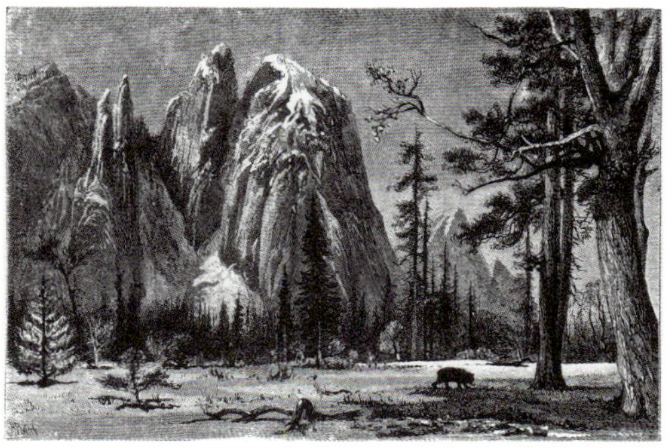

*Chapter XVI., page 376.* THE CATHEDRAL ROCKS IN THE YOSEMITE VALLEY. (*From a Sketch by* A. BIERSTADT.)

Figure 111

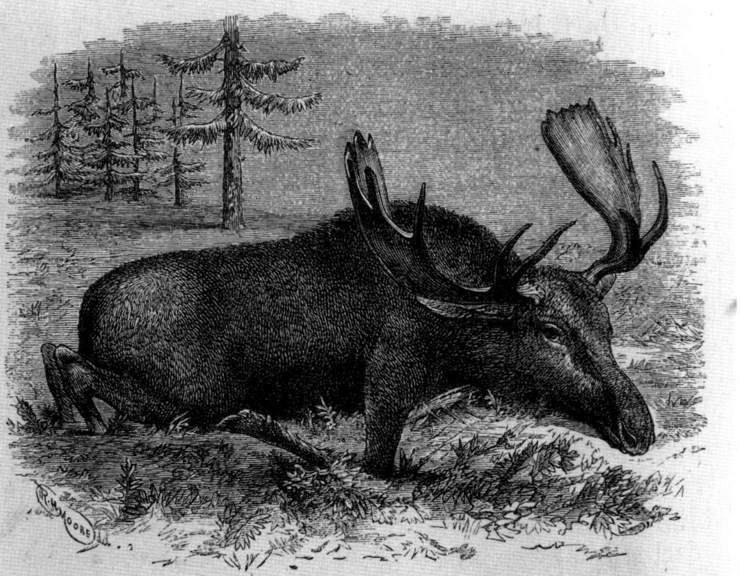

THE DEAD MOOSE.

*From a Sketch by Albert Bierstadt.*

Figure 112

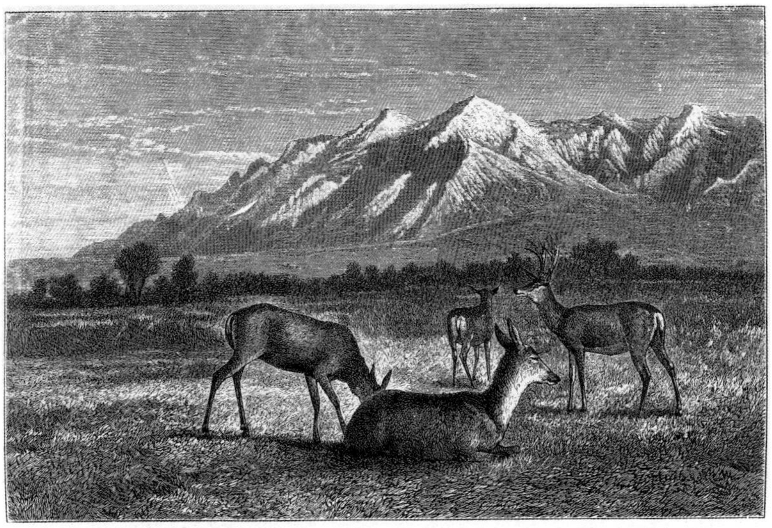

*Chapter XIII., page 305.* A MOUNTAIN RANGE, WITH BLACK-TAILED DEER. (*From a Sketch by* A. BIERSTADT.)

Figure 113

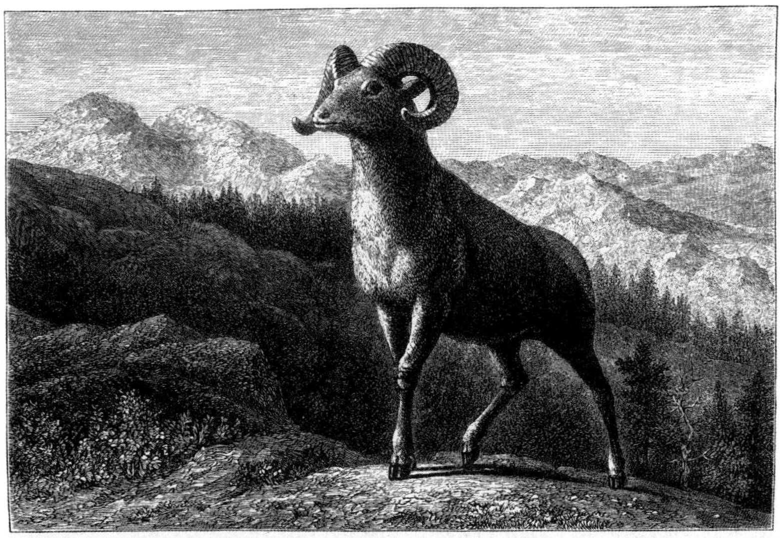

*Chapter XI., page 261.* THE "MOUNTAIN SHEEP" (OVIS MONTANA). (*From a Sketch by* A. BIERSTADT.)

Figure 114

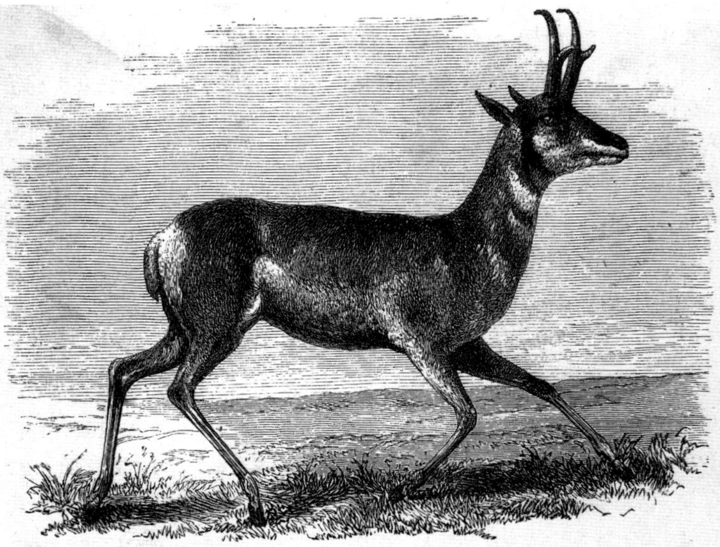

PRONG-HORNED ANTELOPE (*Antilocapra Americana*).

*From a Sketch by A. Bierstadt.*

Figure 115

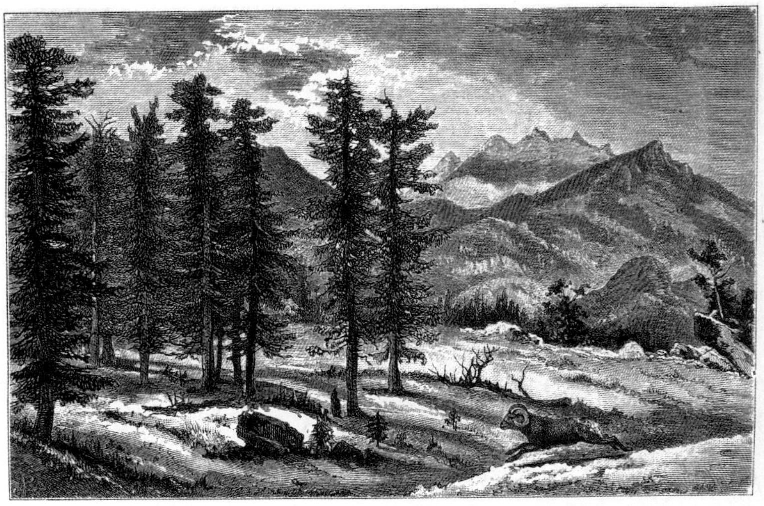

*Chapter VII., page 137.* SCENE IN ESTES PARK. (*From a Sketch by* A. BIERSTADT.)

Figure 116

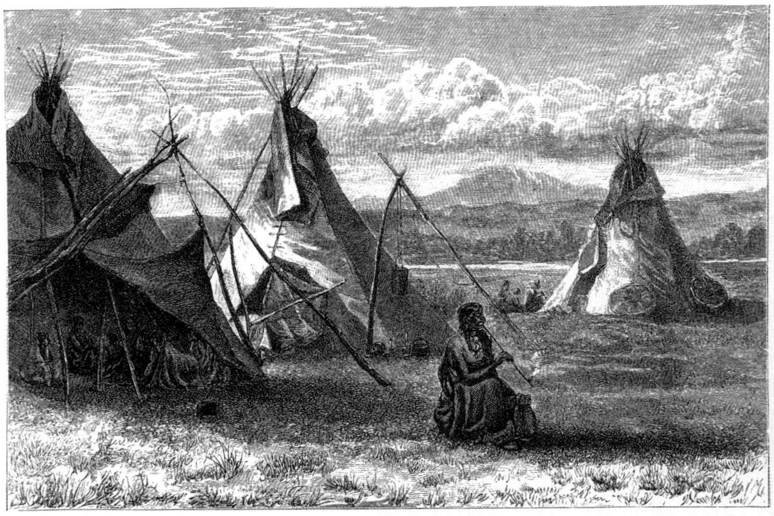

*Chapter IX., page 213.* A SIOUX CAMP NEAR LARAMIE PEAK. (*From a Sketch by* A. BIERSTADT.)

Figure 117

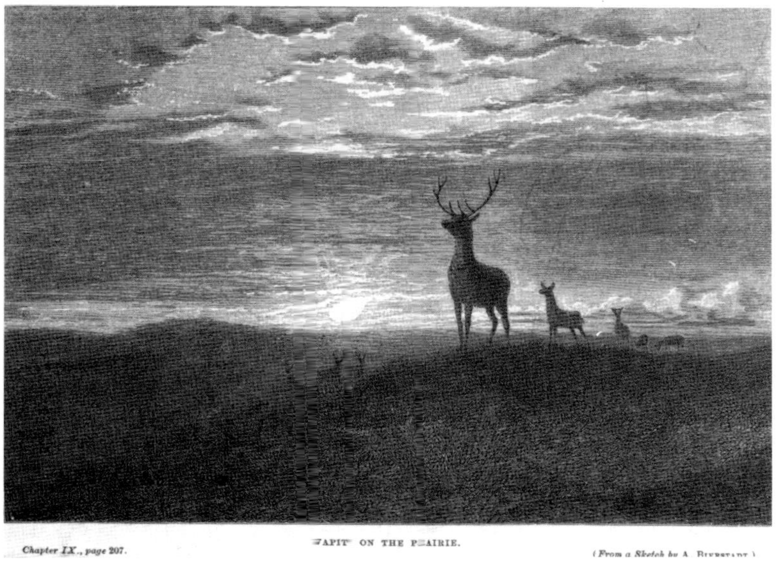


Figure 118

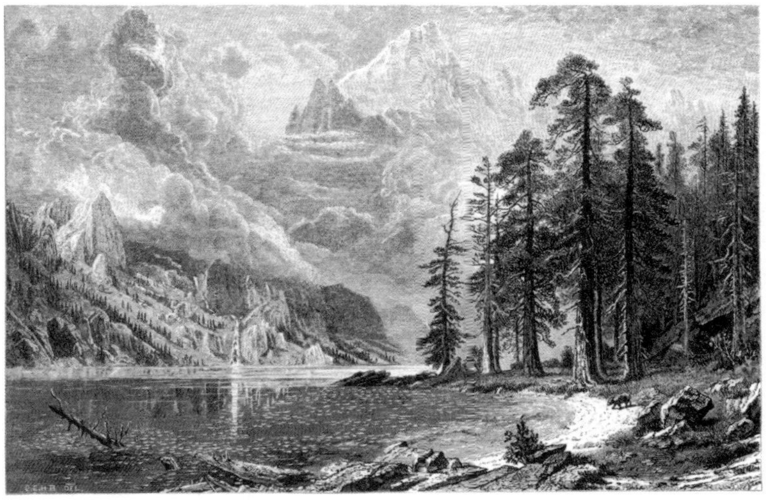

Figure 120

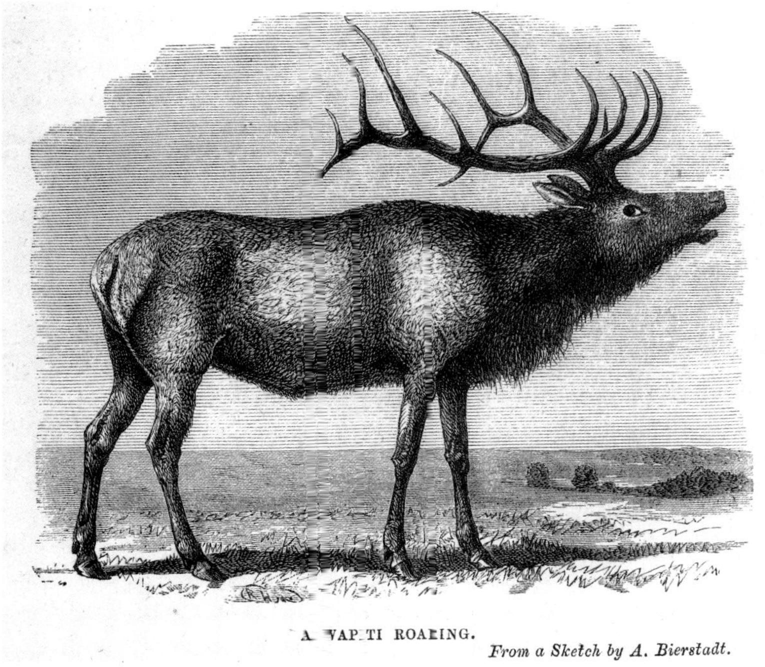


Figure 119

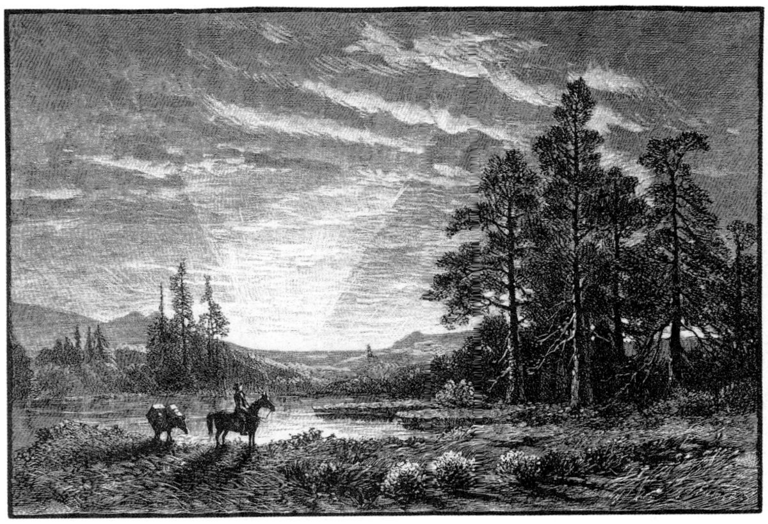

Figure 121

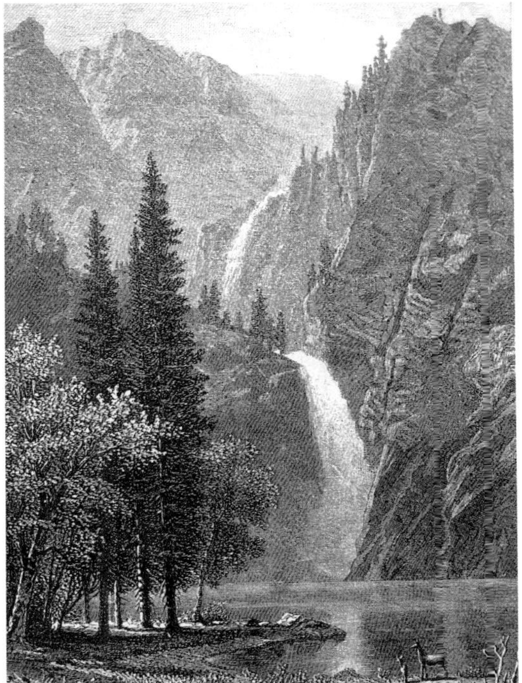

Figure 122

---

"Mount Corcoran, Sierra Nevada" (Fig. 120) and "Near the Black Hills" (Fig. 121). Wood engravings in Sheldon 1879. Reprinted in Montgomery 1889. Another smaller-format wood engraving of *Mount Corcoran* appeared in Faus 1909.

---

"View on the Kern River.—[A. Bierstadt.]" (Fig. 122). Wood engraving in Benjamin 1879.

**This view of a dramatic waterfall in the Sierra Nevada Mountains of California represented Bierstadt's work in a retrospective article, "Fifty Years of American Art," by S. G. W. Benjamin in *Harper's* (Benjamin 1879). Benjamin subsequently published the essay (and the illustration after Bierstadt) as *Art in America* (Benjamin 1880).**

## 1881

*Snow Scene with Buffalo* (Fig. 123). Artotype (collotype) by Harroun & Bierstadt, 1881. 8 × 10⅝ in. (20 × 27 cm) (sheet). Division of Graphic Arts, National Museum of American History, Smithsonian Institution, Washington, D.C.

**One of Bierstadt's buffalo paintings depicted the animals in a snowy landscape. His brother Edward reproduced the image in collotype, but for what purpose or publication is not known.**

**This small, smoothly varnished copy of Bierstadt's painting was issued during the brief (1878–81) partnership of Edward Bierstadt with Gilbert K. Harroun. A decade after Edward had established the Albertype business with Albert's help, he took Harroun as a partner, probably in return for a capital investment. Together they engaged in a complicated business transaction to create the Artotype Company. Edward Bierstadt held the New York City area license for the Artotype process, simply another proprietary form of collotype, which he used until the turn of the century.[35]**

"Sierra Nevada" (Fig. 124). Wood engraving in Charles M. Kurtz, ed., *American Academy Notes . . .* (New York: 1881).

## 1884

"Rocky Mountain Sheep" (Fig. 125). Artotype by Edward Bierstadt for the *Art Union* 1, no. 4 (Apr. 1884). 12⅝ in. (32 cm) (spine height). Library, Museum of Fine Arts, Boston.

**When this print appeared in the monthly journal of the new Art Union, it was noted in the *Boston Transcript* of 26 May 1884 as a "fine copy." Another source ascribed the lateness of the April number to the inclusion of "a representation of Mr Bierstadt's 'Mountain Sheep' which forms the frontispiece." Reproduced by the "new" (actually six-year-old) process of Artotype, the plate was described as a very beautiful and striking picture, "rich and soft as a steel engraving, . . . while probably more true to the original."[36]**

**A wood engraving of this subject appeared in Vivian 1879, along with several other illustrations after sketches by Bierstadt (see entry for 1879).**

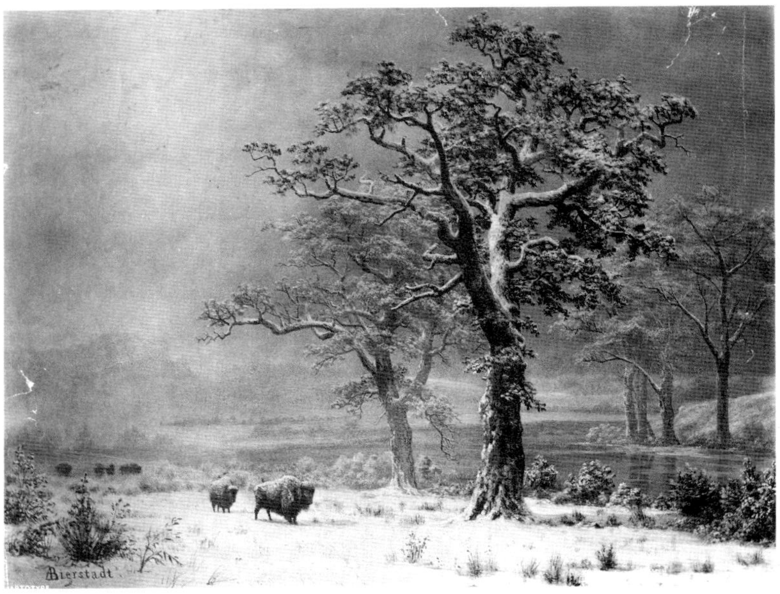


Figure 123

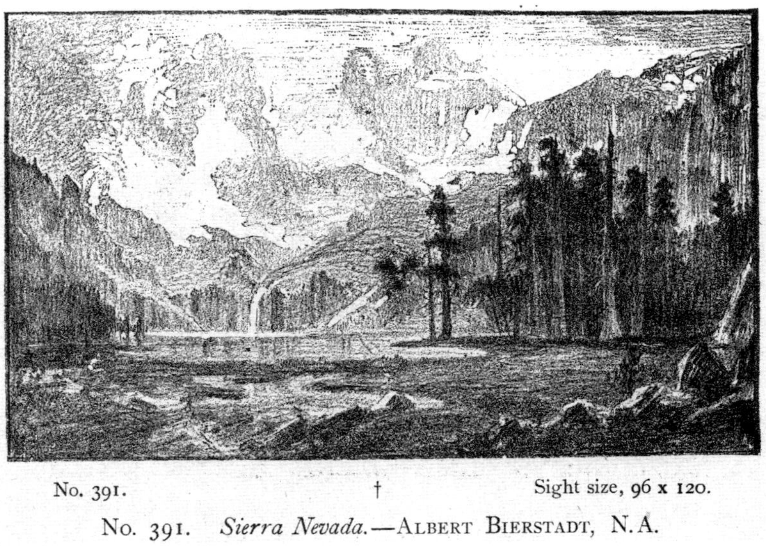


Figure 124

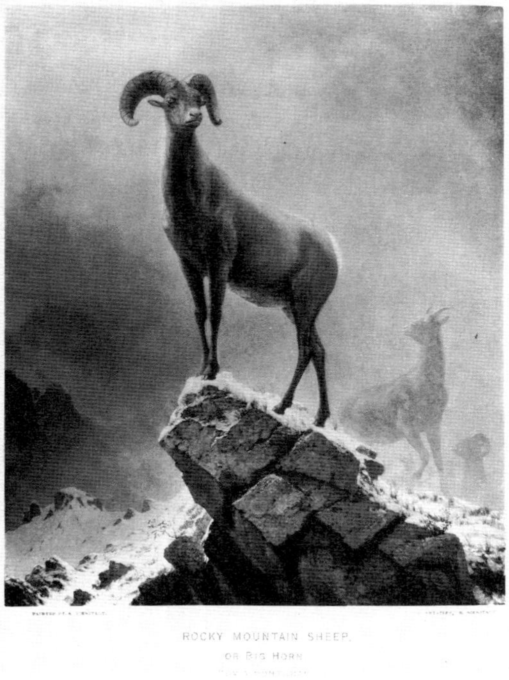


Figure 125

## 1885

In November 1877, five wood engravings after Thomas Moran appeared as illustrations in a *Scribner's Magazine* article on Nassau. One of these, "Tropical Twilight," was republished with an erroneous attribution—as "after Bierstadt"—in William Drysdale's *In Sunny Lands: Outdoor Life in Nassau and Cuba* (New York: 1885). Moran's distinctive monogram appears in the lower right corner of the illustration, and thus it is assuredly his. Bierstadt was associated with Nassau because he had made many visits during his wife's long convalescence there. Rosalie Bierstadt died of tuberculosis in Nassau in 1893.

## 1889

*Mount Corcoran* (Fig. 126). Photogravure by Gebbie & Husson Co. Ltd., 1887, for *One Hundred Crowned Masterpieces . . .* (Philadelphia: [1889]). (Painting, Fig. 32, completed 1877; original title *Mountain Lake*.) 17¾ in. (45 cm) (spine height). Private collection.

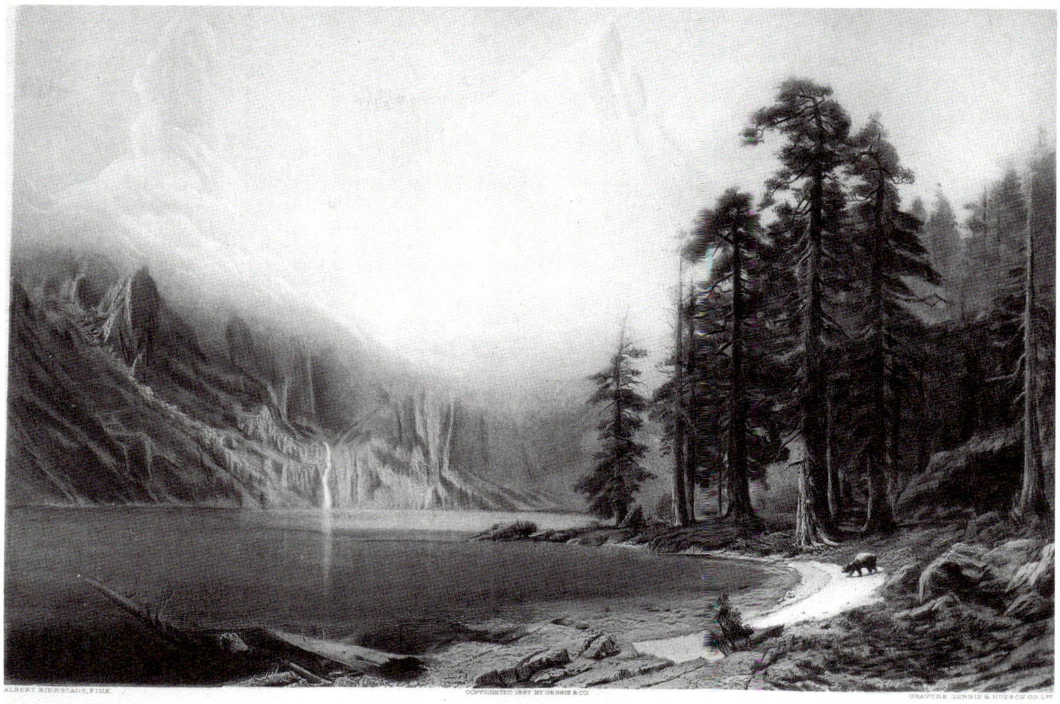

MOUNT CORCORAN.

Figure 126

Gebbie's Philadelphia publishing house followed their successful Centennial publications with a number of related efforts. A series begun in 1887 under the title *One Hundred Crowned Masterpieces: Photogravures from the greatest modern paintings of all nations selected from the public and private galleries of Europe and America* consisted of reproductions issued both bound and in parts, presented loose in portfolios so that the owners could display the art on easels or even frame favorite pictures. Several variants of this work survive with slightly different titles, numbers of parts, and publication dates. All seem to include Bierstadt's *Mount Corcoran*.[37]

Following the Paris Exposition Universelle of 1889, reproductions from that venue as well as from the Paris Salon were added to later editions. Since *The Last of the Buffalo* was rejected for the 1889 Exposition, Bierstadt continued to be represented in these editions by a reproduction of *Mount Corcoran*, completed more than a decade earlier and sold to William Corcoran for his gallery early in 1878.

If Bierstadt was not as up to date as those whose work had been shown in Paris, at least he was very au courant in having his pictures reproduced in photogravure. The age of the steel engraving and the chromolithograph had passed, and Bierstadt was embracing the new technology. One of several evolving photomechanical processes, photogravure was related to collotype. Photogravure plates could produce much larger editions than the more delicate collotype. The plate for *Mount Corcoran* was heavily retouched by hand with an engraver's burin, but Bierstadt's signature was printed. In the "deluxe remarque" edition, a tiny etched bear appeared in the print's margin at left, echoing the small figure on the lake shore at right in the original.

*Mount Corcoran* was reproduced as a full-page wood engraving in two other publications, Sheldon 1879 and Montgomery 1889 (Fig. 127).

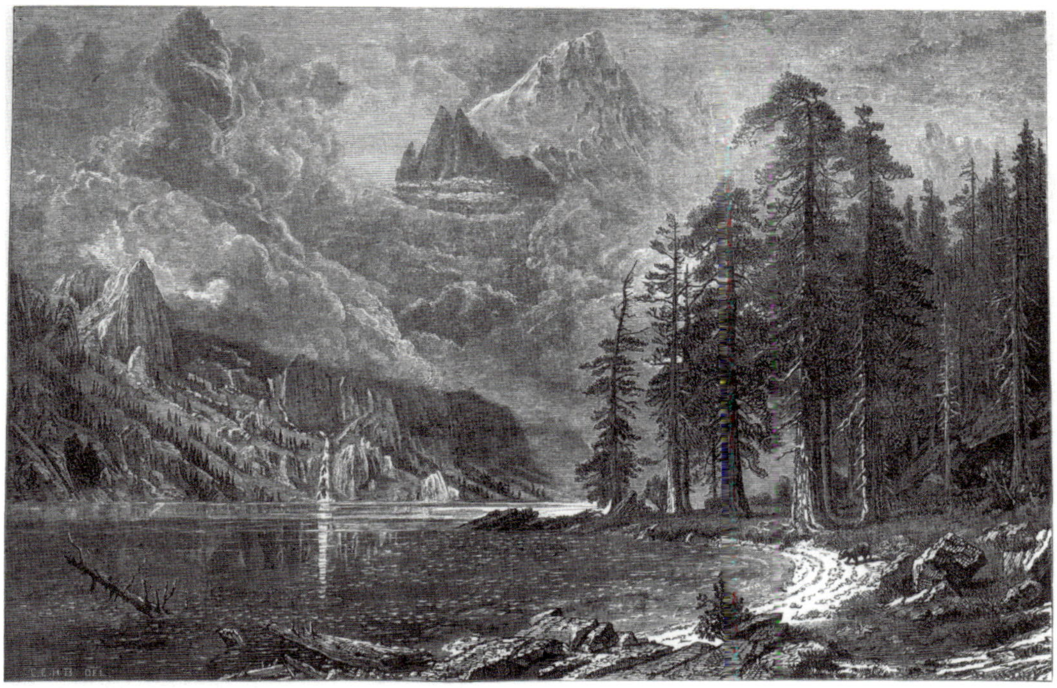

MOUNT CORCORAN, SIERRA NEVADA.

FROM A PAINTING BY ALBERT BIERSTADT.

Figure 127

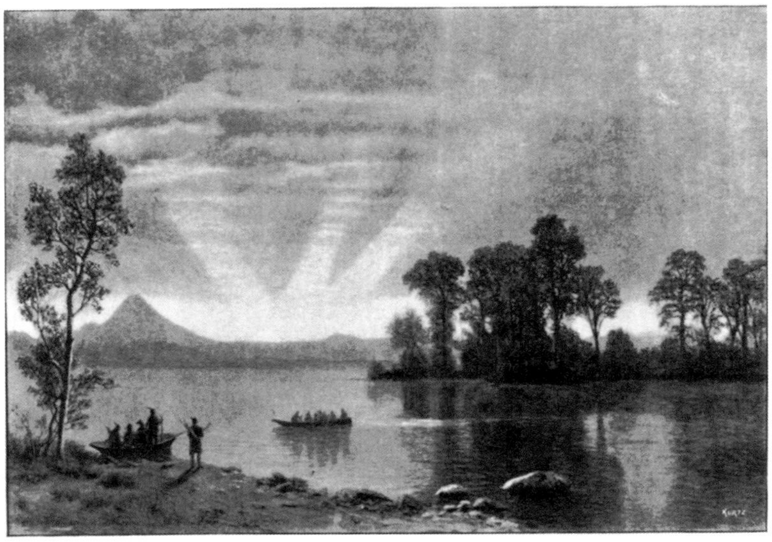

Figure 128

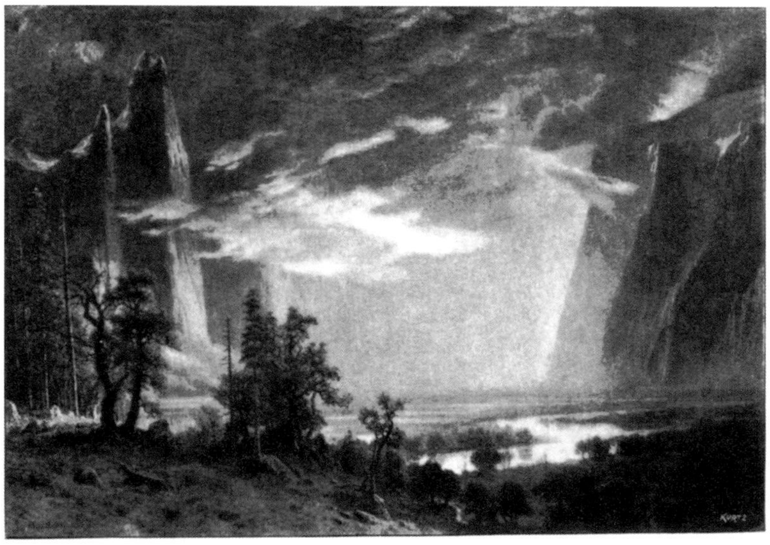

Figure 129

"Mount Hood, Oregon" (Fig. 128) and "Sunset in the Yosemite" (Fig. 129). Photoengravings by William Kurtz for *Catalogue of the Private Collection of Paintings and Sculpture Belonging to Mr. James H. Stebbins, New York*, édition de luxe, 2 vols. (New York: 1889) (Paintings, Fig. 55 and No. 47, completed 1865 and 1868). 4⅞ × 7⅛ in. (12.5 × 18 cm) (mounted on page); 4¼ × 6⅛ in. (10.5 × 15.5 cm) (mounted on page). Library, National Gallery of Art, Washington, D.C.

**The large, lavish volume listing the Stebbins collection served as the auction catalogue for the sale held on 12 February 1889 by Kirby's American Art Galleries in New York. Two of Bierstadt's paintings were among the works represented by small photoengravings. Other artists, such as J.-L. Gérôme, M. Fortuny, and Ernest Meissonier, merited full-page etchings.**

**The smaller prints, including those after Bierstadt's works, were reproduced by William Kurtz's "improved Meisenbach method," a photomechanical relief engraving process also called zinc or line etching. Capable of many thousands of impressions, photoengraving became the standard method used for book and periodical illustration through much of the twentieth century.**

## 1891

*The Last of the Buffalo* (No. 81, Fig. 130). Photogravure. Copyright 1891 by Albert Bierstadt. (Painting, No. 68, completed 1888.) 16⅛ × 27¼ in. (41 × 69 cm) (image). Amon Carter Museum, Fort Worth.

Figure 130

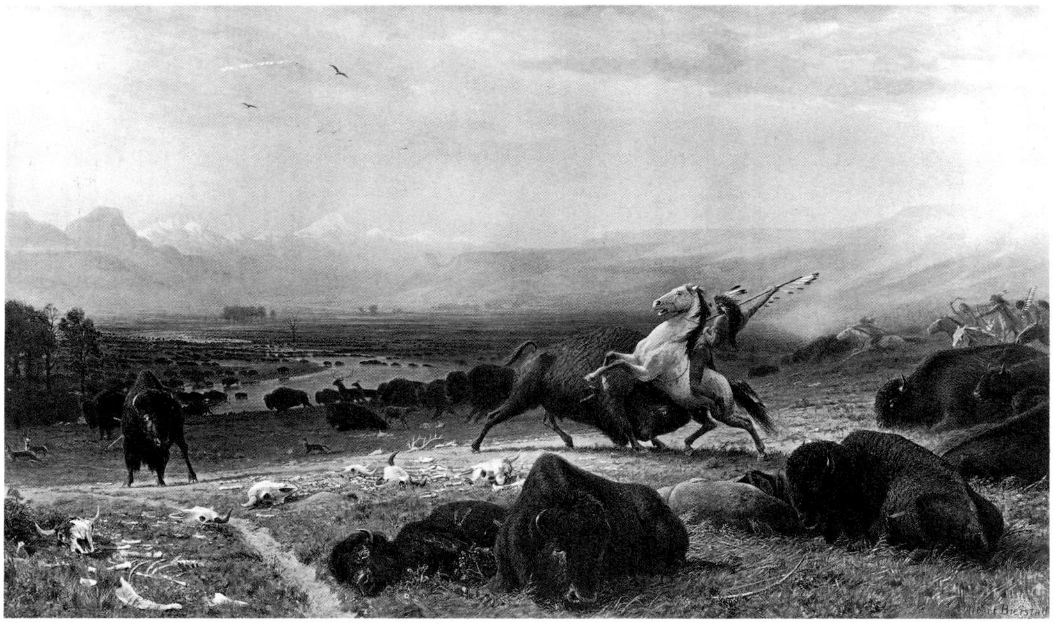

**Albert Bierstadt copyrighted the *Last of the Buffalo* print himself in 1891. Although his brother Edward had registered an earlier copyright under the same title in 1889, perhaps in anticipation of the painting's acceptance for the 1889 Paris Exposition, no copy with that date survives. There are a number of examples that bear the 1891 date, indicating a sizable edition. Neither the printer nor the publisher is known, and no information has come to light concerning the price or distribution of this print.[38]**

**Bierstadt presented copies of what he called "engravings" of "The Buffalo Hunt" to several prominent Canadian Pacific Railway officers in 1891. He sent these prints by way of thanks for favors received.[39] "The Buffalo Hunt" may have been an early or alternative title for *The Last of the Buffalo*, but no impression with that title has been located. Several copies of *The Last of the Buffalo* are proofs before title, however, so a descriptive title such as "The Buffalo Hunt" may well have been supplied.**

# NOTES

1. For information on Bierstadt's early career, see Anderson 1985. Dr. Anderson has provided much additional data and helpful assistance in the course of this project.

2. See Brenda Rix, *Pictures for the Parlour* (Toronto: Art Gallery of Ontario, 1983). Although Rix discusses primarily eighteenth-century English intaglio prints, she offers excellent background information on the engraving medium and includes some nineteenth-century examples.

3. For a full discussion of color lithography in America, see Marzio 1979. Among the most notable examples of landscape lithographs available as models to Bierstadt and other artists were Milbert's *Itineraire pittoresque*, lithographed in Paris 1823–29; August Kollner's *Views of American Cities*, lithographed by Deroy for Goupil in Paris, 1848–51; Edward Beyer's charming *Album of Virginia*, lithographed in the artist's native Germany in 1858; and the English-born Henry Lewis's *Das illustrirte Mississippithal*, lithographed in Düsseldorf between 1854 and 1857 (see H. Lewis 1967). Two recent compendia document these along with hundreds of American landscape prints. See Gloria Gilda Deak, *Picturing America: 1497–1899* (Princeton, N.J.: Princeton University Press, 1988), based on the print collections of the New York Public Library, and John W. Reps, *Views and Viewmakers of Urban America* (Columbia, Mo.: University of Missouri Press, 1984).

Artists of historical and genre subjects also had turned to lithography to reproduce their pictures. For a discussion of the work of George Catlin, one of the few American painters who utilized lithography before 1850, and other prints of western subjects, see Bernard Reilly, Jr., "The Prints of Life in the West, 1840–1860," in *American Frontier Life: Early Western Paintings and Prints* (New York: Abbeville Press, 1987), pp. 167–92.

George Caleb Bingham employed both French and German lithographers to reproduce his paintings during the 1850s. See Joseph L. Tucker, "A Collector's View of the Prints of George Caleb Bingham," *Imprint* 14, no. 2 (Autumn 1989): 2–10; and E. Maurice Bloch, *George Caleb Bingham*, 2 vols. (Berkeley: University of California Press, 1967), especially "Prints After Bingham," in vol. 2, *A Catalogue Raisonné*, pp. 217–25

4. Edward Wilson, *Philadelphia Photographer* 3 (1866): 233–34.

5. Beecher and Stowe 1975, pp. 92–94

6. *Boston Transcript*, 30 Nov. 1863; *Aldine* 2, no. 6 (June 1869): 51.

7. Marzio 1979, pp. 101–29. See also Clarence Cook, *NY Tribune*, 20 Nov. 1866, p. 6; 22 Oct. 1868, p. 4, cited in Peter Marzio, "The Democratic Art of Chromolithography in America: An Overview," in *Art and Commerce: American Prints of the Nineteenth Century* (Charlottesville, Va.: University Press of Virginia, 1978), p. 98.

8. Bierstadt Brothers 1860. No reproductions after Albert's paintings were listed, and none have been located as photographs produced for commercial sale.

9. For a more thorough account of the Bierstadt brothers' interrelated activities as purveyors of landscape views, see Helena E. Wright, "Partners in the Business of Art: Producing, Packaging, and Publishing Images of the American Landscape, 1850–1900," in *Pioneers of Photography* (Springfield, Va.: Society for Imaging Science and Technology, 1987), pp. 274–85.

10. Early experiments with photography included the transfer of an image to a metal plate, which then could be etched and printed, but it was not until about 1880 that the photogravure process offered consistent results suitable for reproducing editions of framing prints. For more information about this and other reproductive processes, see Bamber Gascoigne, *How to Identify Prints: A Complete Guide to Manual and Mechanical Processes from Woodcut to Ink Jet* (New York: Thames and Hudson, 1986).

11. See Jeremy Maas, *Gambart: Prince of the Victorian Art World* (London: Barrie & Jenkins, 1975). Maas's discussion of the nineteenth-century British art scene covers many parallels to developments on this side of the Atlantic, such as the dealer's role in the phenomenal rise in the popularity of living artists, the great sums their works commanded, and the publication of their pictures in many forms, both authorized and pirated.

12. *Post*, New York, 8 July, 11 Aug., 8 Oct., 20 Oct. 1864.

13. By 1864, both Frederic Church and Jasper F. Cropsey had published English chromolithographs of their paintings, and George Caleb Bingham had used both French and German lithographic firms during the 1850s. Storch & Kramer lithographed William Bradford's *Crushed by Icebergs* in 1868 (perhaps at Bierstadt's recommendation), according to the New Bedford *Mercury*, 27 May 1868. John Mix Stanley also had six of his Indian paintings lithographed in Berlin by Storch & Kramer between 1868 and 1870. See Schimmel 1983, pp. 153–56, 412–13. Storch & Kramer also was the choice of the British Arundel Society, which gave its first lithographic commission to a British firm but soon looked to Germany for superior color printing. See Susan Lambert, *The Image Multiplied: Five Centuries of Printed Reproductions of Paintings and Drawings* (London: Trefoil Publications, 1987), p. 106.

14. James Smillie's reputation as the best landscape engraver in America was based upon work he executed after paintings by Thomas Cole, Cropsey, Thomas Doughty, Asher B. Durand, and John F. Kensett, culminating in the four plates for Cole's *Voyage of Life* (1855). Bierstadt's *Rocky Mountains, Lander's Peak* was often noted as the most important work of his career. Smillie was elected to the NAD as the single example of landscape engraver, exemplifying his prominence in that field. For biographical details on Smillie and the other engravers who produced plates after Bierstadt, see W. S. Baker, *American Engravers and Their Works* (Philadelphia: Gebbie & Barrie, 1875), pp. 159–63, and David M. Stauffer, *American Engravers upon Copper and Steel* (New York: Grolier Club, 1907). Smillie's unpublished autobiography, "A Pilgrimage," is among the family papers in the AAA.

15. A good account of the practice of engraving a plate in this period can be found in Basil Hunnisett, *Steel-Engraved Book Illustration in England* (Boston: David R. Godine, 1980), pp. 42–52.

16. Drafts of letters written by James D. Smillie have recently been donated to the AAA.

17. Witthoft 1987 reproduces the entire contract between James Smillie and Albert Bierstadt and provides many details about Smillie's continuing problems during production of the plate. For example, the painting's sale and shipment to England came just when Smillie needed it most in order to study the original. Smillie's autobiographical "Pilgrimage" indicates his plaintive displeasure with Bierstadt's removal of the painting just at the critical juncture for final touches on his engraving. As a result, the engraver never felt fully satisfied with the finished print, but the artist and many other admirers considered it a great achievement of American engraving.

18. Partially filled subscription books prevented other artists from producing proposed prints as well. "Cropsey, like Church, was unsuccessful in securing sufficient pledges for an engraving of his work as readily shown by the subscription book (now in Hastings, N.Y.) that is less than one-third filled" (Peter Bermingham, *Jasper F. Cropsey: A Retrospective View of America's Painter of Autumn* [College Park, Md.: University of Maryland Art Gallery, 1968], p. 26, n. 12; the paintings referred to are not named).

Although it was eventually engraved, Church's *Heart of the Andes* got off to a slow start. The *Chicago Tribune* of 13 Feb. 1861 reported that while visitation to see the painting ran high, "the subscription list for the engraving remained almost blank."

The San Francisco *Bulletin* of 12 June 1865, in a piece titled "California Landscapes at the East," mentioned Bierstadt's praise for Smillie's engraving of *The Rocky Mountains, Lander's Peak* and stated that Bierstadt intended "to have his large picture of *Mount Hood* engraved by the same artist [i.e., Smillie]."

19. *Boston Transcript*, 9 Nov. 1864, and Nancy Anderson, personal communication.

20. Baker, *American Engravers*, pp. 86–87, lists *Silver Lake* among Hunt's engravings. Köhler 1871, p. 363, also named Hunt as the engraver of *Silver Lake*. To maximize production of his prints while his success was current, Bierstadt might well have commissioned both a large and a small plate from the same engraver.

21. For further details about the brothers' photographic enterprises, see Wright, "Partners."

22. L. Prang & Co., *Illustrated Catalogue of Fine Art Studies, Water Color Studies, Pictures, etc.* (Boston: L. Prang, 1890). Division of Graphic Arts, National Museum of American History, Smithsonian Institution. GA 6947.

23. *Putnam's Magazine*, Apr. 1868, p. 514.

24. For a comprehensive discussion of Bierstadt's British patronage, see Carr 1986, pp. 60–71.

25. Carr 1986, p. 64, notes that McLean assumed the role of publisher for Bierstadt's prints but did not do so for Church, yet Church may have introduced Bierstadt to McLean. For more on Church's print-publishing activity, see also Carr 1982.

Both the New York Public Library's copy and the copy in the collection of the late Gordon Hendricks of

*Storm* are identified as having been drawn by M. H. Long, who delineated many prints after Myles Birket Foster. On Long, see Rodney K. Engen, *Dictionary of Victorian Engravers, Print Publishers and Their Works* (Cambridge: Chadwyck-Healey, 1979), p. 128, and correspondence from Susan Lambert, Victoria and Albert Museum print room. Jacob Lutz is identified as the draftsman on a modern label added to the copy in the collection of the late Gordon Hendricks of the *Rocky Mountains, Lander's Peak* chromo. Köhler 1871, pp. 362–63, named Kell Brothers as the printers of both chromos. G. Wakeman and G. Bridson, *A Guide to 19th-Century Colour Printers* (Loughborough: Plough Press, 1975), p. 75, identifies one Thomas McLean as a London lithographer at a different address from the Thomas McLean who published prints and exhibited pictures in his Haymarket gallery. Any connection between the two is not clear.

26. *Anthony's Photographic Bulletin* 3 (1871): 307. The *Bulletin* advertised the prints at a reduced rate of twenty-five dollars for the pair under the titles "Encampment in the Rocky Mountains" and "Storm in the Rocky Mountains: Mt. Rosalie."

Goupil's advertised Church's *Niagara* and Bierstadt's *Rocky Mountains, Lander's Peak* and *Storm in the Rocky Mountains, Mt. Rosalie* as its most celebrated chromos in the New York *Post* of 21 Dec. 1870 but did not mention their prices. A notice in the Philadelphia *Press* of 8 Mar. 1871 for Earle's gallery advertised Bierstadt's four available chromos with their original and "sale" prices. *The Rocky Mountains, Lander's Peak* and *Storm* sold for $18.75 each, reduced from $25 each.

An original label in the Amon Carter Museum files shows *Storm*'s printed title as "'The Storm' in the Rocky Mountains, South America." Bierstadt's work frequently was confused with Frederic Church's South American subjects by the London press, as indicated in the entry for *A Halt in the Yosemite Valley*.

27. On 8 Mar. 1871, Earle's gallery in Philadelphia advertised Bierstadt's chromos for sale in the Philadelphia *Press*. Listed were only four titles, the four major prints produced after 1868: *The Domes of the Yosemite; Sunset: California Scenery; Rocky Mountains;* and *Storm [in the Rocky Mountains]*. *Vesuvius* was not included, nor was his earlier production, *Sunlight and Shadow*.

28. Hendricks 1971, p. 26, mentions this smaller canvas. An oil version of this painting measuring 21½ × 33¼ in. recently was sold by Vose Galleries, Boston. Possibly it is the copy made for use by the lithographer—not an uncommon practice among artists of the time. For details of its exhibition in London, see *Art-Journal*, May 1868, p. 99, and Carr 1986, p. 64.

29. Sarony's gallery in New York advertised the chromo as new in October 1870 but mistakenly added that the original canvas had been destroyed by fire in Philadelphia (*Post*, New York, 19 Oct. 1870). The print was known by several title variants. Anthony's advertised it simply as "Yosemite Valley." A copy in the Oakland Museum has an original label giving the title as "Looking Down the Yosemite Valley." Earle's gallery in Philadelphia and Sarony's in New York both advertised the lithograph as *Domes*.

30. *Anthony's Photographic Bulletin* 1 (1870): 187; 2 (1871): 57–58, 94. William Marder and Estelle Marder, *Anthony: The Man, the Company, the Camera* (n.p.: Pine Ridge Press, 1982) describes the great emporium and its many-faceted sales efforts. The Bierstadt brothers had connections with the Anthony brothers from their earliest days in the photographic business. Anthony may have published some of the brothers' stereographs; Charles and Edward Bierstadt certainly used their photographic supplies; and Edward wrote technical pieces for their publications.

31. S. R. Köhler's list of Bierstadt's works (1871, p. 363) cites *Domes* as having been chromolithographed in London. As Bierstadt exhibited the smaller canvas at McLean's, it is possible that he initially thought to have the print made in London as well but later turned to Düsseldorf.

32. Bierstadt Auction 1905, p. 48. Campbell 1981, p. 17, mistakenly assumed that this was Edward's estate sale, but he did not die until 1906.

33. Adamson 1985, p. 80, n. 231.

34. The *Emerald Pool* now in the Walter Chrysler collection is signed and dated 1871 per Campbell 1981, but as she noted, the exhibition record proves it was completed the year before. Nancy Anderson has found that the painting went on view as early as May 1870 (see Chronology, 23 May 1870).

35. Wright, "Partners," pp. 281–83; Wright, *Imperishable Beauty: Pictures Prınted in Collotype* (Washington, D.C.: National Museum of American History, 1988).

36. Clipping from unidentified source, supplied by Nancy Anderson.

37. The National Union Catalogue lists five variants published between 1887 and 1893. The earliest is *One Hundred Crowned Masterpieces* (1887). There are two variants of *One Hundred Crowned and Laurelled Masterpieces of modern painting: photogravures and etchings from the prize paintings of the Paris Salon, Royal Academy, and Paris Exhibition of 1889 . . .* (Edition de luxe, in portfolios, [1889]). A "grand deluxe remarque edition," limited to 100 copies, is in the library of the Cleveland Museum of Art. Another, the "Royal Aquarelle Edition," was issued as two volumes in four parts, [1890s?]. The other two variants are *The Laurelled Chefs d'Oeuvre d'Art from the Paris Exposition and Salon . . .* (2 vols., 1889) and *The Laurelled Masterpieces of Art, selected from the prize paintings of the best modern artists . . .* (Edition de luxe, 2 vols. in 10 portfolios, [1893?]). Complications in identifying these variants arise from the fact that the titles on the covers often differ slightly from those on the title pages, and it has not yet been possible to examine them all. George A. Smith, B.A., Philadelphia, is credited as the author/compiler in the National Union Catalogue.

38. In a letter to his father, John, dated 11 Jan. 1889, William Sartain mentioned a large painting by Bierstadt, "The Buffalo Hunt," which he had seen at the Union League Club in New York, and suggested that his father might be asked to etch the work. "The picture is quite etchable, [print] to be 26 inches long. The price for etching ought to be $1500." Although William urged his father to pursue this project, it is extremely doubtful that he became involved. John Sartain was a celebrated engraver best known for his mezzotint portraits, and there is no further evidence connecting him with the print (W. Sartain to J. Sartain, 11 Jan. 1889, Sartain Papers, Historical Society of Pennsylvania).

There are two paintings of *The Last of the Buffalo*, but the photogravure was taken from the picture now in the Corcoran Gallery of Art. Some examples of the photogravure have been hand colored.

39. Pringle 1985, pp. 3–27. Pringle also has assembled copies of Bierstadt's correspondence from the CPR Archives, and I am grateful to him for making this useful research available to me.

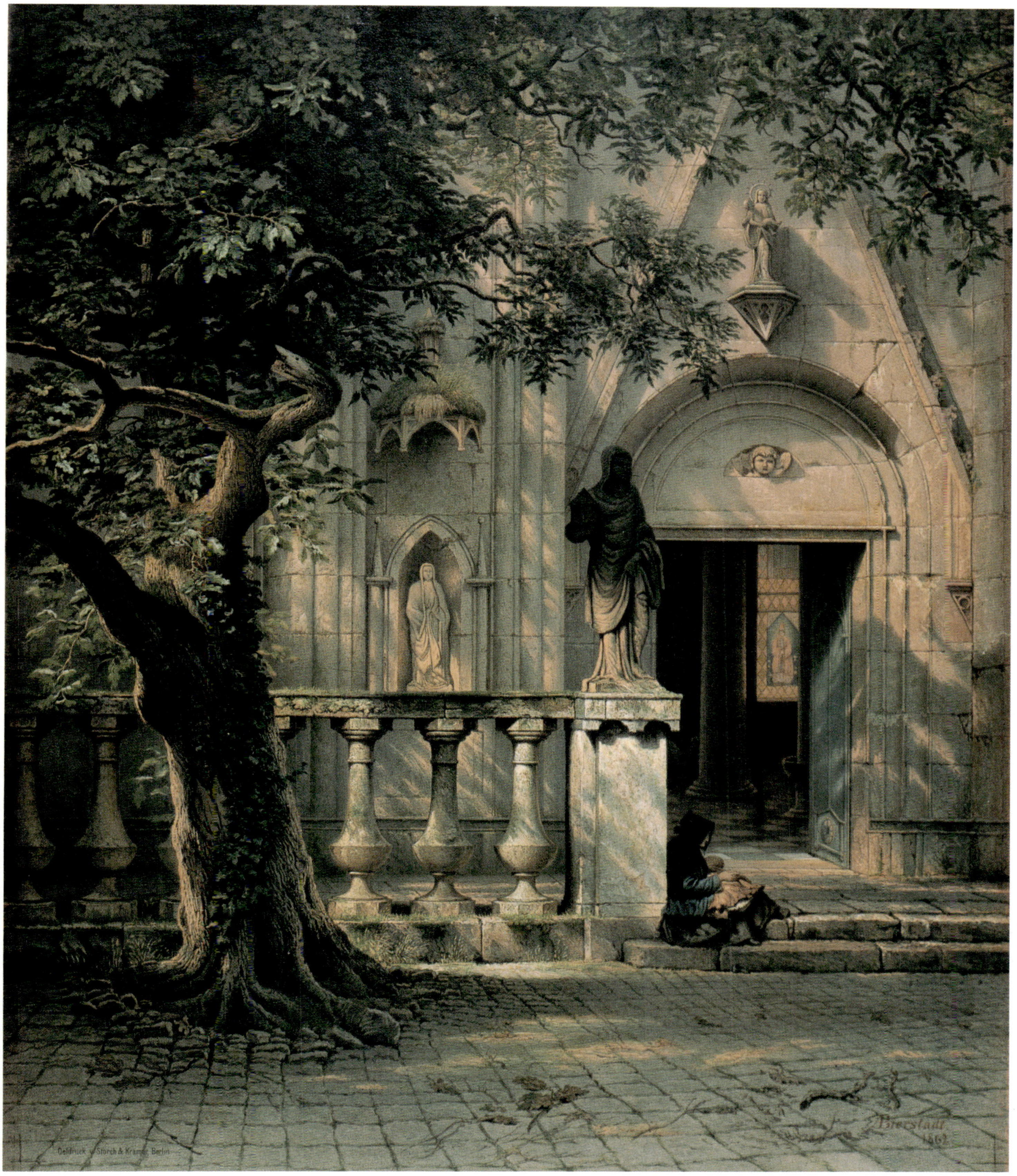

**NO. 76**

*Sunlight and Shadow*, published 1864

Chromolithograph, 22½ × 19½ in. (57 × 49.5 cm) (image)

Division of Graphic Arts, National Museum of American History, Smithsonian Institution, Washington, D.C.

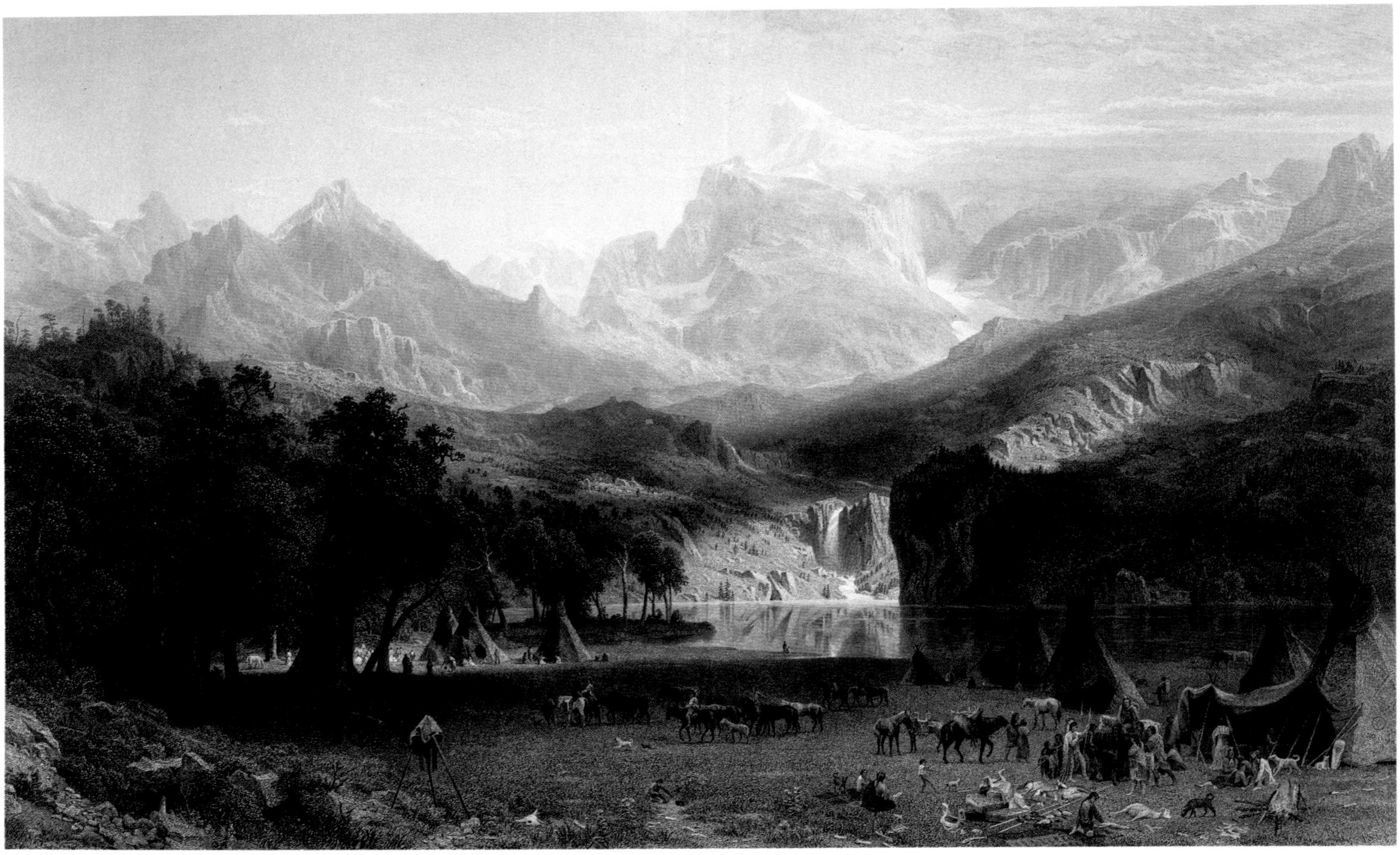

NO. 77

*The Rocky Mountains, Lander's Peak,*
published 1866

Steel engraving, 16¾ × 27¾ in. (43 × 70.5 cm) (image)

Print Collection, Miriam and Ira D. Wallach Division of Art, Prints and Photographs, The New York Public Library, Astor, Lenox and Tilden Foundations

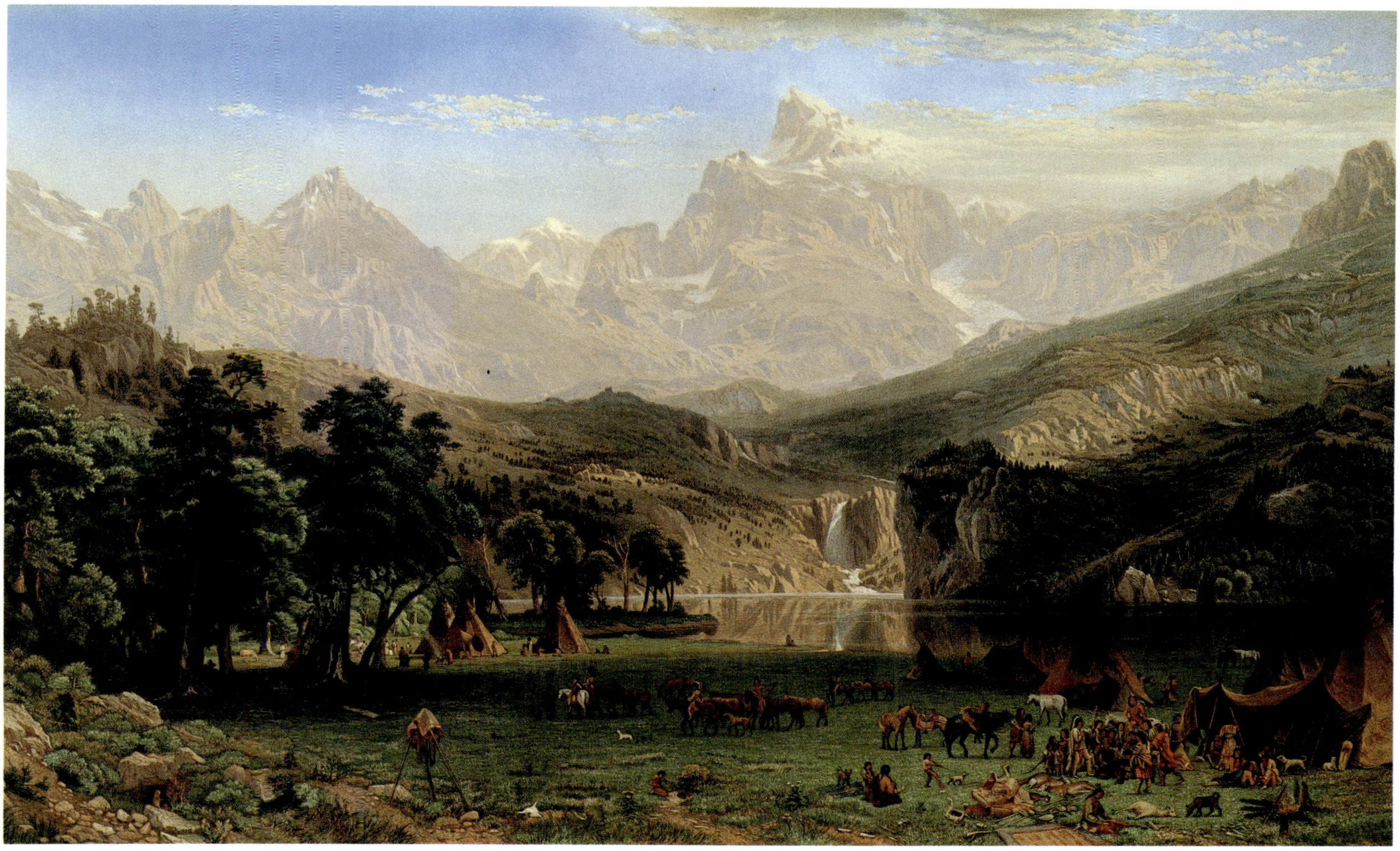

NO. 78

*The Rocky Mountains, Lander's Peak,*
published 1869

Chromolithograph, $21\frac{3}{16} \times 34\frac{9}{16}$ in. (54 × 88 cm) (irregular; image)
Amon Carter Museum, Fort Worth

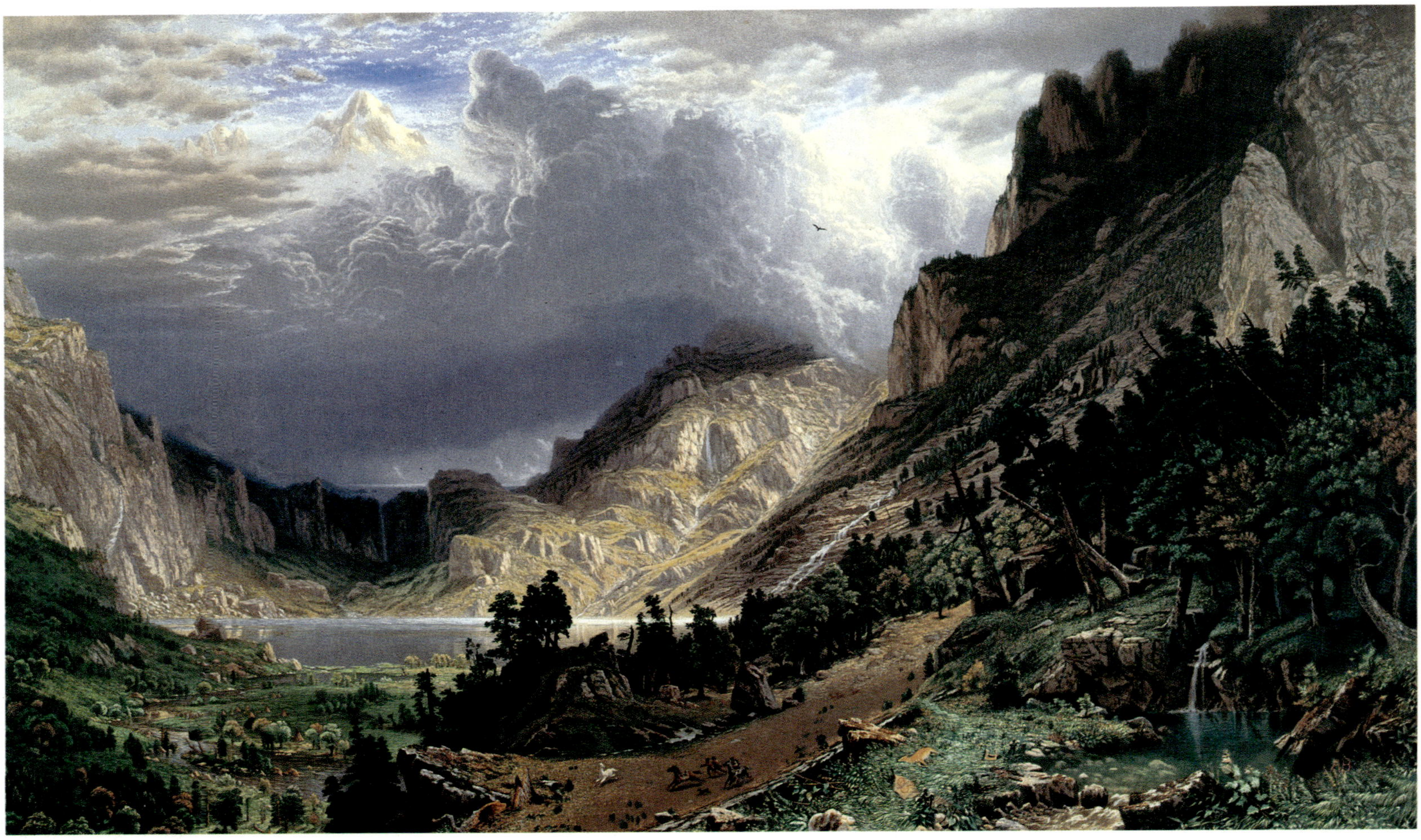

NO. 79

*Storm in the Rocky Mountains, Mt. Rosalie,*
published 1869

Chromolithograph, $20\frac{7}{16} \times 34\frac{3}{16}$ in. ($52 \times 87$ cm) (irregular; image)
Amon Carter Museum, Fort Worth

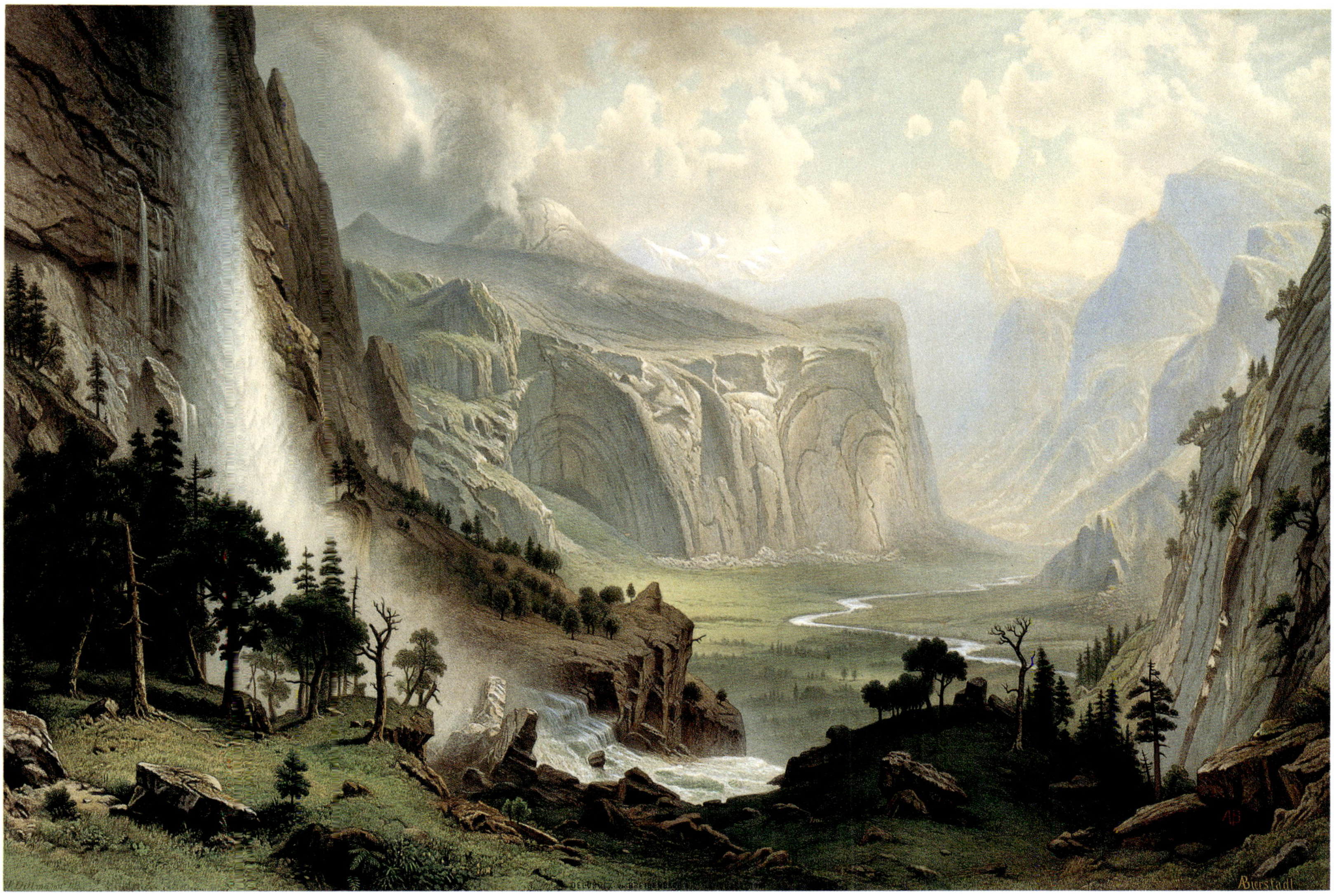

**NO. 80**

*The Domes of the Yosemite*, published 1870

Chromolithograph, 22 3/16 × 33[illegible] in. (56.5 × 84.5 cm) (image)

Amon Carter Museum, Fort Worth

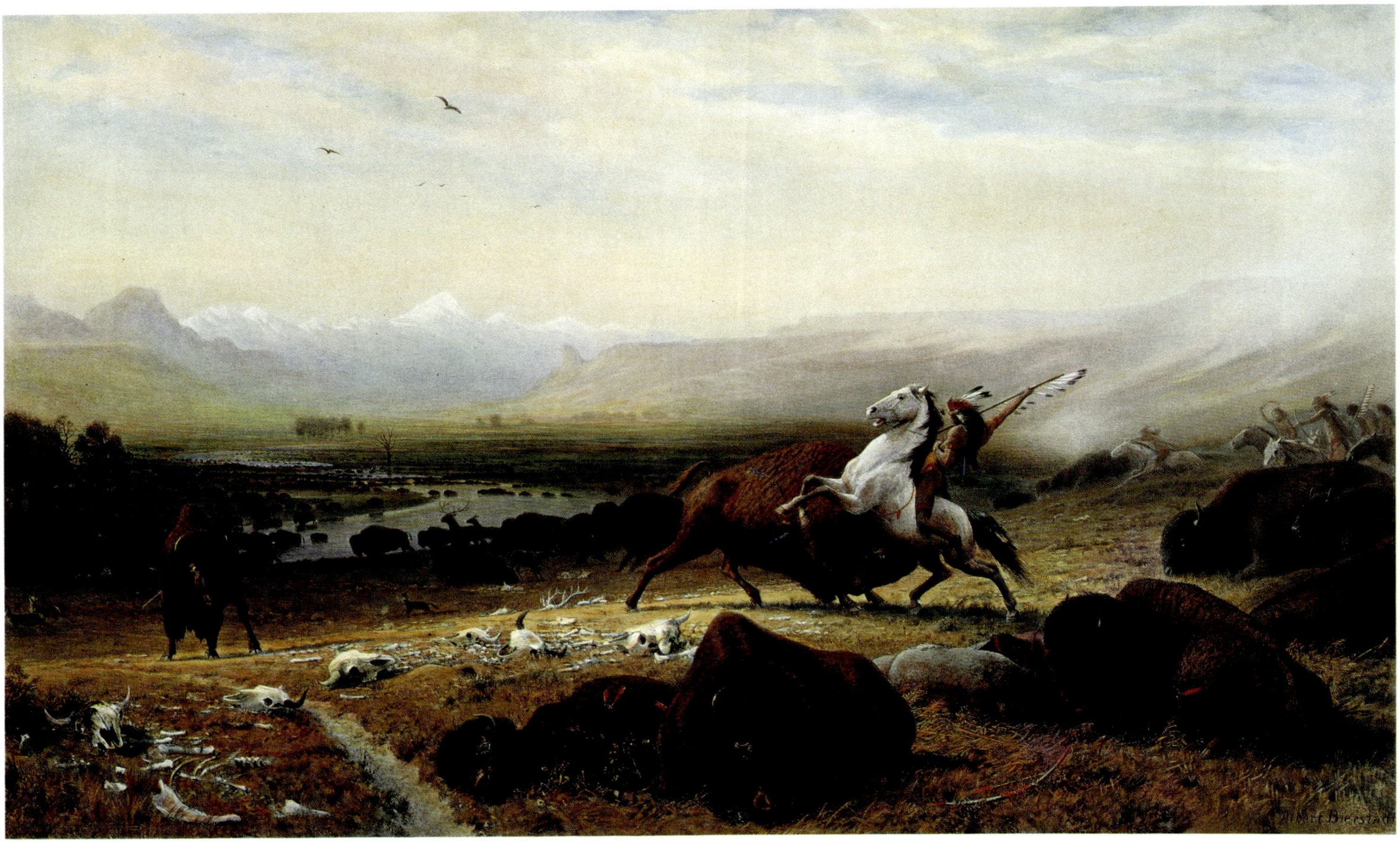

NO. 81

*The Last of the Buffalo*, copyrighted 1891

Photogravure, hand-colored, 16⅛ × 27¼ in. (41 × 69 cm) (image)

Amon Carter Museum, Fort Worth

# SELECTED BIBLIOGRAPHY


## Archival Sources

Archive of California Art. Oakland Museum, Oakland, California.

Baird Archive of California Art. Peter J. Shields Library, University of California, Davis.

John Davis Batchelder Autograph Collection. Rare Book and Special Collections, Library of Congress, Washington, D.C.

Bierstadt Album. National Gallery of Canada, Ottawa.

Bierstadt Album. Private collection, Hannover, Germany.

Bierstadt Correspondence; Curator's Journal. Corcoran Gallery of Art Archives, Washington, D.C.

Bierstadt Correspondence. Records of the Architect of the Capitol, Washington, D.C.

Bierstadt Documents. Evan Hopkins Turner Collection, Cleveland, Ohio.

Bierstadt Documents. Rare Book and Special Collections, Library of Congress, Washington, D.C.

Bierstadt Letters. Manuscript Division, Library of Congress, Washington, D.C.

Bierstadt Scrapbook and Documents. Joyce Randall Edwards Collection, Dobbs Ferry, N.Y.

Bierstadt Sketchbook. Addison Gallery of American Art, Phillips Academy, Andover, Mass.

Canadian Pacific Railway Corporate Archives, Montreal.

Century Association Archives. New York.

Correspondence of Rosalie Osborne Mayer and Mrs. Ross Taggart. Museum of Fine Arts, Boston.

Joseph Downs Manuscript and Microfilm Collection. Henry Francis du Pont Winterthur Museum, Winterthur, Del.

Charles H. Gifford Papers. Archives of American Art, Smithsonian Institution, Washington, D.C.

Robert Swain Gifford Papers, Archives of American Art, Smithsonian Institution, Washington, D.C.

Sanford Robinson Gifford Letters. Archives of American Art, Smithsonian Institution, Washington, D.C.

Ferdinand V. Hayden Papers. National Archives, Washington, D.C.

Gordon Hendricks Papers. Archives of American Art, Smithsonian Institution, Washington, D.C.

Collis P. Huntington Papers. George Arents Research Library, Syracuse University, Syracuse, N.Y.

Anna and Theodore Judah Papers. Private collection, Chevy Chase, Md.

Thomas Starr King Papers. Bancroft Library, University of California, Berkeley.

Frederick W. Lander Expedition Records. National Archives, Washington, D.C.

Frederick W. Lander Papers. Manuscript Collection, Library of Congress, Washington, D.C.

Emanuel Leutze Sketchbooks and Photographs. Prints & Photographs Division, Library of Congress, Washington, D.C.

Henry Lewis Papers. William L. Clements Library, University of Michigan, Ann Arbor.

Fitz Hugh Ludlow Family Papers. New York State Historical Association, Cooperstown, N.Y.

Jervis McEntee Diary. Archives of American Art, Smithsonian Institution, Washington, D.C.

Miscellaneous Bierstadt Documents. Archives of American Art, Smithsonian Institution, Washington, D.C.

Miscellaneous Bierstadt Documents. Manuscript Division, New York Public Library.

National Academy of Design Archives. New York.

William Page Papers. Archives of American Art, Smithsonian Institution, Washington, D.C.

Ferdinand Perret California Art Archive. National Museum of American Art, Smithsonian Institution, Washington, D.C.

Records of the Geological Survey; Records of the Hayden Survey. Letters Received 1871–79, National Archives, Washington, D.C.

William T. Richards Papers. Archives of American Art, Smithsonian Institution, Washington, D.C.

James Smillie Family Papers. Archives of American Art, Smithsonian Institution, Washington, D.C.

Ainsworth R. Spofford Papers. Manuscript Division. Library of Congress, Washington, D.C.

Leland and Jane Stanford Papers. Stanford Archive, Stanford University, Stanford, Calif.

Union League Club Archives. New York.

## Books, Articles, and Dissertations

F. C. Adams 1870. Adams, Francis Colburn. "Executive Document 315: 'Art in the District of Columbia.'" In *Executive Documents Printed by Order of the House of Representatives During the Second Session of the Forty-First Congress. 1869–'70*. Washington, D.C.: Government Printing Office, 1870.

M. E. Adams 1969. Adams, Mary E., ed. *LeGrand Lockwood (1820–1872)*. Norwalk, Conn.: Lockwood-Mathews Mansion Museum of Norwalk, 1969.

Adams, Kelly, and Tyler 1986. Adams, Celeste Marie, Franklin Kelly, and Ron Tyler. *America: Art and the West*. Exh. cat. Sydney, Australia: Art Gallery of New South Wales, 1986.

Adamson 1981. Adamson, Jeremy Elwell. "Frederic Edwin Church's 'Niagara': The Sublime as Transcendence." Ph.D. diss., University of Michigan, Ann Arbor, 1981.

Adamson 1985. Adamson, Jeremy Elwell. *Niagara: Two Centuries of Changing Attitudes, 1697–1901*. Exh. cat. Washington, D.C.: Corcoran Gallery of Art, 1985.

*Aldine* 1873. "Colorado Scenery." *Aldine* 6 (Sept. 1873): 174–75.

L. Aldrich 1920. Aldrich, Lilian Woodman. *Crowding Memories*. Boston: Houghton Mifflin Company, 1920.

T. Aldrich 1865. Aldrich, Thomas Bailey. "Among the Studios, No. 1." *Our Young Folks* 1 (Sept. 1865): 594–98.

Alexander Gallery 1983. *Albert Bierstadt: An Exhibition of Forty Paintings*. Exh. cat. New York: Alexander Gallery, 1983.

Alison [1790] 1968. Alison, Archibald. *Essays on the Nature and Principles of Taste*. Reprint: Hildesheim: Georg Olms Verlag, 1968.

Allen 1973. Allen, Everett S. *Children of the Light: The Rise and Fall of New Bedford Whaling and the Death of the Arctic Fleet*. Boston: Little, Brown & Co., 1973.

American Exhibition Catalogue 1887. *Exhibition of Pictures, etc., in the Art Galleries of the American Exhibition, London, 1887*. London: J. J. Garnett & B. W. Dinsmore & Co., Publishers, 1887.

Amfitheatrof 1980. Amfitheatrof, Erik. *The Enchanted Ground: Americans in Italy, 1760–1980*. Boston: Little, Brown & Co., 1980.

Anderson 1985. Anderson, Nancy. "Albert Bierstadt: The Path to California, 1830–1874." Ph.D. diss., University of Delaware, 1985.

Anderson 1986. Anderson, Nancy. *Albert Bierstadt: Cho-Looke, The Yosemite Fall*. Exh. cat. San Diego, Calif.: Timken Art Gallery, 1986.

Andrews 1964. Andrews, Keith. *The Nazarenes: A Brotherhood of German Painters in Rome*. Oxford: Clarendon Press, 1964.

Anker 1987. Anker, Valentina. *Alexandre Calame: Vie et oeuvre, Catalogue raisonné de l'oeuvre peint*. Fribourg, Switzerland: Office du Livre, 1987.

Appleton 1985. Appleton, Carolyn Mae. "Albert Bierstadt's Early Oil Sketches: 1854–1859." Master's thesis, University of Texas, Austin, 1985.

*Appleton's Cyclopaedia* 1888. "Bierstadt, Albert." *Appleton's Cyclopaedia of American Biography*. Ed. James Grant Wilson and John Fiske. Vol. 1. New York: D. Appleton and Company, 1888.

Arkelian 1978. Arkelian, Marjorie Dakin. "Artists in Yosemite." *American West* 15 (July/Aug. 1978): 34–47.

Arkelian 1980a. Arkelian, Marjorie. *The Kahn Collection of Nineteenth-Century Paintings by Artists in California*. Oakland, Calif.: Oakland Museum, 1980.

Arkelian 1980b. Arkelian, Marjorie. *Thomas Hill: The Grand View*. Exh. cat. Oakland, Calif.: Oakland Museum, 1980.

*Art News* 1963. "Reviews and Previews: Albert Bierstadt." *Art News* 62 (Nov. 1963): 14.

*Art News* 1964. "Reviews and Previews: Albert Bierstadt." *Art News* 63 (Sept. 1964): 12–13.

*Art News* 1968. "Reviews and Previews: Albert Bierstadt." *Art News* 67 (Apr. 1968): 10.

*Art News* 1976. "The Vasari Diary: The Return of 'Rosalie.'" *Art News* 75 (Sept. 1976): 21–22.

*Arts Magazine* 1963. "New York Exhibitions: Month in Review." *Arts Magazine* 38 (Nov. 1963): 30–31.

Aspen Art Museum 1985. "Two Artists of the American West: Albert Bierstadt and Thomas Moran." Exh. checklist. Aspen, Colo.: Aspen Art Museum, 1985.

Athearn 1953. Athearn, Robert G. *Westward the Briton*. New York: Charles Scribner's Sons, 1953.

Atkinson 1880a. Atkinson, J. Beavington. "Düsseldorf: Its Old School and Its New Academy." *Art Journal*, Apr. 1880, pp. 97–100.

Atkinson 1880b. *The Schools of Modern Art in Germany*. London: Seeley, Jackson & Halliday, 1880.

B. Avery 1868. Avery, Benjamin Parke. "Art Beginnings on the Pacific." *Overland Monthly* 1 (July 1868): 28–34; (Aug. 1868): 113–19.

B. Avery 1874. Avery, Benjamin Parke. "Art in California." *Aldine* 7 (Apr. 1874): 72–73.

B. Avery 1878. Avery, Benjamin Parke. *California Pictures in Prose and Verse*. New York: Hurd and Houghton, 1878.

K. Avery 1982. Avery, Kevin J. "Albert Bierstadt." *Arts Magazine* 57 (Sept. 1982): 12.

K. Avery 1984. Avery, Kevin J. "Albert Bierstadt." *Arts Magazine* 58 (Jan. 1984): 14.

K. Avery 1986. Avery, Kevin J. "'The Heart of the Andes' Exhibited: Frederic E. Church's Window on the Equatorial World." *American Art Journal* 18, no. 1 (1986): 56–72.

Baigell 1981. Baigell, Matthew. *Albert Bierstadt.* New York: Watson-Guptill Publications, 1981.

Baigell 1982. Baigell, Matthew. *Oil Sketches by Albert Bierstadt, 1830–1902*. Exh. cat. New York: Davis & Langdale Company, 1982.

Bailey 1865. Bailey, W. P. "Mr. Church's Pictures—Cotopaxi, Chimborazo, and the Aurora Borealis." *Art Journal*, Sept. 1865, pp. 265–67.

A. Baker 1908. Baker, Abby G. "The Art Treasures of the United States Capitol." *Munsey's Magazine* 38 (Feb. 1908): 571–84.

P. Baker 1964. Baker, Paul R. *The Fortunate Pilgrims: Americans in Italy, 1800–1860*. Cambridge, Mass.: Harvard University Press, 1964.

Barker 1950. Barker, Virgil. *American Painting*. New York: Macmillan Company, 1950.

Baro 1975. Baro, Gene. Review of *Albert Bierstadt: Painter of the American West*, by Gordon Hendricks. *Art in America* 63 (Nov./Dec. 1975): 23.

Baur 1949. Baur, John I. H. "Trends in American Painting, 1815 to 1865." In *M. & M. Karolik Collection of American Paintings, 1815 to 1865*. Cambridge, Mass.: Harvard University Press, 1949.

Baur 1954. Baur, John I. H. "American Luminism, A Neglected Aspect of the Realist Movement in Nineteenth-Century American Painting." *Perspectives USA* 9 (Autumn 1954): 90–98.

Beatty 1936. Beatty, Richmond Croom. *Bayard Taylor: Laureate of the Gilded Age*. Norman, Okla.: University of Oklahoma Press, 1936.

Beecher and Stowe [1869] 1975. Beecher, Catharine E., and Harriet Beecher Stowe. *The American Woman's Home*. New York: J. B. Ford and Company, 1869. Reprint: Hartford, Conn.: Stowe-Day Foundation, 1975.

Bendix 1974. Bendix, Howard E. "Discovered!! Early Bierstadt Photographs, Part One: The Lander Expedition." *Photographica* 6 (Oct. 1974): 4–5; "Part Two: Six Photographs Discovered" (Nov. 1974): 7, 10; "Part Three: Bierstadt Brothers, Photographers" (Dec. 1974): 7; "Part Four: Identifying Bierstadt Westerns" (Jan. 1975): 4.

Benjamin 1879. Benjamin, Samuel Greene Wheeler. "Fifty Years of American Art: 1828–1878, III." *Harper's New Monthly Magazine* 59 (Oct. 1879): 673–88.

Benjamin 1879 and 1881. Benjamin, Samuel Greene Wheeler. *Our American Artists*. 2 vols. Boston: D. Lothrop & Co., 1879 and 1881.

Benjamin 1880. Benjamin, Samuel Greene Wheeler. *Art in America: A Critical and Historical Sketch*. New York: Harper & Brothers, 1880.

Benjamin 1887. Benjamin, Samuel Greene Wheeler. "American Art Since the Centennial." *Princeton Review* 5 (July 1887): 14–30.

Benjamin 1914. Benjamin, Samuel Greene Wheeler. *The Life and Adventures of a Free Lance*. Burlington, Vt.: Free Press Company, 1914.

Bestvater-Hasenclever 1979. Bestvater-Hasenclever, Hanna. *J. P. Hasenclever: Ein wacher Zeitgenosse des Biedermeier*. Recklinghausen: Bongers, 1979.

Betthausen et al. 1988. Betthausen, Peter, et al. *The Romantic Spirit: German Drawings, 1780–1850*. Exh. cat. New York: Oxford University Press, in association with Pierpont Morgan Library, 1988.

Bienenstock 1987. Bienenstock, Jennifer A. Martin. *The Forgotten Episode: Nineteenth Century American Art in Belgian Public Collections*. Exh. cat. Brussels: American Cultural Center, 1987.

Bierstadt 1859. Bierstadt, Albert. "Letter from the Rocky Mountains." Letter dated 10 July, in *Crayon*, Sept. 1859, p. 287.

Bierstadt and Bierstadt 1875a. Bierstadt, Charles, and Edward Bierstadt. *Gems of American Scenery Consisting of Stereoscopic Views Among the White Mountains*. New York: Charles and Edward Bierstadt, 1875.

Bierstadt and Bierstadt 1875b. *Pictorial Guide Book: Watkins and Havana Glens*. New York: Charles and Edward Bierstadt, 1875.

Bierstadt Auction 1905. *Catalogue of Choice and Valuable Paintings from the Collection of Mr. Edward Bierstadt and the Estates of the Late Hon. John H. V. Arnold and Edward Dexter*. New York: Anderson Auction Company, 1905.

Bierstadt Brothers 1860. Bierstadt Brothers. *Catalogue of Photographs Published by Bierstadt Brothers*. New Bedford, Mass.: Mercury Job Press, 1860.

Bierstadt Brothers 1865. *Catalogue of Stereoscopic Views*. New Bedford, Mass.: Mercury Job Press, 1865.

Black 1938. Black, Jennie Prince. *I Remember*. New York: Thomas Claydon Printing Co., 1938.

Blaugrund 1987. Blaugrund, Annette. "The Tenth Street Studio Building." Ph.D. diss., Columbia University, 1987.

Blaugrund et al. 1989. Blaugrund, Annette, et al. *Paris 1889: American Artists at the Universal Exposition*. Exh. cat. New York: Pennsylvania Academy of the Fine Arts, in association with Harry N. Abrams, 1989.

Boas 1940. Boas, George, ed. *Romanticism in America: Papers Contributed to a Symposium Held at the Baltimore Museum of Art*. Baltimore: Johns Hopkins Press, 1940.

Boas 1943. Boas, George. "The Critical Practice of James Jackson Jarves." *Gazette des Beaux-Arts* 22 (May 1943): 295–307.

Boetticher 1891. Boetticher, Friedrich von. *Malerwerke des neunzehnten Jahrhunderts*. Dresden: Friedrich von Boetticher, 1891.

Boorstin 1965. Boorstin, Daniel J. *The Americans: The National Experience*. New York: Random House, 1965.

Born 1945. Born, Wolfgang. "Sources of American Romanticism." *Antiques* 48 (Nov. 1945): 274–77.

Born 1948a. Born, Wolfgang. *American Landscape Painting, An Interpretation*. New Haven: Yale University Press, 1948.

Born 1948b. Born, Wolfgang. "The Panoramic Landscape as an American Art Form." *Art in America* 36 (Jan. 1948): 3–10.

Bowles 1865. Bowles, Samuel. *Across the Continent: A Summer's Journey to the Rocky Mountains, the Mormons, and the Pacific States, with Speaker Colfax*. New York: Hurd & Houghton, 1865.

Bowles 1869a. Bowles, Samuel. *Our New West: Records of Travel Between the Mississippi River and the Pacific Ocean*. Hartford, Conn.: Hartford Publishing Company, 1869.

Bowles 1869b. Bowles, Samuel. *The Pacific Railroad—Open*. Boston: Fields, Osgood & Co., 1869.

Bowles 1869c. Bowles, Samuel. *The Switzerland of America: A Summer Vacation in the Parks and Mountains of Colorado*. Springfield, Mass.: Samuel Bowles & Company, 1869.

Britsch 1980. Britsch, Ralph A. *Bierstadt and Ludlow, Painter and Writer in the West*. Charles E. Merrill Monographs, no. 5. Provo, Utah: Brigham Young University, 1980.

Brooks 1947. Brooks, Van Wyck. *The Times of Melville and Whitman*. New York: E. P. Dutton & Co., 1947.

Brooks 1958. Brooks, Van Wyck. *The Dream of Arcadia: American Writers and Artists in Italy, 1760–1915*. New York: E. P. Dutton & Co., 1958.

Broun 1976. Broun, Elizabeth. "American Painting and Sculpture in the Fine Arts Building of the World's Columbian Exposition, Chicago, 1893." Ph.D. diss., University of Kansas, Lawrence, 1976.

Brownell 1880a. Brownell, William C. "The Younger Painters of America, First Paper." *Scribner's Monthly* 20 (May 1880): 1–15.

Brownell 1880b. Brownell, William C. "The Younger Painters of America, Second Paper." *Scribner's Monthly* 20 (July 1880): 321–35.

Bryant 1830. Bryant, William Cullen. *The American Landscape*. New York: Elam Bliss, 1830.

Bryant 1872. Bryant, William Cullen, ed. *Picturesque America; Or, The Land We Live In*. 2 vols. New York: D. Appleton and Company, 1872.

*Bryant Festival* 1865. *The Bryant Festival at "The Century."* New York: D. Appleton and Company, 1865.

Buffalo Fine Arts Academy 1949. Buffalo Fine Arts Academy. *Catalogue of the Paintings and Sculpture in the Permanent Collection*. Ed. Andrew C. Ritchie. Buffalo: Albright Art Gallery, 1949.

*Buffalo Library* 1887. *The Buffalo Library and Its Building*. Buffalo, N.Y.: Matthews, Northrup & Co., 1887.

Bunnell 1911. Bunnell, Lafayette Houghton. *Discovery of the Yosemite and the Indian War of 1851 Which Led to That Event*. Los Angeles: C. W. Gerlichen, 1911.

Burke [1757] 1968. Burke, Edmund. *A Philosophical Enquiry into the Origin of Our Ideas of the Sublime and Beautiful*. Annotated ed.: ed. James T. Baulton. South Bend: University of Notre Dame Press, 1968.

Burroughs 1917. Burroughs, Bryson. "The Hudson River School of Paintings." *Metropolitan Museum of Art Bulletin*, Supplement, 12 (Oct. 1917): 1–11.

Buscarlet 1969. Buscarlet, Daniel. *Alexandre et Arthur Calame*. Neuchâtel: Delachaux et Niestle, 1969.

Bushnell 1903. Bushnell, Horace. *The Spirit in Man: Sermons and Selections*. New York: Charles Scribner's Sons, 1903.

Butler 1973. Butler, Joseph T. "The American Way of Art: Albert Bierstadt Exhibition." *Connoisseur*, Feb. 1973, p. 135.

Byers 1890. Byers, William Newton. "Bierstadt's Visit to Colorado." *Magazine of Western History* 11 (Jan. 1890): 237–40.

Caffin 1907. Caffin, Charles H. *The Story of American Painting. The Evolution of Painting in America from Colonial Times to the Present*. New York: Frederick A. Stokes Company Publishers, 1907.

*California Art Gallery* 1873. "Albert Bierstadt." *California Art Gallery* 1 (Apr. 1873): 49–50.

California Art Research 1936–37. "Albert Bierstadt." In California Art Research, II, First Series, pp. 98–127. Washington, D.C.: Works Progress Administration, 1936–37.

Callow 1967. Callow, James T. *Kindred Spirits: Knickerbocker Writers and American Artists, 1807–1855*. Chapel Hill: University of North Carolina Press, 1967.

Campbell 1981. Campbell, Catherine H. "Albert Bierstadt and the White Mountains." *Archives of American Art Journal* 21, no. 3 (1981): 14–33.

Mrs. Campbell 1979. Campbell, Mrs. Elwyn G. *Artists of This Vicinity*. Fairhaven, Mass.: privately printed, 1979.

Canaday 1972a. Canaday, John. "Art: Shows in Two Cities." *New York Times*, 8 Apr. 1972, p. 26.

Canaday 1972b. Canaday, John. "Art: Bierstadt's Large and Small Work." *New York Times*, 15 Sept. 1972.

Carr 1980. Carr, Gerald. *Frederic Edwin Church: The Icebergs*. Dallas: Dallas Museum of Fine Arts, 1980.

Carr 1982. Carr, Gerald L. "American Art in Great Britain: The National Gallery Watercolor of 'The Heart of the Andes.'" In Studies in the History of Art 12, pp. 81–100. Washington, D.C.: National Gallery of Art, 1982.

Carr 1986. Carr, Gerald. "Albert Bierstadt, Big Trees, and the British: A Log of Many Anglo-American Ties." *Arts Magazine* 60 (Summer 1986): 60–71.

Cary 1952. Cary, Richard. *The Genteel Circle: Bayard Taylor and His New York Friends*. Cornell Studies in American History, Literature, and Folklore. Ithaca, N.Y.: Cornell University Press, 1952.

Caughey and Caughey 1962. Caughey, John, and Laree Caughey. *California Heritage: An Anthology of History and Literature*. Los Angeles: Ward Ritchie Press, 1962.

*Century* 1947. *The Century, 1847–1946*. New York: Century Association, 1947.

B. Champney [1890] 1977. Champney, Benjamin. *Sixty Years' Memories of Art and Artists*. Woburn, Mass.: 1890. Reprint: New York: Garland Publishing, 1977.

L. Champney 1885. Champney, Lizzie W. "The Summer Haunts of American Artists." *Century Magazine* 30 (Oct. 1885): 845–60.

de Chapeaurouge 1979. de Chapeaurouge, Donat. "Zur Ausstellung 'Die Düsseldorfer Malerschule.'" *Kunstchronik* 32 (Aug. 1979): 261–68.

Child 1882. Child, Lydia Maria. *Letters of Lydia Maria Child, with a Biographical Introduction by John Greenleaf Whittier and an Appendix by Wendell Phillips*. Boston: Houghton, Mifflin and Company, 1882.

*Christian Examiner* 1863. "Art & Artists of America." *Christian Examiner* 75 (July 1863): 114–27.

Cikovsky 1970a. Cikovsky, Nicolai, Jr. "George Inness and the Hudson River School: *The Lackawanna Valley*." *American Art Journal* 2 (Fall 1970): 36–57.

Cikovsky 1970b. Cikovsky, Nicolai, Jr. *Sanford Robinson Gifford, 1823–1880*. Exh. cat. Austin: University of Texas Art Museum, 1970.

Cincinnati Art Museum 1972. *Drawings by Carl Friedrich Lessing, 1808–1880*. Exh. cat. Cincinnati: Cincinnati Art Museum, 1972.

C. Clark 1980. Clark, Carol. *Thomas Moran: Watercolors of the American West*. Austin: University of Texas Press, 1980.

E. Clark 1954. Clark, Eliot. *History of the National Academy of Design, 1825–1953*. New York: Columbia University Press, 1954.

K. Clark 1949. Clark, Kenneth. *Landscape into Art*. New York: Harper & Row, 1949.

Clement and Hutton 1880. Clement, Clara Erskine, and Laurence Hutton. *Artists of the Nineteenth Century and Their Works*. Boston: Houghton, Mifflin and Company, 1880, pp. 61–62.

Cobb 1963–65. Cobb, Josephine. "The Washington Art Association: An Exhibition Record, 1856–1860." *Records of the Columbia Historical Society, 1963–65* (Washington, D.C.): 122–90.

Coen 1973. Coen, Rena Neumann. "The Last of the Buffalo." *American Art Journal* 5 (Nov. 1973): 83–94.

Coen 1976. Coen, Rena Neumann. *Painting and Sculpture in Minnesota, 1820–1914*. Exh. cat. Minneapolis: University Gallery of the University of Minnesota, 1976.

Cole 1836. Cole, Thomas. "Essay on American Scenery." *American Monthly Magazine* 1 (Jan. 1836): 1–12.

Conant 1876. Conant, Samuel S. "The First Century of the Republic, Eighteenth Paper." *Harper's New Monthly Magazine* 52 (Apr. 1876): 691–704.

Congdon 1880. Congdon, Charles T. *Reminiscences of a Journalist*. Boston: James R. Osgood and Company, 1880.

Constable 1951. Constable, William George. "The M. and M. Karolik Collection of American Painting, 1815–1865." *Boston Museum Bulletin* 49 (Oct. 1951): 58–65.

Conwell 1881. Conwell, Russell H. *The Life, Travels, and Literary Career of Bayard Taylor*. Boston: D. Lothrop & Company, 1881.

Cook 1888. Cook, Clarence. *Art and Artists of Our Time*. 3 vols. New York: S. Hess, 1888.

Cooper [1836] 1980. Cooper, James Fenimore. *Sketches of Switzerland*. Philadelphia: Carey, Lea & Blanchard, 1836. Reprint (as *Gleanings in Europe: Switzerland*): Albany, N.Y.: State University of New York Press, 1980.

Cornelius 1942. Cornelius, Fidelis. *Keith: Old Master of California*. 2 vols. New York: G. P. Putnam's Sons, 1942.

*Cosmopolitan Art Journal* 1857. "The Düsseldorf Gallery." *Cosmopolitan Art Journal* 2 (Dec. 1857): 43–44.

Cowdrey 1943. Cowdrey, Mary Bartlett. *National Academy of Design Exhibition Record, 1826–1860*. New York: New-York Historical Society, 1943.

Cowdrey 1945. Cowdrey, Mary Bartlett. "The Discovery of Enoch Wood Perry." *Portfolio* 4 (Apr. 1945): 171–81.

Cowdrey 1953. Cowdrey, Mary Bartlett. *American Academy of Fine Arts and American Art-Union Exhibition Record, 1816–1852*. New York: New-York Historical Society, 1953.

Cranch 1867. Cranch, Christopher P. "Art-Criticism Reviewed." *Galaxy* 4 (May 1867):77–81.

Crocker Art Museum 1979. Crocker Art Museum. *Handbook of Paintings*. Sacramento, Calif.: Crocker Art Museum, 1979.

Cropsey 1855. Cropsey, Jasper. "Up Among the Clouds." *Crayon*, 8 Aug. 1855, p. 79.

Cummings [1865] 1969. Cummings, Thomas S. *Historic Annals of the National Academy of Design*. Philadelphia: George W. Childs, 1865. Reprint: New York: Kennedy Galleries, 1969.

Cummins 1893. Cummins, Ella Sterling. *The Story of the Files: California Writers and Literature*. San Francisco: Co-operative Printing Co., 1893.

Current and Current 1978. Current, Karen, and William R. Current. *Photography and the Old West*. New York: Harry N. Abrams, 1978.

*Current Literature* 1902. "Contemporary Celebrities: Albert Bierstadt." *Current Literature* 32 (Apr. 1902): 394.

Curry 1972. Curry, Larry. *The American West: Painters from Catlin to Russell*. Exh. cat. New York: Viking Press, in association with Los Angeles County Museum of Art, 1972.

*Cyclopedia of American Biography* 1897. "Bierstadt, Albert." *The Cyclopedia of American Biography*. Ed. John Howard Brown. Vol. 1. Boston: Cyclopedia Publishing Company, 1897.

*Cyclopedia of Painters and Paintings* 1887. "Bierstadt, Albert." *Cyclopedia of Painters and Paintings*. Ed. John Denison Champlin, Jr., and Charles C. Perkins. Vol. 1. New York: Charles Scribner's Sons, 1887.

Daly 1962. Daly, Mary Lydig. *Diary of a Union Lady, 1861–1865*. Ed. Harold Earl Hammon. New York: Funk & Wagnalls Company, 1962.

Danforth Museum 1982. *American Artists in Düsseldorf: 1840–1865*. Exh. cat. Framingham, Mass.: Danforth Museum, 1982.

Danly and Marx 1988. Danly, Susan, and Leo Marx, eds. *The Railroad in American Art: Representations of Technological Change*. Cambridge, Mass.: MIT Press, 1988.

Darrah 1977. Darrah, William C. *The World of Stereographs*. Gettysburg, Pa.: W. C. Darrah, 1977.

Dengler 1957. Dengler, Dorothy. "The Earl, the Artist and Estes Park." In *1956 Brand Book of the Denver Westerners*, pp. 355–66. Denver: Westerners, 1957.

Dickens 1846. Dickens, Charles. *Pictures from Italy*. London: Bradbury and Evans, 1846.

Dilke 1869. Dilke, Charles Wentworth. *Greater Britain: A Record of Travel in English-Speaking Countries During 1866–7*. Philadelphia: J. B. Lippincott & Company, 1869.

Dixon 1867. Dixon, William Hepworth. *New America*. London: Hurst & Blackett, Publishers, 1867.

Docherty 1985. Docherty, Linda Jones. "A Search for Identity: American Art Criticism and the Concept of the 'Native School,' 1876–1893." Ph.D. diss., University of North Carolina, Chapel Hill, 1985.

Downes 1888. Downes, William Howe. "Boston Painters and Paintings VI. Private Collections." *Atlantic Monthly* 62 (Dec. 1888): 777–86.

Downes 1932. Downes, William Howe. "American Painters of Mountains." *American Magazine of Art* 25 (Oct. 1932): 193–202.

Drachler 1980. Drachler, Carole Simon. "The Gallery and Art Collection of Henry Clay Lewis." Ph.D. diss., University of Michigan, Ann Arbor, 1980.

Draper 1940. Draper, Benjamin Poff. "Albert Bierstadt." *Art in America* 28 (Apr. 1940): 61–71.

Durand 1855. Durand, Asher B. "Letters on Landscape Painting." *Crayon*, 3 Jan. 1855, pp. 1–2; 17 Jan., pp. 34–35; 31 Jan., pp. 66–67; 14 Feb., pp. 97–98; 7 Mar., pp. 145–46; 4 Apr., pp. 209–11; 2 May, pp. 273–75; 6 June, pp. 354–55; 11 July, pp. 16–17.

Düsseldorf 1968. *Die Gemälde des 19. Jahrhunderts*. Düsseldorf: Kunstmuseum Düsseldorf, 1968.

Düsseldorf 1969. *Die Düsseldorf Malerschule. Katalog des Kunstmuseum*. Düsseldorf: Kunstmuseum Düsseldorf, 1969.

Düsseldorf 1976a. *Düsseldorf und der Norden*. Exh. cat. Düsseldorf: Kunstmuseum Düsseldorf, 1976.

Düsseldorf 1976b. *The Hudson and the Rhine: Die amerikanische Malerkolonie in Düsseldorf im 19. Jahrhundert*. Exh. cat. Düsseldorf: Kunstmuseum Düsseldorf, 1976.

Düsseldorf 1979. *Die Düsseldorf Malerschule*. Exh. cat. Düsseldorf: Kunstmuseum Düsseldorf, 1979.

*Düsseldorf Artists* 1854. *Düsseldorf Artists-Album*. London: Trubner & Co., 1854.

Dusseldorf Gallery Catalogue 1849. *Catalogue of Paintings and Original Drawings by the Artists of the Düsseldorf Academy of Fine Arts*. New York: George F. Nesbitt, 1849. (Numerous editions of this catalogue were published.)

Earle 1979. Earle, Edward W. *Points of View: The Stereograph in America—A Cultural History*. New York: Visual Studies Workshop Press, 1979.

Edward Bierstadt Estate Catalogue 1908. *Catalogue of Valuable Oil Paintings, Water Colors, Etchings, Engravings, Color Prints and Drawings Collected by the Late Mrs. A. G. Hunt and a Number of Important Works in Oil Belonging to the Estate of the Late Edward Bierstadt*. New York: American Art Association, 1908.

Eitner 1970. Eitner, Lorenz, ed. *Neoclassicism and Romanticism, 1750–1850: Sources and Documents*. Vol. 1, *Enlightenment/Revolution*. Englewood Cliffs, N.J.: Prentice-Hall, 1970.

Ellet 1867. Ellet, Elizabeth Fries. *The Queens of American Society*. Philadelphia: Porter & Loates, 1867.

Ellis 1892. Ellis, Leonard Bolles. *History of New Bedford and Its Vicinity, 1620–1892*. Syracuse, N.Y.: Mason & Co., 1892.

Emerson and Forbes 1910. Emerson, Edward Waldo, and Waldo Emerson Forbes, eds. *Journals of Ralph Waldo Emerson, 1820–1872*. Boston: Houghton Mifflin Company, 1910.

Engberg and Wesling 1980. Engberg, Robert, and Donald Wesling, eds. *John Muir: To Yosemite and Beyond, Writings from the Years 1863 to 1875*. Madison, Wis.: University of Wisconsin Press, 1980.

Ewers 1965. Ewers, John C. *Artists of the Old West*. Garden City, N.Y.: Doubleday & Co., 1965.

F. J. 1976. F. J. Review of *Albert Bierstadt: Painter of the American West*, by Gordon Hendricks. *American Artist* 40 (Jan. 1976): 30, 87–88.

Fairbanks 1975. Fairbanks, Jonathan L. *Frontier America: The Far West*. Exh. cat. Boston: Museum of Fine Arts, 1975.

Fairman 1913. Fairman, Charles Edwin. *Works of Art in the United States Capitol Building*. Washington, D.C.: Government Printing Office, 1913.

Fairman 1927. Fairman, Charles Edwin. *Art and Artists of the Capitol of the United States of America*. Washington, D.C.: Government Printing Office, 1927.

Farquhar 1948. Farquhar, Francis P. *Yosemite, The Big Trees, and the High Sierra: A Selected Bibliography*. Berkeley, Calif.: University of California Press, 1948.

Faust 1909. Faust, Albert Bernhardt. *The German Element in the United States*. Boston: Houghton Mifflin Company, 1909.

Fenn 1982. Fenn, Forrest. *A. Bierstadt*. Santa Fe: Fenn Galleries, 1982.

Ferber and Gerdts 1985. Ferber, Linda S., and William H. Gerdts. *The New Path: Ruskin and the American Pre-Raphaelites*. Exh. cat. Brooklyn: The Brooklyn Museum, 1985.

Ferlinghetti and Peters 1980. Ferlinghetti, Lawrence, and Nancy J. Peters. *Literary San Francisco*. San Francisco: City Lights Books and Harper & Row, Publishers, 1980.

Fine 1974. Fine, Richard A. "Albert Bierstadt, Fitz Hugh Ludlow and the American Western Landscape." *American Studies* 15 (Fall 1974): 91–99.

Fink 1990. Fink, Lois Marie. *American Art at the Nineteenth-Century Paris Salons*. Washington, D.C.: National Museum of American Art, Smithsonian Institution; Cambridge: Cambridge University Press, 1990.

Fletcher 1872. Fletcher, Robert H. *The Annals of the Bohemian Club*. San Francisco: Press of the Hicks-Judd Co., 1872.

Flexner 1962. Flexner, James Thomas. "The Rocky Mountain School of American Painting." *Antiques* 82 (Oct. 1962): 403–5.

Flexner [1962] 1970. Flexner, James Thomas. *That Wilder Image: The Native School from Thomas Cole to Winslow Homer*. Boston: Little, Brown & Co., 1962. Reprint: New York: Dover Publications, 1970.

Ford 1888. Ford, Sheridan. *Art: A Commodity*. New York: Press of Rogers & Sherwood, 1888.

Frankenstein 1970. Frankenstein, Alfred. "An American Revival . . . of Grandiose Scenery." *San Francisco Sunday Examiner*, 15 Mar. 1970, pp. 46–47.

Frankenstein 1975. Frankenstein, Alfred. Review of *Albert Bierstadt: Painter of the American West*, by Gordon Hendricks. *Art News* 74 (May 1975): 48–49.

Freeman 1971. Freeman, Larry. *Louis Prang: Color Lithographer*. Watkins Glen, N.Y.: Century House, 1971.

Fresno Art Center 1982. *Views of Yosemite: The Last Stand of the Romantic Landscape*. Exh. cat. Fresno, Calif.: Fresno Art Center, 1982.

Friederichs 1979. Friederichs, Yvonne. "Düsseldorfer Malerschule." *Das Kunstwerk* 32, no. 4 (1979): 48–49.

*Gems from the Dusseldorf Gallery* 1863. *Gems from the Dusseldorf Gallery*. New York: Appleton & Co., 1863.

Gerdts 1985. Gerdts, William H. "American Landscape Painting: Critical Judgments, 1730–1845." *American Art Journal* 17 (Winter 1985): 28–59.

Gerdts and Thistlethwaite 1988. Gerdts, William H., and Mark Thistlethwaite. *Grand Illusions: History Painting in America*. Fort Worth, Tex.: Amon Carter Museum, 1988.

Gibbs 1981. Gibbs, Linda Mary Jones. "Enoch Wood Perry, Jr.: A Biography and Analysis of His Thematic and Stylistic Development." Master's thesis, University of Utah, Provo, 1981.

Gilpin 1860. Gilpin, William. *The Central Gold Region. The Grain, Pastoral, and Gold Regions of North America*. Philadelphia: Sower, Barnes, and Company, 1860.

Gilpin 1873. Gilpin, William. *Mission of the North American People, Geographical, Social, and Political*. Philadelphia: J. B. Lippincott & Co., 1873.

Godfrey 1944. Godfrey, Elizabeth H. "Albert Bierstadt." *Yosemite Nature Notes* 23 (May 1944): 49–51.

Goetzmann 1959. Goetzmann, William H. *Army Exploration in the American West, 1803–1863*. New Haven: Yale University Press, 1959.

Goetzmann 1978. Goetzmann, William H. *Exploration and Empire: The Explorer and the Scientist in the Winning of the American West*. New York: W. W. Norton & Co., 1978.

Goetzmann and Goetzmann 1986. Goetzmann, William H., and William N. Goetzmann. *The West of the Imagination*. New York: W. W. Norton & Co., 1986.

Goodrich 1938. Goodrich, Lloyd. *A Century of American Landscape Painting, 1800–1900*. Exh. cat. New York: Whitney Museum of American Art, 1938.

Goodrich 1966. Goodrich, Lloyd. *Three Centuries of American Art*. New York: Frederick A. Praeger, 1966.

Graves 1905. Graves, Algernon. *The Royal Academy of Arts: A Complete Dictionary of Contributors and Their Work from Its Foundation in 1769 to 1904*. London: Henry Graves & Co. and George Bell & Son, 1905.

Gray 1871. Gray, Barry [R. B. Coffin]. "Homes on the Hudson: VIII. Hawksrest. The Residence of Albert Bierstadt." *Home Journal* (1871). Clipping in Bierstadt Scrapbook, Joyce Randall Edwards Collection, Dobbs Ferry, N.Y.

Greeley [1860] 1964. Greeley, Horace. *An Overland Journey from New York to San Francisco in the Summer of 1859*. Reprint: New York: Alfred A. Knopf, 1964.

Green 1972. Green, Janet. "Corcoran Gallery Exhibit Features Albert Bierstadt." *Antiques Monthly* 5 (May 1972).

Greenhalgh 1988. Greenhalgh, Paul. *Ephemeral Vistas: The Expositions Universelles, Great Exhibitions, and World's Fairs, 1851–1939*. Manchester: Manchester University Press, 1988.

Grinnell 1904. Grinnell, George Bird. *American Big Game in Its Haunts: The Book of the Boone and Crockett Club*. New York: Forest & Stream Publishing Company, 1904.

Groseclose 1975. Groseclose, Barbara S. *Emanuel Leutze, 1816–1868: Freedom Is the Only King*. Exh. cat. Washington, D.C.: Smithsonian Institution Press, 1975.

Hansen-Taylor and Scudder 1884. Hansen-Taylor, Marie, and Horace E. Scudder, eds. *Life and Letters of Bayard Taylor*. Boston: Houghton Mifflin Company, 1884.

Harding 1975. Harding, Anneliese. *America Through the Eyes of German Immigrant Painters*. Exh. cat. Boston: Goethe Institute, 1975.

Hardy 1950. Hardy, Ruth Gillette. "A Mountain Traveler." *Appalachia* 16 (June 1950): 63–70.

Harris 1966. Harris, Neil. *The Artist in American Society: The Formative Years, 1790–1860*. New York: George Braziller, 1966.

Harrison 1988. Harrison, Alfred C., Jr. *William Keith: The Saint Mary's College Collection*. Exh. cat. Moraga, Calif.: Hearst Art Gallery, 1988.

J. Hart 1950. Hart, James. *The Popular Book: A History of America's Literary Taste*. New York: Oxford University Press, 1950.

J. Hart 1978. Hart, James. *A Companion to California*. New York: Oxford University Press, 1978.

J. L. J. Hart 1925. Hart, John Lathrop Jerome. *Fourteen Thousand Feet; A History of the Naming and Early Ascents of the High Colorado Peaks*. Denver, Colo.: Colorado Mountain Club, 1925.

Hartman 1901. Hartman, Sadakichi. *A History of American Art*. Boston: L. C. Page, 1901.

Haverstock 1966. Haverstock, Mary S. "White Umbrellas in the Rocky Mountains." *Montana: The Magazine of Western History* 16 (Summer 1966): 65–73.

Hawes 1982. Hawes, Louis. *Presences of Nature: British Landscape, 1780–1830*. Exh. cat. New Haven: Yale Center for British Art, 1982.

Hayden 1876. Hayden, Ferdinand V. *The Yellowstone National Park and the Mountain Regions of Idaho, Nevada, Colorado, and Utah*. Boston: Louis Prang, 1876.

Hays 1871. Hays, William J. "Notes on the Range of Some of the Animals in America at the Time of the Arrival of the White Man." *American Naturalist* 5 (Sept. 1871): 387–92.

Hazelton [1897] 1914. Hazelton, George C., Jr. *The National Capitol: Its Architecture, Art, and History*. New York: J. F. Taylor & Company, 1914.

Hegarty 1959. Hegarty, Reginald B. *New Bedford's History*. New Bedford, Mass.: Reynolds Printing, 1959.

Heller and Williams 1976. Heller, Nancy, and Julia Williams. "Albert Bierstadt: The American Wilderness." *American Artist* 40 (Jan. 1976): 52–57.

Hendricks 1964. Hendricks, Gordon. "The First Three Western Journeys of Albert Bierstadt." *Art Bulletin* 46 (Sept. 1964): 333–65.

Hendricks 1970. Hendricks, Gordon. "Bierstadt's Westward Journeys." *Auction* 3 (Mar. 1970): 42–47.

Hendricks 1971. Hendricks, Gordon. "The Domes of the Yosemite." *American Art Journal* 3 (Fall 1971): 23–31.

Hendricks 1972a. Hendricks, Gordon. *Albert Bierstadt*. Exh. cat. Fort Worth, Tex.: Amon Carter Museum, 1972.

Hendricks 1972b. Hendricks, Gordon. *Albert Bierstadt, 1830–1902*. Exh. cat. New York: M. Knoedler & Company, 1972.

Hendricks 1972c. Hendricks, Gordon. "Bierstadt and Church at the New York Sanitary Fair." *Antiques* 102 (Nov. 1972): 892–98.

Hendricks 1973. Hendricks, Gordon. *Albert Bierstadt: Painter of the American West.* New York: Harry N. Abrams, 1973.

Hendricks 1975. Hendricks, Gordon. "Roaming the West with Albert Bierstadt." *American West* 12 (Jan. 1975): 22–29.

Hillard 1877. Hillard, George Stillman. *Six Months in Italy.* Boston: James R. Osgood and Company, 1877.

Hills 1973. Hills, Patricia. *The American Frontier: Images and Myths.* Exh. cat. New York: Whitney Museum of American Art, 1973.

Himmelberg 1978. Himmelberg, Claudia Joan. "The Oil Sketches of Albert Bierstadt." Master's thesis, University of California at Santa Barbara, 1978.

Hine 1973. Hine, Robert V. *The American West: An Interpretive History.* Boston: Little, Brown and Company, 1973.

Hittell 1863. Hittell, John S. "Art in San Francisco." *Pacific Monthly* 10 (July 1863): 99–107.

Hoeber 1910. Hoeber, Arthur. "The Story of Art in America; Part III—The Close of the Old Regime." *Bookman* 31 (Apr. 1910): 150–60.

Holmes 1863. Holmes, Oliver Wendell. "Doings of the Sunbeam." *Atlantic Monthly,* July 1863, pp. 1–15.

*Home Book* [1852] 1967. *The Home Book of the Picturesque: Or, American Scenery, Art, and Literature.* New York: G. P. Putnam, 1852. Reprint: Gainesville, Fla.: Scholars' Facsimiles & Reprints, 1967.

Honour 1975. Honour, Hugh. *The European Vision of America.* Exh. cat. Cleveland: Cleveland Museum of Art, 1975.

Honour 1979. Honour, Hugh. *Romanticism.* New York: Harper & Row, 1979.

Hoopes 1972. Hoopes, Donelson F. *The Düsseldorf Academy and the Americans.* Exh. cat. Atlanta: High Museum of Art, 1972.

Hoopes 1978. Hoopes, Donelson F. "The American Galleries at the M. H. de Young Memorial Museum." *Antiques* 114 (Nov. 1978): 1076–86.

Hornaday 1889. Hornaday, William T. "The Extermination of the American Bison, with a Sketch of its Discovery and Life History." pp. 367–548. *Annual Report of the Smithsonian Institution for the Year Ending June 30, 1887,* Part 2. Washington, D.C.: Government Printing Office, 1889.

Hudson River Museum 1983. *The Book of Nature: American Painters and the Natural Sublime.* Exh. cat. Yonkers, N.Y.: Hudson River Museum, 1983.

Humboldt 1849. Humboldt, Alexander von. *Cosmos: A Sketch of a Physical Description of the Universe.* London: Henry G. Bohn, 1849.

Huntington 1966. Huntington, David C. *The Landscapes of Frederic Edwin Church: Vision of an American Era.* New York: George Braziller, 1966.

Hutchings 1860. Hutchings, James Mason. *Scenes of Wonder and Curiosity in California.* San Francisco: Hutchings and Rosenfield, 1860; revised ed. 1870.

Hutchings 1886. Hutchings, James Mason. *In the Heart of the Sierras: The Yo Semite Valley, Both Historical and Descriptive.* Oakland, Calif.: Pacific Press Publishing House, 1886.

Huth 1948. Huth, Hans. "Yosemite: The Story of an Idea." *Sierra Club Bulletin* 33 (Mar. 1948): 47–78.

Huth 1950. Huth, Hans. "The American and Nature." *Journal of the Warburg and Courtauld Institutes* 13 (1950): 101–49.

Huth 1957. Huth, Hans. *Nature and the American: Three Centuries of Changing Attitudes.* Berkeley, Calif.: University of California Press, 1957.

Hutt 1964. Hutt, Wolfgang. *Die Düsseldorf Malerschule, 1819–1869.* Leipzig: E. A. Seemann, 1964.

Irving 1835. Irving, Washington. *A Tour on the Prairies.* Philadelphia: Carey, Lea & Blanchard, 1835.

Isham 1905. Isham, Samuel. *The History of American Painting.* New York: Macmillan Company, 1905. Revised ed. with supplemental chapters by Royal Cortissoz, 1927.

Isham 1913. Isham, Samuel. "American Landscape Painters: Albert Bierstadt." *Mentor* 1 (Aug. 1913): 4–5.

Jackson 1964. Jackson, William Turrentine. *Wagon Roads West: A Study of Federal Road Surveys and Construction in the Trans-Mississippi West, 1846–1869.* New Haven: Yale University Press, 1964.

Janson 1975. Janson, Anthony Frederick. "The Paintings of Worthington Whittredge." Ph.D. diss., Harvard University, 1975.

Janson 1976. Janson, Anthony F. "The Western Landscapes of Worthington Whittredge." *American Art Review* 3 (Nov./Dec. 1976): 58–69.

Janson 1989. Janson, Anthony F. *Worthington Whittredge.* Cambridge: Cambridge University Press, 1989.

Jarves 1855. Jarves, James Jackson. *Art-Hints.* New York: Harper & Bros., 1855.

Jarves 1861. Jarves, James Jackson. *Art Studies.* New York: Derby and Jackson, 1861.

Jarves [1864] 1960. Jarves, James Jackson. *The Art-Idea: Sculpture, Painting, and Architecture in America.* New York: Hurd & Houghton, 1864. Reprint: ed. Benjamin Rowland, Jr. Cambridge, Mass.: Belknap Press of Harvard University Press, 1960.

Jarves 1869. Jarves, James Jackson. *Art Thoughts: The Experiences and Observations of an American Amateur in Europe.* New York: Hurd and Houghton, 1869.

Jarves 1870. Jarves, James Jackson. "The Future of Art in America." *Art-Journal* (London), Jan. 1870, pp. 6–8.

Jarves 1883. Jarves, James Jackson. *Italian Rambles.* New York: G. P. Putnam's Sons, 1883.

Johnson 1979. Johnson, Hildegard Binder. "The Framed Landscape." *Landscape* 23 (1979): 27–32.

Kahn 1980. Kahn, Gerrie. "Catalogue of the California Historical Society's Oil Painting Collection." San Francisco: California Historical Society, 1980.

*Karolik Collection* 1949. *M. and M. Karolik Collection of American Paintings, 1815–1865.* Cambridge, Mass.: Harvard University Press, 1949.

Kazin 1988. Kazin, Alfred. *A Writer's America: Landscape in Literature.* New York: Alfred A. Knopf, 1988.

Kelly 1988. Kelly, Franklin. *Frederic Edwin Church and the National Landscape.* Washington, D.C.: Smithsonian Institution Press, 1988.

Kelly 1989. Kelly, Franklin. "Frederic Church and the Enterprise of Landscape Painting." *Antiques* 136 (Nov. 1989): 1110–23.

Kelly and Carr 1987. Kelly, Franklin, and Carr, Gerald L. *The Early Landscapes of Frederic Edwin Church, 1845–1854.* Exh. cat. Fort Worth, Tex.: Amon Carter Museum, 1987.

Kelly et al. 1989. Kelly, Franklin, et al. *Frederic Edwin Church.* Exh. cat. Washington, D.C.: National Gallery of Art, 1989.

Keyes 1986. Keyes, Donald D. "Albert Bierstadt's 'Lower Falls of the Yellowstone.'" *Georgia Museum of Art Bulletin* 11 (1986): 5–20.

Keyes et al. 1980. Keyes, Donald D. *The White Mountains: Place and Perceptions.* Exh. cat. Hanover, N.H.: University Press of New England, 1980.

C. King [1872] 1970. King, Clarence. *Mountaineering in the Sierra Nevada.* Boston: J. R. Osgood and Co., 1872. Reprint: Lincoln, Nebr.: University of Nebraska Press, 1970.

T. S. King 1860a. King, Thomas Starr. *The White Hills; Their Legends, Landscape, and Poetry.* Boston: Crosby, Nichols, and Company, 1860.

T. S. King 1860b. King, Thomas Starr. *Words at Parting: A Sermon.* Boston: Walker, Wise, & Co., 1860.

T. S. King 1877a. King, Thomas Starr. *Christianity and Humanity: A Series of Sermons by Thomas Starr King.* Ed. Edwin P. Whipple. Boston: James R. Osgood and Company, 1877.

T. S. King 1877b. King, Thomas Starr. *Substance and Show, and Other Lectures.* Ed. Edwin P. Whipple. Boston: James R. Osgood and Company, 1877.

T. S. King 1962. King, Thomas Starr. *A Vacation among the Sierras: Yosemite in 1860.* Ed. John A. Hussey. San Francisco: Book Club of California, 1962.

Köhler 1870. Köhler, Sylvester Rosa. "Albert Bierstadt." *Zeitschrift für bildende Kunst* 5 (1870): 65–74.

Köhler 1871. Köhler, Sylvester Rosa. "Albert Bierstadt." *Der deutsche Pionier* 2 (Jan./Feb. 1871): 322–27, 359–64.

Köhler 1880–81. Köhler, Sylvester Rosa. *American Art Review.* Boston: D. Estes and C. E. Lauriat, 1880–81.

Köhler 1882–84. Köhler, Sylvester Rosa. *The United States Art Directory and Yearbook.* New York: Cassell, Petter, Galpin, & Co., 1882–84.

Köhler 1886. Köhler, Sylvester Rosa. *American Art.* New York: Cassell & Co., 1886.

Koke 1982. Koke, Richard J., et al. *American Landscape and Genre Paintings in The New-York Historical Society.* 3 vols. Boston: G. K. Hall & Co., 1982.

Kotowski 1981. Kotowski, Diane Wetmore. "Albert Bierstadt's 'Weeping Oaks, Clear Creek, California' (1880): A Painting in the Collection of the University of Denver." Master's thesis, University of Denver, 1981.

Kozloff 1975. Kozloff, Max. "The Box in the Wilderness." *Artforum* 14 (Oct. 1975): 54–59.

Kugler 1978. Kugler, Richard C. *William Allen Wall: An Artist of New Bedford.* Exh. cat. New Bedford, Mass.: Old Dartmouth Historical Society and Whaling Museum, 1978.

LaFollette 1929. LaFollette, Suzanne. *Art in America.* New York: Harper & Brothers, 1929.

Lamb 1876. Lamb, Martha J. "The Homes of America II." *Art Journal* 2 (1876): 45–48.

Lamb 1879. Lamb, Martha J. *The Homes of America.* New York: D. Appleton & Company, 1879.

E. Lander 1904. Lander, Edward. "A Sketch of General Frederick W. Lander." *Historical Collections of the Essex Institute* 40 (Oct. 1904): 313–20.

F. Lander 1860–61. Lander, Frederick W. "Reports and Maps of the Fort Kearney, South Pass, and Honey Lake Wagon Road." 36th Congress, 2d session (1860–61), House Exec. Document 64: 1–39.

Lanman 1845. Lanman, Charles. *Letters from a Landscape Painter.* Boston: J. Munroe, 1845.

Lanman 1862. Lanman, Charles. *Adventures in the Wilds of North America.* Ed. Charles Richard Weld. London: Longman, Roberts, and Green, 1862.

Larkin 1949. Larkin, Oliver W. *Art and Life in America*. New York: Rinehart & Company, 1949; revised ed. 1960.

Leavitt 1964. Leavitt, Thomas W. *Albert Bierstadt, 1830–1902: A Retrospective Exhibition*. Exh. cat. Santa Barbara: Santa Barbara Museum of Art, 1964.

Leslie 1870. Leslie, Frank. "Report on the Fine Arts." In *Reports of the United States Commissioners to the Paris Universal Exposition, 1867*, vol. 1, pp. 1–43. Washington, D.C.: U.S. Government Printing Office, 1870.

D. Lewis 1976. Lewis, Donald S., Jr. "Herman Herzog (1831–1932), German Landscapist in America." *American Art Review* 3 (July/Aug. 1976): 52–66.

H. Lewis 1967. Lewis, Henry. *The Valley of the Mississippi Illustrated*. Ed. Bertha L. Heilbron. Saint Paul: Minnesota Historical Society, 1967. Originally published as *Das illustrirte Mississippithal*. Düsseldorf: Arnz & Co., 1854; reprint Leipzig: H. Schmidt & Co., 1923.

J. A. Lewis 1972a. Lewis, Jo Ann. "The Bierstadt Retrospective." *Evening Star* (Washington, D.C.), 11 Apr. 1972.

J. A. Lewis 1972b. Lewis, Jo Ann. "Reflections on Bierstadt." *Sunday Star* (Washington, D.C.), 16 Apr. 1972.

O. Lewis 1938. Lewis, Oscar. *The Big Four*. New York: Alfred A. Knopf, 1938.

O. Lewis 1966. Lewis, Oscar. *San Francisco: Mission to Metropolis*. Berkeley, Calif.: Howell-North Books, 1966.

R. W. B. Lewis 1955. Lewis, R. W. B. *The American Adam: Innocence, Tragedy and Tradition in the Nineteenth Century*. Chicago: University of Chicago Press, 1955.

V. E. Lewis 1956. Lewis, Virginia E. *Russell Smith: Romantic Realist*. Pittsburgh: University of Pittsburgh Press, 1956.

Lewison 1964. Lewison, Florence. "The Uniqueness of Albert Bierstadt." *American Artist* 28 (Sept. 1964): 28–33.

Lewison Gallery 1963a. *Bierstadt*. Exh. cat. New York: Florence Lewison Gallery, 1963.

Lewison Gallery 1963b. *The Creative Core of Bierstadt: The Abstract Basis of His Art, An Exhibition of Twenty-four Studies in Oil*. Exh. cat. New York: Florence Lewison Gallery, 1963.

Lewison Gallery 1964. *Man, Beast, and Nature: Oils and Drawings by Albert Bierstadt*. Exh. cat. New York: Florence Lewison Gallery, 1964.

Lewison Gallery 1968. *Bierstadt: His Small Paintings*. Exh. cat. New York: Florence Lewison Gallery, 1968.

Limerick 1987. Limerick, Patricia Nelson. *The Legacy of Conquest: The Unbroken Past of the American West*. New York: W. W. Norton & Co., 1987.

Lindquist-Cock 1970. Lindquist-Cock, Elizabeth. "Stereoscopic Photography and the Western Paintings of Albert Bierstadt." *Art Quarterly* 33 (Winter 1970): 360–78.

Lindquist-Cock 1977. Lindquist-Cock, Elizabeth. *The Influence of Photography on American Landscape Painting, 1839–1880*. New York: Garland Publishing, 1977.

Listokin 1980. Listokin, Barbara Cyviner. "A Bierstadt Sketchbook." *Master Drawings* 18 (Winter 1980): 376–78.

Lloyd 1876. Lloyd, Benjamin E. *Lights and Shades in San Francisco*. San Francisco: A. L. Bancroft & Co., 1876.

Low 1910. Low, Will Hicok. *A Painter's Progress*. New York: Charles Scribner's Sons, 1910.

Ludlow 1864a. Ludlow, Fitz Hugh. "Among the Mormons." *Atlantic Monthly*, Apr. 1864, pp. 479–95.

Ludlow 1864b. Ludlow, Fitz Hugh. "On the Columbia River." *Atlantic Monthly*, Dec. 1864, pp. 703–15.

Ludlow 1864c. Ludlow, Fitz Hugh. "On Horseback into Oregon." *Atlantic Monthly*, July 1864, pp. 75–86.

Ludlow 1864d. Ludlow, Fitz Hugh. "Seven Weeks in the Great Yo-Semite." *Atlantic Monthly*, June 1864, pp. 739–54.

Ludlow 1864e. Ludlow, Fitz Hugh. "Through Tickets to San Francisco." *Atlantic Monthly*, Nov. 1864, pp. 604–17.

Ludlow 1870a. Ludlow, Fitz Hugh. *The Hasheesh Eater: Being Passages from the Life of a Pythagorean*. New York: Hurd & Houghton, 1870.

Ludlow 1870b. Ludlow, Fitz Hugh. *The Heart of the Continent: A Record of Travel Across the Plains and in Oregon, with an Examination of the Mormon Principle*. New York: Hurd & Houghton, 1870.

Lurie [1960] 1988. Lurie, Edward. *Louis Agassiz: A Life in Science*. Chicago: University of Chicago Press, 1960. Reprint: Baltimore: Johns Hopkins University Press, 1988.

MFA 1969. *American Paintings in the Museum of Fine Arts*. 2 vols. Boston: Museum of Fine Arts, 1969.

McClinton 1973. McClinton, Katherine Morrison. *The Chromolithographs of Louis Prang*. New York: Clarkson & Potter, 1973.

McCoubrey 1965. McCoubrey, John W., ed. *American Art, 1700–1960: Sources and Documents*. Englewood Cliffs, N.J.: Prentice-Hall, 1965.

McCracken 1952. McCracken, Harold. *Portrait of the Old West*. New York: McGraw-Hill Book Company, 1952.

McGrath and MacAdam 1988. McGrath, Robert L., and Barbara J. MacAdam. *"A Sweet Foretaste of Heaven": Artists in the White Mountains, 1830–1930*. Exh. cat. Hanover, N.H.: University Press of New England, 1988.

McShine 1976. McShine, Kynaston, et al. *The Natural Paradise: Painting in America, 1800–1950*. Exh. cat. New York: Museum of Modern Art, 1976.

Magoon 1856. Magoon, Elias Lyman. *Westward Empire: Or, The Great Drama of Human Progress*. New York: Harper & Brothers, 1856.

Manthorne 1989. Manthorne, Katherine. *Tropical Renaissance: North American Artists Exploring Latin America, 1839–1879*. Washington, D.C.: Smithsonian Institution Press, 1989.

Marlor 1970. Marlor, Clark S. *A History of the Brooklyn Art Association with an Index of Exhibitions*. New York: James F. Carr, 1970.

Marx 1964. Marx, Leo. *The Machine in the Garden: Technology and the Pastoral Ideal in America*. London: Oxford University Press, 1964.

Marzio 1979. Marzio, Peter C. *The Democratic Art: Chromolithography, 1840–1900, Pictures for a 19th-Century America*. Boston: David R. Godine; Fort Worth, Tex.: Amon Carter Museum of Western Art, 1979.

Masteller 1981. Masteller, Richard N. "Western Views in Eastern Parlors: The Contribution of the Stereograph Photographer to the Conquest of the West." *Prospects* 6 (1981): 55–71.

Mayor and Davis 1977. Mayor, A. Hyatt, and Mark Davis. *American Art at the Century*. New York: Century Association, 1977.

Mellow 1972. Mellow, James R. "Bierstadt: 'Moments of Quite Beautiful Painting.'" *Art News* 71 (Oct. 1972): 62–63.

Mendelowitz 1960. Mendelowitz, Daniel M. *A History of American Art*. New York: Holt, Rinehart and Winston, 1960.

Merk 1966. Merk, Frederick. *Manifest Destiny and Mission in American History*. New York: Vintage Books, 1966.

H. Merritt 1969. Merritt, Howard S. *Thomas Cole*. Exh. cat. Rochester, N.Y.: Memorial Art Gallery of the University of Rochester, 1969.

J. Merritt 1985. Merritt, John I. *Baronets and Buffalo: The British Sportsman in the American West, 1833–1881*. Missoula, Mont.: Montana Press Publishing Company, 1985.

Metropolitan Fair 1864. *Catalogue of the Art Exhibition at the Metropolitan Fair, U.S. Sanitary Commission*. Exh. cat. New York: U.S. Sanitary Commission, 1864.

Metropolitan Fair Record 1867. *A Record of the Metropolitan Fair in Aid of the United States Sanitary Commission, Held at New York in April, 1864*. New York: Hurd & Houghton, 1867.

Metropolitan Museum 1981. *German Masters of the Nineteenth Century*. Exh. cat. New York: Metropolitan Museum of Art, 1981.

Metropolitan Museum 1987. *American Paradise: The World of the Hudson River School*. Exh. cat. New York: Metropolitan Museum of Art, 1987.

D. Miller 1975. Miller, Dwight C. *California Landscape Painting, 1860–1885: Artists Around Keith and Hill, 1850–1900*. Exh. cat. Stanford, Calif.: Stanford University Museum and Art Gallery, 1975.

L. Miller 1966. Miller, Lillian B. *Patrons and Patriotism: The Encouragement of the Fine Arts in the United States, 1790–1860*. Chicago: University of Chicago Press, 1966.

P. Miller 1965. Miller, Perry. *Errand into the Wilderness*. Cambridge, Mass.: Harvard University Press, 1965.

P. Miller 1967. Miller, Perry. *Nature's Nation*. Cambridge, Mass.: Harvard University Press, 1967.

Mills 1985. Mills, Shelley. "Albert Bierstadt: An Observer of Air, Light and the Feeling of a Place." Exh. checklist. San Francisco: Fine Arts Museums of San Francisco, 1985.

Mitchell 1981. Mitchell, Lee Clark. *Witnesses to a Vanishing America: The Nineteenth-Century Response*. Princeton, N.J.: Princeton University Press, 1981.

Monk 1935. Monk, Samuel H. *The Sublime: A Study of Critical Theories in XVIII-Century England*. New York: Modern Language Association, 1935.

Montgomery 1889. Montgomery, Walter, ed. "Albert Bierstadt." In *American Art & American Art Collections*, vol. 2, pp. 578–81. Boston: E. W. Walker & Co., 1889.

*Month at Goodspeed's* 1938. "This Artist Went Overland." *Month at Goodspeed's* 10 (Oct. 1938): 27–29.

C. Moore 1889. Moore, Charles H. "Materials for Landscape Art in America." *Atlantic Monthly*, Nov. 1889, pp. 670–81.

J. Moore 1974. Moore, James Collins. "The Storm and the Harvest: The Image of Nature in Mid Nineteenth-Century American Landscape Painting." Ph.D. diss., Indiana University, Bloomington, 1974.

Moure 1973. Moure, Nancy Dustin Wall. "Five Eastern Artists Out West." *American Art Journal* 5 (Nov. 1973): 15–31.

Muir 1888. Muir, John. *Picturesque California and the Region West of the Rocky Mountains, from Alaska to Mexico*. New York: J. Dewing Company, 1888.

Murray 1853. Murray, John. *A Handbook for Travellers in Central Italy, Part II: Rome & Its Environs*. 3d ed. London: John Murray, 1853.

Muther 1907. Muther, Richard. *The History of Modern Painting*. Revised ed., 4 vols. New York: E. P. Dutton & Co., 1907.

F. Myers 1985. Myers, Fred A. "Bierstadt's Small Paintings: The Intimate Aspect of Grand Opera." *Gilcrease Magazine of American History and Art* 7 (Sept. 1985): 1–9.

K. Myers 1987. Myers, Kenneth. *The Catskills: Painters, Writers and Tourists in the Mountains, 1820–1895.* Exh. cat. Yonkers, N.Y.: Hudson River Museum of Westchester, 1987.

Naef 1975. Naef, Weston. "Artists and Photographers of the Western Expeditions." *Art News* 74 (Dec. 1975): 62–64.

Nash 1969. Nash, Roderick. "The Cultural Significance of the American Wilderness." In *Wilderness and the Quality of Life*, ed. Maxine E. McCloskey and James P. Gilligan. San Francisco: Sierra Club, 1969.

Nash 1982. Nash, Roderick. *Wilderness and the American Mind.* 3rd ed. New Haven: Yale University Press, 1982.

Naylor 1973. Naylor, Maria, ed. *The National Academy of Design Exhibition Record, 1861–1900.* New York: Kennedy Galleries, 1973.

Neuhaus 1931. Neuhaus, Eugen. *The History and Ideals of American Art.* Palo Alto, Calif.: Stanford University Press, 1931.

New Bedford Catalogue 1858. *Catalogue of the New-Bedford Art Exhibition.* New Bedford, Mass.: A. Bierstadt and J. Hopkins, 1858.

New Bedford Library 1965. "A City and Its Painters." Exh. checklist. New Bedford, Mass.: New Bedford Free Public Library, 1965.

New Bedford *Standard-Times* 1960. "Two Artists from New Bedford." *Sunday Standard-Times* (New Bedford, Mass.), 24 Apr. 1960.

*New Path* 1864a. [Clarence Cook]. "Bierstadt's 'Rocky Mountains.'" *New Path* 1 (Apr. 1864): 160–61.

*New Path* 1864b. "The Essential Differences Between the True and the Popular Art Systems." *New Path* 2 (July 1864): 33–35.

*New Path* 1865. "The Mutual Art Association.—Bierstadt's Mount Hope [Hood]." *New Path* 2 (May 1865): 74–77.

Newhall 1949. Newhall, Beaumont. *The History of Photography from 1839 to the Present Day.* New York: Museum of Modern Art, 1949. Revised and enlarged ed. 1964.

Nicholls 1893. Nicholls, Charles Wilbur de Lyon [Shelton Chauncey]. *The Greek Madonna.* New York: G. W. Dillingham, Publisher, 1893.

Nickerson 1984. Nickerson, Cynthia D. "Artistic Interpretations of Henry Wadsworth Longfellow's 'The Song of Hiawatha,' 1855–1900." *American Art Journal* 16 (Summer 1984): 49–75.

Nicolson 1959. Nicolson, Marjorie Hope. *Mountain Gloom and Mountain Glory: The Development of the Aesthetics of the Infinite.* Ithaca, N.Y.: Cornell University Press, 1959.

*Nineteenth Century* 1977. "The Cinemascopic West of Albert Bierstadt." *Nineteenth Century* 3 (Autumn 1977): 55–59.

Noble 1859. Noble, Louis Legrand. *Church's Painting, "The Heart of the Andes."* New York: D. Appleton, 1859.

Noble 1861. Noble, Louis Legrand. *After Icebergs with a Painter: Summer Voyage to Labrador and around Newfoundland.* New York: D. Appleton, 1861.

Nordhoff 1872. Nordhoff, Charles. *California for Health, Pleasure, and Residence. A Book for Travellers and Settlers.* New York: Harper & Brothers, 1872. Revised ed. 1882.

Nordhoff 1874. Nordhoff, Charles. *Northern California, Oregon, and the Sandwich Islands.* New York: Harper & Brothers, 1874.

*North American Review* 1866. "The Conditions of Art in America." *North American Review* 102 (Jan. 1866): 1–24.

Norton 1860. Norton, Charles Eliot. *Notes of Travel and Study in Italy.* Boston: Ticknor and Fields, 1860.

Novak 1969. Novak, Barbara. *American Painting of the Nineteenth Century: Realism, Idealism, and the American Experience.* New York: Harper & Row, 1969.

Novak 1971. Novak, Barbara. "Grand Opera and the Small Still Voice." *Art in America* 59 (Mar./Apr. 1971): 64–73. Reprinted in Novak 1980b.

Novak 1972. Novak, Barbara. "American Landscape: The Nationalist Garden and the Holy Book." *Art in America* 60 (Jan. 1972): 46–57.

Novak 1975. Novak, Barbara. "Landscape Permuted: From Painting to Photography." *Artforum* 14 (Oct. 1975): 40–45.

Novak 1980a. Novak, Barbara. "The Meteorological Vision: Clouds." *Art in America* 68 (Feb. 1980): 102–17.

Novak 1980b. Novak, Barbara. *Nature and Culture: American Landscape and Painting, 1825–1875.* New York: Oxford University Press, 1980.

Novak and Blaugrund 1980. Novak, Barbara, and Annette Blaugrund, eds. *Next to Nature: Landscape Paintings from the National Academy of Design.* Exh. cat. New York: National Academy of Design, 1980.

Novotny 1970. Novotny, Fritz. *Painting and Sculpture in Europe, 1780–1880.* 2d ed. Harmondsworth: Penguin Books, 1970.

Nygren 1986. Nygren, Edward J. *Views and Visions: American Landscape Before 1830.* Exh. cat. Washington, D.C.: Corcoran Gallery of Art, 1986.

Oakland Museum 1964. *The Yosemite Valley by Albert Bierstadt, N.A.* Oakland, Calif.: Oakland Museum, 1964.

Old Dartmouth Historical Society 1976. *New Bedford and Old Dartmouth: A Portrait of a Region's Past.* New Bedford, Mass.: Old Dartmouth Historical Society and Whaling Museum, 1976.

F. L. Olmsted 1952. Olmsted, Frederick Law. "The Yosemite Valley and the Mariposa Big Trees: A Preliminary Report (1865) by Frederick Law Olmsted." *Landscape Architecture* 43 (1952): 12–25.

R. Olmsted 1962. Olmsted, Roger R., ed. *Scenes of Wonder and Curiosity from Hutchings' California Magazine, 1856–1861.* Berkeley, Calif.: Howell-North, 1962.

*Outlook* 1902. "A Self-Made Artist." *Outlook* 70 (1 Mar. 1902): 507.

*Overland Monthly* 1869. "Our Art Possibilities." *Overland Monthly* 2 (Mar. 1869): 248–54.

Palmquist 1981. Palmquist, Peter E. "Soule's California Stereographs." *Stereo World* 8 (Mar./Apr. 1981): 4–10.

Palmquist 1982. Palmquist, Peter E. "Speak Up!" *Stereo World* 9 (Mar./Apr. 1982): 33, 35.

Palmquist 1983. Palmquist, Peter E. *Carleton E. Watkins: Photographer of the American West.* Albuquerque: University of New Mexico Press, 1983.

Pancoast 1989. Pancoast, Virgilia Heimsath. "The IFAR Report: Bogus Bierstadts." *Art & Auction* 12 (Sept. 1989): 122.

Parker 1943. Parker, Barbara N. "George Harvey and His Atmospheric Landscapes." *Bulletin of the Museum of Fine Arts Boston* 41 (Feb. 1943): 7–9.

Parkman 1849. Parkman, Francis. *The California and Oregon Trail.* New York: G. P. Putnam, 1849.

A. Parry 1960. Parry, Albert. *Garrets and Pretenders: A History of Bohemianism in America.* New York: Dover Publications, 1960.

E. Parry 1974. Parry, Ellwood. *The Image of the Indian and the Black Man in American Art, 1590–1900.* New York: George Braziller, 1974.

E. Parry 1988. Parry, Ellwood C. III. *The Art of Thomas Cole: Ambition and Imagination.* Newark, Del.: University of Delaware Press, 1988.

Patent Office Gazette 1896. "559,962. Railway-Car. Albert Bierstadt." *Official Gazette of the United States Patent Office* (Washington, D.C.: U.S. Government Printing Office) 75 (1896): 905–12. (Includes 7 Apr.–30 June 1896.)

Patent Office Gazette 1897. "566,127. Railway-Car. Albert Bierstadt." *Official Gazette of the United States Patent Office* 76 (1897): 1057. (Includes 7 July–29 Sept. 1896.)

Patent Office Specifications 1896a. "559,962. Railway-Car. Albert Bierstadt, New York, N.Y." *Specifications and Drawings of Patents Issued from the United States Patent Office for May 1896, Part 1–2.* Washington, D.C.: U.S. Government Printing Office, 1896. (Part 1: 1118–34, Part 2: 260–63.)

Patent Office Specifications 1896b. "559,962. Railway-Car. Albert Bierstadt, New York, N.Y." *Specifications and Drawings of Patents Issued from the United States Patent Office for August, 1896, Part 1–2.* Washington, D.C.: U.S. Government Printing Office, 1896. (Part 1: 2149–51, Part 2: 521–22.)

Perkins and Gavin 1980. Perkins, Robert F., Jr., and William J. Gavin III. *The Boston Athenaeum Art Exhibition Index, 1827–1874.* Boston: Library of the Boston Athenaeum, 1980.

Perl 1976. Perl, Jed. "The Vertical Landscape: 'In the Redwood Forest Dense.'" *Art in America* 64 (Jan. 1976): 59–63.

Pevsner 1940. Pevsner, Nikolaus. *Academies of Art Past and Present.* Cambridge: University Press, 1940.

*Philadelphia Photographer* 1867. "Stereographs." *Philadelphia Photographer* 4 (9 Sept. 1867): 332–33.

Plowden 1947. Plowden, Helen Haseltine. *William Stanley Haseltine: Sea and Landscape Painter (1835–1900), Notes and Recollections from His Life Collected by His Daughter.* London: Frederick Muller, 1947.

Porter 1989. Porter, Bruce. "Bierstadt: On the Trail of the Great Propagandist of the American West." *Connoisseur* 219 (Aug. 1989): 49–55.

Posner 1964. Posner, Russell M. "Thomas Starr King and the Mercy Million." *California Historical Society Quarterly* 43 (Dec. 1964): 291–307.

Post 1976. Post, Robert C., ed. *1876: A Centennial Exhibition.* Washington, D.C.: National Museum of History and Technology, Smithsonian Institution, 1976.

Pringle 1985. Pringle, Allan. "Albert Bierstadt in Canada." *American Art Journal* 17 (Winter 1985): 3–27.

Pumpelly 1870. Pumpelly, Raphael. *Across America and Asia: Notes of a Five Years' Journey Around the World and of Residence in Arizona, Japan, and China.* New York: Leypoldt & Holt, 1870.

Rae 1871. Rae, William. *Westward by Rail: The New Route to the East.* New York: D. Appleton Company, 1871.

Rasmussen 1942. Rasmussen, Louise. "Artists of the Explorations Overland, 1840–1860." *Oregon Historical Quarterly* 43 (Mar. 1942): 56–62.

Ratcliff 1972. Ratcliff, Carter. "New York Letter." *Art International* 16 (Dec. 1972): 58.

J. E. Reed 1888. Reed, J. E. *One Hundred Crowned Masterpieces of Modern Painting.* Vol. 1. Philadelphia: Gebbie & Co., 1888.

Reiger 1975. Reiger, John F. *American Sportsmen and the Origins of Conservation.* New York: Winchester Press, 1975.

A. Richardson 1867. Richardson, Albert Deane. *Beyond the Mississippi: From the Great River to the Great Ocean.* Hartford, Conn.: American Publishing Company, 1867.

E. Richardson 1944. Richardson, E. P. *American Romantic Painting.* New York: E. Weyhe, 1944.

E. Richardson 1956. Richardson, E. P. *Painting in America: The Story of 450 Years.* New York: Thomas Y. Crowell, 1956.

Richardson and Wittmann 1951. Richardson, Edgar P., and Otto Wittmann, Jr. *Travelers in Arcadia.* Exh. cat. Detroit: Detroit Institute of Arts, 1951.

Ricketson 1858. Ricketson, Daniel. *The History of New Bedford, Bristol County, Massachusetts.* New Bedford, Mass.: privately printed, 1858.

RISD Bulletin 1977. "Selection VII: American Paintings from the Museum's Collection, c. 1800–1930." *Bulletin of Rhode Island School of Design* 63 (Apr. 1977): 34–36.

Robertson 1984. Robertson, David. *West of Eden: A History of the Art and Literature of Yosemite.* Yosemite National Park, Calif.: Yosemite Natural History Association and Wilderness Press, 1984.

Robinson 1937. Robinson, Mary Turlay. "William Allen Wall of New Bedford." *Magazine of Art* 30 (Feb. 1937): 108–11.

Rockwell 1867. Rockwell, Charles. *The Catskill Mountains and Region Around, their Scenery, Legends, and History; with Sketches in Prose and Verse.* New York: Tainton Brothers & Co., 1867.

Roper 1973. Roper, Laura Wood. *FLO: A Biography of Frederick Law Olmsted.* Baltimore: Johns Hopkins University Press, 1973.

Rosenblum 1975. Rosenblum, Robert. *Modern Painting and the Northern Romantic Tradition: Friedrich to Rothko.* New York: Harper & Row, 1975.

Rosenblum and Janson 1984. Rosenblum, Robert, and H. W. Janson. *19th-Century Art.* New York: Harry N. Abrams, 1984.

Runte 1979. Runte, Alfred. *National Parks: The American Experience.* Lincoln, Nebr.: University of Nebraska Press, 1979. Revised ed. 1987.

Ruskin 1847. Ruskin, John. *Modern Painters.* 5 vols. New York: Wiley and Putnam, 1847.

Rutledge 1955. Rutledge, Anna Wells. *Cumulative Record of Exhibition Catalogues: Pennsylvania Academy of Fine Arts, 1807–1870; The Society of Artists, 1800–1814; The Artists' Fund Society, 1835–1845.* Philadelphia: American Philosophical Society, 1955.

Saunders 1988. Saunders, Richard. *Collecting the West: The C. R. Smith Collection of Western American Art.* Austin: University of Texas Press, 1988.

Schimmel 1983. Schimmel, Julie. "John Mix Stanley and Imagery of the West in Nineteenth-Century American Art." Ph.D. diss., New York University, 1983.

Schwarz 1981. Schwarz, Ellen. *Nineteenth-Century San Francisco Art Exhibition Catalogues: A Descriptive Checklist and Index.* Davis, Calif.: University of California Library Associates, 1981.

C. Sears 1947. Sears, Clara Endicott. *Highlights Among the Hudson River Artists.* Boston: Houghton Mifflin Company, 1947.

J. Sears 1989. Sears, John F. *Sacred Places: American Tourist Attractions in the Nineteenth Century.* New York: Oxford University Press, 1989.

Sebastian 1931. Sebastian, Hugh Charles. "A Biographical and Critical Study of Fitz Hugh Ludlow." Ph.D. diss., University of Chicago, 1931.

Sexton 1974. Sexton, Nanette. "Toward the Definition of Process: Photography and the Yosemite Paintings of Albert Bierstadt." Master's thesis, Harvard University, 1974.

Sheirr 1876. Sheirr, Rodman J. "Thomas Thompson and His Art Mania." *Potter's American Monthly: An Illustrated Magazine of History, Literature, and Art* 6–7 (1876): 141–43.

Sheldon [1879] 1972. Sheldon, George William. *American Painters.* New York: D. Appleton and Company, 1879. Reprint: New York: Benjamin Bloom, 1972.

Sheldon 1885–86. Sheldon, George William. *Selections in Modern Art.* New York: D. Appleton and Co., 1885–86.

Sheldon 1888–90. Sheldon, George William. *Recent Ideals of American Art.* 2 vols. New York: D. Appleton and Co., 1888–90.

Shelley 1948a. Shelley, Donald S. "George Harvey and His Atmospheric Landscapes of North America." *New-York Historical Society Quarterly* 32 (Apr. 1948): 104–13.

Shelley 1948b. Shelley, Donald S. "George Harvey, English Painter of Atmospheric Landscapes in America." *American Collector* 17 (Apr. 1948): 10–13.

Shepard 1967. Shepard, Paul. *Man in the Landscape: A Historic View of the Esthetics of Nature.* New York: Alfred A. Knopf, 1967.

Sherman [1895] 1968. Sherman, John. *Recollections of Forty Years in the House, Senate and Cabinet. An Autobiography. Volume II.* Chicago: Werner Company, 1895. Reprint: New York: Greenwood Press, 1968.

Simonds 1917. Simonds, William Day. *Starr King in California.* San Francisco: Paul Elder and Company, 1917.

Simoni 1952. Simoni, John P. "Art Critics and Criticism in Nineteenth-Century America." Ph.D. diss., Ohio State University, Columbus, 1952.

Simpson, Mills, and Saville 1990. Simpson, Marc, Sally Mills, and Jennifer Saville. *The American Canvas: Paintings from the Collection of The Fine Arts Museums of San Francisco.* New York: Hudson Hills Press, 1990.

Slotkin 1973. Slotkin, Richard. *Regeneration Through Violence: The Mythology of the American Frontier, 1600–1860.* Middletown, Conn.: Wesleyan University Press, 1973.

Slotkin 1985. Slotkin, Richard. *The Fatal Environment: The Myth of the Frontier in the Age of Industrialization, 1800–1890.* New York: Atheneum, 1985.

D. Smith 1967. Smith, David Loeffler. "New Bedford Artists of the Nineteenth Century." *Antiques* 92 (Nov. 1967): 689–93.

H. Smith 1950. Smith, Henry Nash. *Virgin Land: The American West as Symbol and Myth.* Cambridge, Mass.: Harvard University Press, 1950.

Smyth 1896. Smyth, Albert H. *Bayard Taylor.* Boston: Houghton, Mifflin & Company, 1896.

Snell 1958. Snell, Joseph W. "Some Rare Western Photographs by Albert Bierstadt Now in the Kansas Historical Society Collections." *Kansas Historical Quarterly* 24 (Spring 1958): 1–5.

Snell 1975. Snell, Joseph W. Review of *Albert Bierstadt: Painter of the American West,* by Gordon Hendricks. *American West* (May 1975): 51.

Soby and Miller 1943. Soby, James Thrall, and Dorothy C. Miller. *Romantic Painting in America.* Exh. cat. New York: Museum of Modern Art, 1943.

Société des Artistes français 1869. Societé des Artistes français. *Explication des Ouvrages de Peinture, Sculpture, Architecture, Gravure, et Lithographie des Artistes Vivants Exposés au palais des Champs-Elysées.* Exh. cat. Paris: Charles de Morgues Frères, 1869.

Soria 1982. Soria, Regina. *Dictionary of Nineteenth-Century American Artists in Italy, 1760–1914.* Rutherford, Pa.: Fairleigh-Dickinson University Press, 1982.

Spassky et al. 1985. Spassky, Natalie, et al. *American Paintings in The Metropolitan Museum of Art.* Vol. 2, *A Catalogue of Works by Artists Born Between 1816 and 1845.* New York: Metropolitan Museum of Art, 1985.

Spieler 1945. Spieler, Gerhard G. "A Noted Artist in Early Colorado: The Story of Albert Bierstadt." *American-German Review* 11 (June 1945): 13–17.

Starr 1973. Starr, Kevin. *Americans and the California Dream, 1850–1915.* New York: Oxford University Press, 1973.

Starr 1977. Starr, Kevin. "Albert Bierstadt: The Civilizing Eye." *Sierra* 6 (Nov./Dec. 1977): 27–30.

Stebbins 1973. Stebbins, Theodore E., Jr. "The Bierstadt Exhibition and Catalogue." *American Art Journal* 5 (May 1973): 90–92.

Stebbins 1976. Stebbins, Theodore E., Jr. *The Hudson River School: 19th Century Landscapes in the Wadsworth Athenaeum.* Exh. cat. Hartford, Conn.: Wadsworth Athenaeum, 1976.

Stebbins 1983. Stebbins, Theodore E., Jr., et al. *A New World: Masterpieces of American Painting, 1760–1910.* Exh. cat. Boston: Museum of Fine Arts, 1983.

Stehle 1964. Stehle, Raymond L. "Washington Crossing the Delaware." *Pennsylvania History* 31 (July 1964): 269–94.

Stehle 1972. Stehle, Raymond L. "The Life and Works of Emanuel Leutze." Unpublished manuscript, 1972.

Stehle 1974. Stehle, Raymond L. "The Düsseldorf Gallery of New York." *New-York Historical Society Quarterly* 57 (Oct. 1974): 304–17.

Stein 1967. Stein, Roger B. *John Ruskin and Aesthetic Thought in America, 1840–1900.* Cambridge, Mass.: Harvard University Press, 1967.

Stein 1968. Stein, Roger B. *The View and the Vision: Landscape Painting in Nineteenth-Century America.* Exh. cat. Seattle: Henry Gallery, University of Washington, 1968.

M. Stevens 1978. Stevens, Mark. "Art: A Rockefeller Bonanza." *Newsweek,* 30 Jan. 1978, pp. 60–61.

M. L. Stevens 1976. Stevens, Moreland L. *Charles Christian Nahl: Artist of the Gold Rush, 1818–1878.* Exh. cat. Sacramento, Calif.: E. B. Crocker Art Gallery, 1976.

Stewart [1936] 1960. Stewart, George R. *Ordeal by Hunger: The Story of the Donner Party.* New York: H. Holt and Company, 1936. Reprint: Boston: Houghton, Mifflin Company, 1960.

Strahan 1876–78. Strahan, Edward [Earl Shinn]. *The Masterpieces of the Centennial International Exhibition Illustrated.* 3 vols. Philadelphia: Gebbie & Barrie, 1876–78.

Strahan 1880. Strahan, Edward [Earl Shinn]. *The Art Treasures of America.* 3 vols. Philadelphia: G. Barrie, 1880.

Strong 1975. Strong, Donald S. Review of *Albert Bierstadt: Painter of the American West,* by Gordon Hendricks. *American Art Review* 2 (Sept./Oct. 1975): 132–44.

Swain School of Design 1960. *Selection of Paintings by Albert Pinkham Ryder and Albert Bierstadt.* Exh. cat. New Bedford, Mass.: William W. Crapo Gallery, Swain School of Design, 1960.

Swan 1940. Swan, Mabel Munson. *The Athenaeum Gallery, 1827–1873.* Boston: Boston Athenaeum, 1940.

Sweeney 1975. Sweeney, J. Gray. "The Artist-Explorers of the American West: 1860–1880." Ph.D. diss., Indiana University, Bloomington, 1975.

Sweeney 1977. Sweeney, J. Gray. *Themes in American Painting.* Exh. cat. Grand Rapids: Grand Rapids Art Museum, 1977.

Sweet 1945. Sweet, Frederick A. *The Hudson River School and the Early American Landscape*. Exh. cat. Chicago: Art Institute of Chicago, 1945.

Taft 1938. Taft, Robert. *Photography and the American Scene: A Social History, 1839–1889*. New York: Macmillan Company, 1938.

Taft 1953. Taft, Robert. *Artists and Illustrators of the Old West, 1850–1900*. New York: Bonanza Books, 1953.

Taragin 1976. Taragin, Davira Spiro. "William Wilson Corcoran." In *Corcoran: The American Genius*, pp. 17–22. Exh. cat. Washington, D.C.: Corcoran Gallery of Art, 1976.

B. Taylor [1850] 1949. Taylor, Bayard. *Eldorado, Or Adventures in the Path of Empire*. New York: G. P. Putnam, 1850. Reprint: New York: Alfred A. Knopf, 1949.

J. Taylor 1976. Taylor, Joshua. *America as Art*. Exh. cat. Washington, D.C.: Smithsonian Institution Press, 1976.

R. Taylor 1929. Taylor, Rose Schuster. "Another Rare Accession for the Yosemite Museum." *Yosemite Nature Notes* 8 (July 1929): 71–74.

R. Taylor 1930. Taylor, Rose Schuster. "The Life of Albert Bierstadt." *Yosemite Nature Notes* 9 (Sept. 1930): 81–82.

R. Taylor 1936. Taylor, Rose Schuster. *Yosemite Indians and Other Sketches*. San Francisco: Johnck & Seeger, 1936.

P. Thomas 1976. Thomas, Phillip Drennon. "Bierstadt of Düsseldorf: The Painter of America's Western Vision." *Montana: The Magazine of Western History* 26 (Spring 1976): 2–17.

S. Thomas 1937. Thomas, Stephen. "The American Career of Albert van Beest." *Antiques* 31 (Jan. 1937): 14–18.

Tillim 1976. Tillim, Sidney. "The Ideal and the Literal Sublime: Reflections on Painting and Photography in America." *Artforum* 14 (May 1976): 58–61.

Todd 1870. Todd, John. *The Sunset Land: Or, The Great Pacific Slope*. Boston: Lee & Shepard, 1870.

Townley 1872. Townley, D. O. C. "Living American Artists: Albert Bierstadt, N.A." *Scribner's Monthly* 3 (Mar. 1872): 605–8.

Trachtenberg 1977. Trachtenberg, Alan. "Myth, History, and Literature in Virgin Land." *Prospects* 3 (1977): 125–33.

Trachtenberg 1985. Trachtenberg, Alan. "Albums of War: On Reading Civil War Photographs." *Representations*, no. 9 (Winter 1985): 1–32.

*Transactions* AAU 1844–49. *Transactions of the American Art-Union*. New York, 1844–49.

*Transactions* Apollo Association 1839–43. *Transactions of the Apollo Association*. New York, 1839–43.

Trenton 1975. Trenton, Patricia. *Harvey Otis Young: The Lost Genius, 1840–1901*. Denver: Denver Art Museum, 1975.

Trenton and Hassrick 1983. Trenton, Patricia, and Peter H. Hassrick. *The Rocky Mountains: A Vision for Artists in the Nineteenth Century*. Norman, Okla.: University of Oklahoma Press, 1983.

Troyen 1984. Troyen, Carol. "Innocents Abroad: American Painters at the 1867 Exposition Universelle, Paris." *American Art Journal* 16 (Autumn 1984): 2–29.

Truettner and Bolton-Smith 1972. Truettner, William H., and Robin Bolton-Smith. *National Parks and the American Landscape*. Exh. cat. Washington, D.C.: Smithsonian Institution Press, 1972.

Trump 1963. Trump, Richard Shafer. "Life and Works of Albert Bierstadt." Ph.D. diss., Ohio State University, Columbus, 1963.

Tuckerman 1847. Tuckerman, Henry T. *Artist-Life: Or, Sketches of American Painters*. New York: D. Appleton & Company, 1847.

Tuckerman 1866. Tuckerman, Henry T. "Albert Bierstadt." *Galaxy* 1 (15 Aug. 1866): 678–83.

Tuckerman [1867] 1967. Tuckerman, Henry T. *Book of the Artists*. New York: G. P. Putnam & Sons, 1867. Reprint: New York: James F. Carr, 1967.

Univ. of Kansas Museum 1972. *The Arcadian Landscape: Nineteenth-Century American Painters in Italy*. Exh. cat. Lawrence: University of Kansas Museum of Art, 1972.

Unruh 1979. Unruh, John D., Jr. *The Plains Across: The Overland Emigrants and the Trans-Mississippi West, 1840–1860*. Urbana, Ill.: University of Illinois Press, 1979.

Van Nostrand 1980. Van Nostrand, Jeanne. *The First Hundred Years of Painting in California, 1775–1875*. San Francisco: John Howell Books, 1980.

Van Rensselaer 1881. Van Rensselaer, Mariana Griswold. "The New York Art Season." *Atlantic Monthly*, Aug. 1881, pp. 193–202.

Van Zanten 1969. Van Zanten, David T. "Jacob Wrey Mould: Echoes of Owen Jones and the High Victorian Styles in New York, 1853–1865." *Journal of the Society of Architectural Historians* 28 (Mar. 1969): 41–57.

Vaughn 1980. Vaughn, William. *German Romantic Painting*. New Haven: Yale University Press, 1980.

Vivian 1879. Vivian, Arthur Pendarves. *Wanderings in the Western Land*. London: Sampson Low, Marston, Searle, & Rivington, 1879.

Walker 1939. Walker, Franklin. *San Francisco's Literary Frontier*. New York: Alfred A. Knopf, 1939.

Wall 1828. Wall, William Guy. *The Hudson River Portfolio*. New York: H. I. Megarey, 1828. (With aquatints by John Hill based on drawings by Wall.)

Wallace 1955. Wallace, E. S. "Albert Bierstadt, Artist." *The Westerners: New York Posse Brand Book* 2 (1955): 1, 20–21.

Wallach 1977. Wallach, Alan. "Trouble in Paradise." *Artforum* 15 (Jan. 1977): 28–35.

Walther 1981. Walther, Susan Danly. *The Railroad in the American Landscape: 1850–1950*. Exh. cat. Wellesley, Mass.: Wellesley College Museum, 1981.

Weir 1877. Weir, John F. "Painting and Sculpture." In *International Exhibition, 1876. Reports and Awards*, vol. 5, pp. 2–45. Philadelphia: J. B. Lippincott, 1877.

Weiss 1977. Weiss, Ila. *Sanford Robinson Gifford (1823–1880)*. New York: Garland Publishing, 1977.

Weiss 1987. Weiss, Ila. *Poetic Landscape: The Art and Experience of Sanford R. Gifford*. Newark, Del.: University of Delaware Press, 1987.

Welling 1977. Welling, William. *Photography in America: The Formative Years, 1839–1900*. New York: Thomas Y. Crowell Company, 1977.

Wendte 1921. Wendte, Charles W. *Thomas Starr King: Patriot and Preacher*. Boston: Beacon Press, 1921.

Wermuth 1973. Wermuth, Paul C. *Bayard Taylor*. New York: Twayne Publishers, 1973.

Whitman [1882] 1982. Whitman, Walt. *Specimen Days*. Reprint: In *Whitman: Poetry and Prose*. New York: Library of America, 1982.

Whitney 1870. Whitney, Josiah Dwight. *The Yosemite Guide-Book*. Sacramento, Calif.: Published by Authority of the Legislature of the State of California, 1870.

Whitney Museum 1938. *A Century of American Landscape Painting*. Exh. cat. New York: Whitney Museum of American Art, 1938.

Whittredge [1942] 1969. Whittredge, Worthington. *The Autobiography of Worthington Whittredge*. Ed. John I. H. Baur. In *The Brooklyn Museum Journal* (1942): 3–68. Reprint: New York: Arno Press, 1969. (Manuscript completed 1905.)

Wilkins 1966. Wilkins, Thurman. *Thomas Moran: Artist of the Mountains*. Norman, Okla.: University of Oklahoma Press, 1966.

Wilkins 1988. Wilkins, Thurman. *Clarence King: A Biography*. Revised and enlarged ed. Albuquerque, N.M.: University of New Mexico Press, 1988.

Williams 1876. Williams, Henry T. *The Pacific Tourist*. New York: H. T. Williams, 1876.

Willis 1840. Willis, Nathaniel Parker. *American Scenery: Or Land, Lake, and River*. London: George Virtue, 1840.

Wilmerding 1968. Wilmerding, John. *A History of American Marine Painting*. Boston: Little, Brown, & Company, 1968.

Wilmerding 1969. Wilmerding, John. *William Bradford: Artist of the Arctic*. Exh. cat. Lincoln, Mass.: De Cordova Museum, 1969.

Wilmerding 1976a. Wilmerding, John. *American Art*. New York: Penguin Books, 1976.

Wilmerding 1976b. Wilmerding, John. Review of *Albert Bierstadt: Painter of the American West*, by Gordon Hendricks. *Art Bulletin* 58 (June 1976): 310–12.

Wilmerding et al. 1980a. Wilmerding, John, et al. *American Light: The Luminist Movement, 1850–1875*. Exh. cat. Washington, D.C.: National Gallery of Art, 1980.

Wilmerding et al. 1980b. Wilmerding, John, et al. *An American Perspective: Nineteenth-Century Art from the Collection of Jo Ann and Julian Ganz, Jr.* Exh. cat. Washington, D.C.: National Gallery of Art, 1980.

Wilson 1982. Wilson, Raymond L. "The First Art School in the West: The San Francisco Art Association's California School of Design." *American Art Journal* 14 (Winter 1982): 42–55.

Winthrop 1859. Winthrop, Theodore. *A Companion to "The Heart of the Andes."* New York: D. Appleton and Company, 1859.

Winthrop [1862] 1955. Winthrop, Theodore. *Canoe and Saddle*. Portland, Oreg.: Binfords & Mort, Publishers, 1955.

Witthoft 1987. Witthoft, Brucia. "The History of James Smillie's Engraving After Albert Bierstadt's 'The Rocky Mountains.'" *American Art Journal* 19 (1987): 40–51.

Wittmann 1958. Wittmann, Otto. "Americans in Italy." *College Art Journal* 17 (Spring 1958): 284–93.

Wolf 1982. Wolf, Bryan Jay. *Romantic Re-Vision: Culture and Consciousness in Nineteenth-Century American Painting and Literature*. Chicago: University of Chicago Press, 1982.

Wordsworth, Jaye, and Woof 1987. Wordsworth, Jonathan, Michael C. Jaye, and Robert Woof. *William Wordsworth and the Age of English Romanticism*. New Brunswick, N.J.: Rutgers University Press, 1987.

Wunderlich 1960a. Wunderlich, Rudolf. "Albert Bierstadt (1830–1902)." *Kennedy Quarterly* 1 (Apr. 1960): 29–33.

Wunderlich 1960b. Wunderlich, Rudolf. "Albert Bierstadt (1830–1902)." *Kennedy Quarterly* 1 (Oct. 1960): 106–10.

Yarnall and Gerdts 1986. Yarnall, James, and William H. Gerdts, compilers. *The National Museum of American Art's Index to American Art Exhibition Catalogues: From the Beginning Through the 1876 Centennial Year*. Vol. 1. Boston: G. K. Hall & Co., 1986.

# APPENDIX A

In September 1857, Albert Bierstadt returned to New Bedford, Massachusetts, following four years of study and travel abroad. Ten months later, he organized (with the assistance of his friend and patron John Hopkins) the first art exhibition ever held in New Bedford. A major undertaking that included 150 works by European as well as American artists, the exhibition marked Bierstadt's debut as a technically mature painter and a skilled promoter. The catalogue that accompanied the exhibition is a particularly revealing document for it testifies not only to Bierstadt's organizational and entrepreneurial skills, but also to his ambition and confidence: among works by such revered masters as Andreas Achenbach, Emanuel Leutze, Asher B. Durand, and Thomas Cole, the young artist hung fourteen of his own paintings.

The exhibition catalogue, an important and rare document, is reproduced here through the courtesy of the New Bedford Public Library.

CATALOGUE

OF THE

**New-Bedford Art Exhibition,**

COMMENCING

**July 1st, and closing August 7th, 1858.**

**Open from 8 A. M., till 7 P. M.,**

**And from 8 till 10 in the Evening.**

PRICE LISTS OF THE PAINTINGS FOR SALE, MAY BE FOUND WITH A. BIERSTADT, OR J. HOPKINS.

**ADMISSION 25 CENTS. SEASON TICKETS $1.00.**

5

| No. | Subjects. | Possessors. | Artists. |
|---|---|---|---|
| 44. | Last hours of the Abbess. | C. C. Perkins. | Toermer. |
| | Scene in the Cloisters of San Giovauni di Laterano. | | |
| 45. | The returned Crusader at the Tomb of the Abbess, San Giovauni di Laterano. | C. C. Perkins. | Toermer. |
| 46. | Rydal Falls. | | J. F. Kensett. |
| 47. | At the Window. Candle Light. | | W.H. Furness,Jr |
| 48. | Robin Goodfellow and the Peasant. | | G. H. Hall. |
| 49. | Venice. San Georgio after Sunset. | | E. W. Perry, Jr. |
| 50. | Roman Fish Market. Arch of Octavius. | | A. Bierstadt. |
| 51. | The Nativity. After Rembrandt. | | M. Wight. |
| 52. | Landscape. | Mrs. Cole. | Thomas Cole. |
| 53. | Landscape, with Cattle. | | J. W. A. Scott. |
| 54. | The Rescue. | | J. E. Craig. |
| 55. | The Fisher Boy. | H. Earl. | Schussele. |
| 56. | Alpine Scenery. | H. Earl. | W. T. Richards. |
| 57. | View in White Mountains. | H. Earl. | E. D. Lewis. |
| 58. | Moonlight. Italian Coast near Gaeta. | | A. Bierstadt. |
| 59. | Water Fall, Charlestown, N. H. | | S. T. Darrah. |
| 60. | Marine View. Frigate Constitution. | H. Earl. | Thomas Birch. |
| 61. | Study from Nature. Hemlock, &c. | | James M. Hart. |
| 62. | View from Manchester Beach. | | S. T. Darrah. |
| 53. | View in Adirondack Mountains. | | W. T. Richards. |
| 64. | View on the Susquehanna. | H. Earl. | E. D. Lewis. |
| 65. | View near Dusseldorf after Sunset. | | A. Bierstadt. |
| 66. | The Lazy Lesson. | J. F. Kensett. | Louis Lang. |
| 67. | Spring. (Drawing.) | | J. A. Oertel. |
| | Innocence and Love: foundation of all virtue. | | |
| 68. | Summer. | | J. A. Oertel. |
| | Peace and prosperity, the time of ripening for the harvest of Heaven. | | |
| 69. | Autumn. | | J. H. Oertel. |
| | Affliction; the blessing of the Cross. Seed sown for eternity. | | |
| 70. | Winter. | | J. A. Oertel. |
| | Rest and Hope; a foretaste of blessedness. Faith rewarded. | | |
| 71. | Jeremiah. | | J. A. Oertel. |
| 72. | Daniel. | | J. A. Oertel. |
| 73. | Isaiah. | | J. A. Oertel. |

6

| No. | Subjects. | Possessors. | Artists. |
|---|---|---|---|
| 74. | Ezekiel. | | J. A. Oertel. |
| 75. | Niagara Falls, from Goat Island. | | Paul Weber. |
| 76. | Crayon Portrait. | | A. Hartwell. |
| 77. | View on the Pemigewasset River. | | S. W. Griggs. |
| 78. | Bay of Salerno. | C.B.H.Fessenden | A. Bierstadt. |
| 79. | Crayon Portrait. | | R. M. Staigg. |
| 80. | Evening. | | D. C. Johnston. |
| 81. | Italian Coast Scene. | Rev. H.W.Parker | J. F. Cropsey. |
| 82. | Scotch Stag Hound. | Gideon Nye. | Sir E. Landseer. |
| 83. | Echo Lake, Franconia, N. H. | | S. P. Hodgdon. |
| 84. | The Basket of Chips. | | J. B. Stearns. |
| 85. | Jack in the Country, from Life. | | A. Fisher. |
| 86. | On the Weser. Afternoon. | J. Hopkins. | A. Bierstadt. |
| 87. | Cavalier. | J. M. Hart. | J. H. Cafferty. |
| 88. | The Page. | | R. M. Staigg. |
| 89. | Young Quails. | J. M. Hart. | A. F. Tait. |
| 90. | The Course of True Love never runs smooth. | | A. F. Bellows. |
| 91. | Sandwich range of Mountains from West Campton. | G. H. Chickering. | W. A. Gay. |
| 92. | View from the Flume House. | G. H. Chickering. | W. A. Gay. |
| 93. | Upper Glacier of Rosenlaui. | J. Hopkins. | A. Bierstadt. |
| 94. | Italian Scenery. | | R. S. Gifford. |
| 95. | Domine Sampson, the Bookworm. | | G. H. Hall. |
| 96. | Blue Grotto, Island of Capri. | C.B.H. Fessenden | A. Bierstadt. |
| 97. | Lake Lucerne. | H. Earl. | A. Calame. |
| 98. | Alpine Scenery | H. Earl. | B. Girscher. |
| 99. | Wild Pigeons. | | S. W. Griggs. |
| 100. | Down in the Meadow. | | Wm. Hart. |
| 101. | Delaware Water Gap. | | D. C. Johnston. |
| 102. | View in North Wales. Copy from Nesfield. | | D. C. Johnson. |
| 103. | Virgil and Dante meeting Homer, Horace, Ovid and Lucan. | C. C. Perkins. | Conzoni. |
| | "When thus my master kind began: 'Mark him Who in his right hand bears the falchion keen The other three preceding, their lord.'" | | |
| 104. | Portrait. | J. Ricketson, 2d. | Ernst Amthor. |
| 105. | The Height of the Ridiculous. | | D. C. Johnston. |
| 106. | Bas relief, Mercury and Pandora. | | P. Stevenson. |

# CATALOGUE.

| No. | Subjects. | Possessors. | Artists. |
|---|---|---|---|
| 1. | Rheingrafenstein on the River Nahe. | | H. Lewis. |

Destroyed by the French in 1689. Martin Luther was concealed here many years.

| No. | Subjects. | Possessors. | Artists. |
|---|---|---|---|
| 2. | View in the Adirondack Mountain. | Harrison Earl. | T. W. Richards. |
| 3. | Portrait of a Lady. | | A. Ordway. |
| 4. | On the Look-out. | | S. W. Griggs. |
| 5. | Sunrise on the Strand. | M. P. Kennard. | Wm. Bradford. |
| 6. | The Wreck. | A. Ricketson. | A. Van Beest. |
| 7. | The Shrimp Fishers. | H. Earl. | A. Achenbach. |
| 8. | View in North Conway. | H. Earl. | E. D. Lewis. |
| 9. | Portrait. | J. Ricketson, 2d. | Ernst Amthor. |
| 10. | Baron Von Humboldt. | | M. Wright. |
| 11. | View of New Castle on the Delaware. | H. Earl. | E. Moran. |
| 12. | Pæstum. | J. Hopkins. | A. Bierstadt. |
| 13. | View on Lake George. | J. B. Congdon. | Paul Weber. |
| 14. | South American Sketch. | H. W Parker. | F. A. Church. |
| 15. | Mountain Scenery. | | W. A. Gay. |
| 16. | Chocorua Peak, Pond, and adjacent scenery as seen towards Evening. | | Alvin Fisher. |
| 17. | The Little Page. | J. H. Clifford. | Geo. H. Hall. |
| 18. | Portrait. | H. W. Parker. | F. B. Carpenter. |
| 19. | Portrait of a Lady. | F. Carnes. | E. D. E. Greene. |
| 20. | Sketch. Stratton Notch, Vt | John Durand. | A. B. Durand. |
| 21. | River Scene. | J. F. Kensett. | J. W. Casilear. |
| 22. | View near Berwick. | H. Earl. | Paul Weber. |
| 23. | Bay of Naples. | | A. Bierstadt. |



| No. | Subjects. | Possessors. | Artists. |
|---|---|---|---|
| 24. | Miranda. | | G. W. Conarroe. |

"If by your art, my dearest father, you have
Put the wild waters in this roar, allay them :
* * * * O, I have suffer'd
With those that I saw suffer ! a brave vessel,
Who had no doubt some noble creature in her,
Dash'd all to pieces. O the cry did knock
Against my very heart."—*Tempest.*

| No. | Subjects. | Possessors. | Artists. |
|---|---|---|---|
| 25. | Italian Peasantry. | H. Earl. | Majound. |
| 26. | Bay of Gaeta. | | A. Bierstadt. |
| 27. | The Unwelcome Visitors. | H. Earl. | Carpenter. |
| 28. | King's Oak at Kirn, on the River Nahe, Prussia. | | H. Lewis. |
| 29. | Washington, after Stuart. | | T. Sulley, senior. |
| 30. | Sir Charles Fox. | | M. Wright. |
| 31. | The Dutch Homestead, after Verschure. | H. Earl. | Wilson. |
| 32. | Green Mountain Scenery. | | A. B. Durand. |
| 33. | The Reverie. | | G. C. Lambdin. |
| 34. | Sybil. | | Louis Lang. |
| 35. | White Mountains from Lake Umbagog. | | F. S. Frost. |
| 36. | Catskill Creek. | | Paul Weber. |
| 37. | Off Havre. | | A. Van Beest. |
| 38. | Endicott and the Red Cross. | | Wm. A. Wall. |

"Before God and man I will avouch the deed," answered Endicott. "Beat a flourish, drummer! Shout soldiers and people! in honor of the ensign of New England. Neither Pope nor Tyrant hath part in it now!"

With a cry of triumph, the people gave their sanction to one of the boldest exploits which our history records. And, forever honored be the name of Endicott! We look back through the mist of ages, and recognise, in the rending of the Red Cross from New England's Banner, the first omen of that deliverance which our fathers consummated, after the bones of the stern Puritan had lain more than a century in the dust." *Vide Hawthorne's Twice-Told Tales.*

| No. | Subjects. | Possessors. | Artists. |
|---|---|---|---|
| 39. | Frederick the Great. | | E. Leutze. |

Frederick indignant at the harsh treatment of his father, attempted to escape to England, to the Court of George Second, his mother's brother. He was overtaken and imprisoned in the fortress of Custrin. At the expiration of two years, after an interview and reconciliation with the King, he was permitted to appear at Court on the occasion of a ball given in honor of the marriage of his sister. The artist has chosen the moment when Frederick is kneeling to his mother and the King approaches with his daughters, crying, "See! Madam, there is Fritz again."

| No. | Subjects. | Possessors. | Artists. |
|---|---|---|---|
| 40. | Moonlight. Lake Melopack, Putnam Co., N. Y. | | Louis Lang. |
| 41. | New Bedford Harbor. | Thos. Nye, Jr. | Wm. Bradford. |
| 42. | Girl Sewing. | | E. W. Perry, Jr. |
| 43. | Mephistophiles Serenading Margaret. | | Geo. H. Hall. |



| No. | Subjects. | Possessors. | Artists. |
|---|---|---|---|
| 107. | Summer Afternoon. | C.B.H. Fessenden | Geo. Inness. |
| 108. | On the Hudson River. | | J. Kummer. |
| 109. | Fishing by Torch Light. Lake Lucerne. | J. Hopkins. | A. Bierstadt. |

The remaining pictures will be on Exhibition from the 20th of July.

| No. | Subjects. | Possessors. | Artists. |
|---|---|---|---|
| 110. | Bebecca and Rowena. | | Wm. A. Wall. |

"Farewell," she said, "may He, who made both Jew and Christian, shower down on you his choicest blessings."—*Vide Ivanhoe.*

| No. | Subjects. | Possessors. | Artists. |
|---|---|---|---|
| 111. | The Darent. Kent, England. | | S. R. Gifford. |
| 112. | West branch of the Delaware. | G. F. Daniels. | S. R. Gifford. |
| 113. | Grassy Pool. | | S. L. Gerry. |
| 114. | Kenilworth. | Miss Brooks. | S. R. Gifford. |
| 115. | The White Mountains, from North Conway. Winter Sunset. | | B. Champney. |
| 116. | May's Pond, Roxbury. | | S. L. Gerry. |
| 117. | Ruins of the Claudian Acqueduct. | R. Goodman. | S. R. Gifford. |
| 118. | Lake Winnepissogee. | G. F. Daniels. | S. R. Gifford. |
| 119. | Lock Awe, with Kilchurn Castle. Highlands of Scotland. | J. A. Griswold. | S. R. Gifford. |
| 120. | Stable Interior. | | A. Atwood. |
| 121. | Kitten. | | Wm. H. Beard. |
| 122. | Among the Alps. | | Wm. H. Beard. |
| 123. | Rembrandt. | | R. M. Staigg. |
| 124. | Daniel Webster. | | R. M. Staigg. |
| 125. | Crayon Portrait. | | J. Pope. |
| 126. | Wm. H. Prescott. | | J. Pope. |
| 127. | Frost Pencilings. | | A. F. Bellows. |
| 128. | Portrait. | G. Hussey. | M. Wilson. |
| 129. | Portrait. | | J. B. Stearns. |
| 130. | Pool in the Wood. Water Color. | | J. M. Falconer. |
| 131. | Sunset on the Creek. Water Color | | J. M. Falconer. |
| 132. | Valley of the Pemigewassett. | | S. L. Gerry. |
| 133. | Lake in the Hills. | | Wm. Hart. |
| 134. | The Rabbit Hunt. | | W. J. Hays. |
| 135. | The Wayfarers. | | J. F. Bellows. |
| 136. | Lake Lucerne. | | A. Bierstadt. |
| 137. | A Weedy Nook. | | S. L. Gerry. |
| 138. | Death and the Gambler. | | J. W. Ehninger. |
| 139. | Palace and Garden of the Elector of Hesse-Cassel. | | H. Lewis. |



| No. | Subjects. | Possessors. | Artists. |
|---|---|---|---|
| 140. | Portrait. | F. Parker. | G. P. A. Healy. |
| 141. | Storm among the Alps. | J. C. Kent. | A. Bierstadt. |
| 142. | Wm. H. Seward. | | F. B. Carpenter. |
| 143. | Portrait. | James Arnold. | Wm. A. Wall. |
| 144. | Ecce. Homo. Copy from Guido. Crystalograph. | James Arnold. | E. D. Marchant. |
| 145. | Josiah Quincy. Crystalograph. | James Arnold | E. D. Marchant. |
| 146. | Fruit Piece. | Mrs. E. Hawes. | B. B. Bucklin. |
| 147. | Canadian Snow Storm. | Mrs. E. Hawes. | C. Kriookoff. |
| 148. | Old Mill, Westphalia. | | A. Bierstadt. |
| 149. | English Fishing Boat. | A. Ricketson. | R. S. Gifford. |
| 150. | Hill Top. | | R. W. Hubbard. |

EVENING STANDARD STEAM PRESS,
7 North Water St., New-Bedford.

# APPENDIX B

In 1859, when Bierstadt traveled west for the first time, he kept friends and family abreast of his progress through personal letters as well as those published in the New Bedford *Daily Mercury* and the *Crayon* (see Chronology, 1859–1862). In 1863, however, when he made his second trip west, he ceded (happily, one senses) all promotional responsibilities to his traveling companion, Fitz Hugh Ludlow, a professional writer. Lacking first-hand commentary from Bierstadt, we are thus dependent upon Ludlow's reports and recollections for information about the trip. Fortunately, Ludlow assumed the role of scribe and publicist with great enthusiasm. Shortly after departing from Saint Joseph, Missouri, Ludlow began sending "Letters from Sundown" to the New York *Evening Post* (see Chronology, 1863–1870). Additional letters appeared in the *Golden Era*, a San Francisco weekly, beginning in February 1864. Following his return east, Ludlow contributed a series of articles about the journey to the *Atlantic Monthly* (see Chronology, 1863–1870), and in 1870, seven years after he had returned from the West Coast, Ludlow recast his recollections in a book-length account, *The Heart of the Continent: A Record of Travel Across the Plains and in Oregon, with an Examination of the Mormon Principle*.

Ludlow's letters to the *Post*, his articles in the *Atlantic Monthly*, and *The Heart of the Continent* are all readily available to modern readers. His "Reminiscences of an Overlander," the fresh and spirited reports published in the *Golden Era*, are, however, relatively inaccessible.

Because Ludlow's "Reminiscences" contain important information regarding Bierstadt's activities and experiences on the crucial 1863 trip, the articles are printed below in their entirety. As contemporary documents, they reflect contemporary concerns and prejudices. Thus, two of the six articles are devoted to the burgeoning Mormon settlement in the valley of the Great Salt Lake, a subject of much interest at the time. (Ludlow later discussed the Mormon community at even greater length in *The Heart of the Continent*.) Perhaps the most revealing of the articles, however, is the last. In harrowing detail, Ludlow describes the desert journey he and Bierstadt endured after they left Salt Lake City. Fighting heat, dust, and the constant threat of Indian attack, the two travelers were so exhausted by the time they reached the foothills of the Sierra Nevada mountains that Ludlow later declared he would not make the journey again for $10,000. Bierstadt may have held a similar view, for he did not venture west again until well after the completion of the transcontinental railroad.

Fitz Hugh Ludlow's "Reminiscences of an Overlander" have been transcribed from original copies of the *Golden Era* at the California State Library, Sacramento.

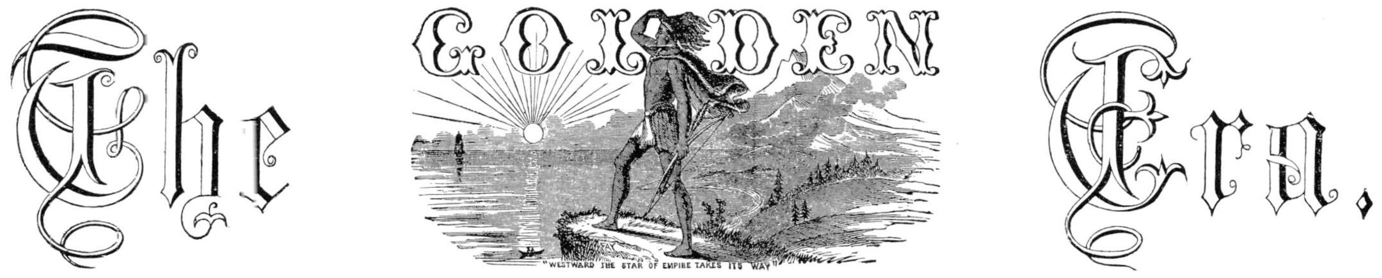


# REMINISCENCES OF AN OVERLANDER

BY FITZ HUGH LUDLOW

*Author of "The Hasheesh Eater;" "The New Partner in Clingham & Co.;" "Little Brother;" "Cruise of the Two Deacons;" "Regular Habits;" "Little Good for Nothing;" "The New Soul of John Markham;" "Battle and Triumph of Doctor Susan;" Etc., Etc.*

**PART I.**

## *From the Missouri to the Rocky Mountains*

*Written for the* Golden Era *(Sunday, 21 Feb. 1864)*

The distance between Atchison, on the Missouri river, and Denver, the base of the Rocky Mountains, is, in round numbers, 700 miles. For nearly one-third of this distance, the Overland road runs through as charming a tract of rolling prairie as can be found on the continent. Thus far we are within the region of summer rains. The grass is high and green to the very horizon edge, and swarms with life endlessly varied in kind and beauty. Unobstructed by fences, the great elk and dainty antelope rove through their limitless park, co-tenants with the strutting prairie-cock and that almond-eyed oriental beauty, the plover; the former hourly bounding across our road—in pairs or herds on their way to water—the latter hardly moving from under our horses' feet, where they throng to pick up grains from the stage's feed-bag, or crumbs from the traveler's haversac. These, to say nothing of the lesser tribes of squirrel and gopher, dove, meadow-lark, quail, and red-headed woodpecker, make populous a vast meadow land worthily adorned for their decoration with every variety of flower beautiful and curious to the traveler from the East. Through the very dust of the road-side spring the gorgeous cups of the prairie poppy—making patches of vivid crimson and delicate fragile green close to the ground where they creep, unlike their eastern brethren, three or four yards in circumference. But the great land owners of the vegetable world, are in this prairie-country, the peas and beans. No body here, with the slightest regard for veracity, could sing the nursery song—

> "You nor I nor nobody know
> Where oats peas beans and barley grow!"

The peas and beans grow everywhere. I myself have found over twenty different varieties within the compass of a good sized garden, and I believe that at least eighty exist in Kansas alone. They grow on tall straight stems and low drooping ones; they twine, they climb, they creep, they stand up independently for themselves; their blossoms are of the faintest flesh-pink, the deepest crimson, flaming scarlet, pure white, blue, purple, and every conceivable tint or combination of yellow. But the loveliest flower of all that divinely free and hedgeless meadow, dawns like unobtrusive virtue only on the eye that seeks it. Or, may be, it comes on you unawares. You are stooping low beside some quiet pool, to drink or pluck a brilliant scarlet pea, when your senses are touched by the faintest suggestion of orange flower odor mingled with tuberose, and looking forth you perceive a cloud of delicate white blossoms, like the water lily in shape, but less than the smallest violet in size, floating at the ends of slender green tendrils upon the bosom of the water. Having never seen this flower described, and finding it too fragile to press, I was compelled to name it myself without the aid of the botanists. It is a lotus, I think—but it seems the spirit of the ordinary lotus, which died and went to Heaven when it was a baby.

So peopled and beautified—refreshed by frequent streams of pure water whose banks are timbered with cottonwood and elm developed into more magnificent tree-forms than I have ever witnessed in my life—this tract of country reaches from Atchison to Fort Kearney—from the Overland Road to the Republican Fork of the Kansas river. I should have had little opportunity to know its value, but for the fact that I stopped on the second day out from Atchison, 80 miles east from Fort Kearney, for a buffalo hunt, which led me into the very midst of the finest portion.

Our resting place was the ranche of a man named Comstock, who had lived in almost every new State in the Union, and now found himself at 60 years and over a Nebraska pioneer with a fine family of boys and girls about him—some of them married and possessing children—but all living together under one log roof. Every individual Comstock was a character—and there were well nigh twenty of them. Character seemed catching in that house—for the half dozen rancheros, not of the family, who lodged there, were only less individual than old Comstock himself. The odd sayings of the latter were innumerable—nor did I have occasion to remember any of them more vividly than the following. We were talking about Overland feeding arrangements.

"D'ye know," struck in old Comstock, "what is a *hot meal* on the Overland Road?"

"No. What is it?"

"Wa-all—a hot meal on the Overland Road is a piece of hard bread and pepper-sas."

At Comstock's we lived more pleasantly than ever happened to people out of civilization yet in-doors. It was the nicest possible compromise between Delmonico's and camping out. We slept on our blankets in a great loft, ate buffalo and antelope, and saw the stage come in daily from the seat of war. This kind of thing was however very temporary, for beating together a company of eleven, we presently set off by saddle horses and farm wagons to the Republican Fork of the Kansas, thirty miles distant, where for ten days we camped, and hunted on the very flank of the main buffalo herd of North America. When I remember that I have chased on horseback and slain a brace of giant bulls; that I have helped to hold one of those royal monsters at bay for half an hour while the Artist Bierstadt made a color study of his death charge; beyond all, when I recall the memory of that black moving mass of savage life, reaching without gap to the horizon's edge on every side of me—that main herd only to be counted by hundreds of thousands—I can almost forgive myself the suffering endured later in the Overland trip. After our fill of hunting—after living on buffalo-hump, antelope steak, and prairie chickens, for which our rifles had marketed and our own genius had done the cuisine, we returned to Comstock's and resumed our journey westward by the Overland stage.

The happiest hours of the trip were those which I spent on the box. This was a place where legs were stretchable and faculties wide awake. If, as often happened, we had a nice driver, I learned from him an hour more of the popular character of the plains than any book of statistics could have told me in a week. What quaint speeches I heard and what original men I saw there! No conventionalism exists on a Nebraska coach-box, you may be sure. In the large busy world we all get an average flavor through perpetual mixture and mutual contact. We are like boarding-house dinners where the beef is muttony and the mutton beefy, through their both getting cooked in the same range; where the milk has a taste of cucumbers and the butter reminds you of yesterday's cold veal, by reason of their all passing a night together in one refrigerator. Out on the plains all the individual man's original and distinguishing flavor is preserved. He has been, so to speak, pickled in solitude—hermetically sealed from his ripening time, under the great lid of the blue firmament of Nature. On the box I first heard a word which amused me much in its specific application though you may have it in California—and in such it won't strike you as it did me. On the plains all emigrants are "pilgrims." The first time I heard a driver say it, I turned to look at him, thinking him an exceptional wag—but his face was perfectly honest, and I presently discovered the universality of the term. I had always coupled pilgrims with religion—that too of a very poetical sort and belonging to the crusades. If my driver had referred to the wind's blowing by the assertion that a balmy zephyr was fanning o'er the verdant dewy mead, I should not have been more startled than when I heard him transfer the title always in my mind associated with a russet gown, a prodigious curly-headed staff, a cockle-shell, and eminent piety to a gentleman from Pike who drove bulls with a black snake, swore blood-curdlingly and chewed literal pounds of plug tobacco. A tobacco-chewing pilgrim! A profane, bull-whacking palmer! Oh, what do you think of that, Peter the Hermit, my boy? After that shock to preconceived opinions I should not have been staggered if a turn of the road had brought me on a prophet playing penny-poker or an apostle shooting prairie-hens.

One thing did surprise me. I rarely saw one of our drivers the worse for liquor and frequently saw one who did not drink it at all. In such a wild country, where no society-restraints exist and excitements are scanty, this is quite remarkable. To be sure, our journey was once varied by the little drama of having to put a pistol to the head of one Jehu who was howling drunk, and thus not open to the usual line of arguments which people choose to demonstrate that difficult proposition, the impropriety of running them off bridges and breaking their necks; but having hoisted him to the ground and driven to the next station of ourselves, we closed the book of unpleasant experiences in that direction. Many of our drivers were as temperate (though none in other respects so charming) as the redoubtable William Trotter, famous along the whole line between Denver and Atchison as the driest of wags and the best of natures, who drove us the first stage west of Fort Kearney. "When I first came out from Ameriky," said Trotter, (and that's the universal phrase for getting west of the Missouri River) "I found lots o' bad liquor here. It 'curred to me that ef I pitched right in, I might help him to drink it all up shortly. But after tryin' that on a matter o' three year, I found they had kept a gainin' on me and that the folks had a dam sight more of it than I supposed. They kept a bringin' and a bringin' of it on—and finally, when I began to see the turkeys a walkin' round with little green hats on, I reckoned it was time to quit. So I did—and I haint touched liquor this eleven years. Do you know," continued Trotter, fixing on me a gaze of impressive solemnity, "that they haint drunk down to the bottom of that 'ere bad liquor yet? I shouldn't wonder if some old sucker had died and gone round under and drunk out the bottom, so that there 'aint none now nor never will be. In which case it was almighty well I stopped when I did."

Just as I was telling him I agreed with him precisely, he drove up to his stopping place and shouted to the hostler who asked him how many passengers he'd got.

"Seven, by thunder—and if you want any more you must buy 'em yourself."

I have dismissed him summarily, not because the above is any sample of his unique conversation, but, ungenerous as it may seem, because it isn't. I have, metaphorically speaking, a cart-load of his drolleries in my journal, but if I told them now they wouldn't be fresh in my book of travels. A trick of the trade, you see.

Beyond Fort Kearney you travel along the Main Platte as far as Cottonwood (about ninety miles) and there find the meanest of all rivers in the Atlas make a fork—the North Platte going up to, or rather coming down from the Fort Laramie part of the Rocky Mountains, while the South is a circuitous line which you follow to Denver. Bierstadt and I, before leaving New York, had had our little joke about toasting a Buffalo on the Fork of the Platte, but if that gigantic form of devilled bones had been prepared by it, it could have been the first use it had been put to since it was made. It is the stingiest shallowest-hearted and most pretentious stream on the Continent. If it were banked up within limits fifty yards apart it would make a tolerable mill-stream; as it is, it varies from an eighth of a mile to eight miles wide (counting the islands between which it struggles in channels of street-gutter size as within its banks), and nowhere save in an occasional treacherous hole or quicksand has it water enough to wet a short man's knees in fording. You cannot resist the impression that it is an accident—was spilled on the surface of the prairie from a hogshead a few moments ago—and will presently be mopped up or trickle away to be seen no more. Yet thus it flows forever—too shoal to swim in—unpleasantly warm to drink—adding no beauty to the landscape—containing no fish but a few pensive suckers who having been dissipated in early life on fog-weed have come here to spend the remainder of their days in a penance which they resolutely refuse to terminate by being caught out. On the banks of this seductive flood, for the most part, there abounds between Fort Kearney and Denver a short dry grass, curious for its tight and wooly spiral mode of growth—which makes the plain look on close inspection like the head of

Nature who had just come from the hands of a barber with too much heat in his enthusiasm and his tongs and too little coolness in his judgment. Thank Heaven that here and there in spots there still springs many a lovely flower among the frizzed and faded grass; that it is good nourishment for the vast cattle herds of the ever-roaming "pilgrim"—and that it is loved by that loveliest of all wild four-footed creatures, the antelope, who never ceases bounding over even its driest tracts save when he stands statue-like for a moment to gaze at that strange phenomenon, the stage, before whisking his white tail and going off with a canter fleet as the wind itself.

Ah! If *he* wonders at the stage, what does he suppose *we* think of it by this time? I, for my part, am so incredibly sleepy and exhausted that when I nod for a minute between jolts, I dream of beds as the traveler dying of thirst dreams of fountains. I am in, oh *such* a glorious old family bed! with a spring mattrass [*sic*] eight feet square and sheets that seem like first-quality slumber spread on linen backs in the poor-man's plaster style. Just as it feels the heavenliest, and every nerve is relaxing from the tension of five madly open-eyed nights and days, a chambermaid who seems strangely like the clerk who booked me at Atchison, dressed in woman's clothes, rushes in to say that its all a mistake. The gentleman's bed is not this bed but some other bed, a little matter of ten stories up and six galleries off. I am dragged out and away; I totter half inanimate through interminable corridors; find the bed that is *not* a mistake and get into it. I am just as near unconsciousness as occurred in bed the first, when a dreadful thump comes at the door, and from a voice outside I discover myself to be what in my waking moments of greatest despondency and self-abasement I never heretofore suspected—a Member of Congress—whose vote is imperatively necessary to pass a bill compelling stages to stop every night and let their passengers sleep eight full hours—a bill which I am still further assured by the voice, will be eternally lost unless I reach the House within ten minutes, as there is now every prospect of a tie, and the Speaker, besides being a man who in childhood used to pull flies legs off, owns fifty shares in the Overland Road. Desperately staggering out of bed in a haste which admits of no additions to my rather airy costume, I wish to seek our national chamber of Legislation—am detained on the way by those thousand dreadful hindrances which belong to nightmare, and finally drag into the house a pair of feet, each one of which seems to have a fifty-six pounder hung to it, just as an Absentee from the Anti-Sleep party enters by the opposite door! Oh Horror! The vote is taken—there is a tie after all—the Speaker, who owns Overland Stock and used to pull flies legs off, smiles fiendishly as he gives his casting vote in the negative—the Anti-Sleep party utter a yell of triumph, and just as they begin carrying me off on their shoulders like a Guy Fawkes, singing as they march:

> "*He* shan't go home till morning,
> Till daylight doth appear!"

I wake up to find myself jolted down upon the floor of the stage where I set astride of the hardest carpet-bag stowed there in a perspiration of agony. I lift myself and remember what Bob Barnum told me in St. Louis—dear old Bob, who like most prophets, got laughed at, at the time—"many people become insane crossing to California overland."

The dreadful fear that this is coming upon *me* rouses all that is Yankee and self-conservative in my nature. I beat my brains. I ransack my resources. I presently smile. It is the resolved smile of a man who has been up and dressed five nights handrunning. I dismount at the next station where the stage stops. I ask the ostler if he has any spare rope about the stable. Perhaps I look so resolved that he fears I want to hang myself—a proceeding which it is more than likely he has grown familiar with in the case of overland passengers. I casually arrange a postage-stamp along his opened palm. It is the east side of the Rocky Mountains where that act corresponds to four bits—where people know their privileges and wouldn't lug around the silver millstones you carry in your pockets here if they could get them. The ostler finds a sudden light shed on the recondite subject of spare ropes—says he will see, and retires to do so. He presently returns with about ten yards of line, various as to length and diameter of pieces. I knot these into two very respectable cables, both of which I tie around the roof of the coach, passing the ends through the windows and uniting them above. I roll my overcoat into a pillow and lay it on top, just back of the hinder loop. Through this loop I squeeze my shoulders—fasten them securely to it by a pair of gaskets in the form of shawl straps—insinuate my feet between the foremost loop—lay my head on the coat—and thus trussed to the top of the coach, am ready for an old-fashioned horizontal sleep by the time it starts. Oh, the bliss of being stretched out flat! No unfortunate man who had just found a friend in adversity ever so revelled in being put on his legs again, as I did in being taken off mine! It was not feathers nor curled hair nor moss; not even straw. But it was lying down!

How I slept only Epemenides or the slumberous seven or the sleeping woman of Islington or Mr. Wardle's fat boy could ever understand or appreciate. Over jolts through ruts—between changes—past Sioux lodges and all sorts of things I ought to have been up and chronicling in my journal; hardly opening my eyes if all my party inside called out at once "Just look at that!" not in danger of keeping them open long if the fabled Gyascutus had been discovered within gun-shot I slept, and slept, and slept—then woke and said, "Heaven be praised for Horizontality!"—then stretched still flatter and slept again.

Borne thus beneath my blessed hold-fasts—a sort of voluntary Overland Mazeppa, roped to an oak ribbed steed with a varnished cloth hide, who pranced madly through the wilderness five miles an hour—I rode for fifty miles successfully, and many more after that at intervals. When at a little place called Beaver Creek the first faint blue of the Rocky Mountains were visible in the far western verge, less like earthly prominences, than like an undefined stain where the fresh azure paint of the sky had run down and dried darker than the rest—I dismounted to shoot a few of the myriad ducks with which a neighboring slough was peopled, and eat a breakfast prepared by the newly married wife of the station man. She was a young looking woman but the driver told me the station man was her third husband. When I ate the breakfast she had prepared I saw satisfactorily how she might have had thus many. I was glad to see, that number three, who looked pale and uncertain about the legs, did not join us in our semi-raw ham, sloppy coffee, and hot bread which appeared to be a preparation of salaeratus raised with flour. He was a sensible man and took such good warning by number one and two that I gave him the dollar which we were justly fined for eating such a breakfast with more patience than if he had been a fool as well as a knave. After that, aided by occasional sleeps, I stood it pretty well to Denver, which with Colorado in general, the way to Salt Lake City and that delectable seraglio itself will be the subject of my next remarks.

**PART II.**

## *Denver to Salt Lake—Both Inclusive*

*Written for the* Golden Era *(Sunday, 28 Feb. 1864)*

Denver has suffered, like a young minister coming to a new place with one year's stock of sermons ahead, first from too much reputation and then as the inevitable reaction from too little. In the early Pike's Peak excitement, people came to Denver with the impression that nice little fortunes lay tucked away for them under flat stones—and that immediately upon rolling these away there would be apparent eight or ten ingots of 800 ounces apiece, as good as refined already and needing nothing but a microscope to read the mark "Kellogg & Hewston" on one of their faces in a rectangle. One hundred thousand people came to Denver and the Colorado mines during the first year—'59—'60—of the great revelation—and wofully [*sic*] were most of them disappointed. Gulch and placer mining was the only kind with which nine-tenths were acquainted, and that is the very kind which can hardly be said to exist in Colorado. Russell, of Pony Express notoriety, took out a neat little sum from a gulch named after him near Central City—but his case was an exceptional one, and though you can still see men sluicing in Colorado ravines, it is only for the purpose of getting daily bread or a capital to make the first start in rock-mining, and there are no such fortunes to be won after that method as were accumulated (or squandered) in the earlier days of California. Of the hundred thousand who came to the Colorado mines at least nine-tenths went away in penury and despair, spreading abroad reports (if they lived to get home to the States) that "Pike's Peak" was a humbug. Pike's Peak is 70 miles south of Denver, and nobody has yet discovered gold enough there to make a set of chemisette-studs for Mrs. General T. Thumb. Nevertheless because it is the most ostentatious mountain seen by travelers approaching Denver across the plains, it gave its name to the whole region.

But Pike's Peak was *not* a humbug. Science, Capital and Enterprise came to the territory bringing quartz-mills. Funny looking things were the earlier sorts, I can assure you—great logs of wood shod with stove-plates are the nearest approach to a just simile for the stamps of that period—while the first mills, manufactured entirely of iron, were about as colossal and effective engines of trituration as a dozen tack hammers worked by cams. Nevertheless, the indomitable miners succeeded in extracting enough gold with them to buy better mills, and now there isn't a busier mining town east of the Sierra Nevadas than Central City, 40 miles from Denver. There is much more ostentation in Virginia City—the mills there are more expensively built than those of Colorado—and the Ophir mine has been driven to a greater extent than any I saw near Denver. But the Virginia ore is no richer and the lodes no more numerous in Washoe than occurs in the Colorado mines which I explored. All the pay—or nearly all—lies, in the latter district, in sulphurets; decomposed pyrites of iron and copper being the richest ore of the famous Gregory lode, while the equally valuable and closely neighboring Bobtail carries its riches in a harder pyrites diffused lead through rock of closer grain. None of it lies in virgin quartz after the California fashion.

But the idea of my talking to California people about gold-mining is something absurd. It is the most barefaced kind of endeavor to instruct in the art of egg-sucking, a grandmother who since '49 has been doing nothing else but suck the eggs of the goose who lays the golden ones. So, away with Metallurgy, and let us talk about people and landscapes. After all, there are other uses for the former than to dig into the latter—other uses for the latter than being dug into.

I have seen prettier places than Denver. It might be made a great deal more picturesque by shoving it twenty or thirty miles up the mountains from that flat plain where it lies at their feet. Last spring its principal business street had been ravaged by fire, and it was just closing up its scars with a new brick epidermis when I got there. But for all its disheveled look, I would not have it change one atom, if by gaining beauty it had to lose any of the people I knew there. I made some friends whom I hope I shall keep all my life—and the three weeks' stay of our party was one continual manifestation of kindness and thoughtful cordiality on the part of the inhabitants. Governor Evans came to our rescue when the journey to Pike's Peak was hindered for lack of proper vehicles—contributing out of the generosity of his heart and the Executive stables, a fine ambulance and an excellent team. The Surveyor General of the Territory, John Pierce, Esq., further added to our equipment a buckboard and pony, which proved the very thing for Bierstadt, who was forever rushing around as a light skirmisher among the forces of Nature, and needed just such a means of conveyance for himself and his armory of colors. Mr. Pierce did still more: he gave to our excursions not only the buckboard, but himself; and I am not flattering him, when I say that without making any pretensions to science as a profession, he is one of the first scientific men among my acquaintance. As a close student and clear-sighted theorizer, he was an invaluable friend to me in my geological researches; and I need not tell any scientific man here, how much the new-comer needs such assistance among the wonderfully jumbled and complex formations between Denver and the Pacific. No man has done more than Pierce for the development of a Geology of Colorado. I know no one who has come nearer attaining a complete system for its tangled rocks, and not the least of his successes, as Geologists will quickly see, is the discovery of that long-missing link in our American chain of Old World history, the true Cretaceous Deposite—a chalk as indubitable and genuine as the Cliff of Dover, and so far as I examined, to all appearances identical and synchronous with the British. I speak of Mr. Pierce at this length, not only because his kind and tireless companionship gives him a large place both in Bierstadt's memory and my own, but in order that visitors to Colorado may know their best source of information in the scientific field.

Another friend who contributed all sorts of assistance to our investigations and did the honors of Denver royally to all our party, was George Tappan—one of the earliest pioneers and foremost merchants of the place. To this gentleman, above all, did we owe it that Denver in one week seemed more like home to us, through the number of our pleasant acquaintances, than any other new place I have lived in for two months. Everywhere his introductions were invaluable—securing us all sorts of attention and information at the mines and mills. Shall I add, with the hope of being understood as not altogether sordid, that after the privation and poisoning of the Overland Commissariat, he seemed to us a peculiarly munificent benefactor, in that through his agency we enjoyed for the first time in many weeks, what at Denver is lovingly entitled "*A good square meal.*"

Ah! ye happy ones who here in the very heart of a sturdy young civilization enjoy that blessing tri-diurnally, deride us not when we say that the friend who invited us to dinner—*a real dinner*—seemed quite angelic in our Overland eyes. I used to laugh at the lithographic Gabriel who in New York apothecary shops comes sprawling down from Heaven with Moffat's Life Pills, to raise a dying man by three doses from the bed where his weeping family have crowded to sob their last farwell [*sic*]. But 700 miles of staging on the plains quite prepared me for the serious reception of an angel who bore messages of steak and mushrooms, and scattered frogs in batter from his balmy wings. Blessed be the man who while one with his friend in spirit, knows that nature has provided bodies for two and orders dinner for them!

Still another friend of ours to whom we were indebted for many facilities was Mr. Elbert, the Territorial Secretary. I do not recollect a more delicate kindness than I received from him when regretting one night that I had left at home that almost indispensable book, "Dana's Mineralogy." I was handed by him a neat parcel as I bid him good-by, which on reaching my hotel I discovered to be the identical volume I had needed only less than sleep all the way from St. Louis, and that, too, the only copy in Colorado. This was a sample of the kindness which we received from everybody in the Territory. For the benefit of future visitors to the Rocky Mountains, I must not omit to mention another valuable friend of ours, and fellow-craftsman of my own, Mr. W. N. Byers, proprietor and editor of the *Rocky Mountain News*, whose guidance into the region of the Snow Range gave Bierstadt opportunity for some of the finest color studies he made along that chain—among others an exquisite series of lakes on a mountain to whose very top he ascended with his color-box, a height of over 15,000 feet, or considerably taller than Mont Blanc.

These lakes are three in number, and connected with each other by precipitous falls of from three to five hundred feet. I never, even in a dream, saw such miracles of pure shining color as were contrasted with each other at the summit of that lofty mountain. The blue of the sky was so intense that if Bierstadt paints it up to its exact truth, no dweller in the plains will believe him, while against this azure were relieved grand roseate masses of granite with dazzling fields of virgin snow, no less positive in hue, and executed with such breadth by the Divine Artist that every fleck or line of light and shade was a surface measurable only by miles of travel. Sparkling in fir-sheltered niches upon the bosom of this giant distance, nestled the three lakes, fed with pure molten crystal from the snow crown of the peak—fonts and chalices of holy water resting against the mighty fire-carven wall of God's most glorious out-door Cathedral. Earthquake and Flood—these were the Michael Angelo and Raphael of that wonderful temple, and when we thought through what patient centuries they had wrought, counting each as we reckon a single labor-hour; what giant tools they had wielded, what measureless masses handled—and how the result of wild convulsion had come to be a beauty like the face of the Divine, sweet peace, tenderness, and purity brooding over the very scars of rage and fire, self and its low aims sank utterly out of sight from us, and we were alone with the Omnipotent Love and Power. That glorious roseate mountain stood nameless among the peaks in its virgin vail of snow; so Bierstadt, by right of first portrayal, baptized it after one far away from our sides, but very near and dear to our hearts—a gentle nature who had followed us clear to the verge of our Overland wanderings at Atchison, and parted from us bravely lest she should make our purpose fainter by seeming moved. Henceforth that shining peak is MONTE ROSA.

**PART II.**

## *Denver to Salt Lake—Both Inclusive*

*Written for the* Golden Era *(Sunday, 6 Mar. 1864)*

I wish that I had time to dwell upon the details of an excursion which we made from Denver to Pike's Peak—rather to Colorado City which lies at the base of that mountain. Never was a journey of 70 miles packed fuller of novelties, beauty, and interest. But I am not now writing a book, and must condense my subjects. I hope this will be accepted as my apology for referring those who care to know more of that trip (if any such there be) to files of the *Evening Post* kept at the Mercantile Library, wherein sometime during the next month my Colorado letters will probably be found. The region through which we journeyed in the Governor's ambulance and the surveyor General's buckboard where Bierstadt rode, accompanied by its genial owner, is, I believe, described at considerable length in one of Fremont's narratives, though no book or books could hope to do justice to it, and those ponderous hippopotami of bibliography, the Mexican Boundary and Pacific Railroad Survey volumes, like most Government jobs, are distinguished for the inadequacy of their performance. As the Hon. Benjamin F. Hall, present U.S. Chief Justice of Colorado, accompanied the remaining two gentlemen of our party, Messrs. Hill and Durfee, who occupied the Governor's ambulance with myself, we may be said to have visited Pike's Peak under the most solemn official sanction. I will briefly sketch at a hand gallop the interesting region through which we slowly and lovingly wandered for a week.

Most of the journey consists in a very gradual ascent from the plains of the South Platte where Denver lies, to the lofty table-land, more than a thousand feet higher, which forms the divide between the last named river and the Arkansas. From the eastern end of this divide springs the most beautiful stream of the plains, the Republican or Main Fork of the Kaw—the same upon whose banks but a few weeks before and several hundred miles farther east we had been chasing the buffalo. The first attraction which strikes us on reaching this divide is the endless variety in hue and species of flowers almost without exception unknown to our Eastern botany. The yellow pink, and scarlet cactus, together with the tall thorny-leaved lily, which in Florida I used to hear called "Spanish Bayonet," (*Vucca Filamentosa*,) but whose Colorado name of "Soap Weed" I am surprised to hear explained by the assertion that the Mexicans use it for cleansing purposes, never in my own experience having learned that they employ anything with that object—these plants are plenty and familiar. I also identify a variety of *asclepias*, whose immense flesh-colored spikes of blossom are very fragrant, quite unlike our milk-weed at the East. But the ground is scarlet with little tongues and tufts of fire which I never saw in any garden, wood, or herbarium, and fifty other blossoms, purple, blue, pink, golden, all conceivable shades, are equally unfamiliar to me.

Coming to the "Pretty Woman's Ranch"—justly so called from the personal claims of the Ranchero's wife, in accordance with the frank significant nomenclature of all new countries, I find myself on the borders of a forest of petrified stumps. With their roots still clinging to the earth, whole acres of decapitated oaks, pines, and cotton-woods have been changed by the slow infiltration of silex into agate, chalcedony and jasper. Not only stumps, but here and there an entire giant trunk which has fallen prostrate in situations favorable for the process, lies transformed into a finer piece of arboreal statuary than Phidias or Palmer or Thompson could execute with fifty years allowed for the filling of the order. Though all the once live material of the tree has been replaced by what we call inorganic matter (as if anything could be inorganic in a world which is all one network of systematic relations!) the work has been so gradual, accomplished by such infinitesimal accretions, that the stone tree has obeyed all the laws once vital in the wood, and retains every pore, concentric ring, medullary ray, scar in the bark, knot, bud, or twist which it had when it was a vegetable. A child would recognize it as a former tree from any fragment split off at random. You acknowledge to yourself (though you are ashamed to say it aloud and be called visionary) that the tree has a soul which survived immortal after its body was dead, and controlled the new atoms by the same law with which it governed the old ones, marshalling them around it into a nobler body which should express its invisible essence by the same character as of old. There is a great lesson of immortality in petrified trees. But as I am not bringing you out into Colorado to moralize to you, I merely call attention to the exquisite translucency and beautiful color of some of the specimens. I sent home several billets of this fossil wood from each of which a gross of seal rings might have been carven worthy of an Emperor's finger.

Still further on we come to "The Dirty Woman's Ranch," a title which my friends inform me was as faithfully significant at the time of its bestowal as the Pretty Woman's. But to our disappointment the dirty woman has departed. Whether because the winds which swept down into the hollow from the pine-clad heights proved such an effectual besom to the log-shanty floor that she got sick of the unequal struggle and emigrated to some more sheltered haven where she could keep her home dirty at less expense of effort as years multiplied upon her stalwart form—whether she died of her own untidiness—or how, report vouchsafes me no certain information. I think, however, that she lives in Colorado City, where I saw several houses which might have belonged to her—and as a native there volunteered the intelligence that a young woman on horseback who dashed gustily through the town was "The Dirty Woman's Gal," unless that charming Amazon be an orphan, which I am reluctant to believe, the Dirty Woman herself could not have been far off. At present the Dirty Woman's Ranch is occupied as a tavern for men and baiting places for horses, by a sanguine person who hopes to live down the title (*too* sanguine! for it will be the Dirty Woman's Ranch while a log holds together)—a person stated in large letters to be "P. Garlick," though whether his Christian name be Pill, I hesitated to inquire.

Shortly after leaving the Dirty Woman's, we came upon Monument Creek—a stream famous for the remarkable formation which crops out along its banks, a friable white conglomerate of sand, lime, clay, iron-stones and pebbles from the granite range, which the wind and the weather have cut into all imaginable fantastic shapes simulating funereal architecture. At even a short distance from them, you can hardly believe that you are not in the midst of an ancient Laurel Hill or Greenwood belonging to the aborigines; some deserted cemetery-sepulchring people whose survivors, as an Irishman would say, were themselves dead a thousand years ago. Through the dwarf cedars and pines rises every variety of monument—the pillar crowned by an urn—the truncated column and pyramid—the plain tablet—the Egyptian vault—the pompous sarcophagus lifted on four round legs like a petrified piano. The least imaginative person needs no help to see these astonishing resemblances. But the architecture is not all funereal. There are ruins there which might make you believe yourself in Luxor, Pompeii, Palmyra, Paestum, Phylae, or the Cave of Elephanta. Long corridors with half their pillars standing at regular distances apart in most artistic symmetry, their shattered entablatures still resting on them, and the tumbled ruins lying disposed in their most natural positions prostrate on the ground; porches almost perfect, with the suggestion of crumbled edifices behind them; silent summer houses like the ancient domed buildings which covered a consecrated fountain; every variety of ruin so astoundingly like the time-smitten work of man, that you are almost afraid to believe them Nature's, lest the inevitable corollary should be a faith in gnomes and genii. And not far from Monument Creek upon the level summit of a low butte, there stands such a life-like fac simile of Windsor Castle, done in a grayer stone and on a grander scale, that I need hardly have sketched it, but might have told the engraver for my book to make a rough copy of any photograph from the British original, with the certainty that he would create a recognizable portrait of the Colorado Windsor.

From Monument Creek we gradually wind through a rising series of foot-hills a little south of westward toward the base of that old giant, Pike, who all day long has seemed just as near us as now, when we have approached within fifteen miles. The closer we come, the less we see of him. And now, as the settlement of Colorado City lies just at our feet, he retires behind the lesser hills, so that we can barely see his frost crowned head. Between ourselves, this far famed Pike is what the vulgar denominate, "no great shakes" to see. The best view is a far-off one. The old Cheyeane—plainly visible just south of Colorado City, though perhaps four thousand feet lower—is on the other hand, for abrupt rise, magnificent breadth of mass, light and shadow, the finest mountain I ever saw.

The great attractions of the country about Colorado City are these:

1. The Garden of the Gods. This is a narrow plain among the foot-hills, where alternate strata of red clay and sand-stone (a genuine natural *brick* of fine grain and occasional jasper-like polish) and a white calciferous sand-rock have been lifted from their planes of deposition through an entire quadrant by the upheaval force of the granite range. The brilliant red and almost dazzling white of these bare upended rocks would make them strikingly picturesque, even were they low and shapeless. You must additionally conceive them not as boulders, but as a flat slab or rock, whose thickness bears an insignificant ratio to their height. In fact, the thin upright marble tablet which is our plainest form of tombstone, gives you an exact idea of their proportions. Still further, think of such a tablet rising out of the dead level plain from two to six hundred feet in height, the white and the red following two nearly straight lines three or four miles long and five hundred feet apart; the edge of each tablet sculptured by the weather into grotesque shapes, among which the most conspicuous are Liberty in her Phrygian cap, a wonderfully life-like dolphin and eagle facing each other across an heraldic shield, a griffin, and an owl—you will then have an idea of one of the most singular open-air collections of natural curiosities which the world possesses. Close by this Garden of the Gods, is the finest gypsum bed I ever saw. I should ask no other fortune than to have it at the East. Whether for the purposes of the Plaster-of-Paris-maker—the sculptor—or the cabinet collector, it would be an inexhaustible mine of wealth to its possessor. It rises as abruptly as the red slabs, (whose following stratum it everywhere seemed to be where I could get an out-crop) to the height, in this particular bed, of three hundred feet, and contains every variety of gypsum known to mineralogy, from the powdery plaster, through the laminated, fibrous and crystalline forms, to the purest white, rosy and translucent alabaster, susceptible of carving into the most delicate shapes with a common penknife, and a polish unsurpassed by the finest Parian. When the cloudless setting sun of Colorado falls slanting on this hill of alabaster, and the gorgeous red and snowy slabs beyond—the Garden of the Gods is a brilliant place to wander through.

2. Camp Creek Canon—two miles northward from the Garden—besides containing some splendid specimens of terraced trap, mounting from the valley bottom in a regular giant staircase two thousand feet at least in perpendicular height, and a number of slabs hardly surpassed by the Garden itself, has one isolated obelisk of the red rock between three and four hundred feet high. This colossal pillar is a greater curiosity than any leaning tower of Pisa. For it not only deviates from the perpendicular as widely as that structure, but after curving boldly out and back again to nearly four-fifths of its previous stature, it suddenly narrows to one-half its previous

diameter—remains pinched in for a few feet farther up—and again as suddenly swells to a prodigious bulb equal in circumference to its pedestal. The simile is not poetical—but I think that an onion-top will give you some faint idea what I mean, though the bulb, unlike the onion-top, is a prolate, not an oblate spheroid. Considering its utter isolation, height, and independence of props, I think I may call this obelisk the most singular curiosity I saw among the eccentric formations of the Sierra Madre.

3. The stream that runs through Colorado City comes down the Ute Pass from the very base of Pike's Peak, and is called, in writing at least, the "*Fontaine qui Bouille*." The nearest approach made by the natives to a French pronunciation of it is "*Fonten kee bu-yeh*." The title derives its origin from a series of powerfully ebullient mineral springs, which rise along the stream at a distance of two and half miles from the town. There is unquestionable evidence in their basins that they formerly rose on a level with the stream and mingled with its waters, but they have now lifted themselves to a height of ten feet above the bed by concentric deposits of the sulphate of soda with which they are impregnated. They are very pungent and sparkling; all of them charged with carbonic acid, but differ among themselves as to the proportion of this ingredient, as well as of iron, sulphur, magnesia, &c. One of them is strongly chalybeate—another quite sulphurous—but the two main springs are the most piquant and reminded me strongly of a very favorite foreign water, the Vichy. I had no facilities for any analysis more delicate than that of taste. For inflammatory diseases, especially the cutaneous and rheumatic types, they are highly regarded by the scattered population of this district. The land they rise on, like that occupied by the Garden of the Gods, has never yet been taken up—but if Colorado ever becomes settled the lucky man who stakes his claim here will have one of the most popular pieces of Spa property in America, not to say the world. Could I make up my mind to wait for Civilization and the Pacific Railroad, those springs should be mine to-morrow. I would telegraph to Surveyor-General Pierce to record the claim immediately.

4. In the clay slates which border the Fontaine qui Bouille below Colorado City are fossil beds which fill the heart of the geologist with delight. He finds here baculites, ammonites, and oysters of the same period in such perfect preservation that their pearly layers are as brilliantly irridescent, their fair proportions as free from nick or scar as the day they closed their fond eyes on all that is dear to mollusks in the shallow inland sea. Their quantity in some situations is as rich as their quality. I know no place comparable to this for the collection of a cabinet of kainozoic shells.

Not to lose time, I must skip abruptly from the base of Pike to the Overland Stage upon which we resumed our journey toward Salt Lake, after our delightful three weeks' stay in Denver. From this latter place the road is most inexplicably erratic. The extent of the circuit which we made will be understood by those taking the trouble to look at a map, when I say that we crossed the South Platte 70 miles north of Denver—the next afternoon passed over both the Big and Little Laramies—continued on past the Medicine Bow and Elk Mountains—(the former one of the grandest and most abrupt of all the ridges in the Rocky Snow Range)—then crossed the North Platte, and having made our triumphal passage from the Atlantic to the Pacific slope of the Continent through Bridger's Pass, came down by way of Fort Bridger to Salt Lake City. Although this eccentric and lawless style of travel added days to the time and at least two hundred miles to the distance of our shortest practicable route, now that it is all over, I am not sorry for the circuit. It carried us within 50 miles of the South Pass, the opening by which the old northern road penetrates the Rocky Mountain barrier. It brought us back again out of Colorado into Nebraska—took us through a portion of the New Territory of Idaho, and led us nearly to the edge of Washington. It sent us traversing the Laramie plains—perhaps the loftiest plateau of equal size in North America, where every breath of air seems pure from the laboratory of nature, and you long to bring it by a system of pipes into New York and "lay it on" in every house, like Croton, that on your return you may sit an hour or so every day at a faucet and do nothing but drink oxygen. It showed us the two crystal clear Laramie Rivers, fresh from the distant snow-peaks, and fringed along their banks with a wealth of exquisite and novel flowers, purple, crimson, scarlet, violet and golden. It brought us face to face with the everlasting snows of Medicine Bow Mountain, and showed us far away but gloriously distinct the Wind River Range, and Lander's peak, its monarch, so that I could make the long desired comparison of Nature's reality with Bierstadt's famous portrait of it. It led us down to the North Platte over a country so demoniacally wild that Gustave Dore should have seen its vast basaltic cliffs, its heaped up mass of trap rock seeming the foundations of some colossal city long since dead, its strange precipices carven into ghastly profiles—before he drew the horrid solitudes through which he sent his wandering Jew. It showed us the most wonderful similation of human building we had seen in all our strange mountain pilgrimage through many such in the "Church Buttes"—a series of Cathedrals, carven by nature in sand-stone, with domes, arches, butments and statued niches of such wonderful beauty and grandeur, that human art might well journey hither to make humble studies for a new order of ecclesiastical architecture. At Fort Bridger it introduced us to the only remnant of truly powerful savage tribes who of their own free will still preserve friendship with the white man; that band of Shoshones, headed by Washki, the only really noble Indian I ever saw, with whom your brave Connor lately made treaty. The remaining 124 miles were full of weariness and suffering from the thirst which nothing but salt or brackish water came to slake. Yet enduring all we did, (and I will not dilate on it) we found admiration for the grandeur of the tremendous canons by which we pierced the Wasatch Range to enter the Salt Lake Valley. As we drew near the Mormon City on the evening of the seventh day from Denver, a wonderful change in all the face of nature proclaimed the approaching presence of mankind.

## *First Impressions of Mormondom*

*Written for the* Golden Era *(Sunday, 20 Mar. 1864)*

It is so hard for even the experienced imagination to avoid doing that poetic justice which exists nowhere in the real world, that I had always pictured to myself the Mormons dwelling in some such physical waste as the wilderness they abide in spiritually. Geography ought to have taught me better—though I think Utah was not a part of that charming science when I learned it—but I had an idea that Salt Lake City was much nearer Salt Lake than it really is, and that great saline cracks ran across the principal streets of Brigham's Metropolis. It was thus a growing astonishment to me when I found the dreadful sage-brush disappear more and more as we approached the City; saw it replaced by glorious meadows of deep green grass, and fields of nestling golden grain. The only jar in all this rising melody of nature, was the evident proof how little *home* was to any of the industrious tillers of the soil compared with orchards, vines and harvests. The most luxuriant farms had no such cheerful homestead as we build on [the] flintiest New England hill-side—but in its stead, among the rich green herbage or the thriving corn, was ever visible a shabby, neglected house with children of harmonious garb and countenance clustered like pigs around the cheerless door—perhaps a series of such houses, strung along in formal line, without shade, ornament or any sign that they were retreats which human hearts came tenderly to or were happy in. On every side the vegetable life seemed all that anybody lived for. Not till nearly sunset, when we stopped at "Kimball's," a station 29 miles east of Salt Lake City, did I see anything that looked like the dwelling of a civilized or Christian household. Kimball's was a neat low farm-house, in the midst of a finely cultivated plantation through which the road ran, and had an attempt at flower-beds before its door. I was both thirsty and hungry—so, while the horses were changing I ran into the house, and asked for some bread and butter with a bowl of milk. I was over my first Mormon threshold. Two young women of prepossessing aspect were dandling babies of the same size—and till I saw that they had no bonnets near them, I could not rid myself of the idea that one was the hostess and the other a neighbor who had just run in to gratify her maternal pride by comparing youngsters. Working fresh golden butter at a table was a gray haired matron of strikingly commanding countenance, who must have been a very handsome woman twenty years ago, and was now an unquestionably strong minded and influential one. I asked if Mr. Kimball was in, and the matron answered me in quaint scriptural phrases that, by the blessing of the Lord Almighty he was now across the sea whither he had gone upon a mission—to carry the glorious revelation to them that were scattered abroad through Great Britain. Both the young women sighed and unconsciously kissed their babies—then looked curiously at me as I sat down on a proffered chair and waited for the bread, milk and butter which I had asked for the nourishment of my Gentile system. I had hardly finished it, when the driver called "all aboard!" As I was tipping my bowl up to get the last spoonfull, I heard the striking-looking matron speak to a new comer of the pretty women as "my son's wives"—and realized that I stood in the presence of the famous Heber Kimball's first wife and his two daughters-in-law. For the next ten miles I was asking myself how that venerable matron of the unquestionably commanding intellect could stand by and see all that kind of thing going on, with such ardently sincere approbation and satisfaction—how those two young creatures could sit there so demurely looking at their own and each others' babies without jumping up to tear each others' hair and scratch each others' eyes out. I afterward learned from Heber Kimball himself, that the secret consisted in "a large outpouring of Divine Grace." When that kind of outpouring comes, God grant all our American women stout umbrellas! It would have relieved my mind for the future of Utah to have seen that happy family clawing each other like tigers. Anything—anything—but the awful lethargy of smiling shame and unconscious degradation.

## THE CITY OF THE SAINTS

It was late at night when we arrived in the Mormon City, but after the barren sage-plains of the past few days, I could not but pry open my weary eyes to see that beautifully cool, shady, and well-watered town, gleaming in the white moonlight. It was a magician's miracle. The irrigating ditches were leading their shiny, tinkling streams along the silent streets on either side; and through all the silver of the moon I could see that the dense foliage which brooded around every hushed dwelling was green as meadow-grass in May. Could this be the home of Mormonism? No worm at the roots—no ashes on the leaves—while Christian people were hourly pining in deserts and garrets? It was such a mixed up problem that I fell asleep from puzzle as much as exhaustion, the moment I tumbled into bed at that quaint caravanserai, kept by the Mormon Brother Townsend, the only hotel in town.

I must here acknowledge with all cordiality the great debt of kindness owed by me and my party for every comfort and entertainment we enjoyed during our stay, to the Agent for the remaining portion of the route, Mr. H. S. Rumfield. No friend who had known us from boyhood could have placed more unselfishly at our disposal his time, his office and every facility for a visit to objects of interest which he himself possessed.—Among other excursions, he contrived and managed throughout, the trip to Salt Lake. It is unnecessary to repeat what other travelers have said about the strength of that vast expanse of pickle. No artificial brine ever could be made to carry so much salt to the pint. The water is fairly worn out with its load and like a tired porter tumbles it down as a precipitate at the very earliest opportunity. After coming out from a ridiculous attempt to dive, which resulted very much as it would if the lake had been an india-rubber air-bed, I was unable to laugh or give facial expression to any emotion whatever until I had scrubbed my features with fresh water and a towel—so had the salt crystallized on me, rigidly and instantaneously. I lay on my back, and, the wind being shoreward, was blown gradually in until I reached a place where the lake was four inches deep—yet never knew it by touching bottom until I put down my hand. To the travelers' tales so far I give my hand and seal—but I must beg to correct all whose narratives I have read before me in this one point—pungent as is this pickle, it is not void of animal life. I collected a bottle full which was fairly squirming with minute maggots or larvae and after keeping it a few days, I saw these turn into flies hardly distinguishable from the larger buffalo gnat. All along the shore we saw myriads of these same insects—but when at the lake I did not know their parentage.

## SALT LAKE.—CHURCH ISLAND.

I have never heard justice done to the beauty of the lake. It is more than a mere natural curiosity. It is a glorious sheet of water to the artist's eye. When its intense blue is ruffled by the winds into foamy streaks and combing surges, the contrasts of its color, and its light and shade with the delicate pink tint of the lofty mountain-island which rises abruptly out of its depths a few miles from the southern shore, is one of the loveliest things I ever saw in nature. For a moment you forget the sullen mystery of its origin, the acrid flavor of its waves—and yearn toward it as toward our own sea teaming with rich life. The island I speak of belongs to the General Corporation of the Saints in common. Its name is "Church Island," and thither all the ecclesiastical herds which come of confiscation and tithing are sent to fatten on sweet grass.

There is no need of *calling* it Church Island—"*Church*" is written in large letters athwart the brow of every man and every thing in Utah. The Mormon system owns its believers—they are for it, not it for them. I could not help regarding this "Church" as a colossal steam engine which had suddenly realized its superiority over its engineers and seeing the absurdity of a creature 10,000 horse power strong being bullied, led on, and choked off by a weak pigmy with an oil-pot, had declared once for all not only its independence but its despotism. "Stop stoking me and my fly-wheel shall fall on you! If you don't keep my rods bright and my stuffing-box well packed, I'll draw you through my cogs and bring you out mince meat!" That is the language of the great ecclesiastical steam-engine, which it was reserved for this nineteenth century and the great salt basin of the continent to see setting up its supremacy over nearly one hundred thousand souls.

## THE MORMON SYSTEM.

You may say, perhaps, that external pressure from the Gentiles has contributed much to the conservation of this devotion to the church; that men who believe themselves persecuted always gather more desperately around their central idea and live for it, die for it even, until it has acquired the solidity of a fixed and tolerated fact among mankind. There is a measure of truth in this—but it is not the whole truth. If the Mormons were left utterly free to work out their own problem to-morrow, the secret chamber of the Inquisition or the Superior of the Jesuit Order would never have had such a grasp upon the souls and bodies of men as that Engine "The Church."

Brigham Young lives within a high walled enclosure of many acres, situated in one of the pleasantest portions of the town and just across the street from that temple whose magnificent foundations (185 feet by 125, if I remember rightly,) are now rising in colossal blocks of bird's eye granite. He has two dwellings—the handsomest and largest in Utah—directly adjoining one another. One—called the "Lion House" from a sculptured figure of that animal which adorns the pediment, is his own favorite residence—contains the apartments of his first wife—and is moreover, divided by ten or twelve lateral partitions, making as many separate suites, each with its own gable, where subsequent matrimonial ventures of his are kept in happy seclusion from each other, with their children. The other residence, called the "Bee House" in virtue of a hive appearing on the point of its middle gable, is cut up into apartments for still further additions to the capital stock. Of wives acknowledged and possessed for this world's uses, the best opinion seems to be that Brigham has seventy—though no one knows exactly, or if any know, they are "forbid to tell the secrets of that prison-house." But the Great Marrier has wives spiritual, set apart for eternal purposes, more than he himself, as he has said, can keep any account of. I do not know whether I need tell you that the Mormon doctrine of marriage is this: the true Mormon may (nay, *must*, under pain of distrust and disapprobation) take as many women to himself as he can persuade or support; but there are two distinct classes among these, some being married to him for time, merely—others, united to him for eternity. The former, at death, lose all hold upon the slippery gentleman to whom their mortal lives have been devoted with all the jealously guarded constancy of the Seraglio; the latter have a right to pounce on him the moment he enters Heaven, and rely on him for all husbandly protection till the crack of doom. Now, as the unmarried have a very wretched time of it in the world to come, and are compelled to perform all sorts of menial offices to the married, if indeed, by a magnanimous stretch of grace they ever get within the garden-fence of Bliss at all, it becomes a very serious consideration with women that they should be "sealed," as the phrase for this everlasting knot runs, to some reputable patriarch who will look after them in Eternity. Regarding Brigham Young as the most efficient and desirable match for that long session, they come to him secretly and propose for an infinitessimal but inalienable share of his hand. He, I must not omit to say, as the visible head of the Church on earth, is the only man empowered to "seal" in Christendom. I believe he never refuses to grant the request of these women. He has no idea how many he has sealed to himself. Frequently a woman comes to him, gets sealed, goes away, and never sees him again. Frequently that woman is already the earthly and temporary wife of somebody else. I suppose that the wives with whom Brigham has thus contracted for eternity may be numbered by hundreds, many of whom he has forgotten, even as to names and faces. He thus looks forward to spending his first years in Heaven in a state of perpetual suspense and twitter at every new arrival from the earth, expecting to hear announced by the celestial usher: "*Another* Mrs. Young."

## THE ENGINE.

Within the same enclosure as his residences stands the Tithing Office. As the secret chamber wherein Brigham, alone of all human beings, has the right to "seal" men and women, is the spot where all the heart-strings or chords of passion in Utah are gathered up into one single hand—so here converge the lines of every Mormon fortune, the purse-strings of the universal Mormon pocket, which that same sole arbiter can bind or loose without appeal. Suppose yourself—or say myself, since even the hypothesis for illustration's sake may be disagreeable to you—driven by some inward craze to emigrate to Utah—with twenty thousand dollars in my carpet-bag, and a cabinet-maker's trade in my head. I join the Mormon church—and from that moment become a slave of the Engine. I own nothing. The twenty thousand dollars—the cabinet-maker's trade—my tools, my hands, my life—belong to the Engine. Brigham is that Engine's voice—and to rebel against its fiat, is as hopeless as kicking at the Wasatch mountains with a view to tip them over. First, I must confess how much money I am worth. Well, $20,000 is more than can be advantageously used in the cabinet business here—one half of that must be considered "*surplus.*" I will please hand that over at my earliest convenience, never to be accounted for to me, or owned by me again. Mind now, that I am not stating an exceptional case; this process invariably occurs with every new convert; and Brigham is the sole judge of the sum proper to be considered "surplus." He can take every cent I have, should he so decide, and put it irrevocably into the Church till. He never does this, of course; for in that case, the Church must support me as a pauper—but he *could* do it, and I should be without remedy. Having permitted me to set up shop with the remaining $10,000, he expects a quarterly visit from me at the Tithing Office. Let us say that I have made twelve hundred dollars during my first year in Utah. Without a murmur, I bring $120 of it to his treasurer. Unless I become a pauper, I never receive one cent of *quid pro quo* for that, any more than for my surplus. Or, suppose I am no cabinet maker, but a farmer. I have made ten tons of hay—one ton I must carry to that all-converging vortex, Brigham's enclosure, and deposit it in the Church barn. I am a miller, with five hundred barrels of flour—a vast storehouse within that same enclosure waits for fifty barrels. Fancy me the poorest, meanest provided laborer, getting a bushel of potatoes for my day's work—one-tenth by weight of these tubers, belongs to Brigham's enclosure. So far, in getting rid of my "surplus" and "tithes," I have contributed to the wheels of the Engine only my normal amount of grease. But the Engine is not without its methods extraordinary—it can squeeze me in a hundred other ways. One of the innumerable spies in its employ reports to Brigham that I was last night the worse for liquor, under my own roof. I am cited by summons before a secret tribunal of the Apostles. I come out—go to my corral—and send the best cow I have to the herd which is going down to Church Island to-morrow. Nobody asks me why—everybody knows why, and keeps mum. Again—if money is wanted for one of the Engine's sudden exigencies—Brigham has it in his power to assess me to any extent on my well known amount of property—and I had better pay without a murmur.

## BRIGHAM OMNIPOTENT.

I have said that the city is irrigated by ditches running along the sides of the street. These communicate with private gardens by small channels across the sidewalk and running under the fences. The water, which is pure, clear and generally plenty, is this year somewhat scant—the snow which supplies it having been unusually light last winter.—Brigham's water-warden accordingly lets on to each garden only a few hours for two days in the week, leaving a card at the house to inform the master when he may expect it among his vegetables. This water flows from what is called City Creek Canon—and where do you think it enters the city? Through Brigham Young's enclosure. If he chose he could shut it off, dam it back, or turn it aside in twenty-four hours and leave the Mormon metropolis mad with thirst—for there are not more than half a dozen wells in the city and those bad and brackish.

There is only one spot where fire-wood can be obtained—and that is this same City Creek Canon. The family-man goes to Brigham and asks permission to pass through the gates of his enclosure up the only road to the canon, and bring down his winter's supply of fuel. "Yes," answers the President, "but every other load you will please deposit in my enclosure."

Thus, it will be seen the Mormon cannot earn his daily bread, quench his thirst, warm his hands, or secure anything but a scullion's place in the external world, without saying to Brigham and the Engine "By your leave." If that Mormon be a woman, she cannot hope to go to Heaven at all, unless some husband saves her—and no one can give her to that husband except Brigham only. The Apostles and Bishops can tie her for this world—but there their power ends. If she has made a bad match however, for ten dollars paid the Engine, per Brigham as usual, either she or her husband can get the knot sundered, provided they have not been sealed. Divorce is very easy in Utah—but Brigham only can grant it.

TALES OF A TRAVELER.

Perhaps I shall hardly be believed in a Christian Community—but The Engine—per B. Y. again—possesses not only the property, happiness, and eternal disposition of the Mormon—but holds within its grasp the power of his physical life and death. It is very well known in Salt Lake City that no man lives there who would not be dead to-morrow if Brigham willed it so. This is an inevitable corollary of the Engine System. If the Mormon lives for the glory of the Engine, when his life ceases to glorify the Engine it must terminate. In the Mormon writings—in their Sunday sermons at the Tabernacle, this doctrine has been openly preached. It is even now declared by their head-men in moments of anger or incaution. "The enemy of the church must perish." "The best service you can do God is to cut off the Gentile enemy or the Mormon apostate." How long do you think that your noble Connor and his little handful of brave men would remain alive on that hill behind the city, if expediency permitted their assassination? Do you think that any conscience, regarding the crime of murder, would restrain the hands of the destroyer? Not five minutes!

As to the Mormon himself he knows perfectly that he can never escape from his vows—not even from his residence if he be suspected of a desire to run away—except through a bloody chink in his own body. A frequently-preached doctrine of the Church is that some sins (those against the Engine, mainly) are only to be washed away by the offender's own blood. "There are some of you," said Brigham on one occasion in the Tabernacle, "who have made the blood of Christ of none effect, and if you realized your dreadful condition you would come to us and ask us to slay you, that your death might expiate your crimes, and save you from hell." Within two years past he has thus addressed one of the Bishops from the pulpit on Sunday—(spiritual rulers of the city wards): "Brother—, there is a man in your jurisdiction who has fallen away, and become a child of hell. He must be disposed of during the coming week. *Send him to California across lots and see that you don't leave the bars down*." With that he drew his hand significantly across his throat. Scarcely twenty-four hours after, the person signified was found lying in one of the lonely streets at dawn with a bullet hole through his head. So much a part of the system is this assassination, that there is a body of men, picked and trustworthy, whose sole function it is to see that the Church is pruned of her human excrescences. These are the *Danites* of whom you have so often heard. I became very well acquainted with their famous head, Porter Rockwell, the Destroying Angel. Twenty-five men at least, have fallen by his hand. He is the personification of the frank, hearty, bluff man of action. The kindest-hearted and most obliging murderer I ever knew. I don't believe that Porter Rockwell ever bore a particle of malice to any living being. But if Brigham Young should tell him to kill me, I should just as much expect him to do it as to eat his dinner. It would not be a matter of reflection with him beforehand or of remorse afterward. Perhaps he wouldn't even remember it next month: I need to look at his broad, pleasant, good-humored face, his mastif head and neck with his long hair braided into twenty little pig tails and tied behind in a knot like a woman's, his powerful, stubby form and massive hands—then say to myself, "There's no moral responsibility in that man—no conscience. He is simply an incarnation of force. When he shoots a Gentile or an Apostate, accountability doesn't begin at the finger which pulls the trigger. The breech of the revolver is as accountable as he. He is a mere instrument—he is part of the Engine." On the Fourth of July he called with a great stage which it had been his fancy to buy "for the old woman and children," and took me out riding to the Hot Springs behind four horses. He was just as bluff and jolly as he could be: wore an immense pair of buckskin gauntlets though it was a hot summer day; and having celebrated the 4th a little incautiously went to sleep with his neck over the middle seat strap in the midst of a description of the great grasshopper plague of '53. I scarcely kept my sides from bursting with merriment as I looked at him and thought of a Destroying Angel in liquor.—What a country of inconsistencies that could produce elevated Angels and profane Pilgrims? I afterwards dined at his house, on my way to California. He keeps the second station out from the Mormon City. Neither from me or Bierstadt could he be persuaded to accept a particle of pay. He had asked us to dine with him, he said. And a very nice dinner it was—got up by two Mistresses Rockwell in concert. These destroying Angelesses seemed to pull together very amicably. The Angel himself was overflowing with good humor, and I parted from him sure that if I needed a friend in distress I should never have to look farther than this amiable murderer—while, if Brigham happened to find that I owed the Engine a life, his vision would be just as little taxed for a collection of the debt. I have seen so many curious incongruities in human nature throughout the world at large that I found the Mormon one far from unintelligible. I have known such devout passers of Sunday's plate who sold light-weight and put the specked potatoes at the bottom of the bushel all the remainder of the week; such disinterested newspaper philanthropists who went home from the editor's to frost-bite their wives with stern tyranny and dry up the loving blood in their little children's hearts by cruel severity or cold indifference.

PART II.

## *From Denver to Salt Lake*

*Written for the* Golden Era *(Sunday, 27 Mar. 1864)*

BRIGHAM YOUNG.

Brigham Young is a distinguished looking man, apparently about fifty, but in reality over sixty years of age—with a very firm mouth and exceedingly protruding chin—a high forehead, slightly grizzled flaxen hair, and a narrow line of beard of the same color which he trains like a cap-strap all around his face from ear to ear. He was very polite to me, and spent a long time in conversing with us about the war and the Indians on one particular evening when we met at a great Mormon ball to which as a distinguished honor we Gentiles were invited. By the way, every Mormon I talked with and all I heard talk in the tabernacle on Sunday inevitably fell back on "the war" as his conversational staple—nor could any of them conceal the glee which he felt in thinking that the United States were now "getting growedy" for the blood of Joseph Smith and driving out the Mormons. There was almost a chuckle in the tone with which Heber Kimball used to ask us, "Now you really don't mean to say you believe the Unions were coming together again!" I may as well record for the benefit of your Copperheads, who, I understand, are a very small crowd and need all the sympathy which they can get, that all the influential Mormons spoke of them to me with warm affection—said that they were the only men in the States they could ever agree with—and entirely coincided with them in the view that this war was began by "the d—d abolitionists" and kept up by "the despotic administration."

HEBER KIMBALL.

Heber Kimball is an interminably jolly old gentleman, at the hale and hearty age of sixty-five—with a ministerial coat, nankeen pantaloons, and a tall, conical leghorn hat. His stature is about six feet, his figure erect and portly. He always talked with us very frankly about Mormonism and his own part in it—using the Bible with a vast knowledge of its weapons, but employing that armory after a manner so original that I was as much amused as if I had seen him trying to stab his enemy with a horse-pistol or do execution at a hundred yards with a small sword. His manner is very cogent if not convincing, for he slaps his collocutor on the back with a force which would prevent the largest size crumb from causing suffocation. His very fluent addresses to Bierstadt and me were of a kind and scope which always made me feel that I was listening to a sincere Chadband compounded with a religious Jack Bunsby. It took me sometime to get accustomed to the frank way in which he said "*my wives*."—There was not a particle of Polygamistic apology about him. As we stood in the big theatre when they were getting it ready for the ball, he asked Bierstadt if he was a German. "By descent," was the reply. "I love the Germans," continued Heber—"I've got a German wife. You remember Christine!" (interrogatively to a carpenter at work near him.) "Oh, yes—I know Christine." Pretty soon I happened to ask what language was spoken by some women who chattered briskly away as they worked at the ropes of evergreen which were to festoon the cornice.—"Those are Danes," answered Heber, "Good people, those Danes—I've got two Danish wives." Not long after he told us as straight forwardly that he had an Irish wife. In all, I believe, he has about as many as Brigham. Bierstadt and I passed a morning in his most luxuriant garden, where he fairly loaded us with fruit—telling us all the time to notice what magnanimity it was on his and his friends' part to get such a beautiful place ready for their enemies, the Gentiles—"You poor fellows who will be all coming out here presently from your broken Union to ask an asylum with the Saints of the Lord. You laugh—you don't believe it, I know." I told him I believed that he believed it (so I do), which is the next best thing—and begged him to remember and save me that particular strawberry patch and apricot clump I was then standing by against the appointed day, as my share of the asylum.

THEATRE—BALL.

The theatre, where the ball was held on the 3d of July evening, is built much after the pattern of the New York Academy of Music, holds three thousand, and is decorated (entirely by Mormon craftsmen) with a taste which took me quite by surprise. It is in fact the handsomest and most commodious place of public amusement I know in this country, out of New York and Philadelphia. The painting on the arch over the stage and the moulding about the proscenium boxes, is as elegant as any thing in our Eastern cities.

All through the great concourse which attended the ball, I looked in vain for one *high-toned* womanly face. There were pretty girls there—there were many kindly feminine countenances—but there was nothing belonging to that *spiritual* type, that lofty beauty which breathes the pride of purity and delicate sweetness, so admired and so constantly found in our American society here and at the East. Everywhere I saw women whom the voluptuary would select for his slave; now and then one whom the sick man would choose for his nurse or the quiet recluse for his housekeeper, but nowhere in all that vast assembly one woman whom the refined, cultivated and spiritually natured man could take to his bosom as a companion, friend or equal. I saw one poor faded woman sitting apart, weeping silently, as she looked at the dancers, where her husband might perhaps be gambolling with a fresh wife—but contrary to all my expectations, no look of shame, and very little of sullenness or seeming dissatisfaction.

AN OPINION.

I know that I am writing a sketch—not a philosophical essay, yet I may be pardoned for expressing an opinion. I had unusually good opportunities for getting acquainted with the Mormons, and I came to a very different conclusion about them from that which I had formed at the East. In their insane error they are *sincere*, as I fully believe, to a much greater extent than is generally supposed. Even their leaders, for the most part, I regard not as hypocrites, but as fanatics. Whatever they may have once questioned in the Mormon system, they have now at least, from long habit, brought themselves to believe in it all, with implicit faith. There are some selfish natures who espouse every canon merely for the temporary gain they can make out of it, and such doubtless here and there exist in Utah. But the sacrifices demanded of the individual by the church; the utter annihilation of personal rights ownership, everything the proud man holds dearest; and the horrible irrevocability of the obligations which a man shuts behind him like tenfold gates of brass, when he becomes a Mormon; with the awful, barbaric penalty certain to overtake the Apostate—these considerations stand guard at the threshold to drive away the hypocrite. A dozen wives are but small compensation for being slave to a system which cuts your throat if you rebel, and fleeces you of all you possess if you don't. Brigham Young has undoubtedly made money by his politics—he is now probably one of the richest men in the world. Heber Kimball is very well off. None of the apostles, bishops or head men of any clan are poor. Yet they cannot get away to enjoy their wealth. The civilized world is barred to them. If Brigham Young should try to run away to-morrow, his own fanatic myrmidons would blow his brains out before he got through Parley's Canon.

MORMON SINCERITY.

The hypothesis of hypocrisy appears still more untenable to me when I consider what the Mormons have done and suffered for their ideas. Hypocrisy, it seems to me could not have come for a haven into the most inaccessible wilderness of the world; and abandoning the fertile slopes where vice may revel in prosperity on the mere condition of cloaking itself in unobtrusive forms, wring from the unwilling breast of a parched desert at once subsistence and the freedom to incorporate immortality into a creed. See by how slight a compromise with conventional decency—by merely keeping their vice secret and abstaining from the promulgation in theory of the evil which they practice in life, bad men enjoy in the very heart of civilization immunity for a crime virtually identical with that which has made Mormonism's stench in Christendom. But the Mormons have fled to a desert where life itself would be a burden to most of us; by incredible labor have replaced the sage brush and the alkali plains with smiling gardens, green meadows, luxuriant orchards and golden harvest fields; have never ceased to wage battle with hostile nature, knowing that armistice means defeat to them of the sorest kind, and that one year's neglect of their laborious system of artificial irrigation would blot out the triumphs of the past painful years; they stand thus, holding the desert from their doors by main force—and all, that they may do as religion what other men practice as crime. If this be hypocrisy it bears most anomalous fruits.

But it is nothing of the kind. The whole secret of their fanaticism is intelligible the moment that you understand one fact—they are saturated through and through with a love of the Old Testament civilization as understood by them. You cannot talk with one of their strongest men, like Young or Kimball, for an hour without seeing that their national model is the Jewish people. Like the Jews, they are grossly sensuous and physical in all their ideas of religion and a future state. Like them they have no notion of the pure conjugal relation and consider Polygamy its highest form. Like them, they believe themselves the constituted rulers of the Gentiles and will "compass heaven and earth to make a proselyte." Like them, they think themselves doing God service by assassinating such as have made defection from their creed; and murder the enemies of their faith with as little compunction as the old Israelitish barbarians were wont to slay the Canaanites. Like them, they extort involuntary contributions for the support of their ecclesiastical organization, and exact the same blind obedience to a privileged priesthood as under pain of death was paid to the Levitical behests. But I might run the parallel interminably. It only remains necessary for me to add that in spite of their being like the Jews, shameless polygamists, assassins, bigots, inquisitors, delighters in massacre, extortioners and zealots, they claim to do all these things under the sanction and by the order of God Almighty—in fact to be "His chosen people." They are an attempt to revive the Israelitish Civilization in the 19th Century.

GENERAL CONNER.

I have dwelt so long upon the subject because I am sure that the prevailing belief in Mormon hypocrisy is a dangerous mistake. The hypocrite will not fight to death—the fanatic will. Secure in the confidence that the Mormons were not heartily committed to their ideas, our people have always made inadequate preparations for the treatment of their case. We have now sent out for the protection of our national officers the noble Conner and a little handful of men who are still further weakened by the necessity of sprinkling them all along the Overland Road for three hundred miles, at the rate of four or five in each station house, these stations being fifteen miles apart. It is well enough known in Utah who has compelled the still further enfeeblement of an adequate force; that the Mormon himself has stirred up the savage to massacre and arson, for the very purpose of breaking Conner's band to atoms. The few hundred who are still left in Camp upon that hill commanding the town occupy the place by the sufferance of Brigham Young. They have a few field-pieces and howitzers, to be sure; and if need be they might burn the town or batter down the President's Houses; but if Brigham said the word there are enough of fanatics in Utah to walk up Conner's hill in the face of his fire, and climbing over the dead bodies of their comrades, slaughter his men at the doors of their tents. Hypocrites are never desperate while they have the alternative of recantation. Fanatics are always desperate. They are men to be feared. And till the Mormons are feared as such, the Laws of the Nation will be as much a dead letter in Utah as they are in South Carolina.

California is represented in Utah by one of the truest and most fearless men who ever lived. He deserves not only the admiration which he gets but the reinforcement he does not get. He should be at the head of at least four regiments to-day. I knew him and learned to love and respect him while in Utah. And I wish I could appeal to all America as I now appeal to California, not to let him perish with his dauntless little band, at the hands of fanatics and savages who may some day catch fire at a word.

PART III.

## *Salt Lake City to San Francisco*

*Written for the* Golden Era *(Sunday, 17 Apr. 1864)*

I wince like Eneas when I approach the third part of our journey across the plains. With the slight alterations of putting you, O ERA, for Queen Dido, and the ride from Salt Lake to Washoe for the Trojan war, I can exclaim:

> *"Me, Requia, jubes infandum renovare dolorem."*

Or liberally rendered—O ERA, you are compelling me to live over a most miserable period of my existence.

Weeks have elapsed since I concluded the last published, or second, portion of this narrative. Then I stopped. Partly because I had spun a yarn which for newspaper purposes was already pretty long—but chiefly because the last stage of our journey was so well nigh unmixed suffering, and because such horrible things occurred during its progress, that I almost despaired of making its recital more attractive to a reader than its memory was to me. I must not, however, leave the ERA with Bierstadt and myself in Salt Lake City, for lack of pluck to face in recollection a desert which I braved in bodily presence. So here goes—with a prayer that I may prove neither dull nor appalling—I shall not be long at any rate.

LES MISERABLES.

I do not know who own the Overland Line from Salt Lake City to Carson. The manner of packing passengers upon this part of the line evinces intellects accustomed to close stowage and large profits. I believe that if the thirteen men whom the proprietors stuffed into our stage (by artistic degrees) so as to accustom us to "scrooging" (and make us think that we had large intervals between us) had been thirteen mild men, instead of thirteen very truculent and self-defensive men, they would have unblushingly proceeded to take out the seats and lay us crosswise, like a cob-house—piled thirteen more mild men on top of us—and at the end of the route have charged us an extra hundred dollars for having packed us so close that we wouldn't bounce.

We were promised by the Stage Company all sorts of facilities. For a part of the way they might not be able to give us a coach entirely to ourselves, but if we would let one other gentleman into the stage with us, that one should certainly be the last. This arrangement gave us a little chance to stretch our legs and prevented the knee-joints from becoming permanently anchylosed by a position whose resemblance to that of negroes on the "middle passage" would have made an abolitionist of me if I had never tended strongly in that direction through my whole previous life.

Delusive dream! Nothing but the use of our six-shooters could have prevented us from reaching at every third or fourth station accessions to our wretched community—and as two parties can play at the revolver game—and we even after all our Overland Stage experience, had still some ghostly hope of reaching California alive, we preferred acquiescence under protest to sending on to Carson City a stage empty or full of mangled remains.

A PERFECT GENTLEMAN.

The Agent of the road at Salt Lake City was so perfect a gentleman, and did for our comfort so many things which he was by no means bound to do and only could have done out of pure natural refinement and goodness of heart, as to convince me that if any guarantees of proper treatment had lain in his power he would most gladly have accorded them to us. On the morning [of] the 6th of July, he sent a very neat, elegant and comfortable coach out of Salt Lake City, containing Mr. Bierstadt and myself. (Our two companions had preceded us by a couple of days to avoid crowding.) At the last moment our consent was asked for the admission of a third passenger, and obtained by the representation of the fact that his business was pressing. Before we had gone thirty miles from Salt Lake City our neat and comfortable stage was taken away from us, and without even the pretence of a necessity for the change, a vastly inferior vehicle, very disagreeably crowded, was substituted in its place.

THE DESTROYING ANGEL!
CAMP FLOYD.

The afternoon of the day that we left Salt Lake, and a few hours after dining with the Destroying Angel, Porter Rockwell (who keeps the second station from Brigham's metropolis); after winding down a long precipitous dug-away and getting a glimpse of that beautiful fresh water lake, Utah, which runs into the Mormon Dead Sea like an American Gennesaret by a river Jordan which we crossed on a rope ferry, and fancied strikingly like its biblical namesake—we came to one of America's characteristic yet unfrequent ruins.

During that belligerent fizzle and humbug known as the "Mormon War," there sprung up about General Johnson's army a straggling adobe village only less populous than Salt Lake City itself. To this, in compliment to that arch-traitor who has lately followed his reputation out of human existence, the gallant commander gave the name of Camp Floyd.

Its present title is Fort Crittenden. Its only occupied dwellings are those used for barracks and military store-houses by a small detachment from Conner's army—posted here mainly for the preservation of the stages from Indian attacks. On every side of their little bustling quarters stretch long silent, treeless, shelterless streets of adobe houses—some of them standing as they were left by their dying inhabitants at the departure of Johnson's army—but the majority unroofed, with the window frames extracted, and gutted of all their wood-work—even second-hand timber in this country being too valuable to be dismissed from active life before fire or rot has utterly terminated its period of usefulness. At sunset I could hardly ride through these straggling lines of livid lead-colored house-ghosts without a shudder. It must be terrible to walk alone with them by moonlight! Their inhabitants seem to have gone away at once and without warning—as if they had strolled out some day to take their air and been licked up into the sky all together with a tongue of whirlwind or fire. What if such an unexpected class of citizens should come whirling back all at once while you stood there—as quickly as they departed? How it would startle you!

SOLDIERED TO DEATH.

At this place we took aboard our first escort of soldiers. It was a fine sample of Conner's troopers. One man especially—a blue eyed, flaxen-haired sergeant of the purest Saxon type who rode with me past two or three stations, was without exception the best informed person regarding the questions at issue in our civil war whom I have met in the army. His name I think was St. John. The others were sturdy-looking, dignified men—a splendid contrast with the finely systematized but unthinking tools, usually resulting from regular army discipline.

From that time on we were be-soldiered to death. Just beyond Fort Crittenden, or just this side (I forget which), we came to a sharp turn between two rough crags of granite with an immense back-ground of sage-brush, where in June, the copper-faced devils, whom Longfellow meanders about in Hiawatha poetry; Cooper in Leatherstocking prose, and all the ministers of my boyhood's acquaintance in Sunday prayers about our "cruelty to the poor Red-Man," rose up with arrow and rifle balls, riddled the driver through and through, and, after killing one passenger, drove the rest trembling back to Salt Lake behind the Providentially turned-round horses. I say "Providentially" but Providence took the form of giving one of the passengers bravery enough to snatch the lines and take the box in place of the murdered driver. I have now in my trunk the arrow which gave the driver his death wound.

In order to preserve us from the repetition of such a disaster, we thenceforth carried as many blue-jackets as we could hold. Bierstadt and I had a blue-jacket stuffed beside us so tight that we had no interstices left—but were like crockery in a crate packed with some blue and military variety of straw. There was another pair of soldiers divided by the young passenger whom we had tolerated because of his pressing business—his countenance steadily indicating that the pressure increased till we got to Washoe. Three more soldiers sat on the remaining seat inside the stage, and one was always beside the driver—both he and his companion in a particularly melancholy state of mind and talking to me through the window, when we stopped, like a sort of twin-target arrangement without any expectation of being appreciated by its country.

IN TERROREM.

We rode all night, sleeping no more than is natural for people not yet utterly exhausted or fainting (as we would be to-morrow) and quite unable to keep our heads on the middle strap, when those members were momently getting shot up against the coach top by the stage's leaping from a rut like a bomb going out of a mortar. When the red-eyed dawn over the Wasatch Mountains broke on us still more red-eyed than itself, we began to hear faint rumors of evil work ahead. At one station, near what in civilized countries is called breakfast-time, we saw with our glass a red fiend skulking through the sage a couple of miles away to eastward. Meeting the stage coming the other way, we got rumors of a more substantial character. There had been murder—burning—awful atrocity—three or four stations ahead. With this subject for reflection we traveled moodily all day—scarcely speaking to each other, and the desert growing more savage.

## ALKALI PLAINS. MORE MISERY.

After winding through chalky dug-ways—a limy sort of slate scaling off from the hill at our side, and the ground beneath us all one ash-heap of white powder, we descended into what I may call a typical Alkali-Plain. As far as the eye could reach in all directions, till the horizon was bounded by a low black range of volcanic mountains, the earth was as white and as sparkling as snow. It was a marble pavement, ninety miles in diameter, each way as the crow flies. So pure was the air above this leafless, burning desert, that the solitary station houses which we must visit during the next twenty-four hours, fifteen and twenty miles apart, were plainly visible one after another, strung along the road like the balls which in old-fashioned schools we used to see spitted on wire frames for the purpose of scholars studying Numeration. (I notice that the Chinese merchants of San Francisco use this same apparatus in keeping their accounts—*"Abacus"* is its name, I believe.)

Here began our chiefest miseries. The road was a crust of alkali, broken into pits from a foot to three feet deep, these situated on the average, ten yards apart—a state of things which results in the alternate lulling to rest of jolted bodies (on the smooth road); a fearful plunge into unknown depths, (in the ruts) and a tremendous leap, sending the inmates of the stage only not through the stage-roof (up the ridge at the further end of the rut.) I cannot dwell on this portion of our experience. It was spread over several days and nights. It produced black and blue bruises—serious abrasions of the skin—ulcers when these last became irritated with omni-present alkali-dust; it made every passenger sore from head to foot as to his body, wretched beyond all measure as to his mind; and worse than all, it rendered anything like true, normal, refreshing sleep impossible to the agonized sitters-up, for six whole days and nights.

About five o'clock one afternoon in July, among the very barrenest hills of the hostile *Goshoot* country, where the stinted cedars—the sharp, castellated crags—the dust-drowned sage, grease-wood and artemisium—were at their very culmination of sombre gloom and loneliness—we came to the authentication of all the road's long-past flying rumors. It was a dreadful place around that Canon Station.

## CANON STATION.

We entered an ampitheatre walled by lofty rocks of green-gray porphyry—nearly a thousand feet high at their outer rim—the whole space about two hundred rods in diameter. Our approach to the basin was a black defile—floored with impalpable alkali dust a foot deep—fenced by successive tiers of ragged crags on either side, all of them the most admirable natural breast-works for an ambushed foe. The dust, as we toiled through it, we could see here and there marked with the deep trail of mocassins [*sic*] too hurried or defiantly careless to blot their sign out. A thousand torn slabs of burnt granitic rock, standing on edge, were strewn over the whole rising floor of the amphitheatre. Military art could not have developed natural advantages so as to make a fortress for guerilla purposes comparable with this collection of ready-made strongholds.

A practical wisdom and knowledge of Indian methods not uncommon on the Overland Road had placed the Canon Station right in the middle of this amphitheatre. I suppose that the proprietors felt anxious to win the Indian's confidence by this experimental proof that they did not distrust them—and to avoid hurting their feelings by acting as if they were suspicious, built their little wooden station-house in a place where their employees could not by any possibility know of the presence of savages till the latter had summoned them.

Of course, we were to have changed horses at Canon Station. We were very anxious to do so, as our poor animals with froth dried on their tongues like baked tiles, were almost worn out with their tug through the burning soda of the last twenty miles between porphyry walls which radiated heat like an oven arch.

## HORRIBILE DICTU!

As we came round the sharp turn which should have revealed to us the station house, what a sight met our eyes! Under a heavy cloud of black, clinging smoke, lay the charred beams and smouldering rafters of the house—while a little further on the ruins of great trusses of hay were still steaming above the conflagration of the stables. On that further pile lay the mangled remains of all the stage stud—ten or a dozen fine animals who had perished with their halters unloosed; and nearer by, among the burning planks of the house, were stretched the bones of six horribly mutilated men, the flesh still partly adhering to them, and the whole mass rapidly becoming undistinguishable, roasting into our nostrils with the smell of mingled man and beasthood, a loathsome holocaust to the Demon of *"Primeval Innocence."* The Leatherstocking novels—the Hiawatha song—the pretty, sentimental, philanthropic prayers—were all made about the beautiful creatures who on this hot July day came down upon Canon Station and left six brave men torn to pieces as by wolves, charring on the flaming rafters! To say nothing of horses, who being "steeds," are much more important to poetry than these poor fellows of the Overland Company and Conner's force, with no pretensions to plumes and "Primeval Innocence!"

So we rolled on fifteen or twenty miles further, expecting every moment to be surrounded by the devils who had murdered our poor countrymen and destroyed the station. With their noses nearly down to the alkali dust, our half-dead team got into the next station, only to bring me within range of still more frightful rumors concerning fire and slaughter at the next station beyond. "The Antelope Station was burned down!" "Every body there was killed!" A party of soldiers going upon the housetop, had seen dense smoke in that direction all the morning. Such was our soothing after our great horror!

## SILENCE—TERRIBLE SUSPENSE—THE NOBLE SAVAGE—GEN. CONNER.

That horror now reached its culmination. Since we entered the Goshoot Country, eighty miles back, we had ridden with our rifles in our hands, their muzzles sticking out of the windows—our fingers never off the triggers, night or day. I had a Ballard's rifle, which in buffalo or antelope hunting had never failed me. It fired seven times in one minute, with perfect accuracy. Bierstadt's double-barreled musket, loaded with buckshot, was in his hands; and across our knees lay our loaded six-shooters. The seven Sharp's rifles of our escort and the two cavalry revolvers of our other passenger and the driver, completed our armament. We had made up our minds that we were to be attacked by the vilest, cruelest set of murderers who ever took advantage of an unprepared stage-coach full of innocent men; but we were ready to sell ourselves dear. I think that I never knew such horrors of suspense as we endured while travelling toward Antelope Station, and expecting momently to be attacked; or, if that danger failed, to be surrounded by the devils who had finished their Canon massacre by burning Antelope Station, the moment we should reach the latter place. This agony was not *fear*. We knew *that* earlier—before we saw the horrors of Canon Station. *This* was worse than fear. It was a suspense which choked our breaths. No man spoke to his neighbor—not knowing but his very whisper might be the signal for a horde of shrieking devils to leap out with a volley of two hundred muskets and bows from the dark, undefined sage brush—lying all spectral, like an illimitable night-bound sea, bordering the powdery road. So we rode in dead silence—our hands on our rifles—the windows bristling with their muzzles, as before. From all signs, I believe that perfect preparation was what saved us. The fiend known as an Indian—the inconceivable devil, whom statesmen and fools *treat* with, but whom brave and practical men shoot and scalp—(that being *their* treaty with demons who spare neither age, a sex nor feebleness—who come without warning and torture without mercy)—this fiend never attacking even the passengers stalled, cooped and hampered in an Overland stage, where there is the slightest possibility that the first of their gang may fall before the shot of this forewarned white man. Oh, sentimentalist!—whiners about the noble savage! if it *can* be possible that there be such in a State like California, be converted and strengthen the arms of your Conner before it be too late for him and you!

HAPPY DELIVERANCE—RUBY VALLEY.

Thank God! Half way between Antelope Station and the one where we had heard the dreadful rumor, a heavy sound of wheels broke the awful stillness of the powdery road and our suspense at the same time!

The stage coming from the other way! We met and learned that the rumor was a false one—built out of the Canon massacre and burning straw—destroyed to get it out of the way of danger. On board the Eastward stage was Major Gallagher of Conner's original regiment, and Dr. Kilpatrick, its surgeon—the former on the way to lead a foray against the murderers—the latter (until we told him of his mission's uselessness) to bind the wounds of the murderers' victims.

After a few moment's talk, we rolled on toward Antelope Station, taking the Doctor with us—and blessing God—oh, how fervently! None can know who have not, like us, ridden out of the *finale* of one horrible tragedy through the desert, into what we honestly expected should be the first act of another!

Two days more of horrible desert—all the same black green weeds, like the funeral trappings of a dead world—black rocks, like the walls of its tomb—alkaline dust, like the fathomless forgetfulness of the Universe, covering it over forever—all stretching without change or break to the very sky line—and then we let the Doctor down at a faint spot of green, called "Ruby Valley," which looked as if God had dropped a tear here, pitying the awful desolation, and longing that He might some day visit it in mercy, were it only thus written on the Eternal memorandum! Here Conner has established one of his posts—here, the poor vacillating wretches who cannot be ever content with Reese River as far enough from God, man and life's gentleness, to hunt gold in and be miserable, have come of late—the papers tell me, seduced by stories of great "ledges." *I* would live on a crust of bread before I would accept nine chances out of ten to come here and be wealthy!

MORE IMPRECATIONS.

A day or two more—we growing madder all the time through deprivation of sleep and frightful jolting—no timber, no green shrub but the sage and grease-wood sprouting out of the alkali—no bird flying over the awful waste—no beast living on it—the water a bitter poison-draft which brought frightful sores out all over the bodies which it touched by washing or entered by drinking—a day or two more of crazy plunging in alkali ruts, amid dense clouds of flying dust or alkaline;—of climbing up barren mountains where the dry, thirsty stars looked down on us pitilessly, like the eyes of fiends tortured in a like alkali hell with us—a day or two more of horrible cannibalistic food, cooked by filthy Indian Squaws or as filthy Station Keepers, but utterly inedible by mouths which gasped only for fresh air and water. Every time we got comfortable a convertible stage—a stage where we could lie down at full length—stretch ourselves—and forget our miseries in sleep—the employees of the company took it away from us at the first station where there could be obtained an old ramshackle coach of narrow dimensions, whose seats could not be moved or extended. I am certain, that if I should be so unfortunate as to find the punishments of the next world arranged after the orthodox Tartarian fashion, the first thing I should be compelled to do after death would be to ride with the Overland Co. (who would certainly be there themselves,) from Ruby Valley to Reese River.

For that latter was the station I got to after those two or three days just sketched.

SUICIDE!

Then came a ride still more horrible, if that can be conceived. We were not stuffed with soldiers any longer, for we had passed the limit of Goshoot danger—but (in spite of all those previous solemn guarantees regarding a coach reserved nearly to ourselves) we were packed three upon a seat which was uncomfortably crowded by two—and thus jammed we rode two more days and nights to Washoe. If we had not found the very best, kindest, and most obliging of men in those enthusiastic Reese miners, with their pockets full of ounce buttons of silver cooked out of two ounces of chloride, bromide or iodide ore—we had indeed given up the ghost by liquefaction under pressure!

Oh, it was horrible—that hydraulic packing. Words utterly give out in the attempt to express our suffering. Still, we lived to Virginia City. The morning before we got there—the young man whose pressure of business had persuaded us to let him ride with us, *(as the only other one!)* though a slight young man, a farmer, with immemorial ploughing, pork-and-beans-eating, ancestors behind him, became quite insane, and had to be kept in the stage at one time by force—seeming to think (as was very natural,) that the stage-owners were plotting to murder him. I had heard before I started, from friends in St. Louis, that this sometimes happened—but had not believed it until this case of irresistible eye-witness. (The other day it happened again, but with a much more funereal ending—the wretched victim of Overland Stage abuse having committed suicide at a station by shooting himself through the head.)

SAVED!

The moment I got into a warm bath at Virginia City, I fainted dead away and was with great difficulty resuscitated. But a splendid constitution was in my favor. I managed to revive sufficiently to reach Lake Tahoe, where the glorious air and scenery additionally benefitted me. After two days there, I risked my life down the slope of the Sierra with one of those reckless drivers who so nearly killed your Ex-Mayor Teschemacher—and finally got to San Francisco via Folsom and Sacramento, but with a constitution so frightfully undermined by the Overland Journey that I never expect to recover fully from it as long as I live. I suffer from it intensely even while I write.

# INDEX

*Page numbers in italics indicate illustrations.*


Achenbach, Andreas, 112, 113, 117, 119, 123, 186, 304
Adams, Alvin, 26, 48, 61–62, 65 n.13, 93, 106 n.76, 113, 124, *124*, 174, 188, 246, 250
Adams, Francis Colburn, 42, 43–45, 183
*After a Norther Off the Bahamas (A Wave Breaking on the Bahamas Coast)*, 251, 252
Agassiz, Louis, 148, *148*
Albert, Joseph, 274, 284
Albertype process, 223, 274, 284
Alexander Gallery (New York), 11
Alexis, Grand Duke of Russia, 220, 223, 224, *224*
American Art Association, 250
American Art Union, 246, 250–51, 284
American Exhibition, London (1887), 246, 252
American school of painting, 60–62, 113
American Society of Painters in Water Colors, 49
Amon Carter Museum, 11
*Among the Sierra Nevada Mountains, California*, 24, 45–46, 48, 61, 65 n.14, 66 n.117, *93*, 93–94, 97, 99, 174, 185, 186–87, 188, 208, *209*, 246, 250, 255
*Among the Wind River Mountains*, 149
*Ancon*, S.S., 104–5, 253, *253*, 263
Anderson, Nancy K., 11–12, 13
"Antelopes" (wood engraving), 274, *275*, 277
*Arch of Octavius, The (The Roman Fish Market)*, 54, 69, 113, 123, 124, 135, *135*, 143, 257
Armstrong, David Maitland, 59–60, 232
*Arrival of a Market Boat, Capri* (engraving), *121*
Arthur, Chester A., 250
*Artist Painting in Yosemite, The*, *82*
*Artist's Camp, Lake Tenaya, The*, 249
*Art-Journal* (London), 94, 208, 240, 279
Artotypes, 274, 284
art-tariff controversy, 250, 255
"Attack of Panther" (wood engraving), 277, *277*
*Autumn, Westphalia*, 143
*Autumn in the Sierras (Kings River Canyon)*, 50, *51*, 51–52, 54–55, 67 n.141, 220, 221, 227, 228
*Autumn Woods, Oneida County, State of New York*, 252
Avery, Kevin, 65 n.14
Avery, Samuel P., 46

Baigell, Matthew, 11
Baird, Spencer, 223
Balch, Vistus, 277
Bancroft, George, 50, 179, 194, 228
Banks, Nathaniel P., 43–44, 51
Barbizon school, 21, 27, 64
*Base of the Rocky Mountains, Laramie Peak*, 24, *24*, 25, 54, 74, 140, 146–47, 148
Baur, John I. H., 11
*Bavarian Farmyard*, 177
*Bay of Salerno*, *122*
*Bay of Sorrento*, 135
Beard, William H., 120–21, 141, 148
*Bebigio—Scene in Italy*, 148
Beecher, Catharine, 268
Beecher, Henry Ward, 177
*Bellemont, Kansas* (stereograph), *144*
Belmont, August, 229
Beniczky, K. W., Ludlow carte de visite, *78*, *177*
Benjamin, Samuel G. W., 61, 167, 283
Benson, Eugene (Sordello), 29, 200
Berlin: International Exhibition (1891), 255; Royal Academy of, 45–46, 93, 185–86
*Bernese Alps, as Seen Near Kusnach, The*, 143
Bierce, Ambrose, 87, 187–88
Bierstadt, Albert, *22*, *257;* carte de visite (Sarony), *177;* engraving by Neumann, *188;* 1859 photograph of, *143;* 1861 photograph of, *146;* 1872 stereograph of, *226;* 1888 photograph of, *252;* photograph with wife Mary, *256*
Bierstadt, Charles, 36, 106 n.13, 115, 140, 145, 146, 188, 228, 230, 272, 274; stereographs by, *81*, *96*, *179*, *181*, *189*, *225*, *250*
Bierstadt, Christina Tillmans, 112, 115, *115*, 181
Bierstadt, Edward, 106 n.13, 115, 140–41, 145, 146, 147, 178, 223, 228, 249, 257, 267, 269, 272, 274, 279, 286, 288 n.32; Artotypes by, *251*, 274, 284
Bierstadt, Eliza, 115, 249, 274
Bierstadt, Henry, 112, 115, *115*, 182
Bierstadt, Mary Stewart, 64, 247, 256, *256*
Bierstadt, Rosalie Osborne Ludlow, 34, *35*, 38–39, 46, 55, 89, 173, 182, *182*, 220, 222, *229*, 285; death of, 64, 247, 255
*Bierstadt at the Piccola Marina, Capri* (Gifford), *122*
Bierstadt Brothers, 140, 146, 147, 149, 182, 267, 269, 270, 272, 274, 288 n.30; stereographs by, *80*, *116*, *146*, 147, *147*, *148*, *149*, *180*, *187*, *189*, 269, 271
*Big Tree of California*, 227
Bingham, George Caleb, 287 ns.3 and 13
Blodgett, William T., 26, 55, 143
Bobbett and Hooper, 273
Bodmer, Karl, 70, 106 n.3, 230
Boston Athenaeum, 54, 113, 117, 123, 124, 137, 147, 257
Bradford, William, 123, 183, 184, 189, 226, 252, 287 n.13
Brady, Mathew B., 141; studio of, *Frederick West Lander*, *77*
Brevoort House (New York), residence of Bierstadt, 229, 249, *249*, 250
Brewer, William H., 56, 226
*Bridal Veil Falls, Yosemite*, *237*
Broadway (New York) studios of Bierstadt, 228, *228*, *229*, 250
Brooklyn Art Association, 148
Brooklyn Museum, 13
Brown, J. G., 62, 63
Browning, Robert, 47
*Brunnen—Lake Lucerne*, 123, 143
Bryant, William Cullen, 32
"Buffalo Calves" (wood engraving), *189*, 277, *277*
"Buffalo Charge" (wood engraving), 274, *275*, 277
Buffalo Fine Arts Academy, *24*, 54, 149, 151, 177, 251
*Buffalo Head*, *261*
"The Buffalo Hunt" (engraving), 286
*Buffalo Trail: The Impending Storm*, *210*
"A Bull Buffalo (Bison Americanus)" (wood engraving), 281, *281*
*Burning Ship, The (Burning Whalers off the Island of Ascension)*, 184, 223, *223*, 229
*Butterfly* (two versions), 265, *265*
Byers, William N., 88–89

Calame, Alexandre, 106 n.20, 119, 123, 174, 205
*California Forest*, 227
*California Landscape*, 187
*California Oaks*, 251, 252
*California Spring*, 68 n.167, 228, *228*
Campbell, Catherine, 11
*Canadian Rockies*, *262*
*Canoes*, *215*
Capitol (Washington, D.C.), paintings for, 40–45, 49–53, 58, 173–74, 182, 183, 221, 227, 228, 231, 232
*Capri* (1857), *133*
*Capri—Bay of Naples* (1859), *see Marina Piccola, Capri, The*
Carleton, Henry Guy, 258
Carnegie, Andrew, 255
Carr, Gerald L., 11, 12, 65 n.14, 67 n.144
Casilear, John W., 164, 273
*Cathedral Rocks, Yosemite Valley, California* (oil on paper), *236*
"The Cathedral Rocks in the Yosemite Valley" (wood engraving), 281, *281*
*Cathedral Rocks in Winter*, 226
Catlin, George, 70, 92, 106 n.2, 173, 287 n.3
Centennial Exposition, Philadelphia (1876), 52, 55, 59–60, 64, 99, 220–21, 229, 281; Art Gallery at, *229*
Century Association and Club (New York), 65 n.2, 172, 177, *177*, 246
*Cerfs d'Amérique*, 250
Chase, William Merritt, 63
Chicago, 250; Crosby Art Gallery, Opera House, and lottery, 182, 183, 188, 224; *see also* World's Columbian Exposition
*Chimney Rock*, 273
*Chimney Rock, Ogalillah* [sic]. *Sioux Village in the Foreground* (steel engraving), 273, *273*
*Cho-looke, The Yosemite Fall* (oil on canvas), *83*, 83–84, 198, *198*, 276, 277
"Cho-Looke, The Yo-Semite Fall" (wood engraving), 276, *276*, 277
chromolithography, 12, 267, 268–69, 271, 285, 287 ns.3 and 13
Church, Frederic Edwin, 12, 22, 27, 36, 42, 54, 58, 59, 60, 65 n.3, 99, 130, 140, 172, 189, 246, 279, 288 n.26; comparisons with Bierstadt, 24–25, 29, 33, 46, 60, 74–77, 84–85, 93, 99, 146, 178, 183, 185, 194, 201, 204, 246, 249, 252, 268, 279; *Cotopaxi*, 84, *86; Heart of the Andes*, 25, 26, 32, *33*, 60, *75*, 75–77, 85, 93, 143, 173, 194, 201, 287 n.18; *Icebergs*, 25, 26; *Niagara*, 26, 29, 45, 46, 55, 60, 183, 184, 279; Olana, home on the Hudson, 34, 35, 39; prints, 268, 287 ns.13, 18, and 25; *Tropical Landscape*, 252
Cincinnati, 102, 182; 1888 Annual Exposition, 227
Civil War, 80–81, 141, 147, 148, 172, 181; Bierstadt drafted and excused, 178, 179
Clarke, Edward, 50, 227
Claude Lorraine, 122, 194, 207
Cleveland, Grover, 255

Coen, Rena, 11
Coffin, R. B. (Barry Gray), 37, 116, 177, 193
Cole, Thomas, 25, 32, 35, 36, 54, 113, 287 n.14, 304
Colfax, Schuyler, 43
collotype, 267, 269, 274, 281, 285
Columbus (Ohio) Academy of Fine Arts, 230
"Comstock's Ranche" (wood engraving), *178*, 277, *278*
*Conway Meadows, Mohawk River*, 181
Cook, Clarence, 27, *28*, 28–29, 30, 31–32, 35, 48, 49, 65 n.34, 67 n.133, 186
Cooper, James Fenimore, 72, 74, 92
Corcoran, William Wilson, 54, 56–57, 285
Corcoran Gallery of Art, 54, 55–57, 58, 227, *227*, 231, 254
Cornelius, Peter von, 120
*Costume Study of Seated Woman*, *134*
Cranch, Christopher P., 30, 33–34
Cropsey, Jasper F., 49, 54, 287 ns.13–14 and 18
*Crossing Green River, California*, 232
"Crossing the Plains" (wood engraving), *144*, 271, *271*
"Crossing the Platte" (wood engraving), *145*, 271, *271*

Dana, Richard Henry, 70
"The Dead Moose" (wood engraving), 281, *282*
*Departure of Hiawatha*, 46, *47*
*Destruction of Pompeii and Herculanaeum*, 257
Dillman, T. J., 276
*Discovery of the Hudson River*, 40, *40*, *43*, 43–44, 45, 50, 52, 53, 221, 227–28
Dodworth's Hall Artists' Receptions, 146, 179
Dole, William P., 149
*Domes of the Yosemite, The* (chromolithograph), 189, *276*, 276–77, 288 n.27, 288 n.29, 288 n.31, *293*
*Domes of the Yosemite, The* (oil on canvas), 24, 25, 27, *27*, 29, 30, 35, 43, 45, 46, 48, 49, *90*, 90–92, 173–74, 183, 184–85, 225, *225*, 226, 276; smaller version, 276, 288 ns.28 and 31
*Donner Lake from the Summit*, 37, 58, *95*, 95–97, 107 n.87, 220, 226–27
Donner Party, 96, *96*
Doughty, Thomas, 287 n.14
Downes, William Howe, 21, 62, 64
Drysdale, William, 285
Dufferin, Lord, 229, 231
Dunraven, Earl of, 55, 99, 222, 229, 230, *230*, 231
Durand, Asher B., 32, 113, 164, 273, 287 n.14, 304
*Dusseldorf*, 148
Dusseldorf Gallery (New York), 65 n.31, 117
Düsseldorf school of painting, 21, 23, 28–29, 30, 41, 46, 49, 60, 61, 64, 112, 117, 120, 129, 147, 167, 183

Eakins, Thomas, 49
*Early Snow Lake in Nova Scotia*, 253
*Echo Lake, Franconia Mts, N.H.*, 147
*Emerald Pool, The* (oil on canvas), 58–59, *59*, 65 n.27, 175, 188, 189, 223, 224, 227, 252, 279, 288 n.34
*Emerald Pool, The* (photograph finished in crayon), 279
*Emigrants Camping*, 147
*Emigrants Crossing the Plains*, 183, 184, 186
*Emigrants Waiting for the Ferry, Saint Joseph, Missouri* (stereograph), *71*
engravings, 12, 267–68; *see also* steel engraving; wood engraving
*Entrance into Monterey*, see *Settlement of California, Bay of Monterey, 1770*
*Escape from an Indian Attack*, 252
*Estes Park, Colorado*, 230, 231, 251; *see also Rocky Mountains, Longs Peak, The*
Exposition Générale des Beaux-Arts, Brussels (1870), 187
Exposition Universelle, Paris: of 1867, 29, 45, 46, 58, 174, 183, *183*, 275; of 1878, 59, 63, 232; of 1889, 58, 62–63, 100, 102, 247, 253, *253*, 258–59, 281, 285

*Falls of the Yosemite*, 274
*Farm Scene in Westphalia*, 118
Farragut, David, 46
*Farrallone Islands*, 252
*Farrallone Islands off the Coast of California*, 252
Ferber, Linda S., 13
Field, Cyrus W., 46–47
*Figure Studies*, *119*
Fine Arts Academy, Buffalo, *24*, 54, 149, 151, 177, 251
Fine Arts Museums of San Francisco, 13
*Fir Trees and Storm Clouds*, *168*
*Fishing Boats at Capri*, 121, *132*
*Five Indians*, *161*
Floyd, John B., 143
*Ford on the Little Blue River, Kansas* (stereograph), *144*
*Forest Glen*, 272
Fortuny, Mariano, 286
*Four Indians*, *162*
Frémont, John C., 35, 70, 106 n.1, 181
Frost, Francis Shedd, 71, 106 ns.6 and 13, 140, 143–45, 146
Furness, William Henry, 119

Gardner, Isabella Stewart, 64, 256
Gautier, Théophile, 174, *187*, 205
*German Costume Study*, *119*
Gérôme, Jean-Léon, 286
*Geyser of the Yellowstone, A*, 252
Gifford, Sanford Robinson, 113, 119, *120*, 120–22, 132, 133, 140, 146, 147, 164, 273; *Bierstadt at the Piccola Marina, Capri*, *122*
*Glen, The*, 249
Godwin, Parke, 46–47
*Golden Era*, 12, 82, 87, 201; *see also* Ludlow, Fitz Hugh
*Golden Gate, California, The*, 181, 225, 257
*Gosnold at Cuttyhunk, 1602*, 93, 137, *137*, 143
Gould, Charles, Jr., 148
Gould, Jay, 35
Goupil's gallery (Paris and New York), 79, 141, 147, 182, 188, 276, 281
Grant, Ulysses S., 249
Gray, Barry, *see* Coffin, R. B.
"Great Picture" exhibitions, 23, 24–26, 31–32, 65 n.14, 74
*Great Trees, Mariposa Grove, California, The*, 222, 229, *229*, 232, 240, *241*
*Great Trees of California, Mariposa Valley (Washingtonia Gigantia)*, 252
Greeley, Horace, 30
*Grizzly Bears*, *159*
Grizzly Giant painting, *see Great Trees, Mariposa Grove, California, The*
Gudin, Théodore, 186
*Guerrilla Warfare (Picket Duty in Virginia)*, 61, 80, *80*, 141, 147, 148, 167, *167*

*Halt in the Yosemite Valley, A* (steel engraving), 279, *280*, 288 n.26
Hamilton, Gail, 94
Hamilton, James, 13
*Happy Hunting Ground*, 224
Harrison, Benjamin, 254
Harroun, Gilbert K., 284
Hart, James, 147
Hart, William, 63
Harvey, George, 23, 35, 116
Haseltine, William Stanley, 119, 120, 140, 146; portrait by Stone, *120*
Hasenclever, Johann Peter, 112, 117
Hassrick, Peter, 11
Hay, John, 141, 148, 178, 257
Hayden, Ferdinand V., 49, 52, 53, 58, 223, 231
Hayes, Rutherford B., 42, 53, 182, 222, 249, 265
Hayes, Webb, 53, 222, 231
*Haying, Conway Meadows*, *191*
*Headwaters of the Black River, Wind River Mountains, California, The*, 189
*Heart of the Continent, The*, see Ludlow, Fitz Hugh
Hendricks, Gordon, 11
Henry, Joseph, 54, 227
Hicks, Theodore F., 247, 256
Hill, James J., 254
Hill, Thomas, 274
Hinshelwood, Robert, 280
Historic Art Association, 255
Holmes, Oliver Wendell, 79
Homer, Winslow, 49
Hopkins, John, 23, 118, 119, 120, 122, 123, 143, 181, 186, 304
Hornaday, William T., *101*, 101–2
Hubbard, Richard William, 164
Hudson River School, 28, 30, 35, 49, 63, 255; Metropolitan Museum exhibition, 12
Hunt, Samuel Valentine, 273, 274, 287 n.20
"Hunter of the Prairie" (wood engraving), 273, *273*
Huntington, Collis P., 48, 58, 95, 97–98, 107 n.91, 220, 223, 226, 233
Huntington, Daniel, 164, 258
Huntington, David, 12

*Indian Pony, Kansas* (stereograph), *144*
"Indians on the Move" (wood engraving), 277, *278*
*Indians Traveling near Fort Laramie*, 148, *163*, 277
*Indian Summer, New Hampshire*, 123
Inness, George, 27
*In the Sierra Nevada Mountains*, 223
Irving, John Beaufain, 119, 146
Irving, Washington, 35, 70, 92, 106 n.1
Isabey, Jean-Baptiste, 186
*Island of Capri*, 146
*Italian Costume Studies*, 121, *134*

Jackson, William Henry, 101
Jarves, James Jackson, 22, 27–28, *28*, 29–30, 33, 75, 77, 189
Jay, John, 223
"Jean Baptiste Moncrévié" (wood engraving), 277, *278*

Johnson, David, 147
Johnson, Eastman, 13, 23
Johnston, John Taylor, 55, 67 n.167

*Kallenfels Among the Hills, Germany,* 119, *119*
Karst, John, 274
Kelly, Franklin, 12
Kennard, Thomas William, 26, 44, 92, 173, 182, 275
Kensett, John F., 42, 54, 55, 164, 273, 287 n.14
Keyes, Donald, 12
King, Clarence, 48, 49, 51–52, 56, 98, 207, 220, 226
King, Thomas Starr, 79–80, *80*, 170, 191
*Kings River Canyon,* see *Autumn in the Sierras*
*King's River Grove—California,* 232
Köhler, Sylvester R., 30, 45, 66 ns.70 and 117, 276, 279
Kurtz, William, 286

*Lake Esther* (painting), 280
*Lake Esther Seirra* [sic] *Nevada Mts. Cal.*: steel engraving, 280, *280;* wood engraving, 280, *280*
*Lake Louise,* 254
*Lake Lucerne (Switzerland),* 26, 41, 61, 65 n.13, 106 n.76, 113, 123, 124, 130, *131,* 135, 143, 174, 246, 250
Lamb, Martha, 36, 66 ns.69–70
Lambdin, George C., *Enoch Wood Perry, 178*
Lander, Frederick W., 55, 71, 76–77, *77,* 106 n.7, 140, 141, 143
Lander expedition (1859), 71–72, 140, 143–45, 267, 268
*Landing of Columbus, The,* 247, 255
*Landscape,* 180, 189, 231
*Landscape—Autumn—Westphalia,* 123
Landseer, Sir Edwin, 47, 123
Lanman, Charles, 166
*Laramie Peak, Rocky Mountains,* 149, 252
*Last of the Buffalo, The* (oil on canvas), 58, 62–64, *100,* 100–105, 247, 253, 254, 255, 258–59, *259,* 285, 286, 288 n.38
*Last of the Buffalo, The* (photogravure), 62, 269, 286, *286,* 288 n.38, *294*
Latham, Milton S., 232
Legion of Honor award, 46, 58, 62, 187, 247
Leighton, Sir Frederick, 255
Leslie, Frank, 45
Lessing, Karl Friedrich, 117
Leutze, Emanuel, 23, 26, 30, 41–42, 43, 45, 54, 112, 113, 117, 118, 120, 123, 129, 140, 141, 143, 146, 147, 164, 304; *Self-Portrait, 117; Westward the Course of Empire Takes Its Way, 41,* 41–42
Lewis, Henry, 23, 113, 118, 119, 123, 124
Lewison (Florence) Gallery (New York), 11
Lincoln, Abraham, 86, 94, 141, 180
Lindquist-Cock, Elizabeth, 11
lithography, 267, 268–69, 287 ns.3 and 13
Lockwood, Le Grand, 27, 43, 44, 48, 90, 183, 225, 276; rotunda of mansion of, *27*
London, 46–47, 58; American Exhibition (1887), 246, 252; Royal Academy of, 58, 66 n.117, 186–87, 226, 227, 232, 249, 254
Longfellow, Henry Wadsworth, and Longfellow Dinner, 46–47, 58, 185, *185*
*Looking Down Yosemite Valley, California,* 24, 29, 85–87, *87,* 88, 89, 91, 93, 97, 98, 173, 181, 182, 183, 200–201, *201,* 224
Louisville, 100; Southern Expositions, 251, 252
Ludlow, Fitz Hugh, 26, 34, 78–82, 85–89, 91, 98, 172, 177–80, 182, 189, 277, 306; *Atlantic Monthly* articles of, 78, 85, 179, 180, 181, 202, 306; carte de visite by Beniczky, *78, 177; Golden Era* "Reminiscences of an Overlander" of, 12, 78, 88, 172, 179–80, 306, 307–21; New York *Evening Post* "Letters from Sundown" of, 26, 85, 172, 177, 178, 179, 306; *The Heart of the Continent,* 78, 86–87, 152, 172, 175, *178,* 189, *189,* 197, 198, 237, 240, 260, 261, 274, 277, *277–79,* 279, 306
Ludwig, Heinrich, 120

McEntee, Jervis, 59, 67 n.167, 229
McHenry, James, 26, 35, 42, 44, 88, 92, 173–74, 181, 182, 183, 275
McKinley, William, 257
McLean, Thomas, 46, 92, 182, 183, 184, 187, 188, 223, 275, 276–77, 287–88 n.25
MacLeod, William, 54, 56–57, 231
Malkasten (Bierstadt home on Hudson River), 34–39, *34–36, 38–39,* 173, 181, *181, 183,* 246, 250
Manthorne, Katherine, 12
*Marina Piccola, Capri, The (Capri—Bay of Naples),* 54, 143, 149, 151, *151,* 177, 252
Massachusetts Academy of Fine Arts, 117
Mauge, Hangard, 276
*Meadow in Westphalia,* 231
Meigs, Montgomery C., 41
Meissonier, Ernest, 286
Metropolitan Fair (New York, 1864), 32, *32–33,* 173, 179–80, *180*
Metropolitan Museum of Art, 174, 188, 223, 249; *American Paradise: The World of the Hudson River School* exhibition, 12
Miller, Alfred Jacob, 70, 106 n.3
Millet, Frank D., 63
*Mill Near Altena in Westphalia, A,* 118
Milwaukee, 100, 182; Art School, 251
Minneapolis, 100; Industrial Expositions, 252, 254
*Mirror Lake, Yosemite Valley,* 184, 277; steel engraving resembling, 277, *277*
*Misty Morning in Westphalia,* 231
*Moat Mountain, Intervale, New Hampshire, 170*
modernism, 248
*Montmorency Falls, Quebec,* 251
*Moose, 264*
*Moose Head, A,* 253
Moran, Thomas, 48–49, 51–53, 56, 58, 59, 63, 221, 223, 231, 232, 274, 285; *Chasm of the Colorado,* 49–50, *50,* 52, 221; *The Grand Canyon of the Yellowstone,* 49, *50,* 52, 62 n.133, 221; *Ponce de Leon in Florida,* 52, *53*
Morgan, J. P., 255
Moser, James Henry, 102; *The Still Hunt,* 102, *103; Where the Millions Have Gone,* 102, *103*
Mould, Jacob Wrey, 36
Mount, William Sidney, 13
*Mount Adams, Oregon,* 179; *see also* 226
*Mount Adams on the Columbia River, Oregon,* 54, 227, 229; *see also* 226
*Mountain Brook, The,* 177, 193, *193*
*Mountain Lake,* 55, 222, 230, *231;* drawing after, *56; see also Mount Corcoran*
*Mountain Landscape,* 57
"A Mountain Range, with Black-Tailed Deer" (wood engraving), 281, *282*
*Mountain Scene, 234*
"The 'Mountain Sheep' (Ovis Montana)" (wood engraving), 281, *282,* 284
*Mount Baker,* 254
*Mt. Chicorua* [sic], *N.H.,* 181
*Mount Corcoran* (oil on canvas), *55,* 55–57, *57,* 222, 230, 231, 285; *see also Mountain Lake*
*Mount Corcoran* (photogravure), 269, 281, 285, *285*
*Mount Corcoran* (wood engraving), 285, *285*
"Mount Corcoran, Sierra Nevada" (wood engraving), 283, *283*
*Mounted Trapper, 158*
*Mount Hood, Oregon* (oil on canvas), 24, 42, 43, 85, 86, *86,* 172, 173, 179, 181, 182, 184, 187, 188, 223, 226, 229, 272
"Mount Hood, Oregon" (photoengraving), 181, 286, *286*
*Mount Sir Donald,* 254, *254*
*Mount Tacoma,* 254, 255
*Mount Vesuvius at Midnight* (chromolithograph), 30, 276, *276*
*Mount Vesuvius at Midnight* (painting), 30, 65 n.14, 174, 185, 186, 187, 276
*Mount Washington, 31*
*Mt. Washington from Shelburne, N.H.,* 143
*Mount Whitney (Sierra Nevada),* 99, *99,* 249, 251, 252
Muybridge, Eadweard, stereographs by, *225, 226*

Napoléon III, Emperor, 46, 187
*Nassau Harbor,* 244, *244*
National Academy of Design, 22, 26, 32, 41, 55, 63, 85–87, 99–100, 140, 141, 143, 146–47, 148, 173, 177, 178, 180, *180,* 181, 182, 184, 189, 200, 221, 222, 223, 224, 225, 227, 228, 230, 232, 246, 249, 251, 252, 253, 258; Bierstadt's debut and membership in, 113, 123, 147, 246
National Art Association, 255
National Convention of Artists, 41, 124
National Gallery of Art, 13
National Museum of American Art, 53
*Natural Park and Lake, Southern California,* 65 n.27, 252
*Near Monterey, California,* 251
*Near San Rafael, California,* 228
"Near the Black Hills" (wood engraving), 283, *283*
*Near Troy, Kansas* (stereograph), *143*
*Nebraska [Territory]: Wasatch Mountains, 155*
Neumann, August, *Albert Bierstadt, 188*
*Nevada Falls,* 251
New Bedford Art Association, 1858 exhibition, 12, 23, 65 n.11, 113, 123, 304; Catalogue, 304–5
*Niagara, 212*
*Niagara Falls,* 253
Nordhoff, Charles, 238, 239
North, John Thomas, 63, 254–55
*North Fork of the Platte, Nebraska,* 177, 197, *197*
Novak, Barbara, 11

*Ogalillah Sioux, Horse Creek, Nebraska* (stereograph), *145*
*Old Mill, The,* 117, 128, *128*
*Olevano, Italy,* 252
*On the Coast Near Nassau, Bahamas,* see *Shore of the Turquoise Sea, The*
*On the Passaic River, New Jersey,* 252
*On the Plains, 196*
*On the Saco, New Hampshire,* 251

*On the way to Cervara. Artists' Festival in Rome* (engraving), *121*
*On the Weser*, 123
*Oregon Trail, The*, *211*
Osborne, Esther, 39
O'Sullivan, Timothy, 84
"The Overland Mail Coach" (wood engraving), *178*, 277, *278*
*Ox*, *160*

Page, William, 120, 224
Paris Salon, 58, 62; of 1869, 46, 174, 186–87; of 1875, 228; of 1879, 232; of 1880, 249; of 1882, 250; of 1889, 62, 247, 253, 285
Parkman, Francis, 70
Parton, Arthur, 63
*Passing Storm over the Sierra Nevada*, *213*
patents held by Bierstadt, 255, 256, *256*, 257
Pennsylvania Academy of the Fine Arts, 54–55, 143, 183–84, 229
Perry, Enoch Wood, 81, 119, 172, 178; Lambdin portrait of, *178*
Peto, John F., 13
Philadelphia, 182, 183; *see also* Centennial Exposition
photoengraving, 267, 286
photography, 267–269, 287 n.10
photogravure, 267, 269, 281, 285, 287 n.10
*Pike's Peak Emigrants, Saint Joseph, Missouri* (stereograph), *71*
"A Pike's Peaker" (wood engraving), *145*, 271, *271*
*Pioneers of the Woods*, 106 n.20, *127*
*Pirate Shenandoah Burning Whalers*, see *The Burning Ship*
*Platte River,—Indians Encamped*, 147
*Platte River, Nebraska*, 182
"Portrait of Comstock" (wood engraving), *178*, 277, *278*
Powell, John Wesley, 49, 56
Powell, William Henry, 41, 42, 45, 52
Powles, Louis D., 244
"Prairie Dogs" (wood engraving), 274, 277, *279*
Prang, Louis, 185, 186, 187, 268–69, 274
Pre-Raphaelites, 27, 28, 48, 65 n.34
Prime, William Cowper, 72
Pringle, Allan, 12
printmaking, 12, 267–70; *see also* chromolithography; collotype; photoengraving; photogravure; steel engraving; wood engraving
"Prong-Horned Antelope (Antilocapra Americana)" (wood engraving), 281, *282*
*Puget Sound, on the Pacific Coast*, 214, *214*

*Quebec Citadel*, 251
Quidor, John, 13
*Quiet Valley, A*, *113*

railway car patents of Bierstadt, 255, 256, *256*, 257
*Rainbow in the Sierras*, 225
*Rain Storm on the Lake*, 252
*Recollections of Capri*, 147
Renwick, James, 54
Richards, William T., 13, 46, 49
Robinson, Theodore, 13
*Rockey Mts. with Buffalo, Bierstadt (Harper's* cartoon), *177*
*Rocky Mountain passages*, 146
*Rocky Mountains, Lander's Peak, The* (chromolithograph), 186, 187–88, 274–76, *275*, 288 ns.25–27
*Rocky Mountains, Lander's Peak, The* (oil on canvas), 24–29 *passim*, 31–32, *32*, 42, 44, 45, 46, 52, 55, 58, 61, 65 ns.14 and 25, *74*, 74–78, 85, 86, 88, 89, 92, 93, 94, 103, 141, 172–74, 177–84 *passim*, 194, *195*, 204, 251, 272
*Rocky Mountains, Lander's Peak, The* (steel engraving), 31, 75–76, 177–78, 179, 182, 183, 184, 268, *272*, 272–73, 287 ns.14 and 17, *290;* prospectus for, *272*, 272–73
*Rocky Mountains, Longs Peak, The (Estes Park, Colorado)*, 56, 99, *99*, 230, 231, 232, 251
"A Rocky Mountain Scene" (wood engraving), 274, *274*
*Rocky Mountain Scenery*, 106 n.14, 146
"Rocky Mountain Sheep" (Artotype), 251, *251*, 284, *284*
*Roman Fish Market, The*, see *Arch of Octavius, The*
Rosa, Salvador, 122
Rothermel, Peter Frederick, 121
Royal Academy, Berlin, 45–46, 93, 185–86
Royal Academy, London, 58, 66 n.117, 186–87, 226, 227, 232, 249, 254
*Ruins of Carthage*, 116
*Ruins of Paestum (The Temples of Paestum)*, 106 n.20, 123, *123*, 143
Ruskin, John, 27, 29, 32, 48, 151, 204
*Rustic Mill, A*, *125*
Ryder, Albert, 223

Saint-Gaudens, Augustus, 59, 63, 232
Saint Louis, 182, 228; Exposition of 1877, 231
*St. Peters and the Castle of St. Angelo—Sunset*, 143
Salon, *see* Paris Salon
San Francisco Art Association, 223–24, 226, 227
Santa Barbara Museum of Art, 11
Sarony, Napoleon, 189, 276; Bierstadt carte de visite, *177*
Sartain, John, 54, 62, 229, 252, 288 n.38
Sartain, William, 62, 253, 288 n.38
"Scene in Estes Park" (wood engraving), 281, *282*
*Scene in the Tyrol*, 118
Scott, General Winfield, 147
*Seal Rock* (oil on canvas), *239*
*Seal Rock, California* (oil on paper), *238*
*Seal Rock, San Francisco*, *27*, 65 n.27, 252
Seitz, Emil, 271–72
*Sentinel Rock after a Snow Storm, Yosemite Valley*, 252
*Settlement of California, Bay of Monterey, 1770*, 40, *40*, *43*, 52–53, 54, 67 n.144, 221, 228, 229, 232
Seymour, Samuel, 106 n.4; *View near the base of the Rocky Mountains*, 70, *70*
Shattuck, A. D., 273
Shaw, Albert, 265
Sheldon, George W., 26, 60
Sheridan, General Philip, 224
Sherman, General William T., 223, 253
Shinn, Earl (Edward Strahan), 60, 65 n.27, 229, 281
*Shore of the Turquoise Sea, The (On the Coast Near Nassau, Bahamas)*, 69, 231, 242, *243*, 249
*Shoshone Children* (stereograph), *145*
*Shoshone Village*, 147
*Shoshone Warrior, Nebraska* (stereograph), *145*
*Sierra Nevada* (painting), *see Mount Whitney*
"Sierra Nevada" (wood engraving), 282, *284*
*Sierra Nevada—Morning*, 252
*Sierra Nevada Mountains, California*, 189
*Sierra Nevada Mountains, The*, 240
*Sierra Nevada Mountains Near Yo Semite Valley*, 184
*Sierras near Lake Tahoe, California, The*, *202*
*Silver Lake, California* (painting), 181, 274, 277
*Silver Lake, California* (steel engraving), *273*, 273–74, 287 n.20
"A Sioux Camp near Laramie Peak" (wood engraving), 281, *282*
*Sioux Village*, 146
*Sioux Village near Fort Laramie, Na.* (stereograph), *145*
"Site of Gosnold's Fort" (wood engraving), *281*
*Sketch after "Sunlight and Shadow,"* *148*
Smillie, James, 75, 177–78, 179, 182, 184, 268, 272–73, 275, 287 ns.14 and 17–18
Smillie, James David, 272
Smith, Caleb, 149
Smith, David D., 101
Smith, Russell, 60
Smithsonian Institution, 54, 101–2, 227; Buffalo Exhibit (1886–1911), *101*
*Snowcapped Mountains (Pacific Northwest)* (two versions, undated), *217*
*Snow Scene with Buffalo* (collotype), 284, *284*
Sordello (Eugene Benson), 29, 200
*South Pass, Rocky Mountains*, 147
*Spearing Fish by Torchlight, Lake Lucerne*, *122*
Spofford, Ainsworth R., 52, 58, 232
Stanford, Leland, 48, 223, 224, 230
Stanley, John Mix, 70, 106 ns.3 and 7, 287 n.13
Stanton, Edwin M., 141, 148
Stebbins, James H., 253, 286
Stedman, Edmund Clarence, 102–3
steel engraving, 267–68, 281, 285
Stewart, A. T., 26–27, 65 ns.25–27, 252; Picture-Gallery of, *27*
Stewart, David, 64, 247, 256
Stieler, Karl, 121
Stoddard, William O., 225, 226
Stone, William O., 120
Storch & Kramer, 271, 287 n.13
*Storm in the Rocky Mountains, Mt. Rosalie* (chromolithograph), 186, 187–88, 274–76, *275*, 288 ns.25–27, *292*
*Storm in the Rocky Mountains, Mt. Rosalie* (oil on canvas), 13, 24, 26, 29, 30, 42, 46, 53, 55, 60, 66 n.117, *88*, 88–90, 92, 93, 173–74, 181–87 *passim*, 204–5, *205*, 251, 252
*Storm on Laramie Peak*, 251
*Storm on the Matterhorn*, 252
*Stormy Lake Scene (Pacific Northwest)*, *216*
Story, William Wetmore, 135
Stowe, Harriet Beecher, 268
Strahan, Edward (Earl Shinn), 60, 65 n.27, 229, 281
*Street Scene in Rome*, 135
Strong, Donald, 11
*Studies of Bison*, *260*
*Study for "The Domes of the Yosemite,"* *91*
*Study of a Ewe*, *119*
*Summit Lake, Colorado*, 253
Sumner, Charles, 141, 148
*Sunlight and Shadow* (chromolithograph), 180–81, *271*, 271–72, *289*

*Sunlight and Shadow* (oil on canvas), 148, 166, *166*, 180–81, 184, 200, 249, 252, 271
*Sunlight and Shadow: Study*, 126, *126*
*Sunrise in the Sierras*, *235*
*Sunrise on the Matterhorn, Switzerland*, 252
*Sunset* (exhibited 1877), 231
*Sunset* (exhibited 1887), 252
*Sunset: California Scenery* (chromolithograph), 185, 186, *186*, 187, 268, 274, *274*, 288 n.27
*Sunset, Cypress Point, California*, 253
*Sunset in California* (painting), 186, 187, 268, 274
*Sun Set—In the Prairies*, 148
"Sunset in the Yosemite" (photoengraving), 286, *286*
*Sunset in the Yosemite Valley* (oil on canvas), 65 n.14, 174, 185, 207, *207*, 253
*Sunset on the Prairies (Le coucher du soleil, sur les prairies)*, 228
*Sunshine and Shade*, 252; *see also Sunlight and Shadow*
*Surveyor's Wagon in the Rockies*, 49, 72–73, *73*, 104, *157*
*Sweetwater River, Wind River Mountains, Wyoming Territory*, *154*
*Swiss Lake*, 149

Taylor, Bayard, 70, 184, *185*, 200
*Temple of Paestum, The*, see *Ruins of Paestum*
Tenth Street Studio Building (New York), 24, *24*, 38, 40, 41, 73, 74, 81, 90, 106 n.14, 140, 143, 146, *146*, 148, 172, 177, 189
Terry, Luther, 120
Thompson, Thomas, 117, 174–75, 188
*Three Views of "A Railway Car,"* *256*
*Thunderstorm in the Rocky Mountains*, 152, *152*
Timken Art Gallery (San Diego), 12
*Towards the Setting Sun*, 228
Townley, D. O. C., 95–96, 233
*Trappers' Camp, The*, 148, 149, 164, *164*
Trenton, Patricia, 11
Trump, Richard Shafer, 11
Tuckerman, Henry T., 32, 35, 45, 65 n.25, 116, 117, 126, 128, 135, 277
*Tuolumne River, California*, *224*
Turner, J. M. W., 27–28, 48–49, 184, 194
Twain, Mark, 91–92
*Twilight View of Boston from the Harbor, A*, 188

Union League Club, 174, 188, 223, 246, 252, 253, 254, 255
*Unpacking Goods for the Indians, Nebraska* (stereograph), *71*
*Upper Glacier of Rosenlaui, The*, *122*, 123
*U.S. Train in Camp, Na.* (stereograph), *143*

*Valley of King's River, California*, 228
*Valley of the Yosemite*, 180, *199*
*Valley of Zermatt, Switzerland*, 251
Vanderbilt, Cornelius, 48, 231, 255
Vanderlyn, John, 52, 113
Van Horne, William C., 252, 253, 254, 256
Van Rensselaer, Mariana Griswold, 61
Victoria, Queen, 46, 174, 184, 275
Vienna Exposition (1873), 58, 227
*View from Gaeta*, 123
*View from Government House, Ottawa*, 251
*View from the Glen House*, 184
*View in the Sierras*, 225
*View in the Yosemite, California*, *83*
*View Near Minden, Westphalia*, 143
*View Near Newport*, 143
*View of Cologne on the Drachenfels from Altenberg, A*, 118
*View of Donner Lake, California*, 233, *233*
*View of Dusseldorf, on the Rhine*, 148
*View of the Hudson Looking Across the Tappan Zee Towards Hook Mountain*, 36, *37*, 66 n.70
*View of the Weser near Minden*, 118
"View on the Kern River" (wood engraving), 283, *283*
*View on the Weser*, 143
*Village of Brunnen*, 143

Walters, William T., 54
*Wanderings in the Western Land* (Vivian): title page, *281;* wood engravings, 281, *281–83*
"Wapiti Feeding" (wood engraving), 281
"Wapiti on the Prairie" (wood engraving), 281, *283*
"A Wapiti Roaring" (wood engraving), 281, *283*
Ward, Samuel, 56
Washington Art Association, 41, 124, 143, 146
*Washington Gigantia (Great Trees of California, Mariposa Valley)*, 252
Watkin, Edward William, 26, 47
Watkins, Carleton E., 79–80, 141, 189, 225; albumen silver prints by, *79;* stereographs by, *229*
*Watson's Weekly Art Journal*, 29, 35, 89, 200, 204
*Wave Breaking on the Bahamas Coast, A (After a Norther Off the Bahamas)*, 251, 252
Weed, Charles Leander, 79
*Weeping Oak, California, The*, 251
Weir, J. Alden, 63
Weir, John Ferguson, 59, 60
*Wellingtonia, The*, 240
*Western Kansas* (painting), 60, 229, 281
"Western Kansas" (steel engraving), *280*, 280–81
*Westphalian Landscape*, *118*
*Wetterhorn, The*, 106 n.20, 120, 122, 129, *129*, 180
*Wharf Scene with Ship at Dock*, *136*
White House, Bierstadt paintings in, 222, 247, 249, 250, *250*, 252, 253, 254, 255
*White Mountains, New Hampshire* (oil on board, 1863), *192*
*White Mountains, New Hampshire* (oil on paper, undated), *169*
Whitney, Anne, 47
Whitney, Josiah Dwight, 56, 226
Whittredge, Worthington, 23, 26, 28, 30, 63, 65 n.3, 67 n.167, 112, 117–21 *passim*, 127, 132, 140, 146, 147, 164, 174, 230; portrait by Leutze, *117; View of Kallenfels*, *119*
Williams, Henry T., 96
Williams, Virgil, 81, 120, 172, 178, *178*
Willmore, Arthur, 279
*Wind River Country*, *156*
*Wind River Mountains, Nebraska Territory* (oil on canvas), 148, *149*
*Wind River Mountains, Nebraska Territory* (oil on composition board), *165*
Winthrop, Theodore, 76, 77, *77*, 84–85
*Wolf River, Kansas, The*, *153*
*Wolf River Ford, Kansas* (stereograph), *144*
"Wolves Attacking a Wounded Buffalo" (wood engraving), 277, *279*
wood engraving, 12, 267–68, 281
Worcester Art Museum, 257
World's Columbian Exposition, Chicago (1893), 58, 247, 255
*Wreck of the "Ancon" in Loring Bay, Alaska*, 49, 69, *104*, 104–5, *263*
Wright, E. W., 253

Yale School of Fine Arts, 184
"The Yo-Semite Fall" (wood engraving), *179*, 276, *276*
*Yosemite Valley* (1865), *see Looking Down Yosemite Valley, California*
*Yosemite Valley* (1866), *203*
*Yosemite Valley* (1868), *206*
*Yosemite Valley* (unidentified), 224, 229, 231
*Yosemite Valley, Glacier Point Trail*, 98, *98*
*Yosemite Winter Scene*, *225*
Yvon, Adolphe, 186

# PHOTOGRAPH CREDITS

*Unless otherwise stated below, credits are given in the captions.*

No. 2 Sarah Wells

Nos. 22, 28 P. Richard Eells

No. 26 Dirk Bakker

No. 27 Regina Monfort

No. 30 Scott Bowron Photography, New York

No. 42 Owen Murphy

Nos. 46, 47 M. Lee Fatherree

No. 53 Patricia Laymon Bazelon

No. 64 E. Irving Blomstronn

No. 65 Jeffrey Nintzel

No. 70 Devendra Shrikhande

No. 81 Linda Lorenz

Fig. 6 Scott Hyde

Fig. 12 Deborah A. Bryk

Fig. 16 Malcolm Varon

Fig. 47 Scott Bowren Photography, New York

Fig. 50 Jose A. Naranjo

Fig. 58 Jenks Studio

Fig. 64 Joseph Szaszfai

Fig. 66 James Milmoc

p. 120 (*William Stanley Haseltine*) David Allison, Photography

p. 122 (*Bay of Salerno*) Hirschl and Adler Galleries, Inc., New York

p. 149 (*Wind River Mountains, Nebraska Territory*) Spanierman Gallery

p. 225 (*Yosemite Winter Scene*) Colin McCrae